D1573277

Modern principles of athletic training

ANCIENT TRAINING ROOM

The palaestra, a sandcovered open courtyard, was surrounded by small rooms where athletes bathed, oiled, and dressed. Right figure, a youth leaves his outer garment with an attendant; center figure, a competitor oils his body before entering the palaestra; left, an attendant removes a thorn from an injured athlete.

Modern principles of athletic training

The science of injury prevention and care

CARL E. KLAFS, Ph.D., F.A.C.S.M.

Professor of Physical Education, California State University at Long Beach

DANIEL D. ARNHEIM, D.P.E., F.A.C.S.M., F.A.C.T.A.

Professor of Physical Education, formerly Head Athletic Trainer, Coordinator, Athletic Training Curriculum, California State University at Long Beach

THIRD EDITION

with 595 illustrations

THE C. V. MOSBY COMPANY

SAINT LOUIS   1973

VH/VH/VH   9   8   7   6

To the training profession

Preface

The ten years since the publication of this text have seen significant strides in the field of athletic training as well as its expansion into the high schools and into female athletics. The advent of sports medicine has given new insight into and interpretation of the many, varied facets of conditioning the athlete and reestablishing his fitness for performance following injury. Training has attained dignity, responsibility, and recognition to which, as a profession, it has long been entitled. The recent surge of girls and women into the competitive athletic programs has further enhanced the role of the trainer.

As in previous editions, the intent of this text is to provide a comprehensive and up-to-the-minute presentation of the many aspects involved in training, recognition, evaluation, management, and rehabilitation of athletic conditions. The approach is again in terms of *prevention*. Although a background in anatomy, physiology, kinesiology, and physiology of exercise, such as is usually offered in the physical education or physical therapy programs, would be desirable, sufficient introductory information in those areas is presented when and where pertinent in order to assist students whose background may be limited. An extensive glossary will assist in the understanding of those technical terms not delineated in detail in the text itself.

The role of the trainer, his qualifications, relationships, and his responsibilities—legal and implied—as they relate to the athlete, team physician, coach, and the community are detailed and stressed. The comprehensiveness, readability, and uniqueness of this text has found wide acceptance, and this edition has been rewritten to conform to the many helpful comments and suggestions of students, teachers, trainers, and friends in the field. It is our hope that the present edition will serve as a valuable source of information, stimulation and inspiration and as a guide at all levels of athletic training to assist the reader in acquiring a more effective grasp of the broad and diverse aspects of this important profession.

We wish to express our appreciation to Mrs. Helene Arnheim for the excellent art work, which has added materially to amplifying and clarifying the text. Our special thanks to Richard Thorsen, team physician at California State University, Long Beach, whose suggestions and criticisms have contributed so much to this revision. Grateful acknowledgement and appreciation is also given Mrs. Ruth E. Johnson, Department of Home Economics, and Mr. Thomas E. Oxley, Head Trainer and Assistant Professor, both of California State University, Long Beach.

Carl E. Klafs
Daniel D. Arnheim

Contents

ix

General principles of athletic training

PART ONE

This section introduces the field of athletic training and its attendant administrative problems, the type of scientific knowledge necessary for instituting a program of injury prevention, and the various special considerations with which the trainer must become familiar if he is to conduct a successful program. The keynote in this unit is *prevention* of injury.

CHAPTER 1

An introduction to athletic training

HISTORICAL BACKGROUND

Primitive man was concerned solely with survival. To exist in his world demanded the utmost in survival skills, for which he needed a body trained to make effective use of each physical ability. Since he could not afford to be incapacitated in any way, he relied upon the soothsayer, medicine man, or shaman to assist him in maintaining his physical well-being. This was usually attempted through the media of prayer, fasting, and/or medication. The use of herbs, either for ingestion or for anointment, was the "stock in trade" of the medicine man. Anodynes of various types were handed down from father to son, and in this way the science of pharmacology may be assumed to have begun.[1]

Although archaeological findings have contributed greatly to our knowledge of sports and athletics in Egypt, Mesopotamia, and other culture centers of early times, it was not until the rise of the Greek civilization that a strongly organized athletic picture began to evolve. Establishment of the Panhellenic Games, the most famous of which were the Olympic Games, in time produced coaches and trainers to assist athletes in achieving a peak of physical perfection.[2-4]

Subsequently, with the appearance of the professional athlete in Athenian society, the *gymnastes* came into existence. These men trained their pupils in the skills and techniques of the sports of their day and employed a rudimentary knowledge of anatomy, physiology, and dietetics to keep the athletes in good condition. Later, the medical *gymnastai* appeared on the scene. Their concern[3,8] was conditioning the athlete and maintaining him at a high peak of physical efficiency. Possessing some knowledge of diet, rest, and exercise and the effect that each has on physical development and performance, they made use of hot baths, massage, anodynes, and other measures.[5] The *paidotribai* (literally "youth or boy rubbers") and the *aleiptes* (anointers) were also professional trainers, and the techniques of massage, the prescription of diet, and the general fitness of the athlete were their particular concern.[3,6]

Professional trainers were very much a part of the scene in ancient Rome. Early in his career Galen, who later served as court physician to Marcus Aurelius, had been physician to the gladiatorial school at Pergamum.[7] He and others of his time wrote at considerable length about the salutary effects of proper diet, rest, abstinence (from strong drink and sexual indulgence), and exercise as prerequisites for physical conditioning. Perhaps the greatest of all the Greek trainers, Herodicus of Megara, was considered a physician as well as a trainer. He performed his duties almost 300 years before Galen, and his chief claim to fame

Fig. 1-1. Ancient shower. The athlete removes sand, dust, and oil with a strigil (small bronze instrument at left) before showering. The strigil and oil bottle were part of the athlete's equipment.

is that he was the teacher of Hippocrates, who was to become the "father of modern medicine."[5,7,8] As far as can be determined Herodicus was the first physician to recommend exercise as a method of treatment for disease. Asclepiades, in the time of Christ, utilized exercise along with massage as a method of treatment. In the sixteenth century Mercuriale was the first physician known to have classified exercise as either "preventive" or "therapeutic"; Pare, another sixteenth century physician, postulated that exercise was a most necessary corollary to the rehabilitation of a fracture following the administration of primary treatment.[9]

For many centuries following the fall of the Roman Empire there was a complete lack of interest in sports activities. It was not until the beginning of the Renaissance that these activities slowly gained an increasing popularity. Training, as we know it, came into existence during the latter part of the nineteenth century with the firm es-

tablishment of intercollegiate and interscholastic athletics in the United States. The first trainers of this era were hangers-on who "rubbed down" the athlete. Since they possessed no technical knowledge, their training techniques usually consisted of a rub, the application of some type of counterirritant, and occasionally the prescription of various home remedies and poultices. Many of those earlier trainers were persons of questionable character. As a result, it has taken a good many years for the trainer to attain the status of a bona fide member of the athletic staff. Today the professional trainer is a well-qualified individual, often possessing an advanced academic degree, who has a thorough understanding of and special skill in the many facets of training and in the care of athletic injuries. Ideally, he works in a team approach with the physician and the coach.

There is a definite trend today toward establishing training as a legitimate area of high school athletic programs, although legal measures providing for the budgeting of salaries and for equipment and facilities are not generally in effect in most states. In the past the coach has been content to confine training to management of preliminary conditioning and the use of preventive strapping. Today, in keeping with the advances in techniques and equipment, the high school coach finds that he must become more familiar with the broader aspects of the athletic training program.

The founding of the National Athletic Trainers Association in Kansas City, Missouri, in 1950 for the express purposes of establishing professional standards and exchanging and disseminating information, was a big step forward. In 1954 the American College of Sports Medicine was founded. This organization is dedicated to the promotion of research in medical problems encountered in physical exercise and sports. It has made numerous contributions to the area of training and has increased the understanding and knowledge of coaches and trainers so that they can more adequately train and care for their athletes.

INCIDENCE OF ATHLETIC INJURIES

By their very nature sports activities invite injury. The "all-out" exertion required, the numerous situations requiring body contact, and play that involves the striking and throwing of missiles establish hazards that are either directly or indirectly responsible for the many and varied injuries suffered by athletes. Although there is no overall estimate of the number of persons injured in sports activities annually in the United States, insurance companies over the years indicate that annually tens of thousands suffer fractures, sprains, strains, cuts, and concussions.

More than 900,000 boys participate in high school football annually, and 30,000 participate at the college level. A high school athlete participating in a full season of practice and games has a 20% chance of being injured during the season and an 8% chance of incurring a serious injury. More players are injured in practice than during

a game. There is no team sport anywhere in the world in which injury occurs more frequently than in American football.[10]

The annual survey of football fatalities, which has been conducted since 1931 by the Committee on Injuries and Fatalities of the American Football Coaches Association, reveals pertinent information that should be kept in mind by trainers and coaches in planning for football[11] (Fig. 1-2). This committee conducts its study on a nationwide basis. All the facts on every known football fatality are collected from newspaper reports. Follow-up questionnaires are sent to the educational and medical authorities who are most qualified to give the desired information. The data are carefully interpreted and coordinated and then are published in an annual report. A partial summary of some of the findings of the 40th (1971) annual report indicates the following*†:

1. A total of twenty fatalities *directly* related to football were reported in 1971— fifteen in high school; three in college.

2. Twelve fatalities were associated with *indirect* causes (heat stroke, heart failure, etc.).

3. Football fatalities have averaged 19.10 per year over the past 40 years.

4. When reported on a per 100,000 player exposure basis, fatalities directly related to football have averaged 1.41 per 100,000 participants for 1971.

5. Most fatal injuries (48%) occur during the regularly scheduled games.

6. Fifty-five percent of the direct fatalities occurred to players between the ages of 16 and 18 years.

7. During the past 40 years the greatest number of fatalities (37%) have occurred during the second and third weeks of October.

---

*All percentage values are interpreted in terms of *recorded* fatalities and are rounded off to the nearest whole number.
†*Direct* refers to deaths resulting directly from football participation. *Indirect* refers to those fatalities caused by systemic failure or secondary complications engendered by football participation.

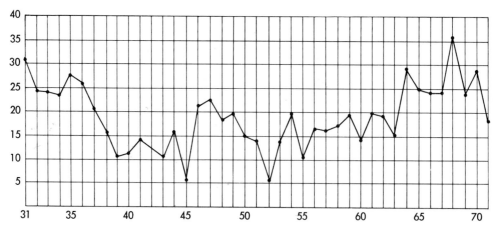

Fig. 1-2. Direct fatalities 1931-1971 (no study was made in 1942). The incidence of direct fatalities for 1971 was 1.41 per 100,000 participants for high schools and colleges combined. There were 18 fatalities among 1,275,000 players (1,200,000 high school players plus 75,000 college players). (From Fatalities directly due to football. Courtesy the American Football Coaches Association, the National Collegiate Athletic Association, and the National Federation of State High School Athletic Associations.)

8. Tackling incurred 32%, carrying the ball 16%, and blocking 10% of the total fatal injuries.

9. Slightly more fatal injuries occur to defensive players than to offensive players.

10. In 1971, sixteen injuries to the head, neck, and spinal cord resulted in death.

11. Since 1931 approximately 33% of all fatalities have resulted from indirect causes (34% of these were from heart and circulatory accidents; 25% were caused by infection).

12. Since the specific locations of injury have been tabulated the head and face area has accounted for 66%, the spine 19%, and the abdominal-internal area for 11% of the fatalities.[11]

In view of these findings the Committee has made a number of recommendations that trainers and coaches would do well to heed. Among other things, these recommendations stress the need for a thorough and comprehensive medical examination, an intensive preconditioning program, lengthening of the preseason training program, attendance of a physician at all games and practice sessions, strict enforcement of game rules, condemnation of "spearing" (using the head and neck as a

ram), proper and ample conditioning exercises to strengthen the neck, and properly fitted helmets.[10]

A 5 year epidemiological study of football injuries, which seeks to get at the causal factors through the use of a standard health research approach, is currently under way at the University of North Carolina under the direction of Robey, Blyth, and Mueller.[12] Some of the preliminary findings from the first 2 years of study indicate the following:

1. Athletes with a history of prior football trauma sustain a higher injury rate than those with no prior history of trauma.

2. No significant difference in the rate of injury for players based on the time exposed to risk in participation is apparent.

3. Injury risk increases with age.

4. Players with a history of training in physical education tumbling and gymnastics indicated a much lower injury rate than those with no such background.

5. A greater frequency of fractures, concussions, and lacerations were found than had previously been reported in the literature on the incidence of high school football injury.

6. More serious injury was associated

Table 1-1. Incidence of football injuries*

Injuries by practice activity exclusive of scrimmage			
Activity	Frequency	Percent	Percent of all injuries
Wind sprints	21		
Reaction drills	15		
Other conditioning	6		
Total, conditioning	42	16.2	3.5
Monkey rolls	11		
Coffee grinder	4		
Total, agility drills	15	5.8	1.2
Alabama drill	16		
One-on-one	52		
Sideline drill	15		
Form tackling	6		
Total, tackling drills	89	34.4	7.4
One-on-one blocking	19		
Two-on-one	11		
Two-on-two	4		
Blocking on end	3		
Half-speed blocking	3		
Total, blocking drills	40	15.4	3.3
Blocking on 7-man sled	12		
Blocking on 2-man sled	2		
Holding dummies	9		
Hitting dummies	13		
Buckaroo machine	9		
Total, equipment	45	17.4	3.7
Other	28	10.8	2.3
Total	**259**		**21.4**

Injuries by offensive play: activity and disability			
Offense activity†	Frequency	Percent	Average disability, days
QB tackled moving laterally	21	5.9	2.1
QB tackled on drop-back	28	7.8	4.7
Ballcarrier tackled			
LOS	22	6.2	2.3
Downfield	41	11.5	5.5
Sideline	37	10.4	2.1
Head-on	24	6.7	3.0
Running ball, nec	31	8.6	1.9
Blocking			
LOS	63	17.6	3.2
Downfield	65	18.2	5.8
Sideline	15	4.2	3.1
Pass blocking	10	2.8	1.8
Total	**357**	**99.9**	**2.8**

*Courtesy J. M. Robey, C. S. Blyth, and F. O. Mueller, Laboratory of Applied Physiology, Department of Physical Education, University of North Carolina, Chapel Hill, N. C.
†LOS signifies line of scrimmage; nec, not elsewhere classified.

with certain phases of play or practice activity.

7. Certain types and makes of protective equipment were shown to be associated with higher injury rates than others.

Some of the data of this study is presented in Table 1-1.

Basketball has the second highest rate of injury. Most of the injuries in this sport in-volve the wrists, elbows, and/or head. They occur as the result of either colliding with other players or attempting to ward off an impending collision with walls, bleachers, or other obstacles. Ankle and knee injuries occur in under-basket play or as the result of change-of-direction actions. The body build of basketball players is typically such that a high center of gravity induces relative

Fig. 1-3. Underbasket play may lead to injury.

instability, resulting in heavy falls to the floor. This is particularly obvious in rough under-basket play when a player must leap off the floor to play the ball (Fig. 1-3). In this situation even slight bodily contact with an opponent or a teammate anywhere below the hips tends to upset him. Another rather common source of injury is demonstrated when an opponent brings his arm forcefully down across the extended arm or arms of a player who is in the act of shooting. Although strictly an illegal maneuver, it is frequently employed and may result in severe bruising of muscle or fracture of the radius.

Compared with football and basketball, baseball has a low accident rate. Considering the fact that there are about 770,000 high school and 205,000 college players—not to mention the hundreds of thousands of Little League, Pony League, and sandlot participants—the low incidence of injuries is quite remarkable. Approximately 96% of the injuries occur in the arm and hand, leg and foot, and head and neck. Spiked shoes, improper sliding techniques, improper hand postures, and the unevenness of playing surfaces account for the majority of the limb injuries. Collisions and blows from either a bat or a ball are most often responsible for the head and neck injuries. Recently, there have been several deaths among the younger players, resulting from their being struck in the head or in the chest with a pitched ball. In one victim hit in the chest the sternum was crushed and forced into the thoracic cavity, which resulted in cardiac involvement and subsequently in death.

Track, which has a tremendous number of participants, is almost free of fatalities and has a relatively low injury rate. Muscle pulls, knee and ankle injuries, puncture wounds from shoe spikes, and abrasions are the most common injuries associated with this sport. Investigation of fatalities has usually indicated the presence of some organic impairment that directly or indirectly contributed to the fatality. In other cases death has occurred as a consequence of a freak accident because the individual was accidentally struck with an implement.

Other sports have relatively low injury rates—with the exception perhaps of skiing, which is becoming increasingly popular as a sport in a number of high schools and in a considerable number of colleges. Most skiing injuries are confined to the knee and ankle joints and manifest themselves as strains, sprains, or fractures. Skiing probably has a higher ratio of leg injuries than any other sport.

More shoulder, elbow, and wrist injuries are reported in gymnastics and wrestling than in any other sport. A recent survey conducted at the world amateur wrestling championships revealed that of injuries suffered by wrestlers 22% were to the head, 15% to the neck, 12% to the arm, 11% to the shoulder girdle, and 10% to the knee. Injuries to other body segments and to the thorax had values of 5% or less.[13] In tennis the incidence of ankle, knee, and wrist injuries is sporadic.

The use of individually fitted mouth protectors as recommended by a joint committee of the American Dental Association and the American Association for Health, Physical Education, and Recreation has reduced dental injuries almost 100% in contact sports.[14]

Since 1931, fifty cases of heatstroke resulting in death have been reported. Most of these deaths were preventable. Coaches and team physicians are becoming increasingly aware of the danger involved when athletes participate in full uniform performance during periods of excessive heat and/or humidity. Careful observation of environmental conditions coupled with a sensible approach to acclimatization during training will prevent heat exhaustion or heatstroke.[16,17] Heat stress is discussed in considerable detail in Chapter 23.

PREVENTION OF INJURIES AT THE HIGH SCHOOL LEVEL

The majority of high schools do not have access to the services of a qualified trainer. Consequently either the coach or a student will handle this responsibility. It is the purpose of this book to provide such a trainer-coach with information regarding the adequate conditioning of athletes and the proper care of any injuries that fall within his province. The primary responsibility of the trainer is the prevention and care of injuries in athletes under his jurisdiction. With reasonable foresight, many accidents can be prevented. Careful and constant supervision of all playing facilities and areas, with respect to maintaining safety factors at a constant level by eliminating any potential or existing hazards, is mandatory. The institution of a carefully planned, scientific program of conditioning the athlete *the year round* will assist greatly in reducing the number of injuries. The athlete who enters competition after insufficient preseason training or who begins preliminary training in a state of physical unfitness is an excellent prospect for injury. It is therefore mandatory that the trainer plan a conditioning program and see that his athletes follow such a program during off-season as well as in-season periods. A player who is unable to participate in competition because of injury is of no use to the team. Attention paid to the role conditioning has in preventing injuries will pay excellent dividends indeed.

Careful attention to the selection and fitting of all gear and equipment will also minimize the probabilities of injury. Procuring the best equipment possible with the funds available should be considered a guiding rule. Good equipment, properly and carefully fitted, should be a guaranteed right of every athlete.

In instances in which it may be necessary for an injured athlete to enter into competition before complete healing has occurred, protective strapping can protect the injury and prevent further injury. In such instances careful consideration of all factors and medical consultation as necessary should precede any decisions.

Finally, the trainer should at all times be cognizant of the physical and psy-chological condition of the athletes under his care, both in and out of competition. Counseling in regard to adequate rest with proper nutrition and exercise, a carefully planned program of physical conditioning, and a good emotional climate will greatly enhance the odds in favor of accident prevention and/or reduction.

SYNTHETIC TURF

Artificial turf has been introduced by a number of companies who claim that their product offers a number of advantages over natural turf, especially in respect to the weather and use factor. Such synthetic turfs have been used for a number of seasons at all levels of competition. Professional football players have been especially critical of some facets of synthetic turf. They claim that skin burns incurred on such a surface are not only more severe than a corresponding burn from natural turf but are more liable to become infected and difficult to heal. Another serious criticism involves the surface applied as a base under the turf. This is often an asphalt compound, which lacks the resiliency of earth. Players claim that head contact, in spite of helmet protection, is more severe. A higher incidence of concussions seems to bear out this contention.

At the high school level the injury rate for artificial surfaces is considerably higher than for natural turf under all field conditions. The injury rate revealed under wet conditions is one third higher, and that incurred under dry field conditions is almost double the rate for natural turf.[15] Synthetic turf is currently undergoing intensive study and research. Improvements may soon be developed that will eliminate the above objections.

IMPLICATIONS

In recent years the number of injuries and fatalities resulting from participation in sports activities has increased steadily. There appears to be a general consensus among top trainers and coaches that the rate of injury can be substantially decreased by proper *preventive* measures. Appropriate and adequate conditioning and the careful fitting of athletic gear and equipment according to individual needs are prerequisites to injury prevention. In addition careful treatment and consideration of the injured athlete will assist greatly in preventing further injuries and in eliminating the dangers of permanent sequelae.

An athlete participates in sports because of his personal interest in the sport and his loyalty to the school. When he is sidelined because of injuries, he is neither deriving personal satisfaction nor benefiting his school. Hence, it is the obligation of the trainer to get him back into competition as soon as it is safely possible. The high school coach and the high school trainer share a mutual obligation in this respect. They should work closely with the school officials and/or the team physician in making their decisions.

According to clinical records, inadequate conditioning is a contributing factor in a high percentage of athletic injuries. The most dangerous period in any sport is the first 3 to 4 weeks of the season. Often the boys are somewhat overweight and generally out of good physical condition. In addition, their lack of familiarity with most fundamentals of the game results in their being awkward and therefore accident-prone in situations that have injury-provoking potential. Undoubtedly, the incidence of injury could be markedly reduced if the various conference and scholastic rules were modified or amended to permit a longer precompetition period devoted to physical conditioning. Such a provision would enable the trainer to prevent many of the injuries that now occur. The extension of the preseason period for the express purpose of conditioning the athlete should in no way be assumed to indicate a desire on our part to extend the competition season. Body contact, scrimmage, and other forms of all-out performance should be limited, by rules and careful regulation, to the last 2 weeks of the preseason period. By that time, assuming that from 3 to 4 weeks of carefully graded conditioning work has been carried on, the athlete is ready for more strenuous effort. By developing more strength, endurance, flexibility, and speed, he is able to meet and surmount accident-provoking situations, which perhaps a month earlier would have had serious implications. He is able to recuperate increasingly more rapidly and effectively from vigorous bouts of activity, and his reflexes have been sharpened and his general kinesthetic sense is more sharply defined. The increase of flexibility and range of joint motion, coupled with the strengthening of the supporting muscles, enables him to withstand more severe strain, impact, and twisting than he could have previously.

During the preseason period as well as during the regular season, strict adherence to the general principles underlying training must be observed. For this reason, knowing the important facts about the principles of use and disuse, intensity of use, alternation of rest and exercise, persistence, and drive is of the utmost concern to trainer and coach. Repetitive bouts of work that are progressively more concentrated induce permanent organic changes, which in turn enable the individual to perform more work and to do so more skillfully and efficiently.

REFERENCES

1. Woody, T.: Life and education in early societies, New York, 1949, The Macmillan Co.
2. Rice, E. A., Hutchinson, J. L., and Lee, M.: A brief history of physical education, New York, 1958, The Ronald Press Co.
3. Harris, H. A.: Greek athletes and athletics, London, 1964, Hutchinson & Co.
4. Vogt, M.: Die Olympische Spiele in Altertum, München. Med. Wschr. 30:1199, 1936.
5. Van Dalen, D. B., Mitchell, E. D., and Bennett, B. L.: A world history of physical education, Englewood Cliffs, N. J., 1956, Prentice-Hall, Inc.
6. Durant, W.: The life of Greece, New York, 1939, Simon & Schuster, Inc.
7. Morehouse, L. E., and Rasch, P. J.: Scientific basis of athletic training, Philadelphia, 1958, W. B. Saunders Co.
8. Durant, W.: Caesar and Christ, New York, 1944, Simon & Schuster, Inc.

9. Ryan, A. J.: The physician and exercise physiology. In Falls, H. B., editor: Exercise physiology, New York, 1968, Academic Press, Inc.

10. Larson, L., editor: Encyclopedia of sports medicine, New York, 1971, The Macmillan Co.

11. Blyth, C. S., and Arnold, D. C.: 40th annual survey of football fatalities, 1931-1971, 1971, American Football Coaches Association.

12. Robey, J. M., Blyth, C. S., and Mueller, F. O.: Athletic injuries; application of epidemiologic methods, J.A.M.A. **217**:184, 1971.

13. Reid, D. C., Cuthbertson, A. N., and Kelley, R. R.: World amateur wrestling championships (F. I. L. A.) injury report, J. Nat. Athl. Train. Ass. **5**:14, 1970.

14. Stenger, J. M., Lawson, E. A., Wright, J. M., and Ricketts, J.: Mouthguards, protection against shock to head, neck, and teeth, J. Amer. Dent. Soc. **69**:273, 1964.

15. Murphy, R. J.: The problem of environmental heat in athletics, Ohio Med. J. **59**:799, 1963.

16. Mathews, D. K.: Recognition and prevention of heat stroke, Mich. Osteopath. J. **31**:10, 1966.

17. Bramwell, S. T., and Garrick, J. G.: High school football injuries: a comparison of playing surfaces, Med. Sci. Sports **3**:s, 1971.

RECOMMENDED READINGS

Adkinson, J., and Garrick, J.: High school football injuries—a comparison of playing surfaces, Med. Sci. Sports **4**:62, 1972.

Clarke, K. S.: Calculated risk of sports fatalities, J.A.M.A. **197**:894, 1966.

Garrick, J., Requa, R. K., and Adkinson, J.: Traction, playing characteristics and injury rates on a synthetic turf field in college football, Med. Sci. Sports **4**:62, 1972.

Haddon, W., Jr.: Principles in research on the effects of sports on health, J.A.M.A. **197**:163, 1966.

Quigley, T. B.: Contributions of sports to medicine, J.A.M.A. **197**:161, 1966.

CHAPTER 2

The trainer: qualifications and relationships

Athletic training involves a great deal more than a knowledge of bandaging techniques, first aid, and conditioning and reconditioning procedures. To conduct an efficient training program, the trainer must also have a knowledge of certain organizational and operational procedures relating to staff relationships, legal implications, budgeting, record keeping, and insurance—to mention a few.

The trainer functions in an unusual situation. Whereas a coach may handle a group of athletes in a specific sport, the trainer deals with all athletes, engaged in all sports, throughout the regular school year. Since athletes usually begin practice immediately following cessation of the daily class schedule, the trainer gets his peak load at that time. On game days there is an additional load—the climate of anticipation, which tends to augment any tension that may usually exist.

To be able to cope with the many complexities that confront him the trainer must develop sound administrative procedures as well as efficient patterns of organization—each based on the cooperative efforts of a number of individuals and on the various factors that are involved in a good training program. Success or failure of the program will be determined by factors such as the type, location, and supervision of the training facilities; the education, professional background, ethics, and experience of the trainer and his assistants; the relationship that exists among trainer, physician, coach, athletes, and other ancillary personnel; and, above all, the trainer's ability to "run a taut ship." Careful organization and planning tend to minimize the number of administrative procedures required and to reduce the many conflicts that can and do arise. The ability of the trainer to earn and retain the respect of coach and athletes reflects his ability in establishing a sound philosophy of training and conditioning, thereby enabling the formulation of policies that will best effect a mutually recognized objective—achieving that which is best for the athlete in terms of preparation for competition, treatment and care of athletic injuries, and reconditioning.

QUALIFICATIONS OF THE TRAINER
Educational preparation

Both educators and the public have become increasingly aware that the conditioning and training of athletes involve much more than simply applying an ankle wrap or administering first aid. With this awareness has come a demand for trainers thoroughly educated and qualified in all phases of the field. Today the trainer is expected to be a college graduate, usually with a major in physical education and emphasis in the area of rehabilitation or a major in physical therapy. If, in addition, he is a certified physical therapist (C.P.T.), he is better qualified and consequently much sought after.

Full-time trainers are usually added to the staff in colleges and junior colleges, whereas the coach generally doubles as trainer at the high school level. There is, however, a decided trend toward employing capable trainers as faculty members in the high school athletic program to serve, as coaches do, in a dual capacity—as teachers of physical education or some other discipline during the regular school day and as trainers in the after-school program. In all probability this trend will continue in the larger school districts.

The awareness of the American Medical Association, the American College of Sports Medicine, the National Athletic Trainers Association, and school administrators in general of the need for better conditioning and training procedures for athletes acts as an incentive, and in recent years both the quality and the quantity of athletic training have shown considerable improvements. A great deal of credit is due the National Athletic Trainers Association for its efforts to improve the standards of training. By formulating and observing a code of ethics and establishing high standards for members, by working continually to improve the amount and quality of professional educational preparation, and by maintaining keen interest and a desire to keep abreast of modern de-velopments, the Association has done much to elevate the profession of training from what was once a rather dubious avocation to the respected status it now enjoys.[1]

Probably a majority of the trainers now serving at the high school level have had most of their undergraduate training in the field of physical education, have a reasonably good basic background in the life sciences, and have had courses in physiology of exercise, kinesiology, and the prevention and care of athletic injuries. However, at the college level there is an increasing trend to hire as trainers those individuals who have completed one of the following programs:

1. Undergraduate major in physical education, science, or nursing with 1 to 1½ years of postgraduate work in an acceptable school of physical therapy
2. Undergraduate degree in physical therapy or certification by a school that meets the standards set forth by the Council on Medical Education and Hospitals of the American Medical Association (In this instance an individual may graduate with a bachelor's degree in physical therapy and then complete the additional work required to obtain certification as a physical therapist.)
3. NATA Approved Program completed at a college or university approved for offering such a program

---

NATA approved educational program*

In the NATA approved program of education, the athlete trainer should be encouraged to act as liaison with the departments of physical education and student health. The program includes a major study in physical education and necessary courses required by the states for a teaching license. Also entered in the degree program are prerequisites for entry to schools of physical therapy as suggested by the American Physical Therapy Association. The basic minimal requirements as recommended by NATA are as follows:

*Reprinted by permission of the National Athletic Trainers Association, Lafayette, Ind.

NATA approved educational program—cont'd

I. A major study including teaching license in physical education and/or health variable, by states
    A. Total of 24 semester hours in laboratory physical, biological, and social sciences
        1. Biology—zoology (anatomy and physiology)—8 hours
        2. Physics and/or chemistry—6 hours
        3. Social sciences (at least 6 hours of psychology)—10 hours
    B. Electives strongly advised
        1. Additional biological and social sciences
        2. Physical education, such as group activities, dancing, etc.
        3. Hygiene
        4. Speech
II. Specific required courses (if not included in I, these must be added)
    A. Anatomy—one or more courses including human anatomy
    B. Physiology—circulation, respiration, digestion, excretion, nerves, brain, and sense organs
    C. Physiology of exercise
    D. Applied anatomy and kinesiology—the muscles: emphasis on their functions in and development for specific activities
    E. Laboratory physical science—six semester hours in physics and/or chemistry, including principles of chemistry
    F. Psychology—six semester hours including personality, intelligence, emotion, memory, thinking, attention, perception, learning
    G. Coaching techniques—nine semester hours
        1. Include football, basketball, and track
        2. Recommend baseball, soccer, wrestling, plus preferred sports by geographic areas
    H. First aid and safety—minimum of Red Cross First Aid
    I. Nutrition and foods
        1. Basic principles of nutrition
        2. Basic diet and special diet
    J. Remedial exercise—exercise for typical and/or temporary and permanent handicaps
    K. Organization and administration of health and physical education programs
    L. Personal and community hygiene
    M. Techniques of athletic training—basic, general course (acceptable course for all coaches)
    N. Advanced techniques of athletic training—special course for athletic training candidates with full academic background
    O. Laboratory practices—six semester hours credit or equivalent work
III. Recommended courses
    A. General physics
    B. Pharmacology—specific side effects of drugs
    C. Histology—tissues and methods of studying them
    D. Pathology—laboratory study of tissues in pathological condition

Personal qualities

The personal qualities of a trainer, not the facilities and equipment, determine his success. Personal qualities may be thought of as the many characteristics that identify the individual in regard to his actions and reactions as a member of society. Personality is a complex of the many characteristics that together give an image of the individual to those with whom he associates. The personal qualities of a trainer are most important since he, in turn, works with many complicated and diverse personalities. Although no attempt has been made to establish a rank order, the qualities discussed in the following paragraphs are essential if one desires to be a good trainer.

Health. Good health is an absolute necessity for the trainer. The work requires abundant energy and vitality. Long, arduous hours of strenuous work will sap the reserve strength of a trainer who is not in the best of health. The trainer must also set an example for his athletes by personally adhering to the rules of good health. Sufficient rest, suitable relaxation, and proper diet will do much toward establishing and maintaining a good level of health.

Sense of fair play. The ethics of training demand that fairness and justice be maintained at all times. A trainer cannot allow himself to become discriminatory in his treatment of athletes. All should be treated on an equal basis regardless of race, color, or creed. A sense of fair play and justice goes a long way toward establishing harmonious relationships.

Maturity and emotional stability. The ability to get along with others and to act properly under duress or pressure is a measure of emotional stability and maturity. A trainer is subjected to much stress and emotional pressure. During the period of competition he moves and works in an atmosphere of constant tenseness. Consequently he must exhibit good self-control at all times. By setting an example he exerts a calming effect on those about him. There is no place in his field for pettiness or immaturity.

Good appearance. "Your appearance as you pass by is your only message to most of the world." This maxim, old though it may be, has never lost its timeliness. It contains considerable truth.

Neatness and cleanliness of person and dress should be the trademark of the trainer. Personal cleanliness, including care of the nails and scalp, should be observed at all times. The cleanliness and sanitation of the facilities and equipment make it imperative that the trainer himself not be remiss in matters of his own cleanliness.

In addition, a clean uniform consisting of a white tee shirt, white duck or drill trousers, and soft crepe- or ripple-soled shoes should be worn. When he is outdoors, a jacket, usually in school colors and with the word TRAINER sewed or embossed across the back may be worn for easy identification. The tee shirt may also bear the word TRAINER over the left breast. If the trainer is a member of the National Athletic Trainers Association, the emblem of that organization may be worn over the left breast or sewed onto the right shoulder of the jacket.

The trainer should also keep in excellent physical condition. If he carelessly permits himself to become excessively overweight or develops a pronounced abdominal ptosis or other manifestations of poor posture, he does not reflect the principles he teaches, nor does he engender trust and confidence among his pupils.

Leadership. The trainer must be a dynamic individual who can lead and motivate those with whom he works, as well as those whom he serves. He must work cooperatively with many people, being able to express his opinions and views without being dogmatic. He must be able to accept, understand, and weigh the views and opinions of others and to transform the abilities of his co-workers into an organized, harmonious whole. Above all, he must be decisive. An equivocal attitude has no place in the training room or on the field where quick, shrewd decisions based on experience and education must be made. Procrastination could prove to be dangerous.

Compassion. Competence must be coupled with compassion—the ability to feel pity for the suffering or distress of others with a real desire to help alleviate such suffering. Empathy combined with compassion for those under his care are qualities that the competent trainer must possess.

Intellectual capacity. In a broad sense intellectual capacity may be defined as the ability to deal with the many problems of life, including those encountered in one's work. It denotes one's ability to adapt himself to constant change, to keep up, as it were, with the times. Consequently, the trainer should possess a lively intellectual curiosity both within and outside his field, which stimulates him to do considerable reading in professional and allied journals and books and to experiment and research in his area. More research concerning athletic injuries is greatly needed, and the trainer is in an ideal position to initiate and to carry through intensive and long-range programs. Many questions still need to be answered.

Sense of humor. Many athletes rate having a sense of humor as the most important attribute of the trainer. The ability to relax others by means of humor and wit is indeed an important asset and can serve to release much of the tension that builds up, particularly prior to competition. An affable trainer who possesses enthusiasm and optimism can do much toward developing a favorable emotional climate in the training quarters.

Kindness and understanding. Among the many traits that a successful trainer possesses, those of being considerate, tactful, and understanding rank high. Athletes often have emotional problems that require understanding, sympathy, and tact on the part of the trainer. A firm belief in athletics and in his own ability to contribute will aid the trainer in solving or ameliorating such problems. At times he functions *in loco parentis,* that is, in lieu of the parent, and must act as both father and confessor in attempting to help the athlete solve his problems. A willingness to listen often goes a long way toward solving many of the problems that arise. Altruism is one virtue a trainer must possess. Unselfishness of time and self is a requisite for becoming a good trainer.

Competence and responsibility. When one speaks of competence, a number of desirable characteristics are implied. A trainer inspires confidence through a quiet competence—knowing what to do, when to do it, how to do it, and then doing it properly and effectively. Self-confidence is a quality that he must exhibit if he expects others to have confidence in him. Versatility in his profession is yet another index of competence. Competence is based upon good scholarship, technical knowledge, and the ability to apply what has been learned.

A competent trainer is a responsible person. He is answerable morally and legally for the discharge of his duties, and he possesses the capacity to perceive the distinctions between right and wrong actions. The competent trainer strives continually for perfection and excellence.

Philosophy. The sum of one's experiences is reflected in one's philosophy. A person's beliefs and his reactions to the world about him reflect his philosophy of life. In addition to a sound philosophy of life, the trainer should possess a good philosophy regarding athletics and the training of athletes. He must believe in what he is doing and must feel that what he is doing has value and serves a purpose—that he is making a vital contribution toward achieving the desired goal. He must be aware that he is dealing with young people and that what he says and does has a part in shaping their philosophies. He functions as confidant, teacher, and friend. If he cannot subscribe to these beliefs and attitudes, he fails both himself and those whom he serves.

DUTIES OF THE TRAINER

The trainer's responsibilities are varied.[2] They are not confined to emergency first-aid treatment and rehabilitation alone but ramify into a number of areas in which he has specific duties, including the following:

1. Working cooperatively with the coaches in setting up and carrying out a program of conditioning for athletes
2. Administering first aid to injured athletes on the field, in the gymnasium, or in the training room
3. Applying protective or injury-preventive devices, such as strapping, bandaging, or braces
4. Working cooperatively with and under the direction of the physician in respect to:
   a. Reconditioning procedures
   b. Operation of therapeutic devices and equipment
   c. Fitting of braces, guards, and other devices
   d. Referrals to the physician, health services, or hospital
5. Working cooperatively with the coaches and the physician in selecting protective athletic equipment and gear and in checking it for safety
6. Supervising the training room, which includes the requisitioning and storage of supplies and equipment, keeping adequate records, maintaining a standing and running inventory, and maintaining an annual budget
7. Supervising and, when necessary, instructing assistant trainers and other staff members under his jurisdiction
8. Counseling and advising athletes and coaches on matters pertaining to conditioning and training, such as diet, rest, reconditioning
9. Conducting himself at all times as a responsible professional person

PROFESSIONAL RELATIONSHIPS
Faculty status and relationships

The trainer is usually a member of either the athletic staff or the physical education staff. At the high school level, as a rule, he is employed as a teacher of one of the school disciplines and performs his training duties on a part-time or an extracurricular basis. He is usually compensated on the same basis as the coaches, that is, in terms of additional release time or a set stipend, on either a semester or a yearly basis. He is considered a bona fide member of the school's faculty and functions accordingly. At the college level, however, his status varies considerably from institution to institution, depending upon the philosophy and the size of the school. Among the smaller colleges and in some states that have enacted legislation to this effect, he is employed in a dual capacity as physical education teacher and trainer. This type of situation commonly prevails where athletics function as a department within the division or school of physical education.

In most colleges and universities, however, athletics is divorced from physical education, and functions as a separate entity. The duties, employment, and release of coaches and trainers generally has no connection with the activities of the teaching faculty. The financing of the athletic program, including salaries, is customarily accomplished through the use of student body and alumnae funds, which may or may not be supplemented by school or tax funds. In such cases the trainer is a member of the athletic staff and functions on a full-time basis with no other duties. He is not usually considered a member of the school's instructional faculty.

Regardless of his status in the school system, the trainer should enjoy good relationships with all of his colleagues. He must develop rapport not only with his assistants and the athletes whom he serves but also with the coaches, the school health personnel, and above all the team physician. He should also make it a point to get around campus and become acquainted with other faculty members and workers and not isolate himself in his own bailiwick. In this way a good understanding of both his work and himself will be engendered, and when problems or needs arise, he will find them easier to solve or fulfill because of a more sympathetic attitude and knowledge on the part of others not necessarily in direct contact with the program.

Good public relations is a vital responsibility of all trainers.

Since the trainer works closely with the coaches, it is necessary that he develop an awareness and an insight into their problems so that he can function as effectively as possible. He must develop tolerance and patience and must earn the respect of the coaches so that his judgment in all matters pertaining to his areas of qualification is fully accepted. In turn, he must avoid questioning the sagacity or abilities of the coaches in their particular fields and must restrict his opinions to those areas in which he is specifically qualified.

Medical personnel relationships

The trainer has administrative and working relationships with the school nurse, members of the school health services program, and the team physician. All these have responsibilities, direct and indirect, connected with the athletic program, and it is well for the trainer to be familiar with the place of each in the program and the relationships of each to the trainer. These relationships and responsibilities must be clearly defined.

The nurse. As a rule, the nurse is not responsible for the recognition of athletic injuries. Her training and background, however, render her quite capable in the recognition of skin diseases, infections, and minor irritations. She works under the direction of the physician and in liaison with the athletic trainer and the school health services.

School health services. Colleges and universities maintain school health services that range from a department operating with one or two nurses and a physician available on a part-time basis, to an elaborate setup comprised of a full complement of nursing services with a staff of full-time medical specialists and complete laboratory and hospital facilities. At the high school level the health services are usually organized so that one or two nurses conduct the program under the direction of the school physician, who may serve

a number of schools in a given area or district. This poses a problem, since it is often difficult to have qualified medical help at hand when it is needed. Local policy will determine the procedure of referral for medical care. If such policies be lacking, the trainer should see to it that an effective method is established for handling all athletes requiring medical care or opinion.

The team physician. The team physician must have absolute authority in determining the physical fitness of an athlete who wishes to participate in the athletic program.[3] He is the final authority in the determination of whether or not an athlete should be permitted to take part in a given sports activity and when, following injury, he should be allowed to reenter competition. The physician's judgment must be based not only upon his medical knowledge but also upon his knowledge of the psychophysiological demands of the sport. For this reason he must be familiar with the elements of intensity, duration, or speed that prevail in the various activities.

It is most desirable that the team physician serve as the athlete's physician in every respect. He must be cognizant of the entire health pattern, including the psychological makeup of the athlete, and should be in a position to advise or treat him for any and all conditions or illnesses whether or not they are directly related to the sport.

When a physician is asked to serve in the capacity of team physician, arrangements must be made with the educational institution employing him as to the specific responsibilities of each. Policies must be established regarding emergency care, legal liability, facilities, personnel relationships, and duties. The physician must work cooperatively with the trainer and the coach in planning a training program for the prevention of athletic injuries, as well as for reconditioning following injury. If it is not possible for the team physician to be in attendance at all practice sessions and competitive events or games, it is sometimes possible to establish a plan of rotation involving a number of physicians. In this plan any one physician need be present at only one or two activities a year. The rotational plan has proved to be quite practical in situations where the school district is unable to afford a full-time physician or has so limited a budget that it must ask for volunteer medical coverage. In some instances the attending physician is paid a per game stipend.

Effective prevention and treatment of athletic injuries require both diagnostic and therapeutic equipment. The physician should have access to x-ray equipment and physical therapy facilities and should avail himself of as many other aids as possible, including a fluoroscope, an oscillometer, and an electrocardiograph, a telemeter, and for use in some sports (e.g., football, wrestling, boxing, and hockey, in which head injuries are not uncommon) an electroencephalograph.

Summary of the team physician's responsibilities. The team physician's various duties and responsibilities may be summarized as follows:

1. To see that a complete medical history of each athlete is compiled and is readily available
2. To conduct the physical examinations
3. To act in a supervisory capacity toward the trainer and the nurse
4. To act, when necessary, as an instructor to the trainer in respect to orientation and instruction in special therapeutic modalities, therapeutic problems, and allied procedures
5. To be in attendance at all games, athletic contests, scrimmages, and practices; if this is not feasible, to arrange for attendance by other qualified medical personnel; when personal attendance is not possible, to be available for emergency call
6. To decide when, on medical grounds, athletes should be disqualified from participation and when they may be permitted to reenter competition
7. To serve as an advisor to the trainer and the coach and, when necessary, as a counselor to the athlete
8. To work closely with the school administrator, the school dentist, the trainer, the coach, and the health services to promote and maintain consistently high standards for the care of the athlete

The team dentist. The role of the team dentist is somewhat analogous to that of the team physician. He serves as dental consultant for the team and should be available for first-aid and emergency care. Heintz[4] indicates that there are three areas of responsibility for the team dentist: (1) he must organize and carry out the preseason dental examination, (2) he must be available to provide emergency care when needed, and (3) he must conduct the mouth protector program.

PHYSICAL EXAMINATION OF PROSPECTIVE ATHLETES

The trainer and physician work closely together for the development of a program for the prevention of athletic injuries and the conditioning of the athlete. This program is based on the thorough examination of the athlete by the physician.[5]

The physical examination must serve as a screening device that permits only those who are physically and psychologically fit in all respects to enter into athletic competition. The various cardiovascular, neurological, orthopedic, and respiratory anomalies or irregularities that may be aggravated by athletic participation or may predispose the participant to injury should be considered disqualifying conditions. Overweight and underweight athletes should be given instructions for correcting their respective weight problems.

Postural or orthopedic conditions that may prove to be a handicap or predispose the participant to injury in a particular sports activity are often revealed during an examination.[6] In some such instances participation in another sport in which the condition will not present a serious problem is recommended. In other instances the condition may prove to be sufficiently serious to warrant a declaration of ineligibility to participate in any sports activity.[7] Individuals can often participate successfully in certain sports even though they may possess some organic anomaly. The physician is the judge as to the type of activity in which the athlete may participate and any limitations necessary within this activity. If, in the physician's considered professional judgment, participation presents certain hazards or may prove deleterious to the health of the athlete, either at the present or in the future, he will disqualify him. The trainer and coach must learn to accept such decisions as being made in terms of what is best for the athlete.

Obtaining a complete medical history should be the first step of the physical examination. Following this, a thorough physical examination, including a careful check of the cardiovascular, respiratory, musculoskeletal, and central nervous systems, should be made (see Appendix B). Care and thoroughness should prevail. Unfortunately, sometimes only a perfunctory examination, limited to cardiac auscultation and a check for inguinal hernia, is made. School administrators and the public must be made aware of the necessity for a thorough and complete physical examination of all prospective participants in school athletic programs.

Because of the hazard in all sports—especially football, track, and baseball—immunization against tetanus should be provided for each player at the time of examination.

Examination of the chest and lungs. The chest and lungs should be examined by means of inspection, palpation, percussion, and auscultation. The general shape and size of the chest, any deformities, any growths or tumors, the distribution of hair, and the condition of the glands are noted. The pulse rate and blood pressure are checked, and the veins are examined to determine the presence of varicosities. The respiratory movements are observed, and the rate and character of respiration noted. By palpation the chest wall is examined for respiratory and cardiac anomalies.

Through percussion (tapping) some abnormal chest conditions can be noted and identified and the size, shape, and position of the heart determined. By means of a stethoscope (auscultation) the examiner carefully listens to the breath sounds (respiratory murmurs) to detect any abnormal or pathological sounds. He then listens to the heart, observing any modifications in sound, intensity, or rhythm. When examining the high school athlete, the physician should be alert to any heart murmurs that may be present. These murmurs may be either functional or organic. Functional murmurs often will disappear as a result of exercise. Organic murmurs are caused by some abnormality in structure resulting from either congenital malformation or disease and usually affect the valves. Exercise will cause an organic murmur to become more pronounced. In the adolescent, heart murmur may signify either incomplete closing of the valves (valvular insufficiency) or narrowing of the valves (stenosis). Organic murmurs are often a residual of rheumatic fever. Many times, detectable heart murmurs found in the adolescent are idiopathic and disappear as the individual advances toward maturity.

Gallagher-Brouha step test: The Gallagher-Brouha step test[8] or similar tests should be given to all examinees and the return of the heart rate and blood pressure to pretest levels carefully noted. Following rehabilitation, the step test may also be used for determining the athlete's fitness to return to competition. The test is easily administered. The subject steps on and off of an 18-inch platform at the rate of thirty times a minute for a total of 4 minutes. Pulse rates are then taken during recovery at 30 seconds, 1 minute, 2 minutes, and 3 minutes. The index is computed as follows:

$$\frac{\text{Duration of exercise in seconds} \times 100}{2 \times \text{Sum of any three pulse rates in recovery}}$$

An athlete scoring 65 or less is unfit for activity. The higher the index the more fit the individual may be assumed to be. Scoring tables have been devised for both high school boys and girls. If at all possible, all athletes should have an electrocardiogram. If this is not feasible, then all potential athletes who have a history of any cardiac anomaly or whose examinations have indicated possible cardiac malfunction should have one.

Examination of the trunk. Using inspection, palpation, and percussion, the examiner notes the size and shape of the trunk, the distribution of hair, the amount of fat present, and the presence of any anomalies of the genitalia, dilated veins, growths, and muscle spasm. He further explores for tenderness, which may be indicative of strains or bruises, enteritis, or appendicitis. He also checks for an enlarged liver or spleen and for hernia.

Abdominal hernias are not uncommon in athletic persons, and the examiner looks carefully for their presence. The protrusion of some of the internal structures through the abdominal wall indicates a hernia, and the name of the hernia is derived from its location.

The most common hernia in males is the inguinal hernia. It occurs at the inguinal canal, located at the extreme lower border of the abdomen. The canal, which lies immediately above the inguinal (Poupart's) ligament and functions as a passageway for the spermatic cord in the male, forms a weak place in the abdominal wall. Weak abdominal musculature, injury, or excessive intra-abdominal pressures, such as those resulting from lifting a heavy object, will predispose a person to hernia. An inguinal hernia may be either direct or indirect. In a direct hernia the intestine protrudes directly through the muscles and into the canal, whereas in the indirect it enters the canal at the internal abdominal ring and follows the course of the spermatic cord.

Femoral hernia, which is more prevalent among women than men, occurs at the femoral ring, an opening in the groin, approximately ½ inch in diameter or usually larger in females, located just below the inguinal ligaments. Femoral hernia is not a particularly common type of hernia.

The rectal area should be inspected for hemorrhoids and cysts (e.g., the pilonidal cyst).

Examination of the head and neck. Examination of the head and neck areas is confined principally to observation for the presence of oral infections, sinus infections (not unusual among athletes), and any abnormal skin, eye, ear, nose, or throat conditions. The eyes are examined and, if practicable, a hearing test is given.

Examination of the mouth. The preseason dental examination can be performed by the team dentist, by a group of school or dental association designated dentists, or by the family dentist. Cases of mouth pathology such as broken teeth, teeth with cavities, or infections should be screened and remedial measures undertaken.

Selection and fitting of the mouth guard can also be done at this time. Athletes with mouth pathology should not be fitted until the mouth has returned to health. Those with mouth anomalies such as cleft palate and those wearing orthodontic appliances, dentures, or bridgework will require special attention. Properly fitted mouth guards will virtually eliminate broken or chipped teeth and will do much toward obviating head or neck injuries.[4,9]

Body structure. Body structure is a definite factor in the degree of efficiency and the level of success an athlete attains. Studies have shown that certain types of body build have definite advantages over other types in certain sports.

Adolescents who are gross in body bulk are often selected to participate in activities that tax them well beyond their physical capacities. However, because their muscles and bones have not yet developed the strength and maturity necessary to adequately meet excessive stresses or above-normal physical demands, boys of this type are prone to serious injury, particularly to the skeletal system, since the epiphysial growth centers can be seriously damaged. Orthopedists often express concern over the tendency of some coaches and physical education teachers to place such individuals in situations in which excessive weight-support demands are placed upon them or in which they are subjected to severe physical contact. Trainers and coaches must be careful never to overmatch an adolescent. Competition kept within the scope of the boy's physical abilities will produce wholesome results, whereas overmatching or placing them in situations for which they are not physically ready can lead to trauma that may have serious permanent consequences.

REFERENCES

1. National Athletic Trainers Association: Constitution and by-laws, Code of Ethics, Palo Alto, Calif.
2. Noonan, J. E., and Reichel, J.: Trainers speak up, Medicine in Sports (Rystan Co.), p. 1, April, 1964.
3. Committee on the Medical Aspects of Sports: Protecting the health of the high school athlete, American Medical Association, 1965.
4. Heintz, W. D.: New man on the team, Medicine in Sports (Rystan Co.), p. 4, April, 1961.
5. Ryan, A. J.: Survey shows up lack of physical exams, J. Nat. Trainers Ass., p. 24, Sept., 1965.
6. Lowman, C. L.: Effects of postural deviations on athletic performance, Proceedings of the Fourth National Conference on the Medical Aspects of Sports, Chicago, 1962, American Medical Association, pp. 8-13.
7. Miles, J. S.: Medical basis for restriction from athletic competition—orthopaedic viewpoint, Proceedings of the Third National Conference on the Medical Aspects of Sports, Chicago, 1961, American Medical Association, pp. 29-30.
8. Mathews, D. K.: Measurement in physical education, Philadelphia, 1963, W. B. Saunders Co.
9. Brotman, I. N., and Rothschild, H. L.: Common dental conditions you should recognize, J. Nat. Trainers Ass. 7:12, 1972.
10. Stenger, J. M., Lawson, E. A., and Wright, J. M.: Mouthguards—protection against shock to head, neck, and teeth, J. Amer. Dent. Ass. 69:273, 1964.

RECOMMENDED READINGS

Bucher, C. A.: Administration of school health and physical education programs, St. Louis, 1967, The C. V. Mosby Co.

Committee on the Medical Aspects of Sports: Protecting the health of the high school athlete, Chicago, 1966, American Medical Association.

Glazer, N.: The physician and the high school football team, Family Physician 5:41, 1963.

Guenther, D.: Problems involving legal liability in schools, J. Amer. Ass. Health, Physical Ed. and Rec. 20:511, 1949.

Hirata, I., Jr.: The doctor and the athlete, Philadelphia, 1968, J. B. Lippincott Co.

La Cava, G.: The value of clinical examination in athletes, J. Sport Med. 2:63, 1962.

O'Donoghue, D. H.: Treatment of injuries to the athlete, ed. 2, Philadelphia, 1970, W. B. Saunders Co.

Reiheld, R. E.: The high school team physician, Proceedings of the Seventh National Conference on the Medical Aspects of Sports, Chicago, 1965, American Medical Association, pp. 50-51.

Schrode, P. F.: The athlete with a chronic condition, J.A.M.A. 197:167, 1966.

Sheldon, W. H., and others: The varieties of human physique, New York, 1940, Harper & Bros.

CHAPTER 3

The trainer: responsibilities

LEGAL IMPLICATIONS IN SCHOOL ATHLETICS

In recent years negligence suits against teachers, coaches, trainers, school officials, and physicians because of sports injuries have increased both in frequency and in the amount of damages awarded.[1] Based on National Safety Council estimates, well over 300,000 accidental injuries have occurred to pupils in elementary and secondary school physical education classes in the school year 1968–1969.[2] An increasing awareness of the many risk factors present in physical activities has had an effect upon the coach and trainer, in particular. A great deal more care is now taken in following coaching and training procedures that conform to the legal guidelines governing legal liability. Therefore, both the athlete and the coach and trainer are more adequately protected.

Inasmuch as athletic training is an auxiliary function of medicine in many respects, many pertinent legal factors are involved.[3,4] The legal liability of the athletic trainer is not always well defined or thoroughly understood. Frequently the trainer or trainer-coach must perform the training duties without the benefit of medical supervision. In such situations he is well advised to confine his duties to routine bandaging and first-aid procedures that can be performed in the absence of a physician. When the nature of athletic training is such that it involves the use of techniques or modalities that require either special training or medical direction a number of legal implications come into play, and it is well that the trainer be cognizant of these before proceeding.

Medical diagnoses, as such, may only be made by a medical doctor, and any final decisions regarding such diagnoses are his alone to make. There is a fine line indeed between the recognition of an injury and its diagnosis. Debating this difference serves no useful purpose other than to further confound the distinction. In situations in which time is of the essence, as is often the case in athletic injuries, the ability to evaluate quickly, accurately, and decisively is of vital importance. In such situations the trainer or coach must remain within the limits of his ability and training and must act in full accord with professional ethics. Complete understanding of what constitutes the framework within which he can safely operate is of paramount importance if he is to avoid pitfalls that may make him legally liable.

Liability is defined in several ways, all of which state in one way or another that it is the legal responsibility of a person in a certain situation to do a particular thing in a reasonable manner; failure to perform such action in a prudent and reasonable manner makes him legally liable for the results of said action. In most cases in which the charge has been negligence the key has been to compare the actions of a hypothetical, reasonably prudent, athletic trainer to the actions of the defendant. This is done to ascertain if the course of action followed by the defendant was in conformity with the judgment exercised by such a reasonably prudent person.[5] The key phrase has been "reasonable care." A trainer who holds certification in any of the ancillary medical services such as physical therapy is in a stronger position, since not only is he trained in the use of the various modalities and techniques, but he also has a more legitimate claim to use these aids under the law than does the trainer who lacks such certification.

Variations in some phases of the interpretation of liability exist among the various states and countries. In most states in this country the rule concept that school districts are not liable for the negligence of their agents while at the same time they act in a governmental capacity in the absence of a statute expressly imposing such liability seems to be well established.[2] This concept has been increasingly challenged in recent years but still holds in most states. The doctrine of immunity in some states has been extended to the university but not to private schools and colleges.[6]

The courts generally acknowledge that hazards are present in athletics through the concept of "assumption of risk." In other words, the individual either by expressed or implied agreement assumes the danger and hence relieves the other individual of legal responsibility to protect him; by so doing he agrees to take his own chances.[7] This concept, however, is subject to many and varied interpretations in the courts. This is particularly true when a minor is involved, since he is not considered able to render a mature judgment about the risks inherent in the situation. Although athletes participating in an athletic program are considered to assume a normal risk this in no way exempts those in charge from exercising reasonable care and prudence in the conduct of such activities or from foreseeing

and taking precautionary measures against accident-provoking circumstances.

The trainer may be held accountable for injuries or accidents resulting from the following:

1. *Torts:* These are legal wrongs that *legal* scholars have considerable difficulty in defining with exactitude. For our purposes a *tort* is defined as legal wrongs, other than breach of contract, for which a court will provide a remedy in the form of damages.[7] Such wrongs may emanate from an act of "omission," wherein the individual fails to carry out a legal duty, or from an act of "commission," wherein he commits an act that is not legally his to perform. In either instance, if injury results, the person can be held liable. In the first case a trainer may fail to carry out a treatment procedure after he has been instructed to do so by a physician. In the second the trainer may attempt to perform minor surgery not within his legal province and from which serious medical complications later develop.

2. *Negligence:* The tort concept of negligence is held by the courts when it is shown that an individual (1) does something that a reasonably prudent person would not do or (2) fails to do something that a reasonably prudent person would do under circumstances similar to those shown by the evidence. Negligence is the failure to use ordinary or reasonable care—care that persons of ordinary prudence would exercise in order to avoid injury to themselves or to others under similar circumstances. The standard as set up takes cognizance of the fact that the individual is neither the exceptionally skillful individual nor is he the extraordinarily cautious one, but rather a person of *reasonable* and *ordinary* prudence. Put another way, it is expected that the individual will bring a common sense approach to the situation at hand and will exercise due care in his handling of it. A case in point might be a training situation in which the trainer, through improper or careless handling of a therapeutic agent, seriously burns an athlete. Another illustra-

tion, occurring all too often in athletics, is one in which a trainer or coach moves a possibly seriously injured athlete from the field of play to permit activity to continue and does so either in an improper manner or before consulting those qualified to know the proper course of action. Should a serious or disabling injury be the result, the trainer or coach has made himself liable to suit.

Knowingly using dangerous or faulty equipment is another type of negligence for which the trainer can be held accountable should an accident result from such use. No equipment is 100% infallible in terms of safety. Never should a trainer or coach state or in any way indicate that a particular piece of equipment is absolutely safe or foolproof or incapable of producing injury, either directly or as an accessory to the fact. If injury in any way results from such equipment and a statement has been made indicating the absolute safety of the equipment, an implied liability could result.

It is expected that a person possessing more training in a given field or area will possess a correspondingly higher level of competence than, for example, will a student. An individual will therefore be judged in terms of his performance in any situation in which legal liability may be assessed. It must be recognized that liability, per se, in all of its various aspects, is not assessed at a universal level nationally but varies in interpretation from state to state and from area to area. It is therefore well to know and acquire the level of competence expected in your particular area.

Summary of legal implications. To safeguard both athlete and trainer the following suggestions are given:

1. Establish and maintain qualified and adequate supervision of the training room, its environs, facilities, and equipment at all times.

2. Exercise extreme caution in the distribution of pills, tablets, and medications at all times. In interscholastic situations age is a definite factor inasmuch as the athlete is a minor. Proper clearance for dispensing

pharmaceutics of any kind must be obtained.

3. Use only those therapeutic methods that you are qualified to use. Certain modalities, by law, must be used only under the direction or supervision of a physician.

4. Do not prescribe except in terms of your own training and limitations.

5. Do not use or permit the presence of faulty or hazardous equipment.

6. Work cooperatively with the coach and the team physician in the selection and use of athletic protective equipment and insist that the best be obtained.

7. Do not permit injured players to participate unless cleared by the team physician. Players suffering a head injury should not be permitted to reenter the game. In some states a player who has suffered a concussion may not continue in the sport for the balance of the season.

8. Do not, under any circumstances, give a local anesthetic to enable an injured player to continue participation. It is dangerous, as well as unethical.

9. Develop an understanding with the coaches that an injured athlete will not be allowed to reenter competition until, in the opinion of the team physician or the trainer, he is mentally and physically able. Do not permit yourself to be pressured to clear an athlete until he is fully cleared by the physician.

10. Follow the expressed orders of the team physician at all times.

11. Make it a point to become familiar with the health and medical history of the athletes under your care so you will be aware of those particular problems an athlete may have that could present a need for additional care or caution on your part.

12. Use common sense.

On-field procedures. The trainer's duties and responsibilities are not confined to the training room but extend to the gymnasium and the athletic field as well. Most injuries occur during games or contests, and devising a proper and legal procedure for the on-the-spot handling of game or competition injuries is a joint responsibility of the team physician, the coach, the administrator, and the trainer. It may be advisable to have the county or district attorney's office check the procedures that you plan to establish to determine whether or not they comply with all legal requirements. Following an approved, standard policy for taking care of athletes injured during competition or practice is sound not only from a legal standpoint but also from the standpoint of therapeutic management. Following are some suggestions that can be used as a basis for establishing standard procedures to be followed by a trainer when an accident occurs and no physician is present.

1. Make an immediate preliminary examination to ascertain the seriousness, type, and extent of the injury.

2. If the injury is recognized as being beyond the scope of your ability, send for the physician immediately.

3. Give first aid if it is indicated.

4. Should the condition of the player be such that he requires removal from the area, determine whether he is in a condition that would warrant medical sanction before attempting to move him. If the player is unconscious or is unable to move under his own power with assistance, use a stretcher. The trainer and his assistants should know the proper methods of transporting injured persons.

5. In some contact sports, particularly football, have an ambulance on call for all games. Some trainers are of the opinion that the presence of an ambulance on or near the field has a negative psychological effect on the players. We believe that an ambulance should be available but out of the view of both spectators and players and that the attendants should be inconspicuously seated where they can be summoned quickly if needed.

6. Use a standard accident report blank upon which all pertinent information may be recorded. A form of this type should contain:

   a. Date, time, and place of the accident

   b. Sport being played

   c. Nature and extent of the injury

   d. Brief description of how the injury occurred

   e. Emergency procedures followed and disposition of the injured athlete

   f. Names and, if possible, signatures of at least two witnesses

An accident report blank of the type described serves as a record for future reference. If the emergency procedures followed are questioned at a later date, one's memory may be somewhat hazy as to the details, but a report filled out on the spot provides specific information. All reports of this nature should be filed in the trainer's office. It is well to make them out in triplicate so that one copy may be sent to the school health office, one sent to the physician, and one retained. Suggested forms for the medical record, the medical examination, and the physician's report to the school are indicated in Appendix B.

Athletic injury insurance. Most states, although recognizing athletics as a bona fide school activity, classify it as extramural and therefore do not extend to it the legal responsibilities they assume for the regular class activities. In recent years there have been considerable advances in making low-cost athletic injury insurance available for high school and college athletes. Such insurance usually covers the athlete against injuries incurred during practice or competition. Most of these plans are sponsored by the state athletic associations. Others are sponsored by private companies.

It is not within the province of this book to detail the various forms of coverage and their advantages and disadvantages, since such information is usually included in texts dealing with the administration of school athletic programs. Nonetheless, insurance is a responsibility of the trainer, to the extent of working closely with the school, the athletic administrator, and the coach to see that every athlete is adequately covered by a good, reliable company. Care should be taken to be certain that the coverage is the best that can be obtained; it should provide a maximum coverage for a minimal cost. This responsibility entails careful study of all available plans.

Records. Some trainers object to the keeping of records, stating that they have neither the time nor the inclination to be bookkeepers. There is, however, a certain amount of paper work that must be done, and, if properly planned, little time need be spent on it. A filing cabinet and desk are as much a part of the trainer's equipment as is a whirlpool bath. Careful records of all serious injuries should be filed and readily accessible. In schools in which there is no permanent health services program the trainer should keep the health appraisal records of all athletes. These would include the results of the physical examination as well as the medical history and other pertinent information. It is important that these records be kept up to date. In schools in which a close liaison exists between the health services and the trainer, the health records of all students, including athletes, are kept in the health services office, and such data as is thought relevant is forwarded to the trainer for his information. Often the school health services are responsible for making out all accident reports. The pertinent information is supplied on a form by either the trainer or the coach and is sent to the health services office where an official transcript is made in triplicate. One copy is sent to the trainer, the second is sent to the school or team physician, and the third is filed in the health services office.

It is not feasible to keep a record of each athlete's visit to the training room, but when an athlete has suffered a handicapping or serious injury and is undergoing reconditioning treatment, a progress record should be kept. Records often have the status of legal documents in that they may be used to establish certain facts should a civil suit, an insurance action, or a criminal action ensue following injury or reconditioning. It is to the trainer's advantage to keep accurate, albeit concise, records at all times.

A good trainer also keeps on file an annual report of the activities in his area.

Such a report should include the number of athletes serviced, a survey of the number and types of injuries incurred, an analysis of the program with recommendations for improvement, a budget record, and any other information that is pertinent. Many schools require that such a report be presented annually to the athletic council or to the department head.

Budget. One of the major problems faced by the trainer is to obtain a budget of sufficient size to permit him to carry out a creditable job of training. Most high schools fail to make any budgetary provisions for training except for the purchase of tape, ankle wraps, and a training bag that contains a minimal amount of equipment. Many fail to provide a room and any of the special facilities that are needed to establish an effective training program. Some school boards and administrators fail to recognize that the functions performed in the training quarters are an essential component of the athletic program and that even if no specialist is employed, the facilities are nonetheless necessary. Colleges are not faced with this problem. By and large, training is recognized as an important corollary of the athletic program, and facilities and specialists are usually available. High school athletes are as much in need of training room services as are college athletes; for that reason high school coaches must strive to convince the school administrators of the need for a training program. Within the last few years there has been a pronounced trend toward wider recognition of this need. More frequently we find not only that well-equipped training rooms are being provided but also that teachers who have had preparation and experience in athletic training are being employed to serve in a dual capacity as teachers and part-time trainers.

Budget needs vary considerably. However, a reasonably good, medium-sized high school athletic training program can be operated at an annual cost of $1,000 to $1,500. The amount spent on building and equipping a training facility, of course, is entirely a matter of local option. In purchasing equipment immediate needs as well as availability of personnel to operate specialized equipment should be kept in mind.

Budget records should be kept on file so that they are available for use in projecting the following year's budgetary needs. They present a picture of the distribution of current funds and serve to substantiate future budgetary requests.

Expenditures for individual items vary in accordance with different training philosophies. Some trainers believe in a considerable amount of strapping and therefore may expend as much as 60% of their annual budget on adhesive tape; others, holding an opposing viewpoint, may spend a rather small percentage of their allotment on tape. The trainer should keep accurate records of his funds and their distribution. Budgets must be justified, and good records aid in substantiating future requests.

PROFESSIONAL ORGANIZATIONS

Professional organizations have a number of purposes: (1) to upgrade the profession by devising and maintaining a set of professional standards and establishing a code of ethics with which to achieve this goal; (2) to bring together professionally competent individuals to exchange ideas and to stimulate research and critical thinking; and (3) to give individuals an opportunity to work as a group with a singleness of purpose, thereby making it possible for them to achieve objectives that, separately, they could not accomplish.

Prior to the formation of the National Athletic Trainers Association in 1950, trainers occupied a somewhat insecure place in the athletic program. Since that time, as a result of the raising of professional standards and the establishment of a code of ethics, there has indeed been considerable professional advancement. The Association accepts as members only those who are properly qualified and who are prepared to subscribe to the code of ethics and to uphold the standards of the Association. It

publishes a quarterly journal, *The Journal of the National Athletic Trainers Association,* and holds an annual clinic in which the members have an opportunity to keep abreast of new developments and to exchange ideas. The organization is constantly working to improve both the quality of training and the status of training.

Another organization that has done much to advance athletic training techniques and knowledge is the American College of Sports Medicine, organized in 1954. This organization is interested in all aspects of sports. Its membership is composed of medical doctors, doctors of philosophy, physical educators, trainers, coaches, scientists, and others interested in or associated with sports. It seeks, through study and research, to improve sports not only from the standpoint of performance but also from the standpoint of injury prevention, conditioning, and reconditioning. It holds national and regional conferences and meetings devoted to exploring the many aspects of sports medicine and publishes a quarterly magazine, *Medicine and Science in Sports.* It maintains a close liaison with the Federation Internationale De Medicine Sportive, which publishes the *Journal of Sport and Physical Fitness.* This journal includes articles in French, Italian, German, and English and provides complete translations in English of all articles. It reports the recent developments in the field of sports medicine on a world-wide basis.

The American Association for Health, Physical Education, and Recreation includes many articles of interest to the trainer in its publications, *Journal of Health, Physical Education, and Recreation* and *Research Quarterly,* the latter reporting current research in a number of fields closely allied to training.

The trainer should belong to at least one professional organization. An organization cannot function successfully through the support of only a few dedicated people. If professional status and advancement, better working conditions, and higher compensation are to be obtained, the trainer must support his professional organizations not only as a dues-paying member but also as an active participant, seeking to reach a higher level of professional recognition.

A CODE OF ETHICS

A code of ethics specifies the acceptable standards of conduct for members of a profession and protects those members, as well as the individuals they serve. It establishes standards that ensure a high level of professional service, and it permits the profession to exercise some control over the conduct of its members.

The National Athletic Trainers Association has developed a "Trainer's Code of Ethics," which indicates the acceptable patterns of conduct.[8] The main qualities stressed in the code are *honesty, integrity,* and *loyalty.* The following suggestions, based upon the code, will help the trainer to build desirable patterns of conduct:

1. Be honest with yourself and with others. Avoid attempting to bluff your way through situations that demand answers you do not possess. Admit your lack of knowledge. Doing so will make you seem more human and increase the athlete's respect for you.

2. Under no circumstances should you attempt to carry out a procedure that is a prerogative of the physician unless you have been given instructions to do so. Do not proceed beyond the limits of your responsibility.

3. Cooperation is a constant watchword. It is your responsibility to create a congenial relationship between yourself and the coaches, parents, administrators, and medical personnel.

4. Be thorough. Administer your respective duties with attention to detail and with professional exactness.

5. Observe the rules of good sportsmanship and fair play in respect to all your associates—colleagues, athletes, and opponents. Avoid making criticisms or speaking disparagingly about coaches or other staff members. Avoid discriminatory practices.

6. Refrain from giving testimonials or endorsements of commercial items. It is unprofessional and unethical and is against the law in some areas.

7. Be courteous and considerate to visiting competitors. Do all you can to render assistance. Remember, they are your guests. Treat them accordingly.

8. Do your best to instill the qualities of good sportsmanship in the athletes by precept and example.

9. Encourage and promote scholastic achievement among the athletes.

10. Use common sense in all public relations. Refrain from making statements that are critical or misleading or that may be misconstrued and so reflect unfavorably upon the school, your colleagues, or the athletic program.

11. Conduct yourself as a responsible, mature member of the community and as one who reflects professional competence and integrity. By your actions, earn the respect and confidence of those about you.

REFERENCES

1. Savastano, A. A.: Tells team physicians how to avoid litigation, Med. Sports **9:**2, 1969.
2. Bird, P. J.: Tort liability, J. Health Phys. Ed. Recreat., p. 38, Jan. 1970.
3. Bergen, R. P.: Law and medicine: problems of school team physicians, J.A.M.A. **195:**279, 1965.
4. George, J. F., and Lehmann, H. A.: School athletic administration, New York, 1966, Harper & Row, Publishers.
5. Liebee, H. C.: Legal bases of liability for athletic trainers, J. Nat. Train. Ass., p. 32, Spring 1971.
6. Salkin, P.: Attorney stresses need for insurance protection of schools, athletes, Med. Sports **6:** 2, 1970.
7. Alexander, R. H., and Alexander, K.: Teachers and torts, Middletown, Ky., 1970, Maxwell Publishing Co.
8. National Trainers Association: Constitution and by-laws, Code of Ethics, Palo Alto, Calif.

CHAPTER 4

Facilities, equipment, and supplies

Essential to any athletic program is the maximum utilization of facilities, the most effective use of equipment, and the best means of buying and storing supplies. This chapter provides the reader with some pertinent and practical information that should enable him to gain a more comprehensive insight into the establishment and administration of a functional training program.

HYGIENE AND SANITATION IN ATHLETICS

The practice of good hygiene and sanitation is of the utmost importance in the athletic program. The greatest number of indirectly caused deaths during the period 1931 to 1967 was attributed to infection. The prevention of infectious conditions is a direct responsibility of the trainer, and it is his duty to see that all athletes are surrounded by as hygienic an environment as is possible and that each man is practicing sound health habits, not only in respect to himself but also in relation to his teammates.

Training room

The use of the training room as a place only for the prevention and care of athletic injuries must be strictly observed. Too often the training facility becomes a meeting or club room for the coaches and athletes. Unless definite rules are established and practiced, room cleanliness and sanitation become an impossible chore. The following are some important training room policies.

1. *No cleated shoes are allowed.* Dirt and debris tend to cling to cleated shoes; therefore, they should be removed before entering the training facility.

2. *Game equipment is kept outside.* Because game equipment such as balls and bats adds to the sanitation problem, it should be kept out of the training room. All coaches and athletes must be continually reminded that the training room is not a storage room for sports equipment.

3. *Shoes must be kept off treatment tables.* Besides the tendency of shoes to contaminate treatment tables, they must be removed before any care is given to the athlete.

4. *Athletes should shower before receiving treatment.* The athlete should make it a habit to be showered before being treated if it is not an emergency. This procedure helps to keep tables and therapeutic modalities sanitary.

5. *Roughhousing and profanity should not be allowed.* Athletes must be continually reminded that the training facility is a place for injury care and prevention. Horseplay and foul language lower the basic purpose of the athletic training room.

General cleanliness of the training room cannot be stressed enough. Through the example set forth by the trainer, the athlete may develop an appreciation for cleanliness and, in turn, develop wholesome personal health habits. Cleaning responsibilities in most schools are divided between the training staff and the maintenance crew. Care of permanent building structures and trash disposal are usually the responsibilities of maintenance, whereas upkeep of specialized equipment falls within the province of the training staff. Division of cleaning responsibilities may be organized as follows:

1. Maintenance crew
   a. Sweep floors daily.
   b. Clean and disinfect sinks and built-in tubs daily.
   c. Mop and disinfect hydrotherapy area twice a week.
   d. Refill paper towel and drinking cup dispensers as needed.
   e. Empty wastebaskets and dispose of trash daily.
2. Training staff
   a. Clean and disinfect treatment tables daily.
   b. Clean and disinfect hydrotherapy modalities daily.
   c. Clean and polish other therapeutic modalities weekly.
   d. Screen foot care powder box weekly and replace it every 2 weeks.

Gymnasium equipment

Sanitation in athletics is a continual battle fought by all who are interested in developing mature young men and women. The total athletic program must direct its efforts toward proper health habits. Such practices as passing a common towel to wipe off perspiration, or using common water dispensers, or failing to change dirty clothing for clean are prevalent violations of sanitation in athletics. The following is a suggested health practice check list, which may be employed by the coach and trainer:

1. Facilities sanitation
   a. Are the gymnasium floors swept daily?
   b. Are drinking fountains, showers, sinks, and urinals and toilets cleaned and disinfected daily?
   c. Are lockers aired and sanitized frequently?
   d. Are mats cleaned routinely (wrestling mats cleaned daily)?
2. Equipment and clothing issuance
   a. Are equipment and clothing fitted to the athlete to avoid skin irritations?
   b. Is swapping of equipment and clothes prevented?
   c. Is clothing laundered and changed frequently?
   d. Is wet clothing allowed to dry thoroughly before the athlete wears it again?
   e. Is individual attention given to proper shoe fit and upkeep?
   f. Is protective clothing provided during inclement weather or when the athlete is waiting on the sidelines?
   g. Are clean dry towels provided each day?
3. The athlete
   a. Is the athlete medically cleared to participate?
   b. Is each athlete insured?
   c. Does he promptly report injuries, illnesses, and skin disorders to the coach or trainer?
   d. Are good daily living habits of resting, sleeping, and nutrition practiced?
   e. Does he shower after practice?
   f. Does he dry thoroughly and cool off before departing the gymnasium?
   g. Does he avoid drinking from a common water dispenser?
   h. Does he avoid use of a common towel?
   i. Does he avoid exchanging gym clothes with teammates?
   j. Does he practice good foot hygiene?
   k. Does he avoid contact with teammates when he has a contagious disease or infection?

THE TRAINING ROOM

The training room (Fig. 4-1) is a special room designed to meet the requirements not only of an athletic training program but also of the general physical education program when the need arises. To accommodate the various functions of a training program, it must be designed as a multipurpose area in which first aid can be administered, physical examinations conducted, pregame and prepractice bandaging and strapping done, and reconditioning carried out. In addition, it must serve as a health center for athletes and as a place from which they may be supervised and treated. A place must be provided too where records pertaining to the health and injury histories of athletes can be kept.

Location. The training room should be located immediately adjacent to the dressing quarters of the athletes and should have two entrances: an inside entrance from the dressing area and an outside entrance from the athletic field. This arrangement makes it unnecessary to bring injured athletes in through the building and possibly through several doors; it also permits access when the rest of the building is not in use. Entrance doors should be at least 44 inches wide, and a double door at each entrance is preferable to allow easy passage of a wheelchair or a stretcher. A ramp at the outside entrance is safer and far more functional than are stairs.

Toilet facilities should be located adjacent to the training room and be readily accessible through a door in the training room.

The training room should be located close to the shower rooms also so that the latter are readily available to athletes coming in for treatment, covered with dirt or mud.

Since the training room is the place where emergency treatment is given, its light, heat, and water sources should be

Fig. 4-1. Modern training room. Wichita State University training facility. (Courtesy John Cramer, Cramer Products, Inc., Gardner, Kansas.)

independent of those for the rest of the building. Some trainers prefer having a compressed air outlet available and find a variety of uses for it.

The trainer's office, which is incorporated in the training quarters, should have an outside telephone line. It is advisable to have a local or campus phone as well. Strict regulations concerning use of the telephones should be established. They should be used only in connection with business pertaining to training and should not be used by students. Because of the nature and character of the training room and of the equipment and supplies within, it should have an independent lock-and-key system so that it is not accessible to everyone who possesses a master key to the building. The trainer alone should possess keys for the training quarters.

Size and construction. A training room 1,000 to 1,200 square feet in size is satisfactory for most school situations. The 1,200 square foot area (40 by 30 feet) permits the handling of a sizable number of athletes at one time besides allowing ample room for the rather bulky equipment needed. A room of this size is well suited for pregame preparation. Careful planning will determine whether a larger area is needed or is desirable. A training area of less than 900 square feet is impractical.

The room should have windows in at least one wall, and the windows should be placed high enough above the floor to provide ample natural light and draft-free ventilation and to ensure privacy. A training room that is not properly equipped with vents can become exceedingly noisome. To supplement natural ventilation, either an exhaust fan or, preferably, an air-conditioning system should be installed.

The walls and ceiling should be of either dry wall or plaster construction and should be painted in a light pastel shade with a washable paint.

The floor should be of smooth-finished concrete, with a nonslip texture. On occasion cleats are worn in the room, and a wooden floor may in time splinter and warp. Vinyl tile, although somewhat expensive, has been used as a floor covering with considerable success. The floors should be graded to slope toward strategically placed drain outlets.

Illumination. The training room should be planned so that good natural illumination comes from high on one side. The trainer should plan his working areas so that the light comes from the left if he is right-handed or from the right if he is left-handed, so that he will not be working in his own shadow. Outdoor diffusers are preferable to shade for eliminating undue glare and controlling illumination.

Artificial lighting should be planned with the advice of a technical lighting engineer. The standard level of illumination recommended for training facilities is 30 footcandles at the height of 4 feet above the floor. Ceilings and walls, acting as reflective surfaces, aid in achieving an equitable distribution and balance of light. Light fixtures may be of several types. Since an even, nonglaring light is desired, a fixture that illuminates indirectly by casting direct light on the ceiling, from which it is reflected down and outward, is an excellent type. Fluorescent lights, when used with a diffuser, also provide a good source of light. Diffusers eliminate the flickering that is otherwise often an objectionable feature.

Special service areas. Apart from the storage and office space, one portion of the training room should be divided into three special service areas separated from each other by walls or partitions: physical therapy and thermal therapy area, electrotherapy area, and hydrotherapy area. Each has functions peculiar unto itself and bears no relationships to the others.

Physical therapy and thermal therapy area: The physical therapy and thermal therapy area should constitute approximately 60% of the total special service area. In addition to being used for physical therapy and heat therapy, it serves as the area in which bandaging and strapping are done and corrective or therapeutic exercises carried out. Equipment should include from six to eight rubbing tables, five or six chairs or stools, several small dispensing tables for holding supplies, shelves and a storage cabinet, and therapeutic and corrective equipment such as shoulder wheels, knee exercisers, exercise weights, and bicycle exercisers. Equipment will vary in amount according to school size.

Electrotherapy area: The electrotherapy area should constitute about 20% of the total special service area and is used for treatment by ultrasound, diathermy, infrared, or other electrotherapy media. Equipment should include at least two treatment tables, several wooden chairs, one or two dispensing tables for holding supplies, shelves, and a storage cabinet for supplies and equipment. The area should contain a sufficient number of grounded outlets, preferably in the walls and several feet above the floor. It is advisable to place rubber mats or runners on each side of the treatment tables as a precautionary measure. This area must be under supervision at all times, and the storage cabinet should be kept locked when not in use.

Hydrotherapy area: The hydrotherapy area should constitute approximately 15% of the total special service area. The floor should slope at a good gradient toward a centrally located drain to prevent water from standing. Equipment should include two whirlpool baths, one permitting complete immersion of the body, a large Roman bath, a needle shower, a steam room or cabinet, several lavatories, and storage shelves. Since some of this equipment is electrically operated, considerable precaution must be observed. All electrical outlets should be placed from 4 to 5 feet above the floor, and all cords and wires must be kept clear of the floor to eliminate any possibility of electrical shock. To prevent water from entering the other areas, a slightly raised, rounded curb should be built at the entrance to the area. When a training room is planned, ample outlets must be provided, for under no circumstances should two or more devices be operated from the same outlet.

Storage facilities. Many training quarters lack ample storage space. Often storage facilities are located a considerable distance away, which is extremely inconvenient. In addition to the storage cabinets and shelves provided in each of the three special service areas, a small storage closet should be placed in the trainer's office. All of these cabinets should be used for the storage of general supplies as well as for the small specialized equipment used in the respective areas. A large walk-in storage closet, 80 to 100 square feet in area, is a necessity for the storage of bulky equipment, medical supplies, adhesive tape, bandages, and protective devices (Fig. 4-2). A refrigerator for the storage of pharmaceuticals, gel packs, and other necessities is also an important and necessary piece of equipment. Many trainers prefer to place the refrigerator in their office, where it is readily accessible but still under close supervision.

Auxiliary areas. Many trainers, while well aware of the necessity of using a powder and benzoin (skin toughener) bench, decry its placement within the training room proper because of the messiness resulting from its use. In such cases it can be placed in an adjacent area.

The trainer's office. A space 10 feet by 8 feet is ample for the trainer's office. It should be so located that all areas of the training room are well under supervision without the trainer having to leave the office. Glass partitions on two sides permit the trainer, even while seated at his desk, to observe all activities. A desk, chair, tack board for clippings and other information, telephones, and a record file are the basic equipment.

EQUIPMENT

The training personnel must be concerned with the equipment the athlete wears. It is just as important in injury prevention to be outfitted with properly fitting equipment as it is to be well conditioned and coached. Too often coaches are more concerned with the outward appearance of

Text continued on p. 42.

Fig. 4-2. Adequate storage facilities are essential to the good training program.

Table 4-1. Suggested basic equipment for individual programs

	Quantities for number of participants per year		
Item	Up to 200	200 to 400	400 to 600
Anatomy charts (set)	1	1	1
Ankle wrap roller	1	2	2
Blankets	3	5	5
Bulletin board	1	1	1
Callus file	6	12	18
Crutches	2 pairs	4 pairs	6 pairs
Diathermy (microwave or shortwave)*	1	1	1
Drinking dispenser	1	1	1
Electric clock	1	1	1
Electric muscle stimulator	1	1	1
Examining table (physician)	1	1	1
Exercise equipment (assorted)	*	*	*
Medicine dropper	3	6	9
Eyecup	1	2	3
Flashlight (pencil type)	1	2	3
Forceps (tweezers)	3	3	3
Hair clippers	2	2	2
Hammer	1	1	1

*Assorted pieces of equipment sufficient for the given number of participants.

Table 4-1. Suggested basic equipment for individual programs—cont'd

Item	Quantities for number of participants per year		
	Up to 200	**200 to 400**	**400 to 600**
Heat lamp (infrared)	1	2	3
Hot pack (hydrocallator)	1	1	2
Ice maker	1	1	1
Mirror (hand)	3	5	7
Nail clippers	1	2	2
Oral screw	(available for each first-aid kit)		
Oral thermometer	1	2	3
Paraffin bath	1	1	1
Plastic pillows	2	4	6
Pliers	1	1	1
Powder and benzoin box	1	1	1
Razor (safety, with blades)	1	1	1
Reconditioning equipment			
Barbells	†	†	†
Chinning bar	†	†	†
Dumbbells	†	†	†
Mats	†	†	†
Pulley weights	†	†	†
Shoe weights	†	†	†
Refrigerator	1	1	1
Resuscitator	1	1	1
Safety pins	200	400	600
Scales and weight chart	1	2	2
Scalpel	2	2	2
Scissors			
All-purpose	1	2	2
Bandage	3	5	7
Surgical	2	2	2
Screwdriver	1	1	1
Shoehorn	3	5	7
Sink and washbasin	1	1	1
Sitz bath	1	1	1
Slings (triangular bandages)	5	10	15
Splints (set of assorted pneumatic)	1	1	2
Steam cabinet (individual)	1	1	2
Sterilizer	1	1	1
Storage cupboards	‡	‡	‡
Stretcher (folding)	1	1	1
Surgical lamp	1	1	1
Tape cutters	5	8	10
Taping tables	2	3	4
Trainer's office			
Bookshelf	1	1	1
Desk	1	1	1
Filing cabinet	1	1	1
Telephone	1	1	1
Training kits	(available for each sport)		
Training tables (massage)	1	2	3
Ultrasound	1	1	1
Waste container	2	3	4
Wheelchair	(should be available)		
Whirlpool baths	1	2	3

†Should be on hand for each participant or funds be available for purchase when need arises.
‡Dry, cool storage areas should be provided to house the bulk of the training supplies.

Table 4-2. Suggested yearly training supplies for individual programs

| Item | Quantities for number of participants per year | | |
	Up to 200	200 to 400	400 to 600
Injury prevention			
Adhesive tape			
½-inch	3 tubes	5 tubes	7 tubes
1-inch	12 tubes	24 tubes	36 tubes
1½-inch	96 tubes	192 tubes	284 tubes
2-inch	48 tubes	72 tubes	144 tubes
Ankle wrap (96 inches long)	20	30	40
Back braces	*	*	*
Elastic bandages			
3-inch	12	24	48
4-inch	36	72	144
6-inch	12	24	48
Elastic knee caps			
Large	*	*	*
Medium	*	*	*
Small	*	*	*
Elastic knee guards			
Large	*	*	*
Medium	*	*	*
Small	*	*	*
Elastic tape (3-inch)	24 tubes	50 tubes	75 tubes
Elastic thigh caps			
Large	*	*	*
Medium	*	*	*
Small	*	*	*
Elastic thigh guards			
Large	*	*	*
Medium	*	*	*
Small	*	*	*
Envelopes for pills	2 dozen	3 dozen	4 dozen
Felt (36 inches by 44 inches)			
¼-inch	1 sheet	2 sheets	3 sheets
½-inch	1 sheet	2 sheets	3 sheets
Flexible collodion	1 pint	2 pints	2 pints
Glare-reduction salve	*	*	*
Heel cups	5	10	15
Knee braces (left and right)			
Large	2	3	4
Medium	2	3	4
Small	2	3	4
Moleskin (12-inch)	2 rolls	4 rolls	6 rolls
Petroleum (grease)	5 pounds	10 pounds	15 pounds
Powdered rosin	*	*	*
Shoulder harness	*	*	*
Skin tougheners and tape adherent			
Aerosol (12-ounce spray can)	18 cans	24 cans	30 cans
Bulk	5 gallons	10 gallons	15 gallons
Sponge rubber (vinyls)			
⅛-inch, 36 by 44	1 sheet	2 sheets	3 sheets
¼-inch, 36 by 44	1 sheet	2 sheets	3 sheets
½-inch, 36 by 44	1 sheet	2 sheets	3 sheets
Waterproof tape	12 rolls	24 rolls	48 rolls

*Should be on hand for each participant or funds be available for purchase when need arises.

Table 4-2. Suggested yearly training supplies for individual programs—cont'd

Item	Quantities for number of participants per year		
	Up to 200	200 to 400	400 to 600
Injury management			
Ammonia ampules (box of 100)	1	1	2
Analgesic balm			
Hot	5 pounds	10 pounds	15 pounds
Warm (regular)	15 pounds	25 pounds	35 pounds
Bandages			
Band-aids (box of 100)			
1 by 3	20 boxes	35 boxes	50 boxes
Butterfly			
Medium	50	100	150
Small	50	100	150
Sterile pads (box of 100)			
2 by 2	5 boxes	10 boxes	15 boxes
3 by 3	5 boxes	10 boxes	15 boxes
Calamine lotion (4-ounce)	4	8	12
Collodion	1 pint	1 pint	2 pints
Combine (roll)	2 rolls	4 rolls	6 rolls
Cotton			
Nonsterile	10 pounds	20 pounds	30 pounds
Sterile	5 pounds	10 pounds	15 pounds
Cotton-tipped applicators	500	1000	1500
Drinking cups (paper, box of 100)	6	8	10
Epsom salt (pounds)	25	50	75
Ethyl chloride (4-ounce)	2	4	8
Fungicides			
Ointments or solutions	1 pint	6 pints	9 pints
Powders (4-ounce can)	4 cans	8 cans	12 cans
Gauze (roll)			
1-inch	25 rolls	50 rolls	100 rolls
2-inch	25 rolls	50 rolls	100 rolls
3-inch	25 rolls	50 rolls	100 rolls
Germicides			
Alcohol	5 pints	10 pints	15 pints
Boric acid (eyewash)	1 pint	2 pints	3 pints
Merthiolate	1 pint	2 pints	3 pints
Nitrotan	1 pint	2 pints	3 pints
Peroxide	1 pint	2 pints	3 pints
pHisohex	1 pint	2 pints	3 pints
Instant cold pack	8	16	32
Internal agents			
Antacid tablets	200	300	500
Aspirin tablets	500	1000	1500
Cold tablets	1000	2000	4000
Dextrose tablets	2000	4000	6000
Salt tablets	2000	4000	6000
Massage lubricant	2 pints	1 gallon	2 gallons
Medicated ointments			
Athletic ointment	1 pound	2 pounds	3 pounds
Ichthyol ointment	1 pound	1 pound	1 pound
Menthol ointment (4-ounce)	1	4	6
Zinc oxide	1 pound	2 pounds	2 pounds
Menthol spray	6	12	18
Rubdown liniment (1-pint)	5	10	15

Continued.

Table 4-2. Suggested yearly training supplies for individual programs—cont'd

Item	Quantities for number of participants per year		
	Up to 200	200 to 400	400 to 600
Injury management—cont'd			
Splints—either:			
Air	1 set	1 set	1 set
Wooden	asst'd sizes	asst'd sizes	asst'd sizes
Cardboard	asst'd sizes	asst'd sizes	asst'd sizes
Stockinette (3-inch roll)	1	3	6
Sun lotion (4-ounce)	4	8	12
Tape adherent (clear)			
Bulk	1 pint	2 pints	3 pints
Spray cans (12-ounce)	10 cans	20 cans	30 cans
Tape remover	1 gallon	2 gallons	3 gallons
Throat gargle, antiseptic (4-ounce)	4	7	12
Tongue depressors	500	1000	1500

Table 4-3. Checklist for trainer's kit*

Item	Amount	Football	Basketball	Wrestling	Baseball	Track and cross country	Water polo and swimming	Gymnastics	Tennis
							Activity		
Adhesive tape									
½-inch	2 rolls	x	x	x	x	x		x	x
1-inch	3 rolls	x	x	x	x	x		x	x
1½-inch	4 rolls	x	x	x	x	x		x	x
2-inch	2 rolls	x	x	x	x	x		x	x
Alcohol	4 ounces	x	x	x	x	x	x	x	x
Ammonia ampules	50	x	x	x	x	x	x	x	x
Analgesic balm	1 pound	x	x	x	x	x	x	x	x
Ankle wraps	3	x	x		x	x			x
Antacid tablets	100	x	x	x	x	x	x	x	x
Antiglare salve	4 ounces	x				x			
Antiseptic powder	4 ounces	x	x	x	x	x	x	x	x
Antiseptic soap	4 ounces	x	x	x	x	x	x	x	x
Aspirin tablets	100	x	x	x	x	x	x	x	x
Band-Aids (1 by 3)	4 dozen	x	x	x	x	x	x	x	x
Benzoin spray	12-ounce can	x	x	x	x	x		x	x
Butterfly bandages									
Medium	1 dozen	x	x	x	x	x		x	
Small	1 dozen	x	x	x	x	x		x	
Combine (material)	6 by 6 sheet	x	x	x	x	x			

*Extra amounts of items such as tape and protective padding are carried in other bags.

Table 4-3. Checklist for trainer's kit—cont'd

Item	Amount	Football	Basketball	Wrestling	Baseball	Track and cross country	Water polo and swimming	Gymnastics	Tennis
Cotton (sterile)	4 ounces	x	x	x	x	x	x	x	x
Cotton-tipped applicators	3 dozen	x	x	x	x	x	x	x	x
Dextrose tablets	200	x	x	x	x	x	x	x	x
Elastic bandages									
3-inch	2 rolls	x	x	x	x	x		x	x
4-inch	2 rolls	x	x	x	x	x		x	x
6-inch	2 rolls	x	x	x	x	x	x	x	x
Elastic tape roll (3-inch)	2 rolls	x	x	x	x	x		x	x
Eyewash	4 ounces	x	x	x	x	x	x	x	x
Felt									
¼-inch	6 by 6 sheet	x	x	x	x	x			x
½-inch	6 by 6 sheet	x							
Flexible collodion	4 ounces	x	x	x	x	x		x	
Foot powder	4 ounces	x	x	x	x	x	x	x	x
Forceps (tweezers)	1	x	x	x	x	x	x	x	x
Fungicide	4 ounces	x	x	x	x	x	x	x	x
Germicide (solution)	4 ounces	x	x	x	x	x	x	x	x
Grease (lubrication)	4 ounces	x	x	x	x	x			x
Gum rosin	4 ounces	x	x		x	x			x
Heel cups	2			x		x		x	
Instant cold pack	2	x	x	x	x	x	x	x	x
Liniment	1 pint	x	x	x	x	x	x	x	x
Medicated ointment	4 ounces	x	x	x	x	x	x	x	x
Mirror (hand)	1	x	x	x	x	x	x	x	x
Moleskin	6 by 6 sheet	x	x	x	x	x		x	x
Nonadhering sterile pad (3 by 3)	12	x	x	x	x	x		x	x
Oral screw	1	x	x	x	x	x	x	x	x
Oral thermometer	1	x	x	x	x	x	x	x	x
Peroxide	4 ounces	x	x	x	x	x	x	x	x
Salt tablets	200	x	x	x	x	x		x	x
Shoehorn	1	x	x	x	x	x			x
Sponge rubber									
⅛-inch	6 by 6 sheet	x	x	x	x	x		x	x
¼-inch	6 by 6 sheet	x	x	x	x	x		x	x
½-inch	6 by 6 sheet	x							
Sterile gauze pads (3 by 3)	12	x	x	x	x	x		x	x
Sun lotion	4 ounces	x	x	x	x	x	x	x	x
Surgical scissors	1	x	x	x	x	x	x	x	x
Tape adherent	12-ounce can	x	x	x	x	x		x	x
Tape remover	4 ounces	x	x	x	x	x	x	x	x
Tape scissors	1	x	x	x	x	x	x	x	x
Tongue depressors	50	x	x	x	x	x	x	x	x
Triangular bandages	2	x	x	x	x	x	x	x	x
Waterproof tape (1-inch)	1 roll						x		

the athlete rather than the extent of protection afforded him. However, it is easy to understand why those given the responsibility for purchasing athletic equipment become confused. Various claims made for a specific piece of equipment and a general lack of knowledge on what constitutes quality merchandise are but two reasons for this confusion. The best rule of thumb is always "you get what you pay for." Safety must never be sacrificed for appearance. In athletic programs with limited budgets, the highest priority must be given to the best quality of protective equipment; outward appearance of the athlete must come second. In most cases the coach has the final word as to which type of equipment he wants his team to have; however, this decision should be made in consultation with the trainer and equipment supervisor.

Another important responsibility of the equipment supervisor and training personnel is the initial fitting of equipment to the individual athlete. Once fitted, the athlete is taught how to wear each protective device properly and to promptly report any malfunctioning or misfit. It is desirable, particularly with young athletes, to check daily the wearing of protective or specialized equipment. Many injuries, which result in loss of sport days, can be avoided by attention to properly fitted equipment (Fig. 4-2).

Recommendations that should prove helpful to the qualified trainer concerning equipment and supplies are indicated in the preceding lists. Table 4-1 itemizes the equipment suggested as basic for individual programs, the quantities listed being applicable to situations in which the number of participants is under 200, 200 to 400, and 400 to 600, respectively.

Table 4-2 lists, yearly training supplies, grouped according to areas of use in injury prevention or injury management. Table 4-3 provides a checklist for the trainer's kit suitable for use in various sports.

RECOMMENDED READINGS

Arnheim, D. D., Auxter, D., and Crowe, W. C.: Principles and methods of adapted physical education, St. Louis, 1973, The C. V. Mosby Co.

Bucher, C. A.: Administration of health and physical education programs, including athletics, St. Louis, 1971, The C. V. Mosby Co.

Forsythe, C. E.: Administration of high school athletics, New York, 1965, Prentice-Hall, Inc.

Forsythe, C. E.: The athletic director's handbook, New York, 1965, Prentice-Hall, Inc.

George, J. F., and Lehmann, H. A.: School health administration, New York, 1966, Harper & Row, Publishers.

Howard, G. W., and Masonbrink, E.: School athletic administration, New York, 1963, Harper & Row Publishers, Inc.

Morehouse, L. E., and Rasch, P. J.: Scientific basis of athletic training, Philadelphia, 1958, W. B. Saunders Co.

CHAPTER **5**

Mechanisms of athletic injuries

If one carefully studies the structure of the human body, it becomes apparent that, from a mechanical standpoint, man was never meant to walk upright. The body must answer to certain laws of physics, which determine what can or cannot be done. At first glance it appears that nature did a rather poor job of designing. Not only must constant gravitational force be overcome, but the body also must be manipulated through space by means of a rather complex system of somewhat inefficient levers, fueled by a machinery that operates at an efficiency level of about 30%. The bony levers that move the body must overcome considerable resistance in the form of inertia and muscle viscosity and must work in most instances at an extremely unfavorable angle of pull. All these factors mitigate the effectiveness of lever action to the extent that most movement is achieved at an efficiency level of less than 25%.

In addition, more than half the total body weight is located in the upper part of the of the body, and this weight is supported by means of rather thin, jointed bones. Thus, the center of gravity, which increases stability as it is lowered, is relatively high in the erect human body.

However, despite these seeming inefficiencies, the body can compensate by making modifications or adjustments that depend upon the task at hand. For example, the center of gravity may be lowered by widening the stance, the segmented body parts may function either as a single unit or as a series of finely coordinated units or an increase in muscle power may be elicited in an effort to offset certain mechanical ineptitudes. Structural changes in bones, resulting from stresses placed upon them, afford broader and more secure muscle anchorage and consequently aid in the development of more power.

Although the bones of the body are not primarily designed to withstand shock, the musculature serves as a shock absorber by absorbing impact and distributing it over a relatively large area, thereby lessening the concentration of the force on a small area of bone. Bones such as the shin and skull, however, which have little or no overlying musculature and thus are more susceptible to injury, should be afforded protection, especially in athletic activities in which they are particularly vulnerable to blows.

In the light of evolutionary changes man has fared reasonably well.[1] As he learned to walk upright and thus bear his weight on the lower limbs, the legs became longer and straighter and the foot became less prehensile and more adaptable for support and propulsion. The pelvis, oddly enough, underwent no significant changes. The spinal column developed three curves in the anteroposterior plane to assist in maintaining body balance by bringing the head, thorax, and pelvis into line—therefore effecting more stability. The articulations of the many small segments of bone (vertebrae) also permit a wider range of movement, without relinquishing too much of the strength afforded by a rigid, rodlike structure.

However, along with the invaluable advantages gained through an upright posture and an increased range of movement, there are, some disadvantages. The mesenteries supporting the abdominal viscera were designed for a quadruped, and the constant gravitational pull plus the weight of the supported organs makes man somewhat prone to have a protruding abdomen unless the abdominal muscles maintain sufficient tonicity to withstand these forces. Also, because of the length and great weight of the torso and head, the lumbosacral area of the spine is subjected to considerable strain and is particularly vulnerable to injury, especially in certain activities. For example, the twisting movements of golf and tennis and the excessive supportive demands sometimes made upon the lumbosacral area in weight lifting or gymnastics often lead to low back strain or injury.

PREDISPOSING FACTORS

A number of factors, either congenital or acquired, may predispose an athlete to a specific type of injury. Certain anomalies in anatomical structure or in body build (somatotype) may make an athlete particularly prone to a certain type of injury.[2] In addition there are kinesiological factor that contribute to the probability of strains, sprains, or fractures. In many instances these factors or mechanisms can be ameliorated or completely eliminated if the trainer recognizes them and takes positive action toward instituting corrective measures to reduce the influence or possible effects of such conditions. In a situation in which a somewhat extreme anatomical condition exists, it may be well to suggest that the individual participate in another type of activity, one in which his handicap does not pose a potential hazard.

The preseason physical examination acquires considerable significance when it is realized that this is when factors that may predispose an athlete to injury are identified and evaluated and a decision is made regarding any existing problem. Both the examining physician and the trainer must learn to look for and recognize such factors. This is of the utmost importance when dealing with the pubescent athlete.

In addition to the foregoing, the growth factor now assumes considerable importance. Although puberty is the time when the greatest physical growth occurs, this growth is accompanied by a slower growth rate in terms of certain other anatomical considerations. For example, closure of the epiphyseal growth centers lags somewhat behind the physical growth pattern.[1] Since these centers are particularly susceptible to injury in the young athlete and since injury to them may lead to osteochondritis, exposing the growing boy to activities that could result in injury to these centers is opposed by orthopedists and by well-informed teachers, coaches, and trainers.[3] In addition the application of unusual stress or torque to the pelvis or the spine of an adolescent athlete may result in injury. Incomplete ossification of bones may also predispose a high school athlete to injury. There is some divergence of opinion as to what, if any, physiological implications are engendered by competing the pubescent boy or girl. Evidence indicates that epiphyseal injuries are more frequent among high school age athletes than among athletes in their early teens.[4] Most authorities believe that if, upon careful examination, no anomalies or factors exist that would predispose the adolescent to injury, heavy competition can be engaged in without serious repercussion. The psychological implications, perhaps, need further study.

Proper conditioning and instruction in correct motor techniques will do much to prevent potential injury. Certain game or play situations, however, may arise that will lead to unavoidable injuries. A disregard of the various mechanical or physiological principles will also lead to injuries, and for this reason the trainer and coach should be familiar with the science of kinesiology—"to be forewarned is to be forearmed." A knowledge of these principles and their application aid materially in reducing the incidence of injury.

ARTICULATIONS

Since the source of all bodily motion is in the joints, an understanding of the structure, strengths, and weaknesses of these articulations is necessary if the trainer is to do a proper job of conditioning to prevent athletic injury or of reconditioning following injury. More complete anatomical analyses are presented later, in introducing discussions of specific joint injuries.

A joint or articulation is defined as the junction of two or more bones. Movement may or may not be present. Joints are classified in various ways by different authorities, but for the sake of simplicity they will be classified here in relation to the amount, type, and variety of movement permitted:

1. *Synarthrodial*—Immovable joint, possessing no articular cavity, united by either cartilaginous or fibrous tissue. Example: the sutures of the skull.

2. *Amphiarthrodial*—A slightly movable joint, possessing a joint cavity and a capsule. Examples: the joints between the bodies of the vertebrae, the sacroiliac joint, the coracoacromial articulation, the articulation between manubrium and body of the sternum, the symphysis pubis.

3. *Diarthrodial*—Freely movable joint, possessing an articular cavity, enveloped within a ligamentous capsule lined with a smooth synovial membrane and lubricated with a synovial fluid. The ends of the articulating surfaces are covered with smooth hyaline cartilage. This type comprises the majority of the joints in the body and is subdivided, on the basis of structure, into the following six types:

a. *Condyloid (ellipsoid)*—Biaxial joint, permitting movement in two planes at right angles to each other. Examples: wrist joint, between the radius and carpals.

b. *Ball-and-socket (enarthrodial)*—Swivel-type joint, having the widest range of motion. Examples: hip and shoulder joints.

c. *Gliding (arthrodial)*—Joint having a relatively free, gliding type of movement. Examples: intercarpal and intertarsal joints.

d. *Hinge (ginglymoid)*—Joint having a hinge action, wherein one articulating surface is concave and fits around the spoollike projection of the other, moving in a gliding action. Examples: elbow, knee, ankle, and interphalangeal joints.

e. *Pivot (trochoid or screwlike)*—Joint permitting rotation only. Examples: radioulnar and atlantoaxial joints.

f. *Saddle (reciprocal in reception)*—Joint having the end of one articu-

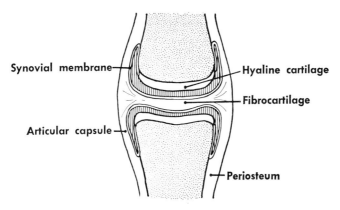

Fig. 5-1. Diarthrodial joint.

lating bone shaped somewhat like a western saddle, the ends being turned up, while the other bone has a reciprocal saddle that conforms to the surface of the first. Movement is biaxial. Example: carpometacarpal joint of the thumb.

MECHANISM OF INJURIES

Spine. The spine or vertebral column consists of twenty-six articulated bone segments called vertebrae, which permit flexion, extension, and rotation of the trunk. To achieve this considerable variety of movement use is made of the intervertebral disks and a number of opposing curves in the anteroposterior plane. These two features permit flexibility and resilience. In addition to permitting a wide range of movement, the spine serves as a place of support and attachment for the ribs and muscles and for the pelvis and head. It also serves as a shock absorber, as a means of distributing body weight, and as a factor in locomotion.

That the spinal column must be carefully strengthened and protected is borne out by the fact that most of the direct fatalities have resulted from injuries to the head and neck. The 1971 Survey of Football Fatalities indicated that over the past 40 years (no study was made in 1942) 78% of the direct fatalities were caused by head or spine injuries.[5]

Most of the serious head and neck injuries occur in football. One cause is the continued practice of "spearing," that is, driving the head directly into an opponent's body when blocking or tackling. Danger of compression, hyperflexion, or hyperextension of the cervical vertebrae with ensuing serious consequences is often the result of this practice. Although spearing is increasingly condemned by trainers, physicians, and many coaches, it is still widely used[5] (see Chapter 20). Many of the head and neck injuries appear to be directly attributable to the use of the combination helmet and face guard, which, because of design, causes the force delivered

to the chin or face guard to be from 30% to 100% greater than the original force. This great increase of force is the result of the combination of levers involved. The force may be exerted in either a horizontal or a rotational pattern. When it is applied in such a manner as to induce severe spinal rotation (i.e., the direction of the applied force is lateral to the recipient), it is applied to the area of least resistance, since the least muscular and ligamentous support occurs on the lateral aspects of the cervical neck. Such lateral force, when coupled with either extension or flexion of the neck, may result in a rotational shear, which is a contributing factor in dislocations and fracture-dislocations[6,7] (see Chapter 20).

The rising popularity of surfing has caused a considerable number of head and neck injuries incurred as the result of the surfer being either struck on the head by a wildly recalcitrant surfboard or propelled headfirst from the board into shallow water. Among aquatic sports diving also contributes its share of head and neck injuries, some of which are fatal.

The pelvis plays an important role in the prevention of injuries to the spine. In sports such as weight lifting, gymnastics, wrestling and pole vaulting, in which force is conveyed to the pelvis in lifting, the abdominal muscles and the thoracic spine oppose the force, thereby reducing the stress on the lumbosacral joint by as much as 30% and that on the lower thoracic spine by as much as 50%. The ability to apply this counterforce is a sign of an experienced athlete and serves to substantially reduce the possibilities of low back injury.

Since the spine must be protected by its surrounding musculature, in the contact sports it is well for the player to keep these muscles in a state of contraction sufficient to support and protect the spine until he is certain that a play has been completed and that no further chance of physical contact is present. Premature relaxation of the muscles may result in a fracture, especially of the transverse processes of the lumbar spine, if unexpected, sudden, and severe force is applied to the spine when the player is not in a state of readiness to receive such force.

Trauma can result from poor postural habits, and the athlete should be made aware of this risk. Again, adequate and proper training and conditioning to develop a strong back musculature are necessary to prevent injury.

Thorax. The thorax—a section of the trunk formed in part by the ribs, costal cartilages, sternum, and thoracic vertebrae—is a resilient cage, which protects the thoracic viscera and aids breathing. It includes also the bones that comprise the shoulder girdle. The thorax is poorly designed for man's upright posture, particularly in regard to protection since several of the organs are relatively unprotected except by a muscle wall. Hence, in rugged contact sports, properly designed and fitted protective equipment should be used.

The more common thorax injuries are cartilage tears and rib strains, which quite often occur in football or wrestling. Compression injuries such as cracked ribs result from a severe external force and are common in these sports. Although a good conditioning program will do much toward minimizing such injuries, both in number and in severity, proper equipment is the best means of prevention. This is especially true in respect to the kidney areas, since these regions are exceptionally vulnerable to injury and can be seriously traumatized if not adequately protected. Equipment that will properly shield these areas should be selected.

Shoulder joint. The shoulder joint plays a most critical role in sports on this continent and injuries to both the soft tissue and to the joint itself are quite common. In many sports the other parts of the body play a somewhat secondary role. Their prime function is to set the stage for the shoulder joint to assume the "star" performance role, for example, in batting, pitching, forward passing, or swinging implements of some type. It is quite possible to identify certain derangements of the shoulder joint as being peculiar to a particular sport.[8]

The shoulder joint is a rather insecure joint formed by articulation of the humerus with the glenoid fossa of the scapula. It possesses a remarkable mobility as a result of the looseness of the capsule and of the ligaments surrounding it. The joint maintains its integrity through the ligamentous structures rather than through the bony structures and is therefore susceptible to severe sprains and luxations.[9]

Many shoulder joint injuries are caused by a descending force or impact that drives the acromion downward and away from the clavicle, which sustains its position.[10] This is a somewhat common injury. In football it occurs when the shoulder is used as a driving force. In tumbling it can occur when there is shoulder point contact with the mat. In wrestling this injury can occur when the wrestler throws his opponent and causes shoulder point contact with the mat, using his own body weight plus the weight of his opponent to provide the force. Another comparatively common cause of shoulder dislocation is demonstrated when the athlete falls on either his hand or his elbow, with the latter in about a 90-degree flexion. In this instance the head of the humerus is driven with great force against both the glenoid fossa and the acromion, forcing them backward and exerting considerable stress upon the coracoclavicular

Fig. 5-2. Mechanism of a rotator cuff strain.

and clavicular ligaments, resulting in a sprain or a rupture.

Soft tissue injuries can result from the repetitious dynamic contraction of the muscle, as in pitching. There is a resultant accretion of microtrauma culminating in a chronic injury. A sudden all-out contraction of a muscle wherein the antagonists fail to function in controlling the effort is another cause. Direct forceful impact to the muscle as from a blow is still another cause of soft tissue injury.

Inasmuch as the shoulder joint is dependent upon the surrounding muscle tissue for additional support and stability, a sound exercise program that will strengthen and maintain these muscles at a high level of fitness is indicated. Following an athlete's injury, the trainer should insist upon his maintaining as much joint mobility as can be obtained at a given time and should seek to increase such mobility as healing progresses.

Elbow joint. The elbow joint is a complex entity in which the radius and ulna articulate with the humerus to form a ginglymus or hinge joint. This permits only two movements, flexion and extension. Flexion is limited either by the locking of the coronoid process on the anterior surface of the humerus or, in some instances, by the bulk of the muscle masses on the forearm and upper arm. The olecranon process, a hooklike protuberance on the ulna, checks extension. The joint is enveloped by an extensive capsule, which is strengthened on all four sides by collateral ligaments: the anterior, posterior, radial, and ulnar, respectively.

Forcible extension, forcible hyperextension, and impact forces are the principal causes of injury to this joint. The momentum of the forearm forcing the olecranon process against the trochlea of the humerus often results in a chipping of the bone or in a partial or complete dislocation. Muscle strains resulting from forcible hyperextension are quite common, as are capsular strains. They usually result either from a fall in which the athlete lands upon an ex-

tended and locked elbow joint or from a situation in which the arm and elbow are in an extended, supportive position and an impact force is directed upon the posterior aspect of the arm in the vicinity of the elbow joint. Throwing, in which the arm is forcefully extended, can result in a painful traumatic elbow. In this type of injury there is irritation of the periosteum, which may become chronic as a result of the calciferous deposits that accrue.

When the elbow or any other hinge joint is flexed at an angle of less than 90 degrees during activity, the component of force that normally acts as a stabilizing factor in essence reverses itself and, instead of acting to thrust the articulating end of the excursioning bone into the joint, tends rather to pull it away and thus decreases the stability of the joint. It is in this position that the joint is most vulnerable to a partial or complete dislocation.

Wrist joint. A diarthrodial, or freely movable, condyloid joint, formed by the articulations of the navicular, lunate, and triquetrum with the radius, and a triangular articular disk interposed between the ulna and triquetrum constitute the wrist joint. The tendons of the extensor and flexor muscles of both the wrist and the hand reinforce the joint, and the capsular ligament that encloses the joint cavity is additionally strengthened by the dorsal and volar carpal ligaments. Basically, movements of the wrist are in two planes; therefore the joint is often classified as biaxial. The wrist joint offers a variety of movements—among them flexion, extension, hyperextension, ulnar duction (adduction), radial duction (abduction), and circumduction. The freedom of action of the wrist joint plus the prehensility of the hand makes this area the most mobile of the body.

Injuries to the wrist are common. Most injuries appear to be the result of force applied when the wrist is in a hyperextended position, thus instituting a severe compression. The lunate bone is frequently injured, often resulting in a chipping of the bone itself. The chip may work itself loose and lodge among other carpal bones causing pain, irritation, and limitation of normal movement.

One of the most important injuries, amounting to approximately 8% of the fractures occurring in organized sport, is fracture of the carpal navicular. This can occur quite easily when the athlete falls on his outstretched hand. Too often, such injuries are rather cursorily dismissed as simple sprains and, as a result, the fracture is neglected.

Wrist injuries are common to all sports but achieve a considerable incidence and significance in wrestling and in gymnastics. Compression injuries are fairly commonplace among tumblers, free-exercise men, and long horse vaulters. In these activities speed is added to mass to increase the resultant force thrust against the hyperextended wrist. Rotatory movements, as performed in tumbling, create an additional hazard, since a rotational shearing action is exerted on the hyperextended wrist if the hand is improperly placed. Severe sprains or fractures are usually the result.

Hip joint. The hip joint is a diarthrodial joint formed by articulation of the head of the femur with the acetabular cavity of the pelvis. A cartilaginous cup or rim further deepens the cavity. The head of the femur is almost completely spherical in shape, permitting a degree of freedom second only to that found in the shoulder joint. However, the accompanying ligaments, capsule, and adjacent muscles serve to restrict this mobility to a considerable degree. Of interest and concern to the trainer is the Y ligament or iliofemoral band, an extremely strong fibrous band that crosses the anterior aspect of the joint and serves to check extension, outward rotation, and inward rotation. As a result, hyperextension of the hip is practically nonexistent. When the thigh is flexed upon the trunk, the Y ligament is slack; but when the thigh is straightened so that it falls into line with the trunk, the ligament is straightened to its full length.

The head of the femur is the main weight-bearing point of the body and, as such, is subjected to much force. Most hip injuries occur as the result of the athlete attempting a sudden change of direction and consequently subjecting the neck of the femur to considerable torque. On occasion injuries occur because the joint is forced beyond the limits of its range of motion. In rare circumstances an impacted fracture may result when force is applied to the leg in such manner that the head of the femur is driven into the acetabulum with great force.

Knee joint. The knee, a hinge joint, permits free flexion and extension and, in some instances, a slight amount of rotation of the tibia. Although formed by the articulation of only two bones, the tibia and the femur, this is not only an exceedingly complex joint but also the largest articulation in the body.

At first glance the joint appears somewhat insecure, but closer observation reveals that it is reinforced on all four sides by ligamentous support and muscle tendons. On the anterior aspect the tendon of the quadriceps fuses with the capsule, which has contained within it the patella or kneecap, a sesamoid bone. Lateral stability is achieved through the fibular and tibial collateral ligaments, the anterior and posterior cruciate ligaments, the articular capsule, and the muscle tendons and tendinous expansions that occur on the lateral and posterior aspects of the joint. Within the joint are the semilunar menisci, two crescent-shaped fibrocartilaginous disks, varying in thickness from their outer rims toward the center and thus providing a concavity into which the femoral condyles fit.

The stress demands made upon the knee joint in all sports are quite severe. Because of the structure of the knee joint, ligamentous injuries are especially common despite the joint reinforcements. The knee is particularly vulnerable to forces delivered either laterally or medially when the joint is in a position of extension. Often the collateral ligaments, most frequently the medial collateral, are either sprained or ruptured. This injury may occur as an isolated trauma. More commonly, however, it is associated with tears of either or both cruciate ligaments and with injury to either or both of the menisci (Fig. 5-3). Such injury may involve various combinations. The menisci may be cracked or may be broken into two or more pieces either as the result of lateral force applied when the joint is in an extended or locked position or as the result of force transmitted through the femur in a downward-angling direction, such as occurs when one lands after a jump and fails to flex the knee joint sufficiently to dissipate the shock of landing. Coaches and trainers must stress the value of the partially flexed knee joint in receiving an impact force if such injuries are to be avoided. A recent study indicates that the cross-body block in football is the major cause of knee injuries in that sport.[11]

Severe twisting of the knee is often encountered, particularly in football, when cleated shoes are worn. The amount of torque engendered when the foot is firmly fixed and the rest of the body continues to rotate longitudinally is of considerable magnitude; consequently, the knee liga-

ments are subjected to tremendous stress and are frequently badly strained or torn.

The search for a football shoe that will not be a considerable factor in knee and ankle joint injuries goes on. One recent study conducted with high school players indicated that low cut shoes with disc heels materially reduced injuries. Players wearing shoes of this type had an injury rate almost one third lower than the rate for players wearing conventional shoes. The study further pointed out that backs incurred double the rate of ankle and joint injuries as compared to lineman, and that the risk of such injuries was ten times greater in a game than in practice.[12,13] A similar study reported that a soccer type shoe with a molded sole with fourteen ⅜-inch soccer cleats markedly reduced both the incidence and the severity of knee injuries among the high school players studied.[14]

Tearing of the tibial collateral ligament usually results in injury to the medial meniscus, since it is attached to the ligament. The action may tend to pull the meniscus out of place and, in some situations, to crack or break it.

Much attention has focused on the need

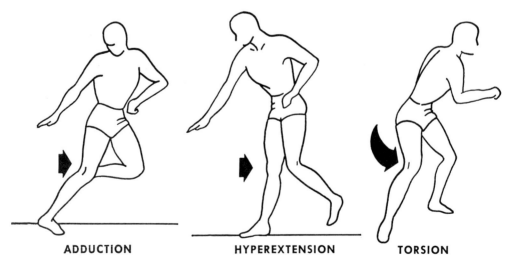

ADDUCTION   **HYPEREXTENSION**   **TORSION**

Fig. 5-3. Mechanisms of knee sprains. Arrow in each case indicates direction of applied force.

to equate the strengths of the muscle groups, particularly those on the anterior and posterior aspects of the thigh, the quadriceps and the hamstring or biceps groups, respectively. It is believed that muscular imbalance between these groups is responsible for many knee injuries, since such imbalance can reduce the stability of the knee or augment ahe amount of force or stress to which the joint is subjected. Attaining a balanced development of the biceps and quadriceps is the best insurance against knee injuries.[12] Among high school athletes the hamstrings are frequently underdeveloped. Therefore the greater strength of the quadriceps puts considerable force into the movement of extension and subjects the tibial tuberosity, where the quadriceps tendon inserts, to pull; this may act as a predisposing factor to the onset of Osgood-Schlatter disease, which is relatively common at this age level.

Evidence indicates that a difference of 10% in the strength between the knee flexors (hamstrings) and the extensors is the critical level. A greater difference results in a tendency for the weaker group to be particularly vulnerable to strain.[15] Muscular imbalance of this type renders the knee less stable and is an invitation to injury.

Inability to predict with some degree of certainty when players will suffer knee or ankle injuries somewhat compounds the situation. Were such prediction reasonably certain, prophylactic exercises could be prescribed for those players having certain characteristics that render them more prone than usual to such joint injuries.[16] Team physicians seem to agree that the strengthening of the hamstrings and the quadriceps bilaterally, to their respective optimums, makes the knee joint stronger and assists the ligaments in maintaining a good level of stability.

Ankle joint. The ankle joint is a freely movable hinge joint formed by the tibia and fibula articulating with the superior aspect of the talus. The tibia and fibula are strengthened by a number of ligaments: the anterior and posterior tibiofibular and talofibular, the calcaneofibular, the lateral talocalcaneal, the deltoid, and the interosseous. All these, together with the capsule that surrounds the joint, ensure its integrity. The strength of the joints is further augmented by the tendons of the long muscles of the lower leg, a number of which traverse the joint. Medial and lateral stability is increased by the extension of the tibial and fibular malleoli, which course down, respectively, the medial and lateral aspects of the talus, completely restricting lateral movement and rotation. The ankle joint has a range of motion from 75 to 80 degrees, moving from plantar flexion to dorsiflexion, and about 50 to 70 degrees from inversion to eversion.

Sprains and bruises occur most often to the ankles and knees. The ankle joint, because of the inadequate support supplied by the muscles and ligaments, suffers frequent and often severe injury. Since the medial malleolus is the shorter of the two, the talus tends to rotate or slide around it in such a manner that the foot is inverted; that is, the foot is turned inward and the lateral aspect of the joint is subjected to a severe pulling or tearing action on the ligaments and surrounding tissues. If the force is unusually severe, the malleolus may break. Since the body weight is transmitted through both fibula and tibia to the talus, the joint is subjected to considerable stress. When the joint is placed in an awkward position, the body weight tends to accentuate the moment of force. Approximately 85% of inversion injuries result in tearing of the lateral ligament.

Generally joints vary in strength based on their skeletal, ligamentous, and muscular arrangement. Table 5-1 indicates the relative strengths of joints in terms of athletic participation.

POSTURAL DEVIATIONS AND INJURY POTENTIAL

Postural deviations are often a primary source of injuries caused by either unilateral asymmetries, bone anomalies, abnormal bone alignments, or poor mechanics of

Table 5-1. General strength grades in selected articulations

Articulation	Skeleton	Ligaments	Muscles
Ankle	Strong	Moderate	Weak
Knee	Weak	Moderate	Strong
Hip	Moderate	Strong	Strong
Lumbosacral	Weak	Strong	Moderate
Lumbar vertebrae	Strong	Strong	Moderate
Cervical vertebrae	Weak	Moderate	Strong
Sternoclavicular	Weak	Weak	Weak
Acromioclavicular	Weak	Moderate	Weak
Glenohumeral	Weak	Moderate	Moderate
Elbow	Moderate	Strong	Strong
Wrist	Weak	Moderate	Moderate
Phalanges (toes and fingers)	Weak	Moderate	Moderate

movement.[2] Many sports activities are unilateral, thus leading to considerable overdevelopment of a body segment. The resulting imbalance is manifested by a postural deviation as the body seeks to reestablish itself in relation to its center of gravity. Often such deviations are a primal cause of injury. Unfortunately, not much in the form of remedial work is done; as a result, an injury often becomes chronic—sometimes to the point that continued participation in a sport must be halted. When possible, the trainer should seek to ameliorate or eliminate bad postural conditions through therapy, working under the direction of an orthopedist or other qualified medical personnel. Remedial work of this type can complement the training program and, in most instances, may consist principally in maintaining sufficient bilateral development to minimize the more obvious undesirable effects of intensive unilateral development. It is well to remember that development of the antagonistic muscles to offset the power and force of the agonistic muscles will reinforce and establish stability and assist in the development and maintenance of good muscular balance. A number of postural conditions offer genuine hazards to an athlete by making him exceedingly prone to specific injuries. Some of the more important will be indicated in the following discussions of foot and leg anomalies, spinal anomalies, and various stress syndromes.

Foot and leg anomalies

Poor mechanics of walking and running. Ligamentous and muscular sprains of the foot, ankle, or knee often result from poor walking or running mechanics. These injuries become chronic when faulty alignment of the foot and leg persists. When such mechanics are observed, it is often well to check the footgear as a first step. Improperly fitting or poorly designed shoes may cause or aggravate an undesirable condition. Therefore, considerable care must be exercised when athletic gear is issued to fit the shoe to the boy and not the boy to the shoe. An orthopedist or corrective therapist can usually assist the trainer and coach in developing an adequate corrective program for remedying foot and leg problems.

The knee joint, by virtue of its anatomical structure, is basically an unstable joint. Thus knee injuries in both contact and noncontact sports are quite common. Pronation or toeing out, in either walking or running, exposes the medial aspect of the knee joint to such an extent that when considerable lateral force is applied (as in being tackled or in changing direction suddenly while moving at a high rate of speed) severe injury can result. Athletes who habitually walk or run in this fashion should be placed on a corrective program to obviate the habit and to reduce susceptibility to knee joint damage.

Valgus knees (knock-knees). Valgus

knees is an orthopedic disorder that presents a serious hazard to the knee joint. The weight-bearing line passes to the lateral side of the center of the knee joint as a result of the inward angling of the thigh and lower leg. This causes the body weight to be borne principally on the medial aspects of the articulating surfaces, thereby subjecting the medial collateral ligament to considerable strain and rendering the joint somewhat more unstable and prone to injury.

Varus knees (bowlegs). Varus knees is the opposite of valgus knees. The extra stress is put upon the fibular collateral ligament. In extreme cases of either of these conditions, it would be well to guide the athlete into a noncontact activity in which he would not be subjected to the conditions of stress and force encountered in the contact sports.

Spinal anomalies

Kyphosis. An abnormal forward curvature of the cervicothoracic spine, commonly termed "round shoulders," characterizes this condition. As a rule it is accompanied by forward-thrust head, abducted scapulae, and flat chest. Usually, activities that make great demands upon the pectoral muscles are a primary cause in fostering this condition among athletes. It has been found that kyphotic athletes who have strong and well-developed but shortened pectoral muscles (such as are found frequently among basketball players, gymnasts, weightlifters, and—as a product of football stances—among football players) are quite susceptible to anterior dislocations of the arm, particularly when the arm is forced into an abducted and extended position accompanied by outward rotation. Exercises designed to stretch the shortened pectoral muscles and to strengthen muscles in the upper back, thus obtaining a more normal shoulder alignment and reducing the possible incidence of shoulder joint injury, are advocated.

Lumbar lordosis. Lumbar lordosis is an abnormal anterior curvature of the lumbar spine, commonly called "hollow back." A tightening of the lower back extensor muscles, a contraction of the lumbar fascia, and a corresponding stretching of the abdominal muscles are involved. Among football players this condition is further aggravated by the postural demands of the offensive stance. Lumbosacral strain, sacroiliac strain, and coccyalgia (pain in the coccygeal area) often may be traced to a lordotic condition as the predisposing cause. During active exercise there may be an overriding of the lumbosacral facets when an excessive lordosis is present; this can and often does result in trauma. The hamstring pull, sometimes suffered by trackmen, is often associated with a lordotic condition in which a lowering of the pubic arch produces a corresponding lift of the ischial tuberosity, where the hamstrings originate. As a result, the latter are constantly in a state of stretch. Correction of the pelvic tilt by means of an exercise program designed to strengthen the abdominal muscles and stretch the lumbar extensor muscles, as well as improving the flexibility of the spine, will do much to ameliorate this condition.

Scoliosis. Scoliosis is defined as a lateral curvature of the spine and is a condition in which there is a rotary, lateral, curving deviation of the vertebrae from the median line of the body. Many of our sports are unilateral, and others have certain phases that tend to develop or aggravate this postural-orthopedic condition. Baseball pitching and high jumping utilizing a one-foot take-off are examples. Scoliotic athletes may be subject to severe epiphysitis or bursitis as a result of the excessive force demands made upon the joint structures of the overdeveloped segment.

When a scoliotic condition is not directly attributable to a sport or a habit, it is usually caused by another structural condition, of which the most common probably is unequal leg length. When this condition exists, a lift built into the shoe will often correct the situation and permit the athlete to function normally. As with other postural-orthopedic conditions, a prescribed exercise program to increase flexibility, to stretch the shortened muscles, and/or to strengthen the stretched muscles should be administered under the direction of a trained therapist or physician.

ABNORMAL AND REPETITIVE STRESS SYNDROMES

Injuries as a result of abnormal and repetitive stress fall into a class with certain identifiable syndromes and result in either limitation or curtailment of athletic performance. Most of these injuries in athletes are directly related to the dynamics of running or throwing. The injuries may result from constant and repetitive stresses placed upon bones, joints, or soft tissues; from forcing a joint into an extreme range of motion; or from prolonged strenuous activity. Some of the injuries falling into this category may be relatively minor; still they can prove to be quite disabling.

Dynamics of running. Since many of the abnormal or continued stress syndromes bear a direct relationship to the act of running, the trainer should have an understanding of what is involved in this gait. Running differs from walking in that the double period of support that occurs in walking is eliminated and a period of flight during which there is no contact with the ground is achieved. Basically there are three phases to the running gait: the push-off, the flight, and the landing. In running the foot strikes the ground almost directly under the center of gravity. This is not the case in walking.[17,18] The resistive force, that is, the body weight and the backward pressure of the foot as it strikes the ground ahead of the body, is almost entirely eliminated in running. The supportive phase decreases, having an inverse relationship to the speed of the gait. In a sprint at a high rate of speed, the supportive phase is almost entirely propulsive. The legs alternate between a swinging phase, a brief supportive phase, and another swinging phase. Since the foot strikes the ground in advance of the body, there is a forward component

of force in the thrust of the foot against the ground, which results in a backward counterpressure of the ground against the foot, slightly checking the forward momentum of the body. Most overuse injuries occur at this moment of impact. The counterpressure exists from the moment of footstrike until the center of gravity has moved beyond the supporting foot. When the center of gravity has moved in front of the supporting foot, a propulsive force is engendered by the forceful thrust of the foot against the ground, resulting from the extension of the hip, knee, and ankle.

The mechanics of running are indeed similar to those of walking, differing, as previously stated, in the fact that the period of double support is eliminated and a period of flight supplants it. The force exerted consists of two components, horizontal and vertical, although the vertical component (unlike that in walking) is negligible because of the great increase in the horizontal component. Since the horizontal force is greatly increased, accompanied by a slight vertical increase, the angle between the leg and the ground during extension is smaller and the pelvis is carried lower. Therefore, the weight is brought closer to the hip. The lowering of the pelvis requires greater flexion of the knee joint of the supporting leg, thus increasing the amount of extensor force developed by the driving leg. The increased knee flexion reduces the amount of time required to carry the leg forward to a position of extension. Since speed is considerably increased in running and since the body undergoes a period of flight, the force is greatly magnified when the swinging leg and foot strike the ground. In walking the heel of the swinging foot strikes the ground; but in running the leg reaches a full extension and has initiated the beginning of a backward movement. This causes the ball of the foot, rather than the heel, to make forceful contact with the supporting surface. In slow running, contact may be made with the heel first, the runner rolling along the lateral border to the ball of the foot as the leg reaches full backward extension. In sprinting, the weight is borne principally by the toes. At the moment of impact the foot may be in either dorsiflexion or plantar flexion, depending upon whether the runner is moving slowly or rapidly. Placement of the foot may be in a neutral position or it may be toed out (pronation) or toed in (inversion). The latter two placements will exert considerable stress on the medial and lateral aspects of the foot, respectively. Pronation, the weakest position of the foot, is usually associated with a decided inward rotation of the thigh, which causes additional strain to be put on the knee and hip joints, sometimes resulting in significant trauma. Continued overuse of the foot, particularly as encountered in distance running, leads to syndromes that are relatively common in activities in which repetitive pounding of the foot occurs in the footstrike and the take-off thrust phases of the gait.

Dynamics of throwing. Throwing activities account for a considerable number of acute and chronic injuries to the elbow and shoulder joints. Throwing is a unilateral action, which, particularly in sports activities such as pitching or javelin throwing, subjects the arm to repetitive stresses of great intensity. Should the thrower employ incorrect techniques, the joints are affected by atypical stresses that result in trauma to the joint and its surrounding tissues. Throwing is a sequential pattern of movements in which each part of the body must perform a number of carefully timed and executed acts. For example, the throwing of a ball or javelin employs one particular pattern of movements; the hurling of the discus or hammer makes use of a similar complex, but with centrifugal force substituted for linear force and the type of terminal movements employed in release being different. Putting the shot—a pushing rather than a throwing movement—has in its overall pattern a number of movements similar to those employed in throwing a ball. Discus and hammer throwing seldom result in significant injury problems. However, hammer throwers, because of improper release of the hammer, on occasion may incur shoulder girdle injuries, particularly of the rotator cuff muscles and the middle and posterior deltoid.

In the act of throwing, momentum is transferred from the thrower's body to the object that is thrown. According to physical laws, the greater and heavier the mass, the greater is the momentum needed to move it. Hence, as the size and weight of the object increase, more parts of the body are utilized to effect the summation of forces needed to accomplish the throw. The same is true in respect to the speed of the object: the greater the speed, the more body parts that must come into play to increase the body's momentum. Timing and sequence of action are of the utmost importance. They improve with correct practice.

In throwing, the arm acts as a sling or catapult, transfering and imparting momentum from the body to the ball. There are various types of throwing, with the overhand, sidearm, and underarm styles being the most common. The act of throwing is fairly complex and requires considerable coordination and timing if success is to be achieved.

In throwing, the shoulder and the elbow seem particularly vulnerable to trauma. Uncoordinated or stress movements can subject either articulation to a considerable amount of abnormal force or torque. In pitching, with considerable speed being engendered, the forearm is the crucial element. The inward or outward rotation that is used to impart additional speed and action to the ball subjects the elbow and the shoulder to appreciable torque, which may become traumatizing if the action is improperly performed over a considerable period of time. The rotator cuff muscles, the long head of the biceps brachii, the pronator teres, the anconeus, and the deltoid are the muscles that are most affected in throwing.

Lesions of the pitching arm are not only quite common, but oddly enough are not restricted to the mature college or professional player. In the adolescent bones are immature; the epiphyses are not closed and appear to be somewhat susceptible to injury. Throwing or pitching involves three distinct phases: a preparatory or cocking phase; the delivery or acceleration phase; and the follow-through or terminal phase. Specific injuries appear peculiar to each phase.[19]

The initial cocking phase may result in decreased internal and increased external humeral rotation, and tendinitis may occur in both the biceps and triceps muscles, as well as in the shoulder rotators. The delivery or acceleration phase can cause tendinitis involving the pectoralis major and the latissimus dorsi muscles. "Little League shoulder," which results in osteochondrosis of the proximal humeral epiphysis or in a fracture of the proximal portion of the humeral shaft can also result.[19] This phase also subjects the elbow joint to considerable torque and stress, which may cause "Little League elbow" (see page 57). Changes at the radiohumeral joint caused by compression forces may result in an aseptic necrosis of the radial head or osteochondritis dissecans of the capitulum of the humerus where it articulates with the radius. Bony spurs on both radius and ulna are not uncommon.

The final phase of the throw, the follow-through, has few problems other than the pronator teres syndrome, wherein pain is felt during the terminal pitching phase.[19] This syndrome appears most frequently among adults, since the forearm pronation is more marked in performing a "breaking" pitch. Tullis and King ascribe this syndrome principally to an ischemia within the pronator teres.[19]

Careful coaching to assist athletes in developing the proper timing and sequence of movement, coupled with a training program for developing the muscles of the throwing arm, will reduce injuries to a minimum.

Dynamics of jumping. In jumping activities the shock of take-off and landing is transmitted to the lower limb or limbs.

Improper take-off or landing is responsible for a great many joint injuries. The force of the take-off can cause a stress fracture to the foot or the ankle. The shock of an improper landing is frequently the cause of injury to the ankle, knee, or hip joint.

Severe torque results when the take-off foot is either toed in or out. In either case the ligaments, particularly in the ankle or the knee joint, are subjected to an intense rotational shear force that usually results in torn ligaments, cartilages, or bone fracture. Improper landings from either the high jump or long jump can cause lower limb injury, but the arms and neck are also vulnerable. The recent introduction of the "Fosbury flop" style of high jumping, wherein the bar is cleared by going over backward and the landing is on the back, has resulted in a rash of cervical injuries, especially to younger jumpers. Inasmuch as this technique requires split-second timing to avoid neck and back injury, its use by junior and senior high school jumpers should be discouraged.

Traumatic forces to the ankle joint frequently occur in jumping. Such twisting or shearing action can be damaging, indeed. Approximately 85% of all ankle injuries result from a forced inversion, which causes a tearing of the lateral ligaments. Eversion injuries usually result in the breaking off of the lateral malleolus with some damage to the connective tissues on the medial aspect of the ankle.[1]

Although the knee is largest joint in the body, its shallowness renders it extremely vulnerable to injury. Medial, lateral, and twisting forces, such as encountered in most sports, subject the supportive ligamentous bands to severe strains. These injuries can occur after one violent traumatic incident, or they may result from the cumulative effects of repeated microtrauma. Such strain can result in the stretching or tearing of the supporting connective tissue. This is particularly the case when the foot is firmly fixed and the body and leg go into or are in rotation. Hyperextension of the knee, wherein the knee is forced into a position beyond the normal 180 degree position, can result in severe joint trauma that may involve the synovial membrane or the deeper periosteal tissue (Fig. 5-3). This commonly occurs in take-off but can occur on landing, especially in gymnastics.

Athletes should be taught proper foot placement as well as the technique of landing with the hips, knees, and ankles partially flexed and relaxed to absorb the landing shock. In some instances the addition of a body or shoulder roll as the initial landing phase is terminated may further mitigate shock.

Enthesitis. Enthesitis applies to a group of conditions that are characterized initially by inflammatory reactions and subsequently by fibrosis and calcification around the tendons, ligaments, and muscle insertions. As the result of muscular imbalance, excessive strength, or incoordination, severe strain may be exerted on the insertions, with enthesitis resulting. Proper conditioning can go a long way toward preventing or eliminating the condition.

Hypertrophy of the second metatarsal. Milers and other distance runners who have engaged in strenuous training and conditioning over a considerable span of time often suffer from hypertrophy of the second metatarsal. It is thought that the condition is caused by the strong thrust of the ball of the foot against the running surface during the phase of pushing off. As the foot begins its thrust, it is in a position of extreme dorsiflexion, usually with the center of gravity passing through or just forward of the ball of the foot. The extensors of the foot and ankle are bringing maximum pressure to bear on the heads of the metatarsals. The resulting forces place great stress on this area, and as a consequence the second metatarsal, which receives a considerable share of the force, tends to enlarge or hypertrophy. This response illustrates the structure-function principle. The length of the first metatarsal apparently has no effect on this anomaly; nor does a condition of flatfoot accompany it or act as a causal factor.

Longitudinal arch strain. Longitudinal arch strain is usually an early season injury caused by subjecting the musculature of the foot to unaccustomed, severe exercise and forceful contact with hard playing surfaces. In this condition there is a flattening or depressing of the longitudinal arch when the foot is in the mid-support phase, resulting in a strain to the arch. Such a strain may appear quite suddenly, or it may develop rather slowly throughout a considerable length of time. As a rule, pain is experienced only when running is attempted and usually appears just below the medial malleolus and the posterior tibial tendon, accompanied by swelling and tenderness along the medial aspect of the foot. Prolonged strain will also involve the calcaneonavicular ligament and move progressively to the talonavicular joint, and then to the articulation of the first cuneiform with the navicular. The flexor muscle of the great toe (flexor hallucis longus) often develops tenderness as a result of overuse in compensating for the stress on the arch ligaments.

Medial epicondyle epiphysis avulsion ("Little League elbow"). Medial epicondyle epiphysis avulsion, seemingly on the increase in recent years, affects young baseball players, particularly those between 10 and 16 years of age. The injury occurs when the medial epicondyle of the humerus breaks loose from the adjacent bone tissue as the result of a severe contraction of the elbow extensors.[20] Youngsters in this age group have muscles that are stronger than their bones, which have not yet reached a stage of complete ossification. The snapping motion of the forearm, commonly employed in pitching a curve ball, occurs as the elbow moves into extension on the forward phase of the throw, just prior to the release of the ball. This is the causal factor of the trauma. Proper conditioning and good warm-up procedures will assist to some extent in the prevention of "Little League elbow", but beyond this there is no known preventive measure other than to delay curve pitching until the late teens.

Metatarsal arch strain. Insufficient conditioning of the foot musculature or incorrect techniques of foot usage are the usual causes of metatarsal arch strain. The athlete who has a high arch is especially susceptible to this type of strain because of the increased stress to which the intermetatarsal ligaments are subjected. Other atypical foot conditions such as flatfoot and hallux valgus (bunion) may predispose to this strain.

Plantar fascia strain. Running the length of the sole of the foot is a broad band of dense connective tissue called the plantar aponeurosis. It is attached to the undersurface of the calcaneus at the back and fans out toward the front, with fibers and their various small branches attaching to the metatarsophalangeal articulations and merging into the capsular ligaments. Other fibers, arising from well within the aponeurosis, pass between the intrinsic muscles of the foot and the long flexor tendons of the sole and attach themselves to the deep fascia below the bones. The function of the plantar aponeurosis is to assist in maintaining the stability of the foot and in securing or bracing the longitudinal arch.

Strains to the fascia commonly occur during the early part of the season in sports that require running. The incidence is fairly high among tennis and basketball players, as well as among runners. The fascia is placed under strain either by extension of the toes or by depression of the longitudinal arch as the result of weight bearing. When the weight is principally on the heel, as in ordinary standing, the tension exerted on the fascia is negligible. However, when the weight is shifted to the ball of the foot (i.e., on the heads of the metatarsals), fascial tension is so increased that it equals approximately twice the body weight. In running, since the push-off phase involves both a forceful extension of the toes and a powerful thrust by the ball of the foot against a relatively unyielding surface, the degree of fascial tension is greatly increased.

Athletes who have a mild pes cavus (high arch) are particularly prone to fascial strain. Modern street shoes, by nature of their design, take on the characteristics of splints and tend to restrict foot action to an extent at which the arch may become somewhat rigid because of shortening of the ligaments and other mild pathologies. The athlete, upon changing from such footgear into a flexible gymnastic slipper or soft track shoe, often experiences trauma when subjecting the foot to stresses. Trauma may also result from running improperly, either as the result of poor techniques or because of lordosis, wherein the increased forward tilt of the pelvis produces an unfavorable angle of foot-strike in which the magnitude of force exerted on the ball of the foot is considerable.

Splints. Splints occur in two areas of the body: the shin and the radial aspect of the forearm. The term "shin splints" is more familiar to the trainer, since the condition occurs frequently among athletes, generally at the start and at the end of the season. It is usually the result of strenuous work on a hard surface, involving sudden changes of direction and starting and stopping. Jumping is also a causal factor, and high jumpers, broad jumpers, and pole vaulters, along with gymnasts, frequently experience this handicapping injury.[21]

"Shin splints" are usually attributed to overuse of the anterior or posterior tibial muscles. The symptoms include a burning or a dull aching pain, somewhat intermittent at the onset but becoming more or less continuous in time. Tenderness, swelling, and heat complete the picture. Attempts to flex or extend the ankle joint elicit pain—sometimes to such an extent that participation in sports may be precluded. In many instances a condition casually diagnosed as "shin splint" may be a periostitis, tenosynovitis, or myositis of the dorsiflexors of the foot; hence, a careful diagnosis is imperative.

"Forearm splints" are quite common among gymnasts and, to a lessor extent, among wrestlers and baseball throwers. Repetitive forceful contact with an unyielding or a lightly padded surface such as is encountered in wrestling, free-exercise performance, tumbling, or side horse work subjects the forearm to considerable punishment and elicits an overuse syndrome in the brachioradialis and attendant forearm muscles. The symptoms, parallel to those of "shin splints," are pain, tenderness, and heat. Flexion or extension of the wrist joint produces considerable pain, often to a degree that will force the athlete to drop out of the activity.

Stress fractures. Fractures caused by stress, overuse, or anatomical anomalies may occur at several places in the foot or leg. An athlete who has an atypical condition such as hallux valgus, flatfoot, or a short first metatarsal is more easily disposed toward incurring a stress fracture than is the individual whose foot is free of pathological or mechanical defects. A short first metatarsal is unable mechanically to make use of its strength and position to properly distribute the weight to the front part of the foot. Therefore, excessive pressure and additional weight are transferred to the second metatarsal, resulting in traumatic changes and, on occasion, fracture. The presence of tenderness or a callus is one of the first indications[22] (Fig. 5-4).

Stress or fatigue fractures may take place in the second, third, or fourth metatarsal, as a result of the pounding to which the ball of the foot is subjected in running. The lower half of the fibula is also prone to stress fractures.[23] It is thought that these fractures occur because of the repeated pulls exerted on the fibula by the plantar

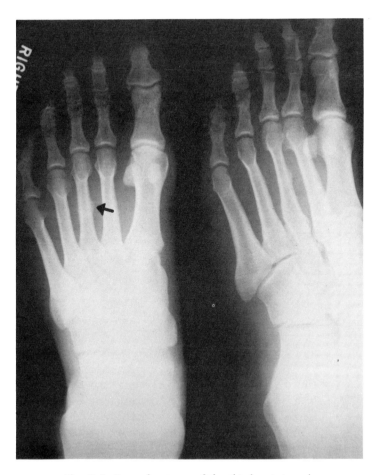

Fig. 5-4. Stress fractures of the third metatarsal.

flexors of the foot and the flexors of the toes during the push-off phase of the stride. Pain, swelling, and tenderness are discernible just above the lateral malleolus, and in time a callus will form.

The squat (deep knee bend). The use of the deep knee bend contributes to an overuse syndrome, which has far-reaching consequences.[24] For that reason it is being considered here. This type of exercise has always enjoyed a great popularity among coaches and has long been employed, ostensibly as a means of strengthening the quadriceps and the hamstrings, through routines involving the deep squat such as the "duck walk," the squat thrust or "Burpee," the "Russian bear dance," or continuous deep knee bends. These activities are sometimes performed with the trainee carrying additional weight in the form of bar bells or other equipment to load the exercise.

The movement employed in the full squat primarily affects the knee and ankle joints and, to a lesser extent, the hip joint. On the initial movement flexion is elicited at the hips, knees, and ankles. It is produced by the force of gravity and controlled by an eccentric or lengthening contraction of the extensor muscles of the thigh. As the athlete reaches the terminal position and is in a full squat, the anterior portion of the knee joint is thrust forward. As a result the extensors are stretched to their full length, thereby forcing the posterior aspect to support the entire weight of the body with the flexors in a state of tension. The knee joint is thus levered into what is tantamount to an open position, exerting an excessive stress on the medial and lateral, as well as on the cruciate ligaments, which may therefore become overstretched and weakened. This reduces the inherent stability of the joint. Using exercises that employ the deep squat contributes to the development of chronic synovitis and may predispose the joint to arthritic changes in later life. In the pubescent athlete the severe pull exerted on the tibial tuberosity by the quadriceps tendon while a deep knee bend is being executed can be a factor in the development of Osgood-Schlatter disease.

Exercises employing the full squat should be eliminated from the conditioning program. The inherent dangers in such exercises far outweigh the values to be gained through performing them. Orthopedists are quite concerned with this problem. Numerous clinical evaluations emphasize the necessity for making this elimination. Substituting either the quarter or the half squat for the full squat, with the heels placed on a lift of from 1 to 2 inches in height, is suggested as better exercise to develop the muscles of the knee and hip joint. An exercise such as recommended here provides ample load for the muscles without subjecting the knee joint to severe strain. Granted that orthopedists seem convinced that one does not need cruciate ligaments to participate in his daily round of normal activities, it is nonetheless advisable that participation in contact sports (especially football) be avoided by the prepubescent individual. Bilaterally strengthening the quadriceps and biceps groups is the best insurance for a stable knee joint.

Traumatic elbow. Traumatic elbow is variously identified as "pitcher's elbow," or "tennis elbow," or "thrower's arm."[25,26] It is rather prevalent in baseball pitching, tennis, golf, and javelin throwing as a result of the continuous forceful extension of the forearm accompanied by a severe twisting motion, such as transpires when a pitcher throws a curve or screwball or when a tennis player applies English in returning a ball. Ball players who have commenced curve ball pitching at too early an age appear especially vulnerable. The constant, repetitive, and violent torsion and extension to which the elbow joint is subjected over a period of time, as in pitching a baseball game, results in the pronator teres muscle being torn from its origin on the lower aspect of the inner condyloid ridge of the humerus. Inadequate warm-up before throwing can also cause this condition. Usually this syndrome appears as the result of continuous abuse, but on occasion it may result from a single incident. (See "Little League elbow.")

Traumatic shoulder. Traumatic shoulder is the condition commonly identified among athletes and trainers as a "glass" arm.[27] It is a syndrome resulting from chronic irritation and degeneration of the tendon of the long head of the biceps. In throwing, the tendon is whipped with considerable force against the outer edge of the bicipital groove, thus causing irritation. Pain is first felt at the site of the irritation, approximately 2 inches below the head of the humerus. As the athlete continues to throw, his throwing effectiveness declines progressively. He loses speed and control; should be persist, function will diminish to the point at which he will be unable to lift his arm. Because of the mechanics involved, pitchers who throw a "roundhouse" type of curve are particularly susceptible to this injury.

Readiness. Muscles serve as pads to cushion and distribute any external force applied to the body. In the contact sports players should be taught to achieve a state of readiness, that is, to "set" themselves a moment before impact by partially tensing the muscles so that the body is prepared to receive the imminent force.[3] Tensing in this fashion aids in preventing bruising and complements the strength of the joints involved, through dissipation of the force by the muscles. This decreases the amount of stress placed on the ligamentous areas. The player who is completely relaxed at the moment of player or ground contact is the one who stands an excellent chance of injury, whereas the player who is in a state of readiness can assume the impact and still be able to continue in the play situation because the muscles are ready to move into instantaneous action.

Reinjury. The problem of reinjury is a serious one for the trainer. Less severe injuries tend to occur and reoccur with increasing frequency and severity. This is usually the result of neglect or of inadequate treatment in terms of reconditioning.

Too often, athletes resume competition before they are completely recovered, thus exposing the condition to reinjury. Treatment takes time. In the long run the athlete will be of more value to himself and to the team if he cooperates in a program of complete rehabilitation.

REFERENCES

1. Rasch, P. J., and Burke, R. K.: Kinesiology and applied anatomy, ed. 3, Philadelphia, 1967, Lea & Febiger.
2. Lowman, C. L.: Effects of postural deviations on athletic performance, Proceedings of the Fourth National Conference on the Medical Aspects of Sports, Chicago, 1962, American Medical Association, p. 8.
3. Stewart, M. J.: Unusual athletic injuries. In Reynolds, Fred C., editor: Instructional course lectures, Academy of Orthopaedic Surgeons, vol. 17, St. Louis, 1960, The C. V. Mosby Co., pp. 377-391.
4. Larson, R. L., and McMahan, R. O.: The epiphyses and the childhood athlete, J.A.M.A. **196**:607, 1966.
5. Blyth, C. S.: Summary and recommendations of the 40th annual survey of football fatalities, 1931-1971, Committee on Injuries and Fatalities, American Football Coaches Association, 1971.
6. Roaf, R.: A study of the mechanics of spinal injuries, J. Bone Joint Surg. **42-A**:810, 1960.
7. Leidholt, J. D.: Spinal injuries in sports, Proceedings of the Third National Conference on the Medical Aspects of Sports, Chicago, 1961, American Medical Association, pp. 12-17.
8. Bateman, J. E.: Shoulder injuries in the throwing sports, American Academy of Orthopaedic Surgeons, Symposium on Sports Medicine, St. Louis, 1969, The C. V. Mosby Co.
9. Symposium: The shoulder in sports, Proceedings of the Sixth National Conference on the Medical Aspects of Sports, Chicago, 1964, American Medical Association, pp. 11-15.
10. O'Donoghue, D. H.: Injuries to the shoulder girdle. In Reynolds, Fred C., editor: Instructional course lectures, Academy of Orthopaedic Surgeons, vol. 17, St. Louis, 1960, The C. V. Mosby Co., pp. 392-405.
11. Peterson, T. R.: The cross body block, the major cause of knee injuries, J.A.M.A. **211**: 449, 1970.
12. Medical Society of the State of New York, Committee on Medical Aspects of Sports: Shoe cuts football injuries, Med. Sports **9**:5, 1969.

13. Klein, C.: Orthopedic aspects of sports medicine, J. Sport Med. **1**:88, 1961.
14. Torg, J. S., and Quedenfeld, T.: The effect of shoe type and cleat length on the incidence and severity of knee injuries among Philadelphia high school football players, Med. Sci. Sports 3:s, 1971.
15. Burkett, L. N.: Causative factors in hamstring strains, Med. Sci. Sports **2**:39, 1970.
16. Clark, J. L., Challop, R. S., and McCabe, E. B.: Predicting lower extremity injuries in high school football players, J.A.M.A. **217** (11):1552, 1972.
17. Napier, J.: The antiquity of human walking, Sci. Amer. **216**:56, 1967.
18. Slocum, D. B., and Bowerman, W.: The biomechanics of running, Clin. Orthop. **23**:39, 1962.
19. Tullos, H. S., and King, J. W.: Lesions of the pitching arm in adolescents, J.A.M.A. **220**:260, 1972.
20. Brogden, B. G., and Crow, N. E.: Little Leaguer's elbow, Amer. J. Roentgen. **83**:671, 1960.
21. Devas, M. B.: Stress fractures of the tibia in athletes or shin soreness, J. Bone Joint Surg. **40-B**:227, 1958.
22. Blazina, M. E., Watanobe, R. S., and Drake, E. R.: Fatigue fractures in track athletes, Calif. Med. **97**:61, 1962.
23. McBryde, A., Jr., and Bassett, F. H., III: Stress fracture of the fibula, M. D. G. P. **38**:120, Oct. 1968.
24. Klein, K. K.: The deep squat exercise as utilized in weight training for athletes and its effect on the ligaments of the knee, J. Ass. Phys. Ment. Rehab. **15**:6, 1961.
25. Garden, R. S.: Tennis elbow, J. Bone Joint Surg. **43-B**:100, 1961.
26. La Briola, J. H.: Athletic injuries from shoulder to wrist, Proceedings of the Fourth National Conference on the Medical Aspects of Sports, Chicago, 1963, American Medical Association, pp. 44-47.
27. Manfredi, D. H.: Baseball pitcher's shoulder and tennis elbow, Med. Sci. **17**:84, 1966.

RECOMMENDED READINGS

Armstrong, J. R., and Tucker, W. E.: Injury in sport, Springfield, Ill., 1964, Charles C Thomas, Publisher.
Badgley, C. E., and Hayes, J. T.: Athletic injuries to the elbow, forearm, wrist, and hand, Amer. J. Surg. **98**:432, 1959.
Brunnstrom, S.: Clinical kinesiology, Philadelphia, 1966, F. A. Davis Co.
Dyson, G. H. G.: The mechanics of athletics, London, 1962, University of London Press, Ltd.
Erskine, L. A.: The mechanisms involved in skiing injuries, Amer. J. Surg. Part II, **97**:667, 1959.
Hirato, I., Jr.: The doctor and the athlete, Philadelphia, 1968, J. B. Lippincott Co.
Kraus, H.: Prevention and treatment of ski injuries, J.A.M.A. **169**:1414, 1959.
Nelson, R. C., Alexander, J. F., Montoye, H. J., and others: An investigation of various measures used in impact testing of protective headgear, J. Sport Med. **4**:94, 1964.
O'Donoghue, D. H.: Head protection with helmet, J. Sport Med. **4**:43, 1964.
Orthopedic aspects of sports medicine, J. Sport Med. **1**:87, 1961.
Rachun, A.: Mechanics of athletic injury, N. Y. J. Med. **61**:2589, 1961.
Ryan, A. J.: Medical care of the athlete, New York, 1962, McGraw-Hill Book Co.
Trickett, P. C.: Athletic injuries: New York, 1965, Appleton-Century-Crofts.
Williams, M., and Lissner, H. R.: Biomechanics of human motion, Philadelphia, 1962, W. B. Saunders Co.

CHAPTER 6

Scientific bases for conditioning and training

Training is usually defined as a systematic process of repetitive, progressive exercise or work, involving also the learning process and acclimatization. The amount of exercise or work performed may be increased in two ways: (1) the weight of the load with which the individual performs exercises may be progressively increased or (2) the total time in which an exercise is performed may be decreased. In interval training, for example, subsequent distances are run within specified decreasing periods of time. Through the use of systematic work increments, improved voluntary responses by the organs are attained; through constant repetition, the conscious movements become more automatic and more reflexive in character, requiring less concentration by the higher nerve centers and thus reducing the amount of energy expended, through the elimination of movements unnecessary for performance of the desired task. Increasing the strenuousness of exercise in the ways suggested is an application of the *overload* principle, which, in essence, holds that an activity must always be upgraded to a consistently higher level through maximal or near-maximal stimulation. In this way the metabolic level and the organic responses can be increased.

PHYSIOLOGICAL EFFECTS OF TRAINING

Increase in body density. Proper training induces specific and identifiable effects. Changes in bones and muscles result as the effect of regular exercise. These physical changes are of definite, recognizable types indicative of the sport for which the training has been designed. The muscles change in girth, showing increases in cross section and in density because of an increase in sarcoplasm. There is a reduction in the amount of adipose tissue in the body, and there is an increase in the development of connective tissue within the muscle bundles, which adds to the general toughness of the muscle and enables it to better withstand the strains and stresses it must undergo.[1]

An immediate, but temporary, weight loss occurs at the onset of training as a result of loss of water. This weight is immediately replaced upon the ingestion of food and water. However, the initial true loss of weight at the start of training is caused by a reduction in the amount of fat and is followed by a slow gain in weight, resulting from an increase in muscle bulk through development.

As a result of the muscle activity involved in training, additional stress is put upon the bones. This results in an increase in the strength of the bones and also a rearrangement of the cancellous plates of the bones in accord with the stresses to which they have been subjected, thus decreasing the susceptibility to injury.[2]

Physiological implications in training for strength. Strength is defined as the capacity to exert force or as the ability to do work

63

against resistance. The most noticeable change that takes place in the muscles as a result of regular and proper exercise is the increase in girth. However, it would be well to remember that this general rule—the girth of a muscle is proportional to the work done by it—does not always hold true. Another consideration to be remembered is that a muscle will grow in size and strength only when a work load over and above any previous demands is placed upon it. This principle of overload is one of the basic premises of strength training. Frequent repetitions, if not coincidental with increases in work load, are in themselves valueless for this purpose, although the total work load may be equal.

Size alone is not an index of the strength of a muscle, since muscles of the same size in an individual may vary considerably in strength because of the difference in the amounts of adipose or fatty tissue each contains. In essence, fat possesses an inhibiting quality with respect to muscle efficiency; it not only lacks contractile power but it also limits the speed and amount of contraction by acting as a friction brake.

Muscular strength can show an increase of three times or more without a proportional increase in muscle bulk necessarily being indicated. However, exercise must be performed against near-maximal and gradually increasing resistance. Such resistance can be obtained either by lifting, pulling, or pushing against some resistive force that requires near-maximal effort for the individual, or by moving the body at an ever-increasing rate of speed that is approaching the maximum level of performance, or by a combination of the two. It is important for the trainer to know that a number of factors are involved in strength training. The speed, the duration, the number of repetitions, and the vigor or force with which exercises are performed will determine the outcome of the program.[3] The variable of individual difference is another factor that will affect the final result. Two men following identical programs will not develop strength at the same rate, in the same man-

ner, and to the same degree, because of varying inherent characteristics.

General consensus favors the current theory that hypertrophy, the increase in muscle cross section, is caused by a development of the existing constituent fibers when strength exercises are employed and by an increase in the total number of capillaries called into play when exercises of endurance are employed.[4,5] In other words, a gain in strength is accompanied by a significant increase in both the size of fibers and the number of capillaries in the muscle and by a resultant gain not only in power but also in speed and endurance.

Cross education: In recent years considerable research has demonstrated the phenomenon of "cross education" to be of some significance.[6-8] "Cross education," or *bilateral transfer of training,* refers to the ability of the nervous system to transfer some of the effects achieved by training one part of the body to the bilaterally opposite part. In some instances, the effects have been transferred to parts other than the bilateral opposite. For example, when a limb on one side of the body is exercised intensively over a period of time, the strength of the corresponding (bilateral) limb on the opposite side of the body also is improved.[9] Improvement of the remaining (ipsilateral) limb on the same side may be noted, too. For the trainer this research holds considerable significance. Following injury or disease, a more rapid return to normal fitness can be obtained if the unaffected contralateral limb or body part is put on an exercise regimen. During any period of reconditioning in which this principle is applied, it is important that the injured or affected part be free of restrictions that would affect its mobility. In this way, following injury or disease, the entire body can be innervated through exercise and the healing process be speeded up.

Planning the strength training program: In setting up a strength training program, the trainer must keep a number of considerations in mind:

1. The "overload principle" must be ap-

plied. All work should be performed with a progressively increased load or resistance or with increasing speed, of near-maximum rate, the maximum resistance being attained when the performer can make no more than ten repetitions with a given load or has reached a plateau at a speed level.

2. Strength should be developed first. Endurance and speed will be developed more readily if strength is already established.

3. The principle of "cross education" should be utilized, particularly in reconditioning.

4. Performance to the point of physical exhaustion is to be avoided. This has a deleterious effect upon the expected daily progression of the training.

5. Exercise having a specific pattern in terms of either movement, force, duration, or speed is used to produce training results that will be peculiar to that exercise alone.

6. The strength training program should be tailored to the individual. The law of individuality will apply. Individuals working on identical programs will not produce the same results.

7. Gains in strength are influenced by several factors. Although the total amount of work load or resistance may be the same, many repetitions performed with a light weight will give far less strength gain than lifting a maximum or near-maximum weight only a few times and holding the terminal position for a few seconds. Detailed instructions for developing maximum strength are given in Chapter 7, which deals specifically with the exercise program.

Physiological implications in training for flexibility. Flexibility is defined as the range of movement about a joint. The degree of flexibility of a given joint is entirely dependent upon the various physiological characteristics of the muscle and collagenous tissues surrounding that joint.[10] Studies[11,12] have indicated that an increase in the flexibility of joints tends to decrease the injuries to those joints. In most instances it is also conceded that an increase

in flexibility contributes to better athletic performance. Both of these considerations are important to the trainer. The flexible athlete, then, is less injury-prone and also is more likely to perform optimally than the inflexible individual.

Good flexibility usually indicates that there are no adhesions or abnormalities present in or around the joints and that there are no muscular limitations of serious import. This allows the body to move freely and easily through the full range of joint flexion and extension without any unnecessary restrictions in the joints or the adjacent tissues.

An increase in flexibility must accompany an increase of strength, or the range of motion may be considerably affected. Studies have shown that exercises of flexibility can achieve their goal without decreasing strength.[13] Conversely, exercises for the acquisition of great strength such as is sought by some weight lifters, without the use of accompanying movements designed to maintain and increase the range of joint motion, can and will result in the condition known as "muscle-boundedness." In this condition, because of the enormous bulk of the muscles, tendons, and ligaments and their inelasticity, there is a decided inability to obtain complete flexibility and freedom of joint mobility.

An increase in flexibility is of importance to the athlete. With more flexibility the runner can increase his stride, the hurdler can effect a more economical flight, and the swimmer can produce a better leg kick and a more efficient arm stroke. The gymnast, the wrestler, and the various other athletes are all dependent to a large degree upon good flexibility and range of motion.

There is some disagreement as to the best type of stretching procedure to use for improving flexibility. The ballistic stretch, in which the body momentum is utilized to force the muscle groups into as much extensibility as can be tolerated, has been used for many years. An example of this procedure is the "hurdler's seat," which employs a bobbing of the trunk toward the extended leg to stretch the hamstrings. Evidence seems to indicate that this type of exercise, although it will increase flexibility, may also induce muscle tears as a result of misjudging the stretch tolerance of the tissues and/or failing to control the force of the body momentum.

The static stretch, in which a position of extreme stretch on a given muscle group is assumed and held for a period of time, is thought by many to be as effective as the ballistic stretch and without the possibility of preactivity muscle strains or tears.[14] The various cultural asanas of the yogic system make excellent use of the static stretch.[15] Users of these postures have been able to achieve remarkable flexibility, apparently without sacrificing other characteristics of body efficiency.

If the ballistic stretch is used, it would be well for the performer to start slowly and confine himself to a limited range of movement. With the increase in capillary circulation and the accompanying increase in heat, range of motion, intensity, and speed may be accordingly increased to the desired amplitude. In this way the possibility of muscle distress or injury may be obviated.

The range of movement in various body parts is improved if the athlete goes slightly beyond the point of pain in such training, regardless of whether he uses the ballistic or the static stretch. Only in this way does he exert significant tension on the fascial ligamentous bands and their attachments. Joint flexibility may be varied or affected by a number of factors; among them are joint pathology, hereditary joint structural differences, elasticity of body connective tissue, reciprocal muscle coordination, and muscle viscosity. There appears to be no one single factor that either increases or decreases flexibility. Several objective methods are available for measuring flexibility. The student or trainer who wishes to utilize such tests should refer to current books on measurement in the fields of physical education, corrective physical education, or rehabilitation.

Physiological implications in training for endurance. Endurance is usually defined as the ability of the body to undergo prolonged activity or to resist stresses set up as a result of prolonged activity. Endurance involves a number of elements, each of which is partially responsible for success or failure in sustaining physical performance. Basically, endurance is primarily dependent upon the various aspects of cardiac efficiency, which in turn exerts influence upon the performance of the other portions of the human organism.[16]

Training or conditioning builds a given economy—an efficiency in body adaptibility —which is important as the body adjusts to the continued and prolonged stresses put upon it in performing an activity that requires all-out or near-maximal performance over a considerable period of time. As a result of careful conditioning, the onset of fatigue is considerably delayed and the athlete is able to maintain a high rate of performance over a long period of time.

Exercises for endurance improve muscle tonus. The improvement is primarily caused by functional involvement of more motor units as a result of work increase. Work increase improves circulation by calling into play more capillaries, thus providing the working muscles with more oxygen and fuel and facilitating removal of the metabolic by-products of exercise.

As a muscle tires, it loses some of its ability to relax. The character of a muscle is indicated not only by its ability to produce power over a protracted period of time but also by its capacity to concurrently maintain its elasticity. As the muscle works, it restores its own oxygen and fuel supplies and disposes of lactic acid and other metabolic products. As long as these two processes continue to operate at basically the same rate, the muscle can continue to work with efficiency. However, when an imbalance is reached in which the rate of waste product accumulation is cumulatively greater than the oxygen and fuel intake, physiological equilibrium (homeostasis) is upset and fatigue sets in. In fatigue the reaction time slows down, accompanied by a stiffening or inability of the muscle to reach a condition of relaxation. This stiffening or incomplete relaxation, coupled with a reduced ability to respond to stimulation, is one of the contributing factors to athletic injury.

According to Hans Selye,[17] noted Canadian physiologist and authority on stress, the degree of ability to withstand fatigue is inherited and the basis of the fatigue pattern is in each individual constitution. Two factors modify a person's capacity for improving his endurance: (1) his ability to endure the pain and concomitant discomforts of fatigue while endeavoring to improve his level of work tolerance, and (2) his body's ability to effect the necessary homeostatic adjustments, which can enable him to increase his energy production to as much as twenty times the resting level when such a demand is made.

Physiological implications in training for speed. Speed differs from endurance in that it requires the expenditure of an enormous amount of energy in a short time. This requires performances of extremely short duration, such as a swim sprint, a dash, or a rope climb, to rely almost exclusively upon the oxygen within the tissues. The anaerobic activity depends upon the immediate chemical release of oxidative energy by phosphocreatine and ATP, a high energy phosphate compound, for instant utilization by the muscles. The amount of energy released, although high, cannot meet the tremendous requirements of prolonged intensive exercise.

Age is a factor in attaining speed. An individual's ability in speed reaches its peak

Fig. 6-1. Sprinting demands great muscular strength.

when he is about 20 years of age. Speed is dependent not only upon a considerable amount of anaerobic activity, but also upon the resiliency and the responsiveness of the circulatory system. Speed ability declines rapidly after 28 years of age because it imposes a considerable task upon the heart and loss of vascular resiliency increases slowly (Fig. 6-1).

As previously stated, the strength gain of muscles is accompanied by a significant increase in both the size of fibers and in the number of capillaries. This gain in strength results in *concomitant gains in speed* and in endurance. Russian studies bear out this contention. In training for speed one should train principally for strength by means of overload and by application of the principles employed for improving strength and endurance.[18,19] Speed activities should be added to the program to enable the athlete to increase his ability to produce energy more rapidly and to accumulate a greater oxygen debt. On this basis it would be consistent to place athletes who participate in activities that require great speed into an intensive strength program, concentrating principally upon the muscle groups most called upon in the particular activity.

As will be indicated in Chapter 7, strength training not only involves weight training or lifting, but also employs running and other activities to achieve the desired results. Therefore, it is good practice, for example, to put a sprinter into cross-country in the off-season, as well as to have him run long distances that will make heavy demands upon him during his regular competitive season. In these activities he will be developing strength and endurance. A strength-endurance program of this kind must be carefully correlated with sufficient sprint activities to develop and maintain a high rate of cardiorespiratory response and efficiency.

Cardiac and circulatory responses to training. Heart size will increase as the result of a training program.[20] This is neither undesirable nor does it indicate any

dangerous or unusual propensity for cardiac anomalies. To the contrary, the increased heart size is believed to be caused by the thickening of the heart muscle. It results in a more powerful contraction and, accordingly, a larger volume output of blood per stroke. In other words, as the result of training or conditioning, the heart becomes considerably more efficient in its operation. Consequently, it is capable of circulating more blood with fewer contractions.

In performing a set amount of work over a period of time, the heart rate becomes slower as training progresses. Training reduces the pulse rate, sometimes by as much as ten to twenty beats per minute, during the period between pretraining and posttraining measurements. The overall efficiency of the heart is high because of the slower heart rate and the more efficient use of oxygen by the coronary arteries, although the consumption of oxygen by the heart itself rises considerably with the increase in work load. One of the advantages of training is that, whereas the heart rate does not show an immediate and rapid increase at the start of severe exercise, it does return to normal more rapidly than the heart of the untrained person.[21] Hence, recuperative power becomes an important factor in proper conditioning. Precluding organic or functional anomaly, there is no evidence that strenuous or severe exercise can injure the heart of a young adult.

Training exerts considerable effect upon blood pressure. Because of the increase in the systemic system, as a result of utilizing blood from the splanchnic pool, there is more volume under higher pressure. This results in better transportation of oxygen to the tissues, when it is needed, and in more efficient removal of metabolites. As the result of prolonged effort in the untrained individual, systolic pressure falls progressively, an indication of approaching exhaustion. On the other hand, training retards this phenomenon and work can be continued for a longer time with scarcely any perceptible changes in blood pressure.

During exercises of endurance, the rise in blood pressure is much greater than during exercises of speed. Many factors tend to modify the response of blood pressure to various forms of exercise. Studies have indicated that the rate, intensity, duration, and state of training of the performer will determine the blood pressure response.

Respiratory responses to training. Training increases vital capacity (the maximum volume of air the lungs exchange in one respiratory cycle) and aids materially in establishing economy in the oxygen requirement.[22,23] The conditioned athlete operates primarily on a "pay as you go" basis as a result of his increased stroke volume and reduced heartbeat. Increase in the contractile power of the respiratory muscles, particularly the diaphragm, results in deeper respiration per breath. This enables the athlete to utilize a greater lung capacity and, consequently, to effect increased economy in the use of oxygen. The untrained individual attempts to compensate by increasing his rate of respiration and soon reaches a state of considerable respiratory indebtedness, which severely encumbers or even halts his performance.

The trained individual, through practice and conditioning, is able to establish a steady state of oxygen consumption at higher rates of work because of his greater mechanical efficiency in performing the required task. This permits him to do more work with a lower expenditure of energy or oxygen consumption. Since he uses much less oxygen for a given task, he has a greater margin of reserve and can continue high-level performance for a longer period of time, without distress, than can the untrained individual.

Intensity of training. In terms of recent research, it appears that most coaches fail to work their athletes hard enough. They are concerned with the problems of staleness and lack of motivation and with the fear of engendering some type of abnormal physiological condition; as a result, they tend to underwork their athletes. High school football players who participate in

an exceedingly intensive preseason conditioning program for 6 to 8 weeks before the start of the playing season have much greater strength and stamina throughout the entire season than do players who begin an identical conditioning program only 2 or 3 weeks prior to the start of the season.

Relatively few men ever approach their maximum in terms of work capacity during training. The various physiological and psychological changes that must necessarily be effected for greater endurance will come about only through an intensive program of work based upon the "overload principle" of progressively increasing the loads, the number of repetitions, and the rate and intensity of these repetitions. This system applies, regardless of the type of activity. There is no short cut to attaining high standards of performance. It is a long, arduous process and one to which the athlete must dedicate himself without reservations if he desires to become a top-flight performer.

Circadian dysrhythmia. The advent of jet power has made it possible to travel thousands of miles in just a few hours. New horizons have been opened, and many athletes have quickly accepted the advantages offered by this form of travel. Athletes and athletic teams are now quickly transported from one end of the country to the other and to foreign lands. For some, such travel induces a particular physiological stress resulting in a syndrome that is identified as a *circadian dysrhythmia* and which reflects a desynchronization of one's biological time clock.

The term *circadian* implies a period of time of approximately 24 hours. The body maintains many cyclic mechanisms that follow a pattern, for example, the daily rise and fall of body temperature or the tidal ebb and flow of the cortical steroid secretion (which produces other effects upon the metabolic system that are in themselves cyclical in nature). Even intellectual proficiency or the ability to think clearly is cyclical in nature. The stress induced in jet travel occurs when flying either east or west at high speed. The changes in time zones, illumination, and environment prove somewhat disruptive to the human physiological mechanisms, particularly when one flies through five or more time zones, as occurs in some international travel.[33] Some people are much more susceptible to the syndrome than are others, but the symptoms can be sufficiently disruptive to interfere with one's ability to perform maximally in a competitive event. The symptoms can be any one or a combination of the following: anorexia, severe headache, blurred vision, dizziness, insomnia, or extreme fatigue. For international travel a full day of recuperation should be allowed before any type of activity is indulged in. Catlett[34] suggests the following preventive measures: (1) depart well rested, (2) choose daylight departures where possible, (3) exercise moderation in eating and drinking both before and during the flight, and (4) plan no strenuous activities for the first 24 hours after arrival.

Acclimatization. An increasing problem in athletics is acclimatization. Today, athletes and athletic teams are traveling farther afield in search of competition. As a result they often encounter abrupt changes in climate. In the United States it is usual for teams to leave severe wintry conditions and engage teams enjoying a subtropical climate in which playing conditions on the stadium floor approach 100° F. Conversely, teams from subtropical areas find themselves engaging in competition on frozen turf and encountering subfreezing temperatures. It is evident that athletes or teams competing under foreign climatic conditions will not perform as well as would be expected unless some preliminary acclimatization takes place. This is probably more evident when the individual moves from a cold to a hot climate.

Evidence is increasing to indicate that an individual can, within a 4- to 5-day period, be completely acclimatized artificially through performing vigorous work in a hot room[24] and that such acclimatization will suffice a minimum of 3 weeks in cold wea-

ther.[25] This would indicate that, when competition is scheduled for a foreign hot climate, it is necessary to provide artificial acclimatization if par performance is expected. Acclimatization of this type results in lower rectal temperatures, more stable blood pressure for any given work load, and lower work-pulse rates.[26] Dietary implications as they affect performance in an unusual environment are discussed in Chapter 8.

The effect of cold upon performance does not produce as marked an effect as heat does. Normally, the increase in metabolic heat is the result of activity, and the necessary heat loss is carried by radiation, convection, and sweating. The important consideration, when performing in a cold environment, is to dress in such a manner as to secure heat retention during warm-up activities and rest periods and still permit heat dissipation during competition.[14]

Training at high altitudes. A considerable amount of research was done concerning the effect of altitude upon training and performance during the XIV Modern Olympiad in Mexico City.[27,30,35-39] The participating countries, aware of performance impairment and the effects of the decreased partial pressure of oxygen at an altitude of 2,300 meters (7,347 feet), trained their athletes at various altitudes either in natural locations or in simulated conditions utilizing hypobaric pressure chambers. Continual testing was carried on throughout the training period and as new knowledge came to light the training programs were modified accordingly.

The ability of an athlete to utilize quickly and effectively the oxygen he takes in is the critical factor in endurance.[36] At an altitude of 2,300 meters the partial pressure of oxygen is approximately 20% less than that at sea level. Therefore, the athlete must take in not only a much greater volume of air, but he must also effect a more efficient extraction and utilization of the oxygen in the ambient air if he is to equal sea level performance in those events in which endurance is a requisite. It has been shown that in running events of 800 meters or more and in swimming events greater in distance than 200 meters a decrease in performance will occur at medium altitude and the greater the performance demand upon endurance the greater the decrement in performance. In events that are basically anaerobic, such as sprints, no significant decrements in performance are found. In fact, the decreased density of the air gives some advantages in the sprints and in the field events. Recovery times in all events are considerably longer than at sea level.

During the Olympics the majority of athletes of both sexes suffered from a number of minor altitude symptoms such as anorexia, dehydration, nose and throat dryness, an increased susceptibility to sunburn, and smog irritation of the eyes, nose, throat, and lungs.

Research indicates that if activities requiring more than 1½ minutes of constant sustained effort are to be performed at an altitude of 3,000 feet or more, the athlete should undergo training for a minimum of 3 to 5 weeks at an altitude comparable to that at which the competition will be held. It has also been shown that some changes in the techniques of performance are needed particulary in reference to breathing patterns.[36,39] This is especially true in swimming where the strokes must be adapted to a different breathing rhythm. One advantage of altitude training has been the decided improvement of performance at sea level.[36] Daniels and Oldridge[36] found that intermittent sea-level stays of as long as 11 days resulted in better performances and did not interfere with altitude acclimatization. There appears to be considerable variability between individuals in respect to acclimatization especially in the ability to tolerate an intense performance tempo for long periods of time at high altitudes.[37] This probably explains the failure of some top athletes to perform as well in long distance events at high altitude as they did near sea level.

Physiological implications of stress. One area that concerns the trainer is the effect

that emotional factors exert upon physical performance. Selye[17] has defined these diverse stimuli, which tend to induce psychological or physiological conditions that upset the internal environment (homeostasis) of the body, as *stressors*. Ulrich,[31] who has done considerable research concerning the effects of stress on physical performance, points out that sport is a stressor; it upsets the homeostatic balance, with physical, psychic, and social stressors acting as an integrated whole to produce response.

The various emotional states are sustained by extensive physiological adjustments comparable to the changes evoked by work and exercise. These changes are controlled to a great extent by the autonomic nervous system and include the acceleration and strengthening of the heartbeat, a rise in blood pressure, a release of glucose from the liver, the secretion of a small amount of epinephrine (adrenaline) from the adrenal glands, and a relaxation of the muscles in the bronchial tubes, which permits easier breathing. These changes permit the body to function more efficiently under conditions of stress.

In addition to the physiological adaptation to the stress of exercise, there is an involvement of the higher centers of the nervous system. Continued repetitive acts become reflex in nature and require less concentration on their performance. This results in improved coordination, which, in turn, is reflected in more skillful and economical performance.

Physiological implications of psychological readiness. Establishing an attitude of readiness or "mind-set" in respect to physical performance is of utmost importance to the athlete. The close relationships between emotions and muscles have long been recognized and have had considerable study.[32] Thinking about a projected physical action affects the muscles involved. Motivational stressors that are based upon *success* can induce a greater work output in the individual and serve to increase the gross mechanical and physiological efficiency, whereas motivational stressors that indicate *failure* may tend to promote an emotional reaction that would circumvent the increased gross mechanical efficiency. If the emotions are developed in intensity and then properly channeled, they can be of considerable aid to physical performance. Trainers and coaches have long recognized this and have employed the "pep talk" and the development of *esprit de corps* among team members as a means of utilizing this relationship. A positive attitude on the part of the athlete as he prepares for competition aids considerably in reducing excess tension. The champion athlete "thinks" like a champion and therefore develops a winning attitude.

REFERENCES

1. Pascale, L. R., and others: Report of changes in body composition of soldiers during paratrooper training, USAMRNL Report No. 156, March, 1955.
2. Rasch, P. J., and Burke, R. K.: Kinesiology and applied anatomy, ed. 3, Philadelphia, 1967, Lea & Febiger.
3. DeLorme, T. L., and Watkins, A. L.: Progressive resistance exercise, New York, 1951, Appleton-Century-Crofts.
4. Denny-Brown, D.: Degeneration, regeneration, and growth of muscle, Amer. J. Phys. Med. 34:210, 1955.
5. Brouha, L.: Training. In Johnson, W. R., editor: Science and medicine of exercise and sports, New York, 1960, Harper & Row, Publishers.
6. Shaver, L. G.: Effects of training on relative muscular endurance in ipsilateral and contralateral arms, Med. Sci. Sports 2:165, 1970.
7. Klein, K. K., and Williams, H. E.: Research: a study of cross transfer of muscular strength gains during reconditioning of knee injuries, J. Ass. Phys. Mental Rehab. 8:52, 1954.
8. Walters, C. E.: The effect of overload on bilateral transfer of motor skill, Physical Ther. Rev. 35:567, 1955.
9. Mathews, D. K., and others: Cross transfer effects of training on strength and endurance, Res. Quart. Amer. Ass. Health Phys. Educ. 27:206, 1956.
10. Johns, R. J., and Wright, V.: Relative importance of various tissues in joint stiffness, J. Appl. Physiol. 17:824, 1962.
11. Mathews, D. K., Shaw, V., and Bohnen, M.: Hip flexibility of college women as related to length of body segments, Res. Quart. Amer. Ass. Health Phys. Educ. 30:352, 1957.
12. Mathews, D. K., Shaw, V., and Woods, J. B.: Hip flexibility of elementary school boys as related to body segments, Res. Quart. Amer. Ass. Health Phys. Educ. 30:297, 1959.
13. Massey, B. H., and Chaudet, N. L.: Effects of systematic heavy resistance exercise on range of joint movement in young male adults, Res. Quart. Amer. Ass. Health Phys. Educ. 27:41, 1956.
14. de Vries, H. A.: Evaluation of static stretching procedures for improvement of flexibility, Res. Quart. 33:222, 1962.
15. Rathbone, J. L.: Corrective physical education, Philadelphia, 1959, W. B. Saunders Co.
16. Rasch, P. J.: Endurance training for athletes, J. Ass. Phys. Ment. Rehab. 13:182, 1959.
17. Selye, H.: The stress of life, New York, 1956, McGraw-Hill Book Co.
18. Smith, L. E.: Influence of strength training on pre-tensed and free-arm speed, Res. Quart. Amer. Ass. Health Phys. Educ. 35:554, 1964.
19. Masley, J. W., and others: Weight training in relation to strength, speed, and coordination, Res. Quart. Amer. Ass. Health Phys. Educ. 24:308, 1953.
20. Raab, W.: Degenerative heart disease from lack of exercise; Exercise and fitness, Chicago, 1960, The Athletic Institute.
21. Morehouse, L. E., and Miller, A. T.: Physiology of exercise, ed. 6, St. Louis, 1971, The C. V. Mosby Co.
22. Consalazio, C. F., Johnson, R. E., and Pecora, L. J.: Physiological measurements of metabolic functions in man, New York, 1963, McGraw-Hill Book Co.
23. Andersen, K. L.: The effect of physical training with and without cold exposure upon physiological indices of fitness for work, Canad. Med. Ass. J. 96:801, 1967.
24. Strydom, N. B., and others: Acclimatization to humid heat and the role of physical conditioning, J. Appl. Physiol. 21:636, 1966.
25. Henschel, A., Taylor, H. L., and Keyes, A.: The persistence of heat acclimatization in man, Amer. J. Physiol. 140:321, 1943.
26. Ruch, T. C., and Fulton, J. F.: Medical physiology and biophysics, Philadelphia, 1965, W. B. Saunders Co.
27. Goddard, R. F., and Balke, B.: The international symposium on the effects of altitude on physical performance, Chicago, 1966, The Athletic Institute.
28. Grover, R., Reeves, J., and others: Exercise performance of athletes at sea level and 3,100 m. altitude, Schweiz. Z. Sportsmed. 14:130, 1966.
29. Klausen, K., and others: Effect of high altitude on maximal working capacity, J. Appl. Physiol. 21:1191, 1966.

30. Schönholzer, G.: Sports at medium altitude, J. Sport Med. 7:1, 1967.
31. Ulrich, A. C.: Measurement of stress evidenced by college women in situations involving competition, Doctoral dissertation, University of Southern California (PE), 1956.
32. Michael, E. D., Jr.: Stress adaptation through exercise, Res. Quart. Amer. Ass. Health Phys. Educ. 28:50, 1957.
33. Schleier, C: How to avoid the time zone blahs, Los Angeles Times, Feb. 27, 1972, H-16.
34. Catlett, G. F.: Circadian dysrhythmia: a jet age malady, Mod. Med. Vol. 36, Aug. 10, 1970.
35. Daniels, J., and Oldridge, N.: The effects of alternate exposure to altitude and sea level on world class middle distance runners, Med. Sci. Sports 2:107, 1970.
36. Malomsoke, J., Csepe, I., and Juhasz, J.: The change of arterial oxygen saturation in voluntary apnea as an indicator of the process of acclimatization to altitude, J. Sport Med. 8: 127, 1968.
37. Astrand, P. O., and Rodahl, K.: Textbook of work physiology, New York, 1969, McGraw-Hill Book Co.
38. Balke, B.: Variation in altitude and its effects on exercise performance. In Falls, H. B., editor: Exercise physiology, New York, 1968, Academic Press, Inc.
39. Ryan, A. J.: The olympic games at altitude. Symposium on Sports Medicine, Academy of Orthopaedic Surgeons, St. Louis, 1969, The C. V. Mosby Company.

RECOMMENDED READINGS

Andrew, G. M., Gusman, C. A., and Becklake, M. R.: Effect of athletic training on exercise cardiac output, J. Appl. Physiol. 21:603, 1966.
Cureton, T. K.: Physical fitness appraisal and guidance, St. Louis, 1947, The C. V. Mosby Co.
Doherty, J. K.: The nature of endurance in running, J. Health Phys. Ed. Rec. 35:29, 1964.
Hammer, W. M.: Physiological and performance changes during periods of football training and de-training, J. Sport Med. 5:72, 1965.
Johnson, W. R., editor: Science and medicine of exercise and sports, New York, 1960, Harper & Row, Publishers.
Mathews, D. K., Stacy, R. W., and Hoover, G. N.: Physiology of muscular activity and exercise, New York, 1964, The Ronald Press Co.
Schulzinger, M. S.: The accident syndrome: The genesis of accidental injury, a clinical approach, Springfield, Ill., 1956, Charles C Thomas, Publisher.

CHAPTER 7

Physical conditioning for the prevention of athletic injuries

Training must be considered principally in terms of *prevention* of injury. Coaches and trainers alike now recognize that a lack of physical fitness is one of the prime causes of athletic injury. Muscular imbalance, improper timing because of poor neuromuscular coordination, a lack of ligamentous or tendinous strength, lack of flexibility, and inadequate muscle bulk are among the causes of injury directly attributable to insufficient or improper physical conditioning. Inadequate nutrition and psychological readiness are also factors and are discussed in considerable detail in Chapters 8 and 9. Physical conditioning is herein defined as the role played by exercise in getting the body ready for sport activity. Many exercises of a general nature aid in developing overall fitness. There are also exercises that are geared to a specific sport, since the demands that different sports make upon the body vary in type, duration, and intensity.

The amount of time spent on preseason and in-season conditioning is relative not only to the type of activity but also to the state of the athlete's physical fitness at the initiation of the conditioning program. The trainer should project the conditioning program on a timetable basis so that desired levels of achievement can be reached by approximately the predicted dates. In this manner a careful check can be kept on the athlete's progress. The athlete who reports for practice at the start of the season 10 pounds overweight or in a flabby condition will require a longer and more intensive schedule than his teammate who reports in a reasonably good state of fitness.

Team physicians and trainers report that the most serious athletic injuries are those to the musculoskeletal system. These injuries can be obviated by proper and thorough physical conditioning. Muscle bulk and strength must be built up to protect the muscles and the underlying soft parts. Tendons and ligaments must be strengthened and toughened to enable them, along with the muscles, to fortify the joints that they traverse, to prevent untoward injuries, and to permit full and effective range of movement and stability. Care must be taken by the athlete to warm up properly to prevent muscle tears or strains and to raise muscle and deep body temperatures to their most effective levels.[1] Flexibility and range of joint motion must be increased to prevent tendon and ligament pulls, as well as to foster body mobility in all aspects. Neuromuscular skills that will effect good motor performance must be developed along with speed and endurance. The awkward, slow, or tired athlete is the one most prone to injury.

GENERAL CONSIDERATIONS

Inadequate conditioning is a contributing factor in a high percentage of athletic injuries.[2] Those who determine national, state, and local conference regulations seem not to recognize the fact that it takes time and careful preparation to bring an athlete into competition at a level of fitness that will preclude early-season injury. The most dangerous period in any sport is the first 3 or 4 weeks of the season,[3] principally because the athlete is usually lacking in flexibility, often overweight, and generally out of good physical condition when he reports for initial practice. In many instances another factor is lack of familiarity with most of the basic fundamentals, resulting in awkwardness and a consequent proneness to potential injury-provoking situations.

Because of the fear of overemphasis, preseason practice schedules are usually severely limited. As a result, many athletes enter competition in a condition far from the optimum level of fitness that is reached, barring injury, at about the third week of competition. There is a considerable difference between training an athlete to reach his peak for a certain performance and training him to reach a good level of fitness to reduce his injury potential. Emphasis in programs for achieving optimum fitness should be on general all-around development, whereas emphasis for peaking should be on all-around development plus gradually intensified, specialized exercise designed to secure maximal performance at the end of a particular time.

TEN CARDINAL PRINCIPLES OF ATHLETIC CONDITIONING

In the following list of variables, briefly discussed, the trainer should identify what might appropriately be termed the "ten cardinal principles of athletic conditioning."

1. *Warming up.* See that proper and adequate warm-up procedures precede all activities.

2. *Gradualness.* Add small daily increments of work. *Remember:* It takes from 6 to 8 weeks for a person to get into top-level condition.

3. *Timing.* Prevent overdoing. Relate all work to the athlete's general condition at the time. Practice periods should extend for 1 hour to 1 hour and 45 minutes, depending upon the sport. *Remember:* The tired athlete is prone to injury.

4. *Intensity.* Stress the intensity of the work rather than the quantity. Usually coaches and trainers fail to work their men *hard* enough in terms of intensity. They make the mistake of prolonging the workout rather than increasing the tempo or the work load. As the degree of training increases, the intensity of training must also increase.

5. *Capacity level.* Expect of the athlete performance that is as close to his physiological limits as health and safety factors will allow. Only in working to capacity will the desired results be achieved.

6. *Strength.* Develop strength as a means of producing greater endurance and speed.

7. *Motivation.* Motivation is a prime factor. Use circuit training and isometric exercises as means for further motivating the athlete.

8. *Specialization.* Exercise programs should include exercises for strength, relaxation, and flexibility. In addition, special exercises geared to the demands made upon the body in specific activities should be used to develop specialization.

9. *Relaxation.* Specific relaxation exercises, which aid in recovery from fatigue and tension, should be taught.

10. *Routine.* A daily routine of exercise, both in-season and off-season, should be established.

PHYSICAL CONDITIONING

Off-season conditioning. It is not essential that the athlete continue an intensive conditioning program during the off-season, although it is usually a good idea for the trainer and coach to encourage him to participate in another sport during this period. Such an activity should make certain physical demands embodying strength, endurance, and flexibility by means of running and general all-around physical performance. This will assist him in maintaining his level of fitness. In other words, the sport must be sufficiently demanding to require a good level of fitness to participate effectively. An excellent off-season sport for the football player would be wrestling or gymnastics. Track, especially cross-country, is a good conditioner. Rope skipping as a conditioning activity lends itself to all sports and makes vigorous demands upon the body.

If it is not feasible for the athlete to participate in an off-season sport, a "detraining" program should be planned. Such a program would permit him to gradually decrease his usual work load and would allow him to exercise less frequently and less intensively. A weekly workout of moderate to strong intensity is usually all that is required, since physical fitness is retained for a considerable length of time after an active program of competition ends. The physically vigorous athlete will tend to be quite active in the off-season too and, as a rule, will stay in reasonably good condition throughout the year.

It must be kept in mind, however, that caloric intake must be decreased accordingly when the exercise load is decreased, since not as much energy is then burned up. The overweight condition of many athletes when they report for preseason training is caused by their having continued a mid-season appetite with an off-season activity load. Establishing regular training routines for the off-season enables the trainer to keep a close check on his men even if he sees them only at 2- or 3-week intervals. In this way he can forestall development of extreme overweight and can further function as a consultant and motivator to the athletes.

Preseason conditioning. The trainer should impress upon his charges the need for maintaining a reasonably high level of physical fitness during the off-season. If such advice is followed, the athlete will find his preseason work relatively rewarding and any proneness to potential injury considerably diminished. The athlete should then experience no difficulty in reaching a state of athletic fitness suitable for competition within 6 to 8 weeks. During this preliminary period stress should be put upon the development of flexibility, endurance, and strength through the use of a carefully graded developmental program. In such a program there must be wise and constant use of established physiological bases for improving physical condition and performance.

The American athlete and coach tend to hurry training. The European athlete is usually confined to a single season of outdoor competition each year. In a precompetition training period of 6 months he follows a carefully controlled approach that permits him to reach the start of his competitive season in superb condition. Most American athletes, particularly in one-season sports, tend to reach their highest level of performance halfway through the season. As a result, they are truly efficient only half of the time. Conference and federation restrictions often hamper or prohibit effective preseason training, especially in football, and therefore compel the athlete to come into early-season competition before he is physically fit for it. At the high school level 4 to 6 weeks of preseason conditioning afford the best insurance against susceptibility to injury and permit the athlete to enter competition in a good state of physical fitness, provided a carefully graded program is established and adhered to conscientiously. Recently, physicians have been adding their voices in the demands for a realistic approach to the problem of proper conditioning, and it may be that school administrators and the general public will see the need and effectiveness of permitting adequate and properly controlled preseason training.

Warm-up. The principle of warm-up is still the subject of considerable debate among serious researchers in the physiology of exercise. Studies by most investigators[1,4-9] have indicated that there are beneficial effects on performance as the result of warm-up. Studies by others seem to cast some doubt on the effectiveness of the warm-up.[10] The term "warm-up" as herein discussed refers to the use of preliminary exercise procedures rather than the use of hot showers, massage, diathermy, counterirritants, and other forms of passive warm-up.

One of the real values of the warm-up is in its use as a preventive measure. It has been shown that adequate warm-up prevents strains and muscle tears that would probably occur if the athlete went into full performance without such a preliminary.[11] The main purposes of warm-up are to raise both the general body and the deep muscle temperatures and to stretch the ligaments and other collagenous tissues in order to permit greater flexibility and thus to generally supple the body. This reduces the possibility of muscle tears and ligamentous strains and helps to prevent muscle soreness. As cellular temperature increases it is accompanied by a corresponding increase in the speed of the metabolic processes within the cells, since such processes are temperature dependent. There is a speed-up in the transmission of nerve impulses as well. The result is an increase in the athlete's physical working capacity. Astrand and Rodahl[7] indicate that following proper warm-up performance improvement ranges from 0.5 to 0.6 seconds in the 100-meter dash to as much as 4.0 to 6.0 seconds in the 800-meter run. The percentage of improvement, from 2% to 5%, is approximately the same for the various distances studied. Similar rates of improvement were noted in swimming by de Vries and Muido.[8,9]

Better performance results when a 15 minute warm-up is employed than when a 5 minute warm-up is used. Depending upon the distance, warm-ups should be of 15 to 30 minutes' duration and should be adjusted in both length and intensity according to the ambient temperature and the

clothing being worn. There is also a psychological effect inherent in warm-up, since it helps the athlete to achieve a state of mental readiness or mind-set.

Warming up through mimicking or using a modified form of the activity in which the athlete is to compete appears to improve coordination by developing the athlete's kinesthetic awareness and thus establishing a neuromuscular pattern of performance. This assists him in determining when he has reached the state of readiness, a state he usually expresses by saying that he feels "right."

Warm-up procedures should consist of jogging or easy running, static stretching, and general body-conditioning exercises. These procedures should mobilize the body for action and make it supple and free. They must be of sufficient duration and intensity to raise deep tissue temperatures without developing marked fatigue. When the athlete attains a state of sweating, he has raised his internal temperature to a desirable level. The nature of the warm-up varies to some degree in relation to the activity. Some procedures lend themselves well to athletic activities of all types and should be performed along with others that are specifically designed for the sport in which the athlete is to participate. After completing the general exercises in his warm-up, the athlete should progress to those that are specific for his event or activity. He should start at a moderate pace and then increase the tempo as he feels body temperature and cardiovascular increases taking place. The effects of warm-up may persist as long as 45 minutes. However, the closer the warm-up period is to the actual performance, the more beneficial it will be in terms of its effect upon the performance.

Most high school athletes fail to warm up sufficiently, intending to "save" themselves for competition. This is a mistaken concept. It takes approximately 20 minutes of gradual warm-up to bring the body to a state of readiness with its attendant rise in body temperature and to adequately mobilize the body physiology in terms of making a greater number of muscle capillaries available for extreme effort and of readying blood sugar and adrenaline. The amount of time necessary to achieve satisfactory warm-up will vary with the individual and will tend to increase with age.

Warm-up differs in relation to the type of competition. It is advisable for the athlete to warm up in activities similar to the event in which he will compete. Accordingly, a sprinter would start by jogging a bit, practice a few starts, and use some stretching techniques and general body exercises. A ballplayer might first use some general body exercises, swing a bat through a number of practice swings, and do some preliminary throwing, alternating these activities with some stretching exercises.

On cool days, warm-up should be increased somewhat in duration and should be performed in sweat clothing. Only when the athlete is fully warmed up and ready to move directly into competition should he remove his sweat clothing. In some events, for example, field events, sweat clothing should be replaced immediately following a competitive effort. If rather long periods of time elapse between trials or events, the performer should use light warm-up procedures during the intervals.

Some trainers advocate massage, whirlpool, diathermy, or warm packs as preliminary warm-up measure. Such passive warm-up procedures have been found effective in laboratory experiments, but for the practical, competitive situations it would appear that active warming-up is more desirable. Using oxygen or taking honey for the purposes of assisting or hastening the warm-up is of little or no value.

Warm-down. This term is applied to exercise of gradually diminishing intensity which follows strenuous work and permits the return of both the circulation and various body functions to pre-exercise levels. From 30 seconds to a minute of jogging, followed by 3 to 5 minutes of walking, permits the body to effect the necessary readjustments.

Flexibility. Most authorities in sports medicine consider flexibility, or the ability to move freely in various directions, one of the most important objectives in conditioning athletes. Good flexibility increases the athlete's ability to avoid injury. Since it permits a greater range of movement within the joint, the ligaments and other collagenous tissues are not so easily strained or torn. It also permits him a greater freedom of movement in all directions. The "tight" or inflexible athlete performs under a considerable handicap in terms of movement, besides being much more injury-prone. Repetitive stretching of the collagenous or fascial ligamentous tissues over a long period of time permits the athlete to obtain an increased range of motion.[12] Such stretching also provides an excellent warm-up.

The athlete who possesses good flexibility can change direction of movement easily, is able to fall properly and with less chance of injury, and physically is more adaptable to almost any game situation. The wise trainer will single out inflexible athletes and have them placed on a regimen of static stretching exercises until they achieve a satisfactory degree of flexibility. This is one way in which a high incidence of injury can be materially reduced.

The athlete who gains improved flexibility and increased range of joint movement is able to use his body more effectively and efficiently, and he is better able to avoid a potential injury-provoking situation. In addition, when such a situation is unavoidable the joints involved are far more stable and can withstand a stress or torque considerably in excess of that which can be resisted by a less flexible person. Increased flexibility further aids in reducing impact shock such as that encountered in the contact sports or in activities in which the body comes into forceful contact with a relatively unyielding surface (for example, the landing phase included in gymnastics, jumping, or vaulting).

Although the end results of static and ballistic stretching may closely parallel each other, static stretching is preferred because it does not result in the small muscle tears and pulls that are so often the result of vigorous ballistic stretching.[1] After a muscle has been thoroughly warmed up through static stretching and through a program of general conditioning exercises, the athlete may proceed to ballistic stretching if he so desires, although it is doubtful that it will contribute anything additional in terms of flexibility.

Muscular soreness. Muscular soreness usually follows early-season or unaccustomed physical work and is ordinarily of two types. A general soreness often appears 4 to 8 hours following exercise. This soreness is of relatively short duration; its disappearance is followed by a localized or specific soreness (myositis) which appears from 8 to 24 hours after the initial period of exercise. As a rule, this soreness persists for several days, gradually diminishing over a period of time. Myositis seldom persists longer than 70 hours.

Commonly held theory relates the secondary specific soreness to tissue damage, such as tears of muscle fibers or of connective tissues. Recent evidence casts some doubt on this theory. de Vries,[1] in an electromyographic study of muscular distress following exercise postulates that such muscular soreness is caused, at least in part, by tonic muscle spasm. He reports that static stretching of both the agonists and the antagonists involved in unaccustomed or severe exercise seems to result in a lessened degree of the soreness. When such soreness occurs, static stretching of the muscles involved will assist materially in reducing the pain and discomfort.

Stiffness. Stiffness often occurs when a group of muscles have been worked hard for a long period of time. The fluids that collect in the muscles during and after exercise are absorbed into the bloodstream at a very slow rate. As a result the muscle becomes swollen, shorter, and thicker; it is therefore more resistant to stretching. Light exercise and massage assist materially in reducing stiffness.

GENERAL WARM-UP PROCEDURES

The following exercises have been selected to provide balance and depth in procedures so that total body warm-up may be achieved. The athlete should begin his daily workout, either for practice or for competition, with running and the static stretches and then proceed to the conditioning exercises. Only when he has completed these should be begin his specific activity warm-up. It is suggested that the exercises be done in the same sequence used in their presentation below.

Running

As the term is used here, running includes running in place, jogging, and easy striding. The type and amount of the running can be individually determined and will be governed somewhat by the type of sport.

Static stretching exercises for general flexibility

1. *Back stretch (the cat stretch)* (Fig. 7-1): Kneeling on both knees, feet extended, sit on the heels, with the trunk bent forward over the thighs, and arch the back as much as possible. Meanwhile retract the abdomen forcefully. Extend arms forward to full length with palms on the floor and force the head down between the arms as far as possible. Hold this position for 60 seconds.

Fig. 7-1. Back stretch.

Fig. 7-2. Trunk stretch.

2. *Trunk stretch (rocker)* (Fig. 7-2): In a prone-lying position reach back and grasp the ankles, arch the back, and hyperextend the head and neck as much as possible. Hold the position for 60 seconds.

3. *Shoulder stretch* (Fig. 7-3): Assume a small side stride stand, arms extended in front of the body and fingers interlaced. Reverse the hand position, maintaining grip (palms now face away from the body), and raise the straight arms overhead, forcing them into as much hyperextension as possible. Be sure to keep the chin firmly tucked in. Hold for 60 seconds.

4. *Hamstring stretch* (Fig. 7-4): Assume a straddle-seat position on the ground, flex trunk forward on the thighs, knees straight, and grasp outer edges of feet. Force the head down between the arms as far as possible. *Note:* When first attempting this position, it may be necessary to bend the knees slightly to grasp the feet. After the grasp is obtained, however, the knees should be straightened as much as possible until you are able to attain and hold the leg-extended position. Hold for 60 seconds.

5. *Lateral stretch* (Fig. 7-5): In a sitting position, fully extend the left leg forward and flex the right leg at the hip, with thigh and lower leg forming approximately a 50-degree angle. Move the right hand as close as possible up under the armpit, with knuckles resting on the ribs and the elbow pointing directly sideward. Position the left hand with heel of the hand on area immediately behind the ear, with elbow pointing directly sideward. Force the trunk as far to the right as possible, assisting the movement by pushing with the left hand. Stabilize the trunk by pushing with the right hand. Hold the position for 60 seconds.

6. *Gastrocnemius stretch* (Fig. 7-6): Stand approximately 3 to 4 feet from a vertical surface such as a wall or upright support. Incline the straight body forward to an angle of approximately 65 degrees, supporting the body with the extended arms, the palms against the surface. *Note:* Stretching may be augmented by having the balls of the feet on a 2-inch elevation such as a short length of a two-by-four. Hold the position for 60 seconds.

Fig. 7-4. Hamstring stretch.

Fig. 7-3. Shoulder stretch.

Fig. 7-5. Lateral stretch.

Conditioning exercises

In performing the conditioning exercises, begin at a moderate tempo and gradually increase the speed and vigorousness of execution. Above all, do the exercises correctly and work up to the maximum number of recommended repetitions.

1. *Side straddle hop* (Fig. 7-7): Starting position—attention. Count 1—jump to a straddle stand while swinging straight arms vigorously overhead. Count 2—return. (20 repetitions.)

2. *Lateral dip* (Fig. 7-8): Starting position—straddle stand, hands on hips. Rebound the trunk 4 times to the left and then 4 times to the right, one count to each sideward-return movement. (5 repetitions of a series consisting of 4 dips to the left and 4 to the right.)

3. *Trunk circling* (Fig. 7-9): Starting position—straddle stand, arms free at the sides. Circle the trunk 4 times to the left and then 4 times to the right. (5 repetitions of a left and right series.)

Fig. 7-6. Gastrocnemius stretch.

Fig. 7-7. Side straddle hop.

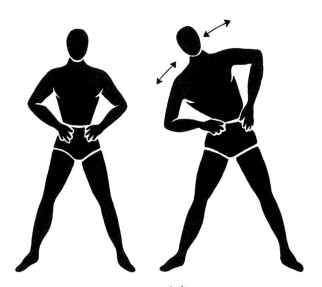

Fig. 7-8. Lateral dip.

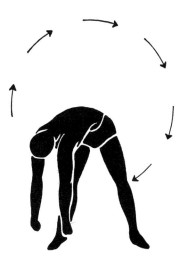

Fig. 7-9. Trunk circling.

4. *Squat thrust* (Fig. 7-10): Starting position—attention. Count 1—bend knees to a full-squat position, hands on floor and arms between knees. Count 2—extend legs backward to a front-leaning rest. Count 3 —return to squat position assumed on Count 2. Count 4—straighten to starting position. (10 to 15 repetitions.)

5. *Abdominal curl* (Fig. 7-11): Starting position—lying on back, knees bent, with feet on the floor and hands clasped back of neck. Count 1—curl upper trunk and head as close to the knees as possible. Count 2—return to starting position. (10 to 20 repetitions.) Vary the exercise by adding a trunk twist on the initial movement, touching the right elbow to the left knee and then returning to the starting position. On the next curl, touch the left elbow to the right knee and return. Alternate these movements for a total of 10 to 20 repetitions.

6. *Arm flinging* (Fig. 7-12): Starting position—straddle stand, both arms side-

Fig. 7-10. Squat thrust.

Fig. 7-11. Abdominal curl.

ward to the left, hands clenched to a loose fist. Swing relaxed arms horizontally to the left as far as they can go, meanwhile rotating the trunk in the same direction. Repeat to the right. Keep feet fixed. (20 to 30 repetitions.)

SPECIFIC EVENT WARM-UP PROCEDURES

It is advisable to use warm-ups involving the same general neuromuscular pattern that is used in the activity. The athlete should start with the general warm-up activities and proceed immediately into the specific warm-up pattern. Depending upon the sport, the specific warm-up may be done individually or, as in certain aspects of football or basketball, it may require working with one or more partners. All warm-up activities should start slowly and work up to a brisk pace so that the athlete will feel an absence of tension and have an awareness of circulatory and respiratory readiness. It is good practice to insist that athletes jog to and from the practice field or area, not only as a means of supplementary conditioning but also as a preliminary warm-up.

The specific warm-up exercises described on the following pages are examples of the types of activity that may be used. A suggested number of repetitions and/or a time span for each activity is indicated. These should be considered minimums.

Specific warm-up exercises

The following exercises are to be used as specific warm-ups following the general warm-up. They serve to localize warm-up in the body areas that receive most use during competition in a particular sport. These exercises, which lend themselves to a number of sports, are described in detail with accompanying illustrations.

1. *Ankle suppler* (Fig. 7-13): Starting position—feet in a small side stride stand. Rock up on the balls of the feet as high as possible, then back on the heels, raising the balls of the feet as much as possible. Next roll over onto the outer borders of the feet and then inward as far as possible onto the inner borders. Repeat the complete sequence from the beginning. (8 to 10 repetitions.)

2. *Arm circling* (Fig. 7-14): Starting position—feet in a side stride stand, hands loosely clenched to a fist. Circle right arm backward for 8 to 10 complete arm circles; then the left arm. Circle right arm forward 8 to 10 circles; repeat with left arm. Continue alternating. (8 to 10 complete repetitions of series.)

3. *Half squat* (Fig. 7-15): Starting position—small stride stand, hands on hips.

Fig. 7-12. Arm flinging.   Fig. 7-13. Ankle suppler.

Keeping the trunk erect and, raising the heels slightly off the ground, bend both knees to a half-squat position. Return to starting position. Complete 15 to 20 repetitions at a moderate tempo.

4. *High kick* (Fig. 7-16): Starting position—attention. Take a small step forward with the left foot, transferring the weight, and kick the extended right leg as high as possible. Step back and repeat the sequence. After 8 to 10 repetitions with the right leg, exercise the left leg.

5. *Hurdle seat* (Fig. 7-17): Starting position—a position assumed on the ground, with the lead leg extended forward and toes pointed; the opposite leg is placed with the thigh at a right angle to the lead leg and the knee is bent, with the lower leg at a right angle to the thigh. Slowly bend the trunk forward, sliding both hands down the lead leg to the toes. Hold this position for at least 30 seconds, preferably for 60 seconds. Return to starting position. (5 to 8 repetitions.) *Caution:* Avoid bob-

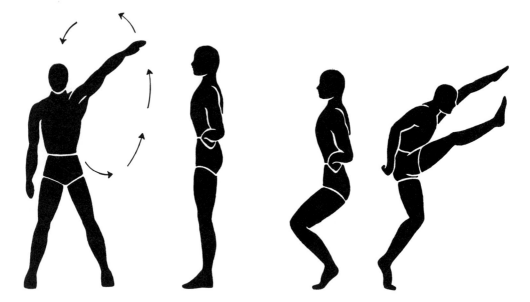

Fig. 7-14. Arm circling.   **Fig. 7-15.** Half squat.   **Fig. 7-16.** High kick.

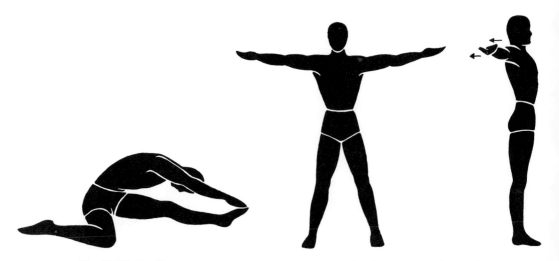

Fig. 7-17. Hurdle seat.   **Fig. 7-18.** Pectoral stretch.

bing or bouncing the trunk in a ballistic stretch. Such bouncing can result in pulled hamstrings.

6. *Pectoral stretching* (Fig. 7-18): Starting position—feet in a side stride stand and arms raised sideward to slightly above shoulder height, palms upward. Slowly and steadily pull the straight arms as far back as possible. Relax the arms momentarily and then repeat the pull. (20 to 30 repetitions.)

7. *Push-ups* (Fig. 7-19): Starting posi-

tion—front-leaning rest with back straight. Bend the arms, lowering the straight body until the chest just brushes the ground. Straighten arms and return to starting position. Execute in a moderate tempo. (6 to 10 repetitions.) *Caution:* Be sure to keep head in line with body and do not permit hips either to sag or to be carried higher than the back.

8. *Shoulder roll* (Fig. 7-20): Starting position—attention. With a preliminary run of 5 or 6 steps, drop the right shoulder and,

Fig. 7-19. Push-up.

Fig. 7-20. Shoulder roll.

Table 7-1. Suggested warm-ups

Sport	Trunk stretch	Back stretch	Shoulder stretch	Hams. stretch	Lateral stretch	Gastroc. stretch	Side strad. hop	Lateral dip	Trunk circling	Squat thrust	Abdom. curl	Arm fling.	Ankle suppl.	Arm circling
Baseball						X	X	X	X			X		X
Basketball						X	X	X	X			X	X	X
Football			X			X	X	X	X					
Gymnastics					X			X	X		X		X	X
Skiing						X		X	X				X	X
Soccer						X	X	X	X				X	
Swimming														
Diving	X	X				X		X	X				X	
Swimming			X			X	X		X			X	X	X
Tennis			X			X		X	X			X	X	X
Track and Field														
Sprinters				X		X	X		X			X	X	
High hurdlers				X		X	X		X				X	
Low hurdlers				X		X	X		X				X	
440 yds./400 m.				X		X	X	X	X					
880 yds./800 m.				X		X	X	X	X				X	
Mile run (1,500 m.)						X	X		X				X	
Two mile run (3,000 m.)						X	X		X				X	

Half squat	High kick	Hurdle seat	Pect. stretch	Push-up	Shoulder roll	Ski stretch	Ant. shoulder stretch	Wrest. br. & pivot	Warm-ups specific to the sport
						X			Warm-up throws with partner. Easy at first, then gradually increasing force of throw.
						X			Warm-up throws. One and 2-hand passing drills, relaxed and easy. Dribbling warm-up drills, pre-game basket shooting practice.
	X				X	X		X	1. Offensive-defensive warm-up. 2. Body contact simulated charge and block.
				X		X			Dip swings on parallel bars; splits. Run through complete routine several times.
X			X		X				
	X								Passing and heading drills.
	X		X			X	X		Warm-up on board with approaches and preliminary bounces, gradually working into dives.
	X		X						Depending upon the event, swim 10-20 laps at moderate rate of speed.
			X			X	X		Following initial warm-ups, warm-up on practice board, then move on court for practice serves and volleys.
	X					X			1. Alternate running at ½ speed and jogging, each for a distance of 50 yards, for a total of 400 yards. 2. Take 6 to 8 starts, running at ½ speed, finally working up to ¾ speed. 3. Several springs at ½ to ¾ speed for 50-60 yards. 4. On competition days, do a few stretching exercises for the legs, such as the ski stretch and side straddle hop during the last 6 to 8 minutes prior to call. This is especially important to warm-up the hamstrings. 5. Take several additional starts sprinting 25-30 yards at ¾ speed.
	X	X				X			1. Take 6 to 8 starts, clearing first hurdle on last 2 or 3 starts. 2. 2/3 maximum speed starts running first 2 or 3 hurdles. 3. Following warm-up keep relaxed, loose, and warm through easy jogging alternated with side straddle hops and trunk circling until called to the mark.
	X	X				X			Same as high hurdlers.
	X	X				X			1. Alternate jogging and running at ½ speed, each for 100 yards, in total 400 yards. 2. Walk 2 to 3 minutes. 3. Run 200 yards at ½ speed. 4. Walk at least 3 minutes. 5. Take a few starts. 6. Finish with some light stretching exercises.
X	X					X			1. Alternate running with jogging at ½ speed, each about 150 yards for 800 m. 2. Walk at least 3 minutes. 3. Run 300 yards at ½ speed. 4. Walk 3 to 5 minutes. 5. Take 6 starts. 6. Finish with some light stretching exercises.
									1. Alternate running with jogging at ½ speed, each for 200 yards—½ mile total. 2. Run ¼ mile at pace race (e.g., 4:20 mile, run 65 sec. 440 yards). 3. Walk 6 to 8 minutes. 4. Jog 220 yards, walk approximately 100 yards and finish with a fast 100-yard sprint. 5. Walk 4 to 5 minutes. 6. Take 2 or 3 starts. 7. Finish with light stretching exercises just prior to the race.
									1. Alternately walk and jog 440 yards. 2. Walk 4 to 5 minutes. 3. Run ½ mile at intended 2 mile pace. 4. Walk 6 to 8 minutes. 5. Jog 440 yards finishing the last 150 yards in a sprint. 6. Finish with some light stretching exercises.

Continued.

Table 7-1. Suggested warm-ups—cont'd

Sport	Trunk stretch	Back stretch	Shoulder stretch	Hams. stretch	Lateral stretch	Gastroc. stretch	Side strad. hop	Lateral dip	Trunk circling	Squat thrust	Abdom. curl	Arm fling.	Ankle supp.	Arm circling
Long distances (5,000-10,000 m.)						X	X		X				X	
Cross country						X	X		X				X	
Weight events			X				X	X	X			X	X	X
Javelin			X	X		X	X		X			X		X
Volleyball			X		X							X	X	X
Water polo			X			X			X			X	X	X
Wrestling	X	X	X	X			X		X	X	X			X

swinging the right arm across the body with chest high, execute a roll forward—landing on the back of the right shoulder, tucking the body by flexing the hips and knees, and rolling up on the feet to a stand. Repeat, rolling on the left shoulder. (4 to 6 repetitions to each side.)

9. *Ski stretch* (Fig. 7-21): Starting position—attention. Move, either by stepping or by sliding the right foot forward into a deep-lunge position, left knee slightly flexed and hand on each side contacting the ground with the fingertips to maintain balance. Hold this position for at least 6 seconds while steadily forcing the body weight downward to increase the stretch. Shift body weight over the forward knee, meanwhile pulling the left leg forward to

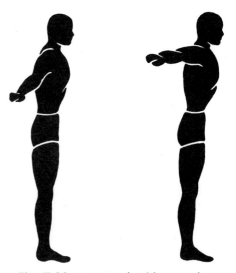

Fig. 7-22. Anterior shoulder stretch.

Fig. 7-21. Ski stretch.

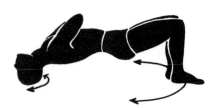

Fig. 7-23. Wrestler's bridge and pivot.

Half squat	High kick	Hurdle seat	Pect. stretch	Push-up	Shoul-der roll	Ski stretch	Ant. shoul-der stretch	Wrest. br. & pivot	Warm-ups specific to the sport
									1. Upgrade specific warm-ups suggested for 2-mile run. 2. Warm-up from 2 to 3 miles—jogging, striding, and walking, terminating with short sprints. Usually jog first mile, stride the second. 3. Finish with some light stretching exercises.
									Follow same warm-up procedures as for long distances.
X			X	X					1. Alternately jog and stride ½ mile. 2. Take 6 to 8 50-yard sprints. 3. Take warm-up throws or puts.
			X						1. Same as for weight events. 2. Warm-up throws from easy to ¾ maximum.
X			X			X	X		1. Circle passing drills and practice serves.
	X		X						1. Same as for swimming. 2. On practice days, swim 6 to 10 laps following general warm-up. 3. Ball-handling drills—deck and in water. 4. Skill drills.
X	X		X	X	X	X		X	1. Sit-outs against token resistance.

starting position. Repeat, moving the left leg forward. (8 to 12 repetitions.)

10. *Anterior shoulder stretch* (Fig. 7-22): Starting position—feet in small side stride stand, fingers hooked together in rear of buttocks (Indian grip). Slowly force the extended arms backward and upward as far as possible. Hold the terminal position for 15 to 20 seconds. (5 to 10 repetitions.)

11. *Wrestler's bridge and pivot* (Fig. 7-23): Starting position—hook-lying position, feet about 18 inches apart. Rock up into a wrestler's bridge and maintain this position for 5 to 6 seconds. Relax to starting position. Repeat 5 or 6 times. Again rock up into a bridge and, in this position, circle the body to the left as far as possible by moving the feet and using the head as a pivot. Repeat, to the right. (4 to 6 repetitions, moving in alternate directions.)

The warm-ups listed in Table 7-1 are designed specifically for the sports indicated. Allow ample time for all warm-up procedures. Do not hurry the exercises but keep at a brisk tempo and give the body time to become ready for the demands that will be made of it. Remember that these exercises are to follow the general warm-up.

WEIGHT TRAINING AND RESISTIVE EXERCISES

The inherent values of weight training are recognized by trainers, physical educators, coaches, and physicians. A cursory review of athletic literature reveals various systems of weight training. It has taken a long time, even for people in the field, to recognize that there is a distinct difference between weight lifting, a sport, and weight training, a system in which series of progressive resistance exercises are used to attain speed, strength, and endurance.

Most weight training systems in use today are based on variations of the De Lorme method.[13] If properly carried out, weight training will contribute to the general physical well-being of the athlete as well as improve his speed, "explosive power," strength, and endurance. The use of a weighted football, soccer ball, baseball, or basketball, the swinging of weighted baseball bats, and the wearing of weighted belts, and other equipment—by runners, jumpers, rope climbers, and other athletes—are simply forms of weight training. Resistive devices, such as those employing friction that can be increased or decreased by means of a dial, have considerable value and are indicated when space and/or finances preclude establishing weight-lifting equipment. These devices can be used either supplemental to or in lieu of barbells and other weights.

Weight exercises are usually categorized, in terms descriptive of the type of contractions they elicit, as either isotonic or isometric. Each type of contraction has considerable value, and a good training program should include exercises from both categories.

An *isotonic* contraction involves a change of length in the muscle, either shortening or lengthening. Isotonic exercises involve the moving of a resistive force, either a part of the body or some extraneous object. This type of contraction is referred to also as a *dynamic* contraction, since definite and easily discerned movement takes place.

An *isometric* contraction involves the generation of heat and energy within the muscles involved, but since the muscle does not or cannot shorten there is no readily discernible movement. Such contractions are identified also as *static* contractions. If a person attempted to lift or push an object that he could not move, his muscles would be in a state of isometric or static contraction. He would be exerting tremendous muscular force but exhibiting no actual movement of the muscles involved or of the object he was attempting to move.

In a weight training program certain fundamental principles must be followed by each athlete:

1. Precede all weight training with the general warm-up.

2. Perform isotonic movements slowly and deliberately, at approximately one-fifth your maximum speed.

3. Hold isometric movements at the terminal position for about 6 to 12 seconds, or longer if desired.

4. Apply the overload principle in all isotonic contractions. When you are able to complete the second or third series with some degree of ease, add additional weight.

5. Maintain good muscular balance by exercising both the agonists and the antagonists.

6. Confine heavy work to the off-season and the preseason period. A light to medium program can be maintained during the regular practice days of the competitive season, provided it is confined to use of the weight schedule after the regular practice and a rest period of approximately 30 minutes before beginning to lift.

7. Work with weights every other day and no more than 4 days a week. This allows ample time for reduction of soreness and stiffness.

8. Initiate your training program first in terms of general body development and then progress to exercises tailored to the specific sport or event.

9. After a general warm-up you may, for purposes of additional warm-up, start a preliminary series of about 10 repetitions, using approximately half of the weight normally used. This is usually sound procedure.

10. Observe proper breathing procedures during lifting to assist in fixing the stabilizing muscles of the trunk and therefore give a firm base from which to work. Inhale deeply just prior to beginning a lift and exhale somewhat forcefully on the return movement. This aids in performing the lift.

General weight training exercises

The following exercises are designed to develop a balanced physique in terms of musculature. These exercises should be done about once a week during the off-season, every other day during the preseason interval, and after regular activity periods during the competition season. It is advised that the beginner start his program during the off-season and concentrate principally on a general body-building program. He should have moved into the preseason period before concentrating on weight training that is specific in terms of his sport. The initial resistance is somewhat arbitrarily determined by ascertaining the athlete's maximum lift in each exercise to be programmed and then by setting the initial resistance at from 75% to 90% of that amount. It is recommended that the exercises be performed for the suggested number of repetitions with near-maximum weight and that a 5-pound increment be added for the arms and a 10-pound increment for the legs when the ultimate series is repeated two workout periods in succession.

Isotonic exercises

1. *Military press* (Fig. 7-24): Starting position—feet in a side stride stand, barbell raised to the bent-arm position in front of chest. Slowly extend arms overhead. Hold. Return to starting position. (3 series of 10 repetitions.)

2. *Two-arm curl* (Fig. 7-25): Reverse or under grip and regular or upper grip. Starting position—feet in a side stride stand, arms extended downward. Slowly flex elbows, bringing the barbell to a bent-arm position in front of chest. Return to starting position. *Note:* Keep elbows close to side of body. Alternate grasp on each series. (3 series of 10 repetitions.)

3. *Half squat* (Fig. 7-26): Heels are elevated approximately 1½ inches and a 20-inch bench is placed behind the buttocks to reduce the possibility of knee injury by

serving as a "stop." Starting position—feet in a small side stride stand, barbell resting on back of neck and shoulders. Slowly bend knees to half-squat position. Hold. Return to starting position. (3 series of 10 repetitions.)

4. *Supine bench press* (Fig. 7-27): Starting position—lying supine on a 20-inch bench, knees bent at right angles, feet flat on the floor, and barbell held at the chest. Slowly extend arms upward. Hold. Return to starting position. (3 series of 10 repetitions.)

5. *Rowing exercise* (Fig. 7-28): Starting position—feet in a small side stride stand, arms extended downward with hands centered and in close proximity on the bar, head resting on a folded towel placed on a table. Slowly pull the bar up to a position in front of the chest. Hold. Return to starting position. (3 series of 10 repetitions.) *Note:* This may also be done with the lifter assuming and maintaining an angle stand, that is, trunk flexed forward at the hips at approximately a right angle.

6. *Side arm raises (prone and supine)* (Fig. 7-29): Starting position—prone or supine position on a bench, arms downward,

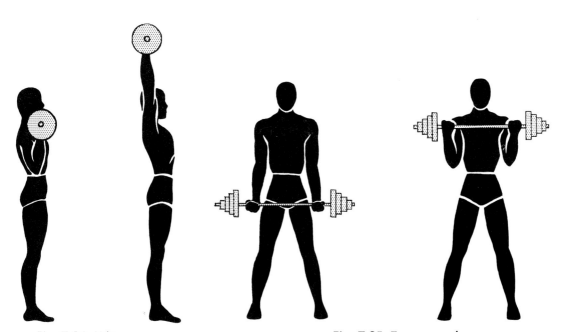

Fig. 7-24. Military press.   **Fig. 7-25.** Two-arm curl.

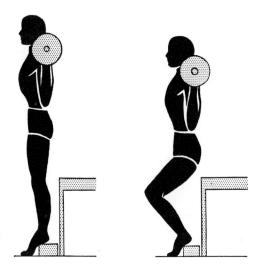

Fig. 7-26. Half squat.

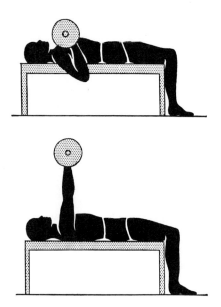

Fig. 7-27. Supine bench press.

Fig. 7-28. Rowing exercise.

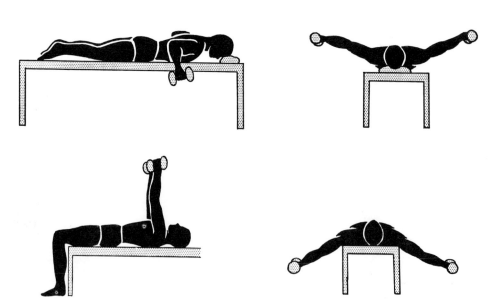

Fig. 7-29. Side arm raise.

hands grasping 10-pound dumbells. Slowly raise arms sideward to a horizontal position. Hold. Return to starting position. *Caution:* Avoid locking the elbow joint in a complete extension, since this exerts severe strain on the joint in this type of exercise. (3 series of 10 repetitions, alternating the prone and supine positions daily.)

7. *Wrestler's bridge* (Fig. 7-30): Starting position—hook-lying position (supine, knees flexed, and feet flat on the floor), barbell held at the chest. Bridge up, supporting self on only the back of the head and the feet. Hold for 5 to 10 seconds. (3 series of 10 repetitions.)

8. *Heel raise* (Fig. 7-31): Starting position—feet in a small side stride stand, balls of the feet on a 2-inch riser, barbell resting on the back of the neck and shoulders. Slowly rise on toes. Hold. Return to starting position. Variations may be performed by having the feet either toed out or toed in. (3 series of 10 repetitions.)

9. *Press bar leg thrust* (Fig. 7-32): Starting position—angle-lying position under the press bar, balls of the feet in contact with the bar or bar platform, legs in a half-flexed position. Slowly extend the knees, keeping the buttocks in contact with the floor. Hold.

Return to starting position. (3 series of 10 repetitions.) *Note:* To provide for better contact, fasten to the bar an 8-inch by 12-inch board. This prevents the feet from slipping off the bar.

10. *Press bar quadriceps strengthener* (Fig. 7-33): Starting position—a half-crouched position under the bar, shoulders and neck in contact with the bar. (A folded towel may be used as a pad.) Slowly extend *knees* to an erect position. Hold. Return to starting position. (3 series of 10 repetitions.) *Caution:* Lift with the knee extensors, not the lower back muscles.

11. *Abdominal curl* (Fig. 7-34): Starting position—hook-lying, feet anchored, and dumbbell weighing 15 to 25 pounds held behind the neck. Curl the upper trunk upward and as far forward as possible. Return to starting position. Maintain a moderate tempo and steady rhythm and avoid bouncing up from the floor. (2 series of 20 repetitions.) Number can be increased as capacity for more work increases.

Isometric exercises

1. *Stationary press bar leg thrust* (Fig. 7-35): Starting position—angle-lying position under the press bar, balls of the feet in contact with the bar or bar platform,

Fig. 7-30. Wrestler's bridge.

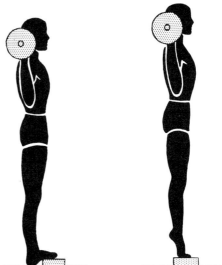

Fig. 7-31. Heel raise.

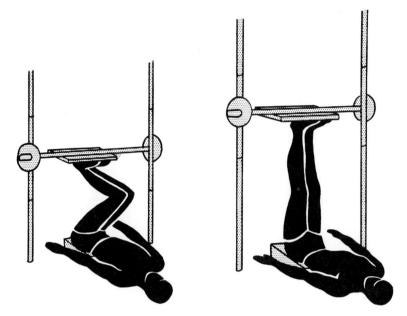

Fig. 7-32. Press bar leg thrust.

Fig. 7-33. Press bar quadriceps strengthener.

Fig. 7-34. Abdominal curl with weight.

legs in a half-flexed position. Press bar is locked into place. Exert maximum force against the immovable bar, sustaining full pressure for 15 to 30 seconds. Following a short period of relaxation (5 to 10 seconds) repeat the procedure. (2 series of 5 to 15 repetitions.) (*Note:* Hips may be elevated by a 2-inch pad.)

2. *Stationary press bar leg tensor* (Fig. 7-36): Starting position—a half-crouched position under the bar, which is locked into place, shoulders and neck in contact with the bar. Exert maximum pressure against the bar by using the leg extensors and sus-

tain full pressure for 15 to 30 seconds. Following a momentary relaxation, repeat the exercise. (2 series of 5 to 15 repetitions.)

3. *Straight arm lift* (Fig. 7-37): Starting position—hook-lying, arms extended, with hands grasping the barbell, which lies on the mat. Raise barbell no more than 4 inches from the mat and hold this position for approximately 10 seconds. Return to starting position. (3 series of 10 repetitions.)

4. *Wall press* (Fig. 7-38): Starting position—stand in a small stride stand in either the corner of a room or a doorway, plac-

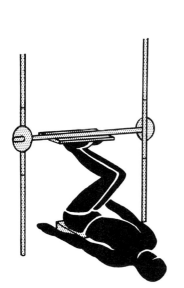

Fig. 7-35. Stationary press bar leg thrust.

Fig. 7-36. Stationary press bar leg tensor.

Fig. 7-37. Straight arm lift.

Fig. 7-38. Wall press.

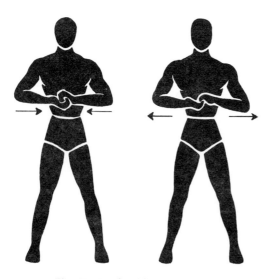

Fig. 7-39. Shoulder-arm tensor.

ing the hands against the walls or the sides of the opening at about shoulder height. The elbows should be bent to about the halfway point in the normal range. Exert maximum force against the opposing surface, holding the position for at least 10 seconds. Relax pressure momentarily. Repeat. (2 series of 15 repetitions.)

5. *Shoulder-arm tensor* (Fig. 7-39): Starting position—feet in a small side stride stand. Hook the fingers of the hands together, elbows bent so that hands are above waist height. Push the hands together forcefully, at the same time tensing the arm, shoulder, neck, and abdominal muscles. Hold for 10 seconds. Relax momentarily and then repeat the tensing action but reverse the hand action by pulling against the fingers with as much force as possible. (2 series of 10 repetitions.)

Weight training in terms of specific activities

Following the general program of weight training, exercises specifically designed to develop the muscle groups that are most important for successful performance in a given activity should be assigned. A thorough knowledge of kinesiology is of the utmost importance if the trainer or coach is to intelligently prescribe suitable activities. Careful analysis of an activity in terms of the types and kinds of movement employed gives clues as to which muscle groups are most prominent in effecting the desired patterns of movement. It is then relatively simple to select routines that have been devised to properly exercise those muscles. It should be kept in mind not only that exercises must be selected on the basis of their development construction but also that some must be selected that are mimetic, motor-wise, in terms of activity. For example, arm swings similar to the crawl stroke might be employed while holding a 5-pound dumbbell in each hand. Throwing a weighted ball could be one means used in strengthening a throwing arm. Mimetic activities of this type assist materially in establishing the neuromuscular pattern of movement desired. Exercises useful for specific purposes are listed below.

Baseball

1. *Upper extremity exercises:*
   a. *Military press*
   b. *Two-arm curl*

Fig. 7-40. Supination-pronation

c. *Rowing exercise*
d. *Side arm raises*
e. *Press bar shoulder shrug*
f. *Wall press*
g. *Supination-pronation* (Fig. 7-40):
   Start with feet in small side stride
   stand, elbow bent at a right angle
   to upper arm, and hand grasping
   a 20-pound dumbbell. Rotate the
   dumbbell alternately left and
   right, using the muscles of the
   forearm and wrist only. (3 series
   of 10 repetitions.)
h. *Wrist roll* (Fig. 7-41): Begin with
   feet in a small side stride stand.
   Slowly wind up a cord to which
   a 25-pound weight has been attached. Reverse the action, slowly
   unwinding the full length of the
   cord. (3 series of 5 repetitions.)
   Note: A wrist roller is easily constructed by securing one end of
   a 30-inch length of sash cord to
   the center of a 12-inch length of
   broomstick or dowel of a somewhat thicker diameter and the
   other end to a 25-pound weight.
   Commercially manufactured rol-
   lers of a friction type, which are
   fastened to the wall, may also be
   used.

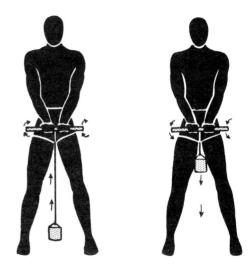

Fig. 7-41. Wrist roll.

i. *Finger strengthening:* Using a
   small sponge rubber ball or a
   commercially manufactured grip
   strengthener of either the spring
   or the hard rubber type, squeeze
   and hold for 10 to 30 seconds. (20
   to 40 repetitions.) It is a good idea
   to carry a ball or strengthener
   with you at all times and to exercise as indicated, throughout the
   day, whenever a few moments are
   available.

j. *Throwing a weighted ball:* Practice throwing, as described earlier, but use a specially prepared ball. A baseball seam can be opened, a ⅜-inch hole be drilled to the center of the ball, and a few ounces of soft spun lead wool (such as that used for sealing pipe joints and obtainable at most plumbing supply stores) be pounded in. The remainder of the hole can then be filled with kapok, cotton, or some other soft material and the cover be resewed.

k. *Swinging a weighted bat:* For trunk twisting use a bat in which a hole has been drilled lengthwise at the top of the bat and 4 or 5 ounces of lead inserted.

2. *Lower extremity exercises:*
   a. *Half squat*
   b. *Heel raise*
   c. *Press bar leg thrust, isotonic and isometric*
   d. *Boot exercise* (Fig. 7-42): Sit on plinth or table with lower legs hanging free over the edge and clear of the floor. A 20-pound boot is strapped to the foot. Do exercises involving knee flexion and extension and inversion, eversion, flexion, and extension of the ankle. The weight should be increased in terms of your ability to handle it. Each exercise should should be done for 3 series of 10 repetitions each.

Basketball

The exercises suggested for baseball players, with the exception of those involving use of a weighted ball or bat, will also serve as specific exercises for basketball players. In addition, passing drills that utilize a 4-pound or 6-pound medicine ball further serve to strengthen the wrists, fingers, forearms, and shoulders. One-hand and two-hand shooting drills in which the shooter uses a medicine ball in lieu of a basketball and goes through the pattern of making a shot to a partner are also excellent for developing strength where it is needed for the sport.

To further develop the explosive power that is so vital in backboard play, players should practice rebound play while wearing a weight belt. Such belts are easily made of canvas and should be of double thickness so that several pounds of lead shot may be placed between the layers. They are secured by a small tongue and buckle. The local shoemaker can construct weight belts at a nominal charge.

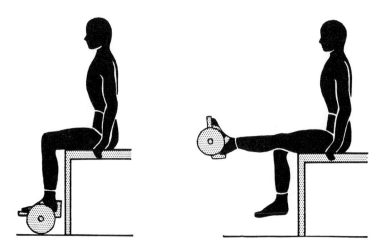

Fig. 7-42. Boot exercise.

Football

Football players should follow the general weight training program to obtain as much overall development as possible. In addition, the practice of the high kick, while using weighted shoes, is of benefit to punters and place kickers. The use of a weighted ball for passing, punting, and centering helps to develop the muscles employed in performing these skills. Such a ball can be easily constructed by stuffing an old ball with cotton waste or, preferably, sponge rubber scraps. The ball should weigh approximately 3 pounds. Passers can further develop the throwing arm by using the same arm, wrist, and shoulder exercises advocated for baseball and basketball players. Linemen can use the press bar to considerable advantage by doing additional work with the shoulder shrug and leg lift, both isotonically and isometrically. The wrestler's bridge and pivot, executed while holding on the chest a weight of 20 to 40 pounds, is also an excellent exercise.

Gymnastics

Exercises for the arm and shoulder joint and for the leg, which have been indicated as part of the general weight training pattern, will serve well as specific exercises for gymnasts if the concentration is increased. In addition, abdominal curls with a weight and the wrist rolls should be included. The use of a weight belt, both by vaulters and by rope climbers, has great value. One of us has had considerable success in developing rope climbers through the use of the weight belt and the strapping of additional weights, ranging from 2½ to 5 pounds, onto each thigh. Chinning, either with the weight belt or with weights attached to the feet, is also an excellent exercise for gymnasts.

Skiing

Exercises for skiing should emphasize strengthening and increasing the flexibility of the hip, knee, and ankle joints, in particular.

The following exercises will be found to be of value:
1. *Press bar quadriceps strengthener*
2. *Press bar leg thrust*
3. *Stationary press bar leg thrust*
4. *Stationary press bar leg tensor*
5. *Half squat*
6. *Boot exercise*
7. *Ski stretch*

These exercises, coupled with general conditioning of the trunk, arms, shoulder girdle, and neck, should bring the skier into good physical condition for participating in his sport.

Soccer (football)

Weight training for soccer football players offers the opportunity to strengthen the vitally important knee and ankle joints and the musculature of the shoulder girdle and the neck. Both isometric and isotonic exercises should be employed. The following are particularly good for this sport:
1. *Press bar leg thrust*
2. *Press bar quadriceps strengthener*
3. *Half squat*
4. *Rowing exercise*
5. *Wrestler's bridge*
6. *Heel raise*
7. *Boot exercise*
8. *Horizontal arm swing*

The use of weighted shoes will be of some benefit and should assist in developing leg strength. The addition of other isometric and isotonic exercises couple with a regimen general conditioning and a challenging jogging or cross country running program should enable conscientious athletes to get into excellent physical condition.

Swimming

Swimmers can use both isotonic and isometric exercises to advantage. In addition to the general weight training exercises, the following ones should be done:

1. Hold a 15-pound dumbbell in each hand and while in a prone position on the exercise bench, and with the head and neck extending over the edge, swing both arms

slowly downward and backward as far as they will go, keeping them close to the body. Hold the terminal position for 6 to 10 seconds. Now swing the arms downward and as far foreupward as they will go. Hold the terminal position for 6 to 10 seconds. (3 series of 10 repetitions.) *Caution:* Keep the elbows extended at all times but not locked. Increase the load when indicated.

2. Repeat the foregoing exercise in a supine position.

3. To strengthen the kick, start in a prone position on the exercise bench with pelvis at the edge and legs extended out over the floor and, using a boot on each foot, alternately move the legs slowly in a crawl kick pattern. (20 to 30 repetitions.) *Caution:* Avoid locking the knee.

4. Repeat the foregoing exercise in a supine position. *Note:* This and the preceding exercise can be varied by raising and lowering both legs simultaneously.

5. Exercises have been developed that involve wall weight and triplex machines to be used while simulating arm and leg swimming motions. However, most such devices do not have sufficient weight to offer serious resistance. If additional weight can be added so that exercising entails real effort, they can be used with some promise of success.

Tennis

The following exercises should be stressed in addition to the general weight training program:

1. *Two-arm curl*
2. *Supination-pronation*
3. *Alternate presses (using dumbbells)*
4. *Horizontal arm swings* (Fig. 7-43): Starting position—small side stride stand, a 20-pound dumbbell in each hand, arms raised directly sideward to shoulder height. Slowly swing the arms forward in a horizontal plane, continuing until each arm has progressed across the other and is carried as far as possible. Arms are extended, but elbow joints should not be locked. Return slowly toward the starting position, carrying the arms horizontally as far backward as possible. (3 series of 10 repetitions.)
5. *Heel raise*
6. *Half squat*
7. *Wrist roll*
8. *Finger strengthening*
9. *Boot exercise*
10. *Practice with a weighted racket:* For use in strengthening the forearm, wrist, and shoulder a racket can be weighted by inserting lead into a hole drilled into the long axis of the handle and wrapping lead tape (used for sinkers in fishing and obtainable at sporting goods stores) or solder around the frame.

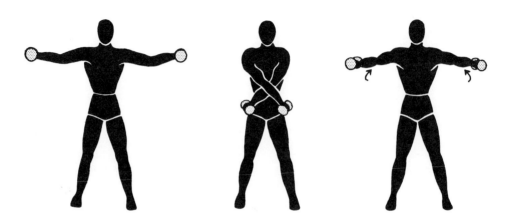

Fig. 7-43. Horizontal arm swing.

Track and field

Sprinters, runners, and hurdlers. Emphasis for these athletes is primarily on leg development. The following exercises should be stressed in addition to the normal weight training program:

1. **Abdominal curl:** Use a weight held behind the head; done in the hook-lying position.
2. **Half squat**
3. **Heel raise**
4. **Press bar leg thrust, isotonic and isometric**
5. **Boot exercise**

Weight men. It is good practice for these athletes to work with their competitive implements weighted to values somewhat above the official weight. In particular, this group must stress the various arm and leg presses and lifts, as well as the abdominal curls. The following should be done additionally:

1. **Supination-pronation**
2. **Wrist roll**
3. **Finger strengthening**

Jumpers and vaulters. The events in which these athletes engage are in some respects quite similar to phases of other events. Yet they have certain other characteristics inherently their own. Broad and high jumpers should follow the same pattern laid down for the sprinters and hurdlers but in addition should wear a weight belt some of the time while practicing. The Russians have had considerable success in developing jumpers and attribute most of their success to the use of the weight belt and the use of weighted footgear as a means of developing the explosive power needed in the take-off.

Pole vaulting, although it has some of the characteristics of sprinting, is a gymnastic event that requires primarily great strength in the abdominal, shoulder, and back muscles. In addition to intensive work on the general weight training program, the vaulter should follow the programs indicated for sprinters and those for weight men. Rope climbing and pull-ups are excellent adjuncts to the weight program.

Although not usually considered weight exercises, they do involve the lifting of the performer's body weight and are mimetic, in that they incorporate a basic movement in vaulting. The use of a weight belt during pull-ups and rope climbing is an excellent means of developing arm strength. Doing abdominal curls, with a weight held behind the head is an excellent exercise, particularly when alternating trunk twists are added, since the oblique abdominal and rectus femoris muscles are brought into active participation. These muscles are very important in executing the pull-up and the turn.

Volleyball

Exercises that strengthen the fingers, wrists, and arms and which will develop the lower extremities for jumping are the prime exercise requisites for this sport. The strength training exercise pattern should be coupled with a program of general conditioning exercises and plenty of running and jumping to develop endurance. The following exercises are suggested:

1. **Press bar leg thrust**
2. **Press bar quadriceps strengthener**
3. **Military press**
4. **Two arm curl**
5. **Half squat**
6. **Heel raise**
7. **Straight arm lift**
8. **Supination-pronation**
9. **Wrist roll**
10. **Boot exercise**

Water polo

Although this sport is primarily an aquatic activity, it has many of the elements of basketball. Polo players should follow the program outlined for swimmers and in addition should work on strengthening hands, wrists, and shoulders by using the basketball exercises that involve these body parts. Dry land passing drills, using a medicine ball, are quite effective as a means of developing good throwing ability.

Wrestling

Wrestling is an activity that requires excellent all-around development. In addition to the general weight training exercises the following should be stressed:

1. *Supination-pronation*
2. *Wrist roll*
3. *Finger strengthening*
4. *Kick strengthening*
5. *Boot exercise*
6. *Wrestler's bridge and pivot:* This should be performed while holding a weight on the chest, as has been previously indicated. It may also be done while holding a barbell overhead in an extended arm press.

CIRCUIT TRAINING

Circuit training is a method of physical conditioning that employs both weight training and conditioning exercises. In some forms apparatus stunts have been added as a third kind of activity. The method has achieved considerable popu-

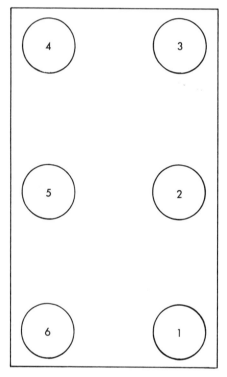

Fig. 7-44. Circuit A—general conditioning. Station **1**, squat thrusts, ¾ maximum number of repetitions performed in 1 minute; **2**, general flexion exercise, performed for 2 minutes; **3**, abdominal curls with weights, ¾ maximum number of repetitions; **4**, two arm curls, ¾ maximum number of repetitions; **5**, vertical jump (Sargent), ¾ maximum number of repetitions performed in 1 minute; **6**, half squat, heels raised, exercise with weight, ¾ maximum number of repetitions.

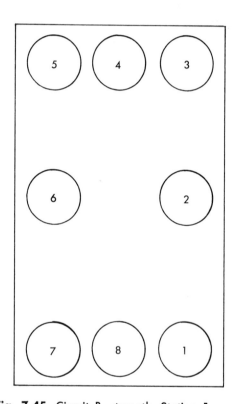

Fig. 7-45. Circuit B—strength. Station **1**, rowing exercise, 70% maximum number of repetitions; **2**, chinning, 70% maximum number of repetitions; **3**, abdominal curls with weights, ¾ maximum number of repetitions; **4**, two arm curls, 70% maximum number of repetitions; **5**, heel raising, toes elevated, 70% maximum number of repetitions; **6**, military press, 70% maximum number of repetitions; **7**, press bar leg thrust, 70% maximum number of repetitions; **8**, rope skipping, 1 minute, 70% maximum number of repetitions performed in 1 minute.

larity in England[14] and is finding favor in this country as a means of achieving optimum fitness in a systematized, controlled fashion. The method was originally introduced by Morgan and Adamson in the late 1950s at the University of Leeds, England. It was immediately accepted by physical educators, coaches, and trainers as an excellent and self-motivating means of increasing strength, flexibility, and endurance in an orderly fashion, within a group. The intensity and vigor of circuit training is indeed challenging and enjoyable to the performer. Studies in various areas of athletics have indicated not only that this system produces positive changes in motor performance but also that general fitness, muscular power, endurance, and speed have shown decided improvement.[15-18]

Circuit training is based on the premise that the athlete must do the same amount of work in a shorter period of time or must do considerably more work within the limits of an assigned training period. Numerous variations of this system are in use, but all employ certain common factors: (1) the use of progressive resistance exercises; (2) the use of physical conditioning and apparatus exercises, the former being performed either with or without weights; (3) a circular arrangement of the activities that permits progression from one station to another until all stations have been visited, the total comprising a "circuit"; and (4) a limiting time factor within which the circuit must be concluded.

The circuit is usually set up around the perimeter of the exercise area. When a circuit is set up, the number and types of stations desired should be selected for their value in stressing development of the body parts most commonly called into play in a particular athletic activity, as well as for their worth as activities promoting all-around body fitness. Six to twelve different stations can be set up, each with a specific exercise. The circuit should be so planned that the trainee can complete a circuit without becoming excessively fatigued.

After a thorough orientation period to familiarize the trainee with the procedure and with the exercise to be done at each station, he is given a time trial to ascertain the length of time he requires for completing one to three laps, depending upon the number of stations and the intensity and design of the various exercises. He progresses from one station to the next immediately upon completing the assignment at the first station. A "target" time, which is one third lower than his initial trial time, is then assigned. The weight exercises are usually performed at 50% to 70% of the athlete's maximum number of repetitions, and the resistance is usually arbitrarily determined by the trainer, in accordance with the athlete's capability. Two sample circuit programs that may serve as guides in developing programs to meet various requirements are shown in Figs. 7-44 and 7-45.

• • •

We have used circuit training with considerable success at California State University, Long Beach, as a method of conditioning basketball players and track men and in the weight training and conditioning classes.[19] This system easily lends itself to handling large groups efficiently and productively. It is a practical method, entailing some preliminary planning, but beyond that it needs little coordinating. Athletes find it motivating since it makes conditioning fun and challenging through competition against teammates and against time.

INTERVAL TRAINING

For developing athletes to participate in endurance sports, interval training appears to be the most successful method in bringing them close to their potential. Improvements in training methods have enabled man to significantly reduce his times in the running events. Hard, intensive work is the key to the top conditioning that makes near-record and record-breaking performances possible. Resistance to the various effects of fatigue can be accomplished only through intensive, rigorous training that loads the circulorespiratory system to a level above an established threshold. In this way improvement in training, notably, endurance, can occur. Below the training threshold no training effect is visible. Here we have application of the *overload principle* to the cardiorespiratory system, wherein sufficient stress in the form of a specific workload and time factor is applied in order to develop endurance. Karvonen and others[20] have established a threshold (working pulse rate) as an increase from the resting value to a heart rate at least 60% of the maximum value. This level must be achieved and maintained before training effects can result. Others have suggested 160 b/m (beats per minute) as a rule-of-thumb threshold. (A 10-second value of 27 b/m may be used.)

The program of interval training must be set up to permit the athlete to achieve the greatest possible workload with the least amount of fatigue. That the body can achieve and tolerate a workload, when done intermittently, well over three times that done continuously has been well established by physiologists.[21,22]

Four factors are significant in interval training: (1) a specified distance that is repeated a given number of times, (2) a recovery period during which the athlete jogs slowly and relaxes, (3) a predetermined pace, carefully timed, at which the athlete covers the set distance, and (4) a predetermined number of repetitions in running the distance. Alternating 30-second intervals of work with rest intervals, which terminate when the pulse rate reaches 120 b/m, appears to be the best pattern.

It is best to start the program 6 to 8 months prior to the opening of the competitive season. A relatively slow pace is used in the beginning and is sufficiently increased every 4 weeks to bring the runner to his desired time peak at the start of competition.

This type of conditioning program is quite flexible and permits adaptation. However, it is best not to tamper with the pace factor, since this is the key to a successful, planned performance. The number of repetitions should be increased if one wishes to intensify the workout, but the pace, the recovery period, and the distance should remain unchanged.

REFERENCES

1. de Vries, H. A.: Physiology of exercise for physical education and sports, Dubuque, Iowa, 1966, William C. Brown Co., Publishers.
2. Ryan, A. J.: The role of training and conditioning in the prevention of athletic injuries, Health and fitness in the modern world, Chicago, 1961, The Athletic Institute.
3. Committee on Sports Injuries and Safety, National Collegiate Athletic Association, Kansas City, Mo., 1960.
4. Asmussen, E., and Bøje, O.: Body temperature and capacity for work, Acta Physiol. Scand. **10:**1, 1945.
5. Burke, R. K.: Relationship between physical performance and warm-up procedures of varying intensity and duration, Doctoral dissertation, University of Southern California, 1957.
6. Massey, B., Johnson, W. R., and Kramer, G. F.: Effect of warm-up exercise upon muscular performance using hypnosis to control the psychological variable, Res. Quart. **32:**63, 1961.
7. Astrand, P. O., and Rodahl, K.: Textbook of work physiology, New York, 1970, McGraw-Hill Book Co.
8. de Vries, H. A.: Effects of various warm up procedures on 100 yard times of competitive swimmers, Res. Quart. **30:**11, 1959.
9. Muido, L.: The influence of body temperature on performances in swimming, Acta Physiol. Scand. **12:**102, 1946.
10. Karpovich, P. V., and Sinning, W. E.: Physiology of muscular activity, ed. 7, Philadelphia, 1971, W. B. Saunders Co.
11. Start, K. B., and Hines, J.: The effect of warm-up on the incidence of muscle injury during activities involving maximum strength, speed, and endurance, J. Sport Med. **3:**208, 1963.
12. Johns, R. J., and Wright, V.: Related importance of various tissues in joint stiffness, J. Appl. Physiol. **17:**824, 1962.
13. De Lorme, T. L., and Watkins, A. L.: Progressive resistance exercise, New York, 1951, Appleton-Century-Crofts.
14. Morgan, R. E., and Adamson, G. T.: Circuit

training, New Rochelle, N. Y., 1958, Sport-shelf & Soccer Association.
15. Nunney, D. N.: Relation of circuit training to swimming endurance, unpublished Master's thesis, University of California, Los Angeles, 1959.
16. Thompson, H. L., and Stull, G. A.: Effects of various training programs on speed of swimming, Res. Quart. 30:479, 1959.
17. Rahn, S.: Kreisbetrieb (circuit exercises), Körpererziehung 16:445, 1966.
18. Thomas, G.: Erfahrungen mit dem Kreisbetrieb im Unterricht, Körpererziehung 16:195, 1966.
19. Arnheim, D. D.: Preventing basketball injuries, coaching clinic, Englewood Cliffs, N. J., 1963, Prentice-Hall, Inc., pp. 10-11.
20. Karvonen, M. J.: Effects of vigorous exercise on the heart. In Rosenbaum, F. F., and Belknap, E. L., editors: Work and the heart, New York, 1959, Paul B. Hoeber, Inc.
21. Shephard, R. J.: Standard tests of aerobic power. In Shephard, R. J., editor: Frontiers of fitness, Springfield, Illinois, 1971, Charles C Thomas, Publisher.
22. Astrand, P. O., and Rodahl, K.: Textbook of work physiology, New York, 1970, McGraw-Hill Book Co.

RECOMMENDED READINGS
Barney, V. S., Hirst, C. C., and Jensen, C. R.: Conditioning exercises, St. Louis, 1965, The C. V. Mosby Co.
Berger, R. A.: Comparison between static training and various dynamic training programs, Res. Quart. 34:131, 1963.
Berger, R. A.: Effects of isometric training, Physical Educator 22:81, 1965.
Clarke, H. H.: Muscular strength and endurance in man, Englewood Cliffs, N. J., 1966, Prentice-Hall, Inc.
Doherty, J. K.: Training for running, Englewood Cliffs, N. J., 1964, Prentice-Hall, Inc.
Falls, H. B., editor: Exercise physiology, New York, 1968, Academic Press, Inc.
Frey, G. E.: Interval exercises for wrestlers, Coaching Clinic, Englewood Cliffs, N. J., 1963, Prentice-Hall, Inc., pp. 12-13.
Holland, G. J.: Physiology of flexibility, a review of the literature, unpublished paper presented to the Southwest District Conference, AAHPER, April, 1966.
Massey, B., and others: The kinesiology of weight lifting, Dubuque, Iowa, 1959, William C. Brown Co., Publishers.
Ricci, B.: Physical and physiological conditioning for men, Dubuque, Iowa, 1966, William C. Brown Co., Publishers.
Rich, G. Q., Ball, J. R., and Wallis, E. L.: Effects of isometric training on strength and transfer of effect to untrained antagonists, J. Sport Med. 4:217, 1964.
Spackman, R. R.: Two-man isometric exercise program for the whole body, Dubuque, Iowa, 1964, William C. Brown Co., Publishers.
Wessel, J. A., and Van Huss, W.: Therapeutic aspects of exercise in medicine. In Johnson, W. R., editor: Science and medicine of exercise and sports, New York, 1960, Harper & Row, Publishers.
Wilt, F.: Training for competitive running. In Falls, H. B., editor: Exercise physiology, New York, 1968, Academic Press, Inc.
Zateorskii, V. M.: The meaning and maintenance of weight training essential for increase in muscle mass: theory and practice of physical culture, 2:24, 1963 (from the Yessis Translation Review [Russian] 1:19, 1966).

CHAPTER **8**

The influence of ingesta and other aids on athletic performance

Exercise makes metabolic demands on the body. Competitive activities make demands considerably in excess of those made under normal circumstances. The repair of damaged tissues, the recuperation of fatigued muscles, and the regeneration of energy necessitate a balanced and adequate diet. At the high school level the absence of a training table or other means of dietary control presents a problem for trainer and coach. This problem must be solved through developing the athlete's awareness of the elements comprising a good diet. To some extent this problem is encountered at the college level also. Selecting a balanced diet and understanding the values and importance of dietary supplements and food substitutes are the responsibilities of the trainer. New developments in the nutritional field and a bewildering mass of advertising claims and counterclaims, make it difficult to intelligently judge products based on scientific facts. Fallacies and food fads are prevalent, especially at the high school level, and it requires constant education to establish sound dietary habits.

From time to time various foods and drugs have been introduced to athletes for the purposes of improving performance and/or assisting in weight gain or loss. It is the trainer's duty to know what these ingesta contain and whether or not they may be harmful to the athlete. The trainer must also decide if taking such aids would be ethical.

FOODS

The foods commonly ingested are actually chemical substances that can be broken down into simpler substances by digestive enzymes. The body then uses the energy stored in these compounds.

Food is categorized into six basic groups: carbohydrates, fats, proteins, minerals, vitamins, and water. Each is equally important in the diet. In the typical American diet from 50 to 60% of the energy is provided by carbohydrates, from 35 to 45% by fats, and from 10 to 15% by proteins.[1] However, there are variations in these percentages because of cultural, agricultural, economic, and sociological factors. There is also an apparent trend toward using less carbohydrate and more protein.

Carbohydrates, fats, and proteins are responsible for energy production. However, proteins are used primarily for the building and repairing of tissue, and they are essential in the regulation of body processes.

Water, although not a food, is necessary for the various metabolic chemical reactions. It is a component in protoplasm, it assists in the transportation of food and waste materials, it aids in elimination of waste products, and it assists in control of body temperature. Mineral salts aid in maintenance of the internal environment and are basic in formation of many tissues, particularly the bones, blood, and teeth.

Vitamins are organic substances that, although needed in very small amounts, are indispensable for normal functioning of the body.

Carbohydrates. Carbohydrates are organic compounds composed of carbon, hydrogen, and oxygen. The ratio of hydrogen to oxygen is 2:1, the same ratio found in water. Common carbohydrates are the starches and sugars found in foods such as breadstuffs, potatoes, and chocolate. During digestion the complex sugars found in foods are broken down into simple sugars that can be absorbed by the blood and tissues.

The sugars are carried to the liver where they are converted either into glycogen or into glucose (blood sugar). Glycogen is stored in the liver and can be readily reconverted into glucose when the demands of exercise require it. Glucose is carried by the blood to the various cells of the body. Some of the glucose may be stored as muscle glycogen in the muscle cells, but most is utilized immediately as energy at the cellular level. This is especially true of nerve cells, since they cannot utilize any other energy-yielding nutrient.[1] Excess glucose that is not used as energy and has not been converted into glycogen is transformed into fat and is stored as a reserve energy source. Muscles utilize the carbohydrates first during the initial stages of exercise, and they use more for strenuous work than for moderate work. Carbohydrates are usually considered to be the primary body fuels, and fats assume the role of reserve stores.

Fats. Fats and carbohydrates are composed of the same basic elements, but in fat the relative hydrogen content is higher. Fats or fatty compounds are usually referred to as *lipids* and are generally classified as *saturated, monounsaturated,* or *polyunsaturated* fats. In saturated fats each carbon atom in a molecular chain has two hydrogen atoms attached to it. Monounsaturated fats have one carbon atom in the chain that is free of hydrogen. In polyunsaturated fats two or more carbon atoms are free of hydrogen.

Fats provide more energy per gram than either carbohydrates or proteins, but body efficiency appears to be about 4.5% less on a fat diet than on a carbohydrate diet.[2] Following digestion, fats are absorbed and deposited in muscle tissue and in other fat storehouses or depots around the body. These depots supply an energy reserve when needed, particularly if exercise demands are so protracted that they result in a diminution of carbohydrate stores.

Americans consume too much fat. The average diet is approximately 40% fat, and most fats consumed are "hard," or saturated, fats. These fats have a higher melting point (solidification point) and are principally animal fats, dairy products, hydrogenated shortenings, chocolate, and coconut. Saturated fats tend to raise the cholesterol level of the blood.[3] "Soft" or unsaturated fats are classified as monounsaturated or polyunsaturated. Monounsaturated fats are generally free flowing and do not solidify even at low temperatures. Monounsaturated fats are found in fowl, olive and peanut oils, and most nuts. These fats appear to be neutral in their effect on cholesterol. Polyunsaturated fats apparently lower the cholesterol level in the blood. Polyunsaturates are found in fish, various plant oils (corn, soybean, sunflower, safflower), and special margarines.

As caloric intake is increased above normal in preparation for competition or for a heavy bout of work, there is a tendency to overemphasize the fat content of the diet. Generally, athletic diets are too heavy with fatty foods, particularly dairy products and eggs. Investigations[2,3] have emphasized the importance of fatty acid as one of the major causes of atherosclerosis, a common form of arteriosclerosis (hardening of the arteries). Atherosclerosis is characterized by abnormal, cholesterol-containing deposits (plaques) on the inner layers of the blood vessels. It is one of the main causes of hypertension (high blood pressure). Authorities have expressed a need for caution in prescribing an over-abundance of fatty foods in the athletic diet, although fats are recognized as one of the major sources of energy. Current research indicates that not more than 25% of the caloric intake should come from fats. It must be stressed that the bulk of fat intake should consist of the polyunsaturated fats.

Fats are not as quickly digested as are other food elements. However, they must still be considered a basic source of muscular energy, since fats are used when the carbohydrate stores are depleted. More oxygen is needed by the athlete who is on a fat diet than would be required for metabolism were he on a carbohydrate diet. This means that greater demands will be made on the respiratory system. For this reason it would not be feasible to place a distance runner, for instance, on a high fat diet. Slow digestion, then, is characteristic of fat. In some instances the products of fat breakdown prove to be exceedingly irritating to the linings of the stomach and the digestive tract. This can cause a considerable amount of dietary distress and in some cases may cause diarrhea.

Proteins. Proteins are nitrogenous organic compounds that break down into amino acids and are transported by the blood to the tissues. Proteins are somewhat complex substances. Basically, they are composed of a great number of carbon atoms with which atoms of hydrogen, oxygen, and nitrogen are associated. Other elements such as iron, copper, sulfur, and phosphorus are also associated with proteins, but in small amounts.

Food proteins are made up of amino acids in various and complex combinations. Twenty amino acids, usually considered the "building blocks" of proteins, are derived from digested food protein. The food proteins vary considerably in the type and number of amino acids consti-

tuting them. Amino acids are classified as either essential (indispensable) and non-essential (dispensable).[5] Eight of the twenty amino acids are considered essential, because they cannot be synthesized by the body at a rate sufficient to meet its needs for growth and maintenance. They must, therefore, be provided by the diet. The other twelve can be synthesized by the body to build body proteins, provided sufficient nitrogen is available. Such nitrogen (nonessential nitrogen) comes from either an excess of essential amino acids or from nonessential amino acids. Nutritional values of the different protein foods vary also, inasmuch as their values to the diet are determined by their amino acid pattern. Generally, proteins of animal origin are considered more adequate than those of vegetable origin, although within each group the range in biological values is wide.

Amino acids are absorbed from the intestine and transported via the bloodstream to the various parts of the body. Amino acid molecules are deaminized by the liver cells, with a portion forming glucose and the remainder forming urea. Those having the ability to form glucose are termed *glycogenic;* others, which bear a closer relationship to fatty acids, are classified as *ketogenic,* since they break down to acetic acid. Nitrogen is important as one of the key elements necessary for growth and repair. Amino acid not utilized undergoes a process of deamination during which the nitrogen is combined with carbon dioxide to form urea, which is excreted as urine within 4 hours after ingestion of this protein. This necessitates the provision of adequate daily dietary protein amounts to maintain a healthy growing state of the individual. In addition to their building and repairing properties, food proteins have considerable importance in maintaining the body's ability to resist infections and to effect good healing. Protein intake for the athlete should constitute 11% or 12% of the total calories in his diet. More than this does no particular good; on the other hand, it seems to do no particular harm either,[3] although high protein intakes may be converted to fat and stored as adipose tissue.

Inorganic requirements. Inorganic salts are essential for good health and for life itsef. Through metabolization these salts perform a number of vitally important services. As stated earlier, they aid in the formation of tissues, particularly the bones and teeth, and perform the taks of maintaining the homeostatic or internal environment of the body through stabilizing a specific ion concentration. Calcium salts help to sustain the rhythms of heartbeat and intestinal peristalsis in addition to functioning in the formation of bones and teeth, blood clotting, neuromuscular irritability, and nerve transmission. Sodium salts help to maintain the acid-base balance and osmotic pressure of the blood. Some salts trigger certain enzymatic reactions; others activate endocrine secretion.

Most of the necessary elements are present in the common foods, thus obviating the need for supplemental ingesta when a properly balanced diet is followed. The principal mineral elements are calcium, sodium, magnesium, phosphorus, potassium, chlorine, and sulfur. In addition, there are a number of important *trace* elements: cobalt, copper, fluorine, iodine, iron, manganese, molybdenum, selenium, vanadium, and zinc.

Potassium, a soluble salt found in the cells and interstices, is usually present in lean muscle meats, some leafy vegetables, and certain native waters. It is especially significant in the functioning of muscle, and plays an important role in contraction. It seems also to serve as an antifatiguing agent.

Calcium, although considered a common food element, is not readily absorbed from certain foods and is present only in rather minute quantities in others. Calcium phosphate is essential for the good development of teeth and bones. A small amount of magnesium, which is present in leafy vegetables, milk, and fruit, is also necessary for proper bone growth. The bulk of dietary calcium is supplied by dairy products. A very small quantity is supplied by such secondary sources as green leafy vegetables, legumes, egg yolks, nuts, and whole grains. Milk and the various milk products are particularly needed by the growing young athlete.

Sodium chloride (common table salt) is a necessary dietary requirement, since it plays a vital role in maintenance of the osmotic pressure of the blood. Salt is lost through perspiration and urination. Following severe or moderately severe exercise, sodium chloride excretion decreases extremely rapidly and pronouncedly. There is no evidence to support the common practice of increasing the salt intake of athletes in excess of the losses that accompany sweating in normal competitive situations. Salt supplementation may be indicated in cases that involve sudden exposure to considerable heat, such as might be encountered in a climatic change. In this situation supplementation need be carried out only until acclimatization or adaptation is accomplished (usually 1 week). If physical performance takes place under a specific condition of extreme heat, supplementation is indicated. Salt may be administered in several ways. According to Murphy and Ashe,[6] the most advantageous method is a 0.1% sodium chloride solution. Although some athletes may find this unpalatable, most of them become accustomed to it and in time actually prefer it to fresh water in field situations. An alternative is one enteric salt tablet per 6 oz. water. An individual can usually can tolerate from six to twelve 5-grain tablets per day.[7] A lemon-flavored sodium chloride preparation, which seems to be tolerated better by most users, is also available. Enteric salt tablets, although widely used, are often not well tolerated by the athlete, and their ingestion may result in considerable gastric distress and nausea. Supplementation, in such instances, is better effected by increasing the amounts of salt normally used in the diet.

Sulfur and phosphorus, principally obtained from protein foods, are also essential for various body needs. Sulfur assists in the formation of certain amino acids; phosphorus and calcium play an important role in the development of bones and teeth, in the transport of fatty acids, in the functioning of the buffer system, and in energy metabolism.

Anemia will result if there is an iron deficiency in the diet. Iron, along with cobalt and copper, regulates the body's synthesis of hemoglobin (the oxygen-carrying substance of the red blood cells). As the worn-out red blood cells are catabolized in the liver, the greater portion of the iron in the hematin, which is the iron-containing pigment, is conserved and is used again. Iron is found in lean muscle meats, organ meats (particularly liver), egg yolk, seafood, green leafy vegetables, nuts, legumes, and whole wheat.

Manganese, copper, and zinc are activators of certain enzyme reactions and serve some functions in normal metabolism. Manganese, copper, and zinc are present in animal and plant foods. Copper, in sufficient quantity for human needs, is dissolved into foodstuffs and water from pasteurizing machines, copper water pipes, or copper-lined cooking vessels. Iodine, although required in small amounts, is essential to the normal functioning of the thyroid gland. An iodine deficiency can result in goiter. However, today's practice of iodizing table salt and the drinking water has materially obviated this danger, and the athlete is assured of an adequate iodine intake. Another excellent source of iodine is seafood.

Vitamins

More misinformation has been disseminated about vitamins than about any other nutritional factor. Historically, the word "vitamin" is derived from the term "vitamine" (literally, "life amine"), coined in 1912 by Casimir Funk, a Polish chemist who was working in England. Funk isolated a compound from rice hulls, hoping that it would cure beriberi. He applied the name "vitamine" to his discovery, on the mistaken premise that his compound was *vital* to life and also that it was an *amine*.

He was wrong in both assumptions. However, the name has persisted throughout the years, although some time ago the terminal "e" was dropped. Funk's significant contribution to science was the hypothesis that a lack of vitamins was the underlying cause of a number of deficiency diseases. As a result, interest in nutritional research was increased tremendously, and today probably more research in nutrition is carried on in the field of vitamins and their use than in any other single area.

Vitamins are organic compounds, present in varying amounts in natural foods, that act as regulators or catalysts in the body processes. Although they are not chemically related, they do have certain functional similarities, and they assist the body in utilizing other nutrients. In all probability more than 26 vitamins exist. At first it was thought that there were only a few; accordingly, they were named by the letters of the alphabet and were further identified by indicating their preventive nature against a specific disease (for example, vitamin B_1, antiberiberi). This method proved cumbersome, however, and vitamins are currently identified by names that are descriptive of their chemical nature, although the old terms are still recognized and used.

Vitamins are essential for maintaining good health. A lack of vitamins in the diet leads to deficiency conditions, which express themselves in a variety of ways. A problem of vitamin deficiency is rarely caused by the lack of a single vitamin. It is, rather, the result of a multiple vitamin deficiency. A good, varied diet that includes a balance of the "basic four" food categories will supply all vitamin requirements (Table 8-1).

Several vitamins can be made synthetically, and according to the available research it appears that the body is unable to distinguish between the natural and the synthetic vitamins, either is utilized equally well. The body, however, can not manufacture any of the vitamins except D, which is derived from sunshine. Thus, it must obtain its requirements from the diet. Supplementary vitamins are of considerable value during postoperative or recuperative periods following illness or injury and are often prescribed by the physician to aid in the healing process.

Although, many vitamins and vitamin substances are known at the present time, there are some whose functions have been successfully demonstrated on experimental animals but whose effectiveness on man has not been indicated with any degree of validity. Only those vitamins whose actions have been demonstrated to have specific human significance will be considered. Vitamin A, some elements in the vitamin B complex (such as thiamine, riboflavin,

Table 8-1. Daily food guide—the basic four food groups*

Food group	Main nutrients	Daily amounts†
Milk		
Milk, cheese, ice cream, or other products made with whole or skimmed milk	Calcium Protein Riboflavin	Children under 9: 2 to 3 cups Children 9 to 12: 3 or more cups Teenagers: 4 or more cups Adults: 2 or more cups Pregnant women: 3 or more cups Nursing mothers: 4 or more cups (1 cup = 8 oz. fluid milk or designated milk equivalent‡)
Meats		
Beef, veal, lamb, pork, poultry, fish, eggs	Protein Iron Thiamine	2 or more servings Count as one serving: 2 to 3 oz. of lean, boneless, cooked meat, poultry, or fish
Alternates: dry beans, dry peas, nuts, peanut butter	Niacin Riboflavin	2 eggs 1 cup cooked dry beans or peas 4 tablespoons peanut butter
Vegetables and fruits		4 or more servings Count as 1 serving: ½ cup of vegetable or fruit, or a portion such as 1 medium apple, banana, orange, potato, or ½ a medium grapefruit, melon
	Vitamin A	Include: A dark-green or deep-yellow vegetable or fruit rich in vitamin A, at least every other day
	Vitamin C (ascorbic acid)	A citrus fruit or other fruit or vegetable rich in vitamin C daily
	Smaller amounts of other vitamins and minerals	Other vegetables and fruits including potatoes
Breads and cereals		4 or more servings of whole grain, enriched or restored Count as 1 serving:
	Thiamine Niacin Riboflavin Iron Protein	1 slice of bread 1 ounce (1 cup) ready to eat cereal, flake or puff varieties ½ to ¾ cup cooked cereal ½ to ¾ cup cooked pastes (macaroni, spaghetti, noodles) Crackers: 5 saltines, 2 squares graham crackers, etc.

*From Williams, S. R.: Nutrition and diet therapy, St. Louis, 1969, The C. V. Mosby Co.
†Use additional amounts of these foods or added butter, margarine, oils, sugars, etc., as desired or needed.
‡Milk equivalents: 1 ounce cheddar cheese, 3 servings cottage cheese, 1 cup fluid skimmed milk, 1 cup buttermilk, ¼ cup dry skimmed milk powder, 1 cup ice milk, 1⅔ cups ice cream, ½ cup evaporated milk.

niacin, B_{12}), and vitamins C and D fall into this category.

Other vitamins, such as vitamins H and P, folic acid, and inositol, have demonstrated certain actions in laboratory animals only. Since their effects have not been verified on humans as yet, they will not be considered here.

Vitamins are usually identified as either fat-soluble or water-soluble. Fat-soluble vitamins usually persist in the diet in a reasonably intact state; they are found in butter, fortified margarines, and liver and are not usually destroyed in cooking. Vitamins A, D, E, and K are fat-soluble and the others are water-soluble. Water-soluble vitamins are often lost through cooking vitamin-containing foods in water and then disposing of the water in which they were cooked. Some vitamins are categorized as *heat-labile*. These are the vitamins usually destroyed in the cooking process because of their inability to withstand heat. Vitamin C is an example of this group. Most of the vitamins, however, are *heat-stable* and are not easily oxidized. Vitamins act as protein substances in the body.

Vitamin A

Vitamin A is essential for cell building, acts as a stimulus for new cell growth, and is a factor providing for skeletal growth, tooth formation, and formation of epithelial tissue composing the skin, the mucous linings of the digestive, respiratory, genitourinary tracts, and the sinuses. It aids in keeping up resistance to infections through the maintenance of normal epithelium. It also increases longevity, delays senility, and acts as a preventive for nyctalopia (night blindness). If there is a deficiency of vitamin A in the diet, the "visual purple" (rhodopsin) that is required for red vision and the iodopsin required for cone vision are bleached out. Lack of this vitamin may also cause reduced peripheral vision, which often results in accident proneness.

The implications of vitamin A deficiency are important to the trainer. Increased intake improves night vision and should benefit football players and other athletes who play under the lights. It may also be of benefit to players for whom good peripheral vision is a decided asset, for example, pass catchers in football and basketball players.

Sources: Since animals such as fishes have the ability to store considerable amounts of vitamin A in their livers, this organ is one of the best sources of the substance. Codliver oil, which contains fat-soluble vitamin A and D, is one of the most prevalent commercial sources. A precursor of vitamin A, *carotene*, is found in plant foods such as green leafy vegetables, carrots, sweet potatoes, mango, artichokes, and papayas. It is converted into vitamin A in the liver.[1] Other sources of this vitamin are liver, eggs, and dairy fat.

Vitamin B complex

The vitamin B complex group of vitamins is water-soluble. Some are lost in preparation as the water is poured off, and others, being heat-labile, are destroyed by prolonged cooking. The various vitamins are known to be quite closely interrelated and involved in various enzymatic actions. Water-soluble vitamins are stored in the body in limited amounts and must therefore be included in the daily food plan.

Thiamine (vitamin B_1, antineuritic factor). Thiamine is of the utmost importance for the proper and complete utilization of carbohydrates. Only a small amount of thiamine, enough for a few days of normal functioning, is stored in the body. Since this small reserve may readily be depleted by physiological emergencies, it is important that adequate amounts of thiamine be secured daily, preferably through normal dietary means. Thiamine is produced synthetically and thus can be made available for supplementation if indicated by a physician.

Sources: The richest dietary source of this vitamin is pork and pork products. Peas, legumes, and enriched or whole-wheat bread are other good sources of thiamine. Dried brewer's yeast and wheat germ oil, both extremely high in thiamine, are not utilized regularly and so assume little importance in the average diet. In our culture there is a tendency to use refined cereals and flours, with the result that much of the thiamine is lost in the milling process unless the flour is subsequently enriched.

Riboflavin (vitamin B₂ or vitamin G). Found in all living cells and a constituent of many enzymes, riboflavin can also be made synthetically. It is the link between the metabolism of carbohydrates and proteins. Its main functions are to promote growth, general health, and longevity. It is also essential to certain aspects of nerve tissue and cell respiration maintenance.

Sources: Liver is probably the richest source of supply of riboflavin. Kidney, lean meats, chicken, peanuts, eggs, dried yeast, vegetable greens, and carrots are all excellent sources. The most common source of riboflavin is milk. Because riboflavin is easily affected by light, foods such as milk should not be stored in strong light lest they lose their riboflavin content. The body is unable to store this vitamin.

Niacin (nicotinic acid, pellagra-preventive factor). Niacin works quite closely with riboflavin and thiamine and enters into necessary enzyme reactions. This vitamin is quite stable in respect to heat, light, air, acids, and alkalies. As a result, it is not destroyed by ordinary cooking. Like riboflavin, it cannot be stored by the body; therefore, adequate amounts should be included in the daily diet. Niacin is an effective element in promoting and maintaining normal growth, function, and health.

Sources: Liver, dried brewer's yeast, lean muscle meats, whole-wheat bread, enriched bread, milk, fresh vegetables, and fresh fruit are the principal sources of niacin.

Vitamin B₁₂ (antipernicious anemia factor). A group of complex compounds comprise this vitamin, the only vitamin to contain a metal, cobalt, which is found in each of the compounds. This water-soluble vitamin is stable to heat in neutral solutions but is destroyed by heating in dilute acid or alkali.

Its most essential function is in the development and production of red blood cells.

Vitamin B₁₂ serves as an erythrocyte maturation factor and is important in respect to anemia and pernicious anemia. Not only does it act as a preventive and as a specific in treatment, but it also serves to relieve the digestive and nervous disturbances that accompany these diseases. It is effective also in developing appetite and acting as a growth factor in children. It functions by putting weight on children who are underweight.

Since vitamin B₁₂ is essential in the energy metabolism of muscle, it has been postulated that injecting B₁₂ intramuscularly before competition would enable the athlete to perform more effectively. Studies investigating this premise indicate that vitamin B₁₂ supplementation is wholly unnecessary and that any advantage gained is in all probability purely psychological.[8]

Sources: The major sources of this vitamin are liver and kidney. Milk, fish, lean beef, and pork rank as medium in terms of content.

Ascorbic acid (vitamin C, antiscorbutic factor)

Vitamin C or ascorbic acid is the least stable of all vitamins. It is freely soluble in water and is relatively stable in weak acids, but it is neutralized in the presence of alkalies. It is quite sensitive to oxidation; consequently, the drying or storage of foods destroys or materially reduces their vitamin C content. Since it is extremely heat-labile, cooking can easily render it ineffective. Therefore, vegetables or fruits should be eaten raw or, if cooked, should be prepared at low heat with a minimum quantity of water. Since ascorbic acid is stored in the body for extremely short periods, a daily dietary requirement is indicated.

As with other vitamins, ascorbic acid is essential to the formation of the intercellular substance, collagen, that acts as a bonding or cementing force between the cells. In this task it is responsible for maintaining the firmness of tissues such as the gum tissues. It further acts as a factor in maintaining the integrity or soundness of the capillaries and thus preventing the condition known as "capillary fragility," in which a hemorrhagic condition of the capillaries is induced. Vitamin C influences and plays a most important role in tooth and bone formation, development, and repair and in the healing of wounds. Vitamin C also functions in the absorption of iron from the intestinal tract. The callus that is formed in the healing of a fracture is a result of ascorbic acid action. There seems to be some relationship between vitamin C and the production of the adrenocortical hormones, especially with reference to the pituitary gland. This vitamin may also be concerned in the maintenance of normal hemoglobin levels and in the maturation of red blood cells.

Sources: Fresh citrus fruits such as oranges, grapefruit, lemons, and limes are the best sources of ascorbic acid. Tomatoes, raw cabbage, white potatoes (cooked in their skins, and most vegetables and greens, *if eaten raw,* are also good sources.

Vitamin D (antirachitic factor)

Vitamin D is composed of at least 16 known substances of different forms. Of these, D_2 and D_3 are of the greatest importance, although other forms also contribute to the general good health of the individual. Vitamin D is fat-soluble and is stable with reference to both heat and oxidation.

The average athlete obtaining reasonable exposure to sunlight will, in all probability, need no vitamin D supplementation.

Sources: The sources of vitamin D are somewhat limited. Sunlight is an excellent source. Other good sources are irradiated milk; the liver oils of cod, tuna, halibut, and other bony fishes; eggs; and butter. Some activated margarines are also suitable sources.

WATER

Water, one of the three prime necessities of life, comes from several sources to meet the body's physiological needs. Most of it is ingested in the daily diet either as fluid or as the fluid elements contained in the so-called solid foods. The remainder is a result of the oxidation of organic foodstuffs.

Water forms the bulk, about 75%, of all protoplasm, and it acts as a medium for the various enzymatic and chemical reactions. Water functions as a diluent of toxic wastes, thus preventing damage to the body and its organs from some of the toxic by-products of metabolism. This is especially true in respect to the kidneys. Water aids in the transport of body fuels and the elimination of waste materials. It also helps to regulate body temperature, by dissipating excess heat from the body through perspiration (Table 8-2).

A water balance must be maintained. The water loss usually approximates the water intake. If a salt deficit exists, the body will not retain water but will continue to eliminate it at a rate basically the same as that of the intake under normal situations. Dehydration must be prevented. It has been found that moderately severe or even severe exercise can be sustained quite comfortably over extended periods of time if the water intake is regulated to conform to the water loss. Small amounts given often are more effective in maintaining balance under severe heat and exercise conditions than are extremely large amounts given at greater intervals.[9] Deprivation of water

Table 8-2. Typical water balance in adult*

Sources and loss	Milliliters
Sources of water	
Liquid food	1100
Solid food	500–1000
Water of oxidation	300– 400
Total	1900–2500
Loss of water	
Urine	1000–1300
Perspiration and evaporation	
from skin	800–1000
Feces	100
Total	1900–2500

*From Guthrie, H. A.: Introductory nutrition, St. Louis, 1967, The C. V. Mosby Co.

leads to more rapid dehydration, with subsequent impairment of performance. A daily intake of 2,000 ml. of water should be adequate in most instances but should be increased if sweating occurs. Some form of water should be available at all training sessions and games. It should be considered as much a part of the training/competitive regimen as any other phase. The withholding of water from athletes can neither be condoned morally nor can it be justified on physiological bases. Encourage your players to drink all the water that they want. In extremely hot weather even the thirst mechanism may fail to require adequate amounts. A little water sloshing about in the stomach can do no harm.[10,11]

Weight loss during hot weather activity is primarily water loss. It is good practice to weigh athletes nude and dry both preceding and following practice to observe the amount of weight loss. Excessive loss should be noted. A loss of 2.2 pounds (1 kg.) is accompanied by a loss of approximately 2 grams of salt (1 level teaspoonful of salt equals about 4 grams). A loss of 5 pounds requires careful observation, and a loss of 10 pounds or more during a single practice period approaches the danger level.[12]

FOOD SUPPLEMENTS

A number of liquid food supplements have been produced and are being used by college and professional teams with some indications of success. These supplements supply from 225 to 400 calories per average serving, at a cost equal to approximately one fifth that of the pre-game meal, which usually consists of steak. Athletes who have used these supplements, usually in about 925-calorie servings, report elimination of the usual pregame symptoms of "dry mouth," abdominal cramps, leg cramps, nervous defecation, and nausea.[13,15]

Pregame emotional tension often delays the emptying of the stomach, and therefore the undigested food mass remains in the stomach and upper bowel for a prolonged time, even up to or through the actual period of competition. This unabsorbed food mass is of no value to the athlete. According to team physicians who have experimented with the liquid food supplements, one of their major advantages is that they do clear both the stomach and the upper bowel prior to game time, thus making available the caloric energy that would otherwise still be in an unassimilated state.[16,17] It appears that there may be some merit in the use of such food supplements for pregame meals.

VALUES OF SUPPLEMENTATION

The trainer or coach should use vitamin or food supplementation only when it is difficult or impossible for the athlete to obtain a well-balanced diet or when most of the nutrients are lost or destroyed during food preparation. When a meal is low in vitamin content it is usually low in mineral content also. In such cases it would be advisable to administer both vitamin and mineral supplements.

Since vitamin retention by the body is limited and since activity requiring endurance or all-out effort makes demands upon the limited body stores, these stores can easily become seriously depleted during a period of intense work. Deficiency diseases are not as common in the United States today as they are in other parts of the world, since most Americans eat a reasonably well-balanced diet. Despite this, many people suffer from a vitamin shortage of sufficient degree to lessen their effectiveness in work or, in the case of athletes, their capacity for optimum performance.

Athletic performance may increase the need for vitamin supplementation because the body has increased its metabolic demands. This is especially true when meeting weight regulations in such activities as wrestling, boxing, or weight lifting is a problem. The requirements for specific vitamins may increase in a direct proportion with the energy demands. Extremely demanding endurance activities may increase the normal requirements of vitamin B, vitamin C, and others as much as fifteen times.

Coaches and many trainers have long believed that fortifying a normal diet with relatively large dosages of vitamins would improve the athlete's performance and fitness for exercise. In recent years there have been several experiments seeking to substantiate such hypotheses. Experiments concerned with the effects of vitaminization on muscular endurance, running, strength, and speed have, generally speaking, produced no definitive indications of significant gains in performance.

During the 1961 season Rasch, Klafs, and Arnheim[18] conducted an experiment using an entire cross-country team in an attempt to ascertain the effectiveness of ascorbic acid in improving performance. Five hundred milligrams of vitamin C were administered daily to each runner of the experimental group to maintain a saturation level. The control group was given a placebo, and care was taken to eliminate undesirable variables. No significant improvement was noted. On the basis of this and other studies, we believe that supplementing the diet of the athlete with vitamins does not markedly improve performance unless a pre-existing vitamin deficiency was present.

Taking vitamins in excessive quantities is of no particular value and can, in certain circumstances, have deleterious effects and lead to vitamin toxicity. In extreme cases it can prove fatal. It would seem to be more practical to attain desired vitamin levels through intelligent food selection and preparation rather than to rely upon artificial supplements.

NUTRITIONAL REQUIREMENTS

Nutritional requirements can be outlined briefly as follows:
1. Foods used for maintenance, repair, and growth: Foods in this category are the basic protein foods such as milk, eggs, meats, whole grain enriched cereals, peas, beans, and milk products.
2. Foods used as energy: Foods in this category are the fats, starches, proteins, and sugars found in butter, margarine, meat, ice cream, potatoes, and cereals.
3. Vitamins: As previously indicated, these are found in certain foods, and they must form a part of the balanced diet to prevent deficiency diseases. They are necessary also for the transformation of energy and for the regulation of various metabolic functions. Important vitamins and their sources are the following:
   a. Vitamin A—Leafy green and yellow vegetables, butter, enriched or fortified margarine, and liver
   b. Vitamin B—Lean muscle meats, whole grain or enriched breads, spaghetti, and macaroni
   c. Vitamin C—Citrus fruits, tomatoes, broccoli, potatoes, strawberries, and cantaloupe
   d. Vitamin D—Sunlight and fortified vitamin D milk
   e. Vitamin E—Green leafy vegetables, whole grain flour, and vegetable oils
4. Minerals: Calcium and phosphorus are found in milk; iron and sulfur in lean muscle meats and eggs; and iodine, sodium, and chlorine in iodized salt.
5. Water.

It is important that the athlete follow a balanced diet. A varied diet is not necessarily a balanced diet; attention must be given to the type as well as to the quantity of food ingested. The use of a training bulletin board or individual throw sheets containing suggested balanced diets is of value in orienting the athlete. A more effective device is a placard display. Occasional short talks by both the trainer and the coach and incidental suggestions made at an opportune time further serve to emphasize the necessity of a balanced diet. The sample diets shown are indicative of suggested meal patterns rather than of specific meals.

Breakfast

Fruit—fresh citrus fruit, canned or fortified frozen citrus juices, canned tomatoes, or vegetable-tomato juice

Cereal—dry or cooked cereal with milk and sugar

Meat and/or eggs—bacon or ham, broiled crisp; eggs, boiled or poached

Bread—whole wheat or bran; occasionally, sweet rolls

Spreads—jelly, jam, marmalade, or honey

Beverage°—milk, cocoa, tea, or coffee

Luncheon

Soup—choice in terms of preference; greasy soups to be avoided; clear soups preferred

Salad—fresh fruit or vegetable with small amount of dressing

Main course—sandwiches, casseroles, stews, creamed meats, fowl, or fish

Vegetables—choice of two, fresh preferred

Bread—whole wheat, bran, plain or toasted

Dessert—fresh fruit, gelatin, or puddings

Beverage—milk, cocoa, tea, or coffee

Dinner

Soup—choice in terms of preference

Salad—fresh fruit or vegetable, with small amount of dressing

Main course—meat, fish, or occasionally fowl, broiled

Vegetables—choice of two, fresh preferred

Bread—whole wheat, bran, plain or toasted

Dessert—cake, pie, ice cream, gelatin, or puddings

Beverage—milk, cocoa, tea, or coffee

It should be noted that an abundance of fresh fruits and vegetables is recommended. In addition to their nutrient value, such foods also contain indigestible materials such as cellulose, which in the form of

°Milk is the preferred beverage for the high school athlete.

roughage, are of considerable assistance in the process of elimination.

Liquids such as water or milk, taken with meals, should not be used to wash the food down; nor should they be ingested in copious quantities. Large amounts of liquid tend to give a feeling of fullness before an adequate amount of food has been ingested, and they delay digestion.

Fried foods should be avoided, since they take longer to digest and, if eaten to excess, can cause gastric disturbance. The tendency of many people to breakfast on oven-fresh rolls or sweet rolls is also questionable. Freshly baked breadstuffs are difficult to digest properly and, if eaten, should be eaten well in advance of any projected physical activity.

Today's youth is quite "sweets"-conscious. Peer pressure and advertising make it difficult for the high school athlete to adhere to a balanced diet. Snack bars on the high school grounds or in the immediate neighborhood make the substitution of french fries, soft drinks, and candy for a nutritious luncheon quite easy and make between-meal snacks of such foods, which are undesirable from a training point of view, readily accessible. When possible, the athlete should be counseled to substitute fresh fruit or an occasional glass of milk for between-meal snacks rather than to appease his appetite with candy bars or other similar foods.

It has long been an American custom to subsist principally on three meals a day, patterned on a clock-hour basis. Research has indicated the values of the coffee break,

Table 8-3. General approximations for daily adult basal and activity energy needs*

Basal energy needs (av. 1 cal. per kg. per hr.)		Man (70 kg.) calories 70 × 24 = 1,680	Woman (58 kg.) calories 58 × 24 = 1,392
Activity energy needs			
Very sedentary	+20 basal	1,680 + 336 = 2,016	1,392 + 278 = 1,670
Sedentary	+30 basal	1,680 + 504 = 2,184	1,392 + 418 = 1,810
Moderately active	+40 basal	1,680 + 672 = 2,352	1,392 + 557 = 1,949
Very active	+50 basal	1,680 + 840 = 2,520	1,392 + 696 = 2,088

*From Williams, S. R.: Nutrition and diet therapy, St. Louis, 1969, Courtesy The C. V. Mosby Co.

in terms of work efficiency. It may be well to permit a snack between meals, provided such a snack has good nutritive value and does not add to an existing overweight problem. Many authorities advise eating when hungry rather than eating on the clock-hour basis.[19,20] Although such a suggestion may have physiological merit, it is not always feasible in terms of practical management.

EMOTIONAL STATE AT MEALTIME

It is imperative that meals be eaten in an atmosphere of relaxation and in pleasant, cheerful surroundings. Negative emotions tend to upset and retard the digestive processes through shifting the blood mass away from the organs of digestion. Emotional stress over a period of time can result in chronic gastrointestinal disturbances.[21,22] Pre-event stress is transitory in nature but is often severe enough to pose problems. By establishing a near-normal situation, in terms of emotional climate, mealtimes can be pleasant and full of good fellowship and camaraderie.

PRE-EVENT NUTRITION

There is no scientific evidence that performance can generally be improved through control of the athlete's diet.[23,24] Improvement in performance may be attributed to a balanced diet, if there have been previous dietary deficiencies. The main value of proper nutrition lies in preventing the deleterious effects of improper or inadequate nutrition. Too often trainers and coaches concern themselves principally with the meal immediately preceding competition and do not seem to realize that pre-event nutrition begins some time before that. Events that call for sudden bursts of all-out energy, rather than endurance or sustained effort, do not appear to be particularly affected or modified by pre-event nutrition. However, in preparing for moderate or sustained effort that requires endurance, it is well to include consideration of nutrition approximately 48 hours preceding competition, since such events can be significantly affected by ingestion. The usual manifestation of precompetitive tension such as abdominal cramps, "dry mouth," acidosis, and other metabolic symptoms can be either reduced or eliminated to a considerable degree by dietary consideration.

It is also wise to begin to gradually decrease the training program about 48 hours before competition. This is advocated because it enables the body to replenish certain essential stores and to reduce or eliminate various metabolites that might reduce performance. As has previously been shown, the glycogen stores of the body—specifically those in the liver, which normally consist of about 1,500 calories—need to be built up to a full measure if an athlete is to compete in an endurance event and give a good account of himself. In endurance events approximately 1,500 calories are consumed during the first hour of effort, and continued exertion may result in an excessive depletion of the glycogen reserves of the body, with consequent hypoglycemia (marked reduction in blood sugar) and appearance of evident fatigue.

Foods to avoid. Foods of high cellulose content such as lettuce should be avoided, since they tend to increase the need for defecation. The elimination of highly spiced and of fatty or fried foods from the diet is also desirable because of the likelihood of gastrointestinal irritation.

Protein content. It is advisable to limit protein intake during the period just prior to competition, since proteins are a source of fixed acids, which can be eliminated from the body only through urinary excretion. Since water intake is usually somewhat modified prior to and during performance, urinary output may be reduced, with a resulting increased acid load that could have a negative effect on optimal performance. To prevent this, meats, fish, and eggs should be eliminated from the meal that immediately precedes competition. However, during training periods it would be well to advocate generous amounts of protein in the daily diet to allow a more rapid increase in muscle mass without depletion of protein sources elsewhere in the body.

Carbohydrate content. Carbohydrate intake should be significantly increased during the precontest period. Extra helpings of breads, cereals, potatoes, and sugar should be the rule. Bread and potatoes do not deserve their reputation as fattening foods. Potatoes should be eaten plain, that is, baked or boiled without the addition of milk, cream, or butter, which are the fattening agents. Bread, preferably, should be constituted from the less-refined flours or enriched by the restoration of the vitamins and minerals lost through refining. Since carbohydrates are most readily available and most easily absorbed in terms of metabolic demands, they are the first elements utilized for muscular work. Inasmuch as the final by-products of carbohydrate metabolism, carbon dioxide and water, are eliminated from the body through the lungs and the skin, no additional acid load is accumulated in the tissues, which cannot be removed by kidney function (Table 8-4).

Fat content. Since fats are somewhat more difficult to digest than either proteins or carbohydrates and since they often prove to be quite irritating to the gastrointestinal tract, their inclusion in the pre-event diet should be sharply reduced, if not altogether eliminated. For this reason the amount of milk drunk should be restricted unless skim milk is substituted for whole milk.

Liquids. Liquids should be low in fat content and readily absorbable. Above all, they should not cause laxation; therefore fruit juices should be restricted. Items such as prune juice, which has a high laxation factor, should be eliminated from the diet. Water intake should be normal. Cocoa, whether made from milk or water, is an excellent beverage to give some variety and can be substituted for milk, juice, coffee, or tea as the occasion demands.

Coffee, tea, and alcohol. The use of coffee, tea, and alcohol requires specific mention. At the high school level, drinking tea or coffee is not the usual practice among athletes, but it becomes more prevalent at the college level. For many years, tea, a caffeine-containing fluid, has traditionally been a part of the pregame meal. Caffeine induces a period of stimulation of the central nervous system that is followed by a period of depression. Inasmuch as the athlete is usually excited and somewhat nervous during the precontest period, the addition of caffeine to the pregame meal may not be advisable. The same statements apply to the use of coffee. Tea and coffee are also diuretics; that is, they stimulate the flow of urine and thus may cause additional discomfort during the competitive period.

It must be recognized, however, that individual tolerance or reactivity to caffeine-containing liquids varies considerably. At the college level, insistence upon the complete elimination of coffee or tea from a diet wherein drinking such beverages has been customary may result in a psychological effect that militates against the athlete more than would his usual intake of the mild stimulants.

The use of alcohol in the athletic diet cannot be recommended. Here, again, physiological tolerance, aside from moral or religious convictions, is a factor. In small quantities alcohol affects the finer neuromuscular coordinations; if taken in large amounts it affects gross coordinations to a considerable degree. It is a well-known fact that many foreign athletes consume varying amounts of beer or wine as a regular part of both their training and their pre-event diets. There is not enough evidence that such practices sufficiently improve performance to merit the addition of alcoholic beverages to the training or the pre-event diet.

Salt intake. In maintaining an adequate salt content a daily intake of 15 to 20 grams (approximately 1 tablespoon) will meet most needs. As has been previously stated, this is better obtained through the salting of foods than through the issuance of supplementary salt tablets. The consumption of one cup of bouillon and three glasses of

Table 8-4. Energy equivalents of food calories expressed in minutes of activity*

Food	Calories	Walking[1]	Riding bicycle[2]	Swim-ming[3]	Running[4]	Reclining[5]
			Minutes of activity			
Apple, large	101	19	12	9	5	78
Bacon, 2 strips	96	18	12	9	5	74
Banana, small	88	17	11	8	4	68
Beans, green, 1 c.	27	5	3	2	1	21
Beer, 1 glass	114	22	14	10	6	88
Bread and butter	78	15	10	7	4	60
Cake, 2-layer, 1/12	356	68	43	32	18	274
Carbonated beverage, 1 glass	106	20	13	9	5	82
Carrot, raw	42	8	5	4	2	32
Cereal, dry, ½ c. with milk, sugar	200	38	24	18	10	154
Cheese, cottage, 1 tbsp.	27	5	3	2	1	21
Cheese, Cheddar, 1 oz.	111	21	14	10	6	85
Chicken, fried, ½ breast	232	45	28	21	12	178
Chicken, TV dinner	542	104	66	48	28	417
Cookie, plain	15	3	2	1	1	12
Cookie, chocolate chip	51	10	6	5	3	39
Doughnut	151	29	18	13	8	116
Egg, fried	110	21	13	10	6	85
Egg, boiled	77	15	9	7	4	59
French dressing, 1 tbsp.	59	11	7	5	3	45
Halibut steak, ¼ lb.	205	39	25	18	11	158
Ham, 2 slices	167	32	20	15	9	128
Ice cream, ⅙ qt.	193	37	24	17	10	148
Ice cream soda	255	49	31	23	13	196
Ice milk, ⅙ qt.	144	28	18	13	7	111
Gelatin, with cream	117	23	14	10	6	90
Malted milk shake	502	97	61	45	26	386
Mayonnaise, 1 tbsp.	92	18	11	8	5	71
Milk, 1 glass	166	32	20	15	9	128
Milk, skim, 1 glass	81	16	10	7	4	62
Milk shake	421	81	51	38	22	324
Orange, medium	68	13	8	6	4	52
Orange juice, 1 glass	120	23	15	11	6	92
Pancake with syrup	124	24	15	11	6	95
Peach, medium	46	9	6	4	2	35
Peas, green, ½ c.	56	11	7	5	3	54
Pie, apple, ⅙	377	73	46	34	19	290
Pie, raisin, ⅙	437	84	53	39	23	336
Pizza, cheese, ⅛	180	35	22	16	9	138
Pork chop, loin	314	60	38	28	16	242
Potato chips, 1 serving	108	21	13	10	6	83
Sandwiches:						
Club	590	113	72	53	30	454
Hamburger	350	67	43	31	18	269
Roast beef with gravy	430	83	52	38	22	331
Tuna fish salad	278	53	34	25	14	214
Sherbet, ⅙ qt.	177	34	22	16	9	136

*From: Konishi, F.: Food energy equivalents of various activities, J. Amer. Dietetic Assoc., 46:186, (1965). Used by permission.
[1] Energy cost of walking for 150-lb. individual = 5.2 calories per minute at 3.5 m.p.h.
[2] Energy cost of riding bicycle = 8.2 calories per minute.
[3] Energy cost of swimming = 11.2 calories per minute.
[4] Energy cost of running = 19.4 calories per minute.
[5] Energy cost of reclining = 1.3 calories per minute.

Table 8-4. Energy equivalents of food calories expressed in minutes of activity—cont'd

Food	Calories	Minutes of activity				
		Walking[1]	Riding bicycle[2]	Swimming[3]	Running[4]	Reclining[5]
Shrimp, French fried	180	35	22	16	9	138
Spaghetti, 1 serving	396	76	48	35	20	305
Steak, T-bone	235	45	29	21	12	181
Strawberry shortcake	400	77	49	36	21	308

liquid during the pregame meal, followed by an additional glass of water about 1½ hours after the meal, should meet the needs in terms of both salt and liquid requirements.

Time of the pre-event meal. The number and spacing of meals and the effect of food intake has been reported by several investigators.[13,19-22] It is generally conceded that the pre-event meal should be consumed about 3 hours before competition. Eating a meal immediately before competition is not conducive to effective performance. The acute discomfort of attempting to perform physically on a full stomach provides a psychological impediment. Also, the increase in portal circulation required for digestion is achieved by withdrawing from the systemic circulation blood that would otherwise be readily available for the maintenance of physical work.

The amount of time in which different foods are evacuated from the stomach varies considerably. Pure cane sugar, for example, can be evacuated in 1½ hours or less, whereas beef or chicken requires at least 3 hours and cereals and breads 2 hours. Fatty substances require approximately 5 hours and a heavy meal composed of starch, protein, and fats will take from 4½ to 5 hours to leave the stomach. Normally, foods used in the pre-event meal are evacuated from the stomach in 2 to 3 hours. A 3-hour period is ample to ensure adequate digestion and absorption and still not allow the athlete to feel hungry. The feeling of queasiness that often precedes competition may delay gastric emptying. Therefore fats, which tend to delay digestion, should be excluded from the pre-event meal.

WEIGHT CONTROL

Gain or loss of weight in an athlete often poses a problem because the individual's ingrained eating habits are difficult to change. The trainer's inability to adequately supervise the athlete's meal program in terms of balance and quantity further complicates the problem. An intelligent and conscientious approach to weight control requires, on the part of both trainer and athlete, some knowledge of what is involved. Such understanding allows the athlete to better discipline himself as to the quantity and kinds of foods he should eat. Weight control is basically a psychosomatic problem; therefore it requires a psychological approach on the part of the trainer.

The energy requirements of an individual are not at all constant but vary with age, sex, weight, current health status, and occupation. Body weight is determined in part by body build or somatotype. Because of these many variables, there is no short cut or magic formula to weight control.

Overweight is simply the result of putting more energy into the body than is taken out. The principal cause is overeating coupled with inactivity. It is important that the athlete develop good eating habits, restricting his use of fatty foods and modifying his carbohydrate intake. He must learn to eat less—overeating at the training table is a common fault—and to confine his intake to bulky, low-calorie foods.

Exercise and weight control

There has long been a misconception that exercise has little or no effect on caloric balance. Nothing could be farther from the truth. Inactivity is probably the most important factor in weight gain. Eating habits do not readily change but activity habits do. The measured costs, in energy expenditure, of various types of physical activities give an indication of the value of exercise as a means of weight control[23] (Table 8-5). This is exemplified by the added poundage the athlete usually takes on during the off-season. He continues his food intake at substantially the same rate but lowers his activity level; therefore, the energy that is usually burned off through activity remains as adipose accretion.

Since the energy cost of exercise is proportional to body weight, the overweight athlete requires more energy and utilizes more of his body reserves in performing a given activity than does a person who is not carrying excess poundage. If an athlete permits himself to become 20% or more overweight, the energy cost of his performance will go up the same amount and he will be working at an inefficient level. A reduction in surplus weight, even when additional weight appears to be a desirable factor, generally results in a more efficiently functioning individual whose increase in usable energy will more than offset any apparent advantage dead weight would seem to give. If an increase in weight is desirable, it is better achieved through a gain in muscle bulk rather than through a gain in fat. Overnutrition can be a distinct hindrance to many types of performance since the excess caloric intake causes excessive adipose tissue deposits, which tend to restrict body movement, thus adding to the work load and reducing the effective available surface for heat loss.

Weight reduction. To lose weight one must increase physical activity, and maintain a proper diet, for only in this way can caloric expenditure be increased.[24,25] Regular exercise tends to stabilize the weight, once the desired level is attained. In some sports, especially wrestling and weight lifting, it is sometimes necessary for the athlete to lose a few pounds so that he may make a specific weight class. Usually, most of the loss is achieved through dehydration and/or reducing the food intake.

Intense weight reduction during a short period of time may seriously impair performance. Ordinarily, weight reduction is effected within a period that ranges from 2 to 7 days. From 2 to 4½ pounds may be lost during this time. Avoiding fat foods and limiting the fluid intake, coupled with an exercise program to induce sweating, is the method customarily used. Cross-country running in heavy clothing is preferable to the use of steam or hot baths and is far less enervating. Dehydration is marked by an impairment of performance; it has been observed that in some individuals a dehydration of as little as 2% of the body weight causes a significant deterioration of work performance. If at all possible, weight reduction should be avoided. However, should the trainer be faced with someone's need for weight reduction, he should advocate a gradual loss over as long a period of time as is feasible under the circumstances, to ensure the athlete's entering competition in a near-optimal state of fitness.[26,27]

In an attempt to lose weight the athlete

Table 8-5. Calorie adjustment required for weight loss*

To lose 1 pound a week—500 fewer calories daily
Basis of estimation

1 lb. body fat	=	454 grams
1 gm. pure fat	=	9 calories
1 gm. body fat	=	7.7 calories (some water in fat cells)
454 gm. × 9 cal. per gm.	=	4,086 calories per lb. fat (pure fat)
454 gm. × 7.7 cal. per gm.	=	3,496 calories per lb. body fat (or 3,500 calories)
500 cal. × 7 days	=	3,500 calories = 1 lb. body fat

*From William, S. R.: Nutrition and diet therapy, St. Louis, 1969, The C. V. Mosby Co.

may go on a "crash" diet. Diets of this nature fail to recognize the basic problem in weight reduction—that of acquiring a change in eating habits. Athletes should be discouraged from attempting this type of program. The resulting lowered vitality makes the individual susceptible to colds and infections and produces ennui and weakness, which are reflected in a lowering of both the efficiency and the magnitude of physical performance.

Weight gain. Weight gain can be accomplished through diet enrichment and exercise regulation. At times it may be advisable to advocate dietary supplementation between meals to increase caloric intake. Some reduction in the rigor of the daily training program, with an increase in the periods of rest and relaxation, helps in adding extra ounces. Such reductions in the training program should be consistent with maintaining the *status quo* of performance levels.

Weight control in wrestling

Some publicity in recent years has charged that certain coaches were requiring wrestlers to achieve excessive weight loss so that they could make a certain weight class for competition. If this is true, such practices cannot be condoned. They are not only undesirable from the standpoint of maintaining physical effectiveness but are also potentially harmful. A rapid decrease in weight, which is caused by extreme restrictions of caloric intake, is

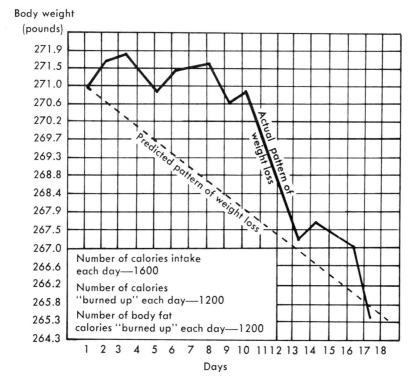

Fig. 8-1. Changes in body weight of a very overweight person on a reducing diet. The progress chart of an actual patient shows how greatly body weight can fluctuate as a result of water retention even though daily calorie intake remains constant. This dieter accumulated water for 10 days while losing fat, then showed a rapid weight loss as water was eliminated. (Courtesy Pennwalt, Prescription Products Division, Pennwalt Corporation, Rochester, N. Y.)

contraindicated immediately prior to or during periods that will require maximal physical effort. Also, weight reduction by high school athletes poses a serious problem because of the growth and maturation factors.[26-28]

Some coaches and trainers advocate "dry-out" and total fasting as initiatory to a program of weight reduction. Usually they suggest elimination of carbohydrates and salt. Such an approach has serious implications to the athlete since salt loss in the urine is greatly increased and this loss, coupled with the additional salt loss incurred through perspiration, greatly increases the possibility of a clinically identified sodium deficiency. When vigorous physical activity is performed, these features are not only magnified, but they may lead to a renal shutdown as well. During such total fasts there is a decrease in heart size, which accompanies these hydrodynamic changes.[26]

As indicated previously in this chapter, weight control is difficult for some individuals and is easier for others. Undoubtedly, the psychological makeup of the person plays a large part in accomplishing the mental discipline for the "long haul" concept of weight reduction. *There is no easy or quick way to lose weight safely.*

It is sometimes difficult to determine whether or not a person is overweight. Some athletes who appear overweight or who tip the scales above average standards are not overweight at all; they usually possess greater musculature and larger bones. A knowledge of somatotyping, in such situations, would be of value to the trainer or coach.

According to Cooper[26] body fat comprising from 5% to 7% of the total body weight is ideal. He suggests a rule-of-thumb method for assessing optimum weight by pinching the skin on the forehead at the outer upper area above the eye and then comparing its thickness to the skinfold over the abdomen and over the back of the arm (center of the triceps). All three measurements should be approximately the same, an average of 6 to 8 mm.

Weight loss during training should not exceed 2 to 5 lbs. a week, and the conditioning program should be started at least 5 to 6 weeks before final decisions are made as to the final weight at which the athlete is to wrestle.[26] Once it is determined, he should not be permitted reduction to wrestle at a lower weight but should let his weight stabilize. Weight fluctuations impair physical performance.[26]

A balanced diet, reduced somewhat in quantity, coupled with an adequate fluid and salt intake and with hard physical work is still the best way to reduce weight. The use of digitalis and other weight-loss drugs is strongly condemned.

ERGOGENIC AIDS

For years there has been considerable interest in finding an agent that would improve athletic performance. Such an aid is classified as an *ergogenic* (literally, "work-producing") aid and is usually defined as any substance or means that improves physical performance through its effect on the body. Substances include drugs, foodstuffs, and physical stimulants such as electricity or thermal packs. A method (means) might be hypnosis or cheering.

From time to time, there are enthusiastic claims for a wonder "aid," which subsequent and more careful research fails to substantiate. In many instances, psychological effects alone are responsible for improved performance. Other substances that do have some ergogenic properties have such deleterious physiological and psychological side effects that their use cannot be tolerated under any circumstances. Aside from the medicolegal aspects of administering various substances, the use of some "aids" poses an ethical problem.[29] Certainly a trainer has no moral right to permit the use of any substance that is potentially harmful. In addition, is it sporting to "soup up" an athlete through the use of a substance that the opposition neither uses nor condones? Are the resulting performances truly indicative of an athlete's potential or are they merely indicative of his reaction to an artificial stimulus? If a trainer encounters potential or actual use of harmful or dangerous ergogens, he should counsel the athletes by explaining to them the agent's action on the body and its effect upon physical performance. Such explanations should be done rationally rather than emotionally. Leaders in athletics and in sports medicine have taken an unequivocal stand against the use of any agent that would fall into the category of dope or that would be used to enhance athletic performance through artificial means.[29,30]

It has often been argued that the use of vitamins, food supplements, gelatin, and the like as possible ergogenic aids carries the same implications. Such measures, however, do no harm to the athlete; nor can they be considered unfair practice. Indeed, they may conceivably reduce a dietary need, although it is improbable that they contribute to the improvement of physical performance.

The trainer is advised to forego the use of questionable materials and to rely upon *ethically* and *morally sound practices*. He should develop the various potentials inherent within the athlete, rather than to resort to artificial means. The more common ergogenic aids, which have been used and have been subjected to considerable research and testing, are discussed below to assist the trainer in developing some knowledge and an awareness of their effects upon human beings and human performance. Since the physiological effects of alcohol, coffee, tea, and salt have been discussed previously in this chapter, they will not be re-examined, although they are ergogenic aids.

Amphetamine (Benzedrine, d-amphetamine sulfate). This synthetic alkaloid is an extremely powerful and *dangerous drug*, contrary to what uninformed individuals may say. It may be taken either in the form of tablets or by means of inhalers. Proprietary forms are Benzedrex, Benzedrine, Dexedrine, Desyphed, Tuamine, and, in Europe, Pervitin. Publicity regarding the use of "pep" pills or "bennies," of which Benzedrine is the active ingredient,

has made the general public quite conscious of the dangers involved in using this drug. Such use in athletics, for the purpose of reducing fatigue, cannot be condoned.

Benzedrine functions as a powerful stimulant to the central nervous system. In most instances its effects are evidenced through increases in blood pressure and the rate of breathing and through a general feeling of alertness, euphoria, and peppiness. It does not seem to have any effect on the higher mental processes. Its use also impairs sleep; for this reason it is often used by students when preparing for examinations and by truck drivers whose long and monotonous journeys frequently compel them to seek some means of remaining awake while at the wheel.

Benzedrine may cause dizziness and a feeling of depression. It appears to have a greater effect on individuals of a slight body build than on those with a heavier build. Individual reaction may be highly specific. In some instances hallucinations have lead athletes to believe that they were performing far better than they actually were. They were guilty of exhibiting extremely poor judgment in critical situations and otherwise not playing up to their usual level of performance. In these instances amphetamines had been taken without the knowledge of the staff.

Since Benzedrine and its derivatives constrict the mucous membranes, their use, under medical direction, for the relief of nasal congestion is quite safe, provided instructions are followed. Prolonged use of amphetamines leads to extreme nervousness and may produce hallucinations and insomnia. Their continued use leads to addiction. Studies reported in the literature are somewhat contradictory in that there is some evidence that *d*-amphetamine sulfate inhibits fatigue[31-33]; on the other hand, evidence that supports the contention that improved performance results from the administration of *d*-amphetamine sulfate is lacking.[34-36] The fact that the drug is inherently dangerous should inveigh against its use.

Androgenic-anabolic steroids. Some athletes, particularly weight lifters, track weight men, and wrestlers, have been using anabolic steroids in an attempt to gain weight and strength. These drugs are categorically condemned for this use since *the dangers associated with their use are most insidious and can lead to effects as serious as those associated with the amphetamines.*[37] Androgenic hormones are basically a product of the male testes. Of these hormones, testosterone is the principal one and possesses the ability to function androgenically (the ability to stimulate male characteristics) and anabolically (the ability through an improved protein assimilation to increase muscle mass and weight, general growth, bone maturation, and virility). When prescribed by a physician to ameliorate or improve certain physiological conditions these drugs have value.

Within the last few years steroids have been synthetically developed that, while related to testosterone, have a decreased androgenic effect. Among the most commonly used are Anavar, Dianabol, Durabolin, Deca-Durabolin, Maxibolin, Nilevar, and Winstrol. As is usual with many such drugs, undesirable side effects, such as reversion of testicular size and function to prepubertal levels, have resulted in a manifestly decreased libido. If these drugs are given to the prepubertal boy, a decrease in the ultimate height, because of the cessation of long bone growth, is a most certain hazard. There is also risk of liver damage and growth of the prostate gland if steroids are taken for any protracted period.[22] There is also a strong possibility of cancer if steroids are taken for any protracted period or in dosage greater than that which is usually medically prescribed.[24]

Most studies have shown that there are significant increases in strength and in weight when steroids are taken. Research indicates that the administration of from 5 to 10 mg. of methandrostenolone (Dianabol) daily will reflect significant increases in strength and weight if accompanied by 30 grams of 90% protein supplement and stressful weight exercises.[38,39] Anabolic steroids act upon the central nervous system and the biochemical processes that are involved in reflex patterns and the contraction of the skeletal muscles. Their use appears to improve the function of these mechanisms.[40] No improvement in aerobic capacity has been noted nor have any significant changes occurred in either skinfold or spermatogenesis.

Studies such as these are conducted under carefully controlled laboratory situations wherein all precautions are taken to obviate undesirable or dangerous side effects. It must be recognized that these drugs are extremely dangerous and must not be given to athletes as ergogenic aids.

Aspartates. Aspartic acid is one of the fundamental amino acids. Aspartic acids and their salts, which appear under a number of pharmaceutical trade names, are used in the abolition or reduction of fatigue at the neuromuscular level. Generally, potassium and magnesium aspartates are used. Some slight controversy has developed concerning the efficacy of aspartates since recent investigations offer some differences of opinion. Rosen and others[41-43] have presented evidence that the administration of aspartates produced marked relief from fatigue, whereas subsequent studies,[44,45] failed to adequately verify all claimed beneficial effects. Before the use of aspartates can be recommended for such use on an unqualified basis, it would seem that additional experimentation is needed. Aspartates pose no particular health problem provided that recommended dosages are followed.

Hypnosis. The use of hypnosis as an ergogenic aid has been explored to some degree but needs much further study before definite conclusions can be drawn. These studies have shown that hypnosis will aid both strength and endurance to some extent. Investigations have shown that untrained individuals generally show a marked improvement in strength as compared with the trained athlete, whereas the athlete shows a much greater improvement in endurance. This may be caused by the release of psychologically inhibiting factors.

One of the dangers in the use of hypnosis is the possibility that untrained operators may attempt to use hypnotism, perhaps with serious results for the athlete. The use of hypnosis for therapeutic purposes, executed under medical supervision, has a bona fide place in the program.[46-48]

Oxygen. Ever since the 1932 Olympic Games in Los Angeles, when Japanese swimmers overran their competition and attributed their success to oxygen inhalation, there have been sporadic outbursts of oxygen use by trainers and athletes in attempts to improve performance or to speed up postexercise recovery. Much evidence has shown that this practice is without value. Any demonstrable effects are purely psychological.

One of the principal limiting factors in any type of physical performance is the amount of oxygen that the organism can take up. Another factor is the inability of the organism to store up oxygen; therefore any of the beneficial effects of oxygen are transitory, being completely depleted within a period of 3 minutes or less after intake.

There is some evidence that oxygen breathing immediately before a short swimming race may be beneficial. This is probably caused by an improved ability to hold the breath longer. When working at high altitudes, the breathing of oxygen has some value, but continued intake is necessary if the activity is of any duration. In general, all the scientific evidence thus far clearly establishes that fact that both the breathing of oxygen prior to performance to improve that performance, and the breathing of oxygen immediately following performance to hasten recovery are of little or no value.

Negative ionization. Results of negative ionization are quite similar to those noted when pure oxygen is inhaled, a feeling of considerable euphoria.

It has long been known that people feel much better following a rain shower or storm or when they are in the vicinity of a waterfall. Conversely, people often feel dull and lethargic and complain of headaches when in the presence of heavy electrical machinery. Military leaders have been concerned about the morale and well-being of men isolated in submarines and space ships, and as a result research has been conducted to ascertain if negative ionization would assist in solving some of their problems. It is generally accepted that ions affect not only our moods but also our circulation and respiration. The negative ions in the bloodstream speed up delivery of oxygen to the cells and tissues, whereas the positive ions tend to slow down such delivery, with subsequent symptoms that resemble anoxia.

Some interest has been shown in the possibilities of utilizing negative ions as an ergogenic aid through their improvement of respiratory function. Only two studies of the subject have been found at this time. One, dealing with strength improvement as measured by grip strength, revealed some significant improvement in performance after subjects had been administered negatively ionized air.[49] de Vries and Klafs[50] hypothesized that trained individuals, after exposure to negatively ionized air, should show significant improvement in physical performance. Subjects were exposed to both negatively ionized and positively ionized air in turn, with careful controls established. No improvement in physical performance was noted, but the subjects complained of headaches and physical distress when subjected to positive ions. Although medical research has established the facts that negative ionization is extremely beneficial to patients with respiratory ailments and that it has marked analgesic and therapeutic effects in cases of severe burns, it appears to have little or no value as a means of improving physical performance.

Smoking. On the basis of various investigations into the relationship between smoking and performance some pertinent conclusions can be drawn:

1. There is individual sensitivity to tobacco that may seriously affect performance in instances of relatively high sensitivity.[51] Since over one third of the men studied indicated tobacco sensitivity, it may be wise to prohibit smoking by athletes.

2. As few as 10 inhalations of cigarette smoke causes an average maximum decrease in airway conductance of 50%. This has been found in nonsmokers as well as smokers.[52]

3. Smoking reduces the oxygen-carrying capacity of the blood.

4. Smoking aggravates and accelerates the heart muscle cells through overstimulation of the sympathetic nervous system.

5. Total lung capacity and maximum breathing capacity are significantly decreased in heavy smokers; this is significant to the athlete since both changes would impair his capacity to take in oxygen and make it readily available for body use.

6. Smoking decreases pulmonary diffusing capacity.

7. After smoking, an accelerated thrombolic tendency is evidenced.[53]

8. Smoking is a carcinogenic factor in lung cancer and is a contributing factor to heart disease.

Certainly the amount of evidence is all on the negative side. Since smoking offers no positive contribution to either health or performance, it should be forbidden.

Sugar. Many coaches and trainers advocate giving sugar, either in the form of lump sugar, dextrose tablets, glucose pills, or honey, as a means of improving athletic performance. Since sugar is a fuel food and therefore is active in muscle contractions, it has been reasoned that the feeding of supplementary sugar should have value. Such sugar feeding, if limited to an intake of several spoonfuls of honey or a few lumps of sugar, may improve performance in an event that is of long duration and is exhausting in nature. However, no favorable effects have been recorded in activities of short duration.

Any beneficial effects evident have been psychological. Physiologically, when an individual is fed sugar, there is a tendency for the fluid required for its digestion to be drawn into the gastrointestinal tract, thus further dehydrating the organism. A more desirable way of feeding sugar is to serve tea, well sweetened and with lemon, to aid in overcoming this dehydrating factor. Sugar feeding must be carried out with some degree of understanding, since indiscriminate or excessive feeding can lead to severe gastric disturbances.

REFERENCES

1. Guthrie, H. A.: Introductory nutrition, St. Louis, 1967, The C. V. Mosby Co.
2. Mathews, D. K., Stacy, R. W., and Hoover, G. N.: Physiology of muscular activity and exercise, New York, 1964, The Ronald Press Co.
3. Durnin, J. V.: The influence of nutrition, proceedings of the international symposium on physical activities and cardio-vascular health, Canad. Med. Ass. J. 96:715, 1967.
4. Williams, R. L., editor: The healthy life, New York, 1966, Time, Inc.
5. Williams, S. R.: Nutrition and diet therapy, St. Louis, 1969, The C. V. Mosby Co.
6. Murphy, R. J., and Ashe, W. F.: Prevention of heat illness in football players, J.A.M.A. 194:650, 1965.
7. Murphy, R. J.: The problem of environmental heat in athletics, Ohio Med. J. 59:799, 1963.
8. Rose, K. D., Mathews, S., and Sullivan, G.: Vitamin B$_{12}$ in athletics, a negative report, J. Nat. Athletic Trainers Ass., p. 3, Winter, 1966.
9. Robinson, S., and others: Rapid acclimatization to work in hot climates, Amer. J. Physiol. 140:168, 1943.
10. Blank, L. B.: An experimental study of the effect of water ingestion upon athletic performance, Res. Quart. Amer. Ass. Health Phys. Educ. 30:131, 1959.
11. Little, C. C., Strayhorn, H., and Miller, A. T.: Effect of water ingestion on capacity for exercise, Res. Quart. Amer. Ass. Health Phys. Educ. 20:398, 1949.
12. Mathews, D. K.: Recognition and prevention of heat stroke, Mich. Osteopathic J., vol. 31, Oct., 1966.
13. Mayer, J., and Bullen, B.: Nutrition and athletic performance, Exercise and Fitness, Chicago, 1960, The Athletic Institute.
14. Rose, K. D., Schneider, P. J., and Sullivan, G. F.: A liquid pregame meal for athletes, J.A.M.A. 178:30, 1961.
15. Roberson, M.: Research gives support to the

liquid pregame diet, J. Nat. Athletic Trainers Ass., p. 12, Winter, 1965-1966.
16. Rose, K. D., and Fuenning, S. I.: Pre-game emotional tension, gastrointestinal motility, and the feeding of athletes, Nebraska Med. J. 45:575, 1960.
17. Johnson, R. D.: Liquid meal called digestive aid, Medicine in Sports (Rystan Co.), pp. 1-2, 1967.
18. Rasch, P. J., Klafs, C. E., and Arnheim, D. D.: Effects of vitamin C supplementation on cross country runners, Sportzärzliche Praxis 1:4, Jan., 1962.
19. Asprey, G. M., Alley, L. E., and Tuttle, W. W.: Effect of eating at various times upon subsequent performances in the one-mile run, Res. Quart. Amer. Ass. Health Phys. Educ. 35:227, 1966.
20. Ball, J. R.: Effect of eating at various times upon subsequent performances in swimming, Res. Quart. Amer. Ass. Health Phys. Educ. 33:163, 1962.
21. Guild, W. R.: Pre-event nutrition, with some implications for endurance athletes, Exercise and Fitness, Chicago, 1960, The Athletic Institute.
22. Van Itallie, T. B., Sinisterra, L., and Stare, F. J.: Nutrition and athletic performance. In Johnson, W. R., editor: Science and medicine of exercise and sports, New York, 1960, Harper & Row, Publishers.
23. Osness, W. H., Balke, B., Gordon, E. S., and Rankin, J.: The metabolic role of lipids in the production of energy during exercise, Physiological aspects of sports and physical fitness, Chicago, 1968, American College of Sports Medicine and The Athletic Institute.
24. de Vries, H. A.: Physiology of exercise for physical education and athletics, Dubuque, Iowa, 1966, William C. Brown Co., Publishers.
25. Mayer, J.: Exercise and weight control. In Johnson, W. R., editor: Science and medicine of exercise and sports, New York, 1960, Harper & Row, Publishers.
26. Symposium: Weight control in wrestling, Proceedings of the Seventh National Conference on the Medical Aspects of Sports, Chicago, 1965, American Medical Association, pp. 52-70.
27. Forum on Interscholastic Wrestling: Weight abuses—how serious are they? Medicine in Sports (Rystan Co.) 7:1, April, 1967.
28. Paul, W. D.: Crash diets and wrestling, J. Nat. Athletic Trainers Ass., pp. 7-12, Winter, 1966.
29. Porritt, A.: Doping, J. Sport Med. 5:166, 1965.
30. Prokop, L.: The problem on doping, final report on the International Doping Conference, Tokyo, 1964, J. Sport Med. 5:88, 1965.
31. Ikai, M., and Steinhaus, A. H.: Some factors in modifying the expression of human strength, J. Appl. Physiol. 16:157, 1961.
32. Rachman, S.: Effects of stimulant drug on extent of motor responses, Percept. Motor Skills 12:186, 1961.
33. Smith, G. H., and Beecher, H. K.: Amphetamine sulfate and athletic performance, J.A.M.A. 170:542, 1959.
34. Blyth, C. S., Allen, M., and Lovingood, B. W.: Effects of amphetamine (Dexedrine) and caffeine on subjects exposed to heat and exercise stress, Res. Quart. Amer. Ass. Health Phys. Educ. 31:553, 1960.
35. Golding, L. A., and Barnard, J. R.: The effects of D-amphetamine sulfate on athletic performance, J. Sport Med. 3:221, 1963.
36. Karpovich, P. V.: Effect of amphetamine sulfate on athletic performance, J.A.M.A. 170:558, 1959.
37. Astrand, P. O., and Rohdahl, K.: Textbook of work physiology, New York, 1970, McGraw-Hill Book Co.
38. Johnson, L. C., Fisher, G., Silvester, L. J., and Hofheins, C. C.: Anabolic steroid: effects on strength, body weight, oxygen uptake, and spermatogenesis upon mature males, Med. Sci. Sports 4:43, 1972.
39. Bowers, R. W., and Reardon, J. P.: Effects of methandostenolone (Dianabol) on strength development and aerobic capacity, Med. Sci. Sports 4:54, 1972.
40. Ariel, G.: The effect of anabolic steroids on reflex components and skeletal muscle contractile force, Med. Sci. Sports 4:54, 1972.
41. Rosen, H., Blumenthal, A., and Agersborg, H. P. K.: Effects of the potassium and magnesium salts of aspartic acid on metabolic exhaustion, J. Pharm. Sci. 51:592, 1962.
42. Kruse, C. A.: Treatment of fatigue with aspartic acid salts, Northwest Med. 60:597, 1961.
43. Shaw, D. L., Jr., and others: Management of fatigue: a physiologic approach, Amer. J. Med. Sci. 243:758, 1962.
44. Consolazio, C. F., and others: Effects of aspartic acid salts (Mg+K) on physical performance of men, J. Appl. Physiol. 19:257, 1964.
45. Matoush, L. O., and others: Effects of aspartic acid salts (Mg+K) on the swimming performance of rats and dogs, J. Appl. Physiol. 19:262, 1964.
46. Johnson, W. R., and others: Effect of posthypnotic suggestion on all out effort of short duration, Res. Quart. Amer. Ass. Health Phys. Educ. 31:142, 1960.
47. Ryde, D.: A personal study of some uses of hypnosis in sport and sports injuries, J. Sport Med. 4:241, 1964.

48. Peck, T. T.: Medical hypnosis and athletics, J. Nat. Athletic Trainers Ass., p. 6, Fall, 1959.
49. Minkh, A. A.: Highly ionized atmosphere as a factor increasing physical work capacity, Vestn. Akad. Med. Navk SSSR **18**:33, 1963.
50. de Vries, H. A., and Klafs, C. E.: Ergogenic effects of breathing artificially ionized air, J. Sport Med. **5**:7, 1965.
51. Karpovich, P. V., and Hale, C. J.: Tobacco smoking and athletic performance, J. Appl. Physiol. **3**:616, 1951.
52. Nadel, J. A., and Comroe, J. H., Jr.: Acute effects of inhalation of cigarette smoke on airway conductance, J. Appl. Physiol. **16**:713, 1961.
53. Engelberg, H.: Cigarette smoking and the in vitro thrombosis of human blood, J.A.M.A. **193**:1033, 1965.

RECOMMENDED READINGS

Anthony, C. P.: Textbook of anatomy and physiology, St. Louis, 1959, The C. V. Mosby Co.
Best, C. H., and Taylor, N. B.: The physiological basis of medical practice, Baltimore, 1955, The Williams & Wilkins Co.
Dagenais, G. R., Oriol, A., and McGregor, M.: Hemodynamics effects of carbohydrate and protein meals in man: rest and exercise, J. Appl. Physiol. **21**:1157, 1966.
De Coursey, R. M.: The human organism, New York, 1961, McGraw-Hill Book Co.
Grossman, M. I.: Digestive system, Ann. Revue Physiol. **12**:205, 1950.
Johnson, W. R.: Hypnosis and muscular performance, J. Sport. Med. **1**:71, 1961.
La Cava, G.: The use of drugs in competitive sports, J. Sport Med. **1**:49, 1961.
Paul, W. D.: Crash diets and wrestling, J. Nat. Athletic Trainers Ass., pp. 6-12, Winter, 1966.
Pargman, D.: Body build and dietary habits in college athletes, Med. Sci. Sports **3**:140, 1971.
Prokop, L.: Adrenals and sport, J. Sport Med. **3**:115, 1963.
Ruff, W. K.: Athletes warned about anabolic steroids, J. Nat. Athletic Trainers Ass., pp. 14-15, Winter, 1965-1966.

CHAPTER 9

Psychogenic factors in athletics

Mens sana in corpore sano, or "a sound mind in a sound body," is one concept of mind-body relationship that we have accepted since the time of the early Greeks. However, in recent years we have become increasingly concerned with the effect of psychosomatic relationships and their applications to physical performance.

Training requires mental discipline, and it is often difficult to motivate the athlete sufficiently for him to attain the goals set. The great athlete becomes a great athlete not only because of his endowed physical equipment but also because of his dedication and tenacity of purpose. The high school athlete often has too many conflicting interests to achieve the singleness of purpose that would aid in making him a stellar performer. This diversification of interests appears to be one of the underlying reasons why it is difficult to maintain a balanced training schedule that brings the athlete to his peak at the proper time.

The interest of the trainer is twofold. He is concerned with the effects of emotional factors upon physical performance and equally concerned with their effects upon the reconditioning of the athlete. To do the best in his position, the trainer must master some of the techniques of psychology and learn how and when to apply them to obtain desirable results.

Psychological conditioning is fully as important and as much the responsibility of the trainer as is physical conditioning or re-

conditioning. Often an individual's psychological condition has a direct bearing on his neuromuscular or physical response. Also, the trainer is a teacher and, functioning in this role, must seek to develop accepted sociological and psychological behavior in his athletes. He can contribute much to the emotional stability and the psychosociological maturity of those who come under his care.

Participation in athletics occurs principally as an effort on the part of an individual to satisfy various psychogenic needs.[1] These needs may consist of desires to achieve social status or to seek prestige; they may manifest themselves in the assertion of certain aggressive tendencies; or they may stem from several other factors. Such patterns are derived from basic activity drives.

In recent years much emphasis has been placed on a need for competition—the fact that life itself is competitive and we therefore need to stimulate and encourage competition. Athletes derive satisfactions from the act of participating in a sport activity. These satisfactions spark or stimulate the competitive drive, although the intensity of the drive tends to vary depending on the individual and/or the type of activity pursued. Because of variations in human temperament, individual differences permit some persons to become more competitive than others. It must be recognized, however, that competition and rivalry are not inherent tendencies but are learned incentives peculiar to our type of society. There are many societies in which competition as we know it is unknown or undesirable.

TRAINER'S RESPONSIBILITIES

Because his work brings him into close personal contact with the athletes, the trainer is often faced with emotional or sociological problems. Athletes, by their very nature, tend to develop tensions. The trainer is in an excellent position to eradicate or prevent such tensions. He must have a knowledge of psychological factors and know what course of action to follow. Some situations require understanding and sympathy, others firmness. Still others require considerable restraint. The right word spoken at the right time can often resolve a situation that could develop into an unfortunate circumstance.

Injury prevention is *psychological,* as well as *physiological.* The athlete who enters a contest when angry, frustrated, or discouraged or when he is host to some other disturbing emotional state is more prone to injury than is the individual who is better adjusted emotionally. The angry player, for example, wants to vent his ire in some way and therefore often loses his perspective of desirable and approved conduct. In the grip of his emotion he sacrifices skill and coordination, with the result that he sustains an injury that otherwise would have been avoided.

Studies have indicated that athletes in certain types of sport tend to manifest some characteristics in common.[2] It may be that these identifiable personality characteristics influence the choice of sport that the athlete makes. Trainers and coaches have long believed that there are "types," readily identifiable by specific personality traits, who gravitate toward specific sports. On the basis of the limited evidence available, such assumptions seem to be reasonable.

In a study of the aggressive tendencies of athletes, Husman[3] found that boxers showed less outward manifestation of aggressiveness than did wrestlers, cross-country runners, and nonathletes.

Athletes usually select an **activity** because they have achieved some degree of success in that activity previously, either as students in general physical education classes or as participants in recreational or sandlot competition. They have developed an interest in the activity, although their actual participation experience may be somewhat limited. Sometimes a coach or trainer, observing a student in some type of physical activity, will suggest that he try out for a particular sport. To the trained eye this student has given evidence of possessing the inherent characteristics, both physical and psychological, that indicate he has an excellent chance for success in that activity.

Through daily contact the observant trainer soon learns to predict the responses of athletes. Generally, such responses follow a consistent pattern. It is through a knowledge and understanding of these patterns that the trainer is able to predict responses and, thus, be prepared to handle situations as they develop in the training room and on the field.

The training room is no place for a display of temperament on the part of the trainer. He must learn to condition and modify his personality so that his behavior becomes a stable element in the midst of a somewhat unstable emotional climate. Students learn by precept and example. The trainer, by making himself a model, can aid considerably in maintaining a fairly consistent level of behavior among those with whom he comes in contact. He must learn to respond to irritability with tranquility, to obstinacy with patience, and to anger with tolerance. To respond with an emotion that is similar to the athlete's tends to increase tensions and may result in feelings of enmity and dislike on the part of the athlete. There may, however, be occasions when the trainer will need to respond with such emotions, feigned to evoke a desired response from the athlete. Patience and understanding are the keys to establishing and promoting desirable relationships with those whom he serves.

PERSONALITY PATTERNS

Personality patterns are seldom found as pure types but, rather, are found in varying combinations, with one or two characteristics being somewhat outstanding in each. The different types are quite recognizable in the training room. They respond differently to treatment, and the trainer must be able to recognize and understand the dominant traits of each so that therapy and reconditioning may proceed at an optimum rate.

One type is the naturally cheerful, confident, and quite optimistic athlete who is exceedingly extroverted. He usually demonstrates good leadership qualities. Often he is a man who needs constant checking, since he tends to slough off or ignore injuries and does not adhere as closely to training procedures as may be desirable. Similarly, an easygoing, sometimes lackadaisical, and not easily excited athlete who lacks drive and seldom uses full vigor in his efforts, is a constant problem to the trainer and the coach because he too requires constant checking to ensure that he is following recommended procedures.

A frequent visitor to the training room is the person who suffers from a host of injuries and ailments, principally psychosomatic in origin. As a rule he is somewhat introverted and hypochondriacal. He can be a difficult problem unless the trainer takes a positive approach and does not become overly indulgent.

The athlete who displays tenacity, stubbornness, and irascibility, and who is usually impatient and quick to anger, often possesses strong leadership qualities. He is usually fiercely competitive and quite aggressive. He is a good competitor but needs careful handling by the coach and trainer to properly channel these characteristics so that they will improve rather than negate his performance.

PREGAME TENSION

Varsity competition at the high school and college levels tends to promote precontest emotional disturbances. Such disturbances do not appear to have deleterious effects on the health of either male or female participants. However, they can and often do have detrimental effects upon the athlete's performance. These disturbances result from tensions built up within the athlete and from the emotional climate that precedes competition. The trainer is in a particularly advantageous position to aid in dispelling such tensions. Despite the bustle and demands of the training room, a word of counsel or a joke may relieve the climate, leaving the athlete relaxed and consequently better able to perform effectively.

Pregame tension is evidenced in a syndrome with which everyone connected with athletics is familiar. Prior to any event that is of significance to the performer, the symptoms manifest themselves in varying degrees. Continued exposure somewhat lessens but does not eradicate the effects, and veteran athletes, public performers, politicians, and others will attest to still feeling one or more of these effects of tension.

The pregame syndrome is one of nature's ways of preparing the individual for maximum effort and is the result of adrenomedullary activity. Epinephrine is released into the system, with dramatic results. (Adrenalin is a proprietary name for epinephrine, a hormone of the adrenal medulla, which was the first hormone identified [early 1900's].) Is is formed by the adrenal gland, located on the superior border of the kidney, and is released into the bloodstream in varying amounts. It is theorized that an epinephrine-like compound stimulates the adjacent dendrites and muscle cells when it is released, as a result of the nerve impulse reaching the synapse or myoneural junctions. The adrenal hormones spread throughout the body and elicit a wide range of effects. These effects are such that they increase the physical performance of an individual in an emergency. This is accomplished through the following means:

1. Speedup of circulation and respiration, which increases the delivery of fuel to the muscles and the removal of metabolites and other wastes

2. Increase in glycogenolytic action, which increases the blood sugar content and supplies more fuel to the muscles
3. Increase in the metabolism of the cerebrum, which results in an increase in alertness and in the neuromuscular responses, thus improving physical performance
4. Increase in the excitability of the neurons, which enhances motor activity and alertness.

With the increase in blood pressure and heart rate and the endocrine stimulation, certain emotional symptoms appear, such as a feeling of anxiety, breathlessness, "butterflies" in the stomach, and trembling. An athlete in a state of readiness for competition will exhibit these signs in varying degrees.

Xerostomia (dry mouth). A dryness of the mouth (xerostomia) often accompanies the above symptoms. It results from a lack of normal secretion and is caused by stress. The use of lozenges, chewing gum, or lemons—in fact, anything that will reactivate salivary action—is indicated. This serves two purposes: (1) to relieve xerostomia and (2) to aid somewhat in relieving the tension. It keeps the athlete occupied, even though to a limited extent.

Diuresis and nervous defecation. Diuresis (increased flow of urine) and nervous defecation are often attendant to pregame tension and may be attributed to the increased hormonal and nerve action. The increase in anxiety appears to increase nerve irradiation and thus activate not only the adrenal glands but also the brain regions and visceral nerves that govern these functions, with the result that both bladder action and bowel action are stimulated.

STALENESS

Athletes who have been training over a long period of time or who have been involved in long periods of competition, with a resultant lack of relaxation and rest, sometimes go "stale." Staleness is evidenced by a wide variety of symptoms, among which are a deterioration in the usual standard of performance, apathy, loss of appetite, indigestion, weight loss, constipation, and inability to sleep or rest properly. Often the athlete will exhibit a lowered blood pressure or an increased pulse rate. All these signs indicate adrenal exhaustion.[4] He becomes irritable and restless, has to force himself to practice, and exhibits signs of ennui and lassitude in respect to everything connected with the activity.

When these symptoms first appear, the trainer should immediately bar the athlete from all activity, prescribing instead ample rest and relaxation. Sometimes having a chat with the individual, explaining what the problem is and how it can be met, helps to get the athlete back to normal a little faster. The main key is the revival and stimulation of interest, motivation, and desire.

CONFLICT ADJUSTMENT

It is not within the scope of this book to discuss the considerable amount of psychological groundwork underlying the various complex mechanisms of human behavior. The reader who wishes to pursue this phase to greater depth is referred to the selected readings at the end of this chapter. However, the trainer must realize that his charges will exhibit many of the incontrovertible evidences of conflict; it is therefore important for him to be able to recognize and be of assistance in handling these symptoms.

Ambivalence is typical of an individual in conflict. To want something and simultaneously to reject it is quite characteristic. As the person achieves more satisfaction from one aspect, the greater is the frustration that he encounters in the other. To express it differently, whatever he does to fulfill one motive opposes the other. Over a long period of time he tends to develop an attitude of "Whatever I attempt to do is wrong or ends in failure." In such cases individuals tend to develop personality patterns that reveal various types of recognizable, overt behavior. Thus the accident-prone athlete, the overly aggressive individual, and the complacent person all indicate outward manifestations of some hidden psychological problem. In some instances overt behavior is indicative of a specific failing or shortcoming that the individual seeks to mask by assuming a defensive posture. Some of the more common behavior patterns encountered in athletics are discussed on the following pages.

Accident-proneness. The acident-prone athlete usually has more than what might be considered an average share of injuries. Injuries seem to seek him out, and normally insignificant or innocuous situations assume significance when this type of athlete appears on the scene. He is easily involved in situations wherein he receives some injury although others emerge unscathed. Ogilvie and Tutko[1] categorize the accident-prone athlete into three types: (1) the bona fide injured, (2) the psychologically injured, and (3) the malingerer. The *bona fide injured* athlete may have a series of rather severe injuries as the result of hostility directed toward himself, which he manifests in reckless and daredevil performances, thus inviting injury. The *psychologically injured* individual constantly complains of injury and pain, but no medically sound evidence is recognizable. The *malingerer* intentionally lies about his injury so that he will get out of work. The latter is discussed in more detail later in the chapter.

Accident-prone individuals are most disposed to suffer an accident toward the end of a long or sustained period of work. Accident-proneness appears to be caused by a lack of ability to coordinate properly, as the result of either fatigue or emotional imbalance. Often the discouraged or apathetic athlete is accident-prone. Trainers and coaches have long observed that the competitor who is not emotionally stable stands an excellent chance of being injured.[7]

Certain characteristics can be recognized in the accident-prone athlete. Usually he is easily distracted and, as implied above, generally exhibits emotional instability. In some instances he becomes extremely aggressive toward and intolerant of others, displaying an attitude of superiority. He actually enjoys some accidents because they serve to make him a focus of attention. Some individuals of this type become almost permanent fixtures in the training room. Their high incidence of injury, plus the fact that they enjoy the ministrations and attention, makes these individuals a real problem for the trainer and the coach alike.

Hostility and overt aggressiveness. Although aggressiveness is a desirable characteristic in athletics, some athletes will manifest feelings of hostility or over aggressiveness not only toward their opposition but also toward team members and associates. Such feelings may be indications of pregame tension or they may be the result of intensive training over a long period of time. Frequently, athletes who display aggressive tendencies falling into the latter category are "drawn fine" and need to ease their rigorous schedules for a while. Often feelings of hostility are released through competition. This is particularly true in contact sports.

The trainer can handle the overly aggressive individual in several ways. He can attempt to channel the tendencies into more desirable avenues through careful counseling; or if the athlete seems amenable to reason, the trainer can show him his problem, getting him to recognize it and to attempt to solve it through changes in his behavior. The latter method is not always effective, particularly when anger or hostility is evidenced during the discussion. A person in this frame of mind soon loses the ability to listen, to reason, and to think coherently and often becomes more symptomatic than usual. When neither the catharsis of competition, channeling, nor reasoning produces favorable results, the individual should be remanded to proper counseling channels for assistance. This type athlete is usually difficult to recondition.

Rationalization. Many times the trainer will encounter an athlete who employs rationalization to a considerable degree. Such an individual advances seemingly plausible reasons for everything he does. Whenever errors, misunderstandings, or problems occur, although it is evident that the fault lies with him, he defends his position with the support of a somewhat credible explanation. His relationship to the trainer and the training program takes the form of projection, usually involving a feeling of persecution. Sometimes he takes the position that the trainer is not interested in him or in his rehabilitation and that this attitude is a result of some misunderstood action that has caused the trainer to develop a feeling of personal animosity.

An individual who shows a pattern of this type is difficult to reach. He fails to follow training or reconditioning instructions, complaining that he cannot see the use of such procedures. He is convinced the procedures are giving him no positive results or are only aggravating his particular problem. Any attempt to point out specifics to him usually results in more rationalization. He not only fails to realize his shortcomings but also, when they are made apparent to him, refuses to accept them. He covers his failures or confusion with specious reasoning which will, in his eyes, justify his actions.

The difficulties in working with this type of individual are well-nigh insurmountable. However, pressuring the athlete and consistently explaining the objectives often bring about positive results. Extreme cases should be referred to the school psychologist.

Sarcasm and criticism. Some athletes seek relief from emotional conflicts by turning to an excessive use of sarcasm or criticism. They carp incessantly about equipment, training facilities, and gear. They are hypercritical of their wrappings and of other preventive or therapeutic actions. When queried, they take refuge in heavy sarcasm rather than attempt to critically evaluate their behavior and then take steps to eradicate or improve their faults. Answering such sarcasm with sarcasm tends

to strengthen rather than attenuate the difficulty. Consequently, such individuals are best dealt with privately in efforts to help them recognize and overcome their shortcomings.

Foul language and profanity. The person who persistently uses foul or profane language often wishes to distract attention from his failings or to compensate for his feelings of insecurity. In some instances profanity may be a means of relieving inner tensions, but under no circumstances should the use of such language be tolerated. It has no place in athletics. The usual, relaxed after-practice atmosphere of the training room may reflect a feeling that the barriers are down and thus induce, in some individuals, a tendency to be careless with their language. Violators should promptly be called to task and told in no uncertain terms that such action is not and will not be tolerated.

Defeatism. Occasionally the trainer will encounter an individual who is a defeatist. This fellow is a quitter. He gives up easily, cannot see the use of continuing, and often employs rationalization in an attempt to cover his shortcomings. It is difficult to ascribe a specific reason for this attitude, since it often has rather deep psychological implications. This type of individual is completely unreliable in competitive situations, since it is difficult to predict just when he will give up. Because he will not persist in treatment procedures, he is difficult to handle in reconditioning.

The trainer may attempt to help this individual develop a more positive attitude through counseling, but such attempts are not usually successful. It is better for the individual to secure the services of someone trained in the complexities of psychological diagnosis and treatment. As a rule, the defeatist or quitter does not last long in athletic competition. He is either dropped by the coach or gives up athletics voluntarily because of his preconceived ideas about his inability to succeed.

Complacency. The complacent athlete is so satisfied with his own abilities and merit that he does not endeavor to improve. This type of individual presents a trying problem both to the trainer and to the coach, for it is difficult to find adequate means of motivating such an athlete. Methods that work for others are seldom effective with the complacent athlete. Constant needling by the trainer or coach may occasionally effect some motivation but it is usually sort-lived. It is dispiriting when one recognizes that such an individual is performing well below his optimum. It is difficult to get him to recognize his full potential, shake off the shackles of lethargy, and so become an efficiently functioning, contributing member of the team.

In the training room the complacent athlete casually accepts all ministrations but beyond this makes little or no effort to assist with his own reconditioning. This necessitates constant checking to ensure that he is following instructions and to provoke him into action. This is time-consuming and also can prove vexing. The complacent athlete who makes no effort to respond is a detriment and should be dropped from the team.

Malingering. Certain athletes seek to escape practice and other responsibilities or to gain sympathy by feigning illness or injury. In many instances such an action may be difficult to detect. However, a history of repeated questionable incidents bears thorough investigation. When a case of malingering is evident, the trainer can usually handle it by direct means, that is, by letting the athlete know that his acting has been detected and that henceforth his complaints had better be legitimate. Should the conduct continue, a conference between trainer and coach is indicated. A persistent malingerer is of no value to the team and should be dropped.

Pain tolerance. Recent investigations have turned up an interesting and somewhat significant relationship between the type of sport an individual chooses to participate in and his ability to stand pain.[5,6] The athlete who participates in contact sports is able to tolerate more pain than

the one who participates in the noncontact sports such as golf or tennis.[6] The latter, however, are able to endure more pain than nonathlete. The contact sport athlete tends to reduce the intensity of his perception and so evinces a greater pain tolerance. He also tends to be more extroverted than the noncontact sport athlete. The noncontact sport athlete tends to augment his perception somewhat but not to the degree that the nonathlete does. Experienced trainers are well aware of the differences in pain tolerance exhibited by athletes in various sports, and these studies tend to verify the empirical observations heretofore made.

MOTIVATION

There appears to be a specific relationship between the voluntary motor system and emotion. Kinesthetic skills and performances are affected by the state of emotion existing at a given time.[8] Motivation is facilitated when emotion is channeled so that it acts as an energizing force rather than as an impediment. Such factors as cheering, excitement, pep talks, and the like are motivational influences that assist the athlete in performing at his optimum, calling up his reserves to sometimes exceed his known ability, or staving off the onset of fatigue or exhaustion. This type of motivation is usually not within the realm of the trainer.

The trainer deals with motivation in terms of developing desirable patterns of response and attitudes toward training and its various procedures and in terms of instilling in the athlete a desire to participate in therapy and reconditioning with a positive attitude. To want to get well is extremely important in any therapeutic process. Thus, good motivation enables the athlete to assist the trainer, as it were, and so he becomes an asset rather than a liability.

By planning and maintaining his premises and facilities in such a manner that they convey an atmosphere of pleasant efficiency, the trainer can motivate those he serves. He and his staff should maintain an air of cheerfulness and confidence but still appear businesslike and competent. From factors such as these, the athlete derives an emotional climate and a personal relationship conducive to proper motivation.

WINNING ATTITUDE AND LEVEL OF ASPIRATION

A champion thinks like a champion. A positive attitude toward a competitive situation materially aids the performer.[9] His mind is not hindered or cluttered with

Fig. 9-1. Determination to succeed is vital for a champion.

doubts and countless little nagging thoughts couched in terms of failure. Rather, he is determined to succeed and can concentrate all his conscious efforts, physical and phychological, toward achieving his goal. Studies have shown that players will react emotionally to the importance of a contest.[10,11] If they are competing against a team that they believe will not give them much trouble, it is difficult for the coach and trainer to get them "up" psychologically for the contest. An underrated team will often play far above its usual rated level of performance simply because it aspires to win. The players are determined. Conversely, their opponents, unquestionably the better team in terms of previous performances, cannot seem to get going. Psychological readiness or mind-set—call it what you will—is as important to performance as is physical conditioning.

Successful players and competitors have high levels of aspiration. They constantly raise these levels and maintain hopes of success even if at times they repeatedly experience failure. On the other hand, the unsuccessful player tends to lower his level of aspiration. An individual who has a low level of aspiration and then experiences failure tends to escape by removing himself from the failure situation through various means such as rationalization, or defeatism. If he is neither favorite nor underdog, he has a 50/50 chance of being successful.

The level of aspiration of either an individual or a team can be raised through pep talks, slogans, and various audio-visual materials in the training and locker rooms. The trainer can play an important role both in maintaining and in raising the level of aspiration by utilizing his position as a means of adding to the motivation and encouragement so necessary in athletics.

PSYCHOLOGICAL FACTORS IN RECONDITIONING

Reconditioning in athletics can pose problems that tax the trainer's patience and ingenuity. A highly motivated athlete begrudges every moment he must spend out of action and can become somewhat difficult to handle if the desired ends are to be attained. At the other end of the scale, the malingerer presents a problem in that he persists in treatment when it is no longer necessary. Between these extremes are problems of varying difficulty and complexity. To reduce problems in reconditioning to a minimum, the trainer must establish a preliminary pattern of contact with his charges so that they will work cooperatively and confidently with him. It is necessary, first, to make certain that the athlete understands his condition, especially the prognosis. He must be made aware that the results will largely be determined by the energy and enthusiasm that he puts into his reconditioning program. Second, the athlete's interest in his own recovery must be aroused, and he must be strongly impressed with the fact that shirking any of the procedures, either by omission in whole or in part or by decrease in intensity, will result in cheating himself—not the trainer. Many injured athletes lack patience. Recovery is usually a rather slow and often a tedious process. Patience and desire are therefore necessary adjuncts in securing a reasonable rate of recovery. Some athletes are unenthusiastic and consequently will require continued motivation. The athlete must be made to realize that recovery depends upon his attitude, as well as upon the physiological healing processes and that he can indeed aid by means of conscientious and persistent effort. Third, the trainer must know both the pathology of the case and his patient to be successful in motivating, couseling, and guiding him along the road to recovery.

RELAXATION

Relaxation is usually defined as the elimination or diminution of tension. For our purposes, we will define it as the constructive use of tension, or the ability of the muscles to release contractual tension. Tension of a muscle may be introduced in two ways: physiologically through exercise or psychogenically through anxiety, uncer-

tainty, or other mental-emotional stressors. Emotional disturbances are reflected in muscle action, and situations that tend to increase such emotional tensions are thus indicated by increased muscular tensions. There are many causes of tensions. Generally, normal fatigue, chronic fatigue, and overactivity are the principal ones. Before relaxation can be obtained, the causes for being tense must be studied. In athletics, we are chiefly concerned with the release of tensions within the muscles, tensions introduced either physically or psychogenically.

As muscles tire they lose some of their ability to relax, to give up some of their contractual tension. As a result, the elasticity of the muscle is considerably diminished. The endurance of a muscle is characterized by its ability to retain its elasticity as well. Hence, the degree of elasticity determines the degree of muscular efficiency. A muscle carefully conditioned for endurance will assume its maximum length after a long series of repeated actions. As a muscle fatigues, it steadily diminishes in irritability (its ability to respond to a stimulus) and in elasticity because of the presence of increased metabolites. It loses its ability to readily give up eccentric (lengthening) contraction. The capability of a muscle to recuperate following a bout of exercise is considerably enhanced by the ability of the athlete to consciously relax.

Tension is a natural concomitant of any form of competitive endeavor. Properly channeled it proves an asset rather than a liability. Excessive tension, however, is detrimental not only to physical performance but to the health of the athlete as well.

Hypertension, usually as the result of overwork and/or extreme anxiety, is sometimes evident in athletes. Evidences of hypertension are seen in increased tendon reflexes, increased mechanical muscle irritability or excitability, occasional mechanical nerve excitability, spasticity of certain muscle groups, and a somewhat abnormal excitability in terms of cardiac and respiratory responses. Extreme irritability, restlessness, and tremor complete the syndrome. Relaxation eliminates these symptoms of stress.

To eliminate undesirable tensions athletes should be trained to employ one of the various recognized techniques of relaxation, since reducing muscular tension leads to a lessening of nervous tension and vice versa. A number of techniques for inducing relaxation have been advanced. Each has its proponents. Jacobson[12] has developed a technique that employs a principle of progressive relaxation. He recognizes two types of relaxation: general and differential. General relaxation is that obtained only when the subject is lying down and practically all voluntary muscles are completely relaxed. Differential relaxation is the absence of any unnecessary degree of contraction in the muscles not involved in the act while other muscles actually perform the act. The Jacobson technique requires, as do other techniques, considerable practice before mastery is achieved. One hour, two to three times a week, is recommended. Practice can be carried out on either a group or an individual basis. Once the basic principles are acquired, the athlete can use them at his convenience and, in most instances, achieve a reasonable degree of success.

de Vries[13] has developed a technique combining some of the principles of Jacobson, Yogic *shavasana*, and kinesthesis. He has achieved some excellent results. Both of these methods should be given consideration since both methods produce positive results that have been measured electromyographically. Most techniques employ the principles utilized for teaching kinesthesis so that the sensations of muscle and body awareness are established. The trainer should familiarize himself with one or more techniques and become proficient in using them when necessary.

It behooves the trainer to learn to recognize the symptoms of stress early in their development. It is much easier to develop relaxation in an individual before muscle spasticity and other physiological anomalies manifest themselves in any degree of severity. Normal precontest tension can generally be handled by maintaining, insofar as possible, the usual training room atmosphere and equanimity. Athletes should be instructed to take advantage of moments of respite and to develop habits of relaxation at such times. Conservation of energy should be the byword.

REFERENCES

1. Ogilvie, B. C., and Tutko, T. A.: Problem athletes and how to handle them, London, 1965, Pelham Books, Ltd.
2. Johnson, W. R., and Hutton, D. C.: Effects of a combative sport upon personality dynamics as measured by a projective test, Res. Quart. 26:49, 1955.
3. Husman, B. F.: Aggression in boxers and wrestlers as measured by projective techniques, Res. Quart. 26:421, 1955.
4. Prokop, L.: Adrenals and sport, J. Sport Med. 3:115, 1963.
5. Ryan, E. D., and Foster, R. L.: Athletic participation and perceptual augmentation and reduction. In Morgan, W. P., editor: Contemporary readings in sport psychology, Springfield, Ill., 1970, Charles C Thomas, Publisher.
6. Ryan, E. D., and Kovacic, C. R.: Pain tolerance and athletic participation, Percept. Motor Skills 22:383, 1966.
7. Ryde, D.: The role of the physician in sports injury prevention, J. Sport Med. 5:152, 1965.
8. Howell, M. L.: Influence of emotional tension on speed of reaction and movement, Res. Quart. 24:22, 1953.
9. Pierce, C. M., and Stuart, H. J.: Mental readiness in sports, Proceedings of the Seventh National Conference on the Medical Aspects of Sports, Chicago, 1965, The American Medical Association, pp. 27-29.
10. Johnson, W. R., Hutton, D. C., and Johnson, G. B.: Personality traits of some champion athletes as measured by two projective tests: the Rohrschach and H-T-P, Res. Quart. 25:484, 1954.
11. La Place, J. P.: Personality and its relationship to success in professional baseball, Res. Quart. 25:313, 1954.
12. Jacobson, E.: Progressive relaxation, Chicago, 1938, University of Chicago Press.
13. de Vries, H. A.: Neuromuscular tension and its relief, J. Ass. Phys. Ment. Rehab. 16:86, 1962.

RECOMMENDED READINGS

Carroll, H.: Mental hygiene, the dynamics of adjustment, Englewood Cliffs, N. J., 1964, Prentice-Hall, Inc.

Cofer, C. N., and Johnson, W. R.: Personality dynamics in relationship to exercise and sports. In Johnson, W. R., editor: Science and medicine of exercise and sports, New York, 1960, Harper & Row, Publishers, pp. 525-559.

Cratty, B. J.: Psychology and physical activity, Englewood Cliffs, N. J., 1968, Prentice-Hall, Inc.

Deutsch, H.: Neuroses and character disorders, New York, 1965, International Universities Press.

Doherty, J. K.: Physical readiness for sports, Proceedings of the Seventh National Conference on the Medical Aspects of Sports, Chicago, 1965, American Medical Association, pp. 30-35.

Kaplan, L.: Foundations of human behavior, New York, 1965, Harper & Row, Publishers.

Lambertini, G.: Morphological and psychological traits related to the activity of the athlete. In Health and fitness in the modern world, Chicago, 1961, Athletic Institute.

Steinhaus, A. H.: Facts and theories of neuromuscular relaxation. Quest, monograph III, pp. 3-14, Dec., 1964.

Watson, G.: Social psychology: issues and insights, Philadelphia, 1966, J. B. Lippincott Co.

Wolf, S.: Psychosomatic aspects of competitive sports, J. Sport Med. 3:157, 1963.

CHAPTER **10**

Training for girls and women

The fact that girls and women can successfully compete in strenuous athletic activities without physiological or psychological harm is gradually gaining belated acceptance in our society, although Europeans have recognized this for many years. Over the years sociological customs have created a number of differences between the sexes. The cultural conditions under which we have lived have insisted that there are distinct physiological and psychological differences between men and women that preclude the latter from participating in strenuous physical activity, particularly of a competitive nature. Our nation has been built upon a basis of competition, and women have vied successfully with the opposite sex in many endeavors without having suffered psychological trauma. Since the dawn of history, woman has indulged in strenuous physical activity and has thrived upon it. It was, in earlier days, a way of life and was accepted as such.

Our society has seen fit to cast American womanhood, with the exception of the pioneer woman, in a somewhat effete role—quite a different construct from that set forth by our European neighbors, who have long felt that a woman can be both physically active and feminine at the same time. There remains a not inconsiderable group who believe that for a woman to participate in competitive athletics is physically and psychologically harmful and, in some instances, morally wrong, as well. Expert opinion, gathered from doctors of medicine, teachers, researchers, psychologists, and the athletes themselves, is producing an ever-increasing amount of proof that the latter concept does not stand scientific scrutiny. As long as a girl or woman is physically fit, voluntary participation in competitive athletics is not detrimental to either her health or her morals. It is, rather, definitely beneficial.

Women are currently engaging in intensive competitive performances in many sports and have shown no deleterious effects. For example, the half mile has now been run under 2 minutes, a feat comparable to the sub-4-minute mile, considered in terms of woman's physiological capabilities. The remarkable swimming records being produced by young teen-aged girls surpass Olympic winning times of male swimmers of a period not too many years ago. Jokl[1] has selected a women's track and field team (circa 1960) whose records were such that they would have beaten most male opponents at that time.

EFFECTS OF ATHLETIC PERFORMANCE

Body build and masculinity. Contrary to lay opinion, participation in sports does not masculinize women. Within a sex, the secretion of testosterone, androgen, and estrogen varies considerably, accounting for marked variation in terms of muscularity and general morphology among males and females. Girls whose physiques reflect considerable masculinity are stronger per unit of weight than girls who are low in masculinity and boys who display considerable femininity of build.[2] Those who are of masculine type often do enter sports and are usually quite successful because of the mechanical advantages possessed by the masculine structure. However, such types are the exception, and by far the greater majority of participants possess a feminine body build (Fig. 10-1). The consensus of a number of doctors, coaches, and trainers holds that sports competition keeps women looking young in face and figure much longer than would otherwise be the case. They appear to be more vibrant and youthful in their thinking, as well. The present generation is achieving an improved and better-balanced maturation that makes them stronger and more capable of undergoing strenuous activity. One need only to peruse the sports records for the past 20 years to see proof of this.

Running. Girls often have difficulty in

Fig. 10-1. Strength, balance, and skill contribute to a graceful, feminine physique.

running, particularly after adolescence. The female pelvis is broader and shallower, which causes the femur to articulate at a more acute angle than does that of the male, resulting in a mechanical disadvantage; the obliquity of the femur tends to induce a lateral sway of the body in running. Girls frequently fail to lift the knee sufficiently and tend to compensate by casting the lower leg and foot out to the side in the forward-carry phase, causing the femur to be rotated inwardly. The casting accentuates the trunk sway, which becomes quite pronounced. In conditioning and coaching, good knee elevation, directly forward, coupled with straight-forward foot placement, should be stressed.

As girls run they tend to hug the upper arms and elbows tight against the body and swing the forearms out to the sides, meanwhile vigorously rotating the upper trunk and the shoulders in an attempt to offset the inward thigh rotation. In addition to showing the exaggerated trunk rotation, some girls tend to keep the clenched fists tight against the chest, meanwhile alternately thrusting the elbows forward in a vigorous manner. Stressing relaxation and a proper arm swing, linked with a strong high forward knee lift, will increase the efficiency and the speed of the runner.

Jumping. One of the arguments frequently advanced against athletics for women raises the point that activities such as the high jump or broad jump are harmful because they cause internal damage in the pelvic region, as a result of the jarring forces encountered when landing. This, it is argued, subjects the mesenteries and other supportive tissues to tearing, with concomitant trauma to the neighboring organs. Medical findings refute this postulate. The exercise indulged in by a woman athlete in training and in conditioning, as well as in actual competition, tends to strengthen the floor of the pelvis and the surrounding tissues and brings about an improved tonicity of the muscles.

Irritation or strain to the breasts can result, especially if the breasts are pendulous,

unless adequate support and restraint are afforded by means of a properly designed and fitted brassiere.

Women have a lower center of gravity than do men and hence are more stable. Their arms and legs are proportionately shorter than are those of the opposite sex. Both of these factors present disadvantages in jumping.

Throwing and support activities. The shoulder width of the female is narrower than that of the male, and the breadth of the pelvis, augmented by the adipose pads over the hips, usually causes the arm to incline inward. Most women have a pronounced hyperextension of the elbow joint, often coupled with a decided outward angling of the forearm. These skeletal differences create difficulties in throwing, circling, or rotatory movements of the arm as a whole. This is true also in activities involving the support of the body by the arms, as encountered in gymnastics. In the latter the differences provide a distinct handicap, since both elbow and shoulder joints must function at somewhat unfavorable angles for weight bearing.

PHYSIOLOGICAL IMPLICATIONS

Both structural and physiological differences emphasize the fact that women should not be compared with men in terms of performance. They should be judged in terms relative only to the performance standards of their sex. Sex has definite influence on training principally because of the difference in the physiological capacity to perform exercise.

Prepubertal and pubertal periods. During the prepubertal period, girls are the equal of, and often are superior to, boys of the same age in activities requiring speed, strength, and endurance.[3] The difference between the sexes is not too apparent until after puberty. With the advent of puberty the gulf begins to widen, with the males continuing in a slower gradual increase in strength, speed, and endurance. In contrast, the females indicate a decrease and, at times, a termination of the desire and ability to perform well physically. In the second instance the lack of desire may be culturally imposed or it may come about as the result of a general physical ineptness incurred because of a limiting morphology.

Circulatory factors. In the performance of moderate exercise there is little significant difference between young men and women in respect to standards of performance, but the significance increases as the strenuousness of the activity increases. Women are subject to the same physiological laws as are men. However, they have a smaller heart and a faster pulse rate. They indicate a greater and more rapid increase in pulse rate at the beginning of exercise and a much slower recovery following exercise. The pulse rates of trained women athletes are about ten beats per minute slower than those of nonathletes.

At rest the average number of red blood cells in the female is 4,500,000 per cu. mm. as compared to 5,000,000 per cubic millimeter in the male. Postexercise values reflect an increase of approximately 1,000,000 for the male and a comparable rise for the female relative to the lower resting value. This rise is indicative of the compensatory adjustment to meet the demand for an increased oxygen supply. The female also has approximately 8% less hemoglobin.[4]

At a given level of oxygen consumption women indicate a higher heart rate than do men. On the other hand, for a given heart rate men can transport more oxygen during submaximal and maximal work. In both sexes the maximum heart rate bears a linear relationship with an increased work load. Exhaustion, however, is reached at a lower rate of performance in women.

Blood pressure values, both diastolic and systolic, are from 5 to 10 mm. Hg lower in the female. Pubertal systolic values, although reflecting some rise, are less pronounced than those of the male and will often indicate a slight decrease, which is maintained until age 18 or 19. After age 19 there is a slow but steady increase in both the male and female as age advances. Following menopause most women show a systolic increase slightly higher than the comparable male.

Respiratory function. Because of the smaller thoracic cavity, women respire more rapidly. They require less oxygen because of a lower metabolic rate and smaller body size. Trained subjects of both sexes appear to utilize their anaerobic processes to approximately the same level.[8] Women breathe more shallowly, that is, with the upper part of the chest, whereas men tend to breathe deeper and hence more diaphragmatically.

Vital capacity is the volume of air moved through the lungs from a maximal inspiration to a maximal expiration. It varies between the sexes since it bears a direct relationship to body size, area, and height. Although vital capacity is not predictive of performance by itself, it can be enhanced through training, and it determines performance capabilities. The vital capacity of the female is about 10% less than that of a male of the same size and age. The tendency to breathe costally (with the upper part of the chest) rather than diaphragmatically further limits the respiratory volume of the female. However, through training, diaphragmatic breathing can be developed.

The *maximum aerobic power* of the female, the ability to utilize oxygen effectively, is also from 25 to 30% less than that of the male after age 12. Prior to that time both values are about the same. Both men and women peak out at age 18 years, after which there is a gradual decline.[5] A comparison of the oxygen uptake values indicates similar levels per kilogram of body weight and it would seem that women, having a smaller body size, should have a higher value. It may well be that the smaller hemoglobin concentration restricts the full utilization of the cardiac output for oxygen transport. Maximal oxygen uptake values (oxygen accepted by the tissues) are much higher for physically active females than for the more sedentary.

Metabolism. According to Ruch and Fulton[6] the metabolic rate of the female at all ages is from 6% to 10% lower than that of the male of comparable size when related to body surface area. When the basal metabolic rate is related to the muscle mass, however, the sex difference disappears.[7] This would indicate a significance to the resting heat disposition but not to muscular efficiency.

Muscular strength. In proportion to weight and size, women's muscles are weaker than men's, possessing at maturity approximately half the strength of their male counterparts. Muscular strength is related to the size and anatomy of the body and is indicated in terms of its proportionate mass. Among males this constitutes approximately 43% and among women about 36% of the total (Fig. 10-2). Differences in relative amounts of muscle tissue during

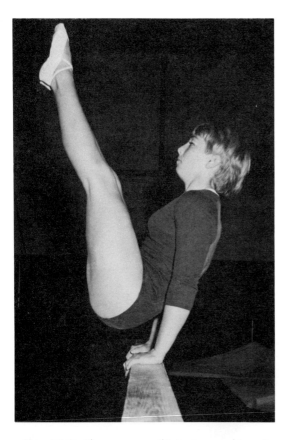

Fig. 10-2. The woman athlete is capable of feats of considerable strength and balance.

puberty are the result of endocrine function, which causes the fundamental sex differences in terms of weight and development. Testosterone produces a marked increase in the weight of muscle tissue and an enlargement of the muscle fibers.[2] Female hormones have a growth inhibiting effect. As with men, muscles develop in relation to the fundamental laws of exercise.

Femininity. Many girls and women fear the development of unsightly, bulging muscles should they exercise vigorously. They point to the pronounced muscular definition of the quadriceps and the gastrocnemius often seen in women who have had intensive and prolonged ballet or dance training. Actually, such overdeveloped musculature is the result of long, arduous, and concentrated training for many years, which cannot be compared to the span of time usually covered in training and competition. In comparison, this period is of relatively short duration. Such excessive development is not a concomitant of athletic competition. One need only observe some of the outstanding girl and women athletes to obtain complete refutation of such a premise. Indeed, physical activity develops femininity and grace. The responsibility for masculinity in the female must be laid on the inherent endocrinological and morphological factors of the individual rather than on the pursuit of physical activity.

Adiposity. Women have about 10% more adipose tissue than do men. The fat is stored at various depots around the body, as well as in a rather thick subcutaneous layer that serves as protection and insulation. Because of the subcutaneous layer, women are better able to withstand heat and cold than are men. The greater amount of adipose tissue may have some effect on the lower metabolic rate. Since fat is inert, it limits athletic performance, representing dead weight that must be carried by the athlete.

Periodicity. For many years medical opinion held that little or no exercise should be taken during the menstrual period. In modern medical opinion the avoidance of strenuous activity is advised for only the first 2 days. During this time, the womb is quite heavy and engorged with blood. It is at this time that the athlete would do well to avoid activities involving torque or jarring forces such as jumping or twisting movements that involve the pelvis. Some athletes, however, are able to participate in heavy training or competition without experiencing any distress or involvement during their menstrual period. The best performances usually appear during the immediate postmenstrual period and the poorest performances are observed during the immediate premenstrual period.[9] It appears that these variations in performance may be induced by the psychological and hormonal factors that normally accompany menstruation and that are indicated by such symptoms as depression, fatigue, irritability, nervousness, and water retention.

Studies[10] indicate that engaging in either heavy training or competition does not affect the onset of the menarche.

Physicians report that exercises ranging from mild to vigorous in nature aid in ameliorating dysmenorrhea (painful menstruation).[11,12] Physicians generally advise a continuance of the usual sports participation during the menstrual period, provided the performance level of the individual does not drop below her customary level of ability. Gymnastics, skiing, swimming, diving, and tennis are sports wherein women athletes reveal a higher percentage of menstrual and inflammatory disease than occurs in other sports. In these they also appear to perform less effectively during the menstrual period than do women in other activities.

Childbearing and athletic performance. Clinical data compiled by a number of medical researchers add up to but one conclusion: athletic participation does not affect childbearing or childbirth in an adverse way but, on the contrary, serves this biological function in a positive way.[13,14] Pregnancy may well be considered a training period for the maternal organism inasmuch as the increases in blood volume and metabolism make rather intensive demands upon the physiological systems. Strenuous to moderate physical activity continuing to the latter months of pregnancy should be viewed as preparatory. Such activity makes pregnancy, childbirth, and post-parturition less stressful.

One statement commonly expressed is that women athletes have pelves which are narrower than normal and that, consequently, they experience various disorders in pregnancy and childbirth. The skeletal measurements of women athletes indicate no departure from normal dimensions. It is a matter of record that they are less subject to uterine disorders than are nonathletes. Fertility and gestation among women athletes are within normal ranges. Athletes have a significantly shortened duration of labor and have fewer disorders and complications during the process of giving birth than do nonathletes. Following childbirth many athletes have recorded better performances; it has been postulated that pregnancy and childbirth activate latent endocrinological forces that manifest themselves in an improved physical efficiency. Many athletes have competed during pregnancy with no ill effects. Most physicians, although advocating moderate activity during this period, believe that especially vigorous performance, particularly in activities in which there may be severe body contact or heavy jarring or falls, should be avoided.

PSYCHOLOGICAL IMPLICATIONS

Women participate and compete in athletic activities because of a need to satisfy certain physiological and psychological needs. Woman's psyche responds not only to certain biological demands but also to social and cultural demands, thus establishing patterns of behavior that are peculiarly hers. Today woman is not leading the sheltered and sequestered life of earlier times but is competing in many areas formerly denied her and on favorable and equal terms with man. This gradually expanding role has led to an increasing amount of participation in the field of sports. Although it is recognized that within this area the differences between the sexes arc far from as extreme as was once thought, it is recognized also that some differences do exist, making it advisable for women to compete only against members of their own sex.

Girls and women participating in athletics develop good emotional control and

Fig. 10-3. Sports help to keep one **vigorous** and youthful.

stability.[15] It is part of the game. They learn to respect and abide by the laws of good sportsmanship, to be gracious in defeat as well as in victory, to work cooperatively as a member of a team, and a to establish and work toward desirable goals. However, participation must be on a voluntary basis. The emotional strains resulting from coercion have been shown to manifest themselves in a number of ways, particularly through menstrual anomalies. Athletic activities provide a wholesome, sensible emotional outlet for the teen-age girl and can substitute for other less desirable activities in meeting this need. Active interest and participation in sports can keep a woman thinking and looking younger throughout her lifetime (Fig. 10-3).

Fears are often expressed that the emotional tension to which athletes are subjected during the precompetitive and competitive periods are detrimental to the emotional health of girls and women. It must be recognized that such periods are transitory. It is doubtful if in any way they measure up to the intense and prolonged emotional bouts, for example, to which adolescents are prone. Sports participation and competition exert a healthy influence upon the socioemotional qualities of the female, and encouragement to take active part in such activities should be given at every opportunity.

CONDITIONING FOR ATHLETICS

The conditioning program for girls and women in preparation for athletic participation varies little from that recommended in Chapter 7 for boys and men. Since women are not as strong or as powerful as men, conditioning procedures in activities in which strength is the prime factor may need to be downgraded somewhat to fit the ability of the trainee. The same policy applies to activities of endurance. Trainers and coaches have often been concerned about the effects of endurance events such as the half-mile race. The nausea and fatigue that follow such a performance are normal and are experienced by many male athletes after strenuous performance of this type. Jokl, who is considered one of the leading authorities on the heart of the athlete, states unequivocally that endurance events of this nature do not overtax the cardiovascular resources of women.

Weight training for women. There has long been a belief that heavy exercise, particularly weight training, will develop unsightly and bulky muscles in women and that such exercises have a tendency to develop masculinity. These beliefs are not sound. One has only to observe outstanding women athletes to see the femininity and grace that have accompanied intensive and prolonged developmental exercise. Proper exercise of this type will do much to improve the figure, since it develops muscles that are in need of growth, improves tonicity, and brings about a beauty of coordination and movement that makes the performance a delightful sight. Those who have had the opportunity to see the women Olympic gymnasts, skaters, or track performers have been impressed with the physical perfection and femininity of these young women. The sociopsychological differences that exist between men and women have been demonstrated to be largely the result of social factors or cultural conditions rather than the result of actual sex differences. A different philosophical approach to female participation in physical activities is indicative of the renewed interest of young women in physical activities that demand considerable physical conditioning as a prerequisite to participation. To ensure proper and adequate conditioning a program of resistive exercises should be planned and carefully followed.

Women can follow the same general and specific training procedures advocated for the men, with the exception that the amount of weight to be handled must be within their capacity to manage. The identical exercise programs, including the recommended number of repetitions should be followed. It is suggested, however, that weight increments be in units of 2½ and 5 pounds, rather than 5 and 10 pounds, unless the individual shows herself fully capable of handling the larger increment. During the menstrual period it might be advisable to curtail the lifting program for a couple of days at the onset, substituting the moderate general conditioning and stretching exercises.

Training considerations in the care and treatment of injuries. The training procedures detailed in the following chapters apply to women and girls as well as to men. The team physician has the responsibility and the authority to make the decisions that involve medical practice. The trainer and the coach work under his direction. Limitations in terms of knowledge and training on the part of the trainer and coach must be recognized and respected. If at all possible, a woman should serve as trainer or coach or in the dual capacity.

The evidence resulting from many studies thus far indicates that competition in athletics by girls and women has a most positive effect on health and well-being and that no adverse effects are encountered later in life. The incidence of injury is not appreciably greater than that of men, although women are considered somewhat more prone to injury. A study on the effects of athletic competition on females, which included a report on a national survey of athletic injuries incurred by college women, indicated both a higher rate and a greater severity index than men. Most injuries have occurred in activities that require explosive effort, such as the long jump or sprints. Injuries involving conditions of overstrain (periosteal, bursae, tendinous, in nature) are reported to occur almost four times as much among women athletes as among men.

Injuries to the female genitalia occur less frequently and are less severe than is the case with the males. Breast injuries, which usually occur in activities where there is physical contact with either an opponent or with equipment, should be guarded against by insisting that the athlete wear a properly designed protective device, such as a plastic cup brassiere.

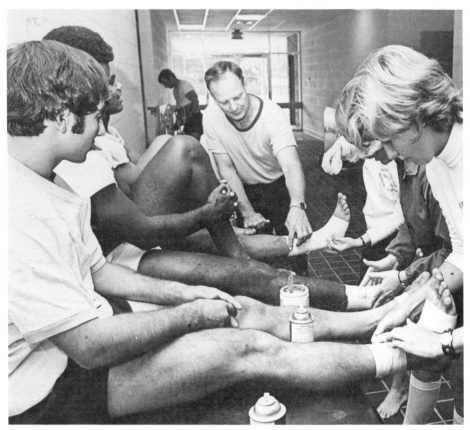

Fig. 10-4. Women are becoming increasingly interested in the care and prevention of athletic injuries. (Courtesy John Cramer, Cramer Products, Inc., Gardner, Kansas.)

Active participation by adequately trained and properly coached girls and women in local, national, and international competition in sports such as track and field, gymnastics, basketball, softball, swimming, and diving has resulted only in the usual types of temporary injuries such as strains and sprains, which are common to all athletics. Over the years no untoward increase in the incidence of these injuries has been noted; nor has there been any indication of the occurrence of serious injuries, such as have been observed in men's athletics (Fig. 10-4).

Because of the great increase in the number of girls and women in sports participation, there is a vital need not only for women coaches who have a greater knowledge of and who are specifically trained to handle the coaching of advanced athletic techniques but also for women who can take over the training of women and girls for such competition. Women trainers should have the same educational and professional backgrounds as do the men. Properly qualified women trainers and coaches can contribute much to the improvement of women's athletics and can instill confidence and interest in young women who enter the field not only for competition but who are, in addition, desirous of becoming trainers and coaches as well.

The few anatomical or physiological considerations that will be encountered in dealing with women in athletics have been discussed in this chapter and will not be detailed later. Where modifications in training procedures need to be made, the trainer should experience no difficulty in making the adjustments.

REFERENCES

1. Jokl, E.: Physiology of exercise, Springfield, Ill., 1964, Charles C Thomas, Publisher.
2. Cress, C. L., and Thorsen, M. A.: Morphological bisexuality as a factor in the motor performance of college women, Res. Quart. Amer. Ass. Health Phys. Educ. **35**:408, 1964.
3. Brouha, L.: Physiology of training including age and sex differences, J. Sport Med. **2**:3, 1962.
4. Astrand, P. O., and Rodahl, K.: Textbook of work physiology, New York, 1970, McGraw-Hill Book Co.
5. Ulrich, C.: Women and sport. In Johnson, W. R., editor: Science and medicine of exercise and sports, New York, 1960, Harper & Row, Publishers.
6. Ruch, T. C., and Fulton, J. F.: Medical physiology and biophysics, Philadelphia, 1965, W. B. Saunders Co.
7. de Vries, H. A.: Physiology of exercise for physical education and athletics, Dubuque, Iowa, 1966, William C. Brown Co., Publishers.
8. Cumming, G. R.: Current levels of fitness, Canad. Med. Ass. J. **96**:868, 1967.
9. Pros, J. R.: A gynecologist's remarks on women's competitive swimming, Teorie A Praxe Tel Vych, Praha **9**:414, 1961.
10. Erdelyi, G. J.: Gynecological survey of female athletes, J. Sport Med. **2**:174, 1962.
11. Pros, J. R.: Physical movement and sports as prevention and therapy of dysmenorrhea, J. Sport Med. **2**:125, 1962.
12. Pros, J. R.: Prevention of climacteric complains by means of sport, J. Sport Med. **2**:125, 1962.
13. Gendel, E.: Pregnancy, fitness and sports, Proceedings of the Seventh National Conference on the Medical Aspects of Sports, Chicago, 1965, American Medical Association, pp. 43-46.
14. Klaus, E. J.: The athletic status of women. In Jokl, E., and Simon, E., editors: International research in sport and physical education, Springfield, Ill., 1964, Charles C Thomas, Publisher.
15. Diem, L.: The olympic sport for women, evaluation of declarations, Rev. Anal. Educ. Phys. Sport. **8**:2, 1966.

RECOMMENDED READINGS

Albright, T.: Sports for teen age girls, Proceedings of the Sixth National Conference on the Medical Aspects of Sports, Chicago, 1964, American Medical Association, pp. 31-33.

American Association for Health, Physical Education and Recreation: Second National Institute on Girls Sports, Washington, D. C., 1966.

American Association for Health, Physical Education and Recreation: Standards in sports for girls and women, Washington, D. C., 1961.

American Association for Health, Physical Education and Recreation: Statement of policies for competition in girls' and women's sports. Washington, D. C., 1964, DGWS Executive Council and AAHPER Board of Directors.

Kita, H.: On professional women skin divers in Japan, J. Sport Med. **5**:43, 1965.

Klafs, C. E., and Lyon, J. M.: The female athlete: conditioning, competition, and culture, St. Louis, 1973, The C. V. Mosby Co.

McGill, F., and Luft, U. C.: Physical performance in relation to fat free weight in women compared to men. In Balke, B., editor: Physiological aspects of sports and physical fitness, Chicago, 1968, American College of Sports Medicine and The Athletic Institute.

Olree, H., and Stevens, W. C.: Evaluation of physical fitness with special reference to girls and women. In Balke, B., editor: Physiological aspects of sports and physical fitness, Chicago, 1968, American College of Sports Medicine and The Athletic Institute.

Bases for managing athletic conditions

PART TWO

Part Two is designed to provide the trainer or coach with the diversified information necessary to perform the duties required in an effective athletic injury management program.

CHAPTER 11

Pharmacology in athletics

Pharmacology may be defined as the science of drugs and their effects on the human body. Generally speaking, athletic pharmacology encompasses those training room supplies that affect a healing or a therapeutic response in the athlete. It must be plainly understood that although trainers or coaches may not legally, ethically, or morally administer harmful drugs, they should have a general knowledge of those substances that are used in first aid and in follow-up care. Such information should include knowledge of (1) legal implications, (2) basic drug preparation, (3) general drug classification, (4) a knowledge of the popular substances under each class of drugs commonly used in athletic training.

LEGAL IMPLICATIONS

Liability during the follow-up care of the injured athlete is dependent upon the school district's philosophy, the extent of the trainer and/or the coach's knowledge, and the scope of the care that is allowed them by the athletic physician. Exceeding any one of these restrictions may result in legal problems.

Most public school districts have definite policies concerning the oral administration of any substance to any student. The taking of aspirin, vitamins, or even dextrose for energy by the athlete may be forbidden by district policy. In this event the team physi-

cian (if he so desires, and with the permission of the school district) may undertake the responsibility of prescribing such medications, which may then be dispensed by the trainer or coach.

DRUG PREPARATIONS

Basic drugs are combined with other substances, called vehicles, which have no action on the body except to contribute toward ease of administration. Vehicles may be either solid or liquid, and the resultant drug preparations also may be so classified.

Solid preparations

1. *Ampule*—a closed glass receptacle containing a drug.
2. *Capsule*—a gelatin receptacle containing a drug.
3. *Ointment (emollient)*—a semisolid preparation that consists of lanolin, petroleum jelly, or lard suspending a drug.
4. *Paste*—an inert powder combined with water.
5. *Pill* or *tablet*—a drug powder compressed into a small oval, circle, square, or other form.
6. *Plaster*—a drug in wax or resin, usually spread on a muslin cloth.
7. *Poultice*—an externally applied, soft and moist paste containing a drug.
8. *Powder*—a finely ground drug.
9. *Suppository*—a medicated gelatin

155

molded into a cone for placement in a body orifice, for example, the anal canal.

Liquid preparations

1. *Aqueous solution*—sterile water containing a drug substance.
2. *Elixir*—alcohol, sugar, and flavoring with a drug dissolved in solution, designed for internal consumption.
3. *Liniment*—an alcohol or oil containing a dissolved drug designed for external application.
4. *Spirit*—a drug dissolved in water and alcohol or in alcohol alone.
5. *Suspension*—undissolved powder material in a fluid medium; must be mixed well by shaking before use.
6. *Syrup*—a mixture of sugar and water containing a drug.

ADMINISTRATION OF DRUGS AND MEDICATIONS

The administration of drugs and medications in athletics, as in any treatment center, may be either internal or external and is based upon the type of local or general response desired.

Internal administration

Drugs and medications may be taken internally by means of inhalation, or they may be administered intradermally, intramuscularly, intranasally, intraspinally, intravenously, orally, rectally, and sublingually.

Inhalation is a means of bringing medication or substances to the respiratory tract. This method is most often used in athletic training to relieve the athlete of the discomfort of upper respiratory involvements, such as colds and coughs. The vehicle for inhalation is usually water vapor, oxygen, or highly aromatic medications.

Intradermal (into the skin) or *subcutaneous* (under the custaneous tissues) administration is usually accomplished by means of a hypodermic needle injection. Such introduction of medication is initiated when a rapid response is needed, but it does not produce so rapid a response as

that following intramuscular or intravenous injection. Tests for allergic sensitiveness are given intradermally rather than below the skin.

Intramuscular injection means that the medication is given directly into the muscle tissue. The site for such an injection is usually the gluteal area or the deltoid muscle of the upper arm. The use of injections to speed the recovery of the athlete is increasing in popularity. Some substance such as procaine, for local anesthesia, combined with cortisone is introduced into areas of inflammation to encourage the healing process.

Intranasal application is varied according to the condition that is to be treated. When head colds or allergies exist, the introduction of decongestants by the use of a menthol salve, a dropper, or an atomizer may relieve discomfort. When it is difficult to control epistaxis (nosebleed), an ephedrine-saturated cotton plug may be introduced to serve as a vasoconstrictor.

Intraspinal injection may be indicated for any of the following purposes: (1) introduction of drugs to combat specific organisms that have entered the spinal cord, (2) injection of a substance such as procaine to anesthetize the lower limbs, or (3) withdrawal of spinal fluid to be studied.

Intravenous injection (into a vein) is given when an immediate reaction to the medication is desired. The drug enters the venous circulation and is spread instantly throughout the body. If large quantities of drugs are introduced into a vein, drop by drop, the process is called *intravenous infusion*.

Oral administration of medicines is the most common method of all. Forms such as tablets, capsules, powders, and liquids are easily administered orally.

Rectal administration of drugs is limited. In the past some medications have been introduced through the rectum to be absorbed by its mucous lining. Such methods have proved undesirable because of difficulties in regulating dosage. Drugs are primarily delivered rectally to effect an enema or to medicate disease conditions of the area.

Sublingual and *buccal* introduction of medicines usually consists of placing easily dissolved agents such as troches or lozenges, tablets, or pills under the tongue or in the cheek. They dissolve slowly and are absorbed by the mucous lining. This method permits slow drug administration into the bloodstream.

External administration

Medications administered externally include inunctions, ointments, pastes, plasters, poultices, and solutions.

Inunctions are oily or fatty substances that are rubbed into the skin and result in a local or systemic reaction. Oil base liniments or petroleum analgesic balms used as massage lubrication are examples of inunctions.

Ointments consisting of oil, lard, petroleum jelly, or lanolin combined with drugs are applied for long-lasting topical medication.

Pastes are ointments with a nonfat base, which are spread on cloth and usually produce a cooling effect on the skin.

Plasters are preparations that have a thicker consistency than ointments and are spread either on cloth or paper or directly on the skin. They usually contain an irritant and are applied as a counterirritant and used for relieving pain, increasing circulation, and decreasing inflammation.

Poultices are applied to skin areas where there is need for decongestion, absorption, stimulation, or a faster localization of suppuration. They consist mainly of a nondrug substance such as a flour paste or a mixture of water and flaxseed, which is heated and placed in a sack and then placed on the affected area. This method of heat therapy is used when other types are unavailable.

Solutions can be administered externally and are extremely varied, consisting principally of bacteriostatics. Antiseptics, disinfectants, vasoconstrictors, and liquid rubefacients are examples.

RESPONSE TO DRUGS

Individuals react differently to the same medication, and different situations can change the effect of a drug. The drugs themselves can be altered through age or improper preservation and through the manner in which they are administered. Response alterations may also be caused by differences in an individual's size or age.

Following is a list of general bodily responses sometimes produced by drugs and medications:

1. *Addiction*—bodily response to certain types of drugs that produce both a physiological need and a psychological desire for the substance.

2. *Antagonistic action*—result observed when medications, used together, have adverse effects or counteract one another.

3. *Cumulative effect*—combination of results, effected when the body is unable to utilize a drug as fast as it is administered. Such drug accumulation may cause unfavorable reactions.

4. *Depressive action*—effect caused by drugs that slow down cell function.

5. *Habituation*—individual's development of a psychological need for a specific medication.

6. *Hypersensitivity*—allergic response to a specific drug. Such allergies may be demonstrated by a mild skin irritation, itching, or a rash, or a drug may cause severe anaphylactic reaction, which could be fatal.

7. *Idiosyncrasy*—unusual reaction to a drug; a distinctive response.

8. *Irritation*—process, as well as effect, caused by substances that result in a cellular change. Mild irritation may stimulate cell activity, whereas moderate or severe irritation by a drug may decrease cell activity.

9. *Side effects*—occurrence that is the result of a medication that is given for a particular condition but affects other body areas or has effects other than those sought.

10. *Specific effect*—action usually produced by a drug in a select tissue or organic system.

11. *Stimulation*—effect caused by drugs that speed up cell activity.

12. *Synergistic effect*—result that occurs when drugs, given together, produce a greater reaction than when given alone.

13. *Tolerance*—condition existing when a certain drug dosage is no longer able to give a therapeutic action and must therefore be increased.

TYPES OF MEDICINALS USED IN ATHLETICS

Certain types of drugs used in athletics are briefly defined in the following list. Some of these, as well as other selected drugs, are discussed in greater detail in the next portion of this chapter.

1. *Analgesics* or *anodynes*—pain-relieving drugs.

2. *Anesthetics*—agents that produce local or general insensibility to touch, pain, or stimulation.

3. *Antacids*—substances that will neutralize acidity; commonly used in the digestive tract.

4. *Anticoagulants*—agents that prevent coagulation of blood.

5. *Antidotes*—substances that prevent or counteract the action of a poison.

6. *Antipruritics*—agents that relieve itching.

7. *Antispasmodics*—agents that relieve muscle spasm.

8. *Antitussives*—agents that inhibit or prevent coughing.

9. *Astringents*—agents that cause contraction or a puckering action.

10. *Bacteriostatics* and *fungistatics*—agents that retard or inhibit the growth of bacteria or fungi.

11. *Carminatives*—agents that relieve flatulence (due to gases) in the intestinal tract.

12. *Cathartics*—agents used to evacuate substances from the bowels; active purgatives.

13. *Caustics*—burning agents, capable of destroying living tissue.

14. *Counterirritants*—agents applied locally to produce an inflammatory reaction for the relief of a deeper inflammation.

15. *Depressants*—agents that diminish body functions or nerve activity.

16. *Diuretics*—agents that increase the secretion of urine.

17. *Emetics*—agents that cause vomiting.

18. *Hemostatics*—substances that either slow down or stop bleeding or hemorrhage.

19. *Irritants*—agents that cause irritation.

20. *Narcotics*—drugs that produce narcosis, or complete insensibility.

21. *Sedatives*—agents that quiet body activity.

22. *Skeletal muscle relaxants*—drugs that depress neural activity within skeletal muscles.

23. *Stimulants*—agents that temporarily increase functional activity.

24. *Vasoconstrictors* and *vasodilators*—drugs that, respectively, constrict or dilate blood vessels.

SELECTED MEDICINALS IN ATHLETICS

The use of drugs and medicines in athletics is similar to their use wherever the injured are cared for. The use and application of some substances are unique to athletics, however.

The purpose of this section is to help the reader to (1) understand the rationale behind giving certain medications, (2) select and use nonprescription medications intelligently, and (3) gain a basic understanding of the drugs used by the physician.

Drugs to combat infection

Antiseptics and disinfectants. An antiseptic is a bacteriostatic substance that is designed to *inhibit* the growth of microorganisms. Disinfectants are germicides or chemical agents that *kill* pathogens.

Antiseptics and disinfectants act on disease-producing organisms by changing the protein structure of the organism, increasing its permeability, and inhibiting its metabolic processes. Chemical agents should be selected for their ability to react selectively against the pathogen and not against the normal cells.

Many chemical agents are used to combat infection in athletics. Basically, they fall into ten categories: phenol, dyes, mercury compounds, silver compounds, halogens, oxidizing agents, alcohols, formaldehyde, boric acid, and soap.

Phenol was introduced to medical science as an antiseptic in 1867 by Sir Joseph Lister. From its inception until the present it has been used to control disease organisms, both as an antiseptic and as a disinfectant, in varying concentrations. It is available in liquids and emollients. Substances that are related to phenol and that cause less irritation are now used more extensively. These substances are resorcinol and thymol.

Dyes are used less extensively since the advent of antibiotics. Their greatest attribute is their ability to be absorbed by protein substances.

Mercury compounds are considered to be bacteriostatic because they inhibit certain enzymatic actions of the bacteria. In some instances mercury compounds are harmful to normal tissue.

Silver compounds have both antiseptic and astringent effects. As with mercury, silver penetrates tissue protein and disrupts the function of the microorganism by inhibiting enzymatic action.

Quaternary ammonium compounds will combat a broad spectrum of bacteria. For example, benzalkonium chloride (Zephiran), a nonirritating, noncorrosive compound, has been found to be highly effective in the sterilization of surgical instruments.

Halogens are a group of chemical substances—chlorine, iodine, fluorine, and bromine—that are used for their antiseptic and disinfectant qualities.

Oxidizing agents include hydrogen peroxide and potassium permanganate and affect disease-producing organisms by freeing oxygen.

Alcohols are some of the most commonly used germicides. Ethyl alcohol and isopropyl alcohol are used as antiseptics and disinfectants.

Formaldehyde is a strong gas that can penetrate cutaneous tissue and is used predominantly for fumigation. In a liquid form it is used for the preservation of biological specimens and as a bactericide.

Boric acid is used in a powder or liquid form as a mild astringent and antiseptic.

Soap is a salt of a higher fatty acid containing an alkali or metal. Soaps are separated into two categories—soluble and insoluble. Soluble soaps are used for cleansing and detergent action. Most soaps disinfect by mechanically removing the microorganism. Some soaps also produce a bacteriological action.

Antibiotics. Antibiotics are chemical agents that are produced with microorganisms. Their useful action is primarily a result of their acting on pathogenic microorganisms by interfering with the necessary metabolic processes. In athletics they are used by the physician as a topical dressing or for systemic medication. The indiscriminate use of antibiotics can produce extreme hypersensitivity or idiosyncrasies and can prevent the acquisition of a natural immunity to succeeding infections. The use of any antibiotics must be carefully controlled by the physician, who selects the drug on the basis of the most desirable type of administration, the amount of toxicity to the patient, and the cost of the drug.

Penicillins, tetracyclines, erythromycin, and bacitracin are at present widely used. Penicillin is a mold that inhibits the metabolism of other bacteria. The group of tetracycline antibiotics have a broad spectrum, or range, and are helpful in treating many pathogenic organisms. In the group are Aureomycin, Terramycin, and Achromycin. Erythromycin has a spectrum similar to that of penicillin in treating pathogens and is often used for penicillin-resistant organisms. Bacitracin has proved to be extremely valuable in athletics in the last few years. Like penicillin, it has a broad spectrum of effectiveness as an antibacterial agent. In addition, it seldom causes sensitivity reactions when used topically in a salve, an advantage over penicillin.

Sulfonamides. The sulfonamides are a group of antibiotics that come from chemical synthesis and are not obtained from natural sources, as are organic antibiotics. All sulfonamides used in treatment contain the substance para-aminobenzene sulfonamide, which invests them with a common characteristic. Authorities indicate that sulfonamides make pathogens vulnerable to phagocytes by inhibiting certain enzymatic actions. The most commonly used drugs are sulfadiazine, sulfamerazine, sulfamethazine, and sulfisoxazole.

Drugs for cutaneous and mucous membrane

Disease control in athletics is primarily effected through the skin. Care includes the use of agents that have the following actions: antipruritic, antiseptic, analgesic and local anesthetic, astringent, irritant and counterirritant, keratolytic, and protective.

Antipruritics. *Pruritus* (itching) is the result of irritation to the peripheral sensory nerve. It is a symptom, rather than a condition in itself, and leads to scratching, which in turn may cause infection. To relieve itching solutions and ointments containing either a mild topical anesthetic such as benzocaine or a cool, soothing agent like calamine or menthol may be applied to the skin.

Calamine is one of the oldest medications used today. It is composed of zinc oxide powder with a small amount of ferric oxide, which gives it a pinkish color. In a lotion form it is combined with glycerin, bentonite magma (a suspending agent for insoluble drugs), and a solution of calcium hydroxide (lime water). Placed on the skin, calamine lotion acts as a soothing, protective coating in cases of itching dermatitis.

Antiseptics. Those agents which arrest microorganisms may be considered antiseptics. Such agents can be introduced in solutions, ointments, or powder form. Each vehicular medium is applicable to different conditions. To be most effective, antiseptics must retard bacteria and fungi without insulting the cutaneous tissue. (Antifungal agents, pediculicides, and scabicides are discussed in Chapter 23). A great many products are on the market. Some of the more effective chemical agents are alcohol, tincture of benzoin, tincture of green soap, hydrogen peroxide, drugs containing mercury or silver nitrate, tannic acid, and boric acid.

Alcohol is one of the most useful substances in the training room. Besides being directly combined with other agents to form tincture solutions, it acts independently on the skin as an antiseptic and astringent. In a 70% solution it can be used for disinfecting instruments. Because of alcohol's rapid rate of evaporation, it produces a mild anesthetic action and, when used as a massage agent, gives a refreshingly cool sensation.

Tincture of benzoin is composed of 20% benzoin in a solution of alcohol. Benzoin is basically a resin obtained from *Liquidambar orientalis*. It may also contain resorcinol, which acts medicinally as a skin dehydrant and antiseptic. Tannic acid may be present in addition to, or in place of, resorcinol; its presence initiates an astringent action on the skin, and it has a tendency to toughen the epidermis. In athletics tincture of benzoin is combined with storax to form tincture of benzoin compound and is used for a protective and adherent base for adhesive strapping or as an antiblister agent.

Tincture of green soap is used in athletics for cleansing contaminated skin areas. It contains a soft soap with added alcohol and thus combines an antiseptic action with a cleansing action.

Hydrogen peroxide is an antiseptic that, because of its oxidation, affects bacteria but readily decomposes in the presence of organic substances such as blood and pus. For this reason it has little affect as an antiseptic. Contact with organic material produces an effervescence, during which no great destruction of bacteria takes place. The chief value of hydrogen peroxide in the care of athletic wounds is its ability to cleanse the infected cutaneous and mucous membranes. Application of hydrogen peroxide to wounds results in the formation of an active effervescent gas that dislodges particles of wound material and debris and, by removing degenerated tissue, eliminates the wound as a likely environment for bacterial breeding. Hydrogen peroxide also possesses a styptic action as a result of encouraging fibrin development in open wounds. Because it is nontoxic, hydrogen peroxide may be used for cleansing mucous membranes. A diluted solution (50% water and 50% hydrogen peroxide) can be used for treating inflammatory conditions of the mouth and throat.

Mercury preparations have been found to be valuable in treating various skin conditions. Together with other ingredients, they act as an antiseptic, a germicide, and a fungicide. Some popular mercury products are Merthiolate, Metaphen, and Mercurochrome.

Silver nitrate is a toxic drug made from silver. In athletics it is most often used as an ointment. It acts as a local astringent and germicidal agent and has the greatest effect on mucous membranes.

Boric acid is a colorless crystal or white powder that is soluble in water. It is used as a liquid for rinsing mucous membranes or bathing an irritated eye, or in an ointment form for use on open skin lesions.

Antifungal agents. There are many medicinal agents on the market designed to treat fungus which is commonly found in and around athletic facilities. The three most common fungi are *Epidermophytosis, Trichophyton,* and *Candida albicans.* New and relatively successful antifungal agents are Tinactin (tolnaftate) and Griseofulvin. Tinactin is a topical medication for superficial fungous infection caused by *Trichophyton* and other fungi. Griseofulvin is an oral fungous medication that combines with the hair, nails, and keratin of the skin.

Analgesics and local anesthetics. The inhibition of pain sensations through the skin is of major concern in athletics. Analgesics

give relief by causing a mild topical anesthesia in peripheral sensory nerve endings. Many chemical reactions on the skin can inhibit pain sensations through rapid evaporation, which causes a cooling action, or by counterirritating the skin. Counterirritants overcome the pain response by irritating the skin with a stronger agent, which contracts the epidermis or arrests hemorrhaging. This in turn causes a mild analgesic action as a result of the prevention of blood engorgement. Used in the training room to produce skin analgesia are cold applications, alcohol, camphor, Ichthyol, menthol, ethyl chloride, and methyl salicylate.

Cold applications immediately act to constrict blood vessels and to numb sensory nerve endings. Application of ice packs or submersion of a part in ice water may completely anesthetize an area. If extreme cold is used, caution must be taken that tissue damage does not result.

Alcohol evaporates rapidly when applied to the skin, causing a refreshingly cool effect that gives a temporary analgesia.

Camphor may be considered a counterirritant when applied to the skin. It has mild antiseptic and skin-irritating qualities. Acting as a rubefacient, it relieves superficial tissue areas of congestion and pressure on sensory pain receptors.

Menthol is an alcohol taken from mint or peppermint oils and is principally used as a local analgesic, counterirritant, and antiseptic. Most often in athletics it is used with a petroleum base for treating cold symptoms and in analgesic balms.

Spray coolants, because of their rapid evaporation, act as topical anesthetics to the skin. Several commercial coolants are presently on the market. Ehyl chloride is one of the most popular spray coolants used in athletics today. Cooling results so quickly that superficial freezing takes place, inhibiting pain impulses for a short time. Athletic trainers disagree as to the effectiveness of spray coolants. Some trainers use them extensively for strains, sprains, and contusions. In our opinion spray coolants are useful only when other analgesics or anesthetics are not available.

Methyl salicylate is synthetic wintergreen used externally in athletics as an analgesic, counterirritant, and antiseptic. Together with menthol and capsicum (red pepper), it is one of the main constituents of analgesic balms and liniments.

Local anesthetics are usually injected by the physician in and around injury sites for minor surgery procedures or to alleviate the pain of movement. Procaine hydrochloride is used extensively as a local anesthetic in athletics, since its anesthesia is more concentrated than cocaines and it does not cause blood vessel constriction.

Astringents. Astringents cause a contraction of cells, arrest capillary bleeding, and coagulate the albumins of local tissues. Astringents applied to mucous membranes will harden tissue cells as well as decrease inflammatory exudates. The most popular astringents in athletics are alum, boric acid, zinc oxide, and tannic acid.

Alum is used in athletics mostly in powder form and is extensively applied as a styptic in the care of mouth ulcerations and in the control of excessive foot perspiration.

Boric acid is used both as an astringent and as a mild antiseptic. As an astringent it is used in powder form; it can be dusted on capillary bleeding areas or be used on the feet to control foot odors and excessive perspiration. Toxic reaction may occur because of its high absorbability.

Zinc oxide in an ointment medium effects a soothing and astringent action. Used in the mass (sticky portion) of the adhesive tape, it helps to prevent undue skin softening when tape is applied. As an emollient, zinc oxide ointment can be applied to denuded skin areas and can effect a mild healing action without softening the skin excessively.

Tannic acid, when administered externally, has both astringent and hemostatic qualities. It is found in many training room preparations designed to toughen skin.

Irritants and counterirritants. Irritating and counterirritating substances used in athletics act as rubefacients and skin stimulants. Their application causes a local increase in blood circulation, redness, and a rise in temperature. Pain can be allayed by the irritating qualities of some preparations, which overcome the pain sensations by producing stronger stimuli. Liniments, analgesic balms, and ichthammol are examples of irritants found in the training room.

Liniments are liquids designed for use in massaging the body when an anodyne (pain reliever) or rubefacient (skin-reddening agent) is desired. These agents may contain—besides the active ingredients of ammonia, camphor, chloroform, methyl salicylate, or turpentine—such vehicles as alcohol, water, oil, or soap. Vehicles such as soap and oil act as a lubrication medium for the hands.

Analgesic balms contain, for the most part, the same ingredients as liniments but are carried in a petroleum base medium.

Ichthammol is an example of a coal tar derivative used as an antiseptic and as an irritant. Tars from various sources have been found to be beneficial for many skin conditions.

Keratolytics. Keratolytics encourage keratolysis, or a loosening of the horny epidermal skin layer. Salicylic acid and resorcinol are the drugs most used for this purpose. They are used for the care of warts, corns, and excessively thick calluses.

Skin coatings (protectives). Coatings may be applied to skin areas where protection from contamination, friction, or the drying of tissues is needed. Protective coatings in athletics consist mainly of substances containing storax or flexible collodion, plus adhesive tape.

Storax is a balsam derived from the trunk of *Liquidambar orientalis* or of *Liquidambar styraciflua*. It occurs as a semiliquid, grayish, sticky, and opaque mass, which is used most often in a compound benzoin tincture as an adherent. Its qualities give a protective coating against tape and friction irritations.

Flexible collodion is a mixture of ethyl oxides, pyroxylin, alcohol, camphor, and castor oil. This solution, when applied to the skin, evaporates rapidly, leaving a flexible cohesive film. Its use in athletics is primarily for covering exposed tissue and protecting lacerated cuts from further irritation.

Adhesive tape offers a highly adaptable means for the protection of athletic affections.

Spray plastic coatings have been developed to cover external wounds, replacing the conventional cloth dressing. The danger of such coatings is that infection may be contained within the wound if it has not been properly cleansed.

Drugs for the gastrointestinal tract

Disorders of the gastrointestinal tract include an upset stomach or formation of gas because of food incompatibilities and acute or chronic hyperacidity, which leads to inflammation of the mucous membrane of the intestinal tract. There is an ever-increasing incidence of ulcers among high school and college athletes, most of which are probably caused by the stress of anticipating athletic performance. Poor eating habits may lead to involvements of the digestive tract, such as diarrhea and constipation. Drugs that elicit responses within the gastrointestinal tract are basically alkalies, carminatives, cathartics, emetics, and hydrochloric acid.

Alkalies. Alkalies taken into the stomach relieve hyperacidity. The most common alkalies are sodium bicarbonate, calcium carbonate, magnesium carbonate, calcium hydroxide (lime water), and bismuth. They may be used in liquid, powder, or tablet form.

Carminatives. Carminatives are drugs that give relief from flatulence (gas). Their action on the digestive canal is to inhibit gas formation and aid in its expulsion. Peppermint and spearmint water are the most commonly used carminatives. They may be combined with alkalies to decrease the acid secretion of the stomach.

Cathartics. The use of cathartics in athletics should always be under the direction of a physician. Constipation may be symptomatic of a serious disease condition. In-

discreet use of laxatives may render the athlete unable to have normal bowel movements. There is little need for healthy, active individuals to rely on artificial means for stool evacuation.

Cathartics are drugs that encourage bowel evacuation. They are classified into two basic types, laxatives and purgatives. Laxatives are mild cathartics and purgatives the severe ones. Bowel evacuation can be encouraged in several ways: (1) by filling the digestive tract with a bulk-type substance, such as fruits and vegetables, and thereby activating peristalsis; (2) by administering a drug to stimulate the mucous membrane, which increases its fluid secretions; or (3) by administering a substance that draws fluid from the mucous membrane. Fluid increase in the intestinal canal softens the feces, allowing it to pass more easily.

Cathartic drugs are classified according to their action on the intestinal tract. *Inorganic cathartics* include magnesium sulfate (Epsom salts), magnesia magma (milk of magnesia), sodium phosphate, and sodium sulfate. These cathartics pull fluid from the intestinal tissues, soften the feces, and increase peristalsis. Mineral oil also is used as a laxative; because of its nonabsorption, it lubricates and expands the feces for ease of evacuation.

Emetics. Emetics are drugs that cause a reverse peristalsis, or vomiting. This is usually a first-aid measure to rid the stomach of poison. In athletics it may be used to rid the stomach of disagreeable food. A glass of warm water with a teaspoonful of powdered mustard or salt, or soapy water can cause regurgitation. A full glass of warm water and bicarbonate of soda will take the acidity from the vomitus. Probably the least time-consuming method to induce vomiting is to have the athlete tickle the back of his throat, at the gag reflex center.

Hydrochloric and citric acids. Hydrochloric and citric acids are seldom used in athletics. Hydrochloric acid is given in a dilute form when there is a decreased amount of acid secretion in the stomach. Citric acid helps to overcome acidosis caused by an alkali reduction within the body.

Drugs for the respiratory system

The most common type of respiratory drugs are expectorants and respiratory stimulants. Each may be found useful in the training room or may be prescribed by a physician for use by an athlete.

Antitussives. Antitussives aid in inhibiting or preventing coughing. Their action may increase the fluid content so that expectoration is made easier, or they may relieve irritated mucous membrane by soothing or healing inflamed mucosa. They are available in liquid, capsule, pill, troche or spray form. *Ammonium chloride* is used in many cough medicines to alleviate symptoms of inflamed mucous membranes. *Terpin hydrate* and *creosote* are substances that help to diminish bronchial secretions. *Codeine* is also commonly used, but must be prescribed by a physician. It is a depressant and affects the reflex cough center in the brain.

Respiratory stimulants. The trainer should have a full understanding of the respiratory tract. Respiration is controlled by a nerve center in the medulla oblongata of the brain. This center is extremely sensitive to the amount of carbon dioxide concentration within the circulatory system. When the carbon dioxide content of the blood rises and the P_{CO_2} ("partial" pressure of carbon dioxide) reaches above 40 mm. of mercury, the inspiratory center is stimulated and the respiration rate increases. However, if the arterial blood P_{CO_2} increases excessively, a servomechanistic phenomenon appears in which the P_{CO_2} acts as a depressant and the respiration rate decreases. Injury to the nerves controlling the repiratory system, an uncontrollable cough, or other conditions resulting in a lack of oxygen may lead to anoxia and suffocation.

The most common respiratory stimulants used in athletics are oxygen and ammonia.

Oxygen is most beneficial where there is an extreme lack of oxygen in the circulatory system, causing a depression of stimuli to the respiratory center. Oxygen is found most valuable in cases of asphyxia. In athletics it has been used for recovery from fatigue and for increased endurance. To date there are no findings that substantially endorse its use in this manner. Any benefits that accrue, athletically, may be considered psychogenic.

Ammonia is a mechanical respiratory stimulant that, when inhaled, causes an irritating stimulation of the respiratory tract and through a reflex action encourages breathing. When an athlete has been knocked unconscious or is stunned from a blow, ammonia may hasten recovery.

Drugs for the circulatory system

There are various drugs and medicines that cause selective actions on the circulatory system—vasoconstrictors, anticoagulants, and nasal decongestants.

Vasoconstrictors. In athletics vasoconstrictors are most often administered externally to sites of profuse bleeding. The drug most commonly used for this purpose is adrenaline, which is applied directly to a hemorrhaging area. It acts immediately to constrict damaged blood vessels and has been found extremely valuable in cases of epistaxis (nosebleed) where normal procedures were inadequate.

Anticoagulants. Drugs that inhibit blood clotting may be used by the athletic physician in cases of recent injury or in cases of blood vessel occlusion by a thrombus. The most common anticoagulants used by physicians in athletics are heparin and coumarin derivatives.

Heparin is a substance that is derived from the lungs of domestic animals. It prolongs the clotting time of blood but will not dissolve a clot once it has developed. Heparin is used primarily to control extension of a thrombus that is already present.

Coumarin derivatives act by suppressing the formation of prothrombin in the liver. Given orally, they are used to slow clotting time in certain vascular disorders.

Nasal decongestants and antihistamines. Drugs that affect the nasal mucous membranes are basically vasoconstrictors, which reduce engorged tissue during upper respiratory involvements. They are often combined with antiseptics or antihistamines. Many decongestants that contain mild vaso-constricting agents such as phenylephrine hydrochloride (Neo-Synephrine) or napha-zoline hydrochloride (Privine) are on the market. These agents, applied topically, are relatively safe. Only when used to excess do they cause undesirable side effects.

Antihistamines are often added to nasal decongestants. Histamine is a protein substance contained in animal tissues that, when released into the general circulation, causes the reactions of an allergy. Histamine causes dilation of arteries and capillaries, skin flushing, and a rise in temperature. An antihistamine is a substance that opposes histamine action. Examples are diphenhydramine hydrochloride (Benadryl hydrochloride) and tripelennamine hydrochloride (Pyribenzamine hydrochloride).

Some antihistamines have been found also to relieve the symptoms of *motion sickness* by depressing the central nervous system and particularly the nerves affecting the labyrinth of the ear. One of the most popular compounds used for motion sickness is dimenhydrinate (Dramamine).

Drugs for the central nervous system

Drugs affect the central nervous system by increasing or decreasing its irritability. in Chapter 8 we discussed the action of stimulants on the central nervous system. In this chapter those drugs that decrease the irritability of the system will be discussed. For this purpose, they are classified as analgesics and antipyretics, hypnotics and sedatives, and anesthetics and narcotics.

Analgesics and antipyretics. Analgesics are those drugs designed to suppress all but the most severe pain, without the patient's losing consciousness. Their main action is on the nerves carrying the pain impulses to the brain. In most cases these drugs also act as antipyretics, inhibiting toxins from affecting the temperature control centers. They consist mainly of acetyl-salicylic acid (aspirin: 5 to 15 grains), ace-tanilid (5 grains), and acetophenetidin (5 grains). Salicylic acid is a remarkable com-

pound in that its as an analgesic, antipy-retic, and anti-inflammatory agent. Propoxyphene hydrochloride (Darvon) is a relatively recent sedative drug used primarily in the relief of pain. Darvon is less habit forming than codeine.

Caution should always be used in dispensing analgesics for headaches and other complaints, since they may disguise symptoms of serious pathology.

Hypnotics and sedatives. Hypnotics and sedatives may be given to the athlete by the physician in cases when an athlete either is under extreme tension, playing in an "away" game and unable to rest properly amid strange surroundings, or is abnormally apprehensive before a big contest. At such times there may be need for sleep or relaxation induced through the administration of hypnotics or sedatives. Such drugs, in most cases, give little relief from pain. They consist mainly of barbituric acid derivatives and bromides.

Barbituric acid is a main ingredient in many hypnotic and sedative drugs. The most common are probably phenobarbital and Nembutal. Each produces a natural sleep and inhibits nervousness. Phenobarbital quiets nervousness, and Nembutal is given orally for sleep.

Bromides give a sedative action, calming anxiety and nervousness.

Anesthetics and narcotics. Most narcotics used in medicine are derived directly from opium or are synthetic opiates. They depress pain impulses and the respiratory centers of the patient. The two most often used derivatives are codeine and morphine.

Codeine resembles morphine in its action but is less potent. Its primary action is as a respiratory depressant and because of this it is found in many cough medicines.

Morphine depresses pain sensations to a greater extent than any other drug. It is also the most dangerous drug because of its ability to depress respiration and because of its habit-forming qualities. Morphine is never used in the following situations: (1) before a diagnosis has been made by the physician, (2) when the subject is unconscious, (3) when there is a head injury, or

(4) when there is a decreased rate of breathing. It is never repeated within 2 hours.

Demerol hydrochloride is often prescribed by the physician for athletes. This drug is used as a substitute for morphine in the relief of pain caused by muscular spasticity.

Drugs for skeletal muscle relaxation

Skeletal muscle relaxants are agents designed to alleviate spasms of the musculature and are used in both acute and chronic conditions. By means of relieving muscle spasms, pain can be diminished and normal function can often be resumed. In recent years they have been given by physicians to athletes immediately following a musculoskeletal injury.

Drugs that produce muscular relaxation are divided into "peripheral" relaxants and "central" relaxants. The peripheral type act on the myoneural junction by blocking the depolarization of the motor end-plate by acetylcholine. The central relaxants inhibit specific neuromuscular reflexes. Common skeletal muscle depressants that act on the central nervous system are mephenesin, methocarbamol (Robaxin), and carisoprodol (Soma).

Most of these relaxants are dispensed in tablet form and ingested orally. These drugs relieve muscle spasm that has occurred from the traumatic injuries of sprains, strains, fractures, or dislocations.

Enzyme drugs

The use of enzymes as therapeutic agents is considered by many as particularly valuable in the care of athletic conditions. It is becoming increasingly popular in the care of traumatic and chronic conditions. Enzymes are catalytic agents that accelerate a chemical response without themselves being affected in the process. Their value is in the specificity of their reactions.

Hyaluronidase is an enzyme found in many organic substances within the body. Its primary contribution to the healing of

injuries is its ability to thin or act as a "spreading factor." Injected into articulations, it reduces the viscosity of the synovial fluid. When injected into tissue, it increases interstitial cell permeability but fails to increase fluid flow.

Trypsin and *chymotrypsin* are pancreatic secretions, which, through enzymatic action, aid in the digestion of proteins, particularly clotted blood, exudate, and necrotic tissue.

Streptokinase and *streptodornase* (Varidase) are enzymes taken from specific strains of streptococci and have the ability to liquefy suppurative material.

Bromelain (Ananase) contains proteolytic enzymes produced by the pineapple plant. It is taken orally and is designed to assist the inflammatory process resulting from trauma.

Anti-inflammatory agents

Anti-inflammatory agents are often used by the physician for subacute and chronic conditions. The most common drug employed by athletic physicians is *cortisone*. Cortisone is a hormone found in the cortex of the adrenal gland, and is used clinically for treating rheumatoid arthritis, rheumatic fever, and various other chronic degenerative diseases. Its contribution to athletic injuries is in its ability to raise the metabolism of connective tissue and increase the process of repair.

RECOMMENDED READINGS

Bergersen, B. S., and Krug, E. E.: Pharmacology in nursing, ed. 12, St. Louis, 1973, The C. V. Mosby Co.

Goth, A.: Medical pharmacology, ed. 6, St. Louis, 1972, The C. V. Mosby Co.

Grollman, A.: Pharmacology and therapeutics, Philadelphia, 1965, Lea & Febiger.

Jordon, E. P., editor: Modern drug encyclopedia and therapeutic index, ed. 7, New York, 1967, The Reuben H. Donnelley Corp.

Martin, E. W., editor: Pharmaceutical science, ed. 13, Easton, Pa., 1965, The Mack Publishing Co.

The pharmacopeia of the United States of America, ed. 17, Easton, Pa., 1965, The Mack Publishing Co.

CHAPTER 12

Therapeutic modalities

Therapeutic modalities may be defined, for our purposes, as all agents used in the treatment of an injury. Only those modalities that have special implications for the athletic training program will be considered in any detail. These consist of (1) mechanical therapies, including massage and mobilization techniques, and (2) cryotherapy, thermotherapy and electrical therapies.

Massage and mobilization

MASSAGE TECHNIQUES

Massage is defined as a systematic manipulation of the soft tissues of the body for therapeutic purposes. It is one of the world's oldest medical modalities. There are indications that it was used in China more than 3,000 years before Christ. Almost every culture uses some form of massage for the care of physical disabilities. From the ancient East massage traveled to Europe where the Greeks, as early as 300 B.C., began rubbing the body for the treatment of disease. From the Greeks the use of massage then passed to the Roman Empire. Galen used massage extensively in conditioning and caring for injured gladiators. With the fall of the Roman Empire and the advent of the Middle Ages came an era in which the practice of massage was considered sinful. Not until the seventeenth century did the rubbing of the body begin to regain favor as part of the healing arts. The "English Hippocrates," Thomas Sydenham (1624-1689), promoted massage as a means to normalize the body processes to cure disease. During the nineteenth century massage began to develop into scientific systems.

Mitzger of Holland and Ling of Sweden are names that stand out in the development of exact methods of exercising and massage. Ling divided his system into three categories: passive, active, and resistive. All Swedish movements are designed to accelerate lymphatic and venous flow. After his death in 1839 the pupils of Ling published his theories and spread the "Ling system" throughout the world. England also made great contributions toward the use of manipulation and massage. A society of physiotherapy was organized in 1894, which later became the allied health profession of physical therapy.

In the United States massage became accepted by the medical profession as a healing modality during World War I, when massage and movement techniques were found beneficial in restoring normal function to handicapped soldiers. It gathered greater impetus during and following World War II, and today in physical therapy it is an important medical modality. Historically, wherever sports were played some form of massage was used. In most cases it was used to prepare the athlete for the contest, to care for his injuries, or to help rejuvenate him after the contest, a practice still used in Europe.

Primarily, athletic massage may be separated into two basic categories: *therapeutic* and *stimulating* massage. Therapeutic massages are those moves performed directly to initiate a healing response. They are referred to as effleurage and friction. *Effleurage* (stroking) is a technique wherein the body or body part is rubbed with the heels and palms of the hands. *Friction* movements are used very successfully on joints and areas where there is little soft tissue and on soft tissue that is indurated. However, it has value in any area in which there may be an accumulation of scar tissue or adhesions. The fingers and thumbs then move in circular patterns, pulling the underlying tissue and thus effecting an increase in circulation to the part.

Stimulating massage is designed to bring about general body stimulation and a sense of well-being or euphoria. The strokes can be classified as percussion, kneading, and vibration. *Tapotement* (percussion), the beating type of massage, consists of a cupping, clapping, or hacking movement of the hands in striking the body to bring about a stimulating response. *Pétrissage* (kneading) is a technique wherein soft tissue, held between the thumb and forefinger, is alternately rolled and twisted to stimulate fluid drainage. *Vibration* massage can be performed by the fingers. However, it is usually given by means of a vibrating machine.

Physiological considerations

Throughout history many claims have been made as to the curative effects of massage, but most of these claims have not been substantiated. Manipulation of the joints and soft tissue is not a panacea but rather is a useful adjunct to other modalities. In athletics massage activates both mechanical and reflex responses that initiate certain physiological changes within the body. Massage also effects psychological responses such as relaxation or invigoration.

Mechanical responses. Mechanical responses to massage are effects that occur as a direct result of the graded pressures and movements of the hand. Such action encourages venous and lymphatic drainage and mildly stretches superficial tissue. Connective tissue can be effectively stretched by friction massage which helps to prevent rigidity in scar formation. When enforced inactivity is imposed on the athlete as the aftermath of an injury, or when edema surrounds a joint, the stagnation of circulation may be prevented by employing certain massage techniques. Massage can also increase nutrition and metabolism of the musculature, and it aids in the speedy removal of metabolites such as lactic acid.[1]

Reflex responses. The reflex effects of massage are processes that, in response to a nerve impulse initiated through rubbing the body, are transmitted to one organ by afferent nerve fibers and then respond back to another organ by efferent fibers. Reflex responses elicit a variety of organ reactions, such as body relaxation, stimulation, and increased circulation.

Relaxation can be induced by slow and superficial stroking of the skin. It is a type of massage that is beneficial for tense, anxious athletes who may profit from gentle treatment.

Stimulation is attained by quick, brisk action that causes a contraction of superficial tissue. The benefits derived by the athlete are predominantly psychological. He feels invigorated after intense manipulation of the tissue. In the early days of American sports, stimulation massage was given as a warm-up procedure but it has gradually lost popularity because of the time involved and the recognition that it is relatively ineffectual.

Increase in circulation is accomplished by mechanical and reflex stimuli. Together they cause the capillaries to dilate and be drained of fluid as a result of firm outside pressure—thus stimulating cell metabolism, eliminating toxins, and increasing lymphatic and venous circulation. In this way the healing process is aided.[1]

Technique of athletic massage

Massage in athletics is usually confined to a specific area and is seldom given to the full body. The time required for giving an adequate and complete body massage is approximately an hour. It is not feasible for a trainer or coach to devote this much time to one athlete; 5 to 10 minutes is usually all that is required for massaging a given area.

Massage lubricants. To enable the hands to slide easily over the body, a friction-proofing medium must be used. Rubbing the dry body can cause gross skin irritation by tearing and breaking off the hair. Many mediums can be used to advantage as lubricants, such as fine powders, oil liniments, or almost any substance having a petroleum base.

Positioning the athlete. Proper positioning for massage is of great importance. The injuried part must be made easily accessible to the operator, and at the same time the athlete must be in a comfortable position.

Confidence. Lack of confidence on the part of the masseur is easily transmitted through inexperienced hands. Every effort should be made to think out the procedure to be used and to present a confident appearance to the athlete.

Effleurage. Effleurage or stroking (Fig. 12-1) is divided into light and deep methods. Light stroking is designed primarily to be sedative, soothing, and relaxing. It is also used in the early stages of injury treatment. Deep stroking is a therapeutic compression of soft tissue, which encourages venous and lymphatic drainage. A particular method of effleurage is used for each body part. By stroking proximally first and then gradually moving distally, proper venous flow is assured.

Light and deep stroking of the back: When stroking the back, the heel of the hand is pushed upward upon the back of the athlete to the heavy trapezius muscle, where the fingers encircle and lift the soft tissue (trapezial milking), and then trail down to where the stroke commenced. The stroke starts in the lower lumbar area and as close as possible to the vertebral column. The hands stroke upward, covering the entire length of the spine and over the tops of the shoulders. When the length of the spine has been covered, the fingers move out from the center about ½ inch and trail down the back to start the succeeding stroke. Progressively the hands move out to the periphery of the back until the whole area has been rubbed. The trainer then proceeds to move inward toward the center. To facilitate relaxation as well as vascular drainage, the hands should maintain a definite rhythm and never lose contact with the athlete's back. Another excellent relaxation technique is to initiate a slow stroking directly over and down the full length of the spinal column.

Stroking of the lower limb: When effleurage is applied to the lower limb, the same principles as those used in back massage must be followed: begin the stroking at about the middle of the thigh, rubbing upward over the buttocks to the lower back, and then trail down to a point below the place where the stroke was initiated. Each stroke starts below and out from the preceding one, until the entire limb has been massaged. A pad should be placed under

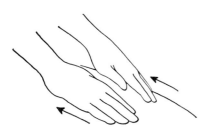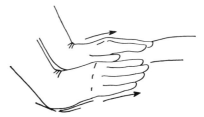

Fig. 12-1. Effleurage.

the knee and the ankle. Pressure should be applied lightly in these areas.

Friction. The friction type of massage (Fig. 12-2) is used primarily on joints and areas where tissue is thin. The action is initated by bracing with the heels of the hands, then either holding the thumbs steady and moving the fingers in a circular motion or holding the fingers steady and moving the thumbs in a circular motion. Each method is adaptable to the type of area or articulation that is being massaged. The motion is started at a central point and then a circular movement is initiated, the hands moving in opposite directions and away from the center point. The purpose is to stretch the underlying tissue, develop friction in the area, and increase circulation around the joint.

Pétrissage. Kneading or pétrissage (Fig. 12-3) is a technique adaptable primarily to loose and heavy tissue areas such as the trapezius, the latissimus dorsi, or the triceps muscles. The procedure consists of picking up the muscle and skin tissue be-

tween the thumb and forefinger of each hand and rolling and twisting it in opposite directions. As one hand is rolling and twisting, the other is commencing to pick up the adjacent tissue. The kneading action wrings out the muscle, thus loosening adhesions and squeezing congestive materials into the general circulation. It should be noted that picking up skin may cause an irritating pinch. Whenever possible, deep muscle tissue should be gathered and lifted.

Tapotement. The most popular methods of tapotement or percussion (Fig. 12-4) are the cupping and the hacking movements.

Cupping: The cupping action is designed to produce an invigorating and stimulating sensation. It is a series of percussion movements rapidly duplicated at a constant tempo. The hands of the trainer are cupped to such an extent that the beat emits a dull thudding sound, quite opposite to the sound of the slap of the open hand. The hands move alternately, from the wrist, with the elbow flexed and the upper arm

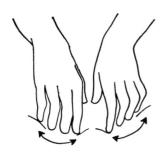

Fig. 12-2. Friction.

Fig. 12-3. Pétrissage.

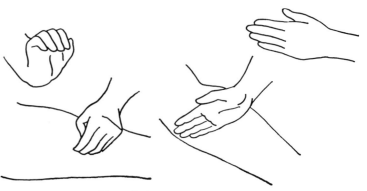

Fig. 12-4. Tapotement.

stabilized. The cupping action should be executed until the skin in the area develops a pinkish coloration.

Hacking: Hacking can be used in conjunction with cupping to bring about a varied stimulation of the sensory nerves. It is done in a way similar to cupping, with the exception that the hands are rotated externally and the ulnar or little finger border of the hand is the striking surface. It should be noted that only the heavy muscle areas should be treated in this manner.

Procedures for effective massage

Besides knowing the different kinds of massage, the trainer should have an understanding of how to give the most effective massage. The following rules should be employed whenever possible:

1. Make the athlete comfortable:
   a. See that he is in proper position on the table.
   b. Pad the areas of the body that may be put under stress while massaging.
   c. Keep the training room at a constant 72° F. temperature.
   d. Maintain the athlete's modesty by draping him with a blanket or towel, exposing only those body parts that are to be treated.
2. Develop a confident, gentle approach when massaging:
   a. Assume a position that is easy both on you and on the athlete.
   b. Avoid using too harsh a stroke, or further insult to the injury may result.
3. To ensure proper lymphatic and venous drainage always stroke toward the heart.
4. Know when to use and when to omit massage:
   a. Never give a massage when there may be a local or general infection. To do so may encourage its spread or aggravate the condition.
   b. Never apply massage directly over a recent injury; keep stroking limited to the periphery. Massaging over recent injuries may dis-

lodge the clot organization and start bleeding. It is desirable to wait 36 hours following injury when applying massage directly to the area.[2]

PASSIVE MOBILIZATION TECHNIQUES

Joint mobilization may be defined as a freeing of encumbered joints to allow a range of motion within anatomical and physiological limitations. Any disturbance in the musculature or connective tissue surrounding a joint can restrict the amplitude of movement. Injuries in athletics can cause muscle weaknesses, poor bony alignments, or abnormal tightness of the connective tissue surrounding the articulations. Abnormal muscle or fascial tightness of the trunk and lower extremities can be reflected in postural deviations. Restoration of normal joint alignment and strength is of the utmost importance to the athlete. Optimal range of motion must be obtained so that the athlete may perform adequately and have the postural balance and elasticity needed to withstand the majority of traumatic forces incurred in his sport.

The human body can be mobilized either through active exercise performed by the athlete himself or through passive measures that are conducted by the trainer. Here our discussion will be confined to the passive approach.

Passive manipulation is defined as the passive movement of a body part by the trainer with no aid on the part of the subject. *Passive stretching* is the extension of the tissue surrounding and adjacent to an articulation so that its range of motion can be increased.

Effective techniques of manipulation and stretching are invaluable as a sequel to massage in the treatment of athletic injuries. Massage increases the healing process of a part, and mobilization methods help to maintain its function. The trainer, to avert additional insult to the injury, should fully understand the *indications* for mobilization, the correct *positioning* for most effective movement of the part, procedures for the proper *execution* of various actions, and, finally, the *precautions* to be observed.

Indications. It is well known that acute or chronic conditions may result in a limited range of motion. After the effects of an internal injury to a joint have subsided, normal movement should be encouraged whenever it is possible without deterring the healing process. Internal scar tissue and adhesions resulting from joint inactivity can often be averted through passive exercising of the part. In chronic conditions there may be a special problem, because overuse or abnormal stresses may have been the etiological factors. Hence, every precaution must be taken to maintain function without additional aggravation. This may require that there be less passive stretching used, thereby sacrificing function for adequate and complete healing.

Positioning. The trainer must have complete understanding of the injury and of the mobilization technique that is to be employed. Poor positioning and improper isolation of the part to be treated may cause increased insult to the injury. The athlete's confidence in the ability of the trainer will be jeopardized if abnormal stresses or strains are manifested outside the injured area.

Execution. When passive mobilization is given, the athlete must be completely relaxed so that the connective tissue, rather than the musculature, may be stretched. If the subject is tense and apprehensive, a lead-up massage combined with soothing conversation may put him at ease. When mobilization is about to begin, the athlete should hyperventilate by taking a series of deep breaths and exhaling slowly each time. When the trainer has decided that the athlete is at ease and thoroughly relaxed, he initiates the manipulation or stretch during one of the exhalations. Exhaling helps the athlete avoid tensing a particular muscle group in anticipation of the mobilization procedure. Quick or extremely harsh moves should be avoided. Emphasis should be placed on steady, progressive movement.

Precautions. To ensure adequate and safe mobilization, the following should be noted:

1. Never attempt mobilization of a suspected fracture.

2. Always wait until internal hemorrhage has subsided before attempting mobilization.

3. Increase the circulation to an area prior to any stretching.

4. Position the athlete to effect the best results without strain to other parts of the body.

5. Before mobilization takes place, have the athlete completely relaxed to ensure the stretching of connective tissue as opposed to musculature.

SELECTED MOBILIZATION PROCEDURES

The following selected mobilization techniques are commonly conducted in athletic training programs by experienced trainers. Additional techniques may be found in Appendix A.

Cervical region
Traction stretch

Indications. When muscle contractures occur in the cervical region, traction may aid in securing relaxation. Traction can be given by manual stretching (Fig. 12-5) or by means of a mechanical traction device. Both have their values. Manual traction is usually given as a follow-up to a rotation stretch and is used for only a short period of time. When traction is needed over an extended period of time, as in a severe neck

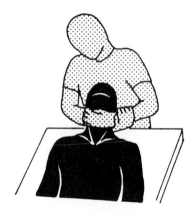

Fig. 12-5. Traction stretch.

strain, progressive mechanical traction may be indicated by the physician.

Positioning. The athlete lies supine and completely relaxed. The trainer stands at the head of the table, cupping his left hand and grasping the point of the athlete's chin. Next, he places his right forearm under the cervical curve of the athlete's neck and grasps the left wrist. In this position the head is securely stabilized and will allow a secure, comfortable pull.

A traction device should be used only under the direction of a physician. The starting weight resistance should be no more than from 10 to 15 pounds. The athlete's tolerance increases progressively with each treatment. Application time may range from 10 to 20 minutes. It is suggested that heat in some form be applied along with the traction to produce muscle relaxation.

Execution. Before passive traction is applied a light effleurage massage is advisable to obtain muscle relaxation. After assuming the traction position, the trainer pulls gently until the athlete's neck is at its greatest length. At this point traction is maintained for approximately 2 minutes.

Precautions. Traction should never be initiated by the trainer if there is any possibility of a fracture. In any severe condition of the neck a physician must be consulted before traction is applied. Massage and relaxation techniques should be applied before traction is given. Sudden movements or excessive elongation of the neck should be avoided. Before stretch is given, the trainer must be sure that the athlete's chin is depressed, keeping the back of the neck as flat as possible. The force of the stretch should be felt along the entire cervical and thoracic spine.

Thoracic region
Chest lift stretch

Indications. The chest lift (Fig. 12-6) is a general thoracic stretch designed to extend the spinalis muscle group lying along the vertebral column. It may be used to advantage for mild strains and for a general loosening of the thoracic cage.

Positioning. The athlete sits with his legs extended and his fingers interlaced behind his head. The trainer stands behind the athlete and places one knee on the table. He then put his arms through the arms of the athlete, placing his hands directly under the posterior rib cage, and instructs the athlete to lie back on his knee.

Execution. While lying with his spine directly over the trainer's knee, the athlete is instructed to take a deep breath and exhale. At this time the trainer pushes downward with his arm on the athlete's arms and presses the athlete's rib cage upward with his hands.

Precautions. Avoid stretching in cases in which possible rib or vertebral fractures are suspected. *Note:* Do not apply too much force to the shoulders.

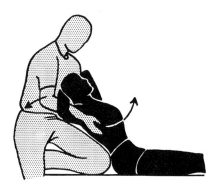

Fig. 12-6. Chest lift stretch.

Fig. 12-7. Trunk rotation stretch.

Trunk rotation stretch

Indications. Limited ranges of motion on trunk rotation may be increased by use of the trunk rotation stretch.[3]

Positioning. The athlete sits on a stool or chair with his hips against the back of the chair and his feet planted firmly on the floor (Fig. 12-7). The trainer stands to one side of the chair, facing the athlete. The trainer then places his outside leg over the knees of the athlete, stabilizing the lower limbs; he reaches around the back of the athlete's upper trunk, grasps the shoulder farthest from him and pulls it toward him. Simultaneously, he places his free hand on the athlete's near shoulder and pushes forward, thus affecting a forced torsion of the athlete's upper trunk.

Execution. The athlete should exhale as the trainer pulls him into trunk rotation, which should be executed with a slow and even pressure, beyond the point of restriction. It is desirable that the athlete have at least a 90-degree range of motion.

Precautions. Make certain that the athlete's hips are maintained in a stabilized position. Do not attempt to stretch when the athlete's lungs are saturated with air.

Lumbosacral region
Low back rotation stretch

Indications. Increasing the range of motion of the low back often relieves the irritation of strain and chronic fibromyositis.

Positioning. The athlete lies in a supine position with his hips turned laterally to the trunk, the upper leg flexed at a 90-degree angle. The trainer stands at the middle of the table, facing the athlete, and places the hand that is on the side of the athlete's feet directly on the sacrum, positioning the other hand on the athlete's shoulder.

Execution. In this position the trainer stabilizes the athlete's shoulder and with a scissors action pushes the pelvis forward, thereby initiating a stretch (Fig. 12-8).

Precautions. Do not stretch if there is a possibility of a fracture. Do not thrust, but stretch with an even and steady movement. Do not stretch beyond normal, relaxed limitations.

Thigh region
Hamstring stretch

Indications. Athletes who have muscle spasm or a limited range of hip motion or who have recently recovered from a strain of the hamstring muscle group require passive stretching.

Positioning. The athlete lies supine on the table with his legs extended. The trainer, facing the athlete's hips, holds down the leg nearest him and gradually raises the opposite leg with the knee straight (Fig. 12-9).

Execution. The leg is lifted gradually and sufficiently to cause a moderate degree of discomfort in the hamstring area. The leg

Fig. 12-8. Low back rotation stretch.

is then returned gradually to the table.

Precautions. Apply massage and heat before stretching. Move slowly to permit complete relaxation. After the stretch, the leg must be lowered slowly to avoid muscle spasm.

Hip flexor stretch

Indications. A recent strain in the hip area or an abnormally tightened hip flexor may require passive stretching.

Positioning. The athlete lies on his back with one knee bent over the end of the table and the other flexed on his chest (Fig. 12-10). The trainer stands transversely at the lower end of the table, facing the athlete's hips. With one hand he stabilizes the leg hanging over the end of the table, and the other hand is placed on the flexed thigh.

Execution. The trainer presses gently on the flexed thigh with a steadily increasing force until there is moderate discomfort.

Precautions. Before stretching of the hip flexors, the area should be well heated by moist hot packs or the whirlpool.

Shoulder girdle
Shoulder joint stretch

Indications. Following an injury to the muscular and capsular tissue surrounding the shoulder joint, the range of motion is

Fig. 12-9. Hamstring stretch.

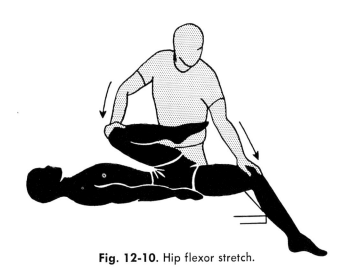

Fig. 12-10. Hip flexor stretch.

Fig. 12-11. Shoulder joint stretch.

quite often hampered. To encourage normal function, active and passive exercise must be taken by the athlete.

Positioning. The athlete lies on his side with the affected shoulder upward. The trainer stands transversely at the back of the athlete and, stabilizing the athlete's shoulder joint with the hand toward the head, he grasps the wrist of the patient with the other hand (Fig. 12-11).

Execution. In this position the trainer forces movement in all directions, up to the point of mild discomfort.

Precautions. The shoulder musculature should be fully warmed up before stretching. Avoid overstretching.

Cryotherapy, thermotherapy, and electrical therapy

Cryotherapy, thermotherapy, and electrical therapies play vital roles in recovery from athletic injuries. There are numerous varieties within each category, making it possible for any athletic program to utilize them in some form. The purpose of the following is to indicate the values of each so that intelligent selections can be made.

CRYOTHERAPY

Cold therapy has been mentioned as a modality in medical reports of past cen-turies. However, there has been a recent revitalization in cryotherapy as a possible adjunct to the treatment of neuromuscular affections.

The physiological basis for using cold therapy is difficult to glean from the literature. Confusion exists as to whether its therapeutic values are primarily neurologi-cal or circulatory or both. Findings indi-cate that vasoconstriction is followed by periods of vasodilation. Moore and others[5] state that the positive effects of ice therapy are primarily anesthetic in nature; cold decreases spasticity, which may accompany musculoskeletal injury. Current research seems to indicate that cold penetrates deeper tissue with greater effect than does heat.[6] There are also indications that cold exposure from 10 to 30 minutes results in vasoconstriction, while longer exposure results in vasodilation and increased cir-culation.[7] In a recent study Morris[8] con-cluded that application of a cryogenic agent immediately following virorous exercise which was designed to induce soreness pre-vented postexercise soreness.

Traditionally, cold application is given in athletic training to constrict superficial blood vessels, producing local inhibition of circulation. Whenever trauma occurs in sports, the immediate use of cold combined with pressure tends to prevent internal hemorrhage and aids in faster clot organiza-tion.

Methods of cryotherapy

Cold can be applied in several ways, depending upon time and the availability of material. The following are four common methods employed by the athletic trainer.

Cold packs are a versatile means for ap-plying cold therapy. They may consist of bags filled with ice, commercial chemical cold packs, or simply toweling saturated in an ice water slush. If placed on the affected part, the cold may control hemorrhage of the fresh injury or diminish pain of sub-acute or chronic conditions.

Ice water immersion in water 65° F. or lower is a simple means for treating a part.

After analgesia, which occurs rapidly, the athlete is encouraged to move the part in a normal manner. A combination of ice water and hydromassage action of a whirlpool has been found to reduce initial swelling and encourage rapid healing.

Spray coolants such as ethyl chloride have been used in athletics for several years. Their primary use has been to reduce local spasm and hemorrhage caused by injury. The trainer holds the ethyl chloride dispenser about 18 inches from the injury and sprays the skin with a back and forth motion until a fine frost appears. Caution must be taken not to freeze the part but to only lightly anesthetize the area. It is doubtful whether using ethyl chloride on acute injuries has any lasting effects other than a psychological one.

Ice massage has been used in athletics to some advantage. The technique calls for massaging the affected part with an ice cylinder obtained from freezing water in a frozen fruit juice can.[9] Grasping the ice cylinder with a towel, the trainer begins to massage the affected part in a circular manner, continuing until the part progresses from an uncomfortable chill sensation to an ache and then numbness. When the part exhibits analgesia and loss of pain, a program of static stretching and mobilization is executed by the athlete. Such a technique allows for simplicity of application, little expense, and a means for carrying on home treatment.

THERMOTHERAPY

Thermotherapy (heat application) for disease and traumatic injuries is as old as mankind. Primitive societies found that heat not only afforded analgesic effects but possessed healing qualities as well. Heat speeds up circulation, encourages venous and lymphatic drainage, and as a result hastens cell metabolism and healing. Many forms of heat can be used: (1) moist heat, as derived from whirlpool or water packs, (2) dry heat, such as that of the infrared lamp, and (3) the penetrating therapeutic agencies of diathermy and ultrasound. Heat is provided through either conduction, convection, or conversion. *Conduction* refers to heating by direct contact with a hot medium, as in whirlpool or hot-water tub baths. *Convection* is a form of heating indirectly, or through another medium; for example, the heated air obtained from a stove. *Conversion* is the production of heat by other forms of energy, such as in diathermy, which produces heat from short-wave radio frequencies.

Heat awakens closed capillary beds, increasing the fluid quantity of the tissue by speeding the blood flow and dilating the vessels in the surrounding area. With the increase of blood and capillary dilation, tissue temperature rises, hastening chemical changes and metabolism. Leukocytes and antibodies become concentrated in the inflamed area, thus helping to clear the area of both microorganisms and toxins. Increased circulation to a part diminishes congestion and will alleviate pain sensations. Pain from trauma is partially the result of local ischemia, which causes anoxia and chemical irritation of pain receptors. Heat also reduces spasm in muscles by temporarily inhibiting the nerve activity to those muscles.

Important contraindications and precautions regarding the use of heat from any source are listed below:

1. Never apply heat where there is a loss of sensation.

2. Never apply heat immediately after an injury.

3. Never apply heat when there is decreased arterial circulation.

4. Never apply heat directly over the eyes or the genital areas.

Hydrotherapy and other superficial therapies

Hydrotherapy is the most widely used modality in athletic training. It is readily available for use in any athletic program. The greatest disadvantage of hydrotherapy devices is the difficulty incurred in controlling the therapeutic effects. This is primarily caused by the rapid dissipation of the heat radiation, which makes it difficult to maintain a constant tissue temperature.

Physiological effects. For the most part moist heat aids the healing process by causing higher superficial tissue temperatures and muscle relaxation. Superficial tissue is a poor thermal conductor, and temperature rises quickly on the skin surface as compared to the underlying tissues. Evidence indicates that cutaneous and subcutaneous circulation is increased by topical heating. However, joint and muscle circulation displays little increase.

Indications for use. Hydrotherapy is best applied to postacute conditions of sprains, strains, and contusions. Hydrotherapy produces mild healing qualities with a general relaxation of tense, spasmed tissue.

Techniques of application. Each hydrotherapy modality has its own technique of application. Basically, the temperature of the water must be kept constant, within a range of 100° to 120° F., with variances that depend upon the texture and pigmentation of the athlete's skin being permitted. A light complexioned individual cannot, as a rule, withstand intense moist heat. Conversely, the darker pigmented athlete is able to endure hotter temperatures.

Precautions. The contraindications and precautions in the use of hydrotherapy are the same as for other types of heat devices. The following considerations must be given:

1. Avoid overheating sensitive skin, the eyes, and the genital organs.

2. Never apply heat to a recent injury until hemorrhage has subsided.

3. Use caution when the athlete is submerged in heated water, since unconsciousness may result as blood is withdrawn from the head and centralized in other areas.

Moist hot packs

Moist hot packs fall into the category of conductive heating, whereby a heated device is brought into direct contact with the skin. Packs, usually commercial, are thermostatically controlled pads that are laid on the skin after having been covered by toweling to prevent burning. Thermo-

statically controlled heat pads containing a silicon gel retain a constant heat for a period of 20 to 30 minutes. Moist heat packs are useful because of their adaptability for positioning anywhere on the body. The trainer can secure the same effect as that obtained with the commercial pack by placing a moist towel on the part to be treated and positioning an infrared lamp so that it radiates directly on the towel.

Immersion baths

Water is a reasonably good conductor of heat with little heat loss to an immersed part. The two types of immersion baths principally used in athletic training are the local bath and the whirlpool hydromassage.

Hydro baths are an adaptable, inexpensive, and readily available method of providing hydrotherapy. Besides increasing circulation, the buoyancy of the water allows mild exercise of painful areas and produces a soothing sensation. Temperatures up to 120° F. can be used with complete safety for 10 to 30 minutes. The heated water soak is often used as a vehicle for selected germicides and medications used to treat infection.

Whirlpool (hydromassage) is a combination therapy, giving the athlete both a massaging action and a hot-water bath (Fig. 12-12). It has become one of the most popular thermotherapies used in athletic training. Through water agitation and the heat transmitted to the injured area, local circulation can be increased, which is usually followed by a reduction in congestion, spasm, and pain. The following general treatment approach is suggested when using the whirlpool in athletics:

Injury situation	Water temperature	Duration of treatment
Phase II of acute injury (see Tables 13-1 to 13-3)	60°- 65°	10 min.
Phase III of acute injury	90°	10 min.
Phase IV of acute injury	100°-105°	10-20 min.
Chronic or old injury	105°-110°	10-20 min.
To warm part before activity	100°-110°	5 min.
Full body immersion	100°	5-10 min.

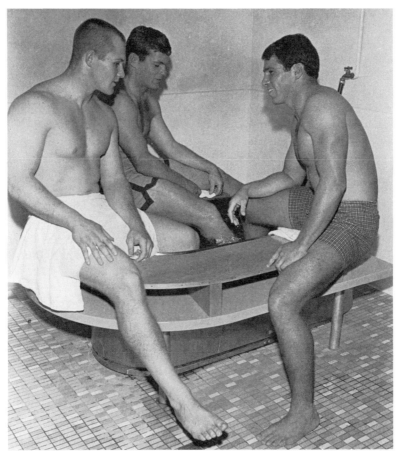

Fig. 12-12. Using whirlpool bath. (Courtesy Kent Henderson, Long Beach Independent Press Telegram.)

When using the whirlpool very early after an injury the water jet should be directed toward the sides of the tank. Directing the stream of water on the injury will only aggravate the condition and perhaps cause additional bleeding. It should be also noted that full body immersion can result in unconsciousness if the immersion period is too long and the water is too hot.

Contrast baths are used by many trainers to relieve swelling and muscle spasm. The affected part is immersed alternately in water that is 110° F. and 60° F. Such alternation causes contraction and relaxation of blood vessels in the area and maintains a constant increase in circulation. The following sequence and length of time of immersion in each temperature is modified from Rusk.[1] The total treatment time is from 20 to 25 minutes.

110° from 5 to 10 minutes, then 2 minutes of 60°
110° for 4 minutes, then 2 minutes of 60°
110° for 4 minutes, then 2 minutes of 60°
110° for 4 minutes, then 2 minutes of 60°
110° for 4 minutes, then 2 minutes of 60°
Complete routine with 5 minutes of 105°

Other superficial thermotherapies. Water percussion, the use of heated air, and water vapor baths are other therapeutic media available for use in the athletic program. *Water percussion* can be given to the body generally, in the form of a brisk shower bath, or specifically, through a water stream from a hose. A shower with a temperature of between 100° to 105° F. for a period of

10 to 20 minutes can produce soothing sedation to a fatigued athlete or relieve the congestion of sore muscles. A water jet from a hose nozzle played directly on a towel that covers a subacute strain or sprain can offer a deep effleurage massage effect to the injured area. The towel should be folded into four thicknesses and laid over the injured area to prevent skin irritation from the heavy water stream. The length of application time should not exceed 10 minutes at a temperature of 110° F.

Heated air and *vapor baths* are ancient instruments for treating ills and for causing loss of body weight through profuse perspiring. Today we see these devices used by athletes who must make a particular competitive weight, such as is specified in wrestling. Often, these individuals attempt to "make" weight the day of the contest. Such extreme heating of the body produces extreme fluid loss, which is fatiguing and is generally harmful to the athlete. Heated air baths are usually taken in cabinets containing electrically heated air. Such baths produce profuse perspiration resulting in a high fluid loss. Such therapy should be given in temperatures ranging from 130° to 160° F. and is most effective at from 10- to 20-minute exposures. Heated air therapy is less fatiguing than vapor therapy, because the slower heating of the tissue allows the skin to cool by perspiration. Vapor baths (steam baths)are similar in function to the heated air baths, with the exception that highly heated water is used in its vaporized form. Temperature is maintained at 105° to 115° F. for 20 to 30 minutes in either a cabinet or a closed room. During the first 10 minutes of heating, the athlete feels physically invigorated because of the stimulation of the central nervous system. If the heating continues for more than 20 minutes, a depression of the system will result. This extreme fluctuation of nervous energy causes greater physical fatigue than that which results from dry heat. Generally speaking, both heated air baths and vapor baths aid in sedating and in producing hyperemia of muscle and articular tissue.

Analgesic balm pack

Application of a petroleum base rubefacient to postacute injuries is one of the most popular therapeutic agents used in athletics. Analgesic balm chiefly contains methyl salicylate (oil of wintergreen), capsium (red pepper) and menthol, It acts as a skin counterirritant. Because it is applied directly to the skin, it allows the athlete freedom of movement while he is receiving a therapeutic increase in local circulation.

Physiological effects. The irritation of the analgesic balm is claimed by many trainers to stimulate peripheral sensory and vasomotor nerves, creating capillary dilation and a mild anesthesia at the injured site. However, the exact nature of the analgesic action of the balm is not known. The sensation of heat may be caused by the rubefacient irritation, which stimulates superficial pain fibers and increases local capillary circulation.

Application. Many and varied methods of applying analgesic balm packs have been devised by trainers and coaches. The following is the most popular procedure (Fig. 12-13).

Materials needed: Analgesic balm, nonsterile cotton, a sheet of paper or plastic, and an elastic bandage.

Procedure:

1. A thin layer of balm, approximately ⅛ inch thick, is spread over the injured site.

2. A layer of nonsterile cotton or cloth is placed over the balm.

3. A sheet of paper or plastic is laid over the cotton or cloth.

4. An elastic bandage from 3 to 6 inches in width (depending on the area covered) is wrapped around the back of the balm pack to hold it in place.

This method ensures an airtight medium that will generate heat for as long as 3 hours.

Indications. The use of the analgesic packs as a treatment is as varied as any other form of heat therapy. Most posttraumatic and chronic conditions can be treated in this manner. Sprains, strains, and muscle

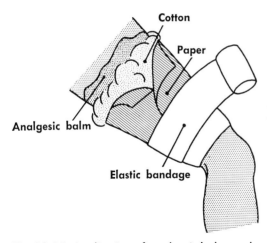

Cotton

Paper

Analgesic balm

Elastic bandage

Fig. 12-13. Application of analgesic balm pack.

contusions will respond adequately to the application of analgesic balm. Because of its pungent wintergreen odor and greasy residue, it is more adaptable in athletics than it is in regular civilan therapy.

Precautions. Blistering does not usually occur from an analgesic pack; but on occasion, when other forms of heat therapy have preceded the balm pack, burns may result. The trainer or coach should be cautious in applying an analgesic immediately after a whirlpool or an infrared treatment. A waiting period of at least 15 minutes should be observed.

ELECTRICAL THERAPIES

Electrotherapy, when *used by qualified personnel,* can add considerably to the rehabilitation of athletic injuries. The devices fall primarily into four types as used in the training room: infrared therapy; muscle stimulators, which stimulate muscle contraction with various speeds and intensities; short wave diathermy, which gives deep, penetrating heat through high-frequency current; and ultrasound therapy, which infiltrates and increases circulation to the intracellular tissue by means of high-frequency sound waves.

Infrared therapy

The term *infrared* pertains to the wavelength of radiant energy beyond the red end of the light spectrum. The waves that are emitted come from objects with a higher temperature than the surrounding environment. Any heated material giving off infrared waves has some therapeutic value. Various lamps have been devised to give off radiant therapeutic energy. Therapeutic heat lamps are classified either as *radiant* or *nonradiant.* Radiant lamps contain materials such as carbon filaments or tungsten that emit visible rays; nonradiant lamps usually consist of coiled wires covered by some refractory material that radiates heat from the wire.

Energy from both types of lamps penetrates the skin and underlying tissue in similar fashion. It has been found that maximum tissue heating without blistering may extend to a depth of 1 inch, but only a small quantity of radiation usually attains this level.

Physiological effects. Infrared heating results primarily in superficial radiations causing dilation of the superficial vessels. Circulation increases in the area being heated but not to any great extent. The main advantage to be gained from superficial heating is that it aids massage and passive or active mobilization procedures. Light exposure, in some instances, will give analgesia to painful areas. Heavy exposure may indicate signs of blanching, giving the skin a mottled appearance.

Operation. The athlete lies on a table in a relaxed position. After the lamp is allowed to warm up for 10 minutes, it is placed at a distance of 18 to 24 inches over the part to be heated. The exposure time can safely range from 20 to 30 minutes. A moistened towel placed over the skin may aid in preventing overheating of the area (Fig. 12-14). A thin film of analgesic balm spread over the injured part will encourage faster counterirritation when desired.

Precautions. Overdosage of infrared heating can cause severe skin irritation and burns. The trainer must allow for the variances in the skin textures and be aware of the differences in individual heat tolerances.

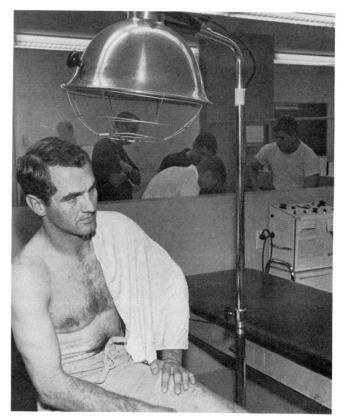

Fig. 12-14. Combining infrared heat with wet towel. (Courtesy Kent Henderson, Long Beach Independent Press Telegram.)

Diathermy

Diathermy is the therapeutic application of high-frequency electrical current to the tissue below the body surface. There are two basic diathermy devices in extensive use today: the shortwave and the microwave. Each offers unique therapeutic qualities to the less dense tissues of the body, such as fat or the more fluid muscle tissues. Generally, the use of a diathermy machine must be under strict control, and a prescription for its use must be obtained from the physician.

Shortwave diathermy

The shortwave diathermy machine applies a high-frequency (of over 10 megacycles), oscillating, electrical current to the deep tissues of the body. The electrical current is converted to give a homogeneous heating effect. The current is brought to the patient through two cords from the machine generator. The cords terminate in loose cables, drum electrodes, or pads, depending upon the operator's preference.

Physiological effects. Shortwave diathermy has been purported to raise the internal tissue temperature as much as 9° F. With this temperature rise there is increased blood flow through the dilated vessels, which in turn accelerates the metabolic processes and phagocytosis.

Indications. Deep diathermy heat is valuable when local hyperemia is needed. Subacute and chronic conditions can be treated equally well with shortwave devices. Acute conditions should be treated after a 24- to 48-hour period to allow for the control of hemorrhage. Low intensity and short duration of current can be applied to acute in-

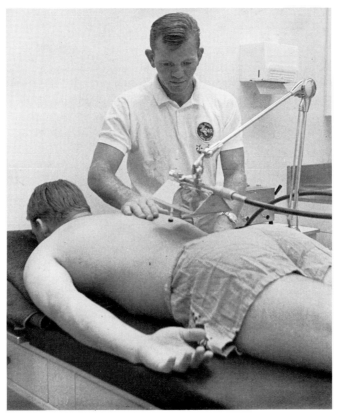

Fig. 12-15. Microwave diathermy to lower back region. (Courtesy Kent Henderson, Long Beach Independent Press Telegram.)

juries, but in most cases such early treatment should be avoided. Wherever practical, a daily administration of 10- to 20-minute treatments should be given for best results.

Microwave diathermy

Microwave diathermy produces 2,450 megacycles per second as compared to approximately 10 megacycles in shortwave diathermy. Shortwave diathermy treats a widespread area, whereas the microwave diathermy can be directed to a specific area (Fig. 12-15). The microwave energy is generated by a magnetron tube, which directs its current through a coaxial cable.

Physiological effects. As in shortwave diathermy, microwave diathermy increases capillary circulation, local metabolism, and phagocytosis and is purported to penetrate

as far as 2 inches and to raise deep muscle tissue temperature to over 104° F. Temperature increase in deep muscle, compared to subcutaneous tissue, is higher with microwave treatment than with shortwave diathermy.

Operation. Dosage varies according to the condition being treated and to the vascularity of tissue involved. The variation ranges from 15 to 30 minutes of exposure. The device is placed approximately 2 inches from the epidermis.

The advantages of microwave over shortwave diathermy are (1) ease of operation, (2) accurate measurement of dosage, (3) more effective deep tissue heating, and (4) relative comfort afforded the patient.

The disadvantages are (1) superficial burns are more likely with microwave than with shortwave diathermy, and (2) only one side of a joint may be radiated at one time (shortwave diathermy can heat completely around a joint).

Indications. Microwave differs little from shortwave diathermy as to the types of conditions it treats. Most success has been had with joints, bursae, tendon sheaths, and muscle tissue conditions in subacute and chronic inflammatory stages.

Precautions. Precautions in the use of microwave diathermy are essentially the same as for the shortwave diathermy. Basically, areas are contraindicated for microwave diathermy if adhesive tape is present or if application would be over (1) clothing, (2) recent traumatic injury, (3) highly edematous swelling, (4) ischemic areas, (5) epiphyseal growth areas, (6) anesthetic areas, (7) areas over metal implants, or (8) moist skin.

Ultrasound therapy

An ultrasonic therapy unit consists essentially of a generator of radio-frequency electrical energy and an ultrasonic applicator that is coupled to the generator by means of a flexible cable. The applicator (sound head) includes a transducer (quartz crystal) that converts electrical energy into mechanical vibration. Vibratory energy of the transducer is transmitted from the face of the sound head into the body through a coupling medium. This medium is a liquid such as heavy mineral oil or water and is essential to ensure that the sonic impulses are directed properly to the affected part. Sonic waves cannot be transmitted efficiently through air.

Most therapeutic ultrasound machines have calibrated meters that indicate both the total oscillator output, which ranges usually from 15 to 30 watts, and the sound head output, which ranges from 0.1 to 3 watts/sq. cm.

Physiological effect. When applied to an injured area ultrasound produces two effects. The high-frequency sound energy is converted into heat energy as it penetrates the tissue. It has been estimated to raise muscle temperature at a level 2 inches below the surface from 7° to 8° F. A micromassage action also takes place as a result of the sound waves.

Localized heating results principally at the region of the interface or at the point where two different types of tissue, such as bone and muscle, meet. Increased permeability of the cell membrane is produced, as well as increased cell metabolism and detoxification.

Operation. Stationary and moving techniques are employed in the use of the transducer head. Some operators place a water cushion device between the head and the part to be treated. The stationary technique is not widely used because of the dangers involved in regulating its direction and intensity. The moving sound head technique is most prevalent and, according to physicians, offers the most thorough and safest therapy. Movement is employed in two basic patterns. In the *circular method* the transducer is applied in small, overlapping circles. In the *stroking method* the transducer is moved back and forth. The type of application is determined mainly by the skin area to be treated. The circular method is best for localized injuries of soft tissue. In larger, more diffused injury areas the stroking method is best employed. When therapy must be given to irregular surfaces, as over joints, ultrasound should be given in an under-water medium. Water presents an airtight coupling agent and allows sound waves to travel at a consistently high velocity.

Dosage of ultrasound is variable in terms of the conditions treated and should be determined by a physician. Basically, 0.1 watt/sq. cm. to 0.8 watt/sq. cm. is regarded as low intensity; from 0.8 watt/sq. cm. to 1.5 watts/sq. cm. is considered medium intensity; and from 1.5 watts/sq. cm. to 3 watts/sq. cm., high intensity.

Indications. Ultrasound has been found to be effective in both subacute and chronic conditions. It can be recommended by the physician for easing pain and for irritations caused by bursitis, fibrositis, arthritis, and inflammatory conditions that occur in muscles and tendons. Nerve conditions also may be treated by ultrasound (Fig. 12-16).

Precautions. The same precautions must be observed in the use of ultrasound as in any form of deep heat therapy. Avoidance of overexposure to anesthesized areas, hemorrhaging, and acute infection must be observed. In addition to these general contraindications, the following specific areas must be avoided: nerve plexuses, brain, spinal cord, eyes, ears, heart, reproductive organs, and growth areas of long bones.

In the hands of a reasonable and prudent operator ultrasound is a safe adjunct in the care of athletic conditions.

Muscle stimulation

The use of electrical muscle stimulation is quite varied in athletics. Electrical current applied to the skin can test isolated muscles, detect specific sore areas, and initiate a therapeutic action. There are three basic types of low-frequency currents used in physical therapy: (1) *galvanic,* which is a primary direct current used for diagnosing and muscle testing; (2) *faradic,* an interrupted electrical current that is used for stimulating muscles and nerves; and (3) *sinusoidal,* and electrical current that rises gradually to a peak and then reverses and falls back to its beginning point.

Galvanic current. Galvanic current is used little therapeutically in athletics. It is used primarily in testing muscle response and in localizing injury sites for specific therapy.

Faradic current. The alternating response of the faradic mechanism is controlled by a breaker device that allows an intermittent flow of current. From these impulses a rhythmic muscle contraction is elicited. The use of this device prevents muscle atrophy and aids in the general care of subacute and chronic conditions.

Sinusoidal current. In contrast to the abruptly alternating faradic current, the sinusoidal currents gradually and rhythmically rise to a crest and fall to starting point. Therapy using this type of current is excellent for athletic strains or sprains, when mild exercise or the relaxation of fatigued muscles is indicated.

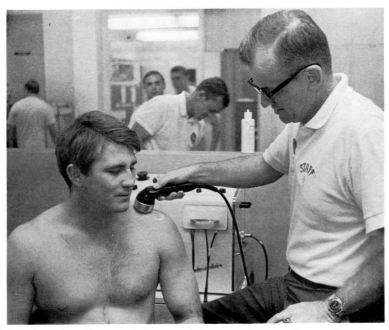

Fig. 12-16. Applying ultrasound therapy. (Courtesy Kent Henderson, Long Beach Independent Press Telegram.)

Physiological effects. Continuous galvanic current is considered by many to result in the following: (1) *vasodilation,* which causes an increase in local circulation; (2) *electro-osmosis,* which brings fluid from the anode to the cathode, thereby increasing osmotic pressure at the cathode and lessening it at the anode; this phenomenon may be effective if the anode is placed over an area of effusion; (3) *electrotonus,* which is caused by galvanic current in the muscles and nerves, thus preventing atrophy and eliminating fatigue; and (4) *counterirritations,* which may relieve pain.

Operation. Current is generated through a machine with a negative and a positive metal electrode leading from it. The metal electrodes are covered by an absorbent material, usually a sponge rubber pad. The pads are moistened and act as a protective divider between the athlete's skin and the electrode. One electrode is set in place over the area to be treated and is secured by a sand bag or an elastic strap. The other electrode is placed in a position in which it will produce the best results from the stimulating electrode.

Current dosage is dependent upon the condition treated. In most cases dosage should be below the point of creating a burning sensation. The length of application can range from 10 to 30 minutes.

Precautions. Muscle stimulation should never be used immediately after an acute injury or where muscle tissues have been torn. Reaching the fatigue stage may aggravate already debilitated muscles. Artificial muscle contraction should never replace voluntary exercise.

REFERENCES

1. Rusk, H. A.: Rehabilitation medicine, ed. 3, St. Louis, 1971, The C. V. Mosby Co.
2. Ryan, A. J.: Medical care of the athlete, New York, 1962, McGraw-Hill Book Co.
3. Billig, H. E., Jr., and Lowendahl, E.: Mobilization of the human body, Palo Alto, Calif., 1949, Stanford University Press.
4. Downey, J.: Physiological effects of heat and cold, J. Amer. Phys. Ther. Ass. 44:713, 1964.
5. Moore, R. J., Jr., Nicolette, N., and Behnke, R.: The therapeutic use of cold (cryotherapy) in the care of athletic injuries, J. Nat. Athletic Trainers Ass. 2:6, 1967.
6. Fisher, E., and Solomon, S.: Physiological responses to heat and cold, Therapeutic Heat and Cold, Baltimore 1965, Waverly Press, Inc. 2:139.
7. Edwards, A. G.: Increasing circulation with cold, J. Nat. Athletic Trainers Ass., 6:1, Spring 1971.
8. Morris, R. J.: An electromyographic investigation of the effect of cold induced muscular soreness, Unpublished master's thesis, California State College, Long Beach, 1972.
9. Hayden, C.: Cryokinetics in an early treatment program, J. Amer. Phys. Ther. Ass. 44:990, 1964.

RECOMMENDED READINGS

Dayton, O. W.: Athletic training and conditioning, New York, 1965, The Ronald Press Co.
Dolan, J. P.: Treatment and prevention of athletic injuries, Danville, Ill., 1967, The Interstate Printers & Publishers, Inc.
Ferguson, A. B., Jr., and Bender, J.: The ABC's of athletic injuries and conditioning, Baltimore, 1964, The Williams & Wilkins Co.
Grant, A.: Massage with ice in the treatment of painful conditions of the musculoskeletal system, Arch. Phys. Med. Rehab. 45:233, 1964.
Krusen, F. H., editor: Handbook of physical medicine and rehabilitation, Philadelphia, 1965, W. B. Saunders Co.
Licht, S., editor: Massage manipulation and traction, New Haven, Conn., 1960, Elizabeth Licht, Publisher.
Licht, S., editor: Therapeutic heat and cold, New Haven, Conn., 1965, Elizabeth Licht, Publisher.
Maitland, G. D.: Vertebral manipulation, London, 1964, Butterworths.
Mennell, J. B.: Manual therapy, Springfield, Ill., 1951, Charles C Thomas, Publisher.
Mennell, J. B.: Physical treatment by movement manipulation and massage, Philadelphia, 1947, The Blakiston Co.
Mennell, J. B.: The science and art of joint manipulation, Philadelphia, 1949, The Blakiston Co.
Moore, R. J., Jr., Nicolette, N., and Behnke, R. S.: The therapeutic use of cold (cryotherapy) in the care of athletic injuries, J. Nat. Athletic Trainers Ass. 2:6, 1967.
Rusk, H. A.: Rehabilitation medicine, St. Louis, 1971, The C. V. Mosby Co.
Tappan, F. M.: Massage techniques, New York, 1961, The Macmillan Co.

CHAPTER 13

Recognition, evaluation, and general care of athletic injuries

Learning to recognize and intelligently evaluate the nature and extent of athletic injuries is of the utmost importance to the trainer or coach. When immediate medical diagnosis is not available, the trainer or coach has the responsibility to determine the extent of specific injuries. He must then make the decisions as to whether or not continued participation would be detrimental to the athlete and whether there is need for medical attention. These questions are among the many that must be answered, and to reach such decisions reasonably and prudently the trainer must be able to distinguish gross pathologies from normal conditions. He must also be able to render immediate and follow-up care of the injury, under the direction of a physician.

Schools accept the responsibility of caring for emergency sicknesses and injuries that occur to the pupils under their jurisdiction. The scope of this responsibility is fairly constant in all school activities with the exception of athletics. The extent of athletic care varies from school to school and among school districts. The range of variations extends from procedures for the handling of minor external wounds to provisions for major physical therapy. It is not our intent to criticize school philosophies on this matter, but we do believe that every effort should be made by schools to provide the best immediate and follow-up care

of athletic injuries that it is possible for them to give.

CLASSIFICATION OF INJURIES

The classification of athletic injuries can be established in many ways. For the sake of simplicity and of clarity, the terms *exposed* and *unexposed* will be used to designate the two classes. Any condition that is external in nature and results in the exposure of superficial and underlying tissue is considered an *exposed* wound. Conversely, any condition that does not break the skin and that is internal in nature is considered to be an *unexposed* wound, even though it may have been caused by an external force. Viewed in a broad sense, athletic conditions result from either acute or chronic occurrences. Acute injuries are the more typical in athletics, since they are incurred suddenly and are usually of short duration. On the other hand, chronic conditions are usually incurred gradually over a long period of time, stemming primarily from a series of acute episodes.

INFLAMMATION; REPAIR AND HEALING

To understand the pathologic conditions incident to athletic contests and the important role that proper management plays in their correction, it is necessary to have a basic knowledge of just how the body responds to an injury.[1]

Inflammation. Inflammation is the local reaction of the body tissues to an irritant. Regardless of causal factors, the basic signs of inflammation are *local heat, swelling, redness, pain,* and *malfunction.* This response takes place either microscopically or macroscopically within the body and is usually followed by repair and healing. The main causative factors of inflammation are (1) trauma, resulting from a blow or mechanical irritation; (2) chemical agents such as insect stings, poison ivy, strong acids or alkalies; (3) thermal extremes of either heat or cold; and (4) pathogenic organisms associated with external and internal infections.

The irritants impose a cellular disruption, which results in metabolic changes, and these changes cause a freeing of substances that begin the inflammatory process. Inflammation is a protective mechanism designed to localize an injury area, rid the body of the irritant, and initiate healing (Fig. 13-1). Essentially, in a localized inflammatory site there occurs a vascular phenomenon that brings about a fluid imbalance, thus causing white blood cells to concentrate at the site; then, by an extravasation of blood in the tissue area, it leads to repair and, finally, to healing.

At the moment an acute injury takes place, blood vessels constrict and cause a diminution of blood at that point. The contraction is transitory; the capillaries then dilate and become engorged with blood.

These reactions disrupt the fluid pressure balance and cause a leakage of blood serum (exudate) into the surrounding tissues. This results in swelling and, possibly, pain caused by pressure on nerve endings. In the opinion of some authorities,[2] the process of attracting leukocytes (white or colorless blood cells) and the increased capillary permeability are caused by the presence of enzymes, which have been given off by the injured tissues.[1-3] The leukocytes form along the sides of the dilated vessel walls (margination), with a fluid stream moving through the center. As the white cells marginate, they press themselves through the capillary walls (diapedesis) and move to the irritant. The multitude of white blood cells surround the irritant by means of a process celled phagocytosis, and begin to engulf and ingest debris. This chain of events is continual until the lesion is healed.

Repair and healing. Fluid and cells accumulate in the areas of tissue insult. This fluid accumulation is known as *exudate* or *edema* and contains many of the ingredients that assist in the healing process.[1] Associated with tissue irritation, and following the vascular and exudative process, are repair and healing (Fig. 13-2). In many cases there is little regeneration of the more specialized living tissues. Few tissues in the human body repair totally; the degree and type of healing that take place are dependent upon the type of tissue involved and

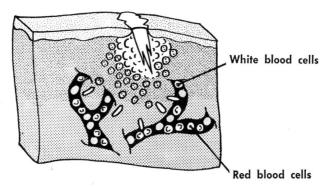

Fig. 13-1. Localized inflammation, with concentration of white blood cells at the injury site. The red cells appear as the nonnucleated bodies, whereas the white cells are nucleated.

the extent of the tissue damage. Repair begins with the exudate of the inflammatory process. Within the exudate are immature connective tissue cells (fibroblasts) together with endothelial cells forming a granular mass called granulation tissue. The granulation tissue gradually replaces the exudate and forms a loose, highly vascularized connective tissue. Eventually, the young connective tissue becomes devoid of blood vessels, leaving a fibrous, inelastic scar tissue.

Two kind of healing will be described. (1) *Primary healing* (healing by first intention) takes place in a wound that has even and closely apposed edges, such as a cut or incision. With this type of wound, if the edges are held in close apposition, a minimum of granulation tissue is produced. (2) *Secondary healing* (healing by secondary intention) results when there are gaping lesions and large tissue losses, which are prone to infection. Union takes place through the formation of granulation tissue. The wound fills in with fibrous tissue and heals from the bottom and sides upward.

INJURY INSPECTION

A logical process must be used if one is to accurately evaluate the extent of an athletic injury. The trainer must be aware of the major signs that reveal the site, nature, and—above all—severity of the injury. Detection of these signs can be facilitated initially in two ways; (1) by understanding the mechanism or traumatic sequence and (2) by methodically inspecting the injury. Knowledge of the mechanism of an injury is extremely important in finding which area of the body is most affected. When the injury mechanism has been determined, the examiner proceeds to the next phase—physical inspection of the affected region. At this point information is gathered by what is seen, what is heard, and what is felt.

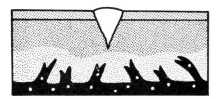

FIVE MINUTES FOLLOWING INJURY

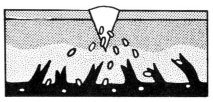

ONE DAY FOLLOWING INJURY

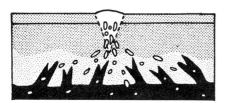

SEVEN DAYS FOLLOWING INJURY

FOURTEEN DAYS FOLLOWING INJURY

NINETY DAYS FOLLOWING INJURY

Fig. 13-2. Healing by secondary intention.

Visual observation. This discloses gross and apparent anatomical distortions such as deformities, swelling, and skin discoloration. These signs, for a trained observer who has seen the actual injury sequence, can indicate the seriousness of the pathology.

Key sounds. Sounds heard by the trainer can often yield valuable information. When the injury is palpated the examiner should be alert for a grating noise or a harsh, rubbing sound that may indicate a fracture. Joint sounds may be detected when either arthritis or an internal derangement is present. When the athlete is questioned about his injury, he should be asked if a noise was heard when the injury occurred. Such sounds as a snap, crack, or pop are often indicative of a bone break.

Feeling or palpation. Feeling or palpating a part with trained fingers can, with the visual and audible signs, give some final clues as to the nature of the injury. While probing the part, the trainer can first determine the scope of the lesion by having the athlete indicate if or where there is irritation present. Palpation also permits the trainer to ascertain the superficiality or depth of the injury as well as its condition.

ACUTE CONDITIONS

Most athletic injuries are acute. Complete understanding of these must be within the province of the physician, the trainer, and the coach if quick and proper treatment and rehabilitation are to be effected.

Acute injuries occur as the result of force that stretches or compresses tissues to the extent that continuity is disrupted. Such trauma usually results in an extravasation of blood in and around the injury site. Therefore, the primary goal of care of an athletic injury is to prevent further insult to the body, to localize and encourage the resolution of the injury, and to allow the normal healing process to take place. Four procedures should be followed in the immediate care of the injury: cold application, compression, elevation, and immobilization.

Cold is commonly applied immediately to injuries with the express purpose of controlling swelling, decreasing muscular spasm, and eliminating some of the discomfort. Duration of cold application may vary from 1 to 72 hours depending on the severity of the injury. *Compression* is often applied to the injury concurrently with cold. Pressure applied in the form of tape or elastic bandage is designed to help control hemorrhage and to localize the injury. *Elevation* of the part also controls edema and encourages hemostasis; *immobilization* in the form of a splint or sling prevents further aggravation of the injury.

Various medical approaches are designed to assist the normal healing process particularly during the very early stages of an injury. One such procedure is to give enzymes either orally or by injection during the first 24 hours of injury. Other approaches include cold, heat, and/or rehabilitative exercises. We believe that cold application should be continued until the injury has stopped hemorrhaging and has begun to organize and heal. When resolution has begun, a gradual increase of heat can be applied to the part (see Table 13-1). *Progressive rehabilitative exercise* also follows the increase of heat. As the injured tissue organizes and consolidates activity can be progressively increased. The best criterion for increasing exercise and heat to any injured part is the extent of palpable point tenderness and indurated thickening.

Exposed wounds

Exposed injuries can be classified primarily into four separate types of skin insults (Fig. 13-3): abrasions, lacerations, incisions, and puncture wounds. The greatest problem these conditions present is their vulnerability to infection through direct exposure to a contaminant. *Abrasions* are conditions wherein the skin is abraded by scraping against a rough surface. The epidermis and dermis are worn away, thus exposing numerous blood capillaries. This general exposure, with dirt and foreign materials scraping and penetrating the skin,

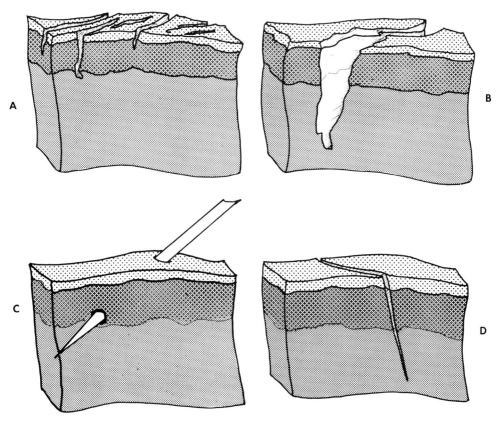

Fig. 13-3. Exposed wound. **A,** Abrasion; **B,** laceration; **C,** puncture; **D,** incision.

increases the probability that infection will result unless the wound is properly debrided and cleansed (see p. 213). *Lacerations* also are common in athletics and occur when a sharp or pointed object tears the tissues, giving a wound the appearance of a jagged-edged cavity. As with the abrasion, the laceration presents an environment conducive to severe infection (see p. 213). *Puncture wounds* can easily occur during physical activities and can be fatal. Direct penetration of tissues by a pointed object such as a track shoe spike can introduce the tetanus bacillus into the bloodstream, thus making the athlete a possible victim of lockjaw. All puncture wounds and severe lacerations should be referred immediately to a physician (see Chapter 14). The cleanly cut or *incised wound* often appears where a blow has been delivered over a sharp bone or one that is poorly padded. It is

not as serious as the other types of exposed injuries (see Chapter 14).

Unexposed wounds

Unexposed or closed wounds in athletics include those internal injuries that do not penetrate the epidermal skin layer. These injuries consist of fractures, joint sprains, muscle strains, and contusions. Recognizing and caring for these conditions present a definite challenge to the trainer and coach, since their actions can mean the difference between a rapid or a prolonged period of rehabilitation.

Contusions

Contusions or bruises are the result of traumatic blows to the body. These blows, depending upon their intensity, can cause injury ranging from superficial ones to deep tissue tears and hemorrhage (Fig. 13-4).

Table 13-1. General management of contusions

Condition	Intensity, symptoms, and pathology	Phase of management	Basic management	Recovery time
Acute contusion—sharp and relatively intense; rapid onset and short duration.	First degree (mild contusion)— blow to body from external force. Mild sprain and transitory point tenderness.	Phase I— immediate	1. Determine extent of injury. 2. Apply cold and pressure for 1 to 2 hours. Static stretch to reduce spasm. 3. Elastic wrap for support.	Variable. May modify workout on second day.
		Phase II— second day	1. If irritation persists, ice massage followed by static stretch or analgesic balm pack, light massage above and below injury, or warm whirlpool (not to exceed 90°F. and for no longer than 10 minutes). 2. Continuous and sustained total body exercises to promote mild general circulation to area.	
	Second degree (moderate contusion)— bruising blow to soft tissue or bone from an external force. Extreme pain, point tenderness, and loss of function. Swelling in soft tissue.	Phase I— immediate	1. Determine extent of injury. 2. Apply pressure and cold; elevate part for 24 to 48 hours. 3. Medication as prescribed by physician.	1 to 2 weeks.
		Phase II— second or third day	Continue Phase I routine if injury has not begun to organize. If organization has begun, conduct the following procedure: 1. Ice massage or cold whirlpool for 10 minutes at 60° F. 2. Static stretch after cold therapy. 3. General calisthenics program to promote total body circulation. 4. Support contusion with a compress bandage.	
		Phase III— third or fourth day	1. Start gradual program of thermal therapy using whirlpool, infrared lamp, moist heat pack, or analgesic balm packs (temperature not to exceed 90° F.). 2. Repeat static stretch and general body calisthenics. 3. Continue compress and/or elastic bandage support.	

		Phase—Time	Procedure	Time
		fourth or fifth day	100° and 105° F. 2. Deep therapy (diathermy, ultrasound) may be employed. 3. Repeat general calisthenics and static stretching. 4. Institute progressive resistive exercise program (PRE) if there is minimum discomfort at the injury site. *Note:* protect contused area with special padding to prevent recurrent insult.	3 weeks to 2 months.
	Third degree (severe contusion)—from violent blow to bone or soft tissue from some external force, severe pain, muscle spasm, loss of function, point tenderness, swelling, extensive hemorrhage, and later discoloration.	Phase I— immediate	1. Determine extent of injury. 2. Apply pressure compress and cold pack; elevate part for 48 to 72 hours. 3. Refer to physician for diagnosis, and medication. Repeat above procedure on second day.	
		Phase II— third or fourth day	See Phase II, second degree acute contusion.	
		Phase III— fourth or fifth day	1. Start a gradual program of thermal therapy using superficial devices such as whirlpool, infrared lamp, moist heat packs, or analgesic balm packs. Temperature of modalities not to exceed 90° F. 2. Repeat Phase II program of static stretch and general body calisthenics. 3. Continue use of compress and/or bandage support.	
		Phase IV— fifth or sixth day	See Phase IV, second degree acute contusion.	
Chronic contusion— long duration, gradual onset.	Result of repeated blows to the same area. Persistent low-grade inflammation, constant irritation, and loss of function. Persistent aggravation may result in myositis ossificans, myositic, fasciatis, and periostitis.	Symptomatic	1. Avoid repeated bruising of an area. 2. Avoid aggravating injury through activity. 3. Support with an elastic bandage. 4. Increase blood circulation. 5. Anti-inflammatory therapy as prescribed by physician.	Variable.

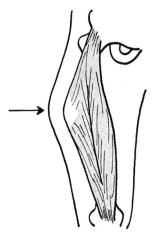

Fig. 13-4. Typical contusion or bruise as it occurs to the quadriceps group of muscles.

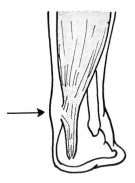

Fig. 13-5. Strain or muscle tear occurring to the Achilles tendon.

Interrupting the continuity of the circulatory system results in a flow of blood and lymph into the surrounding tissues. A hematoma (blood tumor) is formed by the focalization of the extravasated blood into a clot, which becomes encapsulated by a connective tissue membrane. The speed of healing depends upon the size of the lesion and the amount of internal bleeding that has taken place. It should be noted that at every place where there is a clot organization there is also a possibility of scar tissue formation.

Contusion or the crushing of soft tissue can penetrate to the skeletal structures causing a bone bruise (Table 13-1). The ex-

tent to which an athlete may be hampered by this condition is dependent upon the location of the bruise and the force of the blow. Typical in cases of severe contusion are the following: (1) the athlete reports being struck a hard blow, (2) the blow causes pain and a transitory paralysis caused by pressure on and shock to the motor and sensory nerves, (3) palpation often reveals a hard area, indurated because of internal hemorrhage, and (4) ecchymosis or tissue discoloration may take place.

Strains

A strain, sometimes referred to by the layman as a muscle pull, is a stretch tear or rip in the muscle itself or in the adjacent tissue, such the fascia or muscle tendons (Fig. 13-5). The etiology of muscle strain often is obscure because there are many possible causes. Most often a tear is produced by an abnormal muscular contraction. The cause of this abnormality has been attributed to many factors. One popular theory suggests that a fault in the reciprocal coordination of the agonist and antagonist muscles takes place. In essence, the cause of this fault or incoordination is more or less a mystery. However, among the possible explanations advanced are that it may be related to (1) mineral imbalance caused by profuse sweating, (2) fatigue metabolites collected in the muscle itself, or (3) imbalance between agonists and antagonists in muscle strength.

A strain may range from a minute separation of connective tissue and muscle fiber to a complete tendinous avulsion or muscle rupture (graded as *first, second,* or *third degree,* see Table 13-2). The resulting pathology is similar to that of the contusion or sprain, with capillary or blood vessel hemorrhage. Healing takes place in a similar fashion, with organization of a hematoma, absorption of the hematoma, and finally the formation of the cicatrix by fibroblastic repair. Detection of the injury is accomplished by understanding how the injury occurred and the administration of a muscle test to determine the specific locality. The muscles that have the highest incidence of strains are the hamstring group, the gastrocnemius, quadriceps group, hip flexors, hip adductor group, the spinalis group of the back, the deltoid, and the rotator cuff group of the shoulder. The signs that indicate a strain are listed below:

1. The athlete may hear a snap when the tissue tears.

2. He may have complained of muscle fatigue and spasm before the strain occurred.

3. A severe weakness and a loss of function of the part are detected.

4. A sharp pain is felt immediately upon the occurrence of the injury.

5. There is often a spasmodic muscle contraction of the affected part.

6. Extreme point tenderness is apparent upon palpation.

7. An indentation or cavity where tissues have separated may be felt immediately after the injury.

Sprains

The sprain, one of the most common and disabling injuries seen in athletics, is a traumatic joint twist that results in stretching or totally tearing stabilizing connective tissues (Fig. 13-6). When a joint is forced beyond its normal anatomical limits, microscopic and gross pathologies occur. Specifically, there is injury to ligaments, to the articular capsule and synovial membrane, and to the tendons crossing the joint. Effusion of blood and synovial fluid into the joint cavity usually accompanies this lesion, thus presenting all the classic signs of inflammation (joint swelling, local temperature, point tenderness, and—later—ecchymosis). According to the extent of injury, sprains are graded as *first, second,* and *third degree* (Table 13-3). According to statistical incidence, the joints that are most vulnerable to sprains are the ankles, knees, and shoulders. Sprains occur least often to the wrists and elbows. Since it is often quite difficult to distinguish between joint sprains and tendinous strains, the worst possible

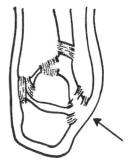

Fig. 13-6. Sprain or ligamentous tearing occurring to the ankle joint.

Fig. 13-7. Dislocation.

condition should be expected and cared for accordingly.

Dislocations

Dislocations are second to fractures in terms of handicapping the athlete. The highest incidence of dislocations involves the fingers and next the shoulder joint (Fig. 13-7). Dislocations, which result primarily from forces causing the joint to go beyond its normal anatomical limits, are divided into two classes: *subluxations* and *luxations.* Subluxations are partial dislocations wherein an incomplete separation between two articulating bones occurs. Luxations are complete dislocations, presenting a

Text continued on p. 201.

Table 13-2. General management of strains

Condition	Intensity, symptoms, and pathology	Phase of management	Basic management	Recovery time
Acute strain—short and relatively intense. Rapid onset and short duration.	First degree (mild strain)—stretch of musculotendinous unit. Spasm, local weakness, transitory point tenderness.	Phase I—immediate	1. Determine extent of injury. 2. Apply pressure bandage and cold pack for 1 to 2 hours. Ice massage with static stretch in mild cases.	Variable. May modify workout for 2 or 3 days.
		Phase II—second day	1. If some mild irritation persists, apply analgesic balm pack, light massage above and below injury, or warm whirlpool (not to exceed 90° F.) for 10 minutes. 2. Static stretch if there is muscle spasm. 3. Continuous and sustained general exercise to stimulate mild general circulation to area.	
	Second degree (moderate strain)—hard stretch to musculotendinous unit. Moderate spasm, point tenderness, and loss of function with swelling, and, in some cases, discoloration.	Phase I—immediate	1. Determine extent of injury. 2. Pressure bandage, intermittent cold pack, and part elevation for 24 to 48 hours. 3. Refer to physician for diagnosis and medication if applicable.	Because of tendency of recurrence 3 weeks may have to be allowed before normal sports activity can be permitted.
		Phase II—second or third day	Continue Phase I routine if injury has not begun to organize. If organization has begun, conduct the following procedure: 1. Apply ice massage or cold whirlpool for 10 minutes at 60° F. 2. Active movement of part but avoid stretching. 3. Sustained general calisthenics program to encourage total body circulation. 4. Elastic bandage to strain area.	
		Phase III—third or fourth day	1. Gradual program of thermal therapy using superficial devices such as whirlpool, infrared lamp, moist heat pack, or analgesic balm packs. 2. Repeat phase II program of mild active exercise of injury site; general calisthenics program for general increased circulation.	

Continued.

	Phase IV—fourth and following days	should be started (intermittent walking and slow running), keeping off toes. 3. Elastic support to injured site. 1. Repeat Phase III or begin deep heat therapy (diathermy, ultrasound). 2. Repeat superficial general calisthenics program. 3. Institute a Phase III progressive resistance program if there is minimum discomfort at injury site. 4. Continue support until full strength and flexibility established.	Several weeks to an entire season.
Third degree (severe strain)—violent contraction and stretch to musculotendinous unit. Severe spasm, point tenderness, and palpable defect or complete avulsion or muscle separation. Loss of function, swelling, extensive hemorrhage, and discoloration; surgical intervention may be required.	Phase I—immediate	1. Determine extent of injury. 2. Pressure bandage, intermittent cold pack, and part elevation for 48 to 72 hours. 3. Refer to physician for diagnosis, X-ray, and medication if applicable.	
	Phase II—third or fourth day	Repeat care procedure on second day. Continue Phase I routine if injury has not begun to organize. If organization has begun, conduct the following procedure: 1. Apply ice massage or cold whirlpool for 10 minutes at 60° F. 2. General calisthenics without moving injured part. 3. Elastic bandage of strain.	
	Phase III—fourth or fifth day	1. Program of thermal therapy using superficial devices such as whirlpool, infrared lamp, moist heat, or analgesic balm pack. Massage above and below injury site. 2. If complete tissue separation has not occurred, begin active movement of affected part avoiding stretch. 3. General calisthenics program to encourage general circulation. 4. Support strain area with an elastic bandage.	
	Phase IV—fifth or sixth and following days	See Phase IV, second degree acute strain.	

Table 13-2. General management of strains—cont'd

Condition	Intensity, symptoms, and pathology	Phase of management	Basic management	Recovery time
Chronic strain—long continued, with gradual onset.	Persistent low-grade inflammation, constant pain, a mild to moderate weakness in part. Condition becomes steadily worse as inflammation process continues. Generalized scarring occurs because of constant fibrocytic re-creation in inflammation, resulting in a myositis, tendinitis, or periostitis at muscle attachment.	Symptomatic	1. Discourage any aggravating activity; complete rest will hasten recovery. 2. Deep heat to increase blood circulation to part. 3. Anti-inflammatory agent if prescribed by physician.	Variable.

Table 13-3. General management of sprains

Condition	Intensity, symptoms, and pathology	Phase of management	Basic management	Recovery time
Acute sprain—sharp and relatively intense. Rapid onset and short course. Occurs primarily to the supportive joint structure.	First degree (mild sprain)—sudden transitory pain in joint. Mild disability with local weakness lasting up to a few minutes. Mild point tenderness. Minimal hemorrhage and swelling with mild stretching of ligamentous tissue.	Phase I—immediate	1. Determine extent of injury. 2. Pressure bandage, cold compress, and elevation of part for 1 to 2 hours. Encourage athlete to move affected part actively if he can do so without discomfort. 3. Tape support and/or elastic wrap to part maintaining mild pressure.	Any injury of this intensity should not force athlete to miss practice.
		Phase II—second day	1. If some irritation persists, apply superficial heat and light massage above and below injury site. Do not exceed 90° F.	

Injury	Phase	Management	Duration
sprain)—Sudden, prolonged pain that results in point tenderness, swelling, localized hemorrhage. Weakness and painful movement of part.	immediate	physician for diagnosis, X-ray, examination and medication if applicable. 2. Pressure bandage with cold pack. Maintain cold intermittently with part elevation for at least 24 to 48 hours. 3. Adhesive strapping when applicable to maintain a constant pressure and support. 4. Prevent weight bearing; where applicable, crutches to be used until initial soreness subsides.	…duration.
	Phase II—second or third day	1. If indications of joint swelling, maintain ice packs, pressure, and elevation for a second day. 2. If hemorrhage is controlled, use ice massage or a cold whirlpool for 10 minutes at 60° F. 3. Apply adhesive strapping for support. 4. General calisthenics for unaffected parts of the body.	
	Phase III—third or fourth and following days	1. Use superficial thermal therapy when hemorrhage has ceased; analgesic balm packs, infrared light, or whirlpool to relax and help to curb pain. Temperature should not exceed 90° F. Two or 3 heat applications per day tend to speed healing; heat therapy should be continued as long as there are symptoms. 2. Normal movement to be increased slowly. Avoid weight bearing until walking can be executed normally. 3. Adhesive strapping until full strength and range of movement are regained. 4. Once full strength and range of movement without pain have been regained, resume normal activity. Apply preventive strapping and padding if there is a chance of reinjury or aggravation.	
Third degree (severe sprain)—sudden severe and constant pain, loss of function, point tenderness, swelling, and hemorrhage. Complete tear of ligamentous tissue.	Phase I—immediate	1. Determine nature and extent of injury and refer to physicians for X-ray diagnosis and medication if applicable. 2. Watch for signs of shock. 3. Apply pressure and cold intermittently for 48 to 72 hours. 4. Elevate part.	From several weeks to entire season.

Continued.

Table 13-3. General management of sprains—cont'd

Condition	Intensity, symptoms, and pathology	Phase of management	Basic management	Recovery time
			5. Constant pressure and support. Prevent weight bearing; crutches to be used until full strength and range of movement are restored. Repeat Phase I procedure on second day.	
		Phase II— third or fourth day	1. Ice massage or cold whirlpool for 10 minutes at 60° F. Limited movement. 2. Adhesive strapping for support. 3. General calisthenics for unaffected body parts.	
		Phase III— fourth or fifth day	1. Apply superficial thermal therapy only after internal hemorrhage has ceased (superficial heat may be applied in combination with massage above and below injured site, temperature not to exceed 90° F.). 2. Normal range of movement to be increased slowly. Avoid weight bearing until it can be done without a limp.	
		Phase IV— fifth or sixth and following days	1. Massage and superficial heat not to exceed 100°-105° F. See Second degree, Phase III. *Note: In every degree of injury, athlete should be encouraged to exercise the uninjured body parts extensively so that he will be ready for competition when injury has healed.*	
Chronic sprain— long continued, having a gradual onset.	Tends to recur. Irritation, lack of stability caused by repeated joint stress. In later stages traumatic arthritis may be apparent, with a persistent, low-grade inflammation.	Symptomatic	1. Discourage any aggravating activity; complete rest hastens recovery. 2. Increase blood circulation to part by use of various therapeutic modalities; ultrasound is of particular value in fibrocytic connective tissue conditions. 3. Maintain full range of joint movement without irritating part. In chronic condition of a lower limb joint, encourage passive nonweight-bearing exercise. 4. Refer any persistent or chronic condition to team physician. 5. Anti-inflammatory agent if prescribed by physician.	Varies with extent of pathology and acceptance of treatment.

total disunion of bone apposition between the articulating surfaces.

There are several important factors to be remembered in recognizing and evaluating dislocations:

1. There is a loss of limb function. The athlete usually complains of having fallen or of having received a severe blow to a particular joint and then being suddenly unable to move that part.

2. Deformity is almost always apparent. Since such deformity can often be obscured by heavy musculature, it is important for the examiner to palpate the injured site to determine the loss of normal body contour. Comparison of the injured side with its normal counterpart often reveals distortions.

3. Swelling and point tenderness are immediately present.

At times, as with a fracture, roentgenography is the only absolute diagnostic measure. First-time dislocations or joint separations may result in an avulsion of the stabilizing ligamentous and tendinous tissues surrounding the joint. Trauma is often of such violence that small chips of bone are torn away with the supporting structures, or the force may separate growth epiphyses or cause a complete fracture of the neck in long bones. This indicates the importance of administering complete and thorough medical attention to first-time dislocations. It has often been said, "Once a dislocation—always a dislocation." In most cases this is true, since once a joint has been either subluxated or completely luxated the connective tissues that bind and hold it in its correct alignment are stretched to such an extent that the joint will be extremely vulnerable to subsequent dislocations. Chronic, recurring dislocations may take place without severe pain, because of the somewhat slack condition of the stabilizing tissues.

A first-time dislocation should always be considered and treated as a possible fracture. Once it has been ascertained that the injury is a dislocation, a physician should be consulted for further evaluation. However, before the patient is taken to the physician, the injury should be properly splinted and supported to prevent any further damage to the area.

Fractures

Fractures are defined as interruptions in the continuity of a bone. Since they can range from partial to complete separations of the bony parts, it is not always necessary that the opposing parts in fractures be completely separated. These injuries are classified into two categories: *simple* and *compound* fractures. A simple fracture consists of a break in a bone, without external exposure present. A compound fracture, on the other hand, is one in which bone has extended through the outer skin layers, with a resultant external wound. Fractures are one of the most serious hazards in athletics and should be suspected and closely searched for in any traumatic condition. Types of fractures are listed below:

1. *Comminuted fractures* (Fig. 13-8) consist of three or more bone fragments at the fracture site. A hard blow or a fall in an awkward position may be the cause. From the physician's point of view, these fractures impose a difficult healing situation because of the displacement of the bone fragments. Soft tissues are often interposed between the fragments, causing incomplete healing. Such cases may need surgical intervention.

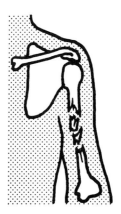

Fig. 13-8. Comminuted fracture.

2. *Depressed fractures* (Fig. 13-9) occur most often in flat bones such as those that comprise the skull. They are caused by falling and striking the head on a hard, immovable surface or by being hit with a hard object. Such injuries result in gross pathology of soft areas.

3. *Greenstick fractures* (Fig. 13-10) are incomplete breaks in bones that have not as yet completely ossified. They occur most frequently in the convex bone surface, the concave surface remaining inact. The name is derived from the similarity of the fracture to the break in a green twig taken from a tree.

4. *Impacted fractures* (Fig. 13-11) can result from a fall from a height, which causes a long bone to receive, directly along its long axis, a force of such magnitude that the osseous tissue is compressed. This telescopes one part of the bone upon the other. This type of injury requires immediate splinting by the trainer and traction by the physician to ensure a normal length of the injured limb.

5. *Longitudinal fractures* (Fig. 13-12) are those in which the bone splits along its length, often the result of jumping from a height and landing in such a way as to impact force or stress to the long axis.

6. *Multiple fractures* (Fig. 13-13) are not often seen in athletics because of the tremendous force required to bring about such injury. Falling in an extremely awkward position may cause such fractures.

7. *Oblique fractures* (Fig. 13-14) are similar in nature to spiral fractures and occur when the causative force is a sudden torsion or twist of the part while one end of the bone is fixed or stabilized.

8. *Serrated fractures* (Fig. 13-15) in which the two bony fragments have a sawtooth, sharp-edged fracture line are usually caused by a direct blow. Because of the sharp and jagged edges, extensive internal damage, such as the severance of vital blood vessels and nerves, often occurs.

9. *Spiral fractures* (Fig. 13-16) give the appearance of a spiral or S-shaped separation. They are fairly common in football

and ski activities wherein the foot is firmly planted and then the body is suddenly rotated in an opposing direction.

10. *Transverse fractures* (Fig. 13-17) occur in a straight line, more or less at right angles to the bone shaft. A direct outside blow usually causes this injury.

In addition, there are *contrecoup fractures*, occurring on the side opposite to the part where trauma was initiated. Fracture of the skull is at times an example of the contrecoup. An athlete may be hit on one side of the head with such force that the brain and internal structures compress against the opposite side of the skull sufficiently hard to cause a fracture.

Spontaneous fractures (stress fractures) can result either when there is a pathological weakness in the bone or when, during strenuous physical activity, there is sudden and forceful muscular contraction on a bone.

All the foregoing can become further complicated by injury to nerves, blood vessels, or internal organs near the site of the fracture. Poor handling of a fracture case can cause additional involvement and injury. Immediate and professional care is important to ensure an uncomplicated condition.

Fracture signs. X-ray films offer the only accurate and positive means of identifying a fracture. Whenever there is some question as to the possibility of a fracture having occurred, the athlete should be referred to a physician. An understanding of the gross fracture signs by the trainer or coach cannot be overemphasized. He should familiarize himself with them sufficiently to be able to make the following examination at the time and place of injury:

1. Determine the mechanism of the injury:
   a. In what sport was the athlete engaged?
   b. How was he hit?
   c. How did he fall?
   d. Did he feel a sudden pain when the injury occurred? *Note:* Often, immediate pain subsides and numbness is

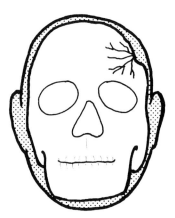

Fig. 13-9. Depressed fracture.

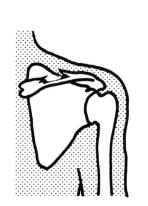

Fig. 13-10. Greenstick fracture.

Fig. 13-11. Impacted fracture.

Fig. 13-12. Longitudinal fracture.

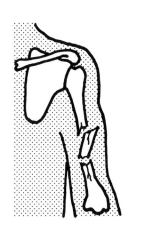

Fig. 13-13. Multiple fracture.

Fig. 13-14. Oblique fracture.

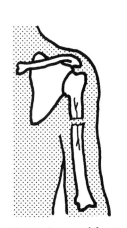

Fig. 13-15. Serrated fracture.

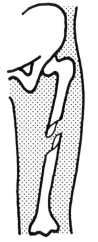

Fig. 13-16. Spiral fracture.

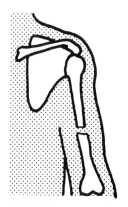

Fig. 13-17. Transverse fracture.

present for a period of 20 to 30 minutes.

2. Inspect the area of the suspected fracture:

a. Deformity. Compare corresponding part to determine deformity.

b. Swelling. Is rapid swelling taking place?

c. Direct tenderness. Ascertain the presence of point tenderness, especially over bony structures.

d. Indirect tenderness. Through palpation, proximally and distally to the injury site, determine if pain can be elicited at the probable fracture point.

e. Bony deviations. Does palpation indicate any irregularity in the continuity of the bone?

f. Crepitus. On examing the body part, is there a grating sound apparent at the fracture site?

g. False joint. Is there an abnormal movement of the part, sometimes giving the appearance of an extra joint?

h. Discoloration. Is there discoloration around the site of injury? *Note:* Often, discoloration does not appear until several days after the injury has occurred.

Fracture pathology and healing. The coach and trainer must fully realize the seriousness of a fracture. Coaches are often impatient for the injured athlete to return to competition and are sometimes unjust in their criticism of the physician or trainer for using a more conservative approach. The coach must be made aware that patience is required to permit proper healing and complete bone repair.[4]

When a bone breaks, there is injury to the periosteum, the membranous covering of the bone, and to the surrounding soft tissues, consisting of muscles, blood vessels, nerves, and connective tissues. Usually there is marked hemorrhaging, which forms an organized clot between the broken bone ends. At the time the clot forms, the body begins to develop the secondary type of healing. Granulation tissue forms as a gelatinous mass, later developing into a fibrous junction between the ends of the bone. This union is commonly known as the soft callus. Gradually, osteoblasts, or the immature bone cells growing out from the periosteum, infiltrate the fibrous tissue and form a hard callus that later develops into rigid bone. If the periosteum has been damaged, bone development is often hampered, because the bone-forming cells cannot be produced.

In the treatment of fractures the bones must be immobilized completely until x-ray studies reveal that the hard callus has been formed. It is up to the physician to know the various types of fractures and the best form of immobilization for each specific fracture. During healing, fractures can keep an athlete out of participation in his particular sport for several weeks or months depending upon the nature, extent, and site of the fracture. During this period there are certain conditions that can seriously interfere with the healing progress. Three such conditions are discussed below:

1. If there is a *poor blood supply to the fractured area* and one of the parts of the broken bone is not properly supplied by the blood, that part will die and union or healing of the fracture cannot take place. This condition is known as aseptic necrosis and can often be seen in the head of the femur, the navicular bone in the wrist, the talus in the ankle, or in isolated bone fragments. The condition is relatively rare among vital, healthy, young athletes, except in the navicular bone of the wrist.

2. *Poor immobilization of the fracture site,* resulting from poor casting performed by the physician and permitting motion between the bone parts, may not only prevent proper union but may also, in the event that union does transpire, cause deformity to develop.

3. *Infection* can materially interfere with the normal healing process, particularly in the case of a compound fracture, which offers an ideal situation for development of a severe streptococcal or staphyloccal infection. The increased used of modern antibiotics has considerably reduced the prev-

alence of these infections coincidental with or immediately following a fracture. The closed fracture is not immune to contamination, of course, since infections within the body or a poor blood supply can render it quite liable. If the fracture site should become and remain infected, the infection could interfere with the proper union of the bone. The interposition of soft parts between the severed ends of the bone—such as muscle, connective tissue, or other soft tissue immediately adjacent to the fracture—can prevent proper bone union, often necessitating surgical cleansing of the area of such tissues by the surgeon.

Whenever a fracture is suspected, the following rules should be applied:

1. Before moving the athlete, splint the area properly and apply traction if indicated.

2. In case of an open fracture, stop the hemorrhaging and then apply a sterile dressing to the wound.

3. In any suspected fracture, treat for shock.

4. Place the athlete on a stretcher and secure the injured part sufficiently so that no motion can occur in it during transportation.

5. Obtain medical attention as soon as possible, particularly in the case of compound fractures, which require prompt surgical cleansing or debridement to prevent severe infection.

In cases of suspected fractures, as in other unexposed injuries, pressure and ice should be applied to the injured area. This should be done in all such cases *with the sole exception of the compound fracture*, which is an exposed wound. If hemorrhage is not controlled, swelling may be so severe that the physician will have to delay casting for several days until the swelling subsides.

Splinting. Proper splint application is of considerable importance when it is necessary to transport the athlete. As has been previously stated, inadequate stabilization of a fracture can often be the cause of increased damage and may delay the healing process. Always stabilize the joint, both above and below the site of fractures. In the case of a fracture of the tibia, for example, the splint should immobilize both the knee and the ankle joint. In cases of long bone fracture apply the necessary traction if the patient is to be transported a considerable distance. This situation arises occasionally in ski injuries. Refer to Chapter 14 for a discussion of splinting procedures.

CHRONIC SOFT TISSUE CONDITIONS

The chronic condition is usually of long onset and duration, but acute injuries, if not properly cared for, can become chronic in nature. As in acute conditions, inflammation plays an important role in chronic injuries, although it does not necessarily present the classic stages of redness, swelling, pain, heat, and loss of function. Because of the constant presence of a low-grade inflammation, there is a proliferation of fibroblasts, which develop a generalized connective tissue scarring. In athletics a chronic condition may have any of several etiological factors: poor performance techniques, sequelae of acute injuries, or constant stress beyond physiological limits.

The use of *improper form* places abnormal strain on joints and tendons, predisposing the athlete to a future chronic condition. Proper form must be stressed! Acute injuries, if improperly handled, can develop into chronic conditions.

The *sequelae of acute injuries* may lead to a chronic condition in which traumatic injuries are superimposed one on the other or incessant reinjury of a part occurs. The healing of an acute injury, if delayed by improper care, may result in chronic inflammation.

Stress beyond the physiological limits of the athlete (overuse syndrome) may occur either grossly, as in heat exhaustion, or—more frequently—in small, insidious micropathologies in the muscles and joints. Such conditions are frequently most difficult to detect as specific single entities and as a result can cause untold loss of competitive time.

General care of chronic injuries in athletics is basically the same regardless of the condition. Of prime importance is rest for the injured part. If this is not feasible, then supportive strapping should be used, particularly if it is necessary for the athlete to continue activity. To encourage healing heat should be applied (see Tables 13-1 to 13-3).

HEMORRHAGE

In any injury situation one must be constantly aware of the danger of hemorrhage. Hemorrhage is the escaping of blood through the walls of the blood vessels or through ruptured blood vessels. There are three basic types of hemorrhage: arterial, venous, and capillary. It is vitally important that hemorrhaging be promptly recognized.

1. *Arterial hemorrhage* is a condition in which the artery has been damaged or severed. There is a very rapid flow of bright red blood, usually escaping in a rhythmical spurting with each heartbeat. Because of the rapidity with which the blood is lost from the body, this type of hemorrhaging is considered the most dangerous. It requires immediate attention. The trainer should promptly elevate the part and apply a compress bandage directly over the site of the hemorrhage. Direct pressure is considered the best means of control and causes the least amount of further damage to the injured area. Only when the use of direct pressure does not appear to be acting as a suitable control should a tourniquet be applied.

2. *Venous hemorrhage* is characterized by a rapid, steady effusion of dark blood from the wounded area. It is controlled by elevation of the part and application of direct pressure over the area. A tourniquet is seldom necessary to control this type of bleeding.

3. *Capillary hemorrhage* is an oozing or very gradual seeping of blood from the wounded area and is easy to control through elevation of the part and direct pressure on a sterile dressing that is placed directly over the wound.

As stated, elevation of the part and direct pressure are considered the best measures in controlling hemorrhage. When the injured area is raised above the level of the heart, there is a diminishing of the pulse pressure, resulting in a reduced amount of blood in the vessels. By applying direct pressure over the wound while the part is elevated it is possible to keep the hemorrhage to a minimum. The pressure should be applied until the blood coagulates or until medical help has been obtained.

If direct pressure fails to control the bleeding, then a tourniquet should be used to cut off the flow of blood above the injured area. The tourniquet has been found to be an inadequate method of controlling hemorrhage. The most common error is applying the tourniquet too loosely, and allowing the blood to seep out slowly. Although a loosely applied tourniquet will constrict the veins, it cannot occlude the deeper arteries; consequently blood will still be lost. It is most important when using a tourniquet to take the pulse rate of the artery *below* the tourniquet to determine if cessation of blood flow has taken place. A tourniquet is seldom used in athletics, and in most cases medical care can be administered in ample time. There are, of course, exceptions such as occur in snow injuries, when the injured person must be transported for a long distance, sometimes under trying conditions, and when there is often only limited help to care for the athlete. Circumstances such as these may necessitate use of a tourniquet. The time of tourniquet application should always be indicated on a card that can be secured to the person of the injured athlete so that an accurate record can be kept of when to release and reset pressure. It must be remembered that if a tourniquet is left on for longer than 10 minutes, or if it is too narrow, a clot may result and the loss of the limb, as a result of gangrene, may be a consequence.

Internal hemorrhage is unexposed and therefore invisible to the eye unless it is manifested through body openings or is identified through x-ray or other diagnostic techniques. Its danger lies in the difficulty of diagnosis. When internal hemorrhaging occurs in an athlete, either subcutaneously or intramuscularly, he may be moved without danger in most instances. However, the detection of bleeding that occurs within a body cavity such as the skull or thorax is of the utmost importance, since it could mean the difference between life and death. Because the symptoms are obscure, internal hemorrhage is difficult to properly diagnose. It has been said that, as a result of this difficulty in evaluating them, internal injuries require hospitalization under complete and constant observation by a medical staff for the nature and extent of the injuries to be determined. It should be noted that all severe hemorrhaging will eventually result in shock and should therefore be treated on this premise. Even if there is no outward indication of shock, the patient should be kept quiet and his body

heat be maintained at a constant and suitable temperature. The preferred shock position is supine with all body parts level with the heart.

SHOCK

In any injury shock is a possibility, but when severe bleeding, fractures, or deep internal injuries are present, the development of shock is assured. Shock occurs when there is a diminished amount of fluid available to the circulatory system. As a result there are not enough oxygen-carrying blood cells available to the tissues, particularly those of the nervous system. This occurs when the vascular system loses its capacity to hold the fluid portion of the blood within its system, because of a dilatation of the blood vessels within the body and a disruption of the osmotic fluid balance (Fig. 13-18). When this occurs, a quantity of plasma is lost from the blood vessels to the tissue spaces of the body,

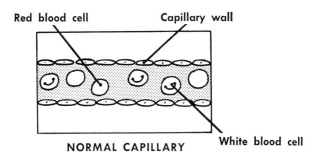

NORMAL CAPILLARY

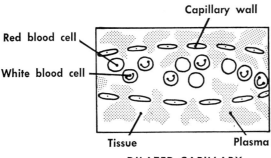

DILATED CAPILLARY

Fig. 13-18. Response of the capillary to shock. The escape of plasma into the surrounding tissue results in lowered blood pressure and a stagnation of blood in the dilated capillary.

leaving the solid blood particles within the vessels and thus causing stagnation and slowing up of the blood flow. With this general collapse of the vascular system there is a widespread death of tissues, which will eventually cause death of the individual unless treatment is given.

Certain conditions, such as extreme fatigue, extreme exposure to heat or cold, extreme dehydration of fluids and minerals, or illness, predispose an athlete to shock.

Symptoms of shock are the following:
1. Blood pressure is low. Systolic pressure is usually below 90 mm. Hg.
2. Pulse is rapid and very weak.
3. The athlete may be drowsy and appear sluggish.
4. Respiration is shallow and extremely rapid.

In a situation in which there is a potential shock condition, there are other signs by which the trainer or coach should seek to assess the possibility of the athlete's lapsing into a state of shock as an aftermath of his injury. The most important clue to potential shock is the recognition of a severe injury. It may happen that none of the usual signs of shock are present. To avoid shock in cases of such injury it is vitally important that immediate care be given to the athlete, as indicated below. These steps should be followed in sequence:
1. *Bleeding,* because it is one of the conditions that causes shock, should receive first consideration. Crowds and curiosity seekers should be kept away from the injured athlete; if the wound is of a disturbing nature, he should not be permitted to see it. He should be handled with patience and gentleness, but firmness, as well.

2. *Body temperature* should be kept at normal, 98.6° F., since extreme variations of temperature serve only to accentuate the condition of shock.
3. The athlete should be placed with his head and trunk level and with lower limbs elevated (Fig. 13-19). If he is unconscious, turn his head to one side so that any fluids, such as mucus or saliva, will drain out of the mouth rather than into the throat; establish an airway; and be sure that he has not swallowed his tongue.
4. *Oxygen,* if available, can be administered to help restore starved tissues.
5. *Pain* is one of the causes of shock and the athletic physician will often administer sedation to enable the athlete to be more at ease.

Shock can also be compounded or initially produced by the psychological reaction of the athlete to an injury situation. Fear or the sudden realization that a serious situation has occurred can result in shock. When an athlete has a psychological reaction to an injury he should lie down and avoid viewing the injury. Spectators should be kept away from the injured athlete.

RECOGNIZING CRITICAL SIGNS

The ability to recognize basic physiological signs of injury is essential to proper handling of critical injuries. When making the evaluation of the seriously ill or injured athlete, the trainer or coach must be aware of nine response areas: heart rate, breathing rate, blood pressure, temperature, skin color, pupils of the eye, movement, the presence of pain, and unconsciousness.[6]

Pulse. The pulse is the direct extension of

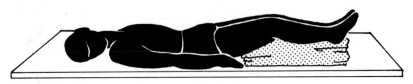

Fig. 13-19. Body position for the management of shock.

the functioning heart. It is normally determined from the radial artery at the wrist or the carotid artery at the neck. A normal pulse ranges between 60 and 80 beats per minute in adults and from 80 to 100 in children.[6] It should be noted, however, that athletes may have a heart rate (pulse) slower than that of the typical population because of the effects of training.

Alteration in pulse may indicate a pathologic condition. For example, a rapid, weak, or thready pulse may indicate shock; the absence of pulse indicates cardiac arrest (heart stoppage).

Respiration. The normal adult breathing rate is approximately 17 breaths per minute. Breathing may be shallow (indicative of shock) or irregular or grasping (indicative of air obstruction), or it may cease (indicative of cardiac involvement). Frothy blood from the mouth indicates an injury to the chest, such as a fractured rib, that has affected a lung.

Blood pressure. Blood pressure as measured by the sphygmomanometer indicates the amount of force that is produced against the artery walls. It is indicated at two pressure levels; systolic and diastolic. Systolic pressure occurs when the heart pumps blood, while the diastolic is the pressure present in the arteries when the heart is between beats. Normal systolic pressure for 15- to 20-year-old males is from 115 to 120 mm. Hg. The diastolic pressure usually ranges from 75 to 80 mm. Hg. At this age, a systolic pressure of 135 mm. Hg and above may be excessive and 110 mm. and below may be considered too low. The outer ranges for the diastolic pressure should not exceed 60 and 85 mm. Hg, respectively. Shock can lower blood pressure; anxiety and/or excitement may raise it.

Temperature and skin reaction. The temperature of the body is normally 98.6° F. Because the skin is directly responsible for temperature regulation, it reacts according to changes caused by disease or trauma. For example, a hot dry skin may indicate disease infection or overexposure to the sun (as in heat stroke). Cool and moist skin is indicative of shock or heat exhaustion.

Skin color. Skin color is a very good indicator of an individual's state of health. (Of course skin color reaction varies according to an individual's pigmentation.) Three colors are commonly identified in specific medical emergencies: red, white, and blue. A red skin color occurs from a lack of oxygen and may be present in high blood pressure and/or heat stroke. A white or overly pale skin is most often seen in shock and in heart disease when blood is not circulating properly. Skin that is bluish indicates that oxygen is not being carried adequately by the circulatory system; it may be the result of heart involvement or air obstruction.

Pupil size. The pupils of the eyes are extremely sensitive to situations affecting the nervous system. Shock, head injuries, and heart involvement can alter the size of pupils. Both pupils may be dilated in the unconscious athlete. However, if the pupils are of unequal size after a head injury, it may indicate neurological problems. It should be noted, however, that some individuals have pupils of unequal size even under normal conditions.

Movement ability. Inability to move a body part may indicate serious central nervous system injury with subsequent involvement of the motor system. Paralysis of arms or legs can result from injury to the neck or back.

Pain reaction. Pain or the lack of pain can assist the trainer or coach in making a reasonable judgment. An immovable body part which elicits severe pain, numbness, or a tingling sensation indicates a probable injury to the nervous system. Any injury that is extremely painful to the athlete but is not sensitive to touch may indicate a lack of circulation.[6]

EVALUATION OF THE UNCONSCIOUS ATHLETE

The state of unconsciousness provides one of the greatest dilemmas in athletics.

Whether it is advisable to move the athlete and allow the game to be resumed or whether to leave him where he lies until the arrival of a physician are problems that too often are resolved hastily and without much forethought.[5] Unconsciousness may be defined as a state of insensibility in which there is a lack of conscious awareness. This condition can be brought about by a blow to either the head or the solar plexus, or it may result from general shock. It is often difficult to determine the exact cause of unconsciousness.

To recognize and evaluate the injury sustained by an unconscious athlete, use the following procedures:

1. Understand the sequence of the accident, either through having witnessed the event or through questioning other players and spectators.

2. After learning how the accident occurred, decide what part of the body was most affected. Often no one is fully aware of just when or how the athlete was hurt. The position or attitude in which the athlete was found may therefore present an important key as to how the injury took place. It is a normal reaction for a person to pull away from an injuring force and to grasp at the painful area.

3. Do not move the unconscious athlete from the position in which he is found, until a thorough examination has been made.

4. Make the examination as follows:

a. First, check carotid pulse for a heartbeat and then determine if the athlete is breathing normally. If breathing is impaired, clear airway and proceed to give mouth-to-mouth resuscitation. If carotid pulse is not detected, closed heart massage should be initiated.

b. Start with the head and determine first if there is bleeding or if there is a straw-colored fluid coming from the nose, eyes, ears, or mouth. Look for bumps, lacerations, or deformities that may indicate a possible concussion or skull fracture.

c. Moving down the body, check each part for deformity and palpate for abnormal movements and uneven surfaces.

It is desirable to have the athlete fully conscious before attempting to move him from the field. When he is in a rational state he can be questioned as to where he has pain and then can be given instructions to tense specific body parts in order to determine possible spinal fracture and paralysis. Placing ammonia under the nose of the injured athlete will often arouse him. Not until the trainer is completely satisfied that no serious injury is present should the athlete be moved. To avoid possible aggravation of an injury, transportation of the injured person from the playing field must be directed by the physician. When such transportation is necessary, it should always be carried out in the manner used for moving a person with a fractured back; that is, by five attendants, with one sup-

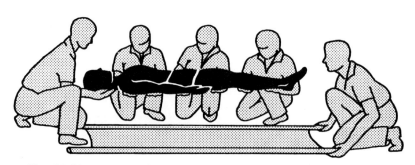

Fig. 13-20. Proper method of lifting an injured athlete to a stretcher.

porting the head and neck, three supporting the trunk, pelvis, and legs, and the fifth sliding a stretcher into place under the patient (Fig. 13-20). *It should also be noted that when a spinal fracture is suspected each curve of the body must be supported. Above all, jeopardize neither the health of the athlete nor your career by making a hasty decision.*

REFERENCES

1. Anderson, W. A. D., and Scotti, T. M.: Synopsis of pathology, ed. 7, St. Louis, 1968, The C. V. Mosby Co.
2. Mills, L. C., and Moyer, J. F., editors: Inflammation and diseases of connective tissue, Philadelphia, 1961, W. B. Saunders Co.
3. McLaughlin, H. L.: Trauma, Philadelphia, 1960, W. B. Saunders Co.
4. Ralston, E. L.: Handbook of fractures, St. Louis, 1967, The C. V. Mosby Co.
5. Shires, G. T., and Jones, R. C.: Initial management of the severely injured patient, J.A.M.A. 213(11):1872, 1970.
6. Emergency care and transportation of athletic injuries, Chicago, Ill., 1971, American Academy of Orthopaedic Surgeons.

RECOMMENDED READINGS

Anderson, W. A. D., and Scotti, T. M.: Synopsis of pathology, ed. 7, St. Louis, 1968, The C. V. Mosby Co.

Ferguson, A. B., Jr., and Bender, J.: The ABC's of athletic injuries and conditioning, Baltimore, 1964, The Williams & Wilkins Co.

Hirata, I., Jr.: The doctor and the athlete, Philadelphia, 1968, J. B. Lippincott Co.

Novich, M. M., and Taylor, B.: Training and conditioning of athletes, Philadelphia, 1970, Lea & Febiger.

O'Donoghue, D. H.: Treatment of injuries to athletes, Philadelphia, 1971, W. B. Saunders Co.

Olson, O. C.: Prevention of football injuries, Philadelphia, 1971, Lea & Febiger.

Ralston, E. L.: Handbook of fractures, St. Louis, 1967, The C. V. Mosby Co.

Ryan, A. J.: Medical care of the athlete, New York, 1962, McGraw-Hill Book Co.

Stimson, B. B.: A manual of fractures and dislocations, Philadelphia, 1956, Lea & Febiger.

Thorndike, A.: Athletic injuries, ed. 5, Philadelphia, 1962, Lea & Febiger.

CHAPTER 14

Selected training methods and techniques

As has been stated in previous chapters, skill in the art of athletic training encompasses many areas. Besides the understanding of injury prevention and the ability to recognize and evaluate injuries, one must have skill in a variety of specialized training techniques. Each requires practice and experience for the development of proficiency. Knowledge and skills should include the numerous techniques of bandaging, the uses of adhesive tape, the buying and fitting of commercial protective and supportive devices, the construction of other devices, and a complete knowledge of lifesaving techniques.

DRESSINGS AND BANDAGES

Dressings and bandages have eight basic uses in the management of athletic conditions:

1. To protect wounds from infection
2. To protect wounds from further insult
3. To control bleeding
4. To act as a compress over exposed or unexposed injuries
5. To immobilize an injured part
6. To protect an unexposed injury
7. To support an injured part
8. To hold protective equipment in place

Wound dressing

Skin lesions are extremely prevalant in athletics; abrasions, lacerations, and punc-

ture wounds are almost a daily occurrence. It is of the utmost importance to the well being of the athlete that open wounds be cared for immediately. All exposed injuries, even those that are relatively superficial, are contaminated. In general, all wounds must be cleansed with an antiseptic soap and dressed with firm dressing. Minor wounds may require antiseptic medication for the control of infection. If a wound requires examination by a physician, it should be cleaned, but no medication should be applied (see Table 14-1). Open wounds are best covered with a nonsticking, sterile dressing.

Basic principles of bandaging

Bandages, when properly applied, can contribute decidedly to the recovery from athletic afflictions. Bandages carelessly or improperly used may cause discomfort, allow wound contamination, or hamper repair and healing. One basic rule is that bandages should never be secured directly over external wounds but should be used to hold dressings in place. In all cases bandages must be firmly applied—neither so tight that circulation is impaired nor so loose that the dressing is allowed to slip.

Materials. Bandages peculiar to athletics consist essentially of gauze, cotton cloth, and elastic wrapping. Each material offers a specific contribution to the care of injuries. *Gauze materials* are used in two forms as sterile pads for wounds, as pad-

Table 14-1. Care of external wounds

Type of wound	Action of trainer	Initial care	Follow-up care
Abrasion	1. Provide initial care. 2. Wound seldom requires medical attention unless infected.	1. Clean abraded area with soap and water; debride with brush. 2. Apply a solution of hydrogen peroxide over abraded area; continue until foaming has subsided. 3. Apply a petroleum-base medicated ointment to keep abraded surface moist. In athletics, it is not desirable for abrasions to acquire a scab. Place a nonadhering sterile pad (Telfa pad) over the ointment.	1. Change dressing daily and look for signs of infection.
Laceration	1. Clean around the wound. Avoid wiping more contaminating agents into the area. 2. Apply dry sterile compress pad and refer to physician.	1. Complete cleaning and suturing are accomplished by the physician; injections of tetanus toxoid are given if needed.	1. Change dressing daily and look for signs of infection.
Puncture	1. Clean around the wound. Avoid wiping more contaminating agents into the area. 2. Apply dry sterile compress pad and refer to physician.	1. Complete cleaning and injections of tetanus toxoid, if needed, are managed by the physician.	1. Change dressing daily and look for signs of infection.

ding in the prevention of blisters of the taped ankle, and as a roller bandage for holding compresses in place. *Cotton cloth* is used primarily for cloth ankle wraps and for triangular and cravat-type bandages. It is soft, is easily obtained, and can be washed many times without deterioration. *Elastic bandage* is extremely popular in athletics because of its extensibility, which allows it to conform to most parts of the body. Elastic wrapping may be considered the "active bandage," which, when applied, lets the athlete move without restriction. It also may act as a compression bandage, in which the regulation of pressure is graded by its elasticity.

A *cohesive elastic bandage* has been de-veloped which exerts constant, even pressure. It is lightweight and contours easily to the body part. The bandage is composed of two layers of nonwoven rayon, which are separated by strands of Spondex material. The cohesive elastic bandage is coated with a substance that facilitates the material in adhering to itself, eliminating the need for metal clips or adhesive tape for holding it in place.[1] *Plastics* are playing an increasing role in athletics. Spray plastic coatings are used to protect wounds. A variety of plastic adhesive tapes are also used because they are waterproof. Many trainers use plastic food envelopes to insulate analgesic balm packs and to protect bandages and/or dressings from moisture.

TYPES OF BANDAGES

Triangular and cravat bandages, usually made of cotton cloth, may be used where roller types are not applicable or available.

Triangular and cravat

The triangular and cravat-type bandages are primarily used as first-aid devices. They are valuable in emergency bandaging because of their ease and speed of application. In athletics the more diversified roller bandages are usually available and lend themselves more to the needs of the athlete. The principal use of the triangular bandage in training is for arm slings. There are two basic kinds of slings, the cervical arm sling and the shoulder arm sling, and each has a specific purpose.

Cervical arm sling

The cervical arm sling (Fig. 14-1) is designed to support the forearm, wrist, and hand. A triangular bandage is placed around the neck and under the bent arm that is to be supported.

Materials needed: One triangular bandage and one safety pin.

Position of the athlete: The athlete stands with his affected arm bent at approximately a 70-degree angle.

Position of the trainer: The trainer stands facing the athlete.

Procedure:

1. The triangular bandage is positioned, by the trainer, under the injured arm with the apex facing the elbow.

2. The end of the triangle nearest the body is carried over the shoulder of the injured arm; the other end is allowed to hang down loosely.

3. The loose end is pulled over the shoulder of the uninjured side.

4. The two ends of the bandage are tied in a square knot behind the neck. For the sake of comfort, the knot should be on either side of the neck, not directly in the middle.

5. The apex end of the triangle is brought around to the front of the elbow and fastened with a safety pin.

Note: In cases in which greater arm stabilization is required than that afforded by a sling, an additional bandage can be swathed about the upper arm and body (Fig. 14-16).

Shoulder arm sling

The shoulder arm sling (Fig. 14-2) is suggested for forearm support when there is an injury to the shoulder girdle or when

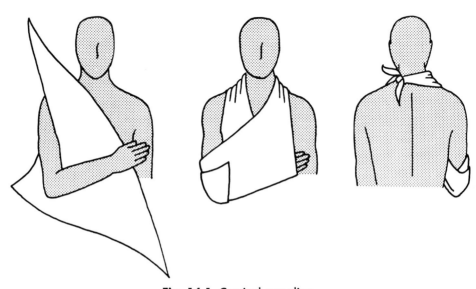

Fig. 14-1. Cervical arm sling.

the cervical arm sling is irritating to the athlete.

Materials needed: One triangular bandage and one safety pin.

Position of the athlete: The athlete stands with his injured arm bent at approximately a 70-degree angle.

Position of the trainer: The trainer stands facing the athlete.

Procedure:

1. The upper end of the shoulder sling is placed over the *uninjured* shoulder side.

2. The lower end of the triangle is brought over the forearm and drawn between the upper arm and the body, swinging around the athlete's back and then upward to meet the other end, where a square knot is tied.

3. The apex end of the triangle is brought around to the front of the elbow and fastened with a safety pin.

Roller bandages

Roller bandages are made of many materials; gauze, cotton cloth, and elastic wrapping are predominantly used in the training room. The width and length vary according to the body part to be bandaged. The sizes most frequently used are the 2-inch width by 6-yard length for hand, finger, toe, and head bandages; the 3-inch width by 10-yard length for the extremities; and the 4-inch or 6-inch width by 10-yard length for thighs, groins, and trunk. For ease and convenience in the application of the roller bandage, the strips of material are first rolled into a cylinder. When a bandage is selected, it should be a single piece that is free from wrinkles, seams, or any other imperfections that may cause skin irritation.

Application

Application of the roller bandage must be executed in a specific manner to adequately achieve the purpose of the wrap. When a roller bandage is about to be placed on a body part, the roll should be held in the preferred hand with the loose end extending from the bottom of the cylinder. The back surface of the loose end is placed on the part and held in position by the other hand. The bandage cylinder is then unrolled and passed around the injured area. As the hand pulls the material from the roll, it also standardizes the bandage pressure and guides it in the proper direction. To anchor and stabilize the bandage, a number of turns, one on top of the other, are made. Circling a body part re-

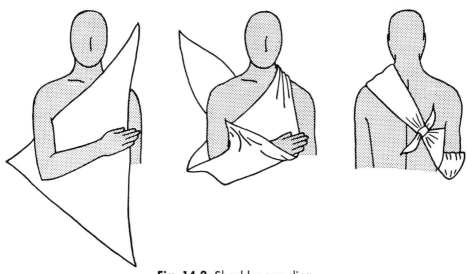

Fig. 14-2. Shoulder arm sling.

quires the operator to alternate the bandage roll from one hand to the other and back again.

To acquire maximum benefits from a roller bandage, it should be applied uniformly and firmly, but not too tightly. Excessive or unequal pressure can hinder the normal blood flow within the part. The following points should be considered when using the roller-type bandage:

1. To ensure unhampered movement or circulation, a body part should be wrapped in its position of maximum muscle contraction.

2. Rather than a limited number of turns applied too tightly, it is better to use a large number of turns with moderate tension.

3. Each turn of the bandage should be overlapped by at least one half of the overlying wrap to prevent the separation of the material while engaged in activity. Separation of the bandage turns tends to pinch and irritate the skin.

4. When limbs are wrapped, fingers and toes should be scrutinized often for signs of circulation impairment. Abnormally cold or cyanotic phalanges are signs of excessive bandage pressure.

The usual anchoring of roller bandages consists of several circular wraps directly overlying each other. Whenever possible the anchor is commenced at the smallest circumference of a limb and is then moved upward. Wrists and ankles are the usual sites for anchoring bandages of the limbs. Bandages are applied to these areas in the following manner:

1. The loose end of the roller bandage is laid obliquely on the anterior aspect of the wrist or ankle and held in this position. The roll is then carried posteriorly under and completely around the limb and back to the starting point.

2. The triangle portion of the uncovered oblique end is folded over the second turn.

3. The folded triangle is covered by a third turn, thus finishing a secure anchor.

After a roller-type bandage has been applied, it is held in place by a *locking technique*. The method most often used to finish a wrap is that of firmly tying or pinning the bandage or placing adhesive tape over several overlying turns.

Once a bandage has been put on and has served its purpose, removal can be performed either by unwrapping or by carefully cutting with a bandage scissor. Whatever method of bandage removal is employed, extreme caution must be taken to avoid additional injury.

Circular bandage

In training procedures the circular bandage (Fig. 14-3) is used to cover a cylindrical area and to anchor other types of bandages.

Fig. 14-3. Circular bandage.

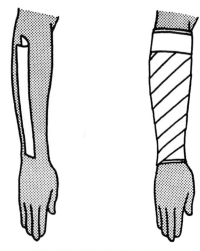

Fig. 14-4. Spiral bandage.

1. A turn is executed around the part at an oblique angle.

2. A small triangle of material is exposed by the oblique turn.

3. The triangle is bent over the first turn, with succeeding turns made over the turned down material locking it in place.

4. After several turns have been made, the bandage is fastened at a point away from the injury.

Spiral bandage

The spiral bandage (Fig. 14-4) is widely used in athletics for covering a large area of a cylindrical part.

1. The spiral bandage is anchored at the smallest circumference of the limb and is wrapped to proceed upward in a spiral against gravity.

2. To prevent the bandage from slipping down on a moving extremity, it is suggested that two pieces of tape be folded lengthwise and placed on the bandage at either side of the limb.

3. After the bandage is anchored, it is carried upward in consecutive spiral turns, each overlapping the other by at least ½ inch.

4. The bandage is terminated by locking it with circular turns, which are then firmly secured by tape.

Recurrent bandage

The recurrent bandage is designed to cover dressings and to place protective material over the injury. In athletics it is primarily used over injuries of the scalp or phalanges and knuckles of the hand.

The *recurrent bandage of the head* (Fig. 14-5) is probably the most difficult type of recurrent bandage to apply. It is used exclusively for holding scalp dressings securely in place.

1. The bandage is anchored by several turns around the head, which are completed posteriorly.

2. The bandage is then twisted one-half turn upward and stabilized by the athlete at the point of the turn.

3. The roll is continued over the center of the scalp to the forehead, folded back and carried back over the head, overlapping the first strip ½ inch.

4. This procedure is continued until the entire head is covered with alternate left and right twists over the center strip.

5. When the strips reach the sides of the head and the scalp is completely covered, two or three circular turns are taken around the head to act as a lock. After this lock is applied, a pin or tape is used to secure it in place.

The *recurrent finger bandage* (Fig. 14-6) is applied with basically the same technique as that described for the head. The bandage is started at the base of the phalanx and carried over the tip of the finger and then down the other side, adjacent to the starting point. The bandage is folded, and the pattern of the underlying bandage is retraced until several gauze pieces have been laid down. The recurrent

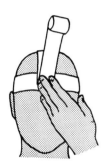 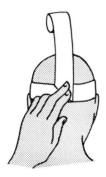  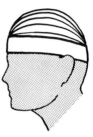

Fig. 14-5. Recurrent bandage of the head.

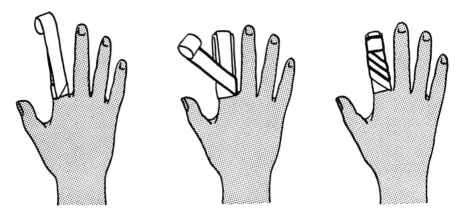

Fig. 14-6. Recurrent bandage of the finger.

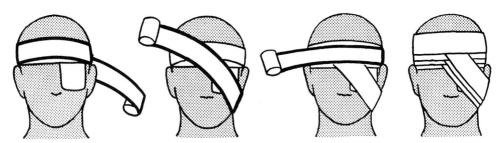

Fig. 14-7. Eye bandage.

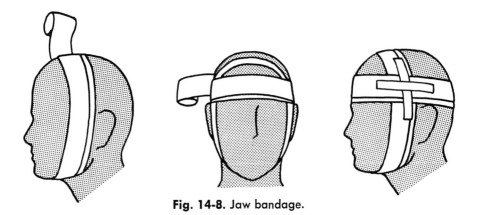

Fig. 14-8. Jaw bandage.

finger bandage is completed and held in place by circular turns. The same recurrent overlapping technique can be used wherever there is a need to protect the padding over dressings.

Eye bandage

For cases in which a bandage is needed to hold a dressing on an eye, the following procedure (Fig. 14-7) is suggested:

1. The bandage is started with a series of three circular turns around the head and then brought obliquely down the back of the head.

2. From behind the head the bandage is carried forward underneath the earlobe and upward, crossing respectively the cheek bone, the injured eye, and the bridge of the nose; it is then returned to the original circular turns.

3. The head is encircled by the bandage, and the procedure is repeated with each wrap overlapping at least two thirds of the underlying material over the injured eye.

4. When at least three series have been applied over the injured eye, the bandage is locked after completion of a circular turn around the head.

Jaw bandage

Bandages properly applied can be used to hold dressings and to stabilize dislocated or fractured jaws (Fig. 14-8):

1. The bandage is started by encircling the jaw and head in front of both ears several times.

2. The bandage is locked by a number of turns around the head.

3. Each of the two sets of turns is fastened with tape strips.

Figure-of-eight and spica

Figure-of-eight and spica bandages are readily applicable in athletic training. They are used both for support and for holding dressings in place near highly movable joints. There is little difference between the two types. The spica has a larger loop on one end, as contrasted to that of the figure-of-eight.

The shoulder, elbow, hip, knee, and ankle joints are well suited for use of the figure-of-eight or the spica bandage.

Shoulder spica

The shoulder spica (Fig. 14-9) is used predominantly for the retention of wound dressings or analgesic balm packs and for moderate muscular support.

1. The axilla must be well padded to prevent skin irritation and constriction of blood vessels.

2. The bandage is anchored by one turn around the affected upper arm.

3. After anchoring the bandage around the arm on the injured side, the wrap is carried around the back under the unaf-

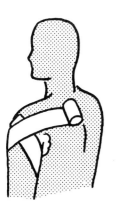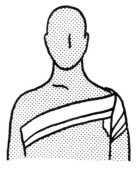

Fig. 14-9. Shoulder spica.

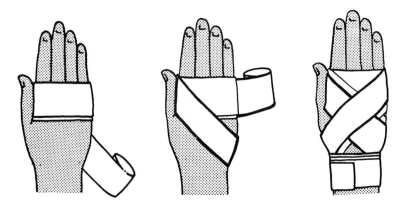

Fig. 14-10. Hand and wrist figure-of-eight.

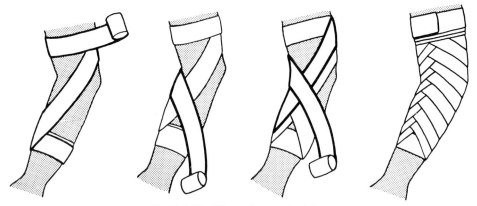

Fig. 14-11. Elbow figure-of-eight.

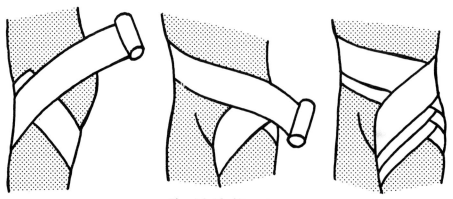

Fig. 14-12. Hip spica.

fected arm and across the chest to the injured shoulder.

4. The affected arm is again encircled by the bandage, continuing around the back. Every figure-of-eight pattern moves progressively upward with an overlap of at least one half of the previous underlying wrap.

Hand and wrist figure-of-eight

A figure-of-eight bandage (Fig. 14-10) can be used for wrist and hand support as well as for holding dressings in place. The anchor is executed with one or two turns around the palm of the hand. The roll is then carried obliquely across the anterior or posterior portion of the hand, depending on the position of the wound, to the wrist, which it circles once; then it is returned to the primary anchor. As many figures as are needed are applied.

Elbow figure-of-eight

The elbow figure-of-eight bandage (Fig. 14-11) can be used to secure a dressing in the antecubital fossa or to restrain from full extension in hyperextension injuries; when it is reversed, it can be employed for conditions on the posterior aspect of the elbow.

1. Anchor the bandage by encircling the lower arm.

2. Bring the roll obliquely upward over the posterior aspect of the elbow.

3. Carry the roll obliquely upward, crossing the antecubital fossa; then pass once again completely around the upper arm and return to the beginning position by again crossing the antecubital fossa.

4. Continue the procedure as described, but for every new sequence move upward toward the elbow one half the width of the underlying wrap.

Hip spica

The hip spica (Fig. 14-12) serves two purposes in athletics. It holds analgesic packs in place and offers a mild support to injured hip adductors or flexors.

1. Start the end of the roll at the upper part of the thigh, anchoring the end by encircling the thigh two times; then move up the thigh to the groin.

2. When the groin has been reached, take the roll around the waist directly above the crest of the ilium.

3. Continue the wrap around the thigh at groin level and again around the waist; secure the end at the waist with adhesive tape.

Ankle and foot spica

The ankle and foot spica bandage (Fig. 14-13) is used in athletics primarily for the compression of new injuries, as well as for holding analgesic heat packs in place.

1. An anchor is placed around the foot near the metatarsal arch.

2. The bandage is brought across the instep and around the heel and returned to the starting point.

3. The procedure is repeated several times, each succeeding revolution ascending upward on the foot and the ankle.

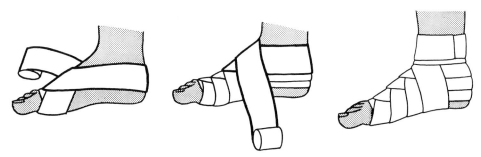

Fig. 14-13. Ankle and foot spica.

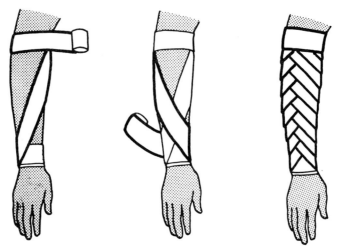

Fig. 14-14. Arm or leg figure-of-eight.

4. Each spica is overlapped by approximately three fourths of the preceding bandage.

Arm or leg figure-of-eight

As with other figure-of-eight bandages, the arm or leg type (Fig. 14-14) is used for keeping dressings in position, for holding splints in place, and for giving mild or moderate muscle support.

1. An anchor is applied by means of circular turns around the wrist or ankle.
2. A spiral strip is carried diagonally upward to a point where one complete circular turn is executed.
3. The roll is then carried downward, crossing the spiral strip, to finish one figure-of-eight.
4. The procedure is repeated until the injury site is thoroughly covered.

Sling and swathe

The sling and swathe combination is designed to stabilize the arm securely in cases of shoulder dislocation or fracture (Fig. 14-15).

Demigauntlet bandage

The demigauntlet bandage (Fig. 14-16) has considerable versatility in athletics. It holds dressings on the back of the hand

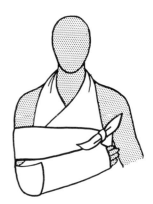

Fig. 14-15. Sling and swathe.

and it also offers support and protection to knuckles.

1. The bandage is anchored by circular turns at the wrist.
2. The roll is carried between the fourth and little finger, encircling the little finger, and is brought once again across the back of the hand to the wrist.
3. The wrist is again encircled by the roll, which is carried to the next fingers consecutively until all digits and thumb are completed.
4. Locking is executed at the wrist.

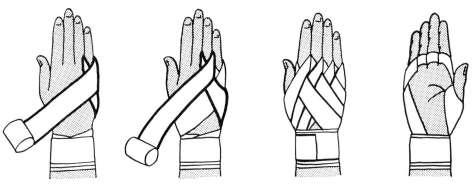

Fig. 14-16. Demigauntlet bandage.

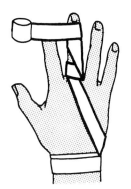 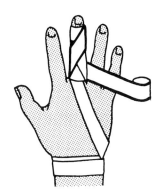 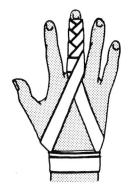

Fig. 14-17. Finger bandage.

Finger bandage

The finger bandage (Fig. 14-17) can be used to hold dressings or tongue depressor splints in place. It is applied in a fashion similar to that used for the demigauntlet, with the exception that a spiral is carried downward to the tip of the finger and then back up to finish around the wrist.

Four-tailed bandage of the jaw

The four-tailed bandage (Fig. 14-18) is most often used for stabilization in cases of possible fracture or dislocation, but it

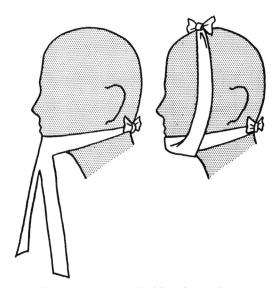

Fig. 14-18. Four-tailed bandage of jaw.

may also be used to hold dressings on the chin.

1. A 3-inch wide and 30-inch long strip of gauze is used and is split lengthwise to a distance of about 3 or 4 inches from the center.

2. The torn ends are tied around the athlete's neck, centering the middle of the strip over the chin. The portion that was not split is allowed to hang down.

3. Next, the remaining strip is split down the middle to approximately 3 or 4 inches from the center, toward the athlete's chin.

4. The torn ends are carried under the chin on each side and then brought upward over the top of the head, where they are tied in a square knot.

ADHESIVE STRAPPING IN ATHLETICS

The use of adhesive substances in the care of external lesions goes back to ancient times. The Greek civilization is credited with formulating a healing paste composed of lead oxide, olive oil, and water, which was used for a wide variety of skin conditions. This composition was only recently changed by the addition of resin and yellow beeswax and, even more recently, rubber. Since its inception, adhesive tape has developed into a vital therapeutic adjunct.[2]

Adhesive tape qualities

Modern adhesive tape has great adaptability for use in athletics because of its uniform adhesive mass, adhering qualities, and lightness, as well as the relative strength of the backing material. All of these are of value in holding wound dressings in place and in supporting and protecting injured areas.

A great many types and sizes of adhesive tape are available. The most popular tape in use today is the type with nonyielding backing. However, elastic tape is becoming increasingly popular because it easily conforms to the contour of a part. When a trainer or coach purchases tape, he must consider several factors such as cost, grade

of backing, quality of adhesive mass, and properties of unwinding.

Tape grade. Linen-backed tape is most often graded according to the number of longitudinal and vertical fibers per inch of backing material. The heavier and more costly backing contains 85 or more longitudinal fibers and 65 vertical fibers per square inch. The lighter, less expensive grade, has 65 longitudinal and 45 vertical fibers.

Adhesive mass. With modern advances in adhesive masses, one should expect certain essentials from the tape that he buys. It should adhere readily when applied and should maintain this adherence despite profuse perspiration and activity. In addition to having adequate sticking properties, the mass must contain as few skin irritants as possible and must also be able to be easily removed without leaving a mass residue or tearing the superficial skin.

Winding. The winding tension that a tape roll possesses is quite important to the operator. Athletics, in particular, places a unique demand on the unwinding quality of tape; if tape is to be applied for protection and support, there must be even and constant tension while it is being unwound. In most cases a proper wind needs little additional tension to give it sufficient tightness.

Injury care. When used in athletics, adhesive tape offers a number of possibilities for the care of injuries: (1) retention of wound dressings in place, (2) stabilization of compression-type bandages that are used to control external and internal hemorrhaging of acute injuries, and (3) support of recent injuries to prevent any additional insult that might result from the activities of the athlete.

Injury protection. Protection of acute, subacute, and chronic injuries is extremely important in reducing the athlete's chances of incurring a more handicapping condition. Protection can often be achieved in one of the following two ways: (1) limitation of joint movement by using a pre-designed strapping or (2) stabilization by securing protective devices.

Using adhesive tape in athletics

Preparation for strapping. Special attention must be given when applying tape directly to the skin. Perspiration and dirt collected during sport activities will prevent tape from sticking properly to the skin. Whenever tape is employed, the skin surface should be cleansed with soap and water to remove all dirt and oil. Hair should be removed by shaving to prevent additional irritation when the tape is removed. If additional adherence or protection from tape irritation is needed, a tincture of benzoin preparation containing storax should be applied. Commercial benzoin or skin tougheners offer astringent action and dry readily, leaving a tacky residue to which tape will adhere firmly.

Taping directly on skin provides maximum support. However, applying tape day after day can lead to skin irritation. To overcome this problem many trainers sacrifice some support by using a protective covering to the skin. A variety of protective coverings can be utilized, such as stockinette, gauze, or a commercial underwrap that is extremely thin and fits snugly to the contours of the part to be taped. Proper use of an underwrap requires the part to be shaved and sprayed with a tape adherent.

Proper strapping technique. Selection of the correct tape width for the part to be strapped depends upon the area to be covered. The more acute the angles present, the smaller the tape width needed to fit the many contours. For example, the hands and feet usually require ½-inch or 1-inch tape, the ankles require 1½-inch tape, and the larger skin areas such as thighs and back can accommodate 2- to 3-inch tape with ease.

Tearing tape. Trainers use various techniques in tearing tape (Fig. 14-19). A method should be employed that permits the operator to keep the tape roll in his hand most of the time. The following is a suggested procedure: (1) Hold the tape

roll in the preferred hand with the index finger hooked through the center of the tape roll and the thumb pressing its outer edge. (2) With the other hand grasp the loose end between the thumb and index finger. With both hands in place, make a quick, scissorlike move to tear the tape.

Rules for tape application. Included below are a few of the important rules to be observed in the use of adhesive strapping. In his practice the trainer will identify others.

1. If the part to be strapped is a joint, *place it in the position in which it is to be stabilized* or, if the part is musculature, make the necessary allowance for contraction.

2. *Overlap the tape at least one half of the width of the tape below.* Unless tape is overlapped sufficiently, the active athlete will separate it, thus exposing the underlying skin to irritation.

3. *Avoid continuous strapping.* Running tape continuously around a part may cause constriction. It is suggested that one turn be made at a time and that each encirclement be torn to overlap the starting end by approximately 1 inch.

4. *Keep the tape roll in hand whenever*

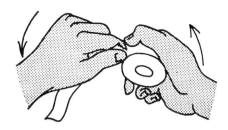

Fig. 14-19. Two methods of tearing tape.

possible and tear it with the fingers. By learning to keep the tape roll in the hand, seldom laying it down, and by learning to use the fingers to tear the tape, an operator can develop strapping speed and accuracy.

5. *Smooth and mold the tape as it is laid on the skin.* To save additional time, tape strips should be smoothed and molded as they are put in place; do this by stroking the top with the fingers, palms, and heels of both hands.

6. *Allow tape to fit the natural contour of the skin.* Each strip of tape must be laid in place with a particular purpose in mind. Most adhesive tape is not sufficiently elastic to bend around acute angles but must be allowed "to fall as it may," fitting naturally to the body contours. Failing to allow this creates wrinkles and gaps that can result in skin irritations.

7. *Start strapping with an "anchor" piece and finish by applying a "lock" strip.* Strapping should commence, if possible, by sticking the tape to an anchor piece that has encircled the part. This affords a good medium for the stabilization of succeeding tape strips so that they will not be affected by the movement of the part. After all the tape has been put in place, a final strip, running crosswise to the basic pattern, should be applied.

8. *Where support is desired, strap directly over skin surfaces.* In cases of sensitive skin, other mediums may be used as tape bases. The most popular mediums are roller gauze, gauze pads, or stockinette. With the use of these artificial bases, one can expect some movement between the skin and the base.

Removing adhesive tape. Tape can be removed from the skin by manual methods, by the use of tape scissors or special tape cutters, or by means of chemical solvents.

Manual removal: When tape is pulled from the body, the operator must be careful not to tear or irritate the skin. Tape must not be wrenched in an outward direction from the skin but should be pulled in a direct line with the body (Fig. 14-20).

Fig. 14-20. Manual removal of tape.

Use of tape scissors or cutters: The characteristic tape scissors have a blunt nose that slips underneath the tape smoothly without gouging the skin. Precautions should be taken to avoid cutting the tape too near the site of the injury, lest the scissors aggravate the condition.

Use of chemical solvents: When an adhesive mass is left on the skin after taping, a chemical agent may have to be used. Commercial cleaning solvents often contain a highly inflammable agent. Extreme care must be taken to store solvents in cool places and in tightly covered metal containers. Extensive inhalation of benzene fumes has a toxic effect. Adequate ventilation when using solvents should be provided.

OTHER PROTECTIVE AND SUPPORTIVE DEVICES

Besides the various bandages and protective and supportive adhesive strapping used in athletic training, there are commercial and self-constructed devices designed to aid the injured athlete. Some of these contrivances have considerable merit, whereas others offer little support or protection and serve only by giving the athlete a psychological crutch.

Commercial devices

It behooves the trainer or coach who must operate within a limited budget to purchase only those items which contribute to his program. It is the purpose of this section to discuss the relative values and applications of certain training devices and to assist in developing more intelligent use of these products.

Foot pads. Commercial foot pads are not usually designed to withstand the rigors of athletics. Their values lie with the walking public and not with the violent activity of the athlete. Those pads which are suited for athletics are not durable enough for the limited budget. If money is no object, the ready-made commercial pad has the advantage of saving time. Commercial pads are manufactured for almost every type of common structural foot condition, ranging from corns and bunions to fallen arches. Indiscriminate use of these aids, however, may result in increasing the pathology or delaying the athlete from seeing a physician for professional evaluation.

Orthopedic footwear. Devices that are built into or placed inside a shoe to permit proper functioning of the foot are defined as orthopedic footwear. The trainer or coach should never presume, without first consulting the team physician, to have an athlete wear orthopedic shoes. Postural imbalance, caused by foot conditions or by improper footwear, can affect the entire body by subjecting the body segments to atypical strains.

Ankle supports. Most commercial ankle supports are of either *elastic* or *spat* type. The elastic type is a flexible, fibered sheath that slides over the foot and ankle, purporting to give a mild support to a weak ankle. It has little use either as a strong support or as a protection to the postacute or chronically weakened ankle in athletics. The spat type is usually less resilient than the elastic and has an open front that permits it to be fitted directly over the ankle and then snugly tied like a shoe. Some spats have vertical ribs to effect added inversion or eversion. No commercial ankle support affords as much protection as does adhesive strapping placed directly on the skin.

Knee supports and protective devices. Knees are next in order to the ankles and feet in terms of incidence of injury in athletics. As a result of the variety and rather high frequency of knee afflictions, many protective and supportive devices have evolved.

The devices most frequently used in athletics today are braces, elastic supports, and elastic pads. Knee braces are probably the most varied, with three major types being employed extensively. These include the wrap-around, the hinge, and the ribbed types, all of which supposedly support weak knee joints. The wrap-around consists of an elastic sleeve with a series of straps that encircle the knee and buckle at different points, giving medial, lateral, anterior, and posterior support. The hinge brace may be an elastic or a laced leather sleeve having on either side of the knee a metal hinge that bends with knee flexion. Athletes often use just an elastic support for mild compression and support. Regardless of the commercial gadget employed, the athlete can expect to gain only moderate support at the most. Adhesive strapping, when properly applied, is far superior to any commercial knee support. For the most part, knee braces can be put into the category of psychological aids.

Elastic knee pads or guards are extremely valuable in sports in which the athlete falls or receives a direct blow to the anterior aspect of the knee. An elastic sleeve containing a resilient material helps to dissipate any anterior striking force but fails to prevent lateral, medial, or twisting trauma.

Abdominal and low back supports. Because low back strain is a national problem, along with problems affecting the feet, there are many gimmicks on the market that claim to give relief. Such devices may be classified as abdominal and low back supports (Fig. 14-21). Where freedom of activity is desired, as in athletics, a rigid and nonyielding material may be handicapping. A material that will permit move-

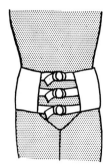

Fig. 14-21. Abdominal and lower back support.

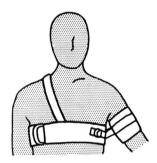

Fig. 14-22. Shoulder brace.

ment and still offer support is desirable. Such material may consist of elastic, rubberized fabric. In most cases of low back strain, supporting the abdominal viscera will alleviate considerable discomfort.

Shoulder braces. The shoulder braces (Fig. 14-22) used in athletics are essentially restraining belts for the chronically dislocated shoulder. Their purpose is to restrict the upper arm from being elevated more than 90 degrees and externally rotated, thus preventing it from being placed in a vulnerable position. Because of the ensuing limitation in range of motion of the arm, the athlete's capabilities are considerably reduced.

Other elastic pads and supports. Elastic pads and supports are varied and can be suited to most body areas. Thigh, forearm, wrist, and elbow devices afford mild support and give protection from direct blows.

Construction of devices

Being able to construct protective and supportive devices is of considerable value to the trainer and coach. The mediums used are sponge rubber, felt, combine (a combination of gauze and cotton), adhesive felt or sponge rubber, gauze pads, cotton, and lamb's wool. All these have special uses in athletic training.

Sponge rubber (foam rubber) is resilient, nonabsorbent, and able to protect the body against shock. It is particularly valuable for use as a protective padding of bruised areas and it can also serve as a supportive pad. It ranges from ½ to ⅛ inch in thickness.

Felt is a material composed of matted wool fibers pressed into varying thicknesses that range from ¼ to 1 inch. Its benefit lies in its comfortable, semiresilient surface, which gives a firmer pressure than most sponge rubbers. Because felt will absorb perspiration, it clings to the skin, and it has less tendency to move about than sponge rubber. Because of its absorbent qualities it must be replaced daily.

Combine is a soft, highly absorbent material that acts in the dual role of a protective pad and a holder for analgesic balms and medicinal emollients.

Adhesive felt or sponge rubber is a felt or sponge rubber material containing an adhesive mass on one side, thus combining a cushioning effect with the ability to be held in a specific spot by the adhesive mass —a versatile material that is useful on all body parts.

Gauze padding is less versatile than other pad materials. It is assembled in varying thicknesses and can be used as an absorbent and as a protective pad.

Cotton is probably the cheapest and most widely used material in athletics. It has the ability to absorb, to hold emollients, and to offer a mild padding effect.

Lamb's wool is a material commonly used by trainers on and around the athlete's toes when circular protection is required.

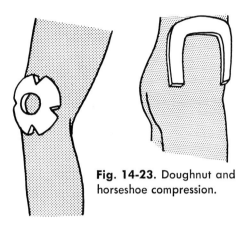

Fig. 14-23. Doughnut and horseshoe compression.

In contrast to cotton, lamb's wool does not pack but keeps its resiliency over a long period of time.

Protective pads can be of varying shapes and sizes, cut to fit the body contours. In addition to the flat and variously shaped compression pads, pads of two other distinct shapes, the *doughnut* and the *horseshoe*, are often used (Fig. 14-23). Each is adapted so that pressure is placed around the perimeter of an injured area, leaving the injury free from additional pressure or

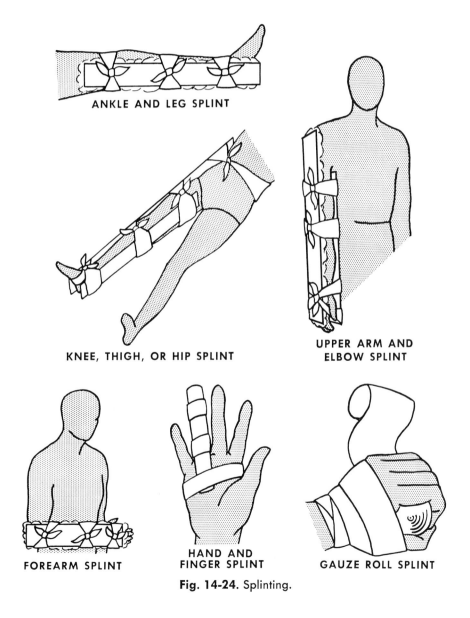

ANKLE AND LEG SPLINT

KNEE, THIGH, OR HIP SPLINT

UPPER ARM AND ELBOW SPLINT

FOREARM SPLINT

HAND AND FINGER SPLINT

GAUZE ROLL SPLINT

Fig. 14-24. Splinting.

trauma. Most of these pads are held in place with tape or an elastic wrap.

Splinting techniques

Any suspected fracture should be splinted before the athlete is moved. Transporting a person having a fracture, without proper immobilization, can result in increased tissue damage, hemorrhage, and shock. Conceivably a mishandled fracture could cause death. Therefore, a thorough knowledge of splinting techniques is important (Fig. 14-24).

In most instances the trainer does not have to improvise a splint, since such devices are readily available in most athletic settings. Commercially sold basswood splints are excellent, as is disposable cardboard or a clear plastic commercial splint, which is inflated with air around the affected part (Fig. 14-25). This excellent innovation provides support and moderate pressure to the part, and affords a clear view of the site for x-ray examination. Whatever the material used, the principles of good splinting remain the same.

Splinting of lower limb fractures. Fractures of the ankle or leg require immobilization of the foot and knee. Any fracture involving the knee, thigh, or hip needs splinting of all the lower limb joints and the trunk on one side.

Splinting of the spine and pelvis. The ideal mode of transporting someone with a fractured spine or pelvis is on a straight board, on which all segments of the body are stabilized. Boards of needed length and width are difficult to find; therefore, transportation in most cases of this type is by stretcher.

Splinting of upper limb fractures. Fractures about the shoulder complex are immobilized by the sling and swathe bandages, with the upper limb bound to the body securely. Upper arm and elbow fractures must be splinted with immobilization effected in a straight arm position to lessen bone override. Lower arm and wrist fractures should be splinted in a position of forearm flexion, supported by a sling. Hand and finger dislocations and fractures should be splinted by use of tongue depressors or gauze rolls.

LIFESAVING TECHNIQUES

Relatively few athletes have died in athletic activity or have been placed in a life-and-death situation as a result of sports

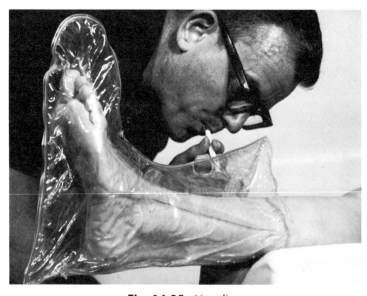

Fig. 14-25. Air splint.

participation. Nonetheless, the trainer and coach must have a knowledge of emergency lifesaving techniques that can be used if needed.

Resuscitation

One type of resuscitation discussed here is the use of artificial respiration, which may revive an individual who has lost the ability to breathe. Artificial respiration techniques are numerous, but the most commonly used manual procedure is the mouth-to-mouth method. It is designed to assist with the rhythmical inhalation and exhalation of the lungs so that the oxygen balance of the body is maintained until normal breathing can be reestablished. A more recent type that is being used is heart-lung resuscitation, which employs the mouth-to-mouth method of artificial respiration and, if necessary, cardiac massage.

Oxygen must be present in the body cells or death will ensue. *Clinical death* is considered to occur when the heartbeat and breathing have ceased. *Biological death* occurs when clinical death has continued from 4 to 6 minutes, after which time there is irreversible brain damage.

Each type of tissue within the body has its own level of oxygen requirement. Nerve cells begin to die when they are denied oxygen for approximately 6 minutes. The brain is especially sensitive to a lack of oxygen. A balance of 21% oxygen and 4% carbon dioxide during inhalation and an exhalation ratio of 16% oxygen and 4% carbon dioxide must be maintained to preserve life.

Artificial respiration must be given immediately to individuals who have ceased to breathe. Never postpone the use of manual resuscitation while waiting for a mechanical resuscitator to arrive. The manual process of artificial respiration is designed to take the place of normal respiration and to maintain the oxygen level within the body until spontaneous breathing is resumed. Life can be maintained as long as the heart continues to circulate blood.

In athletics there are only a few injuries

that may cause breathing to be stopped. These primarily include a severe blow to the solar plexus, which controls the diaphragm, a severe concussion, or a neck fracture that results in a paralysis of the costal muscles and the diaphragm.

Mouth-to-mouth method. The mouth-to-mouth method of artificial respiration (Fig. 14-26) is the most primitive method of maintaining positive pressure in a person who has ceased to breathe. It involves directly forcing air into the lungs of the patient. One operator can continue this method for a prolonged period without extreme fatigue. The one negative factor in the use of the mouth-to-mouth method is the offensiveness that some persons feel when they must breathe directly into another person's mouth. The problem may be solved by the use of a handkerchief placed over the mouth or by a commercial airway.

Heart-lung resuscitation. In some cases of injury, cardiac arrest or heart stoppage may also be present, demanding the dual technique of heart-lung, or cardiopulmonary resuscitation, as suggested by the American Medical Association.[3] This

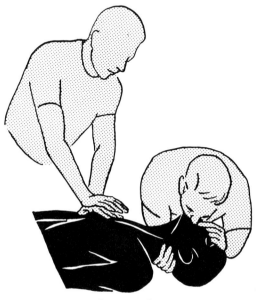

Fig. 14-26. Mouth-to-mouth resuscitation coupled with closed chest heart massage.

method employs both mouth-to-mouth artificial respiration and, when indicated, closed-chest cardiac massage. The following procedures should be initiated:

1. Check athlete's pulse for heartbeat. One of the most prominent pulse sites lies at the carotid artery on either side of the Adam's apple.

2. Check the athlete's respiration. Check shallow breathing by the rise and fall of the patient's abdomen.

3. Check the eyes for dilated pupils. Widely dilated pupils may indicate the lack of a functioning heart or lungs.

4. Where signs of respiration or pulse are not detectable, execute heart-lung resuscitation as follows:

   a. The athlete's mouth is cleared of all obstructions.

   b. The athlete is positioned on his back. The operator uses one hand to lift the athlete's neck, bringing it as far back as possible. In this position a clear airway is made.

   c. After the athlete is in the correct position, the operator takes a deep breath and places his mouth over the athlete's, forming an airtight seal. At the same time he pinches the athlete's nostrils together to prevent air from escaping. Artificial ventilation can also be conducted by a mouth-to-nose or mouth-to-airway device.

   d. When the athlete's chest becomes expanded with air, the operator ceases blowing and removes his mouth from the athlete's, thus permitting air to escape from the lungs.

5. Check carotid artery for pulse. If there is no pulse, closed-chest cardiac massage must be started immediately.

   a. The athlete must be on a firm surface. The operator kneels beside the athlete and places the heel of one hand over the lower third of his sternum and places the other hand on top of the first.

   b. The operator moves his weight over the chest, pushing the sternum downward 1½ to 2 inches and releasing the

pressure quickly after each downward thrust.

   c. The rhythm of the compression should be around 60 per minute for the adult and 80 per minute for the child.

   d. When fifteen chest compressions have been made, two mouth-to-mouth respirations are given filling the lungs to capacity.

It should be remembered that the heart-lung, or cardiopulmonary, resuscitation is continuous until breathing and normal heart rate are restored.

Endotracheal tube: The use of the endotracheal tube should be reserved for a specialist in first aid, since there are several dangers if it is used improperly. Foreign objects may be pushed farther down into the throat or, improperly introduced, it may injure the soft tissues of the throat. The greatest advantage in the endotracheal airway is its ability to bring breath to the lungs without direct mouth-to-mouth contact.

Portable mechanical resuscitator. Most portable mechanical resuscitators are of the "suck-and-blow" type with positive pressure in inspiration and negative pressure for expiration. Most machines of this type use oxygen to encourage breathing and also have the ability to pull mucous secretions from the throat. This device is most valuable when oxygen is needed, as in cases of asphyxiation or cases in which mucus and fluids are blocking normal breathing. Under no circumstances should an untrained person use such a machine. In most situations mouth-to-mouth resuscitation will give the same desirable results.

TRANSPORTING THE INJURED ATHLETE

Transporting the injured athlete must be executed in such a manner as to prevent further injury. First-aid authorities have suggested that improper transportation causes more additional insult to injuries than does any other first-aid procedure. There is no excuse for the use of poor transportation techniques in athletics. Preplanning should take into consideration all

Fig. 14-27. Ambulatory aid.

Fig. 14-28. Manual conveyance.

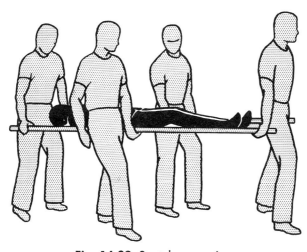

Fig. 14-29. Stretcher carrying.

possible methods that may be necessary for the transportation of any injured athlete. Capable persons, stretchers, and even an ambulance may be indicated to carry out the transportation of the injured athlete. Four modes of assisting in travel are used: ambulatory aid, manual conveyance, stretcher carrying, and vehicular transfer.

Ambulatory aid. Ambulatory aid (Fig. 14-27) is that support or assistance given to an injured athlete who is able to walk. Before the athlete is allowed to be on his feet, he should be carefully scrutinized by the trainer or coach to make sure that the injuries are minor. Whenever serious injuries are suspected, walking should be prohibited. Complete support should be given on both sides of the athlete. His arms are draped over the assistants' shoulders and their arms encircle his back.

Manual conveyance. Manual conveyance (Fig. 14-28) may be used to move a mildly injured individual a greater distance than he is able to walk with ease. As with the use of ambulatory aid, any decision to carry the athlete must be made only after a complete examination to determine the existance of possibly serious conditions. The most convenient carry is done by two assistants, with one standing behind the seated athlete and grasping him around the chest while the other, standing in front and with his back to the athlete, grasps the athlete's legs.

Stretcher carrying. Whenever a serious injury is suspected, the best and safest mode of transportation for a short distance is by stretcher. With each segment of his body supported, the athlete is gently lifted and placed on the stretcher, which is carried adequately by four assistants, two supporting the ends of the stretcher and two supporting either side (Fig. 14-29). It should be noted that any person with an injury which is serious enough to demand use of a stretcher must be examined by a physician before he is moved.

Vehicular transfer. If an injury demands vehicular transfer, the trainer or coach should, if at all possible, use an ambulance. Only in an extreme emergency should other modes of travel be considered. Because of the liability risks involved, it is unwise for a trainer or coach to use his own car. Most vehicles, other than ambulances, are not equipped for carrying a stretcher patient. In cases of moderate injury, when it is inadvisable for an athlete to walk home, his parents should be notified so that they may take him home or to a place where he will receive proper medical attention.

REFERENCES

1. Wagner, M., and others: Clinical and research applications of a new elastic cohesive bandage, Amer. J. Surg. **119:**298, 1970.
2. Therapeutic uses of adhesive tape, New Brunswick, N. J., 1958, Johnson and Johnson.
3. Ad Hoc Committee on Cardiopulmonary Resuscitation of the Division of Medical Sciences, National Academy of Sciences, National Research Council: Cardiopulmonary resuscitation, J.A.M.A. **198:**372, 1966.

RECOMMENDED READINGS

Belilios, A. D., Mulvany, D. K., and Armstrong, K. F.: A handbook of first aid and bandaging, London, 1962, Baillièr, Tindall & Cox.

Cramer's of Gardner, Kansas: The student trainer manual, Gardner, Kansas, Cramer's.

Dixon, D.: The dictionary of athletic training, Bloomington, Ind., 1965, Bloomcraft—Central Printing, Inc.

Dolan, J. P.: Treatment and prevention of athletic injuries, Danville, Ill., 1967, Interstate Printers & Publishers, Inc.

CHAPTER 15

Athletic reconditioning

In a broad sense athletic reconditioning is considered as the restoration of the athlete to the level of his preinjury fitness, after he has received a handicapping injury. The type of reconditioning program followed by the athlete is of vital importance in effecting as rapid a return to competition as possible. The athlete who receives an injury in a sport occupies a rather special position. If he wishes to compete successfully in his activity he must return to action within a relatively short time and must then be able to compete on a par with his teammates or opponents. These requirements pose several problems to the trainer, coach, physician, and the athlete himself. At no time must the immediate or future health of the athlete be endangered as a result of hasty decisions; but at the same time the dedicated athlete should be given every possible opportunity to compete, provided such competition does not pose undue risk. The final decision in this matter must rest with the qualified sports physician. He must decide at what point the athlete can reenter competition without the dangers of reinjury, as well as when the use of supportive strapping or other preventive aids is necessary to prevent further injury. It has been said that a good substitute is always more valuable than an injured star. There must be full cooperation between coach, trainer, and physician—a team approach, as it were—in helping to re-

store the athlete to his previous level of competitive fitness. Working together, they can initiate a therapeutic program of reconditioning that will hasten the recovery period of the athlete.

ACTIVE REHABILITATION

Members of the medical profession are in general agreement that prolonged bed rest and inactivity can delay recovery. This is particularly true with muscular and skeletal involvements. Frequently, intensive exercise programs are scheduled for preoperative preparation of a patient. Such conditioning shortens recovery periods. After surgery, postoperative exercising is encouraged, which further decreases the period of rehabilitation. Controlled exercise during convalescence from a soft tissue injury assists in resolution and healing by decreasing edema and the less viable scar tissue. Reconditioning should be an integral part of the recovery program, and recuperation and rehabilitation will be greatly accelerated if the foregoing principles are remembered when caring for injured athletes.

In addition to the athlete's use of specific exercises assigned for rehabilitation of a part, a level of general physical conditioning must be maintained and improved during the period of incapacitation. When his injuries have fully healed, the athlete should be physically fit and ready to resume normal activity. An extensive conditioning program that contributes to total body fitness but avoids possible aggravation of the injury is advocated.

CONSEQUENCES OF INACTIVITY

Individuals suffering from severe infections are generally debilitated and may have chronic inflammations, organic involvements, or intense pain on moving a part; they may require inactivity. But if injury has been incurred by a healthy and active person, prescribing inactivity may be the placing of insult upon insult. Lack of activity causes a generalized muscle atrophy, as well as a specific degeneration surrounding the injury site. Besides showing muscle atrophy, the body is unable to properly rid itself of waste materials. The athlete therefore loses endurance, strength, flexibility, and coordination and may, as a consequence, forfeit his confidence and his ability in the sport.

PSYCHOLOGICAL CONSIDERATIONS

To understand all of the various psychological implications attending an injury in sports would require extensive analysis, research, and study not within the scope of this book. In training, interest centers more upon the overt signs of maladjustment (see Chapter 9). Many times, an injury causes the athlete to lose his desire to return to athletics. The reasons for such feeling may be manifold: fear of pain, fear of falling, fear of failing those around him, or even the fear of sustaining a handicapping injury. No single answer can describe why some individuals are more psychologically sensitive to injuries than are others. In combating these fears, the total person must be the focus of attention. Whenever possible, the athlete should be kept close to the athletic program, reporting to his team or event as he can, for work within the limits of his injury. This will give him the desire to return to action as soon as possible. The psychological atmosphere that surrounds him following injury is of considerable significance, and at all times a *positive* approach should be used.

Statements such as "You're getting strong fast!" or "You'll be back in the game in no time at all!" and "Keep up the good work, you're making a great improvement!" will create the proper psychological climate.

PROGRAM OF RECONDITIONING

It is apparent that reconditioning after an athletic injury is the combined responsibility of all individuals connected with a specific sport. To devise a program that is most conducive to the good of the athlete, basic objectives consonant with a philosophy that considers his needs important must be developed. In addition to maintenance of a good psychological climate, discussed above, the following are such objectives: (1) prevention of deconditioning of the total body and (2) rehabilitation of the injured part without hampering the healing process.

Preventing deconditioning involves keeping the body physically fit while the injury heals. In establishing a conditioning program, emphasis should be placed on the maintenance of strength, flexibility, endurance, and coordination of the total body. Whenever possible, the athlete should engage in activities of a type that will aid him in his sport but will not endanger recovery from the injury.

Rehabilitating the injured part is of such importance that a program of rehabilitation must be started as soon as possible. An injured part, particularly in an injury to a joint or to the musculature, must be kept from showing disuse degeneration. Disuse will result in atrophy, muscle contractures, inflexibility, and delays in healing because of circulatory impairment. This is not to imply that athletic injuries should be "run off or worked off." Rather, a proper balance between resting and exercising should be maintained. This then is one of the responsibilities of rehabilitation.

THERAPEUTIC EXERCISE

Therapeutic exercises, like conditioning exercises are concerned with four basic components: (1) muscular strength, (2) flexibility, (3) muscular endurance, and (4) coordination and speed of movement.

Muscular strength. Muscular strength allows the athlete to overcome a given resistance. It is one of the most essential factors in the restoration of function following injury. Muscle size and strength can be increased with use and can decrease in cases of disuse. Both isotonic and isometric muscle contraction are used to advantage in reconditioning. Isotonic exercises are preferable because they increase function of a part through a complete range of movement. Isometric exercises involve no movement of the joint, but develop strength primarily in the position exercised.

Most programs of exercise utilizing the overload principle for restoring physical function employ the concept of "progressive resistance exercise" as set forth by DeLorme.[7] This method employs the isotonic principle and basically uses ten repetitions for each exercise bout (set). Exercise bouts are repeated three times. The first bout uses one-half maximum resistance load, the second bout uses three-fourths maximum load, and a full resistance load is performed for the third bout (see Chapter 7).

Isometric exercise as suggested by Hettinger and Müller employs a three-quarter maximum effort to maintain and develop strength. Though generally not preferred as a primary method for strength development, isometrics has proved beneficial in rehabilitation. It is used when the athlete is not allowed to execute isotonic movements. In cases where an injured part is immobilized, static muscle contraction can assist in the prevention of muscle atrophy until movement can be executed.

Flexibility. Flexibility must be present if a part is to be functional. A part that is immobilized in a cast or brace, or is not moved regularly through a full range of movement will eventually become inflexible. An important aspect of the athletic reconditioning regimen are stretching techniques. They are usually instituted if their execution will not aggravate the injury.

Stretching exercises are considered most effective when executed slowly and deliberately without ballistic movements. Bouncing or jerky stretching tends to stimulate the stretch reflex and contracts rather than relaxes the muscle. In actively performing the static stretch, the athlete takes the stretch position and maintains it for 1 to 2 minutes; at the same time he actively contracts the antagonist muscles to those being stretched. This procedure inhibits the stretch reflex of the stretched muscle. A system utilizing this concept of muscle relaxation is called proprioceptive neuromuscular facilitation.[5] Proprioceptive neuromuscular facilitation is being used increasingly in the reconditioning of athletes following injury, particularly where range of motion must be increased or maintained. Proprioceptive neuromuscular facilitation is defined as improving the neuromuscular mechanism through stimulating the proprioceptors. The concept of relaxing and subsequently increasing the extensibility of a muscle or muscle group is based upon the physiological premise that contraction of a muscle is followed by a lengthening, relaxation, and/or inhibition of the antagonistic muscles.[5] There are three techniques that can accomplish this end: contract-relax, hold-relax and slow reversal-hold-relax.

In the *contract-relax* technique the trainer passively moves the affected part until resistance is felt, at which time the athlete is instructed to contract the part isotonically while the trainer resists the movement. Following resistance the athlete is instructed to relax. After the part is relaxed the trainer passively moves the part through range until the limits of the range have been reached, after which the technique is repeated.

The *hold-relax* technique is based on a maximal isometric resistance being given by the trainer. It is similar to the contract-relax technique. The athlete holds at the point where resistance is given rather than pushing or pulling.

The *slow reversal-hold-relax* technique utilizes an isotonic contraction followed by

an isometric contraction of the opposite
or antagonist muscle group.

Muscle endurance. Muscle endurance is
important to the restoration of the injured
part. Muscle endurance is the ability to
sustain muscle contractions at a submaximal
effort over a period of time. Muscle strength
and endurance are indivisible parts of a
continuum. For example, exercises employing progressive resistance at near maximum
effort for between 4 and 6 repetitions effect
mainly strength; decreasing the resistance
and increasing the number of repetitions requires the ability to sustain a movement.

The final stages of reconditioning are
concerned with reestablishing coordination
and the speed of movement. Before an athlete returns to his sport ready to resume
full activity he must be able to perform at
the same level of proficiency and have the
same potential for delaying fatigue as before he became hurt. An athlete who is not
at full capacity or who favors an injury part
will most likely become reinjured or develop associated problems.

Body mechanics. Body mechanics must
always be a concern when considering a
program of physical reconditioning. Athletic affections often produce asymmetrical
behavior. An arm in a sling or the leg in a
cast are examples of situations which dis-
turb the symmetry of the body and place
abnormal stress on the musculoskeletal system. The trainer should insist that the athlete maintain proper postural balance while
recovering from injury.

RECONDITIONING EXERCISES

Reconditioning exercises can be classified into four categories: (1) passive, (2)
assistive, (3) active, and (4) resistive. Each
can be used to advantage in restoring the
athlete to a state of competitive fitness.

Passive exercise. Passive exercise is the
movement of an affected part by another
person or by a device, without effort by the
athlete. This technique can be used to advantage if an injury has hampered the
range of joint motion or if the apprehensive

athlete must be shown that his condition
has been repaired and that there is no need
for fear on his part.

Assistive exercise. Assistive exercise is
movement of an injured part by the athlete,
but with the assistance of another person.
This type is used in conjunction with passive exercise to aid the patient in gaining
confidence.

Active exercise. Active exercise is movement that is executed by the patient without assistance. Exercises falling into this
category are those used for general conditioning and those used remedially for restoring function to an injured part.

Resistive exercise. Resistive exercise is
movement that the athlete performs against
a resisting force. This type is illustrated
in the progressive weight training exercises discussed in Chapter 7. Both isotonic and isometric weight training exercises can be invaluable in effecting rapid
recovery.

Exercises representing each of the four
basic types are suggested in the chapters
that deal with specific athletic conditions.
We consider this a practical and useful approach.

Some general rules for reconditioning are
as follows:

1. Maintain general conditioning.
2. Maintain good body mechanics.
3. Exercise the affected part two to
   three times daily.
4. Execute all exercises smoothly to
   avoid pain.
5. Modify exercises if they cause pain,
   discomfort, or decrease in joint range.
6. Know the reason for a particular exercise and routine.
7. Be certain that full strength, endurance, and flexibility are restored before resuming competition.

Specific reconditioning exercises are discussed in the following section.

SELECTED EXERCISES

The following exercises have been selected for use by the trainer in devising
a specific and individualized program of

reconditioning for the injured athlete. The proposed exercises, in their various groupings, are graded according to difficulty and intensity. It is suggested that the trainer first identify the injury that necessitates reconditioning in terms of the muscles involved, and then make his choice of exercises accordingly. The progression of work should range from passive exercises through those of heavy resistance type, with the number of sets and repetitions employed as suggested in Chapter 7.

Foot, ankle, and leg exercises

1. Plantar flexion and dorsiflexion
2. Ankle suppler
3. Foot arching
4. Tendo achillis stretch
5. Heel raising
6. Lateral stretch
7. Plantar and dorsal resistance against towel
8. Marble pickup
9. Towel gather
10. Plantar flexion and dorsiflexion against resistance
11. Inversion and eversion of foot
12. Grip and spread

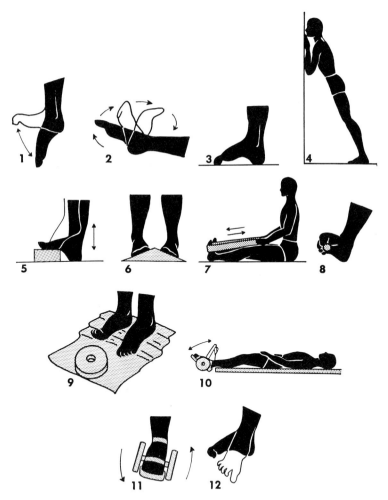

Fig. 15-1. Foot, leg and ankle exercises. **1**, Plantar flexion and dorsiflexion; **2**, ankle suppler; **3**, foot arching; **4**, tendo achillis stretch; **5**, heel raising; **6**, lateral stretch; **7**, plantar and dorsal resistance against towel; **8**, marble pickup; **9**, towel gather; **10**, plantar flexion and dorsiflexion against resistance; **11**, inversion and eversion of foot; **12**, grip and spread.

Fig. 15-2. Knee and thigh exercises. **1,** Isometric (static) exercise, "quad setting"; **2,** knee extension; **3,** wall push; **4,** quadriceps stretch; **5,** hamstring stretch; **6,** hamstring and lower back stretch; **7,** stationary swimming; **8,** bleacher run; **9,** stationary bicycle riding; **10,** quadriceps strengthening; **11,** hamstring strengthening; **12,** press bar leg thrust.

Knee and thigh exercises

1. Isometric (static) exercise, "quad setting"
2. Knee extension
3. Wall push
4. Quadriceps stretch
5. Hamstring stretch
6. Hamstring and lower back stretch
7. Stationary swimming
8. Bleacher run
9. Stationary bicycle riding
10. Quadriceps strengthening
11. Hamstring strengthening
12. Press bar leg thrust

Hip exercises

1. Bicycling
2. Hip lift
3. Hip abduction and adduction against resistance
4. Hip circumduction with boot
5. Hip flexion with boot
6. Hip rotation with boot
7. Hip raise
8. Abduction with boot
9. Hip extension with boot

Fig. 15-3. Hip exercises. **1,** Bicycling; **2,** hip lift; **3,** hip abduction and adduction against resistance; **4,** hip circumduction with boot; **5,** hip flexion with boot; **6,** hip rotation with boot; **7,** hip raise; **8,** abduction with boot; **9,** hip extension with boot.

Fig. 15-4. Abdomen and back exercises. **1,** Alternating leg lift; **2,** trunk circling; **3,** relaxed hang; **4,** abdominal curl; **5,** twist sit-up; **6,** chair stretch; **7,** side raise; **8,** leg crossover; **9,** full bridge; **10,** back arch; **11,** sit-up with weight; **12,** back raise.

Abdomen and back exercises

1. Alternating leg lift
2. Trunk circling
3. Relaxed hang
4. Abdominal curl
5. Twist sit-up
6. Chair stretch
7. Side raise
8. Leg crossover
9. Full bridge
10. Back arch
11. Sit-up with weight
12. Back raise

Neck exercises

1. Sayre sling traction
2. Head up-down, side-to-side
3. Rotary stretch
4. Head lift
5. Half bridge
6. Anteroposterior neck resistance
7. Head-neck rotation
8. Neck raise against resistance
9. Head halter with weight

Fig. 15-5. Neck exercises. **1,** Sayre sling traction; **2,** Head up-down, side-to-side; **3,** rotary stretch; **4,** head lift; **5,** half bridge; **6,** anteroposterior neck resistance; **7,** head-neck rotation; **8,** neck raise against resistance; **9,** head halter with weight.

Shoulder complex exercises

1. Pendulum
2. Shoulder stretch
3. Swimming
4. Arm and shoulder stretch with towel
5. Shoulder wheel
6. Shoulder flexion
7. Shoulder abduction
8. Pectoral strengthening
9. Abduction raise
10. Shoulder shrug
11. Backward extension
12. Rhomboid lift
13. Flexion raise
14. Push-up
15. Parallel bar dips

Fig. 15-6. Shoulder complex exercises. **1,** Pendulum; **2,** shoulder stretch; **3,** swimming; **4,** arm and shoulder stretch with towel; **5,** shoulder wheel; **6,** shoulder flexion; **7,** shoulder abduction; **8,** pectoral strengthening; **9,** abduction raise; **10,** shoulder shrug; **11,** backward extension; **12,** rhomboid lift; **13,** flexion raise; **14,** push-up; **15,** parallel bar dips.

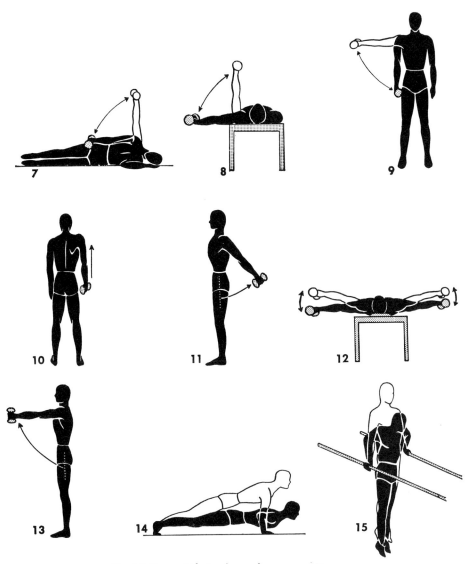

Fig 15-6, cont'd. For legend see opposite page.

Fig. 15-7. Elbow, wrist, and hand exercises. **1,** Wrist circumduction; **2,** grip and spread; **3,** ball squeeze; **4,** towel twist; **5,** supination and pronation against resistance; **6,** wrist roll; **7,** arm curl; **8,** elbow extension; **9,** rope skipping; **10,** push-up; **11,** parallel bar dips; **12,** pull-up.

Elbow, wrist, and hand exercises

1. Wrist circumduction
2. Grip and spread
3. Ball squeeze
4. Towel twist
5. Supination and pronation against resistance
6. Wrist roll
7. Arm curl
8. Elbow extension
9. Rope skipping
10. Push-up
11. Parallel bar dips
12. Pull-up

REFERENCES

1. Ryan, A. J.: Medical care of the athlete, New York, 1962, The McGraw-Hill Book Co., Inc.
2. Hirata, I., Jr.: The doctor and the athlete, Philadelphia, 1968, J. B. Lippincott Co.
3. Rusk, H. A.: Rehabilitation medicine, ed. 3, St. Louis, 1971, The C. V. Mosby Co.
4. Licht, S.: Therapeutic exercise, New Haven, Conn., 1965, Elizabeth Licht, Publisher.
5. Knott, M., and Voss, D. E.: Proprioceptive neuromuscular facilitation, ed. 2, New York, 1968, Harper & Row Publishers.
6. Arnheim, D. D., and others: Principles and methods of adapted physical education, ed. 2, St. Louis, 1973, The C. V. Mosby Co.
7. DeLorme, T. L., and Watkins, A. L.: Progressive resistance exercises, New York, 1951, Appleton-Century-Crofts.

RECOMMENDED READINGS

DeLorme, T. L., and Watkins, A. L.: Progressive resistance exercises, New York, 1951, Appleton-Century-Crofts.

Hittinger, T.: Physiology of strength, Springfield, Ill., 1961, Charles C Thomas, Publisher.

Licht, S.: Therapeutic exercise, New Haven, Conn., 1965, Elizabeth Licht, Publisher.

Prevention and care of the athletic injury

PART THREE

The overall intent of this text has been to take the reader from general to more specific concepts. Part Three is designed to utilize the knowledge imparted in Parts One and Two in the care of specific injuries.

CHAPTER 16

Conditions of the foot, ankle, and leg

The foot

ANATOMY

The foot is designed basically for strength, flexibility, and coordinated movement. It is comprised of 26 bones: 14 phalangeal, 5 metatarsal, and 7 tarsal (Fig. 16-1). The tarsal bones, which form the instep or ankle portion of the foot, consist of the talus (astragalus), the calcaneus (os calcis), the navicular (scaphoid), and the first, second, and third cuneiform bones.

The *talus,* an irregularly shaped bone, is situated on the calcaneus over a bony projection called the sustentaculum tali in such a manner as to permit movement in only a forward and downward direction. It is stabilized by both internal and external ligaments on all four sides.

The *calcaneus* is the largest tarsal bone. It supports the talus and shapes the heel; its main functions are to convey the body weight to the ground and act as a lever attachment for the calf muscles.

The *navicular, cuboid,* and *cuneiform* bones, as a group, are the transverse tarsal bones, which glide upon each other in a combined movement that permits rotation, inversion, and eversion of the foot.

The *metatarsals* are 5 bones that lie between and articulate with the tarsals and the phalanges, thus forming the semimovable tarsometatarsal and metatarsophalangeal joints. Although there is little movement permitted, the ligamentous arrange-

ment gives elasticity to the foot in weight bearing. The metatarsophalangeal joints, permit a hinge action to the phalanges, which is similar to the action found between the hand and fingers. The first metatarsal is the largest and strongest and functions as the main body support during walking and running.

The *phalanges* or toes are somewhat similar to the fingers in appearance but are much shorter and serve a different function. The toes are designed to give a wider base both for balance and for gripping the ground when propelling the body forward.

The *sesamoid bones,* of which there are two, are located beneath the first metatarsophalangeal joint. Their functions are to assist in reducing pressure in weight bearing, to alleviate undue friction during movement, and to act as sliding pulleys for tendons.

The foot is structured, by means of ligamentous and bony arrangements, to form several arches. The arches assist the foot in supporting the body weight in an economical fashion, in absorbing the shock of weight bearing, and in providing a space on the plantar aspect of the foot for the blood vessels, nerves, and muscles. Their presence aids in giving the foot mobility and a small amount of prehensility. There are four arches: the inner longitudinal, the outer longitudinal, the anterior metatarsal, and the transverse (Fig. 16-2).

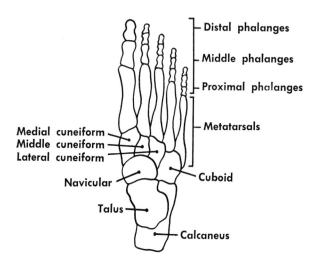

Distal phalanges

Middle phalanges

Proximal phalanges

Metatarsals

Medial cuneiform
Middle cuneiform
Lateral cuneiform

Cuboid

Navicular

Talus

Calcaneus

Fig. 16-1. Bones of the foot.

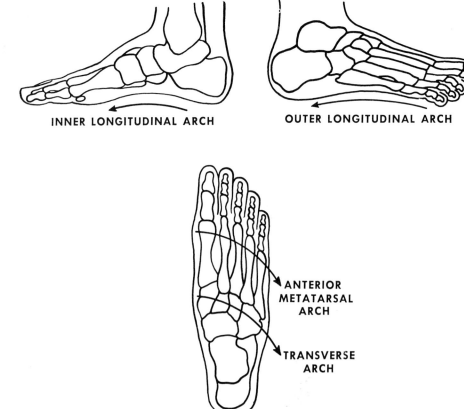

INNER LONGITUDINAL ARCH

OUTER LONGITUDINAL ARCH

ANTERIOR
METATARSAL
ARCH

TRANSVERSE
ARCH

Fig. 16-2. Arches of the foot.

The *inner longitudinal arch* originates along the medial border of the calcaneus and extends forward to the distal head of the first metatarsal. It is composed of the calcaneus, talus, navicular, first cuneiform, and first metatarsal. The main supporting ligament of the longitudinal arch is the plantar calcaneonavicular ligament, which acts as a sling by returning the arch to its normal position after it has been stretched.

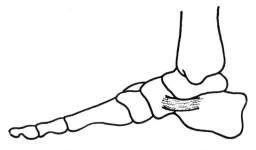

Fig. 16-3. Plantar calcaneonavicular ligament.

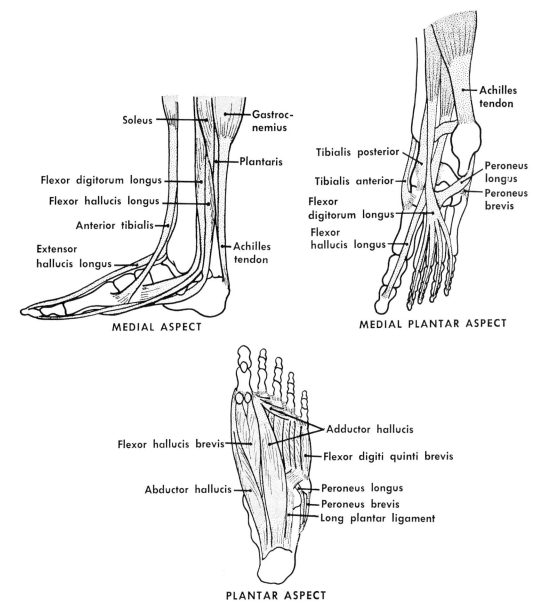

Fig. 16-4. Muscles of the foot.

The tendon of the posterior tibialis muscle helps to reinforce the plantar calcaneo-navicular ligament (Fig. 16-3).

The *outer longitudinal arch* is on the lateral aspect of the foot and follows the same pattern as that of the inner longitudinal arch. It is formed by the calcaneus, cuboid, and fifth metatarsal bones. It is much lower and less flexible than the inner longitudinal arch.

The *anterior metatarsal arch* is shaped by the distal heads of the metatarsals. The arch has a semiovoid appearance, stretching from the first to the fifth metatarsal.

The *transverse arch* extends across the transverse tarsal bones, primarily the cuboid and the internal cuneiform, and forms a half dome. It gives protection to soft tissue and increases the foot's mobility.

Movements of the foot

The movements of the foot are accomplished by numerous muscles (Fig. 16-4). Dorsiflexion and plantar flexion of the foot take place at the ankle joint. The gastrocnemius, soleus, plantaris, peroneus longus, peroneus brevis, and tibialis posterior are the plantar flexors. Dorsiflexion is accomplished by the tibialis anterior, extensor digitorum longus, extensor hallucis longus, and peroneus tertius. The lateral motion of the foot takes place, for the most part, at the subtalar joint, where outward movement (eversion) and inward movement called (inversion) are permitted. The muscles primarily responsible for inversion are the anterior tibialis and the posterior tibialis; eversion is initiated by the peroneals—the longus, the brevis, and the tertius.

The movements of the phalanges are flexion, extension, abduction, and adduction. Flexion of the second, third, fourth, and fifth distal digits is executed by the flexor digitorum longus and the quadratus plantae. Fexion of the middle phalanges is performed by the flexor digitorum brevis, and flexion of the proximal phalanges is by the lumbricales and the interossei. The great toe is flexed by the flexor hallucis longus. The extension of all the middle phalanges is done by the abductor hallucis and abductor digiti quinti, the lumbricales, and the interossei. Extension of all distal phalanges is effected by the extensor digitorus longus, the extensor hallucis longus, and the extensor digitorum brevis. The adduction of the foot is carried out by the interossei plantares and the adductor hallucis; abduction is by the interossei dorsales, the abductor hallucis, and the abductor digiti quinti.

Motor nerve and blood supplies

The tibial nerve, largest division of the sciatic nerve, supplies the muscles of the back of the leg and the plantar aspect of the foot. The common peroneal nerve is a smaller division of the sciatic nerve, and with its branches supplies the front of the leg and the foot.

The major portion of the blood is supplied to the foot by the anterior and posterior tibial arteries.

BASIC CARE AND INJURY PREVENTION

It has been estimated that a majority of the population will at some time in their lives develop foot problems. This is attributed to the use of improper footwear or poor foot hygiene and to anatomical structural deviations that result from faulty postural alignments or abnormal stresses.

Many sports place exceptional demands on the feet—far beyond the normal daily requirements. The trainer should be well aware of potential foot problems and should be capable of identifying, ameliorating, or preventing them whenever possible. A sensible program to prevent foot problems should be instituted and maintained by the athlete as well as by the trainer.

Fitting athletic shoes and socks

Athletic footwear can mean the difference between success or failure in sports. The coach, trainer, and equipment man must take the time and spend the effort needed to fit their athletes properly. Poorly fitting socks cause abnormal pressures and friction to the foot. Socks that are too short will crowd the feet and tend to turn the fourth and fifth toes under. Socks that are too long will cause foot irritations by developing wrinkles and creating abnormal friction sites. Athletic socks are now available that provide a high degree of protection to the wearer by decreasing friction within the shoe. However, these socks are usually too expensive for the typical training budget.

To properly fit an athletic shoe, the athlete should have his game socks on to ensure ample room in the shoe for the bulk of the sock. The length of the athletic shoe should allow some space from the end of the great toe to the front of the shoe. The width should allow free movement for each toe and should permit the shoe to crease evenly at the bend of the phalanges. The shoe will always bend ("break") at its widest part; when the "break" of the shoe and the ball of the foot coincide, the fit is considered to be proper. If the "break" of the shoe is in back or in front of the metatarsophalangeal joint, the shoe and foot will be opposing each other. The first measurement of the foot is taken from the heel to the metatarsophalangeal joint, and the second from the heel to the end of the great toe. An individual's two feet may be equal in length from heel to ball of the foot but differ between heel and toe. Therefore a shoe should be selected for the longer of the two measurements.

Excessive foot perspiration (hyperhidrosis)

Hyperhidrosis increases the possibility of skin irritation. It is essential that the athlete practice good foot hygiene. It is recommended that he apply talcum powder before practice, liberally shaking it on his athletic footwear. After activity he should wipe the feet with alcohol and allow them to dry in the air. He should then apply powder to his feet, his street socks, and his street shoes before putting them on. It has also been found that dusting the shoes and feet with powdered alum or boric acid inhibits and absorbs excessive perspiration.

Excessive foot odor (bromidrosis)

Feet that perspire excessively may emit an offensive odor. To prevent this condition from becoming a source of embarrassment to the athlete, it should be handled in the same manner as suggested for excessive perspiration, with applications of astringents such as alcohol, as well as frequent footwear changes.

Calluses (tylomas)

Excessive callus accumulations on the foot are often the result of constant rubbing of footwear over bony protruberances. They may be caused by shoes that are too narrow or too short, resulting in abnormal skin stresses of the foot. Calluses that develop from these situations can become extremely painful because the fatty layer loses its elasticity and its cushioning effect. Typically, in athletics, calluses develop over the metatarsal heads and around the heel. The callus moves as a gross mass, becoming highly vulnerable to tears and cracks, which results in pain and perhaps infection.[1] This situation can be prevented through proper foot hygiene, which entails (1) wearing two pairs of socks, a thin cotton pair next to the skin and a heavy woolen pair over the cotton pair; (2) wearing shoes that are of a correct size and are in good condition; and (3) developing a preactivity regimen of using skin toughner (astringent) and talcum powder. The athlete should also be encouraged to use an emery callus file after showering to prevent abnormal callus formation. Massaging small amounts of lanolin into the devitalized callus areas once or twice a week after practice has been found to restore tissue elasticity. Once excessive formation has occurred, a keratolytic ointment, such as Whitfield's ointment, may have to be applied. Adhesive-backed felt or sponge rubber provides an excellent means of relieving friction and pain from pressure.[1]

Blister prevention

Blisters are often a dilemma during early season. Soft feet coupled with unyielding shoes combine to give the athlete severe blisters. It has been found that use of a coating of tincture of benzoin followed by a dusting of talcum powder can provide the skin with protection against abnormal friction. (Powder must be applied to eliminate the stickiness of benzoin.) The ritual should be followed daily. Wearing of two pairs of socks, in the manner indicated previously, is also desirable, particularly for athletes who have sensitive feet or feet that perspire excessively. If, however, a friction area ("hot spot") does arise, then the athlete should stop his activity immediately and cover the irritated skin with a "friction-proofing" material such as petroleum jelly or place a "blanked-out" piece of tape (Fig. 16-5) tightly over the area. Another method that has proved successful is the application of ice over skin areas that have developed abnormal friction.[2]

Toenail care

It is important that the athlete's shoes be of the proper length, since continued pressure on a toenail can lead to its loss or cause it to become ingrown. The length of the athletic socks is also at times a factor, since they can cause pressure on the toenails. It is important to know how to trim the nails correctly. Two things must be taken into consideration: first, the nail must be trimmed so that its margins do not penetrate the tissue on the sides (Fig. 16-6) and, second, the nail should be left sufficiently long that it is clear of the underlying tissue and still be cut short enough that it is not irritated by either shoes or socks.

CARE OF COMMON FOOT AFFECTIONS
Skin conditions
Friction blisters

Blisters (Fig. 16-7) are usually caused by some irritating factors within the shoe. As a result of the friction, a separation of the epidermis from the dermis occurs, with fluid accumulating between the two layers. This fluid may be clear, bloody, or purulent.

When caring for a blister, the trainer should be basically conservative in his approach and be aware at all times of the possibility of a severe infection resulting. Whenever a blister appears to be infected it requires medical attention. The care of blisters in athletics makes use of two approaches: the conservative and the radical.[3] The conservative approach should be followed whenever possible. Its main premise is that a blister should not be contaminated by cutting or puncturing but should be protected from further insult by a small doughnut until the initial irritation has subsided. If puncturing is necessary to prevent the blister from tearing, it should be done by introducing a sterilized needle underneath the epidermis, approximately ⅛ inch outside the diameter of the raised tissue. After the fluid has been dispersed a pressure pad is placed directly over the blister to prevent it from refilling, and when the tenderness has subsided the loose skin is cut away. The conservative care of blis-

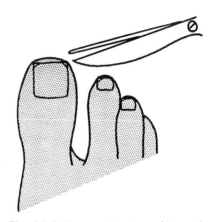

Fig. 16-5. Blanked-out piece of tape.

Fig. 16-6. Proper trimming of toenails.

ters is adequate for cases in which there is little danger of tearing or aggravating the blister through activity.[4]

When a blister has been torn or is in either a vulnerable or a handicapping position and is therefore difficult to protect, the following radical approach may be indicated:

1. Cleanse the blister and surrounding tissue with soap and water; then rinse and wipe with alcohol.

2. Using sterile scissors, cut the blister halfway around its perimeter.

3. Apply antiseptic and a mild ointment such as zinc oxide to the exposed tissue.

4. Lay the flap of skin back over the treated tissue and cover the area with a sterile dressing.

5. Within 2 or 3 days, or when the un-

derlying tissue has hardened sufficiently, remove the dead skin. This should be done by trimming the skin on a bevel and as close as possible to the perimeter of the blister.

6. After removal of the skin, the athlete should begin a daily ritual of toughening feet with an astringent such as tannic acid.

Hard and soft corns

The *hard corn (clavis durum)* is the most serious type of corn. It is caused by the pressure of improperly fitting shoes, the same mechanism that causes calluses. Hammer toes and hard corns are usually associated with the hard corns forming on the tops of the deformed toes (Fig. 16-8). Symptoms are local pain and disability, with inflammation and thickening of soft

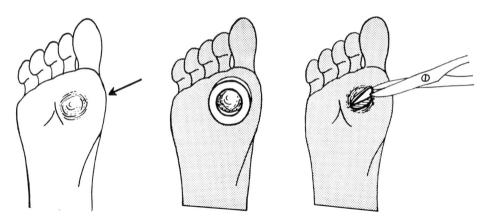

Fig. 16-7. Blister, showing conservative and radical care.

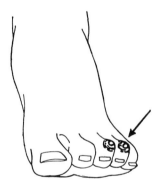

Fig. 16-8. Hard corn.

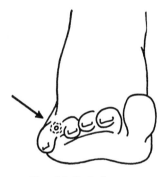

Fig. 16-9. Soft corn.

tissue. Because of the chronic nature of this condition, it requires the care of a physician.

The trainer can ameliorate the situation by issuing the athlete shoes that fit properly and then having him soak his feet daily in warm soapy water to soften the corn. To alleviate further irritation the corn should be protected by a small felt or sponge rubber doughnut.

The *soft corn (clavis molle)* is the result of a combination of wearing narrow shoes and having excessive foot perspiration. Because of the pressure of the shoe coupled with the exudation of moisture, the corn usually forms between the fourth and the fifth toe (Fig. 16-9). A circular area of thickened, white, macerated skin appears between the toes at the base of the proximal head of the phalanges. It displays both pain and inflammation. In caring for a soft corn the best procedure is to have the athlete wear properly fitting shoes, keep the skin between the toes clean and dry, decrease pressure by keeping the toes separated with cotton or lamb's wool, and apply a keratolytic agent such as salicylic acid in liquid or pad form.

Plantar warts (verruca plantaris)

Plantar warts are usually found on the sole of the foot, on or adjacent to areas of abnormal weight bearing. Thus most commonly result from a fallen metatarsal arch or bruises to the ball of the foot, such as may be sustained in excessive jumping or in running on the ball of the foot. Plantar warts are seen as areas with excessive epidermal thickening and cornification (Fig. 16-10). The symptoms are extreme general discomfort and point tenderness in areas of excessive callus formation. Those conditions which resist conservative care may require medical attention by a physician who, in most instances, will perform surgical removal. Until such time as medical care is given, plantar warts should be protected by a doughnut pad.

Ingrown toenails

An ingrown toenail is a condition in which the leading side edge of the toenail has grown into the soft tissue nearby, usually resulting in a severe inflammation and infection. Improper clipping of toenails or use of ill-fitting shoes and socks is often an etiological factor. The care of this foot condition entails the following procedures:

1. Soak the toe in hot water (110° to 120° F.) for approximately 20 minutes, two or three times daily.

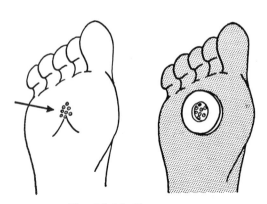

Fig. 16-10. Plantar wart.

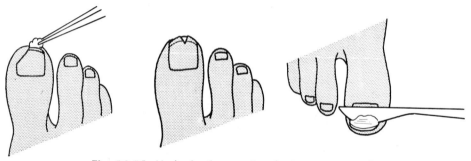

Fig. 16-11. Methods of managing the ingrown toenail.

2. When the nail is soft and pliable, use forceps to insert a wisp of cotton under the edge of the nail and lift it from the soft tissue (Fig. 16-11).

3. Other methods of care include cutting a "V" in the center of the outer edge or shaving the toenail thin, both of which tend to pull the nail from the side.

4. Continue the chosen procedure until the nail has grown out sufficiently that it can be trimmed straight across. The correct trimming of nails is shown in Fig. 16-6.

An ingrown toenail can easily become infected. If this occurs it should be immediately referred to a physician for treatment.

Athlete's foot (dermatophytosis, tinea pedia)

Fungi are the basic cause of athlete's foot but there is often an associated bacterial infection. Because no well-defined cause exists, there appears to be no one cure that will remedy all conditions.

Athlete's foot is usually found in dark moist areas of the foot. It can reveal itself in many ways but appears most often as an extreme itching on the soles of the feet and between and on top of the toes. It is seen as a rash with small pimples or minute blisters that break and exude a yellowish serum. Because of the scratching that usually occurs, the tissue may become inflamed and infected, manifesting itself as a red, white, or gray scaling of the affected area. Basic care of athlete's foot should be instituted in the following manner:

1. Keep the feet as dry as possible through the frequent use of talcum powder.

2. Wear clean white socks to avoid reinfection, changing them daily.

3. Use tincture of benzoin and powder daily before practice.

4. Use a standard fungicide for specific medication. For stubborn cases take counsel with the team physician; a dermatologist may need to make a culture from foot scrapings to determine the best combatant to be employed.

The best cure for the problem of athlete's foot is *prevention*. To keep the condition from spreading the following steps should be faithfully followed by individuals in the athletic program:

1. All athletes who have this condition should avoid contaminating others.

2. Instruct all athletes to powder their feet daily.

3. Dry the feet thoroughly after every shower, especially between and under the toes.

4. Keep athletic shoes and street shoes dry by dusting them with powder daily.

5. Wear clean athletic socks and street socks daily.

6. Clean and disinfect shower and dressing rooms daily.

Structural deviations
Exostoses (over-bone growths)

Exostoses are abnormal bony outgrowths protruding from the surface of a bone. Such outgrowths occur principally at the head of the first metatarsal bone on the dorsum of the foot. The condition is especially common among surfing enthusiasts who propel the surfboard while in a "kneel-sitting" position on one leg, with the foot in plantar flexion and the body weight brought to bear on the instep or dorsum. In certain instances, what may at first appear to be an exostosis is actually a subluxation of the metatarsocuneiform articulation. Should this be the case, referral to the team physician should be made.

Exostoses may also develop as the result of impingement, such as occurs when a joint is continually forced beyond the ranges of normal motion to an extent that actual contact is effected by the bones comprising the joint. This continual contact creates a condition of inflammation and irritation, and eventually activates formation of new bone that will build up to a degree sufficient to cause impingement when the joint is forced to the point where the bones contact each other. Pain and tenderness occur when this transpires, although they may not be present within the normal

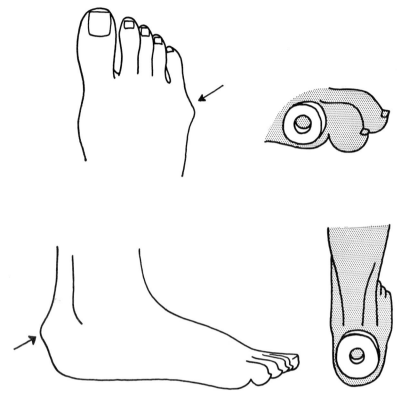

Fig. 16-12. Exostoses (over-bone growths).

ranges of motion. Extreme dorsiflexion, as when the foot is at the end of the support period immediately prior to the forward-carry, may cause exostoses to form on the anterior articular lip of the tibia and the top of the talus as a consequence of the impingement. Pain and tenderness are usually present, accompanied by a marked impairment of performance, especially when the foot is in a position of extreme dorsiflexion. This pain is usually apparent at the anterior aspect of the joint and may be sufficiently severe to weaken the drive from the foot as it thrusts against the ground in the push-off, resulting in a loss of drive and speed.

Poorly fitting shoes or a chronic irritation may also predispose an area to a growth which usually appears either at the head of the fifth metatarsal or as a calcaneal spur (Fig. 16-12). If it becomes chronically irritated or handicapping, it

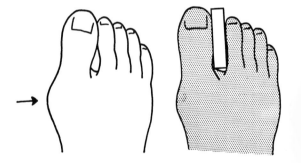

Fig. 16-13. Bunions.

may become a surgical problem and should be referred to a physician. The trainer can sometimes give relief in this condition by making use of protective doughnuts and pads.

Bunions (hallux valgus)

Shoes that are too narrow or too short may cause a condition known as a bunion.

Heredity also has a role in the formation of bunions. A bunion is a prominence and/or growth on the head of the first or the fifth metatarsal (Fig. 16-13) and is often covered by an inflamed adventitious bursa. Because of abnormal pressure and irritation a chronic inflammatory condition develops that causes swelling, redness, pain, and eventually a moderate luxation of the phalanx—a condition known as *hallux valgus* when it involves the great toe and as a *tailor's bunion* when it affects the fifth toe. Both conditions produce burning, tenderness, and pain in their early stages and deformity in the later stages.[6] Early recognition and care such as the following can often prevent these conditions:

1. The athlete should wear properly fitting shoes.

2. Thermal therapy can sometimes help reduce chronic inflammation. This consists of continual heat, applied to the area two or three times daily by means of hot Epsom salt soaks, or whirlpool massage at about 110° F.

3. Wedging of the great toe can help alleviate the irritation.

4. Protective taping (Fig. 16-14) may also be of benefit.

Hammer toes

Hammer toes may be congenital, but more often the condition is caused by wearing shoes that are too short over a long period of time, thus cramping the toes (Fig. 16-15). Usually the second or third toe is involved. The joint protrudes prominently in an upward direction as a result of contraction of the extensor tendons.[6] A fallen anterior metatarsal arch also predisposes the toes to this condition. A deformity such as this eventually results in the formation of hard corns or calluses on the exposed joints. Quite often surgery

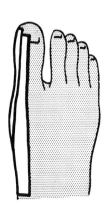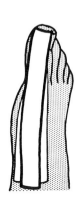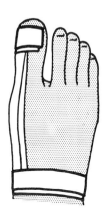

Fig. 16-14. Strapping for the bunion.

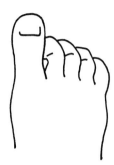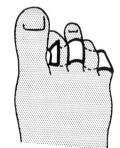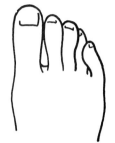

Fig. 16-15. Hammer toes.   **Fig. 16-16.** Strapping for hammer toes.   **Fig. 16-17.** Crooked toes.

is the only cure. However, proper shoes and protective taping (Fig. 16-16) can help prevent irritation.

Crooked toes

Crookedness of the toes (Fig. 16-17) may be congenital or may be brought about by improperly fitting footwear, particularly shoes that are too narrow. The condition at times is an indication of an outward projection of the great toe articulation or of a drop in the longitudinal or the metatarsal arch. As in the case of hammer toes, surgery is the only cure, but physical therapy can assist in alleviating inflammation. Taping (Fig. 16-18) may prevent some of the contractural tension within the athletic shoe.

Arch conditions

Painful arches are usually the result of improperly fitting shoes, overweight, excessive activity on hard surfaces, overuse, faulty posture, or fatigue—any of which may cause a pathological condition in the supporting tissue of the arch. The symptoms in these cases are divided into three stages or degrees, each characterized by specific manifestations. The first-degree pathology shows itself as a slight soreness in the arch. The second-degree pathology is indicated by a chronic inflammatory condition that includes soreness, redness, swelling, and a slight visible drop in the arch. The third degree presents a completely fallen arch accompanied by extreme pain, immobility, and deformity. In caring for

an arch disorder, the following rules should be observed:

1. Shoes should be fitted properly.
2. Hydrotherapy, especially whirlpool, should be given two or three times daily at temperature from 105° to 110° F. until the initial inflammation has subsided.
3. Deep therapy, such as ultrasound, can be used for a condition of this nature.
4. Arch supports may have to be used to ameliorate irritation of the weakened ligaments. If arch pathology can be detected in the first-degree or second-degree stage, arch supports may not be needed.
5. Weakened arches, if detected early, can be aided by an exercise program (see Chapter 15). If the arch is allowed to drop and the condition becomes chronic, exercising can offer little relief other than as a palliative aid.

Fallen anterior metatarsal arch

Activity on hard surfaces or prolonged stresses on the balls of the feet may cause weak or fallen anterior metatarsal arches (Fig. 16-19). When the supporting ligaments and muscles lose their ability to retain the metatarsal heads in a domelike shape, a falling of the arch results, thereby placing pressure on the nerves and blood

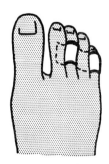

Fig. 16-18. Strapping for crooked toes.

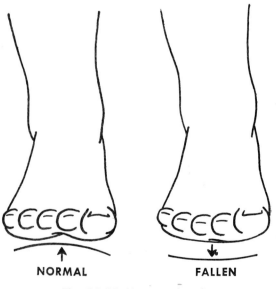

NORMAL   FALLEN

Fig. 16-19. Metatarsal arch.

vessels in the area. With this condition the athlete first notices an irritation and redness on the ball of the foot. As the condition progresses, an increase in pain, callus formation, toe cramping, and often a severe burning sensation develop. Care of fallen anterior metatarsal arch conditions should include the use of hydrotherapy and light friction massage, exercise (see Chapter 15), and metatarsal pads.

Metatarsal pad support. The purpose of the metatarsal pad (Fig. 16-20) is to reestablish the normal relationships of the metatarsal bones. It can either be purchased commercially or be constructed out of felt or sponge rubber.

Materials needed: One roll of 1-inch tape, a ¼-inch felt oval cut to a 2-inch circumference, and tape adherent.

Position of the athlete: The athlete sits on a table or chair with the plantar surface of the affected foot turned upward.

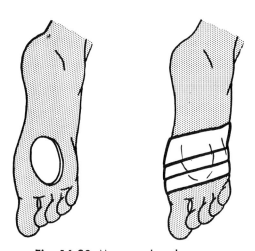

Fig. 16-20. Metatarsal pad support.

Position of the trainer: The trainer stands facing the plantar aspect of the athlete's foot.

Procedure:

1. The circular pad is placed just behind the metatarsal arch.

2. About 2 or 3 circular strips of tape are placed loosely around the pad and foot.

Fallen longitudinal arch

Various stresses weaken ligaments and muscles that support the arch, thus forcing the navicular bone downward. The athlete may complain of tiredness and tenderness in the arch and heel. Ankle sprains frequently result from weakened arches, and abnormal friction sites may develop within the shoe because of changes in weight distribution. This condition may be the result of several factors: shoes that cramp and deform the feet, weakened supportive tissues, overweight, postural anomalies that subject the arches to unaccustomed or unnatural strain, or the overuse syndrome, which may be the result of repeatedly subjecting the arch to a severe pounding through participation on an unyielding surface. Care includes the use of properly fitting shoes that give sufficient support to the arch or permit the normal anatomy of the foot to function; exercise (see Chapter 15), and arch supports and protective taping. In addition, with a chronic condition, emphasis should be given daily hydrotherapy and friction massage until the inflammation has subsided.

Arch strapping with pad support. Arch strapping with pad support employs the following procedures to strengthen weakened arches:

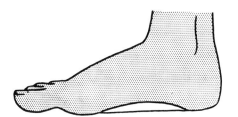

Fig. 16-21. Arch strapping with pad support.

Materials needed: One roll of 1½-inch tape, tape adherent, and a ¼-inch foam rubber pad cut to fit the longitudinal arch.

Position of the athlete: The athlete lies face downward on the table, with the foot that is to be taped (Fig. 16-21) extending about 6 inches over the edge of the table. To ensure proper position, allow the foot to hang in a relaxed position.

Position of the trainer: The trainer stands facing the sole of the affected foot.

Procedure:

1. Place a series of 2 or 3 strips of tape directly around the arch or, if added support is required, around an arch pad and the arch. The first strip should be put on just above the metatarsal arch.

2. Each subsequent strip should overlap the preceding piece about one half the width of the tape.

Caution: Avoid putting on so many strips of tape as to hamper the action of the ankle.

Figure-of-eight strapping for the longitudinal arch. When using the figure-of-eight method for strapping the longitudinal arch, the following steps are executed:

Materials needed: One roll of 1-inch tape and tape adherent.

Position of the athlete: The athlete lies face downward on a table, with his affected foot extending approximately 6 inches over the edge of the table (Fig. 16-22). To ensure proper position, allow the foot to hang in a relaxed, natural position.

Position of the trainer: The trainer faces the affected foot.

Procedure:

1. Lightly place an anchor strip around the ball of the foot, making certain not to constrict the action of the toes.

2. Start the next strip of tape from the medial edge of the anchor, moving it upward at an acute angle, crossing the center of the longitudinal arch, encircling the heel, and descending; then, crossing the arch again, end at the lateral aspect of the anchor.

3. Lock the first "cross" and each subsequent cross individually by means of a single piece of tape placed around the ball of the foot.

Traumatic foot conditions

The feet of athletes are always vulnerable to traumatic injuries. When foot injuries do occur they usually eliminate the

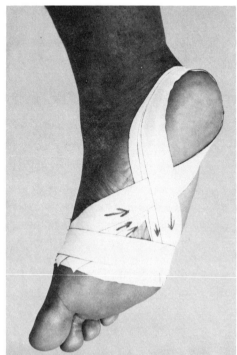

Fig. 16-22. Figure-of-eight strapping for the longitudinal arch.

athlete from his sport for a period of time. The trainer's ability to recognize the injury and to render immediate and follow-up care will hasten the athlete's return to competition.

Calcaneal periostitis (heel bruise)

Of the many contusions and bruises that an athlete may receive, there is none more handicapping than the heel bruise. Sport activities that demand a sudden stop-and-go response (such as basketball, jumping, or the landing action in long jumping) are particularly likely to cause heel bruises. The heel is endowed with a thick, cornified skin layer and a heavy fat pad covering, but even this thick padding cannot protect against a sudden force directed to the area. When injury occurs the athlete complains of severe pain in the heel, which is unable to sustain pressure and has all the signs of an acute injury: swelling, pain, heat, and redness. The general treatment for acute injuries should be used, with special attention paid to the following:

1. Ice applications should be administered for at least 45 minutes immediately after injury.

2. If possible, the athlete's heel should not be stepped on for a period of at least 24 hours.

3. Beginning on the second day, hydrotherapy—preferably a cold whirlpool of 60°

F.—should be applied two or three times daily for several days.

4. On the third and subsequent days warm whirlpool and ultrasound, if it is available, should be administered.

5. If pain on walking has subsided by the third day, moderate activity with the protection given by a heel cup, rubber doughnut, or protective taping (Figs. 16-23 and 16-24) may be resumed by the athlete.

Note: Because of the nature and the site of this injury, it can become chronic and may last throughout an entire season. It is suggested that a conservative approach be taken if the best results are to be obtained.

Athletes who are prone to such injury or who need protection from a bruised heel should either wear a mechanical appliance called a heel cup or use strapping with a foam rubber pad (Fig. 16-24). Surrounding the heel, the heel cup fuses the forces of most trauma, which thus become less concentrated in one area.

Strapping for heel bruise. This strapping (Fig. 16-25) is designed to stabilize the tissue surrounding the heel and can be used conveniently with a heel cup or pad.

Materials needed: One roll of 1-inch tape, tape adherent, and ½-inch sponge rubber pad, having a hollowed-out area for enclosure of the bruised heel.

Position of the athlete: The athlete lies face downward on the table with the foot

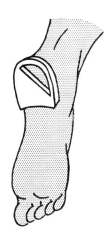

Fig. 16-23. Doughnut for heel bruise.

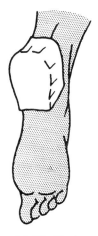

Fig. 16-24. Heel cup.

that is to be taped extending about 6 inches over the edge of the table.

Position of the trainer: The trainer stands facing the affected foot.

Procedure:

1. Place the first strip of 1-inch tape around the base of the Achilles tendon just below the internal and external malleoli.

2. Bring the next strip up from the bottom of the heel, encircling it, and lock on each side of the first strip.

3. After the first and second strips are in place, alternate the tape to produce a basketweave effect.

Sprained toes

Sprains of the phalangeal joint of the foot are caused most often by kicking some object. Sprains result from a considerable force applied in such a manner as to extend the joint beyond its normal range of motion or to impart a twisting motion to the toe, thereby twisting and tearing the supporting tissues. Symptoms of an acute injury appear. Treatment and care involve the following considerations:

1. The injury should be handled as an acute injury.

2. The severity of the injury should be determined through palpation and, if there are signs of a fracture, through x-ray examination.

Strapping for the sprained great toe. The following procedures are used for strapping the great toe after a sprain:

Materials needed: One roll of 1-inch tape and tape adherent.

Position of the athlete: The athlete lies on his back with the injured foot extending over the end of the table and in a relaxed position.

Position of the trainer: The trainer faces the sole of the affected foot.

Procedure:

1. The greatest support is given to the joint by a figure-of-eight strapping (Fig. 16-26). The series is started at an acute angle on the top of the foot, swinging down between the great and first toes, first encircling the great toe and then coming up, over, and across the starting point.

2. The above process is repeated, each series being started separately.

3. After the required number of figure-of-eight strips have been put in position, one lock piece should be placed around the ball of the foot.

Fracture of the talus

A fracture of the talus (Fig. 16-27) is usually the result of a severe ankle twist or of being hit behind the leg while the foot is firmly planted on the ground. There is extreme pain and point tenderness at the distal end of the tibia. For accurate diagnosis an x-ray film is essential. If the fracture is severe, there could be a severance of the blood supply to the area—a condition that results in bone necrosis and may seriously jeopardize future sports par-

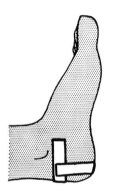
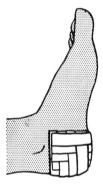

Fig. 16-25. Strapping for a heel bruise.

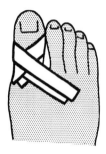

Fig. 16-26. Strapping for sprained great toe.

ticipation by the athlete. The following procedures should be employed:

1. The foot and ankle should be splinted and the athlete transported to a physician.

2. After the fracture has been reduced the physician will usually immobilize the foot in a plaster boot for about 6 weeks and then allow only limited weight bearing on the injured leg for at least another 8 weeks.

Fracture of the os calis

The os calis fracture (Fig. 16-28) is the most common fracture of the tarsus and is usually caused by a jump or fall from a height. There is extreme swelling, but healing takes place readily because there is an adequate blood supply to this area. There is a serious threat that this condition will predispose the athlete to arthritis because of the irregular healing of the articulating surface. Reduction may be delayed for as much as 24 to 48 hours or until swelling has been reduced. In the interval period the following steps should be initiated:

1. Cold and a pressure bandage should be applied.

2. The foot should be elevated immediately after the injury and maintained in this position for at least 24 hours or until definite treatment has been instituted.

Fractures of the metatarsals

Fractures of the metatarsals (Fig. 16-29) are usually caused by direct force,

such as being stepped on by another player. They are characterized by a considerable amount of soft tissue damage and marked swelling.

A fracture of the *fifth metatarsal* (distal end) is normally caused by a sharp inversion of the foot with the body weight carried forward on the front part of the foot. It has all the appearances of a severe sprain. A plaster cast or adhesive strapping is used in caring for this condition. Ambulation is usually possible by the second week.

Fractures of the phalanges

Fractures of the phalanges (Fig. 16-30) are usually of the bone-crushing type such as may be incurred in kicking an object or stubbing a toe. Generally, they are accompanied by swelling and discoloration. If the break is in the bone shaft, an adhesive strapping is usually applied by the physician. However, if more than one toe is involved, a cast may be applied for a few days. As a rule, 3 or 4 weeks of inactivity gives protection and permits healing, although tenderness may persist for some time.

RECONDITIONING OF THE FOOT

In acute injuries of the foot, weight bearing is usually prohibited until the initial pain has subsided. During this period every effort should be made to maintain the normal tendon strength. The muscles that are

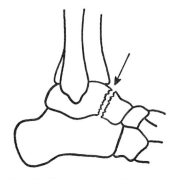 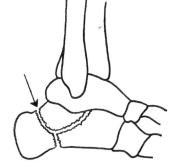 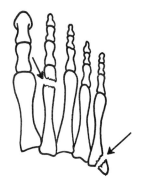

Fig. 16-27. Fracture of the talus.　**Fig. 16-28.** Fracture of the os calis.　**Fig. 16-29.** Fractures of the metatarsals.

particularly affected are the soleus, the gastrocnemius, the posterior tibial, and the peroneal muscles. A graded program, ranging in scope from active to resistive exercises, should be given until weight bearing can be resumed (see Fig. 15-1).

The ankle

ANATOMY

The ankle is a hinge joint (ginglymus), which is formed by the articulation of the tibia and fibula with the talus (Fig. 16-31). The lower ends of the tibia and fibula form a mortise into which the talus fits, thus effecting good lateral stability. The ankle is structurally quite strong because of the bone and ligamentous arrangements.

The lower end of the tibia becomes enlarged as it approaches the ankle and forms a rounded subcutaneous projection, the *internal malleolus*. The border of the internal malleolus is quite rough and provides the attachment of the supporting ligaments. The inferior aspect of the malleolus is concave and is lined with hyaline cartilage for articulating with the talus.

The talofibular articulation is formed by the lower end of the fibula with the talus. At its lower end the fibula develops a long projection, which extends along the lateral aspect of the talus and is called the *external malleolus*. It is located posterior to, and ½ inch lower than, the internal malleolus; like that of the internal malleolus, its border is roughened for ligamentous attachment.

The talus, the second largest tarsal and the main weight-bearing bone of the articulation, rests on the calcaneus and receives the articulating surfaces of the external and internal malleoli. Its almost square shape allows the ankle but two movements: dorsiflexion and plantar flexion.

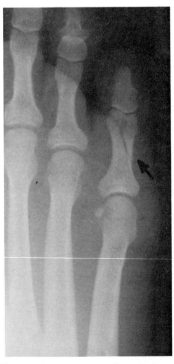

Fig. 16-30. Fracture of a phalanx.

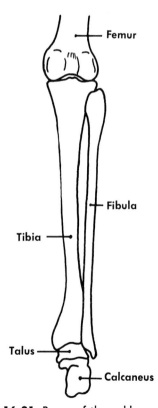

Fig. 16-31. Bones of the ankle and leg.

The ligamentous support of the ankle (Fig. 16-32) additionally fortifies its great bony strength. The medial aspect has greater strength than does the lateral, since the talus is directly over the sustentaculum tali. Laterally, the major ligaments of the ankle are the anterior tibiofibular, the anterior talofibular, the lateral talocalcaneal, and the calcaneofibular. On the medial aspect, the deltoid is the sole ligament, whereas the posterior aspect has two: the posterior talotibial and the posterior talocalcaneal.

By far the weakest aspect of the ankle is its muscular arrangement, since the long muscle tendons that cross on all sides of the ankle afford a maximum of muscle leverage but a minimum of stabilization. The major muscles of the ankle (Fig. 16-33) are as follows: (1) anterior aspect—extensor hallucis longus and extensor digitorum longus; (2) medial aspect—posterior tibialis, flexor hallucis longus, anterior tibialis, and flexor digitorum longus; (3) lateral aspect—peroneus longus and peroneus brevis; and (4) posterior aspect—gastrocnemius and soleus. The muscles of the medial aspect aid in the support of the inner longitudinal arch.

The ankle joint is encased in a thin articular capsule, which is attached to the borders of the bone involved. It is somewhat different from most other capsules in that it is thick on the medial aspect but diminishes into a thin, gauzelike membrane at the back.

The arteries supplying the ankle come from the anterior tibial and peroneal arteries.

Nerves supplying the ankle joint are the deep peroneal and the tibial nerves.

Movements of the ankle joint

Because the talus fits principally into the space formed by the malleoli, little lateral

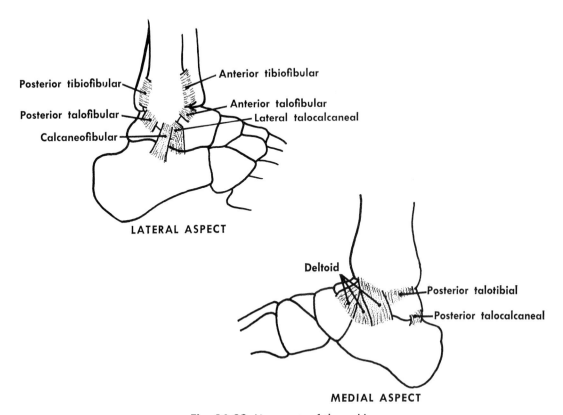

Fig. 16-32. Ligaments of the ankle.

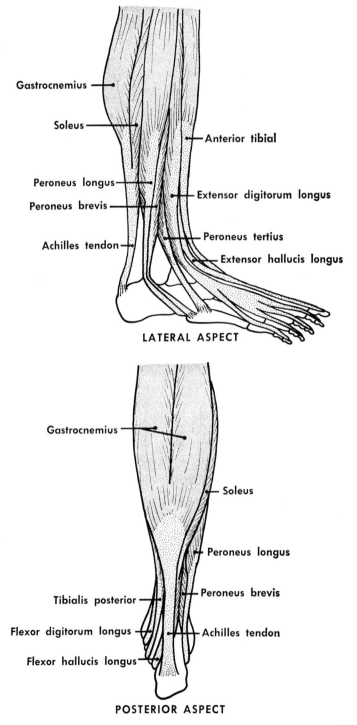

Fig. 16-33. Muscles of the ankle and leg.

movement is present unless the restrictive ligaments have been stretched. Limitation of the backward displacement of the talus results from a narrowing of the malleolar groove, which prevents the leg from moving forward on the foot. Tibiofibular-talar movement is limited to approximately 20 degrees of dorsiflexion and 45 degrees to 60 degrees of plantar flexion; however, these limits may vary.

BASIC CARE AND INJURY PREVENTION

Protecting the ankle is of major concern to the athlete and the trainer, since the ankle is one of the body areas most vulnerable to traumatic injuries. Considerable disagreement exists as to the policy to be adhered to for injury prevention. Several authorities insist that the ankle should be firmly taped in preparation for competition, whereas others insist that taping tends to weaken the normal or near-normal ankle by effecting partial disuse. It is our contention that whenever possible the ankle should not be taped. The athlete be encouraged to develop as much normal strength in the ankle joint as is possible with regular activity. However, for the athlete with a recent sprain or a chronically weakened ankle, taping is the proper way to preclude further injury.

Lacing shoes properly

The first sprain can often be prevented by seeing that shoes are properly laced. In preference to using wraps and strapping, many athletes can avoid that first sprain by having the support of a properly laced shoe, and it is the responsibility of the coach or trainer to teach the correct shoe-lacing technique.

Shoe-lacing technique. The correct procedure for lacing athlete's shoes is as follows:

1. The first 3 eyelets should be laced in an inside-out manner, making sure that the toes have complete freedom of movement.

2. The next 3 or 4 eyelets are laced in an outside-in manner and pulled as tightly as possible without cutting off the blood supply.

3. The last eyelets are laced as were the first, that is, in an inside-out manner.

Note: The reader will observe that this procedure allows freedom of foot action and still offers support.

Cloth ankle wrap

A cloth ankle wrap can give some protection to the ankle at little expense to the athletic program. The athlete can be taught to apply his own wrap over an athletic sock. Each wrap should be 1½ to 2 inches wide and 96 inches long to ensure complete coverage and protection. The purpose of this wrap (Fig. 16-34) is to give mild support against lateral and medial motion in the ankle. It is considered good technique to keep the roll on top and allow it to unwind from the bottom, which offers more control to the operator. Make sure that the athlete wears his socks and that they are pulled tightly, so that the roll may be applied smoothly to decrease the possibility of blisters.

Position of the athlete: The athlete sits on a table, extending his leg and positioning his foot at a 90-degree angle. To avoid any distortion, it is important that the ankle be neither overflexed nor overextended.

Position of the trainer: The trainer stands, facing the sole of the athlete's foot.

Procedure:

1. Start the wrap high on the instep and move it, at an acute angle, to the inside of the foot.

2. From the inside of the foot, move the wrap under the arch, coming up on the outside and crossing at the beginning point, where it continues around the ankle, hooking the heel.

3. From here, move it up, inside, over the instep and around the ankle, hooking the opposite side of the heel. This completes one series of the ankle wrap.

4. Complete a second series with the remaining material, encircling the ankle.

Ankle strapping

Although some coaches and trainers routinely apply tape over packs, stockinette, or special underwrap material (Fig.

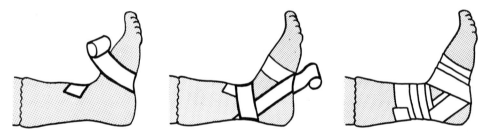

Fig. 16-34. Cloth ankle wrap.

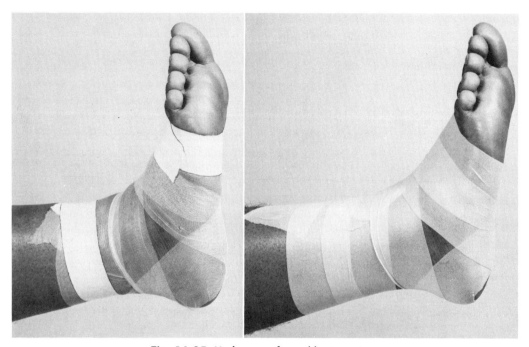

Fig. 16-35. Underwrap for ankle strapping.

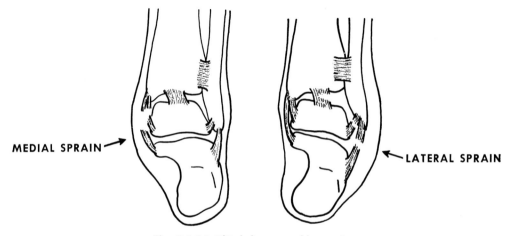

Fig. 16-36. Third-degree ankle sprains.

16-35), ankle strapping that is applied directly on the athlete's skin affords the greatest support. Before strapping, follow this procedure:

1. Shave all the hair off the foot and ankle.

2. Apply a coating of tincture of compound benzoin or plastic material to protect the skin and offer an adhering base.

CARE OF COMMON ANKLE AFFECTIONS
Sprained ankle

The sprained ankle is generally caused by a lateral or medial twist that results in external and internal joint derangement (Fig. 16-36). Subjectively, sprains may be classified as first, second, or third degree. In handling a sprained ankle the following first-aid measures should be applied:

1. Determine the extent of the injury.

2. Apply an elastic pressure bandage around the perimeter of the malleolus at the site of the sprain to decrease internal bleeding.

3. After the pressure bandage has been applied, decrease the temperature of the injury area by use of ice packs or ice-water soaks. An elastic wrap thoroughly soaked in ice water will give a faster cooling action when combined with an ice pack. Ice should be applied only intermittently, allowing the tissue to regain its normal temperature every 10 to 20 minutes. *Note:* Do not expose the tissue to prolonged cooling. If cold is not available, a horseshoe pad that is cut to fit around the malleolus and held in place by an elastic wrap will help confine the internal hemorrhage (Fig. 16-37).

4. When at all practical, promptly elevate the injured limb so that fluid stasis of the internal hemorrhage does not take place.

5. If there is a possibility of fracture, splint the ankle and refer the athlete to the physician for x-ray examination and possibly application of a cast.

Treatment of the sprained ankle should be initiated in the following manner:

1. Pressure, cold application, and eleva-

tion of the ankle should be maintained for at least 24 hours, so that the injury site may be localized and the hemorrhage stopped.

2. In most cases of moderate and severe ankle sprains, cold applications must be continued the second or even the third day.

3. If hemorrhaging has stopped by the third day heating can begin.

Game strapping technique. This type of strapping (Fig. 16-38) is designed for daily protection of weak ankles, giving them maximum support with a minimum use of tape.

Materials needed: One roll of 1½-inch tape and tape adherent.

Position of the athlete: The athlete sits on a table with his leg extended and his foot held at a 90-degree angle.

Position of the trainer: The trainer stands facing the foot that is to be taped.

Procedure:

1. A single anchor is placed around the ankle about 2 or 3 inches above the malleolus.

2. Two stirrups are applied in consecutive order, with care that each one overlaps half the width of the piece of tape it adjoins.

3. After the stirrups have been applied, 5 or 6 circular strips are put on, from the point of the anchor, moving downward until the malleolus is completely covered.

4. Next, 2 or 3 arch strips are applied.

5. The final support is given by a heel lock. Starting high on the instep, bring the tape along the ankle at a slight angle, hook-

Fig. 16-37. Ankle horseshoe.

ing the heel, leading under the arch, then coming up on the opposite side, and finishing at the starting point. At this point the tape is torn to complete one half of the heel lock. To complete the remaining half, execute the same procedure on the opposite side of the ankle (Fig. 16-39).

Closed basket weave (Gibney strapping technique). The closed basketweave technique (Fig. 16-40) offers strong tape sup-

port and is primarily used in athletic training for newly sprained or chronically weak ankles.

Materials needed: One roll of 1½-inch tape and tape adherent.

Position of the athlete: The athlete sits on a table with his leg extended and his foot at a 90-degree angle.

Position of the trainer: The trainer faces the sole of the athlete's foot.

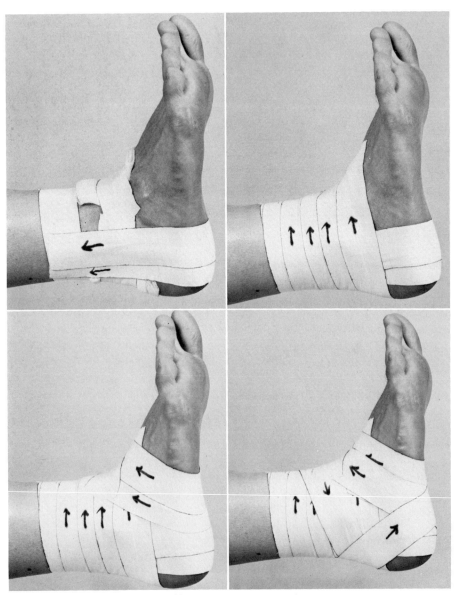

Fig. 16-38. Game strapping technique.

Procedure:

1. One anchor piece is placed around the ankle, approximately 2 or 3 inches above the malleolus, and a second anchor is placed around the arch and instep.

2. The first stirrup is then applied posteriorly to the malleolus and attached to the ankle stirrup.

3. The first Gibney is started directly under the malleolus and attached to the foot anchor.

4. In an alternating series, 3 stirrups and 3 Gibneys are placed on the ankle, with each piece of tape overlapping at least one half of the preceding strip.

5. After the basketweave series has been applied, the Gibney strips are continued on up the ankle, thus giving circular support.

6. For arch support, 2 or 3 circular strips are applied.

7. After the conventional basket weave has been completed, a heel lock should be applied to ensure maximum stability.

Open basketweave strapping technique. This modification of the closed basketweave or Gibney technique is designed mainly to give extra freedom of movement in dorsiflexion and plantar flexion while providing lateral and medial support. Strapping of this design (Fig. 16-41) may be used immediately after an acute sprain in conjunction with a pressure bandage (Fig. 16-41, *C*) and cold applications, since it allows for swelling.

Materials needed: One roll of 1½-inch tape and tape adherent.

Position of the athlete: The athlete sits on a table with his leg extended and his foot held at a 90-degree angle.

Position of the trainer: The trainer faces the sole of the athlete's foot.

Procedure:

1. The procedures followed are the same as for the regular basket weave with the exception of incomplete closures of the Gibney strips.

2. The gap between the Gibney ends should be locked by 2 pieces of tape running on either side of the instep.

Note: Application of a 1½-inch elastic bandage placed over the open basket weave affords added control of swelling; however, it should be removed before retiring.

Ankle tendon conditions
Achilles tendon strain

Achilles tendon strains (Fig. 16-42) are not uncommon in athletics and occur most often as a result of a lack of coordination between the agonists and the antagonists, following ankle sprains or excessive dorsiflexion of the foot. The resulting pathology may be mild to severe. The severe injury is usually thought of as a complete avulsion or rupturing of the Achilles tendon. In the process of receiving this injury, the athlete feels acute pain and extreme weakness on plantar foot flexion. The following are first-aid measures to be applied:

1. As with other acute conditions, pressure is first applied with an elastic wrap together with cold application.

2. In most cases internal hemorrhage is not extensive; thus the pressure and cold need be applied for only 1 to 2 hours.

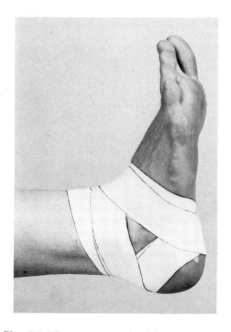

Fig. 16-39. Continuous heel lock technique.

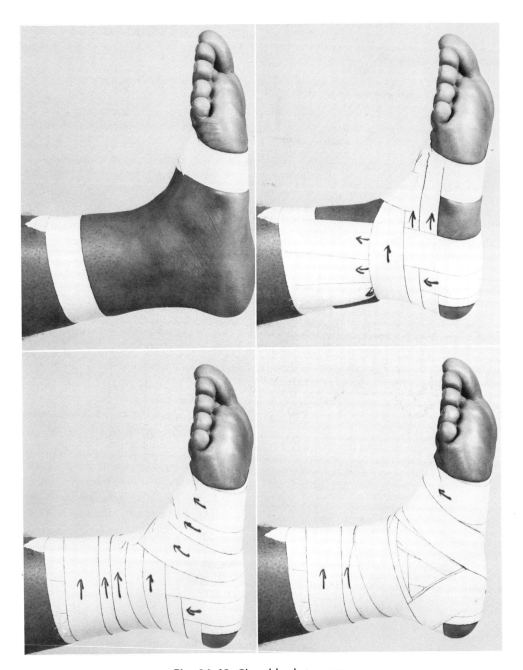

Fig. 16-40. Closed basket weave.

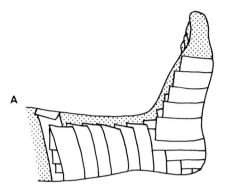

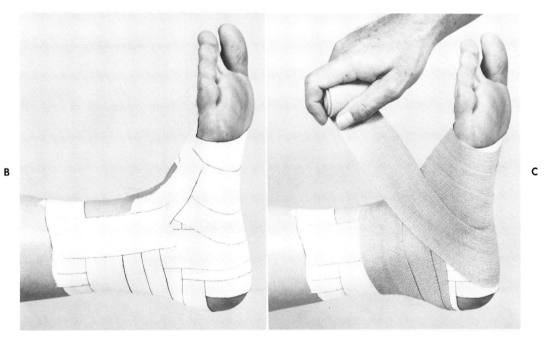

Fig. 16-41. A and **B,** Open basket weave; **C,** open basket weave with pressure bandage.

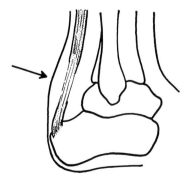

Fig. 16-42. Achilles tendon strain.

3. After hemorrhage has subsided, an elastic wrap can be lightly applied for continued pressure and the athlete sent home. Treatment should begin the following day.

Note: Because of the tendency for Achilles tendon trauma to develop tenosynovitis, a conservative approach to therapy must be taken.

Treatment should be initiated in the following manner:

1. Therapy should be applied on the third and subsequent days by means of hy-

dromassage and analgesic packs until soreness has subsided.

2. Heels should be elevated by the use of a sponge rubber pad placed in the heel of each street shoe, which serves to decrease the extension of the tendon and thereby relieves some of the irritation.

3. In a few days the athlete will be able to return to his activity. The Achilles tendon should be given taped support and a sponge rubber heel lift placed in each athletic shoe.

Achilles tendon strapping. The Achilles tendon strapping (Fig. 16-43) is designed to prevent the Achilles tendon from overstretching.

Materials needed: One roll of 3-inch elastic tape, one roll of 1½-inch linen tape, and tape adherent.

Position of the athlete: The athlete kneels or lies face down, with his affected foot hanging relaxed over the edge of the table.

Position of the trainer: The trainer stands facing the plantar aspect of the athlete's foot.

Procedure:

1. Two anchors are applied with 1½-inch tape, one circling the leg approximately 6 to 8 inches above the malleoli and the other encircling the ball of the foot.

2. Two strips of 3-inch elastic tape are cut about 8 to 10 inches long. The first strip is moderately stretched from the ball of the athlete's foot along its plantar aspect up to the Achilles tendon. The second elastic strip follows the course of the first except that it is cut and split down the middle lengthwise and the cut ends are wrapped around the lower leg to form a lock. *Caution:* Keep the wrapped ends above the level of the Achilles strain.

3. The series is completed by placing 2 lock strips of elastic tape around the arch and 2 strips around the athlete's lower leg.

Achilles tendon bursitis and tenosynovitis

Achilles tendon bursitis and tenosynovitis usually occur from the overstretching

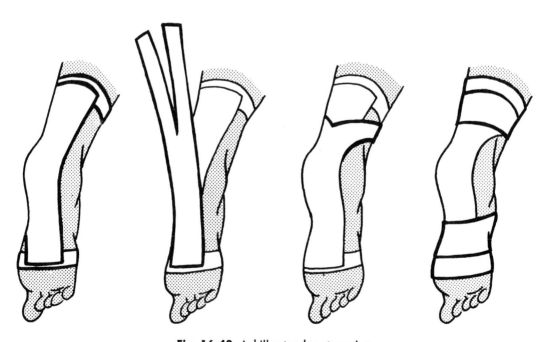

Fig. 16-43. Achilles tendon strapping.

of the Achilles tendon, resulting in a constant inflammatory condition of the Achilles bursa.[6] This condition is usually chronic, developing gradually over a long period of time, and it also takes many days—sometimes weeks—to heal properly. An excellent therapeutic approach is one of using continued heat in as many forms as possible, especially by means of deep therapy such as ultrasound. Activity should be held to a minimum, and heel lifts should be placed in the shoes to relieve the Achilles tendon of as much tension as possible. Static heel cord stretching (Chapter 15) has been found to be an excellent adjunct to heat therapy.

Ankle fractures and dislocations
Fractures of the lateral malleolus

Fracture of the lateral malleolus (Fig. 16-44) is a rather common injury resulting either from a blow from the medial side or from a sudden torsion. There is a point of tenderness over the fracture point, but in several instances pain may occur elsewhere and thus produce a false diagnosis. The medial deltoid ligament may also be torn, resulting in extreme swelling on that side. An x-ray study is the only way in which this condition can be distinguished from a severe sprain. The same first-aid procedures suggested for a sprain should be employed in handling this condition. Splinting is essential, and every effort should be made to keep the swelling down so that a cast may be applied by the physician. In many cases the physician will want early weight bearing. Immobilization is usually continued for 6 weeks.

Fractures of both the lateral and the medial malleolus

Lateral and medial malleoli fractures usually result from severe twisting actions that cause a rotational shear of the joint, such as those incurred in ski injuries. There is marked deformity of the foot, accompanied by extreme swelling and discoloration. Protective first-aid measures only should be given for this condition, and im-

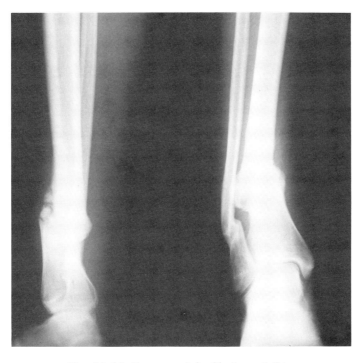

Fig. 16-44. Fracture of the fibula and tibia.

mediate referral to a physician is necessary. When this injury is observed, there is no doubt as to its being a fracture. In most cases the physician will reduce the fracture and apply a walking cast for approximately 6 to 8 weeks. In some cases internal fixation has proved beneficial.

RECONDITIONING OF THE ANKLE

Many physicians are of the opinion that a conservative approach should be taken in the treatment of sprained ankles by placing them in a cast and preventing any weight bearing for a period of at least 2 weeks. On the other hand, many athletic physicians and trainers maintain that the best method is the active approach, wherein the athlete returns to competition much sooner than with the conservative treatment and completes his therapy through activity. The best method for returning an athlete to action should be determined by the physician.

In moderate and severe sprains the athlete should avoid weight bearing for at least 2 days and perhaps longer if there is pain. As the initial soreness decreases, the athlete should be encouraged to move the ankle as normally as possible. If the athlete must go to school or work, it is suggested that he walk on crutches. As the ankle heals the athlete can be graduated from crutch-walking to walking with a cane while the ankle is supported by tape. There should be as much healing as possible before the athlete returns to vigorous activity. A good rule of thumb for determining when the athlete is able to return to his sport is to have him stand, balancing his full weight on the toes of the affected foot and to spring up and down. If he can do so without pain, then it may be presumed that he is strong enough to receive a basketweave ankle strapping and resume running. Maintaining tendon strength will aid the athlete when he returns to his sport. His first concern should be to regain his normal range of motion, after which he may start a graded resistance exercise program (Chapter 15).

The leg

ANATOMY

The portion of the lower extremity that lies between the knee and the ankle is defined as the leg and is comprised of the tibia, the fibula, and the soft tissues that surround them.

The *tibia*, except for the femur, is the longest bone in the body and serves as the principal weight-bearing bone of the leg. It is located on the medial or great toe side of the leg and is constructed with wide upper and lower ends to receive the condyles of the femur and the talus, respectively. The tibia is triangularly shaped in its upper two thirds but is rounded and more constricted in the lower one third of its length. The most pronounced change occurs in the lower one third of the shaft and produces an anatomical weakness that establishes this area as the site of most of the fractures occurring to the leg. The shaft of the tibia has three surfaces, the posterior, the medial, and the lateral. Primarily, the posterior and lateral surfaces are covered by muscle, whereas the medial surface is subcutaneous and, as a result, quite vulnerable to outside trauma.

The *fibula* (calf bone) is long and slender and is located along the lateral aspect of the tibia, joining it in an arthrodial articulation at the upper end, just below the knee joint, and as a syndesmotic joint at the lower end. Both the upper and lower tibiofibular joints are held in position by strong anterior and posterior ligaments. The main function of the fibula is to provide for the attachment of muscles. It serves to complete the groove for the enclosure of the talus in forming the ankle joint.

The *interosseous membrane* is a strong sheet of fibrous tissue that extends between the fibula and the tibia. The fibers display an oblique downward-and-outward pattern. The oblique arrangement aids in diffusing the forces or stresses placed on the leg. It completely fills the tibiofibular space except for a small area at the superior as-

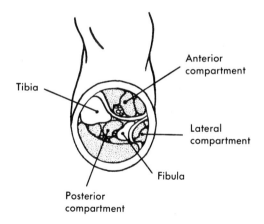

Fig. 16-45. The three compartments of the leg.

pect, provided for the passage of the anterior tibial vessels.

The soft tissue of the leg is contained within three compartments bounded by heavy fascia (Fig. 16-45). The *anterior compartment* holds the major structures for ankle dorsiflexion and foot and toe extension, which are tibialis anterior, extensor hallucis longus, extensor digitorum longus, anterior tibial nerve, and the tibial artery. A *lateral compartment* houses the peroneus longus, brevis, and tertius muscles and the superficial branch of the peroneal nerve. The *posterior compartment* is made up of the gastrocnemius and the soleus. These muscles plantar flex the ankle and control foot inversion and toe flexion.

CARE OF COMMON LEG AFFECTIONS
Shin bruises (traumatic tibial periostitis)

The shin, lying just under the skin, is exceedingly vulnerable and sensitive to blows or bumps. Because of the absence of muscular or adipose padding here, blows are not dissipated as they are elsewhere, and the periosteum receives the full force of any impact delivered to the shin. The periosteum surrounds bone surfaces, with the exception of the cartilaginous areas, and is composed of two fibrous layers that adhere closely to the bone, acting as a bed for blood vessels and bone-forming osteo-

blasts. Severe blows to the tibia often lead to a chronic inflammatory state of the cutaneous and periosteal tissue. The shin is an extremely difficult area to heal, particularly the lower one third, which has a considerably smaller blood supply than the upper portion. An injury to the periosteum that is inadequately cared for may develop into osteomyelitis, a serious condition which results in the destruction and deterioration of bony tissue.

In sports in which the shin is particularly vulnerable, such as football and soccer, adequate padding should be provided. All injuries in this area are potentially serious; therefore, minor shin lacerations or bruises should never be permitted to go untended.

Shin splints

Shin splints, which were discussed in Chapter 5, are an obscure condition that seasonally plagues many athletes. They are characterized by severe pain and irritation on the anterior aspect of the leg. They are usually attributed to an inflammation localized primarily in the tendon of the tibialis posterior or to the interossei between the fibula and tibia. However, the anterior foot and ankle muscles may also be affected. How or why inflammation is produced in this area is something of a mystery, and several theories have been suggested. Speculations advanced as to the cause include faulty posture alignment, falling arches, muscle fatigue, overuse stress, body chemical imbalance, or a lack of proper reciprocal muscle coordination between the anterior and posterior aspects of the leg. All these factors, in various combinations or singly, may contribute to shin splints.[4]

The pathology of this condition is regarded as a myositis or periostitis that occurs either acutely, as in preseason preparation, or chronically, developing slowly throughout the entire competitive season.[5] The trainer should approach this situation through deductive thinking. First, all information as to why a certain athlete may have acquired shin splints must be gathered—his changing from a hard gymnasium floor activity to a soft field sport, for example, or exhibiting general fatigue following a strenuous season. Second, the trainer should examine the athlete for possible structural body weaknesses. From this information an empirical analysis can be made as to the probable cause of this particular shin splint. It should be noted, however, that persistent shin irritation and incapacitation must be referred to the physician for thorough examination. Conditions such as stress fractures, muscle herniations, or acute anterior tibial compartment syndromes (a severe swelling within the anterior fascia chamber) may resemble the symptoms of shin splints.[7]

Treatment of shin splints is as varied as its etiology; therefore, the trainer must manage the condition on a logical basis. Constant heat in the form of whirlpool, analgesic balm packs, and ultrasound therapy have been found to give positive results and, together with supportive strappings and static stretching, afford a good general approach to the problem.[8] Static stretching of the anterior and posterior aspect of the leg has been found to be an effective method of ameliorating or preventing shin splints.

Shin splint strapping. This type of strapping (Fig. 16-46) is designed to give both compression and support to the shin splint region.

Materials needed: One roll of 1½-inch tape, strip of 1½-inch wide firm foam rubber or cardboard, and tape adherent.

Position of the athlete: The athlete sits on a table with his affected leg drawn up toward his chest and with his foot flat on the table. All the muscles of the leg must be completely relaxed.

Position of the trainer: The trainer stands facing the athlete's affected leg.

Procedure:

1. The trainer lays a strip of foam rubber lengthwise over the entire shin splint area.

2. While the athlete holds the pad in position, the trainer applies a series of circular tape strips around the leg and over the pad, starting at the lower aspect of the pad on the side opposite the injury and circling around the back of the leg and over the pad.

3. Many trainers have found it beneficial to apply a figure-of-eight arch strapping or a circular support around the toe tendons.

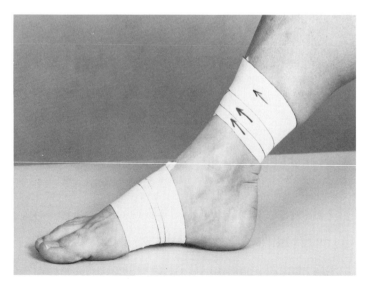

Fig. 16-46. Shin splint strapping.

Leg contusions

Contusions of the leg, particularly in the area of the gastrocnemius muscle, are common in athletics. A bruise in this area can produce an extremely handicapping injury for the athlete. A bruising blow to the leg will cause pain, weakness, and partial loss of the use of the limb. Palpation may reveal a hard, rigid, and somewhat inflexible area because of internal hemorrhage and muscle spasm.

When this condition occurs it is advisable to place the muscle on stretch immediately to prevent spasm and then, for a period of approximately 1 hour, to apply a compress bandage and cold packs to control internal hemorrhaging. Following this, after the initial pain has subsided and hemorrhaging has been impeded, an analgesic balm hot pack may be applied and mild exercise begun.

If analgesics, massage, and whirlpool do not return the athlete to normal activity within 2 to 3 days, the use of deep therapy may be warranted. An elastic wrap or strapping support will serve to stabilize the part and permit the athlete to participate without aggravation of the injury.

Leg muscle spasms

Spasms are sudden, violent, and involuntary contractions of one or several muscles and may be either clonic or tonic. A clonic spasm is identified by intermittent contraction and relaxation, whereas the tonic type is identified by its constant state of muscle contraction without an intervening period of relaxation. Both of these types occur in athletics. How and why muscle spasms happen to athletes is often difficult to ascertain. Fatigue, excess loss of fluid through perspiration, and inadequate reciprocal muscle coordination are some of the factors that may predispose an individual to a contracture. The leg, particularly the gastrocnemius muscle, is prone to this condition. It is usually difficult to predict the occurrence of spasm, since only the aforementioned criteria can be used as a guide.

When a muscle goes into a state of spasm there is severe pain and considerable apprehension on the part of the athlete. Treatment in such cases includes putting the athlete at ease and relaxing the contracted site. Firmly grasping the contracted muscle, together with a mild stretching and use of a counterirritant, has been found to relieve most acute spasms. After relaxation has taken place, a thin layer of analgesic balm spread over the affected part will soothe it and help to preserve a relaxed state. In cases of recurrent spasm, the trainer should make certain that fatigue or abnormal mineral loss through perspiring is not a factor, since the loss of salt or other minerals can result in abnormal motor nerve impulses to skeletal muscles. Salt supplementation should be given to all profusely perspiring athletes.

Leg fractures

Fractures received during athletic participation occur most often to the fingers, hands, face, and legs. Of the fractures that take place in the region of the leg, the fibular fracture (Fig. 16-47) has the highest incidence and occurs principally to the middle third of the leg. Fractures of the tibia occur predominantly to the lower one third.

Fig. 16-47. Fracture of the fibula.

Fractures of the shaft of the tibia and fibula result from either direct or indirect trauma during active participation in sports (Fig. 16-48). There is often a marked bony displacement with deformity, as a result of a strong pull of antagonistic muscles that causes an overriding of the bone ends, particularly if the athlete attempts to move or to stand on the limb following the injury. Crepitus and a temporary loss of limb function are usually present.

The pathology consists of marked soft tissue insult and extensive internal hemorrhaging. The leg appears hard and swollen. If a sharp bone edge has severed a nerve, *Volkmann's paralysis* may be present, with the characteristic drop-foot. Volkmann's paralysis is the result of great internal tension caused by hemorrhage and swelling within closed fascial compartments, inhibiting the blood supply and resulting in necrosis of muscle and in contractures. Fractures of the tibia and fibula may require surgery by a medical doctor because of the interpositioning of soft tissue or a delayed nonunion of the bone as a result of poor circulation. In most cases, reduction and cast immobilization are satisfactory. Immobilization lasts from 3 to 6 months, depending upon the extent of the injury and any resulting complications.

RECONDITIONING OF THE LEG

In most athletic injuries that affect the leg, atrophy and contracture of the leg, thigh, or hip musculature occur. In addition to these conditions, a low back imbalance may also occur and result in a shortening of the injured limb. In dealing with leg injuries, the trainer should strive to maintain strength and complete mobility of the knee, hip, and lower back. Reconditioning depends upon the site of the injury, its nature, and its extensiveness. It is advisable that mobility be attained and encouraged through passive stretching of the plantar

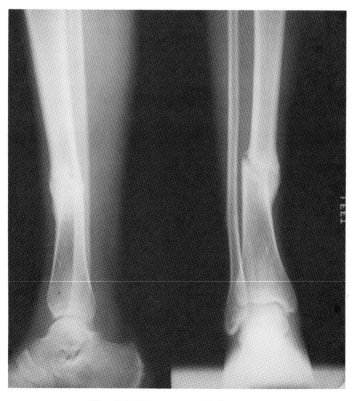

Fig. 16-48. Fracture of the tibia.

and dorsal areas. When pain on movement has decreased, a progressive strengthening program should be established and a daily order of exercise maintained by the athlete (see Chapter 15).

Using the crutch or cane

In most cases, when the athlete has a foot problem, weight bearing may be contraindicated. Situations of this type call for the use of a crutch or cane to assist in locomotion. The proper method of fitting and employing a cane or crutch is more important than is generally realized. To aid the trainer in determining the proper methods the following paragraphs will be of material assistance.

Fitting the athlete

The adjustable, wooden crutch is adaptable to athletics. Fitting should be done by measuring the distance from the underarm crutch brace, which is placed 1 inch below the anterior axillary fold, to the crutch tip position, which is even with the bottom of the shoe heel. The hand brace is placed at a point that is even with the athlete's hand when his elbow is flexed at an approximate 30-degree angle.

Fitting a cane to the athlete is relatively easy. Measurement is taken from the superior aspect of the greater trochanter of the femur to the floor while the athlete is wearing his shoes.

Walking with the crutch or cane

Many techniques of crutch walking are well suited to the vast number of possible conditions that occur to the walking mechanism. The most adaptable technique for use after those injuries which occur in athletics and which require nonweight bearing for one limb is the swing-through-tripod-gait that is executed in the following manner:

1. The athlete stands on one foot with the other elevated, supported by two crutches, thus making the tripod formation.

2. From the tripod stance, the athlete leans forward, locks his elbows, pulls the upper crosspiece firmly against his lateral chest and then swings forward between the stationary crutches.

3. After swinging through, the athlete recovers the crutches and again places them forward in the tripod position.

Cane walking is well suited to lower limb conditions that require limited weight bearing. The cane is used in the hand opposite that of the injured side and swings forward as in a normal gait swing.

REFERENCES

1. Gibbs, R. C.: Calluses, corns and warts, American Family Physician, Vol. 3, No. 4, April 1971.
2. Brown, J., and Childers, P.: Blister prevention: an experimental method, Res. Quart. Vol. 37, No. 2, May 1967.
3. Frank, T. E.: A discriminative study of four methods of preventing blisters, J. Nat. Ath. Trainers Ass. 2:9, 1967.
4. O'Donoghue, D. H.: Treatment of athletic injuries, Philadelphia, 1970, W. B. Saunders Co.
5. Paul, W. D., and Soderberg, G. L.: The shin splint confusion, Proceedings of the Eighth National Conference on the Medical Aspects of Sports, Chicago, 1966, American Medical Association, p. 24.
6. Raney, R. B., and Brashear, H. R., Jr.: Shands' handbook of orthopedic surgery, ed. 8, St. Louis, 1971, The C. V. Mosby Co.
7. Slocum, D. B.: The shin splints syndrome: medical aspects and differential diagnosis, Proceedings of the Eighth National Conference on the Medical Aspects of Sports, Chicago, 1966, American Medical Association, p. 24.
8. Drake, E. C.: Shin splints: the trainers point of view, Proceedings of the Eighth National Conference on the Medical Aspects of Sports, Chicago, 1966, American Medical Association, p. 32.

RECOMMENDED READINGS

Cailliet, R.: Foot and ankle pain, Philadelphia, 1968, F. A. Davis Co.

Dolan, J. P., and Holladay, L. J.: Treatment and prevention of athletic injuries, Danville, Ill., 1967, The Interstate Printers and Publishers, Inc.

McLaughlin, H. L.: Trauma, Philadelphia, 1959, W. B. Saunders Co.

O'Donoghue, D. H.: Treatment of injuries to athletes, Philadelphia, 1970, W. B. Saunders Co.

Ryan, A. J.: Medical care of the athlete, New York, 1962, McGraw-Hill Book Co.

Stamm, T. T.: Foot troubles, London, 1957, Gerald Duckworth & Co., Ltd.

CHAPTER **17**

Conditions of the knee

ANATOMY

The knee, commonly considered a hinge joint (ginglymus), performs two principal actions, flexion and extension. Medial and lateral rotations of the tibia are possible but only to an exceedingly limited degree. Since the knee is extremely weak in terms of its bone arrangement (Fig. 17-1), compensation is provided through the firm support given by ligaments and muscles (Fig. 17-2). It is designed for stability in weight bearing and for mobility in locomotion, however, the knee is extremely unstable laterally.

The knee joint consists of several articulations: those between the two femoral condyles and the menisci, between the tibia and the menisci, and between the patella and the femur. The condyles of the femur move in a shallow depression, formed by the tibia and additionally deepened by two semilunar cartilages (menisci). Collateral ligaments function to stabilize the knee laterally and medially; posteriorly, the floor of the popliteal fossa is formed by the posterior ligament. The menisci, which rest on the tibia, in addition to deepening the tibial receptacle, serve also to tighten the internal cruciate ligament, preventing a forward or backward displacement of the femur on the tibia. An extensive synovial membrane surrounds the knee

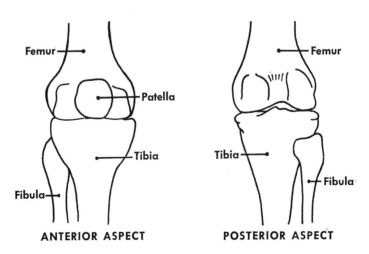

ANTERIOR ASPECT   POSTERIOR ASPECT

Fig. 17-1. Bones of the knee.

286

joint and lines the joint cavity, lubricating the moving structures (Fig. 17-3). More than 18 bursal sacs are located in the knee area, each of which serves to pad it and to prevent abnormal function from taking place. Additional protection is given by fat pads placed anteriorly beneath the patella.

The distal end of the femur expands and forms the convex or *lateral condyle* and the *medial condyle,* which are designed to articulate with the tibia and the patella. The articular surface of the medial condyle is longer from front to back than that of the lateral condyle. Anteriorly, the two condyles form a hollowed-out area to receive

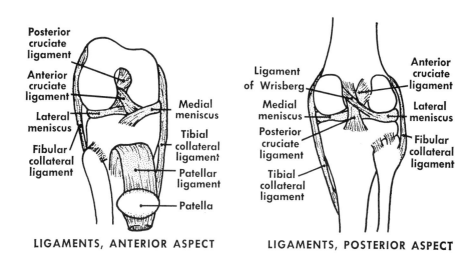

LIGAMENTS, ANTERIOR ASPECT

LIGAMENTS, POSTERIOR ASPECT

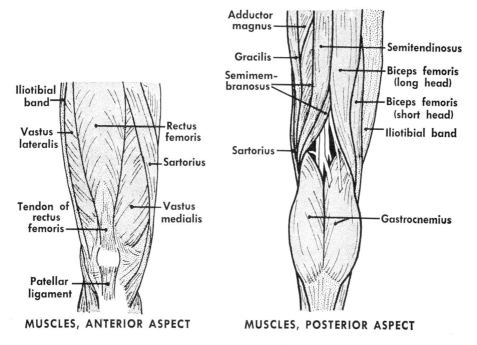

MUSCLES, ANTERIOR ASPECT

MUSCLES, POSTERIOR ASPECT

Fig. 17-2. Anatomy of the knee.

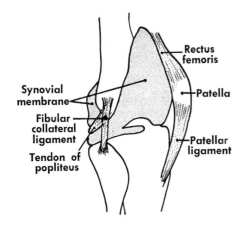

Fig. 17-3. Synovial membrane, lateral aspect of the knee.

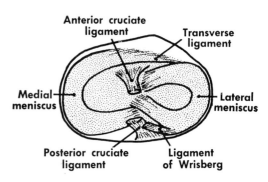

Fig. 17-4. Cross-sectional view indicating relationship of menisci (medial and lateral) to the knee ligaments.

the patella. The upper end of the tibia, designed to receive the condyles of the femur, consists of two *tuberosities,* which are divided posteriorly by a groove called the popliteal notch. Superiorly, the tuberosities have two shallow concavities that articulate with their respective femoral condyles. Separating these concavities or articular facets is a roughened area where the cruciate ligaments attach and from which a process commonly known as the tibial spine arises. The *patella* is the largest sesamoid bone in the body and lies within the tendon of the quadriceps muscles. Its function is to give anterior protection to the knee joint and increased leverage to the knee on extension. All the articular surfaces of the femur, tibia, and patella are covered by *hyaline cartilage,* a smooth and pearly substance that serves particularly to reduce friction.

The *menisci* (Fig. 17-4) are two oval-shaped (semilunar) fibrocartilages that deepen the articular facets of the tibia and cushion any stresses placed upon the knee joint. They are located medially and laterally on the tibial tuberosity. The *medial meniscus* is a C-shaped fibrocartilage, the circumference of which is attached quite loosely to the medial articular facet of the tibia by means of the coronary ligament. The *lateral meniscus* forms an almost com-

plete O and is attached to the lateral articular facet on the superior aspect of the tibia. The consistency of the menisci is much like that of the intervertebral disks. They are held much less rigidly, however, being loose except at the outer edges. Both surfaces of the menisci are articular surfaces and, with the exception of the periphery, they are not directly supplied with blood; their main nourishment comes from the synovial fluid that is contained within the joint cavity.

The *coronary ligaments* attach the menisci at the outer edges of the tibia and are a part of the articular capsule. The *Wrisberg ligament* is that part of the lateral meniscus which projects upward, close to the attachment of the posterior cruciate. The *transverse ligament* joins the anterior portions of the lateral and medial menisci.

The *cruciate ligaments* account for a considerable amount of knee stability and are two ligamentous bands that cross one another within the joint cavity of the knee. The *anterior cruciate ligament* attaches below and in front of the tibia; then, passing backward, it laterally attaches to the inner surface of the lateral condyle. Its function is to prevent posterior displacement of the femur on the tibia. The *posterior cruciate ligament,* the stronger of the two, crosses from the back of the tibia in an upward, forward, and medial direction and attaches to the anterior portion of the lateral surface of the medial condyle of the femur. The function of this ligament is to prevent anterior displacement of the femur on the tibia. The *patellar ligament* is a strong band consisting of a superficial part that is a portion of the quadriceps and an inferior part that extends to the tibial tubercle.

The medial and lateral support of the knee is maintained by two collateral ligaments. The *lateral collateral ligament* stabilizes the lateral aspect of the knee joint and is a round, fibrous cord that is attached to the lateral epicondyle above and to the apex of the head of the fibula below. A fat pad separates the lateral meniscus from the lateral collateral ligament. The *medial collateral ligament* is a broad, flat ligament and is the stronger of the two. The upper end is attached to the medial epicondyle of the femur and the lower end to the upper part of the tibial shaft. Contrary to the nature of attachment of the lateral ligament, the deep fibers of the medial collateral ligament attach directly to the medial meniscus. The *oblique popliteal ligament* is a broad band of fibrous tissue that helps to form the floor of the popliteal fossa. It extends from the upper margin of the intercondyloid fossa to the posterior margin of the head of the tibia.

The *synovial membrane* lines all of the articular surfaces but those of the cruciate ligaments. It is a highly vascularized, tube-like tissue, which extends upward along the anterior aspect of the femur and forms the suprapatella bursa, the largest bursa of the knee. Among the important bursae (Fig. 17-5) are the infrapatellar bursa that lies between the lower portion of the patellar ligament and the tibia, the prepatellar bursa in front of the patella, the pretibial bursa that lies over the tibial tubercle, and numerous popliteal bursae.

The main blood and nerve supply of the knee consists of the popliteal artery and vein and the internal and external popliteal nerves, all of which are protected by the fat that fills the popliteal space.

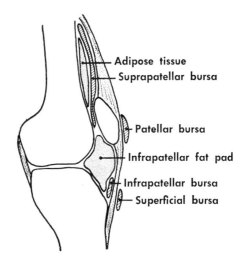

- Adipose tissue
- Suprapatellar bursa
- Patellar bursa
- Infrapatellar fat pad
- Infrapatellar bursa
- Superficial bursa

Fig. 17-5. Important bursae of the knee.

Movements of the knee

The primary actions of the knee are flexion and extension, which involve a rolling and gliding of the femoral condyles on the tibia. Secondary movements consist of a slight internal (medial) and external (lateral) rotation of the tibia. The movements of flexion and extension take place above the menisci, whereas rotation is performed below the menisci. Rotation is caused mainly by the greater length of the medial condyle of the femur, which rolls forward more than does the lateral condyle. The medial meniscus is distorted during rotation as a result of the twisting of its attachment on the tibia, which makes it particularly vulnerable to torsion injuries. In contrast the lateral meniscus is prevented from twisting by the popliteus muscle that pulls it out of the way as the tibia rotates.

In complete flexion, approximately 140 degrees, the range of the knee movement is limited by the extremely shortened position of the hamstring group, the extensibility of the quadriceps group, and the bulk of the hamstrings. In this position the femoral condyles rest on their corresponding menisci at a point that permits a small degree of inward rotation. In full flexion the posterior cruciate ligament is taut; as the knee moves into an extended position the condyles of the femur glide and roll on their respective articulating surfaces, moving together equally. Both cruciates are relaxed when the joint is in the semiflexed position; but as the knee continues forward the condyles move together until, at the point of almost complete extension, the lateral condyle becomes set in the contour of the tibial tuberosity. After the lateral condyle has stopped, the medial condyle continues forward, thus producing a slight external rotation of the tibia. This final external rotation movement is called "knee locking." Throughout flexion, the medial collateral ligament is tight; but it should be noted that the lateral collateral ligament is taut only on full extension.

The actions of the knee joint and the muscles that control them are listed below:

1. Knee flexion is executed by the biceps femoris, the semitendinosus, the semimembranosus, the gracilis, the sartorius, the gastrocnemius, the popliteus, and the plantaris.

2. Knee extension is executed by the quadriceps femoris, consisting of the three vasti—the vastus medialis, the vastus lateralis, and the vastus intermedius—and by the rectus femoris.

3. Outward rotation is controlled by the biceps femoris.

4. Inward rotation is accomplished by the popliteus, the semitendinosus, the semimembranosus, the sartorius, and the gracilis. Rotation of the tibia is quite limited and can occur only when the knee is in a flexed position.

Knee trauma

Although the knee is the largest joint in the body, it is extremely vulnerable to traumatic injuries because of a poor bony arrangement. The shallow joint, with its main stability being derived from muscular and connective tissue, is especially defenseless against force that is applied medially or laterally. Traumatic knee injuries fall mainly into four categories: contusions, lateral and medial sprains, torsion sprains, and hyperextension injuries.

The knee is particularly prone to bruis-

ing (contusion) because of its lack of padding. Contusion trauma comes as the result of falling or receiving a direct blow. Football, basketball, baseball, and wrestling all offer situations conducive to bruising the knee. The cross-body block appears to be the major cause of knee injuries incurred in football. Traumatic forces applied to the knee joint can result in injury to the synovial membrane or to the deeper periosteal tissue.

Sprains of the knee are easily contracted in athletics because the joint is not deeply seated but relies on ligamentous bands for main support. Both direct outside forces and abnormal twisting can bring about a knee sprain (see Fig. 5-2). Over 75% of all knee sprains in athletics are attributable to football; the majority of the remainder occur in wrestling, basketball, and baseball. A direct blow on the lateral or medial aspect of the athlete's knee while his foot is firmly planted will tend to stretch and tear the supporting connective tissue. The extent of pathology will depend on previous knee injuries, position of the knee at the time of the trauma, and the readiness state of the athlete at the time of the injury.

Torsion sprains result from an abnormal wrenching of the knee joint that contorts external and internal supporting structures. In football, basketball, wrestling, or skiing the athlete is often in position for a torsion injury by having the feet fixed while the body is moving in a different direction.

Hyperextension of the knee is not as common as may be thought; most so-called hyperextension injuries are mild muscular strains in the popliteal region. When hyperextension occurs, the knee is extended beyond the normal straight leg position. Such injuries usually occur as the result of a blow delivered to the anterior aspect of the knee while the foot is in a stabilized position. Severe trauma of this nature may result in anteroposterior instability.

EVALUATION OF KNEE INJURIES

It is the responsibility of the team physician to diagnose the severity and exact nature of a knee injury. Although the physician is charged with the final evaluation, the trainer is usually the first person to observe the injury; therefore the trainer is charged with initial evaluation and first aid. The most important item in understanding what pathology has taken place is to become familiar with the traumatic sequence and mechanisms of injury, either through having seen the injury occur or through learning its related history.[2] The athlete should be questioned immediately after the injury as to the severity of pain at the time of trauma and whether a tear was heard or felt. After knowledge as to how the knee was injured has been obtained, an examination should be given by means of visual inspection, first, then palpation of the part, and finally some tests to determine if mobility is normal or abnormal.[3]

When first studying the injury, the trainer should observe whether the athlete is able to support his weight flat-footedly on the injured leg or whether he must stand and walk on his toes. Toe walking is an indication that the athlete is holding his knee in a splinted position to avoid pain or that the knee is being held in a flexed position by a wedge of dislocated menisci. In first-time acute knee sprains, fluid and blood effusion is not usually apparent until after a 24-hour period. Swelling and ecchymosis will occur unless such effusion has been arrested by the use of compression and cold packs.

Palpation of the knee will bring to light the areas of point tenderness. The trainer should proceed with an orderly approach, first feeling the anterior capsular structures, then the posterior popliteal structures, and finally the heavy collateral ligaments. Palpation should be done with a firm but gentle touch, avoiding additional irritation to the athlete.[4]

Tests for abnormal mobility

Knee injuries that are produced by either a twist or a direct blow result in abnormal mobility. The injured and uninjured knees are tested and contrasted to determine any

Fig. 17-6. Collateral ligament test.

Fig. 17-7. Anteroposterior test.

differences of movement between the two. The passive movements that test for abnormal knee mobility are used in the collateral ligament test, the anteroposterior test, and the tibial rotation test.

Collateral ligament test. The collateral ligament procedure (Fig. 17-6) is designed to test the wholeness of the medial and lateral collateral knee ligaments. With the athlete lying in a supine position with both legs extended, the trainer determines the range of lateral mobility of the affected leg as compared to that of the normal leg. To test the medial collateral ligament, the operator holds the ankle firmly with one hand while the other hand is placed on the lower lateral aspect of the thigh. In this position the operator gently pushes medially on the thigh, meanwhile attempting to abduct the leg. An intact ligament offers little movement. After the medial collateral ligament is examined, the operator exchanges hand positions and tests the lateral collateral ligaments in the same manner.

Anteroposterior test. The anteroposterior examination (Fig. 17-7) is designed to test the anterior and posterior stability of the knee. The athlete lies on the training table with the injured leg flexed while the operator, facing the anterior aspect of the athlete's leg, encircles the upper portion of the leg immediately below the knee joint with both hands. The fingers of the operator rest in the popliteal space of the affected knee with the thumbs positioned side by side directly over the tibial tubercle. In this attitude the operator gently pulls the tibia anteriorly and posteriorly. Motion that exceeds ¼ inch may indicate looseness of the cruciate ligaments. This is commonly called the *drawer sign.*

Tibial rotation test. Determining whether or not a knee injury has resulted in a torn meniscus is often difficult. The tibial rotation test (Fig. 17-8) is used in examining for any loose bodies within the knee. The athlete is positioned supine on the table with the injured leg fully flexed. The operator places one hand over the patella, with the fingers and thumb covering the grasped knee, and with the other hand he holds the athlete's ankle. The ankle hand scribes a small circle while the knee hand feels for signs of abnormal clicking, grating vibrations, and pain sites.

Atrophy measurement. A knee injury is almost always accompanied by a marked decrease in the girth of the thigh musculature. The muscles most affected by disuse are the quadriceps group, which are "antigravity muscles" and assist man in maintaining an erect, straight leg position. They are in constant use in effecting movement in activities. Atrophy results when a lower limb is favored and is not used to its potential. Measurement of the circumference of both thighs can often detect the existence of former leg injuries or determine the extent of reconditioning. Measurement in each case should be carried out with a tape

measure placed around the greatest circumference of the thigh at a measured distance from the upper pole of the patella.

CARE OF COMMON KNEE AFFECTIONS
Contusions

Contusions in varying degrees are extremely frequent about the knee in athletics. Lacking fat and muscle padding, the knee is particularly vulnerable to injuries caused by falling or by direct blows from other participants. Contusions about the knee can be discussed in relation to contusions of the knee musculature, capsular tissue, or periosteum.

Contusions of the knee musculature

A blow struck against the muscles crossing the knee joint can result in a handicapping condition. One of the muscles frequently involved is the vastus medialis of the quadriceps group, which is primarily concerned with locking the knee in a position of full extension. Bruises of the vastus medialis produce all the appearances of a knee sprain, including severe pain, loss of movement, and signs of acute inflammation. Such bruising is often manifested by swelling and discoloration caused by the tearing of muscle tissue and blood vessels. If adequate first aid is given immediately, the knee will usually return to functional use 24 hours following the trauma. At that time various forms of heat, combined with massage and mild exercise, may be given. Overuse and irritation of the injury during treatment must be avoided. Muscle contusions require an average of 2 days to 1 week for recovery, depending on the extent of pathological involvement.

Contusions of the knee capsular tissue

Bruising of the capsular tissue that surrounds the knee joint is often associated with muscle contusions and deep bone bruises. A traumatic force delivered to capsular tissue may cause capillary bleeding, irritate the synovial membrane, and result in a profuse fluid effusion into the joint cavity and surrounding spaces. Effusion

Fig. 17-8. Tibial rotation test.

often takes place slowly and almost imperceptibly. It is advisable to prevent the athlete from engaging in further activity for at least 24 hours after receipt of a capsular bruise. Activity causes an increase in circulation and may cause extensive swelling and hematoma at the knee joint. Scar tissue develops wherever internal bleeding with clot organization is present. If this condition is repeated time after time, chronic synovitis or an arthritic sequela may develop.

Contusions of the knee periosteum

The knee presents a multiangular articulation that is especially subject to bruising. A severe penetrating blow that is delivered over the medial or the lateral femoral condyle or over the superior head of the fibula or that is directed toward the patella may result in bruising of the periosteum or the articular cartilage. This condition, although extremely painful on palpation, does not usually restrict the athlete from moving. Compression and cold should be applied immediately after injury and adequate padding should be used.

Care of knee contusions

Care of a bruised knee depends on many factors. However, management is principally dependent on the locus and severity of the contusion. The following procedures are suggested:

1. Apply compression bandages and cold until resolution has taken place.

2. Prescribe inactivity and rest for 24 hours.

3. If swelling occurs continue cold application for 72 hours. If swelling and pain are intensive, refer the athlete to the physician.

4. Gradually begin the use of heat, in the form of whirlpool and analgesic balm packs, when acute phase is over.

5. Allow the athlete to return to normal activity, with protective padding, when pain and initial irritation have subsided.

6. If swelling is not resolved within a week, a chronic condition of either synovitis or bursitis may exist, indicating the need for rest and medical attention.

Bursitis

The anterior aspect of the knee contains three bursae that are particularly vulnerable to recurrent bruising in athletics: the prepatellar, the infrapatellar, and the superficial pretibial. All are subject to chronic irritation when affected by a succession of mild contusions, which can produce a chronic inflammatory condition. The abnormal amount of synovium within the bursa may produce some pain symptoms, but in most cases of knee bursitis activity is not restricted. After the acute stages, heat, compression, and pad protection should be administered to the athlete.

Collateral ligament sprains

Ligament sprains are the most frequently reported injury among the knee injuries that occur in athletics. As mentioned previously, the knee's only lateral and medial stability is achieved by collateral ligaments. The greatest incidence of knee sprains affect the medial collateral ligament as a result either of a direct blow from the lateral side, in an inward direction, or of a severe inward twist. Greater pathology results from medial sprains than from lateral sprains because of their direct relation to the articular capsule and the medial meniscus. Medial and lateral sprains appear in varying degrees, depending on knee position, previous injuries, strength of muscles crossing the joint, force and angle of the trauma, fixation of the foot, and conditions of the playing surface.[5]

The position of the knee is important in establishing its vulnerability in traumatic sprains. Any position of the knee, from full extension to full flexion, can result in pathology if there is sufficient force. Full extension tightens both lateral and medial ligaments. However, flexion affords a loss of stability to the lateral ligament but maintains stability in various portions of the broad medial ligament. The most relaxed position for the collateral and cruciate ligaments is a flexion range of 15 degrees to 30 degrees. Lateral collateral ligament sprains occur most often from a violently adducted and internally rotated knee. The most prevalent mechanism of medial collateral ligament sprain is one of foot eversion with a flexed and abducted knee.

Speculation among medical authorities is that torn menisci seldom happen as the result of a first sprain; most occur after the collateral ligaments have been stretched by repeated injury. Many mild to moderate sprains leave the knee unstable and thus vulnerable to internal derangements. The strength of the muscles crossing the knee joint is important in assisting the ligaments to support the articulation. These muscles should be conditioned to the highest possible degree for sports wherein knee injuries are common. With the added support and protection of muscular strength a state of readiness may be developed through proper training.

The force and angle of the trauma usually determine the extent of pathology that takes place. Even after having witnessed the occurrence of a knee sprain, it is difficult to predict the amount of tissue damage. The most revealing time for testing joint stability is immediately after injury, before effusion masks the extent of derangement.

Foot fixation increases the possibility of the athlete's receiving a severe knee sprain because the knee can flex in only one direction. When the foot is anchored to the ground, as it is when wearing cleats, a sudden and severe blow or twist subjects the ligaments and supporting tendons to severe torque or abnormal strain because the knee cannot give way.

Playing surfaces have a role in the incidence and severity of knee sprains. Irregular surfaces with rocks and holes place abnormal demands on the ankles and knees as they attempt to stabilize the athlete's body. Hard ground surfaces are particularly to blame in cases of collateral sprains, whereas soft surfaces are conducive to torsion injuries. The use of outdoor synthetic

playing fields has revealed a marked increase in ankle and knee injuries.

Care of collateral ligament knee sprains

Collateral knee sprains most often result in profuse internal hemorrhage and an effusion of synovial fluid into articular and tissue spaces. All the signs of acute and subacute inflammation are displayed in this injury. Pain and loss of function appear immediately, with swelling and discoloration following some time afterward. Care of collateral ligament knee sprains varies with the extent of trauma. The trainer should closely follow the management routine previously indicated. General care procedures are listed below:

1. Apply cold and a compression bandage from 24 to 72 hours to reduce fluid effusion and the development of a hematoma.

2. Give the athlete crutches and instruct him to remain off the affected leg until able to walk without a limp.

3. Refer the athlete to a physician for examination and x-ray films.

4. The first day after the athlete has been released to the trainer for physical therapy he is given a cold whirlpool treatment or ice massage. Gradually increased heating of the part takes place over a few days with the use of superficial modalities. *Note:* Neither heat nor massage should be applied until hemorrhaging has ceased.

5. Because the muscles that cross the knee, particularly the quadriceps, lose their strength rapidly, have the athlete start muscle setting exercises immediately after first-aid treatment and continue them until the soreness and swelling have diminished.

6. Allow no athlete to return to his sport until he can demonstrate normal range of joint motion and strength. To enhance normal function, an active program of reconditioning should be instituted (see Chapter 15).

7. Have the athlete, before playing each day, use additional knee support. (Although there is controversy as to the value of any

knee support, the athlete should use any procedure that will possibly provide protection until there is contrary information.) The most satisfactory support for knee sprains in the past has been adhesive strapping. Once a knee sprain has healed and function has been satisfactorily regained, the athlete is still left with weakened structural ligaments. Tape properly applied can assist in stabilizing the knee.[7]

Technique 1—basketweave collateral ligament strapping. No mechanical device is as satisfactory as adhesive strapping when stabilizing weakened knees. Ad-

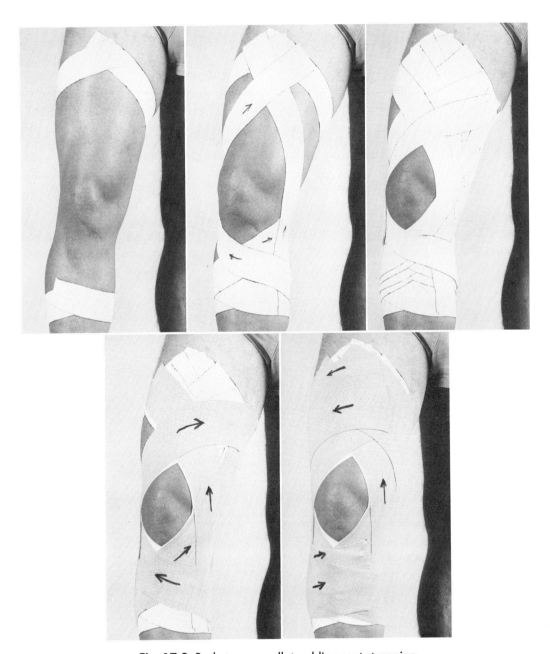

Fig. 17-9. Basketweave collateral ligament strapping.

hesive tape, properly applied against the gravitational pull, can strengthen stretched or torn collateral ligaments immeasurably (Fig. 17-9).[6]

Materials needed: One roll of 2-inch linen tape, a roll of 3-inch elastic tape, 2-inch heel lift, and skin adherent.

Position of the athlete: The athlete stands on a 3-foot table with his injured knee held in a moderately relaxed position by means of a 2-inch heel lift. The hair is completely removed from a point 6 inches above to 6 inches below the kneecap.

Position of the trainer: The trainer stands facing the anterior aspect of the athlete's knee.

Procedure:

1. A circular, 2-inch linen tape anchor strip is placed lightly around the thigh and leg at the hairline.

2. The first linen tape strip is carried from the lateral side of the leg anchor, running obliquely across the tibial tubercle and crossing slightly behind the medial femoral condyle.

3. The second linen strip begins at the medial aspect of the leg anchor and is carried upward across the medial femoral con-dyle, ending on the anterior portion of the thigh anchor.

4. The third linen strip is taken from the medial aspect of the leg anchor, placed obliquely across the tibial tubercle crossing slightly behind the lateral femoral condyle, and ends on the lateral aspect of the thigh anchor.

5. The fourth strip is started from the lateral leg anchor, carried upward across the lateral femoral condyle, and ends on the anterior portion of the thigh anchor. *This first series forms a self-locking X on each side of the knee joint.*

6. The second series is applied in the same sequence as the first but is applied forward, overlapping at least two thirds of the first series' tape width.

7. The third and last series of the linen tape is applied forward, overlapping two thirds of the width of the second series. As this last series is laid in place, it is desirable to tuck ¼ inch of the tape edge nearest the knee cap in for approximately 3 inches on either side of the knee bend to prevent the tape from tearing during activity.

8. Four elastic tape strips are cut, each

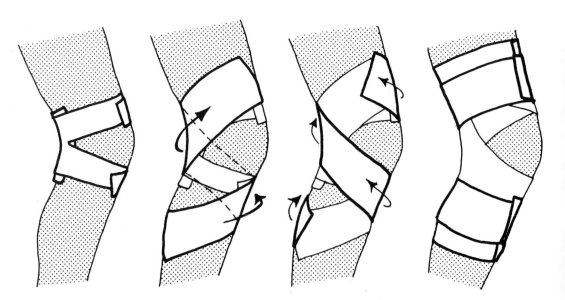

Fig. 17-10. Rotary knee strapping.

about 9 inches in length. Stretched to their utmost, the elastic strips are placed directly over the linen tape series forming an X on both sides of the knee. *Elastic tape provides a flexible reinforcement to the rigid linen tape. It also helps to prevent tearing and loosening caused by perspiration.*

9. Elastic tape is applied as locks for the basket weave. Two or three strips of tape are cut to encircle the thigh and the leg. Some trainers find it advantageous to complete a knee strapping by wrapping it loosely with an elastic wrap, thus providing an added precaution against the tape becoming loose from perspiration.

Technique 2—rotary knee strapping. The rotary strapping method is designed to provide the knee with support when it is unstable from injury to the medial collateral and anterior cruciate ligaments (Fig. 17-10).

Materials needed: One roll of 3-inch elastic tape, skin adherent, 4-inch gauze pad, and scissors.

Position of the athlete: The athlete sits on table with affected knee flexed 15 degrees.

Position of the trainer: The trainer stands facing the side of the athlete's flexed knee.

Procedure:

1. A 10-inch piece of elastic tape is cut with the ends snipped at both ends. The gauze pad is placed in the center of the 10 inch piece of elastic tape.

2. The gauze with the elastic tape backing is placed in the popliteal fossa of the athlete's knee. Both ends of the tape are stretched to the fullest extent and are torn. The divided ends are placed firmly around the patella and interlocked (Fig. 17-10, A).

3. Starting at a mid-point on the gastrocnemius, a 3-inch elastic tape strip is spiraled to the front of the leg, then behind crossing the popliteal fossa, and around the thigh, finishing anteriorly.

4. Procedure 3 is repeated on the opposite side.

5. Three or four spiral strips may be applied for added strength.

6. Once in place, the spiral strips are locked by the application of two circular strips around the thigh and two around the calf (Fig. 17-10, B). *Note:* The trainer may want to provide more rigidity by tracing the spiral pattern with linen tape.

Internal derangements of the knee joint

Internal derangements of the knee joint occur through the same mechanism that causes collateral ligament sprains. The tissues involved are the anterior and posterior cruciate ligaments and the medial or lateral menisci.[5] First-time sprains seldom affect internal structures. These structures are made vulnerable as additional trauma stretches the external supportive tissues.

Lesions of the cruciate ligaments

The anterior and posterior cruciate ligaments are designed to stabilize the tibia on the femur, and they are named in terms of their relationship to the tibia. The anterior cruciate ligament prevents the posterior displacement of the femur on the tibia, while the posterior cruciate prevents anterior displacement of the femur on the tibia. The anterior cruciate is tensed on full extension and the posterior cruciate on full flexion. The cruciates are well protected by their internal position and are extremely strong, they are seldom injured.

The cruciates are extremely valuable to the stability and functioning of the knee, and any injury to them is considered serious. Injury may occur through direct blows (anteriorly, medially, or posteriorly) or through an abnormal twist, usually resulting from an internal rotation of the femur on the tibia. The highest incidence of such injuries is caused by blows to the anterior aspect of the leg. Such blows force the tibia backward while the knee is in flexion, thereby stretching or tearing the anterior cruciate. Medial collateral sprains may also affect the anterior cruciate if they occur to an already unstable knee. Torsion injuries to the knee commonly affect the medial collateral and anterior cruciate ligaments.[8] Injuries to the posterior cruciate may develop as an outcome of overflexion, such as is incurred when repeated deep knee bends or full squats with heavy weights are performed.

When the medial collateral ligament has been stretched or torn by medial and external rotation, the main support of the knee is derived from the anterior cruciate ligament. Therefore, any abnormal movement of abduction, external rotation, or hyperextension may injure the anterior cruciate. A fracture or cracking of the medial meniscus may occur as a corollary to the tearing of the medial collateral and anterior cruciate ligaments. For evaluating a cruciate tear there must be an understanding of the history, which usually includes a severe wrench or an anterior blow directly to the knee. Severe pain, loss of function, rotary instability, and a feeling of weakness on weight bearing are usually involved.

Acute symptoms are marked tenderness and rapid swelling. As soon as possible after the injury has taken place functional tests should be given to determine the anteroposterior stability of the knee. Immediate care of acute cruciate injuries follows the same pattern used for collateral injuries. Athletes who have unstable knees because of a cruciate weakness should be given protective adhesive strapping before engaging in sport activity.

Cruciate ligament and hyperextension strapping. Cruciate ligament and hyperextension strapping (Fig. 17-11) is designed to prevent the knee from hyperextending and may also be used for either strained hamstring tendons or slackened cruciate ligaments.

Materials needed: One roll of 1½-inch tape, felt, cotton or gauze pad cut to approximately 4 inches by 6 inches, tape adherent, and 2-inch heel lift.

Position of the athlete: The athlete's leg should be completely shaved from approximately 6 inches above to 6 inches below the kneecap. He stands on a 3-foot table with the injured knee flexed by means of a 2-inch heel lift.

Position of the trainer: The trainer stands facing the front of the athlete's knee.

Procedure:

1. Place 2 anchor strips at the hairlines, one around the thigh and the other around the leg. These should be applied loosely to allow for muscle expansion during exercise.

2. As shown in the middle view (posterior aspect) in Fig. 17-11, place a gauze pad at the popliteal space to protect the popliteal nerves and blood vessels from constriction by the tape.

3. Start the supporting tape strip on the outside of the anterior part of the leg anchor. Carry it upward and obliquely around the back of the knee at an acute angle, crossing the popliteal space, and continuing upward and around the thigh, and ending on the anterior aspect of the thigh anchor strip.

4. Start the second strip at the same point as the first but carry it obliquely upward on the inside of the anterior aspect of the leg; then bring it back of the leg, crossing the popliteal fossa and continuing upward and around the thigh to finish on the anterior thigh anchor strip. This forms a crisscross over the popliteal fossa.

5. With the third strip of tape, overlap the first strip by at least two thirds and follow the same pattern. The fourth strip is applied similarly to the second strip.

6. Apply an additional series of strips if the athlete is heavily muscled.

7. Lock the supporting strips in place after they are applied. This is done by placing 2 or 3 overlapping circles around the thigh and leg.

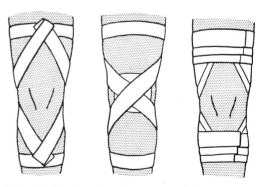

Fig. 17-11. Cruciate ligament and hyperextension strapping.

Lesions of the menisci

Both the medial and the lateral menisci are semilunar (half-moon–shaped) fibro-cartilages that are exceedingly tough and elastic. Their main function is to deepen the joint cavity of the knee and to aid in shock absorption. They are attached by the coronary ligament only at the edges of the tibia and are otherwise free to move. Tibial rotation takes place below the menisci, whereas flexion and extension occur above. The lateral meniscus is more mobile than the medial, because it is controlled by the popliteus muscle that attaches to the arch of the cartilage and draws it out of the way of the rotating tibia. In contrast, the medial meniscus lacks muscle control and becomes distorted during tibial rotation. This makes the medial meniscus extremely vulnerable to sudden and abnormal knee twists.

A tear or complete dislocation of a meniscus can result from either a direct blow or a severe twist. The medial meniscus is affected 90% more in athletes than is the lateral meniscus. The high number of medial tears as compared to lateral tears is basically due to the direct attachment of the medial collateral ligament to the medial meniscus and the resultant distortion of the cartilage during tibial torsion. A blow from the lateral side directed inward forces the knee into a position of adduction that often tears and stretches the medial collateral ligament; meanwhile its fibers twist the medial meniscus outward. Repeated mild sprains reduce the strength of the knee to a state favorable for a cartilage tear through lessening its normal ligamentous stability. The greatest number of medial meniscus lesions are the outcome of a sudden, strong internal rotation of the femur on a partially flexed tibia when the foot is firmly planted. As a result of the force of this action the cartilage is pulled out of its normal bed and levered between the femoral condyles. The most common type of medial meniscus injury is an elongated tear occurring within the cartilage itself. The interior part is cut and lifted from the periphery while it is still held fast at both ends. These tears are commonly called *bucket handle tears* (Fig. 17-12).

Once torn, the meniscus does not heal readily because it lacks a direct blood supply. It acquires its nutriment through the process of osmosis from the synovial fluids that bathe the knee's internal environment. Once a knee cartilage has been fractured, its ruptured edges harden; eventually, complete atrophy may develop. On occasion, portions of the meniscus may become detached and wedge themselves between the articulating surfaces of the tibia and femur, thus imposing a locking action on the joint. In situations of recurring joint locking or in cases where reduction of a lodged dislocated cartilage is impossible, surgical intervention may be necessary.

An absolute diagnosis of cartilage injury is difficult. For determining the possibility of such an injury, a complete history should be obtained, which consists of information

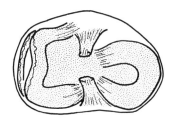

Fig. 17-12. Bucket handle tear.

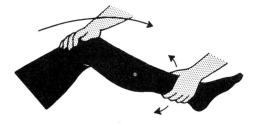

Fig. 17-13. Cartilage click test.

about past knee sprains and an understanding of how the present injury occurred. Diagnosis of menisci injuries should be made immediately after the injury has developed and before muscle spasm and swelling obscure the normal shape of the knee. The injury typically results in severe pain and a loss of motion, with acute tenderness on palpation over the anterior aspect of the meniscus. At this time, all tests for abnormal knee mobility should be given to determine the presence of collateral and cruciate ligament tears. Together with these tests, the *cartilage click test* should be given[9] (Fig. 17-13):

1. One hand is placed over the cap of the flexed knee while the other grasps the ankle.

2. The leg is gently pulled into extension and rotation.

3. A positive sign is established if a click is felt or heard as the joint is moved.

INFRAPATELLAR FAT PAD

The two most important fat pads of the knee are the infrapatellar fat pad and the suprapatellar fat pad. The infrapatellar fat pad lies between the synovial membrane on the anterior aspect of the joint and the patellar ligament, and the suprapatellar fat pad lies between the anterior surface and the suprapatellar bursa. Of the two pads, the infrapatellar is more often injured in athletics, principally as a result of its large size and particular vulnerability during activity. It may become wedged between the knee articulations, irritated by chronic kneeling pressures, or traumatized by direct blows. Repeated injury produces a capillary hemorrhaging and swelling of the fatty tissue; if the irritation continues, scarring and calcification may develop. The athlete may complain of pain below the patellar ligament, especially on knee extension, and the knee may display weakness, mild swelling, and stiffness on movement.

Care of acute fat pad injuries involves rest from irritating activities until inflammation has subsided, heel elevation of ½ to 1 inch, and physical therapy. Heel eleva-

tion prevents added irritation on full extension; it may also be necessary to prevent full extension from taking place by applying a hyperextension strapping. Therapy should include constant heat throughout the day in the form of hydro hot packs, whirlpool, or analgesic hot packs. Massage around the inflamed area may assist lymphatic drainage. However, avoid massaging directly over the joint itself. Quadriceps atrophy may be prevented by assigning a daily program of quadriceps "setting" or isometric exercises. If scarring and bone involvement are noted, surgical removal may be indicated. It is extremely desirable to recognize the acute stages and prevent additional trauma.

PATELLAR CONDITIONS

The position of the patella exposes it to a variety of traumas in athletics. The two most common patellar disorders are dislocations and chondromalacia patellae, an abnormal softness of the knee cartilages.

Dislocations of the patella

Subluxation and dislocation of the patella is prevalent in athletics. The exact reason for this high incidence is not clearly understood. Knock-knees, poor quadriceps tone, lateral insertion of the patellar tendon, and a flattened lateral or medial condyle have been suggested as etiological factors. However, in athletics the primary cause seems to be either a forced rotation of the thigh while the foot is planted or a forced contraction of the patellar tendon while jumping or sprinting.[10] As a rule, displacement takes place outwardly with the patella resting on the lateral condyle (Fig. 17-14).

An acute patella dislocation is usually associated with repeated knee trauma, complete loss of function, pain, and swelling with the patella residing in an abnormal position. The physician will immediately reduce the dislocation by means of a mild pressure on the patella with the knee in full extension. The knee is immobilized in a position of extension for 4 weeks or

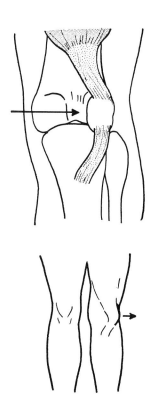

Fig. 17-14. Dislocated patella.

longer, and the athlete utilizes crutches when walking. Reconditioning is designed so that maximum strength is given to the quadriceps muscles.

Chondromalacia patellae

Chondromalacia of this type is defined as a degenerative process that results in a softening of the patella. The softening may develop after several minor or severe injuries to the patella.[14] The symptoms of this condition are chronic pain, weakness, and a catching or locking sensation with accompanying tenderness about the patella. Examination reveals crepitation on movement of the patella, mild swelling, and tenderness.

When diagnosis indicates that an athlete has this condition, protection must be given to the knee in the form of a shock-absorbing pad and an extensive quadriceps-conditioning program (see Chapter 15). Continued neglect of the condition will cause

destruction of portions of the femoral hyaline cartilage and subsequent encouragement of abnormal arthritic bone growth.

Fractures of the patella

Fractures of the patella can be caused by either direct or indirect trauma. Most fractures are the result of indirect violence in which a severe pull of the patellar tendon is executed against the femur when the knee is semiflexed. This position subjects the patella to maximum stress from the quadriceps tendon and the patellar ligament. Forcible muscle contraction may then fracture the patella at its lower one half. Direct injury most often produces fragmentation with little displacement. Falls, jumping, or running may result in a fracture of the patella. The fracture causes hemorrhage and joint effusion, resulting in a generalized swelling. Indirect fracture causes capsular tearing, separation of bone fragments, and possible tearing of the quadriceps tendon. Direct fracture involves little bone separation.

Diagnosis is accomplished by use of the history, palpation of separated fragments, and an x-ray confirmation. As soon as the trainer suspects a patella fracture, he should apply cold and wrap the knee with an elastic compress together with splinting. He should then refer the athlete to the team physician. The athlete will normally be immobilized for 2 to 3 months.

Loose bodies within the knee ("joint mice")

Because of repeated trauma to the knee, loose bodies, which are commonly called "joint mice," may develop within the joint cavity. Joint mice may cause a constant irritation within the joint cavity, which responds with an increase of synovial fluid. The athlete may experience sudden pain and joint locking when a particle becomes wedged between the articulating surfaces. In athletics, loose bodies are developed mainly as a result of the condition known as *osteochondritis dissecans*, a softening and partial fragmentation of the menisci, or by the dislodgment of a particle of synovial tissue as a result of continued and repetitive trauma.

RECONDITIONING OF THE KNEE JOINT

Exercise programs for the knee fall basically into three categories: preoperative, postoperative, and preventive. When examination reveals torn ligaments or a torn meniscus, early surgical repair has been found to hasten the athlete's return to his sport.[11] The preoperative program is concerned with increasing the strength and tone of the muscles surrounding the knee. A well-conditioned knee will experience surgery with fewer negative effects than will one that is deconditioned.

The muscles that surround the knee, particularly the quadriceps and the hamstrings of the thigh, atrophy readily after a knee injury (Fig. 17-15). Joint movement should be avoided until pain has subsided and initial healing is complete. While the knee joint is immobilized, the athlete should engage in static muscle contractions called "quad setting" and graduate to straight leg raises, both from a sitting position with hip flexion and while lying prone. The athlete can also execute toe raises to exercise the gastrocnemius muscle (see Chapter 15). During the period of immobilization a graduated program of isometric contractions can be initiated by applying sandbag weights to the extended leg to afford resistance for periods of 6 to 10 seconds. Active bending of the knee should be avoided until initial pain and soreness have diminished. A gradual program of leg-swinging combined with static stretching of the hamstrings can commence following removal from immobilization. A program of progressive resistance isotonic exercises is usually not begun until pain is minimal and healing has begun. *Note: Caution must*

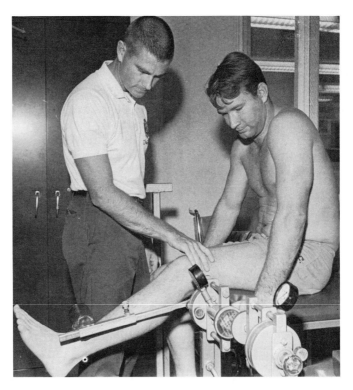

Fig. 17-15. Reconditioning of the knee through the use of a hydraulic resistance device. (Courtesy Kent Henderson, Long Beach Independent Press Telegram.)

be observed when the athlete uses boot weights for resistance. It has been observed in our experience that heavy objects fastened to the foot for resistance purposes may serve to stretch already extended internal structures. Support, therefore, should be given to the leg when it is hanging over the edge of the table. The athlete should begin with light resistance exercises executed several times per day. As strength and range of movement increase resistance may also be increased.

Often the hamstring muscles and gastrocnemius are neglected in reconditioning of the knee. It should be remembered that these muscles contribute a considerable amount of support and stability to the knee; therefore, they should be conditioned along with the quadriceps (see Chapter 15).

When the athlete has reconditioned his knee to the point at which strength and flexibility are adequate for activity, he is encouraged first to jog, graduating to running at half-speed straight ahead, and then to figure-of-eight patterns. When able to run and cut at full speed, the athlete is considered able to return to his sport.[12,13]

REFERENCES

1. Peterson, T. R.: The cross-body block: the major cause of knee injuries, J.A.M.A. **211** (3):449, 1970.
2. Blazina, M. E.: Classification of injuries to the articular cartilages of the knee in athletics. In American Academy of Orthopaedic Surgeons: Symposium on Sports Medicine, 1967, St. Louis, 1969, The C. V. Mosby Co.
3. Reynolds, F. C.: Diagnosis of ligamentous injuries of the knee. In American Academy of Orthopaedic Surgeons: Symposium on Sports Medicine, 1967, St. Louis, 1969, The C. V. Mosby Co.
4. Hughston, J. C.: Diagnosis of internal derangement of the knee. In Proceedings of the Eighth National Conference on the Medical Aspects of Sports, Chicago, 1966, American Medical Association, p. 79.
5. Nicholas, J. A.: Internal derangement of the knee: diagnosis and management. In American Academy of Orthopaedic Surgeons: Symposium on Sports Medicine, 1967, St. Louis, 1969, The C. V. Mosby Co.
6. Tipton, C. M., and others: Current research on ligamentous strength and knee stability. In Proceedings of the Seventh National Conference on the Medical Aspects of Sports, Chicago, 1965, American Medical Association, p. 76.
7. Klein, K. K. and Allman, F. L., Jr.: The knee in sports, Austin, Texas, 1969, The Pemberton Press.
8. Slocum, D. B.: Rotary instability of the knee. In American Academy of Orthopaedic Surgeons: Symposium on Sports Medicine, 1967, St. Louis, 1969, The C. V. Mosby Co.
9. Gardner, R. C.: Diagnosing knee cartilage disease in young and old, Consultant, January 1971.
10. Hughston, J. C.: Subluxation of the patella in athletics. In American Academy of Orthopaedic Surgeons: Symposium on Sports Medicine, 1967, St. Louis, 1969, The C. V. Mosby Co.
11. O'Donoghue, D. H.: Criteria for early (knee) surgery. In Proceedings of the Eighth National Conference on the Medical Aspects of Sports, Chicago, 1966, American Medical Association.
12. Slocum, D. B., and Larson, R. L.: Rotary instability of the knee and its surgical correction, J. Nat. Athletic Trainers Assn., Autumn, 1966, p. 3.
13. Healion, T. E.: The trainer and the knee. In Proceedings of the Seventh National Conference on the Medical Aspects of Sports, Chicago, 1965, American Medical Association, p. 71.
14. Zimny, M., and Redler, I.: An ultrastructural study of patellar chondromalacia in humans, J. Bone Joint Surg. Vol. 51-A, September 1969.

RECOMMENDED READINGS

Dayton, O. W.: Athletic training and conditioning, New York, 1965, The Ronald Press Co.

Hirata, I., Jr.: The doctor and the athlete, Philadelphia, 1968, J. B. Lippincott Co.

Litton, L. O., and Peltier, L. F.: Athletic injuries, Boston, 1963, Little, Brown & Co.

McLaughlin, H. L.: Trauma, Philadelphia, 1959, W. B. Saunders Co.

O'Donoghue, D. H.: Treatment of injuries to athletes, ed. 2, Philadelphia, 1970, W. B. Saunders Co.

O'Donoghue, D. H., and Frank, F. R.: Treatment of acute ligament injuries. In American Academy of Orthopaedic Surgeons: Symposium on Sports Medicine, 1967, St. Louis, 1969, The C. V. Mosby Co.

Smillie, I. S.: Injuries of the knee joint, Baltimore, 1962, The Williams & Wilkins Co.

CHAPTER **18**

Conditions of the thigh, hip, buttocks, and groin

The thigh

ANATOMY

Several important anatomical units of the thigh (Fig. 18-1) must be considered in terms of their relationship to athletics. These involve the shaft of the femur, the surrounding musculature, nerves, and blood vessels and the dense fascia that envelops the soft tissue of the femur.

The *femur* (thigh bone) is the longest and strongest bone in the body and is designed to permit maximum mobility and support during locomotion. The cylindrical shaft is bowed forward and outward to accommodate the stresses placed upon it during the bending of the hip and knee and in weight bearing.

The muscles of the thigh may be divided into four classes according to the type of action for which they are responsible: flexors, extensors, abductors, and adductors. The *adductor* group, for the sake of clarity and for a more functional treatment, will be discussed in connection with hip injuries.

The strongest group of thigh muscles is the *extensor quadriceps* group, which encompasses the anterior aspect of the thigh and consists of the rectus femoris, vastus intermedius, vastus lateralis, and vastus medialis. With the exception of the rectus femoris, which has its origin on the anterior inferior iliac spine of the ilium, the quadriceps muscles arise from along the shaft of the femur. They then converge into a common quadriceps tendon and form the patellar ligament, a continuation of the tendon, inserting on and adjacent to the tibial tuberosity. The three vasti extend the knee. The rectus femoris likewise extends the knee, but because it functions as a two-joint muscle, it also assists in flexing the hip.

The *hamstring* group consists of the biceps femoris, semimembranosus, and semitendinosus. All three arise from the tuberosity of the ischium. The biceps femoris has two heads. The long head originates on the lower and medial aspect of the ischial tuberosity. The short head originates on the lower half of the linea aspera and the outer condyloid ridge of the femur and attaches in the region of the head of the fibula and the lateral condyle of the tibia. The muscle bulk is carried principally along the length of the lateral aspect of the femur, whereas the semimembranosus and the semitendinosus range along the medial side. In addition to being strong knee flexors the hamstrings act also in extension of the hip joint. Assisting the hamstrings in knee flexion are the sartorius, gracilis, popliteus, and gastrocnemius.

The anterior aspect of the thigh is supplied mainly by the *femoral nerve* and the *femoral artery*. The posterior aspect is sup-

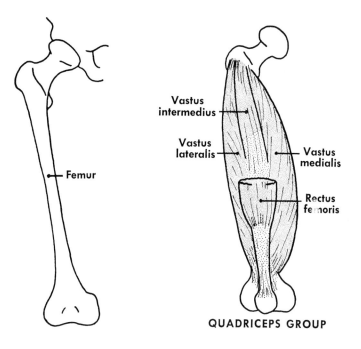

QUADRICEPS GROUP

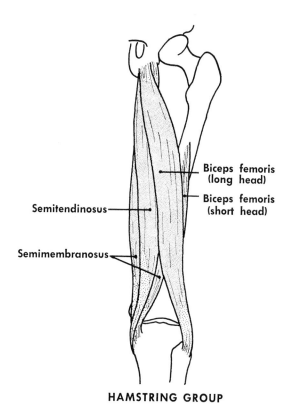

HAMSTRING GROUP

Fig. 18-1. Anatomy of the thigh.

plied by the femoral artery and the sciatic nerve.

Surrounding the muscles of the thigh is a heavy sheath of fibrous tissue called the *fascia lata*. Portions of the fascia form several compartments, one holding the quadriceps, another the hamstrings, and a third the adductor group.

MUSCLE INJURIES

Injuries to the thigh muscles are by far the most common injuries in athletics. Of these conditions, contusions and strains appear most often, with the former having the higher incidence.

Thigh contusion (charleyhorse)

Because of the relative accessibility and bulkiness of the quadriceps group, it acquires the greatest number of contusions. The quadriceps group is continually exposed to traumatic blows, particularly in football, which produces the majority of charleyhorses. However, any active team sport may cause such injury. Contusions of the quadriceps display all the classic syptoms that arise from most muscle bruises and in addition prove to be quite handicapping to the performer. They usually develop as the result of a severe impact to the relaxed thigh (Fig. 18-2); tissue is thus compressed against the hard surface of the femur. At the instant that the trauma occurs there will be pain, a transitory loss of function, and capillary effusion. The extent of the force and the degree of thigh relaxation determine the depth of the injury and the amount of pathology that takes place. Immediate and proper care must be given to the athlete to prevent swelling and inflexibility of the part. Compression by means of a pressure bandage and the application of a cold medium can aid in controlling superficial hemorrhage, but it is doubtful whether pressure and cold will affect a deep contusion. Along with pressure and cold (Fig. 18-3), rest and mild stretching are advocated in varying degrees, according to the extent of the injury, and are much preferred to "running off" a contusion. Early detection and the avoidance of profuse internal hemorrhage are vital, both in effecting a fast recovery by the athlete and in the prevention of widespread scarring. Detection of the charleyhorse is based on a history of injury, palpation, and a muscle function test. The athlete usually describes having been hit by a sharp blow to the thigh, which produced an intense pain and weakness. Palpation may reveal a circumscribed swollen area that is painful to the touch. A function test is

Fig. 18-2. Thigh contusion.   **Fig. 18-3.** Application of a cold compression pack.

given to the quadriceps muscle. Injury to the quadriceps produces varying degrees of weakness and decreased range of motion.

Medical care of a thigh contusion may include surgical repair of a herniated muscle or aspiration of a hemotoma. Some physicians administer enzymes either orally or through injection for the dissolution of the hematoma.[1]

Generally, the rehabilitation of the thigh contusion should be handled conservatively. Heat therapy should not be initiated until there is assurance that the acute phase of the injury has passed. An elastic bandage should be worn to provide a constant pressure and mild support to the quadriceps area. Massage, both manual and hydro, is best delayed until resolution of the injury has begun. Exercise should be graduated from mild stretching of the quadriceps area in the early stages of the injury to swimming, if possible, and then to jogging and running. All exercise should be conducted without pain.

Myositis ossificans (traumatic)

Traumatic myositis ossificans (Fig. 18-4) is an abnormal condition in which mineralization is produced within a muscle as part of the healing process of a hematoma. It occurs most often to the anterior portion of the thigh and the brachialis muscle of the upper arm. Repeated blows to the soft muscular tissue overlying the bone or irritating massage of a recent hematoma can result in the disposition of bony tissue that has replaced blood and fibrous tissue within the muscle proper. Contusions that fail to heal in a normal period of time or that appear as a painful immovable mass deep within the musculature demand medical attention. The ossification site is often accessible to palpation and visible to the physician by x-ray film after 3 or 4 weeks. Without additional irritation, bone growth is self-limiting. When ossification has ceased, surgical removal may be indicated, particularly if it is handicapping. Quite often such bone areas do not hamper activity and pose little problem for the athlete. Adequate protection must be given in this condition to prevent added growth as a result of continued irritation. Active therapy is contraindicated, and massage and sports activity may stimulate additional ossification. Rest and mild heat applied to the site are indicated in most cases.

Quadriceps tape support

The strapping of the quadriceps muscle group (Fig. 18-5) is designed to give support against the pull of gravity. In cases of moderate or severe contusions or strains strapping may afford protection or a mild support and give confidence to the athlete. Various techniques fitted to the individual needs of the athletes can be used.

Materials needed: One roll of 2-inch tape, roll of 3-inch elastic tape, skin toughener, 6-inch elastic bandage, and 2-inch heel lift.

Position of the athlete: The athlete stands on the massage table with a 2-inch elevation under the heel of the injured leg. It is important that the athlete's weight be supported by the normal leg and the affected limb be in a completely relaxed position.

Position of the trainer: The trainer stands facing the anterior aspect of the athlete's injured thigh.

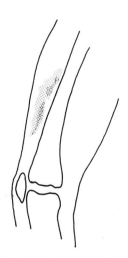

Fig. 18-4. Myositis ossificans.

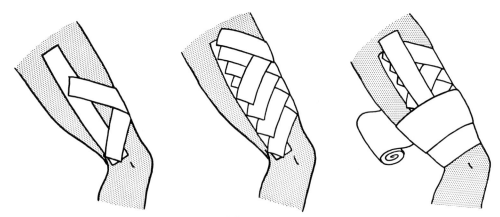

Fig. 18-5. Quadriceps tape support.

Procedure:

1. Two anchor strips, each approximately 9 inches in length, are placed respectively on the lateral and medial aspects of the thigh and are positioned at one half the distance between the anterior and posterior aspects.

2. Strips of 2-inch tape are applied to the thigh, crossing one another to form an X. The crisscrosses are begun 2 or 3 inches above the knee cap and carried upward, overlapping one another. It is important that each tape strip be started from the anchor piece and carried upward and diagonally over the quadriceps, thus lifting against gravity. This procedure is continued until the quadriceps is completely covered.

3. After the diagonal series has been applied, a "lock strip" is placed longitudinally over the medial and lateral borders of the series.

4. To ensure a more effective stability of the quadriceps strapping, it is suggested that the entire thigh be encircled by either a 3-inch elastic tape or a 6-inch elastic bandage.

Hamstring strains

Hamstring strains (Fig. 18-6) rank second in incidence of athletic injuries to the thigh, and of all the muscles of the thigh that are subject to strains, the hamstring

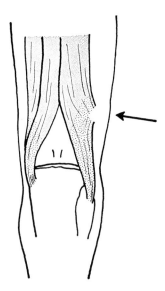

Fig. 18-6. Hamstring strain.

group ranks highest. They are usually from 50 to 60% as strong as the opposing quadriceps muscle group. Participation in any of the active sports can result in strained muscles, but the stresses encountered in running produce the greatest incidence among sports.

As pointed out in Chapter 5, strains occur most frequently in persons with some deficiency in the reciprocal or complementary action of opposing muscle groups. The cause of muscle incoordination is often obscure; but fatigue, poor posture, uneven muscle strength, inflexibility, and poor form in performance can all be considered as possibilities. An imbalance may strain or tear any portion of a specific muscle. There is some indication that an imbalance of 10% or more in the strength of one hamstring group when compared to the other produces a high incidence of strain to the weaker group.[2] Strains involve the muscle at the bony attachment or the belly of the tendon, with the extent of the strain varying from a pulling apart of a few fibers to a complete rupture or avulsion. Capillary hemorrhage, pain, and immediate loss of function vary according to the degree of trauma. Discoloration may occur a day or two after injury.

Strains are always a problem to the athlete and the trainer inasmuch as they tend to recur. This is a result of their healing by inelastic, fibrous scar tissue. The higher the incidence of strains at a particular muscle site, the greater the amount of scar tissue and the greater the likelihood of still more injuries. The fear of "another pulled muscle" becomes to some individuals almost a neurotic obsession, which is often more handicapping than the injury itself. For the trainer the strain presents a difficult task in guidance and management. Before a strain occurs, the athlete may be aware of a feeling of muscular fatigue or of incipient spasm; it would be advisable for the participant to stop activity whenever these symptoms appear. When a hamstring strain occurs, the athlete may feel a sudden snap or a sharp pain. Such a sequence usually indicates a severe strain. On the other hand, if pain is felt only after activity has been completed the strain is probably a mild one.

A *mild* hamstring strain usually is evidenced by muscle soreness on movement, accompanied by point tenderness. These strains are often difficult to detect when they first occur. Not until the athlete has cooled down after activity do irritation and stiffness become apparent. The soreness of the mild hamstring strain in most instances can be attributed to muscle spasm rather than the tearing of tissue. Consequently, ice massage and static stretch may be beneficial. Activity should be cut down until soreness has been completely alleviated. Ballistic stretching and explosive sprinting must be avoided; however, flat-footed jogging may be engaged in with safety.

As with other muscles, tearing of the hamstrings occurs at the point in which the tension is greatest—the mid-range of contraction, when the muscle is at maximum length.[3]

Before the athlete is allowed to resume full sports participation, he should have complete muscular function of the injured muscle.

A *moderate* strain of a hamstring muscle is identified by a sudden snap or tear of the muscle accompanied by severe pain and a loss of function on knee flexion. Pressure and cold should be applied from 24 to 72 hours accompanied by complete rest. Heat treatment should be delayed for at least 72 hours to be certain that hemorrhaging has subsided. Recovery may take from 1 to 3 weeks. Full range of leg and thigh motion are required before resumption of sports participation is permitted.

Severe hamstring strains constitute the rupturing of tendinous or muscular tissue. In such cases pressure and cold applications must be maintained for at least 48 hours, after which the athlete is referred to the team physician. In some instances surgical repair may be needed. The length of time away from competition may range from 1 month to an entire season.

Support of the hamstrings. In contusions or strains of the thigh, support can aid considerably in the protection and recovery of the athlete. Proper support will help to lessen aggravation of the thigh during activity and thus decrease the pain and prevent additional irritation. Various techniques—each specific for a particular degree of injury—can be used to support the hamstring muscle group.

Technique 1:

This first technique (Fig. 18-7) is used for mild hamstring soreness. Flexible, resilient material is applied to the injured area, giving support and confidence to the athlete.

Materials needed: One roll of 3-inch elastic tape or one 6-inch elastic bandage, nonsterile cotton, roll of 1½-inch tape, and 2-inch heel lift.

Position of the athlete: The athlete stands on the training table, facing away from the trainer, with the leg to be strapped maintained in a flexed position and the 2-inch heel lift underneath the heel. The athlete should place his entire weight on the uninjured limb and attempt to relax the injured leg completely.

Position of the trainer: The trainer stands facing the posterior aspect of the injured leg.

Procedure:

1. The injury is palpated by the trainer to determine its scope. A strip of nonsterile cotton is cut to the approximate size of the injury and placed over it.

2. With the cotton held in position by the athlete, the elastic bandage is applied by the trainer in a circular manner, moving diagonally upward. The bandage should be started just above the popliteal fossa and applied with moderate tightness.

3. After completely covering the hamstrings, the wrap is carried diagonally downward, locking the preceding series in place. When the end of the wrap has been reached, it is fastened with a strip of 1½-inch tape.

Technique 2:

It is extremely difficult to completely relieve the injured hamstring muscles by means of any wrapping or strapping technique, but stabilization can be afforded the injury. Technique 2 (Fig. 18-8) is designed

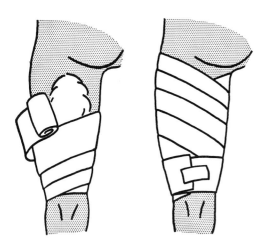

Fig. 18-7. Hamstring support—Technique 1.

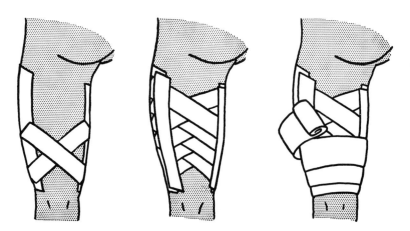

Fig. 18-8. Hamstring support—Technique 2.

to stabilize the moderately to severely contused or torn hamstring muscles, enabling the athlete to continue to compete in his sport.

Materials needed: One roll of 2-inch tape, skin toughener, and a roll of 3-inch elastic tape.

Position of the athlete: The athlete lies face downward on the table, with the affected limb flexed at about a 15-degree angle at the knee so that the hamstring muscle is relaxed and shortened.

Position of the trainer: The trainer stands at the side of the table, facing the athlete's injured thigh.

Procedure:

1. This strapping is applied in a way similar to the quadriceps technique. An anchor strip is placed on either side of the thigh and then strips of approximately 9 inches in length are crisscrossed diagonally upward on the posterior aspect of the thigh, forming an X.

2. After the hamstring area is covered with a series of crisscrosses, a longitudinal lock is applied on either side of the thigh.

3. Three-inch elastic tape may be placed around the thigh to aid in holding the crisscross strapping in place. If elastic tape is not available, an elastic bandage will suffice.

Technique 3:

The third technique (Fig. 18-9) can be used in a dual capacity. It will support and immobilize both the hamstrings and the gluteus maximus on thigh extension and leg flexion.

Materials needed: One roll of 3-inch elastic tape, a roll of 2-inch adhesive tape, and skin toughener.

Position of the athlete: The athlete lies on the table, face downward, with the knee of the affected limb flexed to about 15 degrees.

Position of the trainer: The trainer stands at the side of the table facing the injured thigh.

Procedure:

1. Two anchor strips are applied, using 2-inch adhesive tape. One anchor encircles the thigh approximately 4 inches above the popliteal fossa and the other strip encircles the waist of the athlete.

2. Five 3-inch elastic tape strips, approximately 18 inches in length, are cut. Starting at the inner border of the poste-

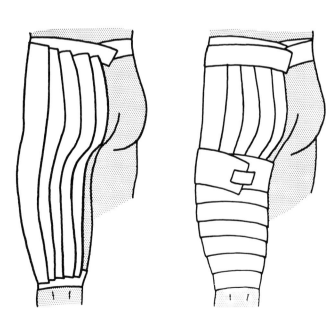
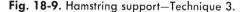

Fig. 18-9. Hamstring support—Technique 3.

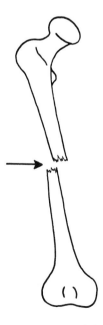

Fig. 18-10. Fracture of the femur.

rior aspect of the thigh, the first elastic strip is applied from the thigh anchor and stretched upward over the buttocks to the waist anchor. The next and succeeding strips are placed similarly, each moving outward and overlapping the preceding strip by one half of its width.

3. After all longitudinal elastic strips have been applied, they are locked in place by a 2-inch piece of adhesive tape that encircles the thigh and waist at the same points as the anchor.

4. To further stabilize this strapping, additional elastic strips may be used to encircle the thigh, or an elastic bandage may be employed in the same fashion.

BONE INJURIES
Fractures of the femur

In athletics fractures of the femur occur most often in the shaft (Fig. 18-10) rather than at the bone ends and are almost always caused by a great force, such as falling from a height or being hit directly by another participant. A fracture of the shaft most often takes place in the middle third of the bone because of the anatomical curve at this point, as well as the fact that the majority of direct blows are sustained in this area. Shock generally accompanies a fracture of the femur, as a result of the extreme amount of pathology and pain associated with this injury. Direct violence produces extensive soft tissue injury with lacerations of the vastus intermedius, hemorrhaging, and muscle spasms. Bony displacement is almost always present as a result of the great strength of the quadriceps that causes an overriding of the bone fragments.

Recognition of the fractured femur is made by means of the classic signs of (1) deformity, with the thigh rotated outward; (2) a shortened thigh, due to bone displacement; (3) loss of function; (4) pain and point tenderness; and (5) swelling of the soft tissues.

To prevent danger to the life of the athlete and to ensure adequate reconditioning, immediate immobilization and referral to the physician must be made.

RECONDITIONING

The quadriceps and hamstring muscle groups have been discussed at length in relationship to knee joint injuries; however, individual consideration must be given to the thigh contusions and hamstring strain. The thigh contusion reconditioning begins with static stretching to control hemorrhage and spasm. To avoid additional hemorrhage at the contused site, muscle tone is maintained by quadriceps tensing and straight leg raising. Jarring movements such as are present in running are avoided to prevent the dislodging of clot formation. With the aid of an elastic support, the athlete gradually resumes sports activity. Conversely, the moderate or severe hamstring tear requires no stretching in its early stage, but with the stabilization provided by an elastic wrap, a flat-footed jogging routine should be encouraged. Jogging, a combination of running short distances and walking, helps to restore the athlete's general thigh circulation and reduces muscle spasm, which has the tendency to form contractures with a subsequent myositis or tendonitis. Within the personal limitations of pain, a lightly resistive, highly repetitive program (20 or more repetitions) should be commenced as early as possible.

The hip

ANATOMY

The hip joint (Fig. 18-11) is formed by articulation of the femur with the innominate, or hip, bone. The innominate bone consists of the ilium, ischium, and pubis. The spherical head of the femur fits into a deep socket, the acetabulum, which is padded at its center by a mass of fatty tissue. Surrounding its rim is a fibrocartilage known as the glenoid labrum. A loose sleeve of articular tissue is attached to the circumference of the acetabulum above and to the neck of the femur below. The capsule is lined by an extensive synovial membrane, and the iliofemoral, pubocapsular, and ischiocapsular ligaments give it strong reinforcement. Hyaline cartilage completely covers the head of the femur,

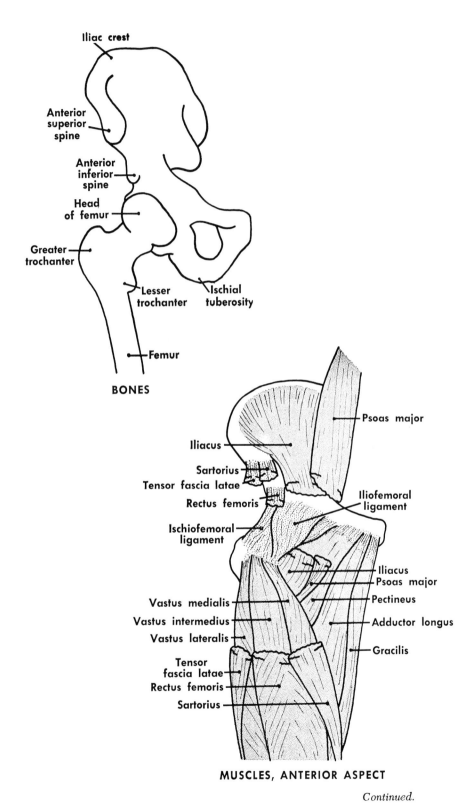

Iliac crest

Anterior superior spine

Anterior inferior spine

Head of femur

Greater trochanter

Lesser trochanter

Ischial tuberosity

Femur

BONES

Psoas major

Iliacus

Sartorius

Tensor fascia latae

Rectus femoris

Iliofemoral ligament

Ischiofemoral ligament

Iliacus

Psoas major

Vastus medialis

Pectineus

Vastus intermedius

Adductor longus

Vastus lateralis

Gracilis

Tensor fascia latae

Rectus femoris

Sartorius

MUSCLES, ANTERIOR ASPECT

Continued.

Fig. 18-11. Anatomy of the hip.

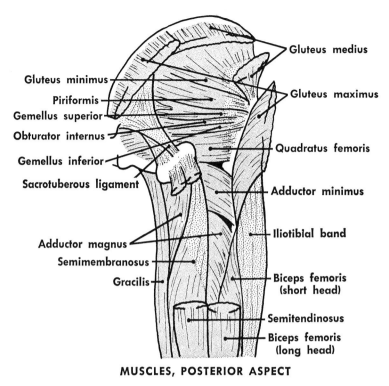

Gluteus medius

Gluteus minimus

Piriformis

Gemellus superior

Obturator internus

Gemellus inferior

Sacrotuberous ligament

Gluteus maximus

Quadratus femoris

Adductor minimus

Iliotibial band

Adductor magnus

Semimembranosus

Gracilis

Biceps femoris
(short head)

Semitendinosus

Biceps femoris
(long head)

MUSCLES, POSTERIOR ASPECT

Fig. 18-11, cont'd. For legend see p. 313.

with the exception of the fovea capitis, a small area in the center to which the ligamentum teres is attached. The ligamentum teres gives little support to the hip joint, having as its main function the carrying of nutrient vessels to the head of the femur. Because of its bony, ligamentous, and muscular arrangements this joint is considered by many to be the strongest articulation in the body.

The *acetabulum*, a deep socket in the innominate bone, receives the articulating head of the femur. It forms an incomplete bony ring that is interrupted by a notch on the lower aspect of the socket. The ring is completed by the transverse ligament that crosses the notch. The socket faces forward, downward, and laterally.

The *femoral head* is a sphere fitting into the acetabulum in a medial, upward, and slightly forward direction.

The *synovial membrane* is a vascular tissue enclosing the hip joint in a tubular sleeve, with the upper portion surrounding

the acetabulum and the lower portion being fastened to the circumference of the neck of the femur. Excepting the ligamentum teres, which lies outside the synovial cavity, the membrane lines the acetabular socket.

The *articular capsule* is a fibrous, sleevelike structure covering the synovial membrane, its upper end attaching to the glenoid labrum and its lower end to the neck of the femur. The fibers surrounding the femoral neck consist of circular fibers that serve as a tight collar. This area is called the *zona orbicularis* and acts in holding the femoral head in the acetabulum.

Many strong ligaments—the iliofemoral, the pubofemoral, and the ischiofemoral—reinforce the hip joint.

The *iliofemoral ligament* (Y ligament of Bigelow) is the strongest ligament of the body. It prevents hyperextension, controls external rotation and adduction of the thigh, and limits the pelvis in any backward rolling of the head of the femur during weight bearing. It reinforces the anterior aspect of the capsule and is attached to the anterior iliac spine and the intertrochanteric line on the anterior aspect of the femur.

The *pubofemoral ligament* prevents excessive abduction of the thigh and is positioned anteriorly and inferior to the pelvis and femur.

The *ischiofemoral ligament* prevents excessive internal rotation and adduction of the thigh and is located posteriorly and superior to the articular capsule.

The hip joint has been described as having many bursae. Clinically, the most important of these are the iliopsoas bursa and the deep trochanteric bursa. The iliopsoas bursa is located between the articular capsule and the iliopsoas muscle on the anterior aspect of the joint. The deep trochanteric bursa lies between the greater trochanter and the deep fibers of the gluteus maximus muscle.

The blood supply to the hip joint includes the obturator, medial femoral circumflex, and the superior and inferior gluteal arteries. The nerve supply to the hip joint consists of the sacral plexus and the sciatic, obturator, accessory obturator (when it is present), and femoral nerves.

Movements of the hip joint

The hip joint is capable of flexion, extension, adduction, abduction, circumduction, and rotation. In the following list muscles are identified with the specific movements in which they are most active. It must be remembered, however, that they may also have other weak or accessory actions:

1. Flexion: psoas major, iliacus, tensor fasciae latae, rectus femoris, sartorius, pectineus, adductor longus, adductor brevis, and gracilis
2. Extension: gluteus maximus, hamstring muscles (biceps femoris, semimembranosus, semitendinosus), and adductor magnus
3. Adduction: hamstring muscles, pectineus, gracilis, adductor magnus, adductor longus, adductor brevis, and psoas
4. Abduction: tensor fasciae latae, gluteus maximus, gluteus medius, and gluteus minimus
5. Inward rotation: gluteus medius, gluteus minimus, tensor fasciae latae, adductor longus, adductor brevis, adductor magnus, and iliopsoas major
6. Outward rotation: gluteus maximus, piriformis, obturator externus and obturator internus, the gemelli (superior and inferior), quadratus femoris, sartorius, and adductor magnus

HIP JOINT CONDITIONS

The hip joint is the strongest and best protected joint in the body. It also has rather extensive ranges of motion. Traumatic injuries of the hip joint are uncommon in athletics but do occur on occasion, and the trainer should be able to distinguish the gross signs of severe injuries.

Sprains of the hip joint

The hip joint is substantially supported by the ligamentous tissues and muscles that surround it; consequently, any unusual movement that exceeds the normal range of motion may result in tearing of tissue. Such an injury may occur as the result of a violent twist, either produced through an impact force delivered by another participant or by forceful contact with another object, or sustained in a situation in which the foot is firmly planted and the trunk forced in an opposing direction. A hip sprain displays all the signs of an acute injury but is best revealed through the athlete's inability to circumduct the thigh.

Dislocation of the hip joint

Dislocation of the hip joint is rarely experienced in athletics, and the few that do occur happen as the end result of traumatic force directed along the long axis of the femur. Such dislocations are produced when the knee is bent. The most common displacement is one posterior to the acetabulum and with the femoral shaft adducted and flexed.

The luxation presents a picture of a flexed, adducted, and internally rotated thigh. Palpation will reveal that the head of the femur has moved to a position posterior to the acetabulum. A hip dislocation causes serious pathology by tearing capsular and ligamentous tissue. A fracture is often associated with this injury, accompanied by possible damage to the sciatic nerve. Medical attention must be secured immediately after displacement, or muscle contractures may complicate the reduction. Immobilization usually consists of 2 weeks of bed rest and the use of a crutch for walking for at least a month or longer.

Synovitis of the hip

Synovitis of the hip is often the result of a sprain or a direct injury. The athlete complains of a general soreness on movement, and point tenderness is present over the greater trochanter, with an apparent muscle sprain about the joint. The signs of synovitis may be mistaken for the more serious pyogenic conditions. Care for both acute and chronic hip synovitis usually consists of rest and daily heat applications of ultrasound or microwave diathermy.

RECONDITIONING OF THE HIP

Reconditioning after a hip injury requires, as for other joints, the resumption of normal range of motion, through use of passive and active stretches and a resistance exercise program. Recovery of the hip from muscle disorders is rapid and usually requires no more than normal activity before the athlete is restored to competion (see Chapter 15).

Conditions of the buttocks

The buttocks consist of the two large fleshy areas that lie posterior to the hip joints and are formed by the muscular bulk of the gluteal muscles. Injuries to this area occur infrequently in athletics because of the adequate natural protection of fat, strong musculature, and relatively invulnerable anatomical location. Of those injuries that do occur to the buttocks, contusions rank first and strains second. The muscles most often involved are the gluteus maximus and the gluteus medius. Injuries to this area usually fall into the mild to moderate category, although occasionally severe injuries to this part will produce a handicapping condition that is difficult to manage. Pressure and cold or heat have little effect on this large tissue mass, and protective support is difficult to apply and permits little movement. Rest, in combination with deep therapeutic heat such as diathermy, has been found to elicit the best response.

Groin strain (inguinal region)

The groin is that depression which lies between the thigh and the abdominal region. The musculature includes the iliopsoas, the rectus femoris, and the adductor group (the gracilis, pectineus, adductor brevis, adductor longus, and adductor magnus). Any one of these muscles can be torn in athletic activity and elicit what is commonly considered a groin strain (Fig. 18-12). Any overextension of the groin musculature may result in a strain. Running, jumping, or twisting with external rotation

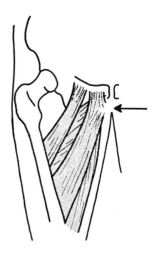

Fig. 18-12. Groin strain.

can produce such injuries. Contrary to some opinions, the adductor group is more often torn than is the iliopsoas.

The groin strain presents one of the most difficult injuries to care for in athletics. The strain can appear as a sudden twinge or feeling of tearing during an active movement, or it may not be noticed until after termination of activity. As is characteristic of most tears, the groin strain also produces pain, weakness, and internal hemorrhage. If detected immediately after it occurs, pressure and cold should be applied intermittently for 48 hours. Often the athlete is unable to pinpoint the exact site of the injury. Therefore, a series of functional tests must be given by the trainer.[4]

FUNCTIONAL GROIN TESTS

Rectus femoris test. The athlete lies face upward on a table, with both legs flexed over one end. He then extends his affected limb against the hand resistance of the trainer applied to the instep. A tendon strain arising from the anterior inferior iliac spine will reflect pain on either a knee extension or sit ups.

Iliopsoas test. The athlete sits on the edge of a table, flexing the affected hip against hand resistance of the trainer applied to the thigh. Pain will occur if the iliopsoas is strained.

Adductor group test. The athlete lies in a supine or face-up position on a table, with the affected hip abducted. The athlete attempts to perform his adduction against the hand resistance of the trainer. If an adductor muscle is strained, the athlete will complain of pain in that general area.

TREATMENT OF GROIN STRAIN

Difficulty is frequently encountered when attempting to care for a groin strain. In these cases rest has been found to be the best treatment. Heat in various forms may be beneficial but is not always successful. Daily applications of whirlpool and analgesic balm packs act as a palliative aid; diathermy and ultrasound offer a more definite approach. It is suggested that exercise be delayed until the groin irritation has disappeared completely. Reconditioning should emphasize static stretching and restoring the normal range of motion. Until normal flexibility and strength are developed, a protective spica bandage should be applied.

Groin support wrap (hip spica). The following procedure is used to support the groin.

Materials needed: One roll of 4-inch or 6-inch elastic bandage, a roll of 1½-inch adhesive tape, and nonsterile cotton.

Position of the athlete: The athlete stands

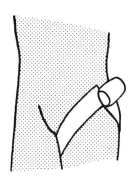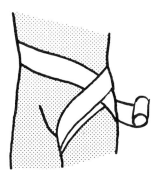

Fig. 18-13. Groin support wrap.

on a table, his weight placed on the uninjured leg. The affected limb is relaxed and internally rotated, if adductors are injured, or semiflexed if the injury is caused by the rectus femoris or iliopsoas.

Position of the trainer: The trainer stands facing the anterior aspect of the injured limb.

1. A piece of nonsterile cotton is placed over the injured site.

2. The end of the elastic bandage is started at the upper part of the inner aspect of the thigh and carried medially around and over the crest of the ilium on the opposite side.

3. The wrap is continued around the waist, resuming the same pattern securing the wrap end with a 1½-inch adhesive tape (Fig. 18-13).

REFERENCES

1. O'Donoghue, D. H.: Treatment of injuries to athletes, ed. 2, Philadelphia, 1970, W. B. Saunders Co.
2. Burkett, L. N.: Cause and prevention of hamstring pulls, Athletic Journal, Vol. LI, February 1971, p. 34.
3. Brewer, B. J.: Mechanism of injury to the musculotendinous joint. In American Academy of Orthopaedic Surgeons: Instructional Course Lectures, Vol, XVII, St. Louis, 1960, The C. V. Mosby Co.
4. Prior, J. A., and Silberstein, J. S.: Physical diagnosis, ed. 3, St. Louis, 1969, The C. V. Mosby Co.

RECOMMENDED READINGS

Adams, J. E.: Outline of orthopedics, Baltimore, 1964, The Williams & Wilkins Co.
Arnheim, D. D., Auxter, D., and Crowe, W.: Principles and methods of adapted physical education, ed. 2, St. Louis, 1973, The C. V. Mosby Co.
Dolan, J. P., and Holladay, L. J.: Treatment and prevention of athletic injuries, ed. 3, Danville, Ill., 1967, The Interstate Printers and Publishers.
McLaughlin, H. L.: Trauma, Philadelphia, 1959, W. B. Saunders Co.
Naylor, A.: Fractures and orthopedic surgery for nurses and physiotherapists, Baltimore, 1964, The Williams & Wilkins Co.
O'Donoghue, D. H.: Treatment of injuries to athletes, Philadelphia, 1962, W. B. Saunders Co.
Prior, J. A., and Silberstein, J. S.: Physical diagnosis, St. Louis, 1969, The C. V. Mosby Co.
Ralston, E. L.: Handbook of fractures, St. Louis, 1967, The C. V. Mosby Co.
Ryan, A. J.: Medical care of the athlete, New York, 1962, McGraw-Hill Book Co.
Strange, F. G.: The hip, Baltimore, 1965, The Williams & Wilkins Co.

CHAPTER 19

Conditions of the pelvic region, abdomen, thorax, and spine

The pelvic region

ANATOMY

The pelvis is a bony ring formed by the two innominate bones, the sacrum, and the coccyx (Fig. 19-1). The innominate bones are each made up of an ilium, ischium, and pubis. The functions of the pelvis are to support the spine and trunk and to transfer their weight to the lower limbs. In addition to providing skeletal support, the pelvis serves as a place of attachment for the trunk and thigh muscles and a protection for the pelvic viscera (Fig. 19-2). The basin formed by the pelvis is separated into a false and a true pelvis. The former is composed of the wings of the ilium, and the true pelvis is made up of the coccyx, the ischium, and the pubis.

The *innominate bones* are composed of three bones that ossify and fuse early in life. They include the ilium, which is positioned superiorly and posteriorly; the pubis, which forms the anterior part; and the ischium, which is located inferiorly. Lodged between the innominate bones is the wedge-shaped *sacrum* composed of five fused vertebrae. The sacrum is joined to other parts of the pelvis by strong ligaments, forming the sacroiliac joints. A small backward-forward movement is present at the sacroiliac junction. The *coccyx* is composed of four or five small, fused vertebral bodies that articulate with the sacrum.

INJURIES OF THE PELVIC REGION
Hernia

The term hernia refers to the protrusion of abdominal viscera through a portion of the abdominal wall. Hernias fall into two main categories, congenital and acquired. A congenital hernial sac is developed before birth and the acquired hernia after birth. Structurally, a hernia has a mouth, a neck, and a body. The mouth, or hernial ring, is the opening from the abdominal cavity into the hernial protrusion; the neck is the portion of the sac that joins the hernial ring and the body. The body is the sac that protrudes outside the abdominal cavity and contains portions of the abdominal organs.[1]

The acquired hernia occurs when a natural weakness is further aggravated by either a strain or a direct blow. Athletes may develop this condition as the result of violent activity. An acquired hernia may be recognized by the following:

1. Previous history of a blow or strain to the groin area that has produced pain and prolonged discomfort
2. Superficial protrusion in the groin area that is increased by coughing
3. Reported feeling of weakness and pulling sensation in the groin area

The danger of hernia to an athlete is in the possibility that the condition may become irritated by falls and blows. Besides

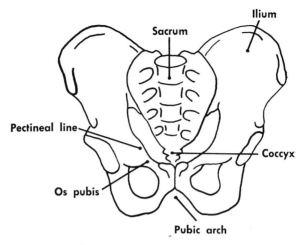

Fig. 19-1. Pelvis.

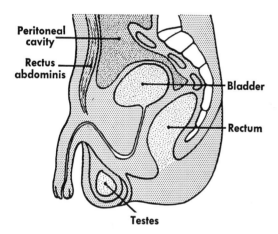

Fig. 19-2. Pelvic viscera.

the aggravations caused by trauma, a condition may arise, commonly known as a strangulated hernia, in which the inguinal ring constricts the protruding sac and occludes normal blood circulation. If the strangulated hernia is not surgically repaired immediately, gangrene and death may ensue.[2]

Hernias resulting from athletics most often occur in the groin area; the inguinal (over 75%) and femoral hernias are the most prevalent types. Externally, the inguinal and femoral hernias appear similar because of the groin protrusion, but a considerable difference is indicated internally. The inguinal

hernia results from an abnormal enlargement of the opening of the inguinal canal through which the vessels and nerves of the male reproductive system pass. In contrast to this, the femoral hernia arises in the canal that transports the vessels and nerves that go to the thigh and the lower limb.

Under normal circumstances the inguinal and femoral canals are protected against abnormal opening by muscle control. When intra-abdominal tension is produced in these areas, muscles produce contraction around these canal openings. If the muscles fail to react or if they prove inadequate in their shutter action, abdominal contents may be pushed through the opening. Repeated protrusions serve to stretch and increase the size of the opening. Most physicians are of the opinion that any athlete who has a hernia should be prohibited from indulging in hard physical activity until surgical repair has been made.

The treatment of choice for the majority of physicians is surgery. Mechanical devices such as trusses, which prevent hernial protrusion, are for the most part unsuitable in athletics because of the friction and irritation that they produce. Exercise has been thought by many to be beneficial to a mild hernia, but such is not the case. Exercise will not affect the stretched inguinal or femoral canal to any extent.

Injuries of the male genitalia

Athletic trauma to the male genital region usually results in an extremely painful condition. The cause of injury most often is a direct blow to the area. See Chapter 10 for a discussion of injuries to the female genitalia.

Scrotum contusion

As the result of its considerable sensitivity and particular vulnerability, the scrotum may sustain a contusion that causes a painful, nauseating, and handicapping injury. As is characteristic of any contusion or bruise, there is a degree of hemorrhage, fluid effusion, and muscle spasm dependent upon the intensity of the impact force. The first responsibility of the trainer is to put the athlete at ease by reducing the testicular spasm that has resulted from the contusion. Two techniques are acceptable for lessening testicular spasm.

Technique 1:

The first technique (Fig. 19-3) is best applied immediately after the injury has occurred. The athlete is placed on his back and instructed to flex his thighs to his chest. This position will aid in reducing discomfort and relax the muscle spasm. After the pain has diminished, the athlete is aided in leaving the playing area and a cold pack is applied to the area.

Technique 2:

The second technique (Fig. 19-4) is designed to reduce muscle spasm of the testes. The athlete sits on the ground with his legs extended and his arms crossed. The trainer stands behind the athlete, grasps him under his arms, and lifts him a few inches from the ground. The trainer then drops the athlete to the ground. This results in a mild jolt to the genitalia, and the shock of the drop often releases painful muscle spasms.

Spermatic cord torsion

Torsion of the spermatic cord occurs as a result of the testicle's revolving in the scrotum or as a result of structural abnormalities that predispose to injury. Such

Fig. 19-3. Relieving testicular spasm—Technique 1.

Fig. 19-4. Relieving testicular spasm—Technique 2.

trauma can cause acute testicular pain, nausea, vomiting, and inflammation in the area. The athlete must receive immediate medical attention to prevent irreparable complications.

Traumatic hydrocele of the tunica vaginalis

Traumatic hydrocele of the tunica vaginalis refers to an excess of fluid that has developed from a severe blow to the testicular region. After trauma the athlete complains of pain, swelling in the lower abdomen, and nausea. Cold packs are applied to the scrotum, and referral to the physician is made.

Varicocele

A variocele, usually occurring on the left side, is a varicosity of the spermatic veins (pampiniform plexus). Twisting of the spermatic cord may present an appearance of a cluster of swollen veins and cause a dull pain combined with a heavy and dragging feeling in the scrotum. This condition may eventually lead to atrophy of the testicle. A physician should be consulted when this condition is recognized by the trainer.

Injuries of the pelvic girdle

The pelvis is an extremely strong structure and fractures from athletic activity are rare. Those which do occur are the result of direct trauma. A force that is directed anteroposteriorly (front to back) can fracture one or both rami and, if sufficiently intense, may even penetrate deeply enough to affect the sacroiliac joint. Severe lateral forces may cause injury similar to the anteroposterior types. A pelvic fracture should be suspected if an athlete has a history of severe injury to the pelvic area or if he is found lying on his back and demonstrates pain or shock. To further substantiate the possibility of a pelvic girdle fracture, the trainer should gently examine the injury in the following manner:

1. Both hands are placed on the anterior superior spines of the ilium and pressed downward and outward. If there is a fracture of the pelvic ring, pain will be elicited with little pressure.

2. Pressure is again gently applied by forcing the iliac spines inward and outward. In cases of pelvic ring fracture, pain will be produced on compression and spreading.

3. The possibility of acetabular and femoral head fractures also should be remembered. The distance between the anterior superior spine and the internal malleolus of both legs should be determined by a careful examination.

4. After measurement is taken, upward pressure should be applied to the femur against the acetabulum. A fracture at this point will produce pain on pressure.

If a pelvic fracture is suspected, the athlete should be immediately treated for shock and expedited to the physician. The seriousness of a pelvic fracture depends mainly on the condition of shock and the possibility of internal injury.

Fracture of the ilium

In athletics, fractures of the ilium are quite rare.[3] Of those which do occur, almost all are caused by direct violence to the crest of the ilium. Fractures may range from large massive breaks to small chips, and in some cases the crest of the ilium may present an epiphyseal separation. There is often a slight bone displacement with local pain, swelling, and point tenderness, and the athlete is usually unable to support his weight comfortably on the affected side. He is unable to perform either hip flexion or hip abduction without considerable pain. X-ray examination is the only means of making an accurate diagnosis.

Hip pointer (contusion of the iliac crest)

Iliac crest contusion, commonly known as a hip pointer, occurs most often in contact sports, principally football (Fig. 19-5). The hip pointer results from a blow to the inadequately protected iliac crest. Hip pads that do not adequately cover the iliac crest make it vulnerable to direct blows.

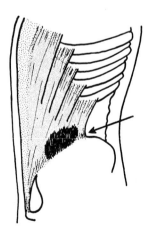

Fig. 19-5. Hip pointer.

The hip pointer is considered one of the most handicapping injuries in athletics and one that is difficult to manage.[4] A direct force to the unprotected iliac crest causes a severe pinching action to the soft tissue of that region. Such an injury produces immediate pain, spasm, and transitory paralysis of the soft structures. As a result, the athlete is unable to rotate his trunk or to flex his thigh without pain. Cold and pressure should be applied immediately after injury and should be maintained for at least 48 hours. In severe cases bed rest for 1 to 2 days will speed recovery. It should be noted that the mechanisms of the hip pointer are the same as those for an iliac crest fracture or epiphyseal separation. Therefore, referral to a physician must be made and an x-ray examination given. Recovery time usually ranges from 1 to 3 weeks. When hemorrhaging has ceased, it is advisable to apply deep-heat therapy and to afford support and protection by the use of an adhesive strapping. When the athlete resumes normal activity, he must wear a protective pad to prevent reinjury.[5]

Iliac crest adhesive support. Iliac crest adhesive strapping (Fig. 19-6) is designed to support, protect, and immobilize the soft tissue surrounding the iliac crest.

Materials needed: One roll of 2-inch adhesive tape, 6-inch bandage, skin toughener, and tape adherent.

Position of the athlete: The athlete stands on the floor, bending slightly laterally toward his injured side.

Position of the trainer: The trainer faces the injured side of the athlete.

Procedure:

1. Two anchor strips, each approximately 9 inches in length, are applied by the trainer. One is placed longitudinally, just lateral to the sacrum and lumbar spine,

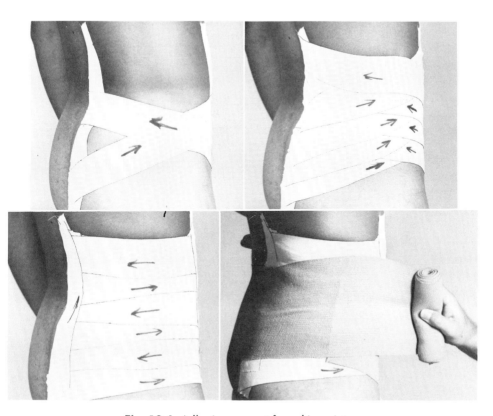

Fig. 19-6. Adhesive support for a hip pointer.

and the other is placed lateral to the umbilicus.

2. Commencing 2 to 3 inches below the crest of the ilium, tape crisscrosses are placed from one anchor to the other, lifting the tissue against the pull of gravity. The crisscrosses are carried upward to a point just below the floating rib.

3. Lock strips are placed over approximately the same positions as the anchor strips.

4. If additional support is desired, horizontal strips should be laid on alternately in posteroanterior and anteroposterior directions.

5. Finally, a 6-inch elastic bandage is applied to additionally secure the tape in place and to prevent perspiration from loosening the strapping.

Injury of the coccyx

Coccygeal injuries in athletics are quite prevalent and occur primarily from direct blows such as are obtained in forcibly sitting down, falling, or being kicked by an opponent. There may be constant pain after an injury. Most injuries to the coccyx are contusions, although fractures and dislocations may be sequelae to direct blows.

Persistent coccyalgia should be referred to a physician for x-ray and rectal examination. Pain in the coccygeal region is often prolonged and at times chronic. Such conditions are identified by the term "coccygodynia" and occur as the result of a bruise over the coccygeal plexus. Treatment is 1 week of bed rest, a crisscross strapping to the buttocks area, which may prove either to aggravate or to relieve pain, and daily sitz baths in the whirlpool baths at temperatures of 105° to 110° F. until the pain and irritation are relieved. The athlete, once healed of the coccygeal injury should be protected against reinjury during activity by means of protective padding.

The abdomen

ANATOMY

The abdominal cavity lies between the diaphragm and the pelvis and is bounded by the margin of the lower ribs, the abdominal muscles (Fig. 19-7), and the vertebral column. Lying within this cavity are the abdominal viscera, which include the stomach and the lower intestinal tract, the urinary system, the liver, the kidneys, and the spleen (Fig. 19-8).

The abdominal muscles are the rectus abdominis, the external oblique, the internal oblique, and the transverse abdominis. They are invested with both superficial and deep fasciae.

A heavy fascial sheath encloses the rectus abdominis, holding it in its position but in no way restricting its motion. The inguinal ring, which serves as a passageway for the spermatic cord, is formed by the abdominal fascia.

The *rectus abdominis* muscle, a trunk flexor, is attached to the rib cage above and to the pubis below. It is divided into three segments by means of transverse tendinous inscriptions and divided longitudinally by the linea alba. It functions in trunk flexion, rotation, and lateral flexion and in compression of the abdominal cavity.

The *external oblique* muscle is a broad, thin muscle that arises from slips attached to the borders of the lower 8 ribs, runs obliquely forward and downward, and inserts on the anterior two thirds of the crest of the ilium, the pubic crest, and the fascia of the rectus abdominis and the linea alba at their lower front. Its principal functions are trunk flexion, rotation, lateral flexion, and abdominal compression.

The *internal oblique* muscle forms the anterior and lateral aspects of the abdominal wall. Its fibers arise from the iliac crest, the upper half of the inguinal ligament, and the lumbar fascia. They run principally in an obliquely upward direction to the cartilages of the tenth, eleventh, and twelfth ribs on each side. The main functions of the internal oblique are trunk flexion, lateral flexion, and rotation.

The *transverse abdominis* is the deepest of the abdominal muscles. Its fibers run transversely across the abdominal cavity, arising from the outer one third of the inguinal ligament, the iliac crest, the lumbar fascia of the back, and the lower 6 ribs. It inserts into the linea alba and the front half of the iliac crest. The main functions of the transverse abdominis are to hold the abdominal contents in place and to aid in forced expiration. All the abdominal mus-

cles work together in performing defecation, micturition, and forced expiration.

The abdominal viscera are composed of both hollow and solid organs. The hollow organs include vessels, tubes, and receptacles such as the stomach, intestines, gall-

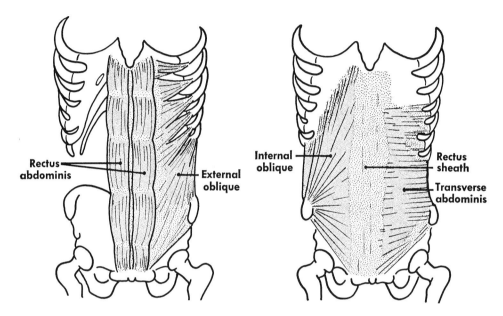

Fig. 19-7. Abdominal muscles.

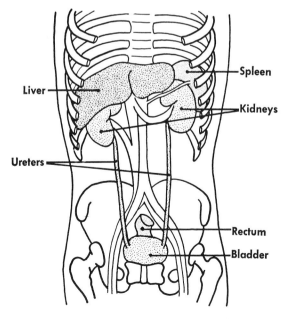

Fig. 19-8. Abdominal viscera subject to athletic injury.

bladder, and urinary bladder. The solid organs are the kidneys, spleen, liver, suprarenals, and pancreas. In those internal injuries of the abdomen which occur in athletics, the solid organs are most often affected. If a hollow organ is distended by its contents, it may have the same injury potential as the solid organ. Therefore, it is desirable for the athlete to eat at least 3 hours before a sports contest and to participate with his stomach and bladder empty. Special anatomical considerations should be given to the kidney and spleen because of their relatively high incidence of injury in athletics.

The *kidneys* are situated on each side of the spine and approximately in the center of the back. They are bean-shaped, about 4½ inches long, 2 inches wide, and 1 inch thick. The right kidney is usually slightly lower than the left because of the pressure of the liver. The uppermost surfaces of the kidneys are connected to the diaphragm by strong, ligamentous fibers. As breathing occurs, the kidneys move up and down as much as ½ inch. The inferior aspect is positioned 1 to 2 inches above the iliac crest. Resting anterior to the left kidney are the stomach, spleen, pancreas, and small and large intestines. Organs that are situated anterior to the right kidney are the liver and the intestines. The peritoneum (the membrane that lines the abdominal cavity) does not invest the kidneys. Rather, the kidneys are surrounded by a fibrous capsule and by a layer of fat that, in turn, is encased in another fatty layer that connects it to the niche in which it lies.

The *spleen* is the largest lymphatic organ in the body. It weighs about 6 ounces and is approximately 5 inches in length. It lies under the diaphragm on the left side and behind the ninth, tenth, and eleventh ribs. It is surrounded by a fibrous capsule that is firmly invested by the peritoneum.

INJURIES OF THE ABDOMEN

The abdominal area is particularly vulnerable to injury in all contact sports. A blow may produce superficial or even deep internal injuries, depending upon its location and intensity.[3] Strong abdominal muscles give good protection when they are tensed, but when relaxed they are easily damaged.

Contusions
Contusion of the rectus abdominis

A contusion of the rectus abdominis is a rare athletic injury. Although it seldom occurs, it should be readily recognized when it does happen because of its handicapping effect on the athlete. A severe blow may cause a hematoma that develops under the fascial tissue surrounding the rectus abdominis muscle. The pressure that results from hemorrhage causes pain and tightness in the region of the injury. The trainer should apply a cold pack immediately after injury and a compression elastic wrap. Signs of possible internal injury must also be looked for in this type of injury.

Contusion of the solar plexus (celiac plexus)

A blow to the sympathetic celiac plexus (solar plexus) produces a transitory paralysis of the diaphragm. Paralysis of the diaphragm results in a stoppage of respiration and in anoxia. When the athlete finds that he is unable to inhale, he may become hysterical because of fear; it is the responsibility of the trainer to allay such fear and instill confidence in the athlete. In dealing with an athlete who has "had the wind knocked out of him," the trainer should adhere to the following procedures:

1. Help the athlete overcome apprehension by talking confidently to him.
2. Loosen the athlete's belt and the clothing around his abdomen.
3. Encourage him to relax by having him initiate short inspirations and long expirations.

If the athlete fails to respond to the above procedures and becomes cyanotic, mouth-to-mouth resuscitation should be given.

It should be noted that an abdominal contusion may result in internal injuries.

Internal abdominal injuries
Rupture of the bladder or urethra

A severe contusion of the lower abdomen or a fracture of the pelvis may also rupture the bladder or urethra. Usually, ruptures take place when the bladder is full and distended. Lacerations of this type may be surgically repaired.

After a severe blow to the pelvic region, the athlete may display these recognizable signs:

1. He may have pain and discomfort in the lower abdomen, with the desire but an inability to urinate.

2. His abdomen may feel rigid.

3. He may indicate nausea, vomiting, and signs of shock.

4. Blood may drip from the urethra.

5. He may pass a great quantity of bloody urine, which indicates possible rupture of the kidney.

In any contusion to the abdominal region, the possibility of internal damage must be considered, and after such trauma the athlete should be instructed to check periodically for blood in his urine. To lessen the possibility of ruptures, the coach or trainer must instruct his players always to empty the bladder before practice or game time.

Rupture of the spleen

Every year there are reports of athletes who suddenly die—hours, days, or even weeks—after a severe blow received in an athletic contest. These deaths are sometimes attributed to delayed spleen hemorrhage. Injuries to the spleen usually occur as a result of a fall or a direct blow to the abdomen. The spleen is the greatest single accummulation of lymphoid tissue in the body. It is located high on the left side within the abdomen, behind the fundus of the stomach, and below the diaphragm. Its main functions are to serve as (1) a reservoir of red blood cells, (2) a regulator of the number of red blood cells in the general circulation, and (3) a destroyer of ineffective red cells. In addition, the spleen produces lymphocytes.

The great danger in a ruptured spleen lies in its ability to splint itself and then produce a delayed hemorrhage. Splinting of the spleen is formed by a loose hematoma formation and the constriction of the supporting and surrounding structures. Any slight strain may disrupt the splinting effect and allow the spleen to hemorrhage profusely into the abdominal cavity. A ruptured spleen requires surgical removal.

The trainer must be able to recognize the gross indications of a ruptured spleen to enable him to refer the athlete to the physician as soon as possible. The injured athlete presents a history of a severe blow to the abdomen and may also display signs of shock, abdominal rigidity, nausea, and vomiting. There is often a reflex pain, called Kehr's sign, which radiates to the left shoulder and one third of the way down the left arm.

Kidney contusions

The kidneys are seemingly well protected within the abdominal cavity. However, on occasion, contusions and even ruptures of these organs occur. The kidney may be susceptible to injury because of its normal distention by blood. A severe outside force, usually one applied to the back of the athlete, will cause abnormal extension of an engorged kidney, which results in injury. The degree of renal injury depends upon the extent of the distention and upon the angle and force of the blow. An athlete who has received a contusion of the kidney may display signs of shock, nausea, vomiting, rigidity of the back muscles, and hematuria (blood in the urine). Any athlete who reports having received a severe blow to the abdomen or back region should be instructed to urinate 2 or 3 times and to look for the appearance of blood in the urine. If there is any sign of hematuria, immediate referral to the physician must be made.

Medical care of the contused kidney usually consists of a 24-hour hospital observation with a gradual increase of fluid intake. If the hemorrhage fails to stop, surgery may be indicated. Controllable contusions usually require 2 weeks of bed rest and close surveillance after activity is resumed. In questionable cases the complete loss of one active playing season may be required.

"Stitch in the side"

A "stitch in the side" is the name given an idiopathic condition that occurs in some athletes. It is best described as a cramplike pain that develops on either the left or right costal angle during hard physical activity. Basketball, track, and other sports that involve running apparently produce this condition in the athlete most often.

The etiology is obscure, although several hypotheses have been advanced. Among these are the following: (1) constipation, (2) intestinal gas, (3) overeating, (4) diaphragmatic spasm consequent to poor conditioning, (5) lack of visceral support because of weak abdominal muscles, (6) distended spleen, (7) faulty breathing techniques leading to a lack of oxygen in the diaphragm, and (8) most logically, ischemia of either the diaphragm or the intercostals.

Immediate care of a "stitch in the side" demands relaxation of the spasm, for which two methods have proved beneficial. First,

the athlete is instructed to stretch the arm on the affected side as high as possible. If this is inadequate, flexing the trunk forward on the thighs may prove to be of some benefit.

Athletes who display recurrent spasms may need study by the trainer. The identification of poor eating habits, poor elimination habits, or an inadequate training program may indicate the athlete's particular problem. It should be noted that a "stitch in the side," although not considered serious, may require further evaluation by a physician if abdominal pains persist.

The thorax

ANATOMY

The thorax is that portion of the body commonly known as the chest, which lies between the base of the neck and the diaphragm. It is contained within the thoracic vertebrae and the twelve pairs of ribs that give it conformation (Fig. 19-9). Its main functions are to protect the vital organs of respiration and circulation and to assist the lungs in inhalation and exhalation during the breathing process. The ribs are flat bones that are attached to the thoracic vertebrae in the back and to the sternum in the front. The upper seven ribs are called

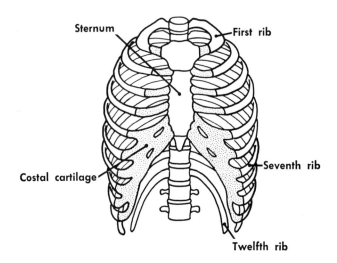

Fig. 19-9. Thorax.

sternal or true ribs, and each rib joins the sternum by a separate costal cartilage. The eighth, ninth, and tenth ribs (false ribs) have cartilages that join each other and the seventh rib before uniting with the sternum. The eleventh and twelfth ribs (floating ribs) remain unattached to the sternum but do have muscle attachments. The individual rib articulation produces a slight gliding action.

INJURIES OF THE THORAX
Rib fracture

Rib fractures (Fig. 19-10) are not uncommon in athletics and have their highest incidence in the contact sports, particularly in wrestling and football. Fracture can be caused by either a direct or an indirect trauma and can, infrequently, be the result of a violent muscular contraction. A direct injury is the type caused by a kick or a well-placed block, with the fracture developing at the site of force application. An indirect fracture is produced as the result of a general compression of the rib cage, such as may occur in football or wrestling.

The pathology sustained in rib fracture varies according to the type of injury that has been received. The direct fracture causes the most serious damage, since the

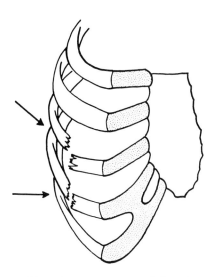

Fig. 19-10. Fractures of the ribs.

external force fractures and displaces the ribs inwardly. Such a mechanism may completely displace the bone and cause an overriding of fragments. The jagged edges of the fragments may cut, tear, or perforate the tissue of the pleurae, causing hemothorax, or they may collapse one lung (pneumothorax). Contrary to the pattern with direct violence, the indirect type usually causes the rib to spring and fracture outwardly, which produces an oblique or transverse fissure.

The rib fracture is usually quite easily detected. The history informs the trainer of the type and degree of force to which the rib cage has been subjected. After trauma, the athlete complains of having a severe pain on inspiration. By placing a hand on the posterior aspect of the athlete's rib cage, the trainer gently pulls the thorax anteriorly, meanwhile stabilizing the alternate shoulder. A fracture of the rib will be readily evidenced by a severe sharp pain and possibly crepitus. After the point of injury is localized, palpation should be initiated to determine point tenderness and swelling. The athlete should be referred to the team physician for x-ray examination if there is any indication of fracture.

An uncomplicated rib fracture is often difficult to identify on x-ray film. Therefore the physician plans the treatment according to the symptoms presented. Care of the rib fracture is managed with an adhesive tape support and rest. Simple transverse or oblique fractures heal within 3 to 4 weeks.

Rib adhesive tape support. Complete immobilization of a fractured rib is extremely difficult. The purpose of rib strapping (Fig. 19-11) is to stabilize and fix the affected side against excessive movement as much as possible and still allow the uninjured side freedom of movement. Many physicians prefer a commercial rib belt instead of tape, particularly for the female athlete or when the splint must be worn for an extended period of time.

Materials needed: One roll of 2-inch adhesive tape or one roll of 3-inch elastic

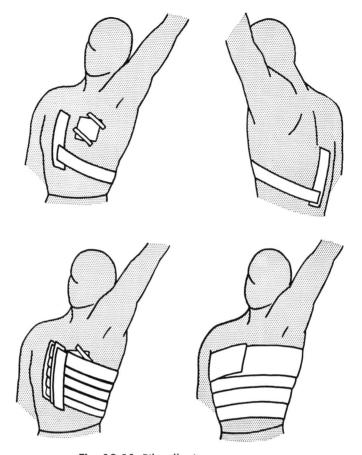

Fig. 19-11. Rib adhesive tape support.

tape, 4-inch elastic bandage, skin toughener, and gauze pad.

Position of the athlete: The athlete stands on the floor with the arm of the affected side raised over his head.

Position of the trainer: The trainer stands facing the athlete's affected side.

Procedure:

1. After a gauze pad is placed over the nipple, 2 anchor strips of tape approximately 6 inches in length are applied, 1 anteriorly and 1 posteriorly, with the anterior strip placed lateral to the sternum and the posterior strip positioned lateral to the spine.

2. From just below the floating rib, a strip of tape 2 inches wide is carried from the spinal anchor strip to the anchor strip of the sternum. The athlete exhales as the tape follows the contour of the ribs.

3. The addition of strips is continued until the injured rib is completely covered. Each strip should overlap the piece preceding it by at least one half its width.

4. Two lock strips are placed over the ends of the rib strapping.

5. The strapping should be encircled by a 4-inch elastic bandage or elastic tape if the athlete is to engage in activity.

Sternal fracture

Fracture of the sternum occurs infrequently in athletics. It can develop from a direct blow to the sternum, from a violent compression force applied posteriorly, or from hyperflexion of the trunk. The most

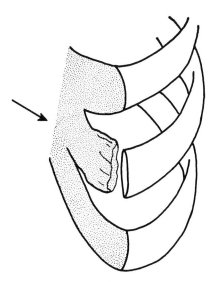

Fig. 19-12. Costochondral separation.

frequently affected area of the sternum is the manubrium. This fracture results in sharp chest pain that occurs particularly on inhalation and is localized over the sternum. The athlete assumes a position in which the head and shoulders are dropped forward.

Palpation indicates mild swelling and, possibly, displaced fragments. An x-ray film must be taken to determine the extent of displacement.

The treatment may require bed rest for 2 to 3 weeks with immobilization by adhesive strapping or the use of a sand weight over the fracture site. After activity is resumed a posterior figure-of-eight bandage is applied to maintain the shoulders in an erect position.

Costochondral separation and dislocation

In athletics the number of injuries involving separations and dislocations of the costochondral region is greater than the number of rib fractures. The most common condition is a fracture-separation at the costochondral junction (Fig. 19-12). This injury has the same mechanisms as do the rib fractures, but it poses a more difficult management problem because it heals slowly. The costochondral separation displays signs identical to those of a rib fracture, with the exception that they are localized in the area of rib cartilage. A separation of this type resulting in a dislocation of the cartilage causes deformity. Such deformities heal without inhibiting the normal functions. Healing time is from 1 to 2 months.

As with rib fracture, the costochondral separation is managed by rest and the use of adhesive tape immobilization. In cases in which dislocation is apparent, a flat compress should be applied before strapping. If there is inadequate cartilage healing or abnormal rib movement as a result of a lack of support, surgery may be necessary.

Muscle conditions of the thorax

The muscles of the thorax are the intercostals and the erector spinae, latissimus dorsi, trapezius, serratus anterior, serratus posterior, and pectoralis major—all of which are subject to contusions and strains in athletics. The intercostals are especially assailable. Traumatic injuries occur most often from direct blows or sudden torsions of the trunk. Their care requires immediate pressure and applications of cold for approximately 1 hour; after hemorrhaging has been controlled, immobilization should be employed.

Internal complications of trauma to the thorax

Internal complications in the thorax resulting from athletic trauma are rare. They pertain principally to injuries of the lung, pleurae, and/or intercostal arteries. Because of the seriousness of internal injuries, the trainer should be able to recognize their basic signs. The most serious of the conditions are (1) pneumothorax, (2) hemothorax, (3) hemorrhaging into the lungs, (4) traumatic asphyxia, and (5) heart contusion.

Pneumothorax is a condition in which the pleural cavity becomes filled with air that has entered through an opening in the chest. As the negatively pressured pleural cavity fills with air, the lung on that side collapses. The loss of one lung may produce difficulty in breathing and anoxia.

Hemothorax is the presence of blood within the pleural cavity. It results from the tearing or puncturing of the lung or pleural tissue involving the blood vessels in the area. As with pneumothorax, difficulty in breathing and cyanosis develop.

A violent blow or compression of the chest without an accompanying rib fracture may cause a *lung hemorrhage*. This condition results in severe pain on breathing, dyspnea (difficult breathing), the coughing up of frothy blood, and signs of shock. If these signs are observed, the athlete should be treated for shock and immediately referred to the physician.

Traumatic asphyxia occurs as the result of a violent blow to or a compression of the rib cage, causing a cessation of breathing. Signs include a purple discoloration of the upper trunk and head, with the conjunctivae of the eyes displaying a bright red color. A condition of this type demands immediate mouth-to-mouth resuscitation and medical attention.

A *heart contusion* may occur when the heart is compressed between the sternum and the spine by a strong outside force. This injury produces severe shock and heart pain. Death may ensue if medical attention is not immediately administered.

The back and spine

ANATOMY

The spine or vertebral column is composed of several individual bones called vertebrae (Fig. 19-13). They total 33, with 24 classified as movable, or true, and 9 classified as immovable, or false. The false vertebrae, which are fixed by fusion, form the sacrum and the coccyx. The design of the spine allows a high degree of flexibility forward and laterally and limited mobility backward. Rotation about a central axis in the areas of the neck and the lower back is also permitted.

The movable vertebrae are separated

into three different divisions, according to location and function. The first division constitutes the seven cervical vertebrae; the second, the twelfth thoracic vertebrae; and the third consists of the five lumbar vertebrae. As the spinal segments progress downward from the cervical region, they grow increasingly larger to accommodate the upright posture of the body as well as to contribute in weight bearing. Physiological curves also are present in the spinal column for adjusting to the upright stresses (Chapter 5). These curves are, respectively, the cervical, thoracic, lumbar, and sacrococcygeal curves. The cervical and lumbar curves are convex anteriorly, whereas the thoracic and sacrococcygeal curves are convex posteriorly. The shape of the vertebrae is irregular, but they possess certain characteristics that are common to all. Each vertebrae consists of a neural

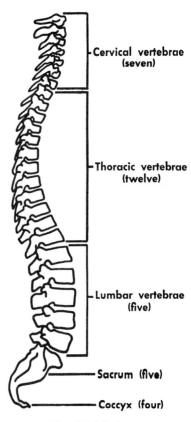

Cervical vertebrae (seven)

Thoracic vertebrae (twelve)

Lumbar vertebrae (five)

Sacrum (five)

Coccyx (four)

Fig. 19-13. Spine.

arch through which the spinal cord passes and several projecting processes that serve as attachments for muscles and ligaments. Each neural arch has two laminae and two pedicles. The latter are bony processes that project backward from the body of the vertebrae and connect with the laminae. The laminae are flat bony processes occurring on either side of the neural arch, which project backward and inward from the pedicles. With the exception of the first and second cervical vertebrae, each vertebra has a spinous and transverse process for muscle and ligament attachment and all have an articular process.

Intervertebral articulations take place between veretbral bodies and vertebral arches. Articulation between the bodies is of the symphysis type. There is an intervertebral disk made up of two components, the *annulus fibrosus* and the *nucleus pulposus*. The annulus fibrosus forms the periphery of the intervertebral disk and is composed of strong, fibrous tissue with its fibers running in several different directions for purposes of strength. In the center is the semifluid nucleus pulposus compressed under pressure. The disks act as important shock absorbers for the spine. Besides motion at articulations between the bodies of the vertebrae, movement takes place at four articular processes that derive from the pedicles and laminae. The direction of movement of each vertebra is somewhat dependent upon the direction in which the articular facets face.

The types of movement allowed by the vertebrae vary considerably. Flexion takes place in the cervical, upper thoracic, and lumbar areas; extension occurs in the cervical and lumbar areas and the lumbosacral joint. The spinous processes in the thoracic region limit hyperextension. Lateral flexion takes place in the cervical and lumbar regions and, to an extremely limited degree, in the dorsolumbar area. Rotation occurs most freely in the cervical region, because of the lack of interlocking articular processes.

The major ligaments that join the vari-ous vertebral parts are the anterior longitudinal, the posterior longitudinal, and the supraspinous. The anterior longitudinal ligament is a wide, strong band that extends the full length of the anterior surface of the vertebral bodies. The posterior longitudinal ligament is contained within the vertebral canal and extends the full length of the posterior aspect of the bodies of the vertebrae. The ligamenta flava connect one lamina to another. The interspinous, supraspinous, and intertransverse ligaments stabilize the transverse and spinous processes, extending between adjacent vertebrae.

DISORDERS OF THE BACK AND SPINE

Back affections, particularly those of the lower back, are next to foot problems in order of incidence. In athletics back problems are relatively common and are most often the result of congenital, mechanical, or traumatic factors. Congenital back disorders are conditions that are present at birth. Evolutionists are of the opinion that man's back is still undergoing structural changes as a result of his upright position and that, therefore, man is prone to slight spinal defects at birth, which later in life may cause improper body mechanics or result in trauma (Chapter 5).

Prevention of back injuries in athletics

All conditioning programs in athletics should include work for the prevention of back injuries. Prevention involves (1) correction, amelioration, or compensation of functional postural deviations, (2) maintenance or increase of trunk and general body flexibility, and (3) increase of trunk and general body strength. The trainer should be aware of any postural anomalies that his athletes possess; with this knowledge, he should establish individual corrective programs. Basic conditioning should include an emphasis on trunk flexibility. Every effort should be made to produce maximum range of motion in trunk rotation and both lateral and forward flexion. Strength should be developed to the ultimate, with stress placed upon developing the spinal extensors (erector spinae) and upon developing abdominal strength, to ensure proper postural alignment.

Mechanical back defects are caused mainly by faulty posture, obesity, or faulty body mechanics—all of which may affect the athlete's performance in sports. Traumatic forces produced in athletics, either directly or indirectly, can result in contusions, sprains, and/or fractures. Sometimes even from minor injuries chronic and recurrent conditions can develop, which may have serious implications for the athlete. To aid fully in understanding a back complaint, a logical investigation should be made into the history and the site of any injury, the type of pain produced, and the extent of impairment of normal function.

Congenital low back anomalies

Anomalies of bony development are the underlying cause of many back problems in athletics. Such conditions would have remained undiscovered had it not been for a blow or sudden twist that created an abnormal stress in the area of the anomaly. The most common of these anomalies are excessive length of the transverse process of the fifth lumbar vertebra, incomplete closure of the neural arch (spina bifida occulta), nonconformities of the spinous processes, atypical lumbosacral angles or articular facets, and incomplete closures of the vertebral laminae. All these anomalies may produce mechanical weaknesses that make the back prone to injury when it is subjected to excessive postural strains.

It should be noted that persons of certain body types have a higher rate of low back problems than do others. The tall, lanky, and relatively thin (ectomorphic) athlete is more susceptible to back injury than is the short and stocky individual— a difference probably caused, in part, by the existence of a sixth lumbar vertebra in the ectomorphic type; the stocky, mesomorphic athlete may possess only four.

An example of a congenital defect that may develop into a more serious condition when aggravated by a blow or a sudden twist in athletics is the condition known as *spondylolisthesis*. This deformity, in combination with a direct blow, a sudden twist, or chronic low back strain, causes the fifth lumbar vertebra to displace itself forward on the sacrum. When this injury happens, the athlete complains of localized pain or a pain that radiates down both legs, stiffness in the lower back, and increased irritation after physical activity. For the most part, these symptoms are the same for the majority of lower back problems; therefore an x-ray film should be made to enable the physician to diagnose accurately.

Treatment in these cases usually consists of rest, mild exercise, and therapy with an emphasis on heat and massage.

Mechanical defects of the spine

Mechanical defects of the spine resulting from faulty body mechanics must be considered as a major cause of spinal problems in athletics.

Maintaining proper segmental alignment of the body during the various activities of standing, sitting, lying, running, jumping, and throwing is of utmost importance for keeping the body equipment in good condition. Habitual violations of the principles of good body mechanics occur in many sports and produce anatomical deficiencies that subject the body to constant abnormal muscular and ligamentous strain.

Postural deviations have been discussed in some detail in Chapter 5. In all cases of postural deformity the trainer should determine the cause and attempt to rectify the condition through reconditioning and mobilization exercises.

Traumatic injuries of the back

Skill in recognizing and evaluating the extent of an athletic injury to the back is of vital importance to the trainer. Every football season stories appear that tell of an athlete who has become paralyzed because of the mishandling of a fractured spine. Such conditions would not occur if field officials, coaches, and trainers would use discretion, exercise good judgment, and be able to identify certain gross indications of serious spine involvement.

General signs of lower back injury

Injury to the lower back produces certain general signs that are readily recognized by the trainer:

1. Muscle spasm may be either bilateral or unilateral. Unilateral spasm of the lower back tends to make the athlete lean in that direction.

2. Point tenderness is indicated at the affected area.

3. Radiating or localized pain is displayed in the lower back region. It becomes more intense upon exercising. Pain may radiate down one or both legs, following the sciatic nerve.

4. Movement is restricted because of the pain and spasm in the lower back region.

Functional mobility tests

Functional mobility tests should be given to the injured athlete to localize the exact site of the injury. The following standard tests may be given to determine abnormal muscle contractures and pain areas present in the lower back.

Posture tests. When first seen in an erect position the athlete may display certain signs. He may complain of leg weakness and lower back pain and may demonstrate poor mobility of the lumbar spine. Contractures at the injury site may be unilateral or bilateral; if unilateral, the athlete may present a lumbar scoliosis, a laterally tilted hip, or one leg shorter than the other.

Sitting tests

1. Sitting in a chair with his feet flat on the floor and his hips well back, the athlete flexes his trunk forward attempting to touch his heels with his fingertips. If there is a sprain of the lower back, pain will be elicited upon flexion; if there is serious pathology of the vertebral disk, flexion will be almost impossible.

2. Sitting in a chair with his feet flat on the floor and his hips well back, the athlete rotates his trunk, first to one side and then to the other, meanwhile stabilizing the lower limbs. Trunk rotation will produce pain in the lower back if an injury is present.

Lying tests

1. Lying supine on a table with both legs flexed over the end, the athlete slowly flexes the hip on the affected side. Pain will be felt if there is pathology of the lower back.

2. Lying supine on a table the athlete hyperflexes both thighs upon his abdomen. This position places stress on the lumbosacral joint and will elicit pain when injury is present.

3. Lying supine on a table with the thighs flexed on his abdomen, the athlete extends first one leg and then the other. This movement stretches the sciatic nerve. Any pathology present will produce pain.

Injuries of the soft tissues of the back

Soft tissue injuries of the back most often occur to the lower back. Those that occur in athletics are produced by acute twists, direct blows, or chronic strains resulting from faulty posture or from the use of poor body mechanics in the sport. Tearing or stretching of the supporting ligamentous tissue with secondary involvement of the musculature occurs. Repeated strains or sprains cause the stabilizing tissues to lose their supporting power, thus producing tissue laxness in the lower back area.

Back contusion

Back contusions rank second to strains and sprains in incidence. Because of its large surface area the back is quite liable to bruises in athletics; football produces the greatest number of these injuries. A history indicating a violent blow to the back could indicate an extremely serious condition. Contusion of the back must be distinguished from a vertebral fracture, which in some instances is possible only by means of an x-ray examination. The bruise causes local pain, muscle spasm, and point tenderness. A swollen area may be visible also.

Cold and pressure should be applied immediately for about 24 hours, followed by rest and a gradual introduction of various forms of superficial heat can be employed. If the bruise handicaps the movement of the athlete, deep therapy in the form of ultrasound or microwave diathermy may hasten recovery. Ice massage combined with static stretching has been found to benefit soft tissue injuries in the region of the lower back. The time of incapacitation usually ranges from 2 days to 2 weeks.

Lower back pain (sciatica; lumbosacral and sacroiliac sprains)

As previously indicated, pain in the lower back is a sign of pathology and not necessarily a condition in itself. Numerous terms are used to designate lower back pain—most of which are either misleading, synonymous, or in some cases false. Among the expressions most often used in athletics are sciatica and lumbosacral or sacroiliac sprains.

The older an athlete is, the more prone he is to lower back injury. Incidence of this injury at the high school level is relatively low but becomes progressively greater at college and professional levels. In most cases, because of postural anomalies and numerous small injuries, a so-called acute back condition is the culmination of a progressive degeneration of long duration that is aggravated or accentuated by a blow or sudden twist. The injury is produced as the result of an existing anatomical vulnerability. The trunk and vertebral column press downward on the sacrum while the lower limbs and pelvis force upward; thus an abnormal strain can be exerted when the athlete's trunk is twisted in one direction while the hamstring muscles pull downward on the pelvis on the opposite side. Such stress, if applied to an inelastic, structurally deformed, or muscularly weak lower back, will produce pathology.

Sciatica is an inflammatory condition of the sciatic nerve. It produces pain that follows the nerve pathway, posterior and medial to the thigh. The term sciatica has incorrectly been used as a general term to describe all lower back pain, without reference to exact causes. The sciatic nerve originates from the lumbosacral plexus and moves down the length of the lower limb, sending out its branches to muscles. The largest sciatic branch is the fifth lumbar nerve, which passes through a minute opening as it leaves the spine. This nerve is particularly vulnerable to torsions or direct blows that tend to impose abnormal stretchings and pressure upon it as it emerges from the spine, thus effecting a traumatic condition. The sciatic nerve is also subject to trauma at the point where is crosses over the ischial spine. There, a muscular spasm or a direct blow can place direct pressure on the nerve. The areas most often affected are those of the lumbosacral joint and the fifth lumbar nerve.

An athlete who has sciatica may feel a localized backache, soreness, pain on movement, cutaneous numbness, or tingling sensations at different points along the sciatic nerve.

The athlete who has a *lumbosacral sprain* will experience a diffused, dull ache in the lower back that is caused by an irritation of the fifth lumbar nerve. He may also display spasm, point tenderness at the lumbosacral junction, and restricted trunk movement. The lumbosacral junction is usually considered to have the greatest number of lower back injuries in athletics. Sprains occur most often to athletes with lordosis. The sports that involve the highest rates of this injury are football, basketball, and baseball. This is attributed to the fact that these sports do not require use of the full range of back motion and, consequently, many athletes become restricted in this area and are unable to withstand abnormal twists or blows.

The sacroiliac is the junction formed by the ilium and the sacrum and it is fortified by ligamentous tissue that allows little motion to take place. It is doubtful that many *sacroiliac sprains* occur as a result of participation in sports. There is much speculation among authorities as to whether the sacroiliac sprain may not, in reality, be a lumbosacral condition.

General care of lower back injuries

Care of injuries of the lower back requires close cooperation between the injured athlete, the physician, and the trainer. The type of care to be administered is based on the extent of the injury and is determined by x-ray study and the physician's physical examination. Most lower back injury care includes the following conservative regimen: (1) limitation of activity, (2) passive lower back stretching, (3) application of heat and massage, (4) use of a bed board, (5) adhesive and brace supports, and (6) reconditioning exercises.

Limitation of activity and, at times, complete rest are the most important factors for healing an injured back. Activity should not be resumed until pain has subsided and movement is restored to normal. *Passive stretching* combined with *heat* and *massage* applied directly to the lower back region will tend to soothe and relax the contracted tissue. Moist heat seems to be most effective, but analgesic balm packs, electric heating pads, and infrared lamp radiations, as well as ice massage have been found beneficial. In cases of chronic inflammatory back conditions, deep therapy has proved of considerable value. Deep massage given daily will aid in loosening tight muscles. It is suggested that heat, massage, and passive stretching be given, in that order, for the most advantageous results.

In the case of a chronic or a subacute lower back condition, placing a ½-inch plyboard underneath the athlete's mattress will afford a much better rest. The ply-

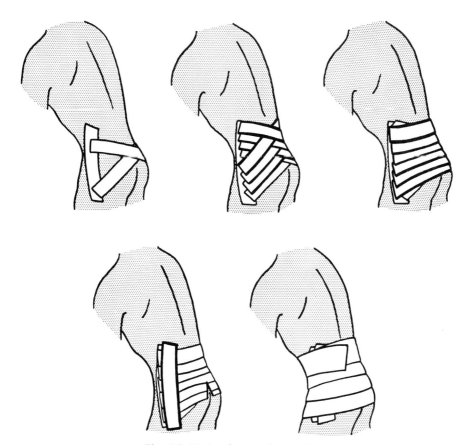

Fig. 19-14. Lumbosacral strapping.

board, which should cover the same area as the bed, prevents sagging and gives a firm, stable surface for the injured back.

Adhesive strapping or brace support

In some cases of lower back injury, the use of support and immobilization by adhesive strapping and/or bracing has proved quite beneficial. A brace, although applicable to everyday activity, is often quite cumbersome during sports participation. The lumbosacral brace can be improvised by the trainer or can be purchased commercially. It should have a rigid back and should fit the entire lumbosacral area of the athlete, being secured in the front by means of straps. It must be recognized that continued dependence on such a device leads to a further weakening of the lower back muscles. If the athlete has a heavy and pendulous abdomen, support may best be given by a girdle that secures the abdominal viscera and thereby removes the strain from the lower back.

Lumbosacral strapping. Adhesive strapping to the lumbosacral region (Fig. 19-14) is useful for mild sprains in some cases after the athlete has been released for participation by the physician. For the greatest support the adhesive tape should be applied from both greater trochanters upward to the ninth rib.

Materials needed: One roll of 2-inch adhesive tape, skin toughener, tape adherent, and 6-inch elastic bandage.

Position of the athlete: The athlete stands with his trunk flexed approximately 20 degrees. Slight trunk flexion tends to straighten out the lumbar curve, making a flat surface for easier application of the tape.

Position of the trainer: The trainer stands facing the back of the athlete.

Procedure:

1. Two anchor strips approximately 12 inches in length are applied laterally, each fanning out from the athlete's greater trochanter toward the ninth rib.

2. Strips of tape are next applied from both trochanters and crisscross one another

in an upward direction. Each strip is pulled tightly, overlapping the previous strip at least one half of its width. The crossing strips cover the entire lumbosacral region.

3. After the crisscross strips are in place, a lock strip is applied vertically over the anchor point, one on each side.

4. Reinforcing tape strips are then applied horizontally, beginning at the tip of the coccyx and continuing upward. Each strip is alternately pulled from one side, then from the other.

5. Lock strips are applied over the horizontal strips, and a slit (approximately 2 inches) is cut in the lower middle of the strapping, to ease tightness over the buttocks.

6. A 6-inch elastic wrap is applied over the strapping, encircling the lower trunk of the athlete. This will hold the tape in position and prevent perspiration from loosening the strapping.

Herniated disk (intervertebral disk syndrome)

Subjected to constant stresses, the intervertebral disks are prone to various degenerations, tears, and cracks (Fig. 19-15). The area most often injured is the lumbar spine, particularly the disk lying between the fourth and fifth lumbar vertebrae. In athletics the mechanism of a disk injury is the same as for the lumbosacral sprain —a sudden blow or twist that places abnormal strain on the lumbar region. Besides injuring soft tissues, such a strain may herniate an already degenerated disk by increasing the size of cracks and allowing the nucleus pulposus to spill out. This protrusion of the nucleus pulposus may place pressure on the cord or spinal nerves, thus causing radiating pains similar to sciatica.[6,7]

The signs accompanying a herniated disk are similar to those of sciatica, lumbosacral sprain, or sacroiliac sprain. Diagnosis of the herniated disk must be made by x-ray examination. Every athlete who suffers a severe twist or blow to the lower back should be referred routinely to the physician.

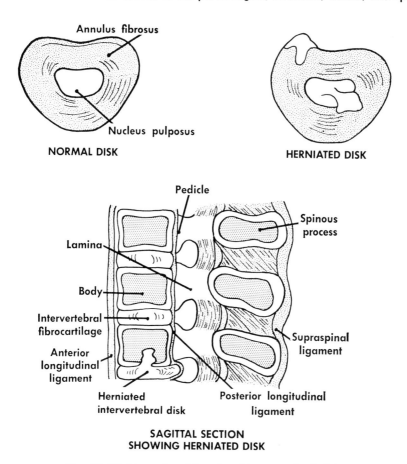

Fig. 19-15. Normal and herniated intervertebral disks.

Vertebral fracture and dislocation

Fractures of the vertebral column, in terms of bone injury, are not serious in themselves; but they pose dangers when related to spinal cord damage. Imprudent movement of a person with a fractured spine can cause irreparable damage to the spinal cord. All athletic injuries involving the back should be considered fractures until proved differently by the physician. It is always advisable to carry the athlete from the playing area, face downward on a stretcher, so that the normal spinal curve is maintained. Lifting and moving the athlete should be executed in such a manner as to preclude twisting, and each body segment (neck, trunk, hips, and lower limbs) should be firmly supported. Vertebral frac-

tures of the greatest concern in athletics are compression fractures and fractures of the transverse and spinous processes.

The *compression fracture* may occur as a result of violent hyperflexion or jackknifing of the trunk. Falling from a height and landing on the feet or buttocks may also produce a compression fracture. The vertebrae that are most often compressed are those in the area of the dorsolumbar curves. The vertebrae usually are crushed anteriorly by the traumatic force of the body above the site of injury. The crushed body may spread out fragments and protrude into the spinal canal, compressing and possibly even cutting the cord.

Recognition of the compression fracture is difficult without an x-ray examination. A basic evaluation may be made with a knowledge of the history and point tenderness over the affected vertebrae.

Fractures of the transverse and spinous processes result most often from kicks or other direct blows to the back. Since these processes are surrounded by large muscles, fracture produces extensive soft tissue injury. As fractures, these present little danger and will usually permit the athlete considerable activity within the range of pain tolerance. Most care and treatment will be oriented toward therapy of the soft tissue pathology.

RECONDITIONING OF THE LOWER BACK

Reconditioning of the lower back after injury primarily involves restoring the normal flexibility, increasing strength, and re-education of posture. Caution should be exercised not to start activity too soon. Reconditioning exercises must not be instituted until pain and irritation have diminished. The first consideration is increasing the lower back range of motion through static flexibility exercises. Static stretches tend to cause less initial irritation than do the ballistic stretches. Suitable exercises may be selected from those in Chapter 15.

Flexion exercises are useful in the acute stages of a low-back condition.[8,9] These may include the following: (1) *pelvic tilt,* in which the athlete lies supine in a hooklying position and tightens the abdominal and gluteal muscles and flattens the lower back firmly against table; (2) *alternate knees to chest,* in which the athlete lies supine and alternately brings the knees toward the chest and pulls them on the chest with both hands. After full movement has been restored, a program of muscle development should be given, with emphasis on abdominal strength and low back flexibility. If faulty posture is an etiological fac-

tor, proper body mechanics in conjunction with strength exercises should be encouraged.

REFERENCES

1. Anderson, W. A. D., and Scotti, T. M.: Synopsis of pathology, ed. 8, St. Louis, 1972, The C. V. Mosby Co.
2. Chisholm, T. C.: What's new with inguinal hernias? Patient Care, September 15, 1970, pp. 61-74.
3. O'Donoghue, D. H.: Treatment of injuries to athletes, Philadelphia, 1970, W. B. Saunders Co.
4. Novich, M. M., and Taylor, B.: Training and conditioning of athletes, Philadelphia, 1970, Lea & Febiger.
5. Dayton, O. W.: Athletic training and conditioning, New York, 1965, The Ronald Press Co.
6. Logan, G. A., and Dunkelberg, J. G.: Adaptations of muscular activity, Belmont, Calif., 1964, Wadsworth Publishing Co., Inc.
7. Taylor, B.: Low back pain, J. Nat. Athlet. Ass. 2:12, 1967.
8. Williams, P. C.: The lumbosacral spine, New York, 1965, McGraw-Hill Book Co.
9. Cailliet, R.: Low back pain syndrome, ed. 2, Philadelphia, 1968, F. A. Davis Co.

RECOMMENDED READINGS

Anderson, W. A. D., and Scotti, T. M.: Synopsis of pathology, ed. 8, St. Louis, 1972, The C. V. Mosby Co.

Cailliet, R.: Low back pain syndrome, ed. 2, Philadelphia, 1968, F. A. Davis Co.

Dolan, J. P.: Treatment and prevention of athletic injuries, Danville, Ill., 1961, The Interstate Printers & Publishers, Inc.

Emergency care and transportation of the sick and injured, Chicago, 1971, Committee on Injuries, American Academy of Orthopaedic Surgeons.

McLaughlin, H. L.: Trauma, Philadelphia, 1959, W. B. Saunders Co.

Novich, M. M., and Taylor, B.: Training and conditioning in athletics, Philadelphia, 1970, Lea & Febiger.

O'Donoghue, D. H.: Treatment of injuries to athletes, Philadelphia, 1970, W. B. Saunders Co.

Ryan, A. J.: Medical care of the athlete, New York, 1962, McGraw-Hill Book Co.

Thorndike, A.: Athletic injuries, ed. 5, Philadelphia, 1962, Lea & Febiger.

CHAPTER 20

Conditions of the neck, head, and face

The neck

ANATOMY

Special study should be devoted to the *cervical spine* so that its vulnerability to athletic injuries may be appreciated. The cervical spine consists of seven vertebrae, with the first two differing from the other true vertebrae (Fig. 20-1). These first two are called the atlas and axis, respectively, and they function together to support the head on the spinal column and to permit cervical rotation. The *atlas*, named for its function of supporting the head, displays no body or spinous processes and is composed of lateral masses that are connected to the anterior and posterior arches. The upper surfaces articulate with the occipital condyles of the skull and allow flexion and extension but little lateral movement. The arches of the atlas form a bony ring sufficiently large to accommodate the odontoid process and the medulla of the spinal cord. The *axis* or epistropheus is the second cervical vertebra and is designed to allow the skull and atlas to rotate upon it. Its primary difference from a typical vertebra is the presence of a toothlike projection from the vertebral body that fits into the ring of the atlas. This is called the odontoid process. The great mobility of the cervical spine is attributed to the flattened, oblique facing of its articular facets and to the horizontal positioning of the spinous processes.

The *spinal cord* is that portion of the central nervous system that is contained within the vertebral canal of the spinal column. It extends from the medulla oblongata upon emergence from the foramen magnum of the cranium and ends at the filum terminale in the vicinity of the first or second lumbar vertebra. The lumbar roots and the sacral nerves form a horse-like tail called the cauda equina.

Thirty-one pairs of *spinal nerves* extend from the sides of the spinal cord: 8 cervical, 12 thoracic, 5 lumbar, 5 sacral, and 1 coccygeal (Fig. 20-2). Each of these nerves has an anterior root (motor root) and a posterior one (sensory root). The two roots in each case join together and form a single spinal nerve, which passes downward and outward through the intervertebral foramen. As the spinal nerves are conducted through the invertebral foramen they pass near the articular processes of the vertebrae. Any abnormal movement of these processes, as in a dislocation or a fracture, may expose the spinal nerves to injury. Injuries that occur below the third lumbar vertebra usually result in nerve root damage but do not cause spinal cord damage.

The *brain* or encephalon is the part of the central nervous system that is contained within the bony cavity of the cranium and is divided into four sections: the

341

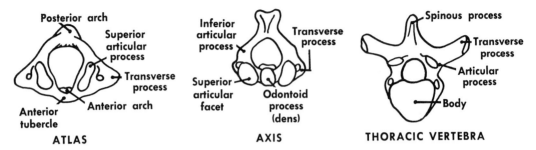

Fig. 20-1. Comparison of the first 2 cervical vertebrae, the atlas and the axis, with a typical thoracic vertebra.

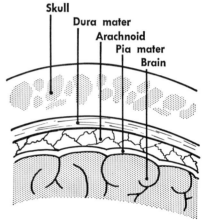

Fig. 20-3. Sagittal section through superior portion of the skull, showing relationship of the meninges to the brain.

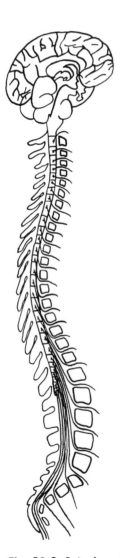

Fig. 20-2. Spinal cord.

cerebrum, the cerebellum, the pons, and the medulla oblongata.

Investing the spinal cord and the brain are the *meninges,* which are three membranes that give protection to the brain and spinal cord. Outermost is the dura mater, consisting of a dense, fibrous, and inelastic sheath that encloses the brain and cord. In some places it is attached directly to the vertebral canal, but for the most part a layer of fat that contains the vital arteries and veins separates this membrane from the bony wall and forms the epidural space. The arachnoid, an extremely delicate sheath, lines the dura mater and is attached directly to the spinal cord by many silklike tissue strands. The space between the arachnoid and the pia mater, the membrane that helps contain the spinal fluid, is called the subarachnoid space. The subarachnoid cavity projects upward and, running the full length of the spinal cord, connects with the ventricles of the brain. The pia mater is a thin, delicate, and highly vascularized membrane that adheres closely to the spinal cord and to the brain—the large extension of the cord that is housed within the skull (Fig. 20-3).

The *cerebrospinal fluid* is contained between the arachnoid and the pia mater membrane and completely surrounds and suspends the brain. Its main function is to act as a cushion, helping to diminish the transmission of shocking forces.

PREVENTION OF INJURIES

Because of the free mobility of the cervical vertebrae, compared with that of vertebrae in the thoracic and lumbar areas, severe neck injuries are relatively uncommon in sports participation. Of those that do occur, most take place in diving and football. Neck conditions that are considered most severe are intervertebral disk ruptures and fractures and/or dislocations or subluxations of the cervical vertebrae. Minor neck injuries primarily affect the soft tissue about the cervical vertebrae and fall into the categories of sprains and strains. The neck suffers injury when it is forced beyond its normal structural limitations. In athletics such effects are usually produced (1) by forced hyperextension, (2) by cervical compression (flexion) caused by a head-on blow, (3) by a sudden backward-forward snap of the head on the neck (whiplash), or (4) by forced rotation of the head (Fig. 20-4).

Prevention of neck injuries depends upon the flexibility of the neck, its muscle strength, the state of readiness of the athlete, and the use of proper protective equipment. A normal range of neck movement is necessary. Therefore, neck flexibility exercises coupled with neck-strengthening exercises should be performed by the athlete daily.

During participation the athlete should constantly be in a "state of readiness" and, when making contact with an opponent, should "bull" his neck. This is accomplished by elevating both shoulders and isometrically contracting the muscles surrounding the neck.

Many authorities have attributed the great increase in severe neck injuries in football to the type of headgear that is being worn. As pointed out in Chapter 5, a face mask, by acting as a lever, can increase the force applied to the cervical region by as much as 30% to over 100%. The back edge of the helmet can be forced into the cervical region, thereby dislocating a cervical vertebra and consequently damaging the spinal cord.

NECK INJURIES
Cervical fractures

Cervical fractures have a low rate of occurrence in athletics because of the wide range of motion possessed by the neck.

Before a fracture takes place, either a subluxation or a complete dislocation of a vertebra usually occurs; quite often, a fracture and a dislocation are closely associated.

A severe force that either hyperextends, compresses by means of a head-on blow, or twists the neck can cause cervical fracture. The hyperextension fracture results from the neck's being forced back, well beyond a normal range of motion. The athlete's head can be snapped backward quite forcibly by a poorly executed block or tackle in football and a fracture may result. These injuries usually affect the spinous processes and particularly the sixth or seventh vertebra. A straight, head-on blow to the top of the athlete's head may cause a compression fracture in the body of one of the cervical vertebrae. In most cases this injury is accompanied by a dislocation and spinal cord damage. Severe torque on the neck places most of the stress on the main rotatory region of the atlas and axis. If the force is great enough to cause a fracture or a dislocation, the injury is usually fatal be-

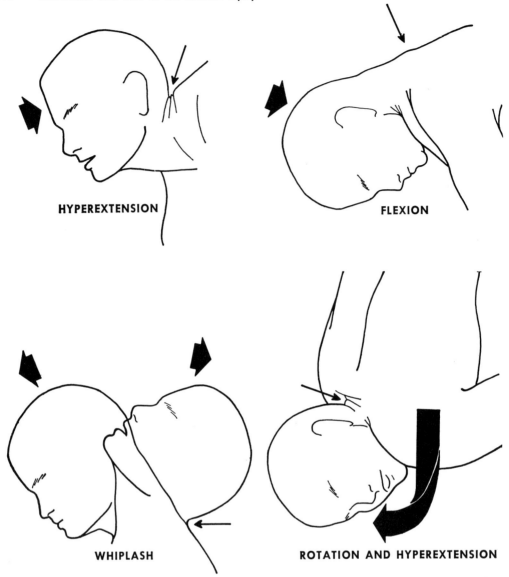

HYPEREXTENSION

FLEXION

WHIPLASH

ROTATION AND HYPEREXTENSION

Fig. 20-4. Mechanisms of neck injuries. (Large arrow in each case indicates direction of force and small arrow the site of injury.)

cause of the proximity of the vital medulla oblongata.

The major symptoms of neck fractures are generalized pain in the cervical region, muscle spasm (stiffness), swelling and tenderness on palpation, inability to move the neck, and evidence of cord damage, indicated by paralysis below the point of fractured.

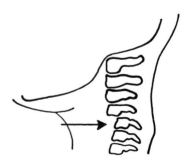

Fig. 20-5. Cervical dislocation.

Cervical dislocations

Cervical dislocations (Fig. 20-5) are not common but occur much more frequently in athletics than do fractures. They usually occur as a result of violent flexion and rotation of the head. Most injuries of this type happen in swimming pool accidents when the diver strikes his head on the bottom of the pool after a dive. The mechanism is analogous to the situation that occurs in football when blocks and tackles are poorly executed. The cervical vertebrae are more easily dislocated than are the vertebrae in other regions, principally because of their nearness to the horizontally facing articular facets. The superior articular facet moves beyond its normal range of motion and either completely passes the inferior facet (luxation) or catches on its edge (subluxation). The latter is far more common and, as in the case of the complete luxation, most often affects the fourth, fifth, or sixth vertebra.

For the most part, a cervical dislocation produces the same signs as a fracture. Both usually result in considerable pain, spasm, deformity, and a degree of paralysis. The most classic difference is the position of the neck in a dislocation. A unilateral dislocation causes the neck to be tilted toward the dislocated side with extreme muscle tightness on the elongated side and a relaxed muscle state on the shortened side. This condition varies from that of wryneck, or traumatic torticollis, in which the tilted side has the spasmed muscle and the elongated side does not evidence contraction.

Spinal cord and nerve injuries

The trainer should always be cautious about neck and back injuries, since they may cause paralysis. Because the spinal cord is well protected by a connective tissue sheath, fat, and fluid cushioning, vertebral dislocations and fractures seldom result in paralysis. Nonetheless, every precaution must be taken to prevent such a situation from developing.

The spinal cord and nerve roots may be injured in four basic ways: laceration by bony fragments, hemorrhage (hematomyelia), contusion, and stretching. These may be combined into a single trauma or may act as separate conditions.

Laceration of the cord is usually produced by the combined dislocation and fracture of a cervical vertebra. The jagged edges of the fragmented vertebral body cut and tear nerve roots or the spinal cord and cause varying degrees of paralysis below the point of injury.

Hemorrhage develops from all vertebral fractures and from most dislocations, as well as from sprains and strains. It seldom causes harmful effects in the musculature, extradurally, or even within the arachnoid space, where it dissipates faster than it can accumulate. However, hemorrhage within the cord itself causes irreparable damage.

Contusion in the cord or nerve roots can arise from any force applied to the neck violently but without causing a cervical dislocation or fracture. Such an injury may result from a sudden displacement of a vertebra that compresses the cord and then returns to its normal position. This compression causes an edematous swelling within the cord, resulting in various degrees of damage.

Stretching (cervical nerve stretch syndrome) or cervical nerve pinch is a condition that has received more recognition in recent years than it did previously. Other terms for this condition are cervical radiculitis, "hot shot," or "pinched nerve."[1] The mechanism of injury is one in which a performer receives a violent lateral wrench of the neck from a head or shoulder block. The player complains of a burning sensation extending from the neck down the arm with some numbness and loss of function. In most cases it is speculated that an overriding of the articular facet has caused the electric-shock–like sensation. However, it also may be an indication of a slipped cervical disk or a congenital vertebral defect. Repeated nerve stretch may result in neuritis, muscular atrophy, and permanent damage. This condition requires immediate medical evaluation. After cervical nerve stretch, medical clearance is required before the athlete can return to sports activity. In some cases pathology is such that the athlete must not participate in certain sports. Conditions for returning to the sport consist of above-average neck strength, wearing of protective neckwear, and proper skill in blocking and tackling.[2,3]

Spinal cord shock

Occasionally a situation arises wherein an athlete, after receiving a severe twist or snap of the neck, presents all the signs of a spinal cord injury. He is unable to move certain parts of his body and complains of a numbness and a tingling sensation in his arms. After a short while all these signs leave; the athlete is then able to move his limbs quite freely and has no other symptoms other than a sore neck. This condition is considered a spinal cord shock and is caused by a mild compression of the spinal cord. Athletes in such cases should be cared for in the same manner used for any severe neck injury.

Emergency care of the severe neck injury

In general, the symptoms of serious cervical injuries are point tenderness, pain on movement, deformity, spasm of the anterior and posterior muscles, and paralysis. One or all of the these signs may be present. Once an injury to the neck has been recognized as severe, a physician and an ambulance should be summoned immediately. Primary emergency care involves maintaining normal breathing, treatment for shock, and keeping the athlete quiet and in the position found until medical assistance arrives. Not until the physician has examined the athlete and given his permission should transportation be attempted. The athlete should be transported while lying on his back with the curve of his neck supported by a rolled up towel or pad. Neck stabilization must be maintained throughout transportation, first to the ambulance and then to the hospital, and throughout the hospital procedure.[5] If sta-

bilization is not continued, additional cord damage and paralysis may ensue.

Cervical strains and sprains

The most common neck injuries in sports —strains and sprains—are caused by the same mechanisms that in more violent degrees produce fractures and dislocations. Typical etiological factors are a sudden twist, forced hyperextension, or a traumatic snap of the head. Cervical strains and sprains have the same pathologies as do other, similar injuries. The force required to affect a cervical strain is considerably less than that required for a sprain. The muscles usually involved are the upper trapezius and the sternocleidomastoideus. The strained neck may appear as a wryneck or acute torticollis, in which the muscles on one side are in a state of spasm. The athlete has marked pain in the area of the contraction and continuing down one shoulder. He has extreme limitation of movement in the cervical region.

The sprain displays all the signs of the strained neck but to a much greater degree. Besides injury to the musculature, the sprained neck also produces tears in the major supporting tissue of the ligamentum nuchae and the interspinous and the supraspinous ligaments. Along with a sprain of the neck, an intervertebral disk may be ruptured.

Care is similar for both the neck strain and the neck sprain. The physician should be consulted in cases of all moderate to severe neck conditions. Often x-ray examination is the only means by which cervical dislocations or fractures can be detected. Basic care of strain or sprain involves rest, traction, heat, massage, manipulation, and the protective support provided by a Thomas collar. The amount of rest required depends upon the extent of injury. In most injuries of this type in athletics a period of 2 days to a week is required for recovery.

Traction has been found invaluable for acute neck conditions. It is best applied two or three times daily and in combination with moist heat. The amount of weight to be applied in traction is executed within the pain tolerance of the athlete.

Massage and manipulation help in relieving congested and spasmed muscles. mild kneading of the deep tissue combined with gentle cervical rotation gives soothing relief.

Heat should be given as needed, as should the other therapies. It should be applied in the form of moist heat or analgesic packs. It serves to relieve pain and to increase local circulation. If the injury continues into the chronic stage, ultrasound has been found beneficial.

If the physician desires immobility of the neck or if protection is needed for sports participation, a Thomas collar should be worn.

Contusions of the neck and throat

Blows to the neck are not prevalent in sports, but occasionally an athlete does receive a kick or blow to the throat that can cause varying degrees of injury. Immediately after the trauma, the athlete experiences severe pain and probably coughs spasmodically. He may speak with a hoarse voice and find it difficult to swallow. A fracture of the throat cartilages is rare, but it is possible and may be indicated by the inability to breathe and expectoration of frothy blood. Cyanosis may be present. Throat contusions are extremely uncomfortable and often are frightening to the athlete.

If the more severe signs appear, a physician should be called. In most situations, cold may be applied intermittently to control superficial hemorrhage and swelling, and, after a 24-hour rest period, heat may be applied in the form of moist packs. For the more severe neck contusions, stabilization by means of a well-padded Thomas collar has been found beneficial.

RECONDITIONING OF THE NECK

Before reconditioning exercises are commenced, pain in the neck muscles should have disappeared completely. The first con-

sideration is to restore the neck's normal range of motion or even to increase its flexibility beyond what it was prior to injury. This is best accomplished at first by mild passive stretchings; the athlete should then carry on an active stretching program. After a normal range of motion has been restored, a muscle-strengthening program is instituted.

The head

HEAD INJURIES

Despite its considerable protection, the brain is subject to traumatic injury, and a great many of the head injuries incurred in athletics have serious consequences. For this reason it is necessary to give special consideration to this part of the body. The need of the brain for blood is vital and critical, and a constant flow of blood must be maintained for its survival.

Cerebral concussions

Most traumas suffered by the head are the result of direct or indirect blows and may be classified as concussion injuries. Literally, "concussion" means an agitation or a *shaking from being hit*, and "cerebral concussion" refers to the agitation of the brain by either a direct or an indirect blow. The indirect concussion most often comes either from a violent fall, in which sitting down transmits a jarring effect through the vertebral column to the brain, or from a blow to the chin. In most cases of cerebral concussion there is a short period of unconsciousness having mild to severe results. There is no agreement as to what is actually involved in the "knocked-out" state, although most do agree that unconsciousness comes from a brain anoxia that is caused by constriction of the blood vessels. There is also disagreement as to whether a blow that can produce unconsciousness will also cause brain damage. For the sake of the athlete, it should be assumed that every "knock-out" in sports causes some pathology.[4] Dependent upon the force of the blow and the tolerance of the athlete to

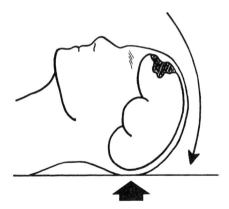

Fig. 20-6. Contrecoup injury of the brain.

withstand such a blow, varying degrees of cerebral hemorrhage, edema, and tissue laceration may occur that in turn will cause pathological changes. Because of the fluid suspension of the brain, a blow to the head can effect an injury either at the point of contact or on the side opposite it. After the head is struck, the brain continues to move in the fluid and may be contused against the opposite side. This causes a *contrecoup type of injury* (Fig. 20-6). An athlete who is knocked unconscious by a blow to the head may be presumed to have received some degree of concussion. Most often the blow simply creates a stunning effect, and the athlete recovers quite rapidly.

In determining the extent of head injury the trainer must be aware of basic gross signs by which concussions may be separated into first, second, and third degrees as follows.

First degree cerebral concussion. A first degree cerebral concussion is considered of mild intensity. An athlete receives a stunning blow to the head or helmet, which causes some temporary amnesia or loss of orientation, and mental confusion. A condition of *automatism* may exist in which the player acts perfectly normal but has no memory of what he is doing at the time. Automatism usually occurs just before there is return to full consciousness. Dizziness, a dull headache, and a ringing in the

ears (tinnitus) may also occur. A groggy player must be taken out of play until free of symptoms.

Second degree cerebral concussion. Considered of moderate intensity, the second degree concussion poses a serious medical problem. The player displays a loss of consciousness for a short interval and fails to relate to events before receiving the head blow. Dizziness, disorientation, tinnitus, transitory neurological signs, and a residual headache are common symptoms. The moderate degree concussion may cause intracranial hemorrhage. Therefore, the athlete must be removed completely from the game and given immediate medical attention. If symptoms persist, the athlete may require 24-hour hospitalization for observation.

Third degree cerebral concussion. The third degree cerebral concussion represents the most serious of the "knocked-out" states. It presents more severe and prolonged signs than do the first and second degrees. Indications may be as follows:

1. *Loss of consciousness* may occur for an extended period, or the athlete may fluctuate between periods of consciousness and unconsciousness.

2. *Retrograde amnesia and disorientation* constitute a condition in which the athlete is unable to remember recent events for a prolonged period or to orient himself to current happenings.

3. *Neurological eye signs* may be present that indicate brain damage. The most prevalent of these are dilated and/or irregular pupils, poor light accommodation by the pupils, blurring of vision, and nystagmus (constant, involuntary movement of the eyeball).

4. *Other neurological signs* include nausea and vomiting, convulsions, coma (deep stupor), and positive Romberg sign. The Romberg test is administered as follows: The athlete is told to stand with his feet together, his arms at his side, and his eyes closed. A positive Romberg sign is indicated if the athlete begins to sway or loses his balance.

5. *Skull fracture signs* that are the most classic are bleeding and the exuding of a clear fluid from the nose and ears.

6. *Paralysis,* the loss of some muscle function or numbness, may indicate brain damage.

Cerebral hemorrhage

A blow to the head can cause intracranial bleeding. It may arise from rupture of an aneurysm or tearing of a sinus separating the two brain hemispheres. Venous bleeding may be slow and insidious, whereas arterial hemorrhage may be evident in a few hours. The athlete may display severe head pains, dizziness, nausea, inequality of pupil size, or sleepiness. Later stages of cerebral hemorrhage display deteriorating consciousness, neck rigidity, depression of pulse and respiration, and convulsions. Of course, this becomes a life-and-death situation necessitating urgent neurosurgical care.

Care of the cerebral concussion

The trainer must be adept at recognizing and interpreting the signs that an unconscious athlete presents. The first concern of the trainer is to clear the athlete's airway and maintain proper breathing. He must then protect the athlete from further injury and treat him for shock.[6] After it has been determined that no fracture of the vertebral column is present, the athlete should be fully awakened as soon as possible to determine the extent of head injury. Applying a cold cloth to the neck and forehead to soothe the athlete and using ammonia fumes directed under his nose are acceptable methods of revival. It may be inadvisable to use ammonia if the athlete is completely unconscious, since the stimulating fumes may cause him to jerk his head and aggravate a spinal fracture. When the athlete becomes conscious, the trainer should proceed to test for orientation by asking him questions about past and present events: "What is your name?" "How old are you?" "Where are we play-

ing?" "What is the score?" "What period is it?" As the trainer talks with the athlete, he should be aware of any pupillary discrepancies, dilation, or irregularities. A check on pupil sizes may be particularly difficult at night and under artificial lights. To ensure accuracy, the trainer should compare the athlete's pupil size with that of an official or player present. It should be remembered, however, that some individuals normally have pupils that differ in size. When he is off the playing field, the athlete should be given the Romberg test.

An athlete with any concussion beyond the first degree might be immediately remanded to the athletic physician for observation. Brain injury may not be apparent until hours after the trauma has been incurred. A postconcussion syndrome can appear gradually with symptoms of prolonged drowsiness, pallor, and neurological signs of injury. The athlete may have to be observed closely throughout the night and be awakened about every 2 hours to check level of consciousness. Any decision dealing with the athlete's immediate disposition lies strictly with the physician.

The first degree concussion, in most cases, requires the athlete to remain out of the contest only until his dizziness and headache have completely subsided. The second degree usually requires that the person have complete rest for 1 or 2 days and no participation in contact sports for 1 to 2 weeks. The athlete with third degree concussion requires rest and close observation for at least 1 week and, depending on medical analysis, no contact activity for a period of 2 weeks to as much as a complete season.

Athletes who have experienced previous episodes of cerebral concussion tend to have a recurrence of this injury. However, it is not fully understood whether this is caused by lack of ability, individual style of play, or other factors.[7] An athlete can be disqualified from his sport if he has suffered two severe concussions that resulted in unconsciousness of 1 minute or longer.

PREVENTION OF BRAIN INJURY

Between the time of the first American football game when Rutgers defeated Princeton on November 6, 1869, and the present, protective game equipment has made a remarkable transition. In its early period, football almost "injured itself out of existence" before the federal government required that preventive measures be taken to reduce the number of injuries. Gear used for head protection has evolved from an inflated rubber crown to the present suspension type of helmet. Each innovation has reduced the number of head injuries and deaths. The suspension helmet holds the head, by a series of straps, within a hard plastic shell and does not come into contact with the cranium. The suspension diffuses each blow to the full shell of the helmet rather than allowing it to be centered at a single point. Current research developments promise to provide even safer helmets than those now in use. A custom-fitting helmet is now available that combines air and liquid in compartments that can be adjusted to individual head characteristics.

SCALP LACERATIONS

Scalp lacerations pose a special problem in care (Fig. 20-7) because of their general inaccessibility. Bleeding is often extensive and makes it difficult to pinpoint the site of the wound. Matted hair and dirt can also disguise the actual point of injury.

Care of the scalp laceration

Materials needed: Antiseptic soap, water, antiseptic, 4-inch guaze pads, sterile cotton, and hair clippers.

Position of the athlete: The athlete lies on the table with the wound upward.

Position of the trainer: The trainer stands at the side of the table facing the injured side of the athlete's head.

Procedure:

1. The entire area of bleeding is thoroughly cleansed with antiseptic soap and water. Washing of the wound is best done lengthwise to remove dirt and debris.

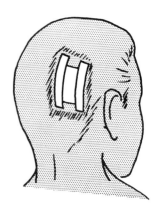

Fig. 20-7. Care of scalp laceration.

2. After cleansing and drying the injury site, it is exposed and, if necessary, the hair is clipped away. Enough scalp should be exposed so that a bandage and tape may be applied.

3. Ethyl chloride or an astringent can be used to reduce bleeding if necessary.

4. Wounds that are more than ½ inch in length and ⅛ inch in depth should be referred to the physician for treatment. In less severe wounds the bleeding should be controlled and an antiseptic applied, followed by the application of a protective coating such as collodion and sterile gauze pad. A tape adherent is then painted over the skin area to ensure that the tape sticks to the skin.

The face

FACIAL INJURIES

Injuries to the face in athletics (Fig. 20-8) are probably exceeded in number only by those conditions that affect the major joints. For discussion here they have been grouped according to the features primarily involved (jaw, nose, eye, ear, etc.).

Injuries to the jaw
Jaw fractures

Fractures of the *lower jaw or mandible* (Fig. 20-9) have their greatest incidence in football and basketball. Because it has relatively little padding and sharp contours,

Fig. 20-8. Situation leading to a serious face injury. (Courtesy Linda Brundige, California State University, Long Beach.)

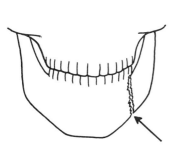

Fig. 20-9. Mandibular fracture.

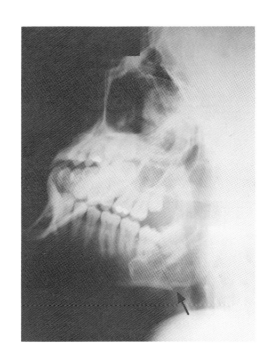

the lower jaw is prone to injury from a direct blow. The most frequently fractured area is that near the frontal angle.

The basic recognition signs for fractures of the lower jaw are bony displacement, abnormal movement, loss of normal occlusion of the teeth (overbite), pain on movement, bleeding around the teeth, and severe point tenderness. Upon recognizing this condition, the trainer should immediately apply ice, immobilize the area by means of a four-tailed bandage, and refer the athlete to the physician.

Fractures about the *upper jaw* usually come from trauma of the crushing type. Football produces the greatest number of these injuries, and the zygoma (cheekbone) is most often involved.

The recognizable signs are swelling, bony displacements, and irregularity on palpation. The trainer should immediately apply a cold compress to the fracture site and refer the athlete to the physician. The athlete should be reminded not to blow his nose because of the possibility of increasing hemorrhage at the injury site.

Jaw dislocations

A dislocation of the jaw, or *mandibular luxation,* involves the temporomandibular joint, which is formed by the condyle of the mandible and the mandibular fossa of the temporal bone. This area has all the features of a hinge and gliding articulation. Because of its wide range of movement and the inequity of size between the mandibular condyle and the temporal fossa, the jaw is somewhat prone to dislocation. The mechanism of injury is usually initiated by a side blow to the open mouth of the athlete, thus forcing the mandibular condyle forward out of the temporal fossa. This injury may occur as either a luxation (complete dislocation) or a subluxation (partial dislocation). The major signs of the dislocated jaw are a locked-open position, with jaw movement being almost impossible, and/or an overriding malocclusion of the teeth.

In cases of first-time jaw dislocation the

main functions of the trainer are to immediately apply a cold compress to control hemorrhage, to splint the jaw by the use of a four-tailed bandage, and to refer the athlete to the physician for reduction. It is not advisable for the trainer to attempt the reduction of a jaw dislocation unless it is of a chronically recurrent type.

Reducing a chronically recurrent dislocation of the jaw. The following method is used to reduce a chronically recurrent jaw dislocation.

Materials needed: Sterile gauze pads to protect the thumbs of the trainer.

Position of the trainer: The trainer faces the athlete. Both thumbs are padded with sterile gauze.

Procedure:

1. The trainer grasps the jaw of the athlete and inserts both thumbs, hooking them over the back molars.

2. The trainer gently presses down on the molars and, depending on the position of the jaw, pushes forward or backward. As the condyles slip back into their fossa, a click may be heard.

Injuries to the nose
Nasal fractures and chondral separation

A fracture of the nose is one of the most common fractures of the face. It appears frequently as a separation of the frontal processes of the maxilla, a separation of the lateral cartilages, or in a combination (Fig. 20-10). The force of the blow to the

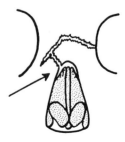

Fig. 20-10. Nasal fracture and separation of cartilage.

nose may either come from the side or be a straight frontal force. A lateral force causes greater deformity than a "straight-on" blow. In nasal fractures hemorrhage is profuse because of laceration of the mucous lining. Swelling is immediate. Deformity is usually present if the nose has received a lateral blow. Gentle palpation may reveal abnormal mobility and emit a grating sound (crepitus).

The trainer should control the bleeding and then refer the athlete to the physician for x-ray examination and reduction of the fracture. Simple and uncomplicated fractures of the nose will not hinder or be unsafe for the athlete, and he will be able to return to competition within a few days if he has adequate protection provided by a tape splinting (Fig. 20-11).

Nose splinting. The following procedure is used for nose splinting.

Materials needed: Two pieces of gauze, each 2 inches in length and rolled to the size of a pencil; 3 strips of 1½-inch tape, cut about 4 inches in length; and clear tape adherent.

Position of the athlete: The athlete lies supine on the training table.

Position of the trainer: The trainer stands facing the athlete's head.

Procedure:

1. The rolled pieces of gauze are placed on either side of the athlete's nose.

2. Gently but firmly, 4-inch lengths of tape are laid over the gauze rolls.

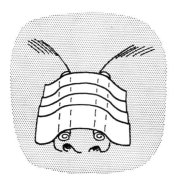

Fig. 20-11. Nose splinting.

Epistaxis (nosebleed)

A nosebleed in athletics is usually caused by a direct blow that effects a varying degree of contusion to the septum. Hemorrhages arise most often from the highly vascular anterior aspect of the nasal septum. In most situations the nosebleed presents only a minor problem, stopping spontaneously after a short period of time. However, there are persistent types that require medical attention and, probably, cauterization.

The general care of the acute nosebleed is as follows:

1. Have the athlete lie on the same side as the bleeding septum, his head comfortably elevated. (In this position the blood will be confined to one nostril.)

2. Place a cold compress over the nose.

3. Have the athlete apply finger pressure to the affected nostril for 5 minutes.

If the above method fails to stop bleeding within 5 minutes, more extensive measures should be taken. With an applicator, paint the hemorrhage point with an astringent or a styptic such as tannic acid or epinephrine hydrochloride solution. The application of a gauze or cotton pledget will provide corking action and encourage blood clotting. If a pledget is used, the ends should protrude from the nostrils at least ½ inch to facilitate removal. After bleeding has ceased the athlete may resume his activity, but he should be reminded not to blow his nose under any circumstances for at least 2 hours after the initial insult.

Foreign body in the nose

During participation the athlete may have insects or debris become lodged in one of his nostrils; if the object is large enough, the mucous lining of the nose reacts by becoming inflamed and swollen. In most cases the foreign body will become dislodged if the nose is gently blown while the unaffected side is pinched shut. Probing and blowing the nose violently will only cause additional irritation. The removal of difficult objects may be aided by placing a few drops of olive or mineral oil into the nostril to soothe and prevent swelling of the mucosa. If oil is unavailable, the application of Neo-Synephrine will help to shrink the mucous membranes.

Injuries to the eye

The eye has many anatomical protective devices. It is firmly retained within an oval socket formed by the bones of the head. A cushion of soft fatty tissue surrounds it, and a thin skin flap (the eyelid), which functions by reflex action, covers the eye for protection. Foreign particles are prevented from entering the eye by the lashes and eyebrows, which act as a filtering system. A soft mucous lining that covers the inner conjunctiva carries and spreads tears, which are secreted by many accessory lacrimal glands. A larger lubricating organ is located above the eye and secretes heavy quantities of fluid through the lacrimal duct to help wash away foreign particles. The eye proper is well protected by the sclera, a tough white outer layer possessing a transparent center portion called the cornea.

If blood is seen in the anterior chamber of the eye a serious condition may exist. Any eye injury deemed serious must be covered with an eye patch and referred immediately to the physician.[8]

Contusion of the eye (orbital hematoma)

Although well protected, the eye may be bruised during sports activity. The severity of eye injuries varies from a mild bruise to an extremely serious condition affecting vision to the fracturing of the orbital cavity. Fortunately, most of the eye injuries sustained in athletics are mild. A blow to the eye may initially injure the surrounding tissue and produce capillary bleeding into the tissue spaces. If the hemorrhage goes unchecked, the result may be a classic "black eye." The signs of a more serious contusion may be displayed in a subconjunctival hemorrhage or in faulty vision.

Care of the eye contusion requires cold application intermittently for at least ½ hour, as well as a 24-hour rest period if the athlete has distorted vision. The following day the trainer may commence heat treatment in the form of hot moist packs, with infrared warming over a moist cloth. Direct exposure to infrared rays must be avoided. Light friction massage will also hasten the absorption of the hematoma. It should be noted that under no circumstances should the athlete blow his nose following an acute eye injury. By doing so he might cause hemorrhaging to be increased.

Foreign bodies in the eye

Foreign bodies in the eye are a frequent occurrence in athletics and are potentially dangerous. A foreign object produces considerable pain and disability. No attempt should be made to rub the body out or to remove it with the fingers. Have the athlete close his eye until the initial pain has subsided and then attempt to determine if the object is in the vicinity of the upper or lower lid. Foreign bodies in the lower lid are relatively easy to remove by depressing

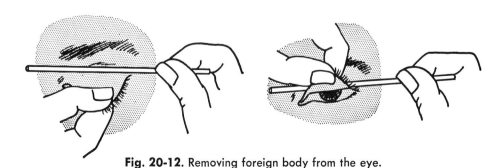

Fig. 20-12. Removing foreign body from the eye.

the tissue and then wiping it with a sterile cotton applicator. Foreign bodies in the area of the upper lid are usually much more difficult to localize. Two methods may be used, the first being quite simple and performed as follows: Gently pull the upper eyelid over the lower lid, as the subject looks downward. This causes tears to be produced, which may flush the object down onto the lower lid. If this method is unsuccessful, the second technique should be used (Fig. 20-12).

Removing a foreign body from the eye— Technique 2. The following is another method that is used for removing a foreign body from the eye.

Materials needed: One applicator stick, sterile cotton-tipped applicator, eyecup, and eyewash (solution of boric acid).

Position of the athlete: The athlete lies supine on a table.

Position of the trainer: The trainer should stand facing the athlete, on the side of the affected eye.

Procedure:

1. Gently pull the eyelid down and lay an applicator stick crosswise at its base.

2. Have the athlete look down; then grasp the lashes and turn the lid back over a stick.

3. Holding the lid and stick in place with one hand, use the sterile cotton swab to lift out the foreign body.

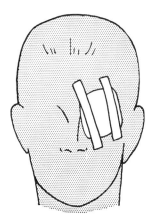

Fig. 20-13. Eye patch.

After the foreign particle is removed, the affected eye should be washed with a boric acid eye solution or with a commercial eyewash. Quite often after debridement there is a residual soreness, which may be alleviated by the application of petroleum jelly or some other mild ointment. If there is extreme difficulty in removing the foreign body or if it has become embedded in the eye itself, the eye should be closed and "patched" with a gauze pad, which is held in place by strips of tape (Fig. 20-13). A complicated eye injury must be referred to the physician as soon as possible.

Protection necessitated by optical defects

The athlete who wears glasses must be protected while he participates. Of course, glasses broken during the heat of competitive battle may pose considerable danger. The eyes of the athlete can be protected by glass guards, case-hardened lenses, plastic lenses, or contact lenses.

A *glass guard* is a metal-rimmed frame that surrounds and fits over the athlete's glasses. The protection the guard affords is excellent, but it does hinder vision in some planes.

Case-hardened lenses are regular glass lenses, of a minimum thickness of 3 millimeters, which have been heat-treated for extra hardness. They are shatterproof and crumble rather than splinter on impact. The cost of this process is relatively low. The only disadvantages involved are that the weight of the glasses is heavier than average, and they may be scratched more easily than regular glasses.

Plastic lenses are made of a hard plastic that can be ground. These lenses are lightweight and nonbreakable. The only drawback is the price; their cost is approximately one half again that of regular glasses.

Contact lenses are one of the most important advances in ophthalmology. Their greatest advantage to the athlete is that they become, in essence, a part of the eye itself and move with it. The main difficulties with contact lenses are their high cost, as compared to regular glasses, and the fact that only certain individuals are able to wear them with comfort and without irritation.[10] Another style of lens—the corneal lens—has been developed that fits more snugly than regular contact lenses. Because there is less chance of loss, these lenses are useful in athletics.

Photochromic lenses are a relatively new development in glasses. These lenses become tinted with a brownish cast on exposure to ultraviolet rays from the sun and then return to clear indoors.

Injuries to the ear

The ear (Fig. 20-14) is concerned with the sense of hearing and equilibrium. It is composed of three parts: the external ear; the middle ear (tympanic membrane) lying just inside the skull; and the internal ear (labyrinth), which is formed, in part, by the temporal bone of the skull. The middle ear and internal ear are structured to carry auditory impulses to the brain. Aiding the organs of hearing and equilizing pressures between the middle and the internal ear is the eustachian tube, a canal that joins the nose and the middle ear.

Athletic injuries to the ear occur most often to the external portion. The external ear is separated into the auricle (pinna) and the external auditory canal (meatus). The auricle, which is shaped like a shell, collects and directs waves of sound into the auditory canal. It is made up of flexible yellow cartilage, muscles, and fat padding, and it is covered by a closely adhering, thin layer of skin. Most of the blood vessels and nerves of the auricle turn around its borders, with just a few penetrating the cartilage proper.

Hematoma auris (cauliflower ear)

Contusions, wrenching, or extreme friction of the ear can lead to the condition of hematoma auris, commonly known as a "cauliflower ear" (Fig. 20-15). This condition usually occurs from repeated injury to the ear and is seen most frequently in boxing and wrestling. However, recently it has been held to a minimum because of the protective measures that have been initiated. Trauma may tear the overlying tissue away from the cartilaginous plate, resulting in hemorrhage and fluid accumulation. A hematoma usually forms before the limited circulation can absorb the fluid. If the hematoma goes unattended, a sequence of coagulation, organization, and fibrosis results in a *keloid* that appears elevated, rounded, white, nodular, and firm, resembling a cauliflower. Quite often it forms in the region of the helix fossa or concha; once developed, the keloid can be removed only by surgery. To prevent this disfiguring condition from arising the trainer should liberally grease with petroleum jelly the ears of the athletes who engage in sports where this condition may occur. He should also insist that they wear ear guards in practice and in competition. If an ear becomes "hot" because of excessive rubbing or twisting, the immediate application of a cold pack to the affected spot will alleviate hemor-

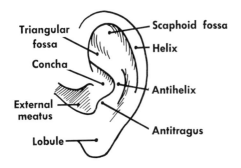

Fig. 20-14. Ear.

Fig. 20-15. Hematoma auris (cauliflower ear).

rhage. Once swelling is present in the ear, special care should be taken to prevent the fluid from solidifying; a cold pack should be placed immediately over the ear and held tightly by an elastic bandage for at least 30 minutes. If the swelling is still present at the end of this time, aspiration by a physician is needed, usually followed by a rigid compress such as the collodion cast, which is worn for approximately 3 days.

Care of the hematoma auris. The following procedure (Fig. 20-16) is designed to prevent the formation of an ear keloid.

Materials needed: Sterile hypodermic needle, sterile cotton, alcohol, 1-inch gauze roll, flexible collodion, 4-inch square of ¼-inch thick felt, and 2-inch elastic wrap.

Procedure:

1. The hematoma is aseptically aspirated by the physician. After the contents of the hematoma have been removed, pressure is applied with sterile cotton for at least 15 to 20 minutes. Pressure with a cold pack may prevent the reentry of fluid more successfully than the use of digital pressure only.

2. After all hemorrhage has ceased, a collodion gauze pack can be applied to effect constant, long-term pressure. A 4-inch square of ¼-inch thick felt is cut to fit around the ear.

3. A collodion-saturated piece of cotton or gauze is packed over and around the injury. The packing should fit smoothly over the ear contours or more irritation may be produced.

4. Cotton is placed over the collodion pack and adjusted to fill the remaining ear spaces.

5. A 2-inch elastic bandage is wrapped around the packed ear and head. The bandage pressure must be both firm and comfortable. The collodion pack should be left in place for at least 3 days for best results. If fluid is still present in the ear after removal of the pack, the pressure should be repeated. Caution must be exercised in the application of a collodion pack, since a poorly applied pack can cause more scarring than no pack at all.

Foreign body in the ear

The ears, as do the nose and eyes, offer an opening in which objects can become caught. Usually these objects are pieces of debris or flying insects. They can become dislodged by having the athlete tilt his head to one side. If removal is difficult, syringing the ear with a solution of lukewarm water may remove the object. Care should be exercised to avoid striking the eardrum with the direct stream of water. Water will also serve to destroy most insects. Probing the ear with various devices will only irritate the mucous lining and cause swelling, thereby lodging the object more tightly. If the above measures are inadequate, referral to the athletic physician should be made.

Swimmers ear

A common condition in athletes engaged in water sports is "swimmers ear," a gen-

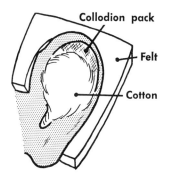
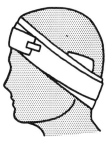

Fig. 20-16. Care of cauliflower ear.

eral expression referring to an ear infection. The athlete may complain of itching, discharge, or even a partial hearing loss. Under these circumstances the athlete should be sent immediately to a physician for treatment. Protection of the athlete with a mild ear infection can be successfully accomplished by plugging the ear with lamb's wool combined with lanolin. Prevention of ear infection can best be attained by drying the ears with a soft towel, cleansing the ears with a mild solution of alcohol, and avoiding those situations that can cause ear infection such as overexposure to cold wind or sticking foreign objects into the ear.[11]

Injuries to the mouth

Athletic injuries to the mouth consist of numerous minor traumas such as contusions, lacerations, and abrasions in and about the lips, and include fractures of the teeth. Although minor in terms of its consequence, the broken tooth not only is disfiguring to the athlete's appearance but also is an expense.

Tooth fracture

The tooth is a composite of mineral salts of which calcium and phosphorus are most abundant. That portion protruding from the gum is called the crown and is covered by the hardest substance within the body, the enamel. The portion that extends into the alveolar bone of the mouth is called the root and is covered by a thin, bony substance known as cementum. Underneath the enamel and cementum lies the bulk of the tooth, a hard material known as dentin. Within the dentin is a central canal and chamber containing the pulp, a substance composed of nerves, lymphatics, and blood vessels that supply the entire tooth. Injuries to the tooth below the gum line may repair themselves because of the abundant blood supply. However, fractures of a tooth below the gum line may not heal if there is an injury to the tooth pulp.

In some cases a tooth that has been knocked out intact can be immediately re-

planted and retained in a healthy state. Teeth in which the enamel or dentin is chipped fail to rejuvenate because they lack a direct blood supply. They may be capped for the sake of appearance. A tooth that is fractured or loosened may be extremely painful because of the damaged or exposed nerve. Immediate relief can be obtained by soaking a piece of cotton in oil of cloves and applying it to the injured tooth. Aspirin gum, when placed over the injured tooth, will also give temporary relief until the athlete can consult a dentist.

Use of mouth protectors

The majority of dental traumas can be prevented by the wearing of a correctly fitted mouth protector (Fig. 20-17). In addition to protecting the teeth it absorbs the shock of chin blows and obviates a possible cerebral concussion. The mouth protector should afford the athlete a proper and tight fit, comfort, unrestricted breathing, and unimpeded speech during competition. A loose mouthpiece will soon be ejected on the ground or be left unused in the locker room. The athlete's air passages should not be obstructed in any way by the mouthpiece. It is best retained on the upper jaw and projects backward only as far as the last molar, thus permitting easy speech. Maximum protection is afforded when the mouth protector is composed of a flexible, resilient material and is form-fitted to the teeth of the upper jaw.

Several commercial protectors are available that can either be self-molded or fitted by a dentist. Many high schools and colleges are now requiring that mouth protectors be worn under certain circumstances.

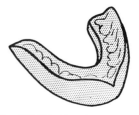

Fig. 20-17. Mouth protector.

Such a protector should be considered as much a part of standard protective equipment as is a helmet or a pad.

Lacerations about the mouth

Lacerations about the mouth usually arise from a blow to the mouth that forces soft tissue against the teeth. The most prevalent lacerations of the mouth occur to the lips and tongue. Deep cuts will need to be sutured by the physician, but most lacerations are minor and will not keep the athlete out of activity.

The trainer, on inspecting this type of injury, should have the athlete rinse his mouth with water and should then examine the teeth for a possible fracture. After the extent of injury has been determined, a solution of hydrogen peroxide is used as an antiseptic and is followed by an astringent-antiseptic solution. Swelling can be controlled by having the athlete suck on an ice cube.

Injuries to the skin

Special consideration must be afforded to skin wounds of the face, as has previously been described for such wounds of the scalp, because of their high vascularity and nearness to the brain. Open wounds may become infected and present extremely serious problems.

Facial abrasions

The many irregular angles of the face make it susceptible to scraping wounds. The face is generally perspiring and dirty during competition and should be cleansed thoroughly with soap and water prior to cleansing and debriding of the abrasion. Debridement is carried out with athletic soap, water, and a brush. Once the wound has been completely cleansed, a mild antiseptic is applied, followed by a medicated ointment to keep the injury moist. A Telfa pad or other nonadhering sterile pad is placed over the ointment and is taped in place. Regular daily checks should be made to ascertain if any infection is present.

Facial lacerations

Because of the many sharp-angled bones of the face, it receives a high percentage of lacerations in athletics. Lacerations especially common to the facial area are those occurring around the orbital socket, particularly at the brow line, and about the chin. As is done with other wounds, the facial laceration is cleansed completely and hemorrhage is controlled by the use of a cold compress, ethyl chloride, or an astringent. Most lacerations about the face can be adequately protected by the trainer until the game is over (Fig. 20-18) and can then be sutured by the physician.

Temporary care of lacerations. The following procedure has been found beneficial in caring for lacerations during competition.

Materials needed: Antiseptic, tape adherent, flexible collodion or plastic spray, butterfly bandages, gauze, and 1-inch tape.

Position of the athlete: The athlete lies on the table, the wound upward.

Position of the trainer: The trainer faces toward the athlete's head, standing alongside the table on the same side as the injury.

Fig. 20-18. Care of facial laceration.

Procedure:

1. After the injury has been washed and dried, it must be shaved if it is in the vicinity of the eyebrow. After the shaving it is again cleansed thoroughly and an antiseptic solution is applied.

2. Tape adherent is painted around the wound, and a coating of flexible collodion is placed directly over the wound.

3. A butterfly bandage stitch is applied across the wound, pulling it together. Two or more butterfly bandage stitches will be needed if the laceration is over ½ inch in length. Each stitch is started below the tear and pulled upward, against gravity, to ensure maximum closure.

4. A gauze bandage is placed lengthwise over the butterfly bandage stitches to give added protection.

REFERENCES

1. Hirata, I., Jr.: The doctor and the athlete, Philadelphia, 1968, J. B. Lippincott Co.
2. Haworth, W. G.: The "nerve pinch" problem—a review, Proceedings of the Eighth National Conference on the Medical Aspects of Sports, Chicago, 1966, American Medical Association, p. 7.
3. Feurig, J. S.: Management of the athlete with a "nerve pinch," Proceedings of the Eighth National Conference on The Medical Aspects of Sports, Chicago, 1966, American Medical Association, p. 13.
4. Van der Noort, G.: Reconditioning and early management of head and neck injuries in football, Proceedings of the Seventh National Conference on the Medical Aspects of Sports, Chicago, 1965, American Medical Association, p. 17.
5. Emergency care and transportation of athletic injuries, Chicago, Ill., 1971, American Academy of Orthopaedic Surgeons.
6. Jackson, F. E.: The treatment of head injuries, Clinical Symposia Ciba, Vol. 19, No. 1, January-February-March 1967.
7. Dickinson, A. L.: The incidence of graded cerebral concussions sustained by athletes participating in intercollegiate football, J. Nat. Athlet. Train. Ass. 2:14, 1967.
8. Allen, J. H.: May's manual of the diseases of the eye, 1968, The Williams & Wilkins Co.
9. Runninger, J.: You can't hit 'em if you don't see 'em, Tennis World, March 1971, p. 54-59.
10. Moyer, S. W.: Contact lens, Tennis World, March 1971, p. 52.
11. Marshall, S.: Ear, nose and throat nursing, London, 1967, Bailiere, Tundall and Lassell.

RECOMMENDED READINGS

Cailliet, R.: Neck and arm pain, Philadelphia, 1964, F. A. Davis Co.

Dolan, J. P., and Holladay, L. J.: Treatment and prevention of athletic injuries, Danville, Ill., 1967, The Interstate Printers and Publishers, Inc.

Emergency care and transportation of the sick and injured, Chicago, 1971, Committee on injuries, American Academy of Orthopaedic Surgeons.

Ferguson, A. B., Jr., and Bender, J.: The ABC's of athletic injuries and conditioning, Baltimore, 1964, The Williams & Wilkins Co.

Hirata, I., Jr.: The doctor and the athlete, Philadelphia, 1968, J. B. Lipincott Co.

McLaughlin, H. L.: Trauma, Philadelphia, 1959, W. B. Saunders Co.

Novich, M. M., and Taylor, B.: Training and conditioning in athletics, Philadelphia, 1970, Lea & Febiger.

Ryan, A. J.: Medical care of the athlete, New York, 1962, McGraw-Hill Book Co.

CHAPTER **21**

Conditions of the shoulder and upper arm

The shoulder

ANATOMY

The shoulder girdle is composed of two bones, the clavicle and the scapula, which form four joints: the sternoclavicular, the acromioclavicular, the coracoclavicular, and the glenohumeral articulations (Fig. 21-1). All except the coracoclavicular are movable joints.

The *clavicle* is a slender bone approximately 6 inches long and shaped like a crank or the letter S. It serves to support the anterior portion of the shoulder, keeping it free from the thoracic cage. It extends from the sternum to the tip of the shoulder where it joins the acromion process of the scapula. The shape of the medial two thirds of the clavicle is primarily circular, whereas its lateral one third takes on a flattened appearance. Also, the medial two thirds bend convexly forward, whereas the lateral third is concave. The point at which the clavicle changes shape and contour presents a structural weakness, and the largest number of fractures to the bone occur at this point. Lying superficially with no muscle or fat protection makes the clavicle subject to direct blows.

The *scapula* is a flat, triangularly shaped bone that serves mainly as an articulating surface for the head of the humerus. It is located on the dorsal aspect of the thorax and has two prominent projections, the spine and the coracoid process. The spine

divides the posterior aspect unequally. The superior dorsal aspect is a deep depression called the supraspinous fossa, and the area below, a more shallow depression, is called the infraspinous fossa. A hooklike projection called the coracoid process arises anteriorly from the scapula. It curves upward, forward, and outward in front of the glenoid fossa, which is the articulating cavity for the reception of the humeral head. The glenoid cavity is situated laterally on the scapula below the acromion.

The head of the *humerus* is spherical with a shallow, constricted neck; it faces upward, inward, and backward, articulating with the scapula's shallow glenoid fossa. Circumscribing the humeral head is a slight groove called the anatomical neck, which serves as the attachment for the articular capsule of the glenohumeral joint. The greater and lesser tuberosities are located adjacent and immediately inferior to the head. The lesser tuberosity is positioned anteriorly and medially, with the greater tuberosity placed somewhat higher and laterally. Lying between the two tuberosities is a deep groove called the bicipital groove, which retains the long tendon of the biceps brachii muscle.

The shoulder complex, consisting of the shoulder girdle and the shoulder joint, is comprised of the four articulations, stabilized and coordinated so that a freely movable unit is produced (Fig. 21-2).

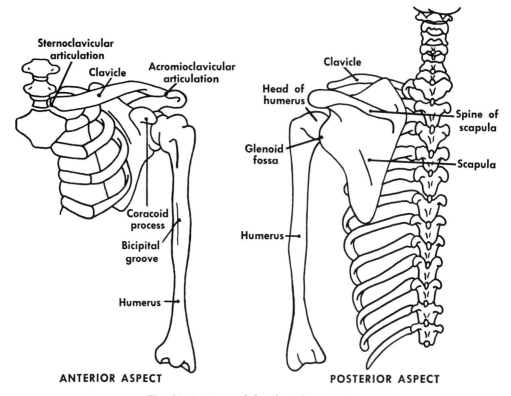

Fig. 21-1. Bones of the shoulder complex.

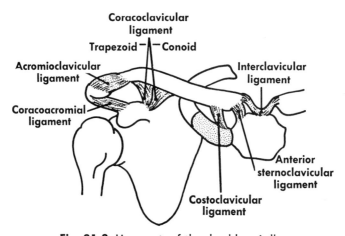

Fig. 21-2. Ligaments of the shoulder girdle.

The clavicle articulates with the manubrium of the sternum to form the *sternoclavicular joint,* the only direct connection between the upper extremity and the trunk. The sternal articulating surface is larger than the sternum, causing the clavicle to rise much higher than the sternum. A fibrocartilaginous disk is interposed between the two articulating surfaces. It functions in the role of a shock absorber against the medial forces and also helps to prevent any displacement upward. The articular disk is placed so that the clavicle moves on the disk, and the disk, in turn, moves separately upon the sternum. The clavicle is permitted to move up and down, forward and backward, in combination, and in rotation.

The sternoclavicular joint is extremely weak because of its bony arrangement, but it is held securely by strong ligaments that tend to pull the sternal end of the clavicle downward and toward the sternum, in effect anchoring it. The main ligaments are the anterior sternoclavicular, which prevents an upward displacement of the clavicle; the posterior sternoclavicular, which also prevents an upward displacement of the clavicle; the interclavicular, which prevents lateral displacement of the clavicle; and the costoclavicular, which prevents lateral and upward displacement of the clavicle.

Some muscular support is given to the sternoclavicular joint by the subclavius, sternocleidomastoid, and sternohyoid muscles.

The *acromioclavicular joint* is a gliding articulation of the lateral end of the clavicle with the acromion process. This is a rather weak junction. A thin, fibrous sleeve surrounds the joint; additional reinforcement is given by the superior and inferior acromioclavicular ligaments and by coracoclavicular ligaments.

The *coracoclavicular joint* is an amphiarthrodial joint, syndesmotic in type, that permits only slight movement. It serves an important function in suspending the scapula and the clavicle and also in giving additional strength to the acromioclavicular joint. The coracoid process and the clavicle are joined by the coracoclavicular ligament, which is divided into the conoid part and the trapezoid part. The coracoclavicular ligament, because of the rotation of the clavicle on its long axis, develops some slack, which permits movement of the scapula at the acromioclavicular joint to take place.

The *glenohumeral joint* (shoulder joint) is an enarthrodial or ball-and-socket joint wherein the round head of the humerus articulates with the shallow glenoid cavity of the scapula (Fig. 21-3). The cavity is deepened slightly by a fibrocartilage rim called the glenoid labrum. Surrounding the articulation is a loose, articular capsule. This capsule is strongly reinforced by the superior, middle, and inferior glenohumeral ligaments and the tough coracohumeral ligament that attaches to the coracoid process and to the greater tuberosity of the humerus. The long tendon of the biceps brachii passes across the head of the humerus and then through the bicipital groove. In the anatomical position the long head of the biceps moves in close relationship with the humerus. The transverse ligament retains the long biceps tendon within the bicipital groove by passing over it from the lesser and the greater tuberosity, converting the bicipital groove into a canal.

Several bursae are located around the shoulder joint, the most important of which is the subacromial (subdeltoid) bursa. This bursa is located between the acromial arch and the capsule and reinforced by the supraspinatus tendon. It is easily subjected to traumatization by the deltoid muscle, which, as it contracts, may force the deeply seated bursa against the acromial shelf.

The muscles that cross the shoulder joint assist in establishing stability to compensate for the weak bony and ligamentous arrangement. They may be separated into two groups, one comprised of the more superficial muscles and the other made up of the deeper muscles. The superficial muscles arise from the thorax and shoulder

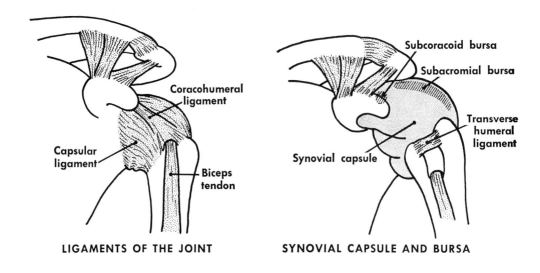

LIGAMENTS OF THE JOINT   SYNOVIAL CAPSULE AND BURSA

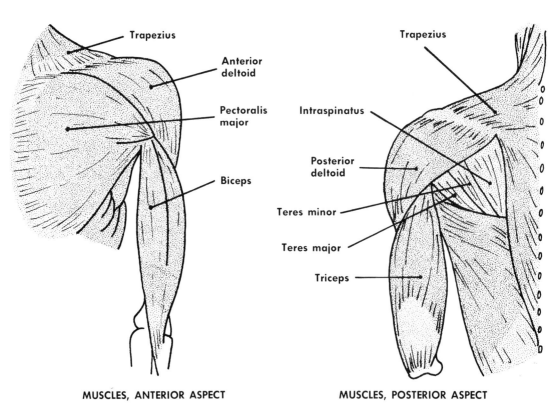

MUSCLES, ANTERIOR ASPECT   MUSCLES, POSTERIOR ASPECT

Fig. 21-3. Anatomy of the shoulder.

girdle and attach to the humeral shaft. They consist of the deltoid, pectoralis major, latissimus dorsi, and teres major. The deeper muscles originate from the scapula and attach to the humeral head. They consist of the supraspinatus, infraspinatus, subscapularis, and teres minor. These four muscles constitute the short rotator muscles, commonly called the *rotator cuff*, whose tendons adhere to the articular capsule and serve as reinforcing structures.

Injuries to the shoulder joint usually result from its structural vulnerability, coupled with its extensive freedom of movement, and a relatively poor correlation between the articular surfaces and the great strength of some of the surrounding musculature.[1]

Movements of the shoulder complex

So that the trainer may have a more comprehensive knowledge of the shoulder and its vulnerability to injury in athletics, there must be an understanding of its complex movements. To assist in the understanding, consider the following analysis of the scapulohumeral rhythm, with the arm moving from the anatomical position through abduction to the vertical position.

All the various components of the shoulder complex must move together rhythmically to perform a specific movement. The ratio of arm movement to scapular movement is considered to be approximately 2 to 1; in other words, 10 degrees of arm movement is comparable to 5 degrees of scapular movement. Although this ratio holds true for a full 0 degree to 180 degrees of scapulohumeral movement, it is variable between individuals. In some persons the scapula will rotate downward before it rotates upward, whereas in other individuals it will remain stabilized for the first 30 degrees. This preparatory period is called "scapular setting."

Throughout the complete 0 degree to 180 degrees of scapulohumeral movement, 120 degrees is attributed to the arm and 60 degrees is considered as being accomplished within the shoulder girdle proper. In the first 90 degrees of movement the arm moves approximately 50 degrees and the shoulder girdle moves 40 degrees, primarily within the sternoclavicular joint. As the arm moves upward it rotates externally to allow the greater trochanter of the humerus to move out of the way of the acromion process; after 135 degrees of move-

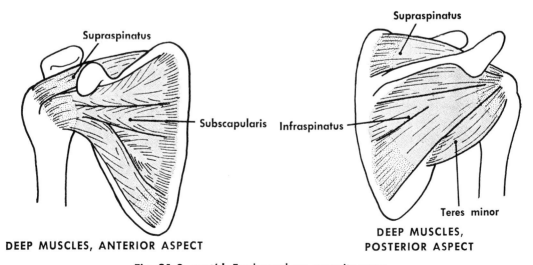

DEEP MUSCLES, ANTERIOR ASPECT

Supraspinatus

Subscapularis

Infraspinatus

Supraspinatus

Teres minor

DEEP MUSCLES, POSTERIOR ASPECT

Fig. 21-3, cont'd. For legend see opposite page.

ment has taken place, or in the last stages of the vertical lift, approximately 20 degrees of motion takes place within the acromioclavicular joint to complete the scapulohumeral rhythm. It also should be noted that the clavicle moves on its long axis posteriorly, in addition to elevating 40 degrees in the sternoclavicular joint and 20 degrees in the acromioclavicular joint. This posterior rotation slackens the coracoclavicular ligament, thus allowing the scapula to move in the acromioclavicular joint.

The muscles moving the arm in the scapulohumeral rhythm of arm abduction are (1) the prime moving muscles of arm abduction: the deltoid, the supraspinatus, and the long head of the biceps when the arm is externally rotated; and (2) the guiding muscles (adductor group): the teres major, the latissimus dorsi, the pectoralis major, the biceps brachii, and the triceps. It is important that the head of the humerus be stabilized and maintained in relationship with the glenoid fossa. This requires application of muscular depression to the head of the humerus by, particularly, the infraspinatus, the teres minor, and the subscapularis, to counteract the upward force of the deltoid muscle. If the depressors were not present, the head of the humerus would be jammed up against the acromion process and would traumatize the soft tissue lying principally between the subacromial bursa and the tendon of the supraspinatus muscle. This depressor action is called a *force couple*.

The muscles moving the shoulder girdle in scapulohumeral rhythm of arm abduction are (1) the prime moving muscles of the shoulder girdle's upward rotation: the upper trapezius, the lower trapezius, and the serratus anterior (considered most important); and (2) the guiding muscles: the rhomboids, major and minor, the levator scapulae, the pectoralis minor, and the subscapularis. The deltoid muscle tends to pull downward on the shoulder girdle when the arm is at the side, and the upper trapezius acts to stabilize the shoulder girdle in the first 30 degrees of arm abduction.

EVALUATING THE SHOULDER COMPLEX

Because of the extreme range of motion produced in the combined action of the shoulder complex, lesions are most easily revealed through mobilization. It must be remembered that 60 degrees of abduction takes place in the shoulder girdle while 120 degrees is executed in the glenohumeral joint. Therefore, to isolate the shoulder girdle and test only the shoulder joint, the scapula must be held steady.[2] Testing should include making a comparison with the normal shoulder to determine individual deviations. Abduction and external rotation are movements that display the most serious limitations from injury, particularly when there is an involvement with the capsular and ligamentous tissue or bursitis. Anterior or posterior flexion of the shoulder joint is seldom limited as a result of injury to surrounding superficial tissue, but the degree of motion will be decreased in respect to internal derangements.[3]

INJURIES TO THE SHOULDER GIRDLE

Injuries to the shoulder girdle in athletics are usually the result of a direct blow or of falling, either on an outstretched arm or upon the point of the shoulder. An outstretched arm, as it strikes the ground, overcomes the protective muscular stability of the shoulder joint and thus transmits a severe force directly against the scapula, causing various pathologies.

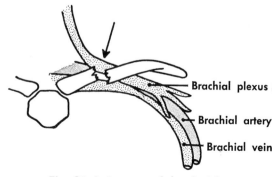

Fig. 21-4. Fracture of the clavicle.

Clavicular fractures

Clavicular fractures (Fig. 21-4) are one of the most frequent fractures in athletics and occur most often to the middle one third, at which point there is a lack of ligamentous support. The cause of the clavicular fracture is either a direct blow or a transmitted force resulting from a fall on the outstretched arm. Fracture of the clavicle in junior and senior high school athletes is most often of the greenstick type.

The athlete with a fractured clavicle usually supports the arm on the injured side and tilts his head toward that side, with his chin turned to the opposite side. On inspection the injured clavicle appears a little lower than the unaffected side. Palpation may also reveal swelling and mild deformity.

The trainer should care for the fracture by immediately applying a sling and swathe bandage (see Fig. 14-15) and treating the athlete for shock, if necessary. He then refers the athlete to the physician, who in most instances will x-ray the area and then apply a shoulder figure-of-eight strapping that will stabilize the shoulder in an upward and backward position.

Fractures of the scapula

Fracture of the scapula is an infrequent injury in athletics (Fig. 21-5). Although the scapula appears extremely vulnerable to trauma, it is well protected by a heavy outer bony border and a cushion of muscle above and below. Those fractures which do occur happen as a result of force applied to the hand, elbow, or shoulder joint. The fracture usually occurs when the humerus carries a force to the scapula, as the serratus anterior muscle violently pulls the scapula forward at the same time. Such a fracture may cause the athlete to have pain on shoulder movement and to display swelling and point tenderness. When this injury is suspected, the athlete should be given a supporting sling and sent directly to the athletic physician.

Sprains of the clavicle
Sternoclavicular sprains

A sternoclavicular sprain (Fig. 21-6) is a relatively uncommon occurrence in athletics, but occasionally one may result from one of the various traumas affecting the shoulder girdle. The mechanism of the injury can be initiated by an indirect force transmitted through the humerus of the shoulder joint, by a direct violence such as a blow that strikes the poorly padded clavicle, or by a twisting or torsion of a posteriorly extended arm.[4] Depending upon the direction of force, the medial end of the clavicle can be displaced upward and forward, either posteriorly or anteriorly. Generally the clavicle is displaced upward and forward, slightly anteriorly.

Trauma resulting in a sprain to the sternoclavicular joint can be described in three degrees. The *first degree* is characterized by little pain and disability with some point tenderness but with no joint laxity. A *second degree* sprain displays subluxation of the sternoclavicular joint with visible de-

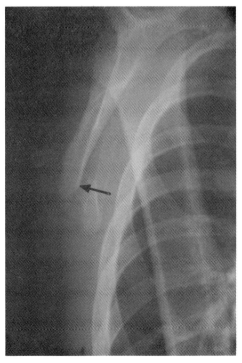

Fig. 21-5. Scapular fracture.

Fig. 21-6. Sternoclavicular sprain.

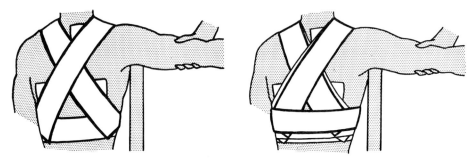

Fig. 21-7. Sternoclavicular immoblization.

formity and swelling, an inability to abduct the shoulder full range or to bring the arm across the chest, indicating disruption of stabilizing ligaments. The *third degree,* which is the most severe, presents a picture of complete dislocation with gross displacement of the clavicle at its sternal junction, swelling, and disability indicating complete rupture of the sternoclavicular and costoclavicular ligaments. If the clavicle is displaced posteriorly, pressure may be placed on the blood vessels, on the esophagus, or on the trachea, causing a life or death situation.

Care of this condition is based upon returning the displaced clavicle to its original position, which is done by the physician, and immobilizing it at that point so that healing may take place. A deformity, primarily caused by the organization of scar tissue at that point, is usually apparent after healing is completed. There is no loss of function. Immobilization (Fig. 21-7) is usually maintained for a period of 3 to 5 weeks and then is followed by graded reconditioning exercises. It should be noted that there is a high incidence of recurrence in this type of dislocation.

Sternoclavicular immobilization. The following is a suggested procedure for the immobilization of the sternoclavicular dislocation.

Materials needed: A felt pad of ¼ inch thickness, cut to a circumference of 4 inches, 3-inch roll of elastic tape, 2 gauze pads, and tape adherent.

Position of the athlete: Reduction of the most common sternoclavicular dislocation is performed by traction with the athlete's arm in an abducted position. With traction and abduction maintained by an assistant, the immobilization strapping is applied.

Position of the trainer: The trainer stands on the affected side of the athlete.

Procedure:

1. An anchor strip is applied around the chest at the level of the tenth rib while the chest is expanded.

2. A felt pad is laid over the sterno-clavicular joint and gauze pads are applied over the athlete's nipples.

3. Depending upon the direction of displacement, tape pressure is applied over the felt pad. With the most common dislocation (that which is upward, forward, and anterior) strapping is started from the back, moving forward over the shoulder. The first pressure strip is taken from the anchor tape on the unaffected side and crosses over the injured site to finish on the front anchor strip.

4. A second strip is taken from the anchor strip on the affected side and crossed over the unaffected side to finish on the front anchor strip.

5. As many series of strips are applied as are needed to give complete immobilization. All series are locked in place by a tape strip placed over the ends.

Acromioclavicular sprain (separated shoulder)

The acromioclavicular joint is extremely vulnerable to sprains among active sports participants. Its mechanism is most often induced by a direct blow to the tip of the shoulder, pushing the acromion process downward, or by an upward force exerted against the long axis of the humerus (Fig. 21-8). The position of the arm during indirect injury is one of adduction and partial flexion.[5] Depending upon the extent of ligamentous involvement, the acromioclavicular sprain is graded as first, second, or third degree (Fig. 21-9).

The *first degree* acromioclavicular sprain reflects point tenderness and discomfort on movement at the junction between the acromion process and the outer end of the clavicle. There is no deformity, indicating only an incomplete tear or stretching of the acromioclavicular ligaments.

A *second degree* sprain indicates rupture of the supporting superior and inferior acromioclavicular ligaments. There is a definite displacement and prominence of the lateral end of the clavicle when compared to the unaffected side. In this moderate

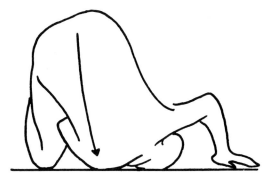

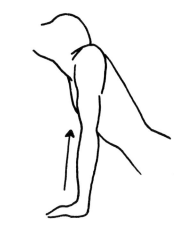

Fig. 21-8. Common mechanisms of the acromioclavicular sprain.

sprain there is point tenderness on palpation of the injury site, and the athlete is unable to fully abduct or to bring the arm across the chest.

Although occurring infrequently, the *third degree* injury is considered a dislocation involving rupture of the acromioclavicular and coracoclavicular ligaments. The mechanics of a completely separated shoulder consist most often of a direct blow that forces the acromion process downward, backward, and inward while the clavicle is pushed down against the rib cage. In such an injury there is gross deformity and prominence of the outer clavicular head, severe pain, loss of movement, and instability of the shoulder girdle.

Immediate care of the acromioclavicular sprain involves three basic procedures: (1) cold and pressure to control local hemor-

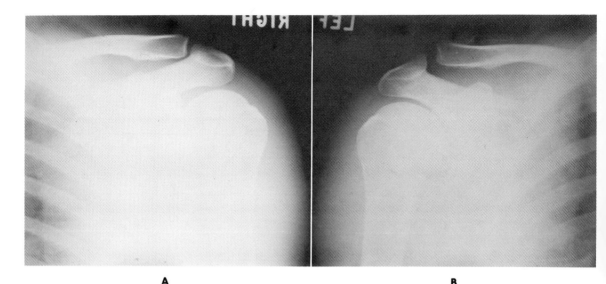

A   **B**

Fig. 21-9. A comparison of a normal, **A**, with a separated, **B**, shoulder.

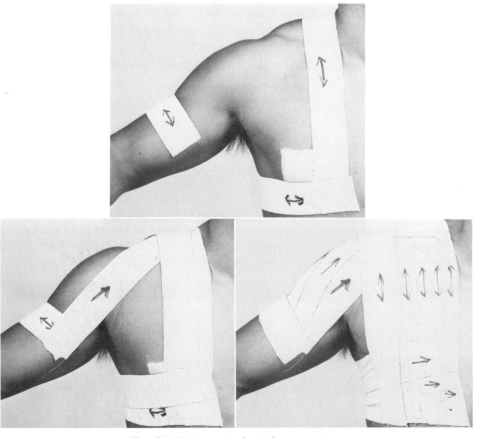

Fig. 21-10. Acromioclavicular strapping.

rhage, (2) stabilization of the joint by a sling and swathe bandage, and (3) referral to the physician for definitive diagnosis and treatment. Complete severance of the coracoclavicular ligament, in most instances, demands corrective surgery. Most second degree sprains require from 4 to 6 weeks for fibrous healing to take place, and an extended period of time is needed for the restoration of general shoulder strength and mobility. A regimen of superficial moist heat will aid in resolving soreness.

Protective acromioclavicular strapping. Protective acromioclavicular strapping (Fig. 21-10) is designed to stabilize the acromioclavicular articulation in proper alignment and still allow normal movement of the shoulder complex.

Materials needed: One ¼-inch thick felt pad, roll of 2-inch adhesive tape, tape adherent, 2-inch gauze pad, and 3-inch elastic bandage.

Position of the athlete: The athlete sits in a chair with the affected arm resting in a position of abduction.

Position of the trainer: The trainer stands facing the athlete's abducted arm.

Procedure:

1. Three anchor strips are applied: the first, a three-quarter circle, is applied just below the deltoid muscle, the second applied just below the nipple and encircling half of the chest, and the third laid over the trapezius muscle near the neck and then attached to the second anchor in front and back.

2. The first and second strips of tape are applied from the front and back of the first anchor, crossing each other at the acromioclavicular articulation and attaching to the third anchor strip.

3. The third support strip is placed over the ends of the first and second pieces, following the line of the third anchor strip.

4. A fourth support strip is laid over the second anchor strip.

5. This basketweave pattern is continued until the entire shoulder complex is covered. It is then followed by a shoulder spica with an elastic bandage.

Contusions about the shoulder girdle

Subcutaneous areas of the shoulder girdle are subject to bruising in contact sports. The most vulnerable to contusion is the enlarged lateral end of the clavicle (acromial end), which forms a projection just before it joins the acromion process. Contusions of this type are often called "shoulder points," and they may cause the athlete severe discomfort. Contusion to the lateral end of the clavical causes a bone bruise and subsequent irritation to the periosteum. On initial inspection this injury may be mistaken for a first degree acromioclavicular separation.

A cold compress is applied for 1 hour, together with mild immobilization exercises. There need be no loss of time from contact activity if the athlete is well protected by a sponge rubber doughnut.

INJURIES TO THE SHOULDER JOINT

Because of the shoulder joint's extreme looseness and lack of structural protection, it is subject to various acute and chronic conditions produced by athletic participation.

Fractures of the upper humerus

Fractures of the upper humerus (Fig. 21-11) pose considerable danger to nerves and vessels of that area. Such fractures can result from a direct blow, a dislocation, or the impact received in falling onto the outstretched arm. Various parts of the end of the humerus may be involved such as the anatomical neck, the tuberosities, or the surgical neck. The greatest number of fractures take place at the surgical neck.

Recognition of a fracture by visual inspection alone may be difficult. Therefore x-ray examination gives the only positive proof. Some of the more prevalent signs that may be present are pain, inability to move the arm, swelling, point tenderness, and discoloration of the superficial tissue. Because of the close proximity of the axillary blood vessels and the brachial plexus, a fracture to the upper end of the humerus may result in severe hemorrhaging or paralysis. Therefore, a suspected fracture of this type warrants immediate support, by the use of a sling and swathe bandage, and referral to the physician. Incapacitation may range from 2 to 6 months.

Epiphyseal fracture

Epiphyseal fracture of the head of the humerus (Fig. 21-12) is much more common in the young athlete than is a bone fracture.[6] It is caused by a direct blow or by an indirect force traveling along the length of the axis of the humerus. This condition causes shortening of the arm, disability, swelling, point tenderness, and pain. There may also be a false joint. The trainer should suspect this type of injury when the above signs appear in young athletes. He should provide splinting and im-

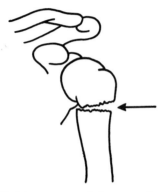

Fig. 21-11. Fracture of the upper humerus.

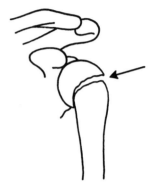

Fig. 21-12. Epiphyseal fracture.

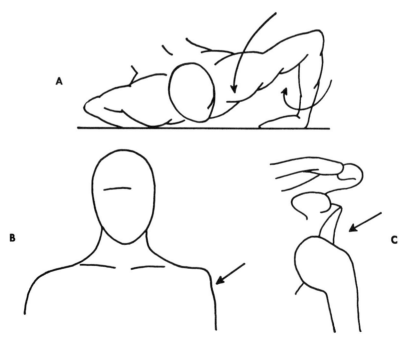

Fig. 21-13. A, Typical mechanism producing an anterior glenohumeral dislocation. **B,** External appearance of the anterior glenohumeral dislocation. **C,** Anterior glenohumeral dislocation.

mediately refer the athlete to a physician. Healing is initiated rapidly; immobilization is necessary for only about 3 weeks. The main danger of an injury such as this lies in the possibility of damage to the epiphyseal growth centers of the humerus.

Dislocations of the humeral head

Dislocation of the humeral head (Fig. 21-13) is second only to finger dislocations in order of incidence in athletics. The extreme range of all the possible movements makes the shoulder joint highly susceptible to dislocation. Displacements usually occur either forward, as a subcoracoid dislocation, or—second—in order of incidence—downward, as a subglenoid dislocation.

Anterior glenohumeral dislocation

The anterior glenohumeral dislocation or subcoracoid dislocation is most often caused when an arm is abducted and externally rotated. An abnormal force to an arm that is executing a throw or an arm tackle can produce a sequence of events resulting in a severe shoulder strain or dislocation. Less often a fall or inward rotation and abduction of an arm may result in serious shoulder joint injury.

The head of the humerus is forced out of its articular capsule in a forward direction past the glenoid labrum and then upward to rest under the coracoid process. The scope of the pathology is quite extensive, with torn capsular and ligamentous tissue, possibly tendinous avulsion of the rotator cuff muscles, and profuse hemorrhage. Additional complications may arise if the head of the humerus comes into contact with and injures the branchial nerves and vessels. The bicipital tendon also may be pulled from its canal as the result of a rupture of the transverse ligament.

The athlete with an anterior dislocation displays a flattened or indented deltoid contour. Palpation of the axilla will reveal a prominence of the humeral head. The athlete carries his affected arm in slight abduction and is unable to touch the opposite shoulder with the hand of the affected arm.

Care of the shoulder dislocation requires immediate reduction, control of the hemorrhage by cold packs, immobilization, and the start of muscle reconditioning as soon as possible. The question often arises as to whether the trainer should reduce a first-time dislocation or wait for medical attention. *Physicians agree that a first-time dislocation may be associated with a fracture, and, therefore, it is beyond the scope of a trainer's duties.* Recurrent dislocations do not present the same complications or attendant dangers as the acute type; however, risk is always involved.

Reduction of the shoulder dislocation

Reduction of the anterior dislocation of the glenohumeral joint usually consists of straight traction on the abducted arm, with a slight external and internal movement as pressure is applied to the axilla by the operator. Because of the possibility of fracture and associated nerves and blood vessels in the shoulder region, only the physician should employ this *heel-in-axilla technique.*

A more conservative method of reduction, which is particularly valuable in the care of subluxation and recurrent dislocations, is the *weight-in-hand technique.* With this method the athlete lies between two tables, his head resting on one and his body on the other. The affected arm is between the tables grasping a 5- to 10-pound weight.[7] As the musculature relaxes about the shoulder from the force of the weight, spontaneous reduction takes place.

After reduction the shoulder is maintained in an immobilized position of internal rotation for a period of 1 to 2 weeks, followed by 1 or more weeks of sling support. Exercise should be started as soon as possible within the limitations of pain, and there should be an avoidance of raising the arm in abduction more than 90 degrees to prevent recurrent dislocation. The athlete may return to competition when his shoulder has regained normal strength and is

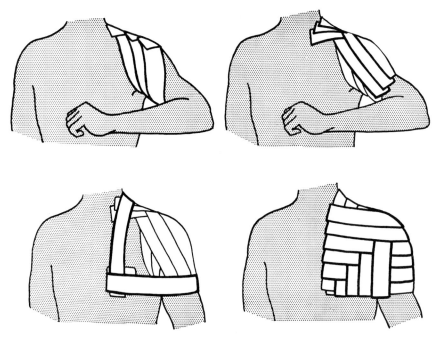

Fig. 21-14. Strapping for shoulder support and restraint.

without pain. It is suggested that a support and restraint strapping be used for the rest of the season to prevent recurrence of the injury (Fig. 21-14).

Strapping for shoulder support and restraint. This strapping is designed to support the soft tissues of the shoulder complex and to restrain the arm from abducting more than 90 degrees.

Materials needed: One roll of 2-inch tape, 2-inch gauze pad, cotton pad, tape adherent, and 3-inch elastic bandage.

Position of the athlete: The athlete stands with the affected arm flexed at the elbow and the shoulder internally rotated.

Position of the trainer: The trainer stands facing the affected arm.

Procedure:

1. The first phase is designed to support the capsule of the shoulder joint. After a cotton pad has been placed in the axilla, a series of 3 loops around the shoulder joint is applied by the trainer. The first loop is started at the top of the athlete's scapula, is pulled forward across the acromion process, around the front of the shoulder, back underneath the axilla and over the back of the shoulder, crossing the acromion process again, and then is terminated at the clavicle. Each of the subsequent strips is begun down the shoulder one half the width of the preceding strip.

2. Strips of tape are next run upward from a point just below the insertion of the deltoid muscle and crossed over the acromion process, completely covering the outer surface of the shoulder joint.

3. Before the final application of a basketweave shoulder strapping, a gauze pad is placed over the nipple area. A strip of tape is laid over the shoulder near the neck and is carried to the nipple line in front and to the scapular line in back.

4. A second strip is taken from the end of the first strip, around the middle of the upper arm and ending at the back end of the first strip.

5. The above alternation is continued with an overlapping of each preceding strip by at least one half its width until the shoulder has been completely capped.

6. A shoulder spica is applied to maintain the strapping in place.

Downward glenohumeral dislocation

Among shoulder joint dislocations the downward glenohumeral or subglenoid dislocation is second to the subcoracoid type, but it is relatively uncommon. It is mainly caused by a hyperabduction of the arm, which forces the head of the humerus to a position below the glenoid cavity. The resultant pathology is a tear on the inferior aspect of the capsule and a rupture of the rotator cuff tendons, accompanied by profuse internal hemorrhaging.

The signs of the downward glenohumeral or subglenoid dislocation are similar to those of the subcoracoid dislocation, except that the arm appears to be longer. Reduction is usually accomplished by upward and outward traction.

Recurrent shoulder dislocations (chronic or "trick" shoulder)

It has been estimated that the majority of anterior glenohumeral dislocations to active persons under 20 years of age will recur. This traumatic repetition can be attributed to the violence that originally injured the glenoid labrum, weakened the articular capsule, and stretched the specific muscle tendon that attaches to the head of the humerus. Every protection should be given to the athlete who may be prone to recurrent dislocation. Restraint by means of adhesive strapping and a harness appliance should be used during any sports activity. Repeated dislocations continue to additionally stretch the supporting structures and damage the articulating hyaline cartilage, sometimes to an extent that may eventually result in an arthritic condition. Corrective surgery is often employed to reestablish joint continuity.

Contusions, strains, and sprains of the shoulder joint

Contusions, strains, and sprains to the soft tissue around the shoulder joint are common in athletics. Injuries of these kinds are usually attributed to either football or wrestling.

Contusions to the shoulder joint most often affect the deltoid muscle. Characteristically, bruises of this type result in pain, swelling, and a mild to moderate disability. Recognition is based on identification of limited function and superficial point tenderness.

Strains to the musculature of the shoulder joint frequently affect the deltoid superficially and affect the tendons of the rotator cuff internally. The principal rotator cuff tendon injured is that of the supraspinatus muscle. The mechanism of shoulder strains occurs mainly as the result of a violent pull to the arm, an abnormal rotation, or a fall upon the outstretched arm, tearing or even rupturing tendinous tissue. A tear or complete rupture of one of the *rotator cuff tendons* (the subscapularis, supraspinatus, infraspinatus, or teres minor) produces an extremely disabling condition in which pain, loss of function (particularly with the arm in abduction or external rotation), swelling, and point tenderness are indicative symptoms. Passive movements in a strained condition seldom yield pain.

Sprains of the shoulder joint involve injury to the articular capsule. Pathology of the sprain is comparable to that of the internal strain and often affects the rotator cuff tendons. The cause of this injury is the same as that which effects dislocations and strains—a violent force transmitted through the long axis of the humerus.

The pathologies resulting from the contusion, strain, or sprain are similar but of different intensities in terms of edema and blood extravasation. Pathology from contusions is usually superficial, whereas that from sprains and strains is internal. There is a fine line of distinction in identifying the strain and the sprain. The only basic difference is that a sprain will result in pain on passive movement, whereas a strain produces pain only on active movement.

Care after acute trauma to the shoulder

joint requires use of a cold pack for at least 24 hours, an elastic or adhesive compression, rest, and immobilization by means of a sling. After hemorrhage has subsided, heat and massage may be added, and mild passive and active exercise is advocated for regaining a full range of motion. Once the shoulder can execute a full range of movement without signs of pain, a resistance exercise program should be initiated. Any traumatic injury to the shoulder joint can lead to a subacute and chronic condition of either synovitis or bursitis, which in the absence of shoulder movement will allow muscle contractures, adhesions, and atrophy to develop, resulting in an ankylosed shoulder joint (see Chapter 15).

Shoulder synovitis; bursitis

The shoulder joint is subject to subacute chronic inflammatory conditions resulting from trauma or from overuse in an abnormal fashion. An injury if this type may develop from a direct blow, a fall upon the outstretched hand, or the stress incurred in throwing an object. Inflammation can occur in the shoulder, extensively affecting the soft tissues surrounding it or specifically affecting various bursae. The bursa that is most often injured is the subacromial, which lies underneath the deltoid muscle and the articular capsule and extends under the acromion process. The apparent pathology in these conditions is fibrous and fluid accumulation developing from a constant inflammatory state.

The recognition of these conditions follows the same course as in other shoulder affections. The athlete is unable to move his shoulder, especially in abduction; rotation and muscle atrophy also may ensue because of disuse.

Care of low-grade inflammatory conditions must be initiated somewhat empirically. In some instances both the superficial heat from moist pads or infrared rays and the deep heat of diathermy or ultrasound are beneficial. In other instances heat may be aggravating, and cold applications by cold pack found more useful.

Whatever the mode of treatment, the athlete must maintain a consistent program of exercise, with the emphasis placed on regaining a full range of motion, so that muscle contractures and adhesions do not immobilize the joint.

The *"frozen shoulder"* is a condition more characteristic of an older person than it is of a young athlete, but occasionally it does occur in the athlete. It results from a chronically irritated shoulder joint that has been improperly cared for. A constant, generalized inflammation causes a degeneration of the soft tissues in the vicinity of the shoulder joint, resulting in an extreme limitation of movement. The main care of the "frozen shoulder" is a combination of deep heat therapy and mobilization exercise. Corticosteroid injections also have been found to be beneficial.

Bicipital tenosynovitis

Tenosynovitis of the long head of the biceps is common among athletes who execute a throwing movement as part of their event. It is more prevalent among pitchers, tennis players, and javelin throwers, for whom the repeated forced internal rotations of the upper arm may, in some cases, produce a chronic inflammatory condition in the vicinity of the synovial sheath of the long head of the biceps.[6,8] A complete rupture of the transverse ligament, which holds the biceps in its groove, may take place, or a constant inflammation may re-

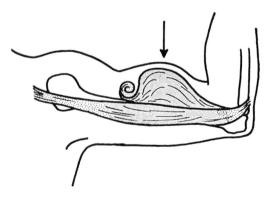

Fig. 21-15. Biceps brachii rupture.

sult in degenerative scarring. The athlete may complain of an ache in the anterior and medial areas of the shoulder; palpation reveals point tenderness in the region of the bicipital tendon.

Such conditions are best cared for by a period of complete rest for 1 to 2 weeks, with daily applications of moist heat, diathermy, or ultrasound combined with massage. After the initial aching has gone, a gradual program of reconditioning is begun.

Biceps brachii ruptures

Ruptures of the biceps brachii (Fig. 21-15) occur mainly in gymnasts who are engaged in power moves on the rings. The rupture commonly takes place near the origin of the muscle. The athlete usually hears a resounding snap and feels a sudden, intense pain at the point of injury. A protruding bulge may appear near the middle of the biceps. When asked to flex his affected arm, the gymnast displays a definite weakness in that area. The trainer should immediately apply a cold pack for hemorrhage control, place the athlete's arm in a sling, and refer him to the physician. Surgical repair is usually indicated.

RECONDITIONING OF THE SHOULDER

Both the shoulder girdle and the shoulder joint acquire contractures of tissue quite readily after injury. Therefore, the program of reconditioning should begin almost immediately after sprains or strains have been incurred. The primary movements of normal abduction and external rotation must be maintained for basic shoulder functions. The exercise program may be divided into three phases. The first phase is concerned with the prevention of rotator cuff atrophy and involves numerous, nongravity, pendular movements daily until all pain and irritation have subsided. The second phase is concerned with utilizing full active movements that not only will restore the complete range of motion but also will strengthen the weakened muscles. The third phase begins after complete mo-

bility has been attained; it consists of a progressive resistance exercise program to continue the reconstitution of muscular strength.

The upper arm

Fractures of the shaft of the humerus

Fractures of the humeral shaft (Fig. 21-16) happen occasionally in athletics, usually as the result of a direct blow or a fall upon the arm. The type of fracture is usually comminuted or transverse, and deformity is often produced because the bone fragments override each other as a result of strong muscular pull.

The pathology is characteristic of most uncomplicated fractures, with the exception that there may be a tendency for the radial nerve, which encircles the humeral shaft, to be severed by jagged bone edges, resulting in radial nerve paralysis and causing a wrist drop and an inability to perform forearm supination.

Upon recognizing this injury, the trainer should immediately apply a splint, treat the athlete for shock, and refer him to the physician. The athlete will be out of competition for approximately 3 to 4 months.

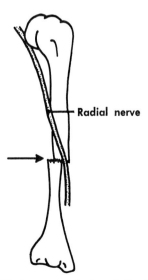

Radial nerve

Fig. 21-16. Fracture of the shaft of the humerus.

Contusions of the upper arm

Contusions of the upper arm are frequent in contact sports. Although any muscle of the upper arm is subject to bruising, the area most often affected is the lateral aspect, primarily the brachialis and portions of the triceps and biceps muscles. Bruises to this area can be particularly handicapping, especially if the radial nerve is contused through forceful contact with the humerus, producing a transitory paralysis and consequently an inability to use the extensor muscles of the forearm.

Cold and pressure should be applied from 1 to 24 hours followed by superficial heat therapy and massage. In most cases this condition responds rapidly to treatment, usually within a few days. If swelling and irritation last more than 2 or 3 weeks, *myositis ossificans* may have been stimulated, and massage must be stopped and protection afforded the athlete during athletic participation.

Strains of the upper arm

Strains of the arm are extremely frequent in athletics, the muscles particularly involved being the biceps and the triceps.[9] Classically, all strains should be treated immediately with cold and pressure to be followed by gradually increased heat therapy.

REFERENCES

1. Markee, J. E.: Anatomy of the shoulder, Proceedings of the Sixth National Conference on the Medical Aspects of Sports, Chicago, 1964, American Medical Association, p. 5.
2. Prior, John A., and Silberstein, Jack S.: Physical diagnosis, St. Louis, 1969, The C. V. Mosby Co.
3. Brewer, B. J.: Injury to the shoulder in throwing sports, Proceedings of the Sixth National Conference on Medical Aspects of Sports, Chicago, 1964, American Medical Association, p. 11.
4. Hoyt, W. A., Jr., and Bailey, S. B.: Etiology of contact injuries to the shoulder, Proceedings of the Sixth National Conference on the Medical Aspects of Sports, Chicago, 1964, American Medical Association, p. 13.
5. Hughston, J. E.: Treatment and rehabilitation of shoulder injuries in athletics, Proceedings of the Sixth National Conference on the Medical Aspects of Sports, Chicago, 1964, American Medical Association, p. 16.
6. Collins, H. R., and Evarts, C. M.: Injuries to the adolescent athlete, Med. Digest, November 1971, p. 50.
7. O'Donoghue, D. H.: Treatment of injuries to athletes, Philadelphia, 1970, W. B. Saunders Co.
8. Tullos, H. S., and King, J. W.: Lesions of the pitching arm, J.A.M.A. **220:**264, 1972. p. 264.
9. Brewer, B. J.: The throwing arm—soft tissue injury. In American Academy of Orthopaedic Surgery: Symposium on Sports Medicine, 1967, St. Louis, 1969, The C. V. Mosby Co.

RECOMMENDED READINGS

Bateman, J. E.: Shoulder injuries in the throwing sports. In American Academy of Orthopaedic Surgeons: Symposium on Sports Medicine, 1967, St. Louis, 1969, The C. V. Mosby Co.

Brewer, B. J.: The throwing arm—soft tissue injury. In American Academy of Orthopaedic Surgeons: Symposium on Sports Medicine, 1967, St. Louis, 1969, The C. V. Mosby Co.

Cailliet, R.: Neck and arm pain, Philadelphia, 1964, F. A. Davis Co.

Colson, J. H., and Williams, J. A.: Sports injuries and their treatment, Philadelphia, 1961, J. B. Lippincott Co.

Ferguson, A. B., Jr., and Bender, J.: The ABC's of athletic injuries and conditioning, Baltimore, 1964, The Williams & Wilkins Co.

Hirata, I., Jr.: The doctor and the athlete, Philadelphia, 1968, J. B. Lippincott Co.

Litton, L. O., and Peltier, L. F.: Athletic injuries, Boston, 1963, Little, Brown & Co.

McLaughlin, H. L.: Trauma, Philadelphia, 1959, W. B. Saunders Co.

Nicholas, J. A.: Athletic injuries to the upper extremity. In American Academy of Orthopaedic Surgeons: Symposium on Sports Medicine 1967, St. Louis, 1969, The C. V. Mosby Co.

Novich, M. M., and Taylor, B.: Training and conditioning in athletic, Philadelphia, 1970, Lea & Febiger.

O'Donoghue, D. H.: Treatment of injuries to athletes, Philadelphia, 1970, W. B. Saunders Co.

Prior, J. A., and Silberstein, J. S.: Physical diagnosis, St. Louis, 1969, The C. V. Mosby Co.

Ryan, A. J.: Medical care of the athlete, New York, 1962, McGraw-Hill Book Co.

Saha, A. K.: Theory of shoulder mechanism: Discriptive and applied, Springfield, Ill., 1961, Charles C Thomas, Publisher.

CHAPTER **22**

Conditions of the elbow, forearm, wrist, and hand

The elbow joint

ANATOMY

The elbow joint is composed of three bones: the humerus, the radius, and the ulna (Fig. 22-1). The lower end of the humerus forms two articulating condyles. The lateral one is the capitulum and the medial one is called the trochlea. The rounded capitulum articulates with the concave head of the radius. The trochlea, which is spool-shaped, fits into an articulating groove, the semilunar notch, provided by the ulna, between the olecranon and coronoid processes. Above each condyle is a projection called the epicondyle. The structural design of the elbow joint is such that flexion and extension are permitted by the articulation of the trochlea with the semilunar notch of the ulna. Forearm pronation and supination are made possible by the fact that the head of the radius rests against the capitulum freely without any bone limitations. The main support band of the radial head is the annular ligament, which forms a cuplike structure. Within the cup of the annular ligament the radius is permitted to move on its long axis but is restricted from anterior and posterior movement.

The reinforcing ligaments of the elbow are the radial and ulnar collateral ligaments. A common synovial membrane invests the elbow and the superior radiolunar articulations, lubricating the deeper structures of the two joints; a sleevelike capsule surrounds the entire elbow joint. The most important bursae in the area of the elbow are the bicipital and olecranon bursae. The bicipital bursa lies in the anterior aspect of the bicipital tuberosity and cushions the tendon when the forearm is pronated. The olecranon bursa lies between the olecranon process and the skin, forming a liquid cushion. Superficial and close to the skin in front of the elbow, lie the veins that return the blood of the forearm to the heart. Deep within the antecubital fossa lie the brachial artery and the medial arteries that supply the area with oxygenated blood. The median and radial nerves also lie within the antecubital fossa. The muscles of the elbow consist of flexor and extensor groups. The main flexors are the biceps, brachialis, and coracobrachialis. The primary extensor is the triceps (Fig. 22-2).

The elbow is subject to injury in athletics because of its broad range of motion, its weak lateral bone arrangement, and its relative exposure to soft tissue damage in the vicinity of the joint.

A slight oblique inclination of the trochlear articulation with the ulna produces an outward angle of 5 degrees to 20 degrees on extension, which is called the carrying angle (Fig. 22-3). In flexion the normal posterior aspect of the elbow creates an

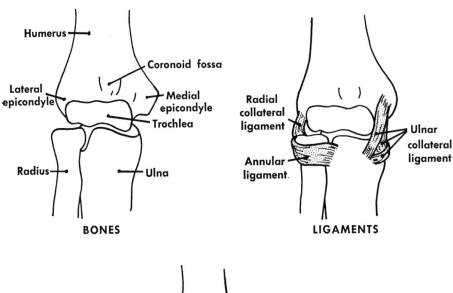

BONES

LIGAMENTS

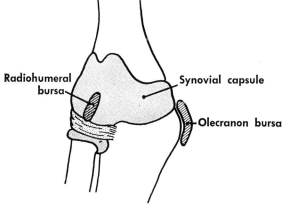

SYNOVIAL CAPSULE AND BURSA

Fig. 22-1. Anatomy of the elbow.

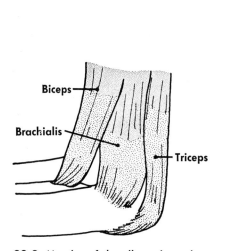

Fig. 22-2. Muscles of the elbow, lateral aspect.

Fig. 22-3. Carrying angle of the elbow.

isosceles triangle and can be shown by drawing a line from the olecranon tip to the superior aspect of each epicondyle (Fig. 22-4).

EVALUATING THE ELBOW JOINT

If the trainer suspects an elbow injury, he should first test the carrying angle of the athlete. If this angle is abnormally increased (cubitus valgus) or decreased (cubitus varus), there may be a fracture or an epiphyseal separation.

Flexion and extension of the elbow should have a range of about 150 degrees, and there should be 150 degrees of full supination and pronation (Fig. 22-5). After the range of motion through flexion and extension has been determined, lateral stability should be tested when the elbow is in full extension. Finally, palpation is used to examine for the presence of a normal or an abnormal triangle formed by the tip of the olecranon and the two epicondyles.

INJURIES TO THE ELBOW
Fractures

An elbow fracture can occur in almost any athletic event and is usually caused by a fall on the outstretched hand or the flexed elbow or by a direct blow to the elbow (Fig. 22-6). Children and young athletes have a much higher rate of this injury than do adults. A fracture can take place in any one or more of the bones that compose the elbow. A fall on the outstretched hand quite often fractures the humerus above the condyles, the condyles proper, or the area between the condyles. The ulna and/or radius may also be the recipients of trauma, and direct force delivered to the olecranon process of the ulna or a force transmitted to the head of the radius may cause a fracture. An elbow fracture may or may not result in visible deformity. There usually will be hemorrhage, swelling, and muscle spasm in the injured area. A possible complication of the humeral fracture

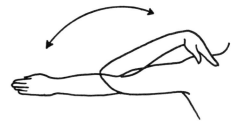

Fig. 22-5. Normal range of elbow movement.

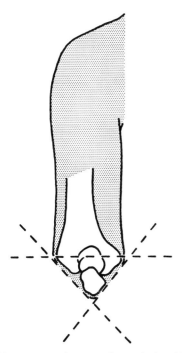

Fig. 22-4. Normal triangular relationship between the humeral epicondyles and the olecranon process.

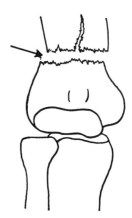

Fig. 22-6. Fracture of the elbow.

is *Volkmann's ischemic contracture or paralysis,* which is caused by muscle spasm or by bone pressure on the brachial artery that results in inhibited blood circulation to the forearm, wrist, and hand. To avoid complications from this fracture the trainer must splint the elbow and immediately refer the athlete to the physician.

Dislocations

Dislocation of the elbow (Fig. 22-7) has a high incidence in sports activity and is caused most often either by a fall on the outstretched hand with the elbow in a position of hyperextension or by a severe twist while it is in a flexed position. The bones of the ulna and radius may be displaced backward, forward, or laterally. By far the most common dislocation is one in which both the ulna and the radius are forced backward. We have handled several conditions that have occurred in football and wrestling, in particular. The appearance of the forward-displaced ulna or radius is one of marked deformity. The olecranon process extends posteriorly, well beyond its normal alignment with the humerus. This dislocation may be distinguished from the supracondylar fracture by observing that the lateral and medial epicondyles are normally aligned with the shaft of the humerus. Elbow dislocations involve rupturing and tearing of most of the stabilizing ligamentous tissue, accompanied by profuse hemorrhage and edematous swelling. The complications of such traumas include injury to the median and radial nerves, as well as to the major blood vessels and arteries, and—in almost every instance—myositis ossificans.

The trainer's responsibility is to immediately apply cold and pressure, then a sling, and to refer the athlete to the physician for reduction. Reducing an elbow dislocation should never be attempted by the trainer. It must be performed as soon as possible to prevent prolonged derangement of soft tissue. In most cases the physician will administer an anesthetic prior to reduction to relax the spasmed muscles. After reduction, the physician will often immobilize the elbow in a position of flexion and apply a sling suspension, which should be used for approximately 3 weeks. While the arm is maintained in flexion, the athlete should execute hand gripping and shoulder exercises. When initial healing has taken place, heat and gentle passive exercise may be applied to help regain a full range of motion. The trainer should, above all, avoid massage and joint movements that are too strenuous before complete healing has been accomplished because of the possibility of encouraging myositis ossificans. Both range of movement and a strength program should be initiated by the athlete. However, forced stretching must be avoided.

Contusions, strains, and sprains
Contusions

Because of its lack of padding and its general vulnerability, the elbow often becomes contused in contact sports. Bone bruises arise from a deep penetration or a succession of blows to the sharp projections of the elbow. A contusion of the elbow may swell rapidly after an irritation of the olecranon bursa or the synovial membrane and should be treated immediately with cold and pressure for at least 24 hours. If injury is severe, the athlete should be referred to the physician for x-ray examination to determine if a fracture exists.

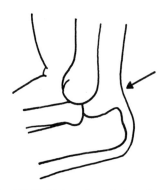

Fig. 22-7. Dislocation of the elbow.

Strains and sprains

Strains and sprains of the elbow must be considered together, since it is difficult to make a fine distinction between the two. Injuries to the tendons that cross the elbow usually injure the joint capsule also to some degree and vice versa. The most prevalent mechanism of injury is a fall upon the outstretched hand with the elbow in extension, thus forcing the elbow into a sudden *hyperextension*. If it does not result in a fracture or dislocation, this will tear the capsular and tendinous tissues anterior to the joint. Another cause of injury may be sudden and forceful abnormal pronation or supination or stretching while the articulation is in a position of full extension. A diagnostic test for hyperextension is the presence of pain in the elbow in a position of 45-degree flexion with a flexed wrist and extended fingers. If severe, the elbow strain or sprain must be suspected of being a fracture or an epiphyseal separation, which is quite probable in athletes under 20 years of age.

Immediate care consists of cold and a pressure bandage for at least 24 hours with sling support fixed at 45 degrees of flexion. After hemorrhage has been controlled, superficial heat treatments in the form of the whirlpool may be started and combined with massage above and below the injury. Like fractures and dislocations, strains also may result in abnormal bone proliferation if the area is massaged directly and too vigorously or exercised too soon. The main interest of the trainer is to gently aid the elbow in regaining a full range of motion and then, when the time is right, to commence active exercise. Until full mobility and strength have returned to the elbow, a strapping that will restrain from hyperextension should be used while the athlete is participating in his sport (Fig. 22-8).

Elbow hyperextension strapping. The procedure for strapping the elbow to prevent hyperextension is as follows.

Materials needed: One roll of 1½-inch tape, tape adherent, and 2-inch elastic bandage.

Position of the athlete: The athlete stands with the affected elbow flexed at 90 degrees.

Position of the trainer: The trainer stands facing the side of the athlete's affected arm.

Procedure:

1. Apply 2 anchor strips loosely around the arm, approximately 2 inches to each side of the curve of the elbow (antecubital fossa).

2. Construct a checkrein by cutting a 10-inch and a 4-inch strip of tape and laying the 4-inch strip against the center of the 10-inch strip, blanking out that portion. Next place the checkrein so that it spans the 2 anchor strips, with the blanked-out side facing downward.

3. Place 5 additional 10-inch strips of tape over the basic checkrein.

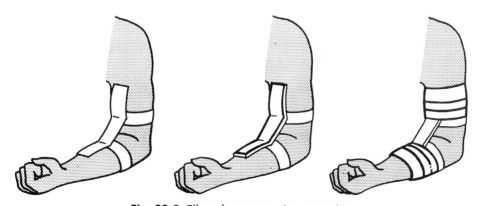

Fig. 22-8. Elbow hyperextension strapping.

4. Finish the procedure by securing the checkrein with 3 lock strips on each end. A figure-of-eight elastic wrap applied over the strapping will prevent the tape from slipping because of perspiration.

Bursitis of the elbow
Olecranon bursitis

The olecranon bursa (Fig. 22-9), lying between the end of the olecranon process and the skin, is the most frequently injured bursa in the elbow. Its superficial location makes it prone to acute or chronic injury, particularly as the result of direct blows. The inflamed bursa produces pain, marked swelling, and point tenderness. Occasionally, swelling will appear almost spontaneously and without the usual pain and heat. If the condition is acute, a cold compress should be applied for at least 1 hour and be followed by superficial heating 24 hours later. Chronic bursitis requires use of constant heat, both superficial and deep. In some cases, aspiration will hasten healing. Although seldom serious, olecranon bursitis can be annoying and should be well protected by padding while the athlete is engaged in competition.

Epicondylitis humeri

Epicondylitis humeri is a chronic condition that may affect athletes who execute repeated forearm pronation and supination movements such as are performed in tennis, pitching, golf, javelin throwing, and fencing.[1] The pathology of this condition is obscure, with radiohumeral bursitis, periostitis, or minute tears of the origin of the extensor carpi radialis or communis being the etiological factor involved. Regardless of the exact location of the injury, the symptoms are similar. Pain around the lateral aspect of the epicondyle of the humerus is produced on pronation and supination. The pain may be centered at the epicondyle or it may radiate down the arm. There is usually point tenderness, and in some cases there is a mild swelling. Passive movement of the arm in pronation and supination seldom elicits pain, although active movement does.

Care of epicondylitis is conservative and usually includes immobilization by adhesive strapping, the use of a sling, rest, deep heat (ultrasound), and injections of an analgesic and corticosteroid by the physician.

RECONDITIONING OF THE ELBOW

While the elbow is immobilized after an acute injury, the athlete should take general body exercises as well as exercises specific to the shoulder and wrist joint. Maintaining the strength of these articulations will speed the recovery of the elbow. After the elbow has healed and free movement is permitted by the physician, the first consideration should be restoration of the normal range of movement. Lengthening the contracted tendons and supporting tissue around the elbow requires daily passive stretching by the trainer and mild active exercises by the athlete. Forced stretching must be avoided at all times. When the full range of motion has been regained, a graded, progressive resistive exercise program should be initiated. Protective strapping must be continued until full strength is restored. Long-standing chronic conditions of the elbow usually cause a gradual debilitation of the surrounding soft tissue, and in conditions of this type the trainer should attempt to maintain the maximum amount of conditioning that can be accomplished without encouraging a postinjury aggravation.

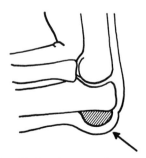

Fig. 22-9. Olecranon bursitis.

The forearm

ANATOMY

The bones of the forearm are the ulna and the radius (Fig. 22-10). The ulna, which may be thought of as a direct extension of the humerus, is long, straight, and larger at its upper end than it is at the lower end. The radius, considered an extension of the hand, is thicker at its lower end than at the upper end. The forearm has three articulations: the superior, middle, and distal radioulnar joints. The superior radioulnar articulation is a pivot joint, moving in a ring that is formed by the ulna and the annular ligament. The middle radioulnar joint, which is the junction between the shafts of the ulna and the radius, is held together by the oblique cord and the interosseous membrane. The oblique cord is a small band of ligamentous fibers that are attached to the lateral side of the ulna and pass downward and laterally to the radius. The interosseous membrane is a thin sheet of fibrous tissue that runs downward from the radius of the ulna and serves to transmit forces directly through the hand from the radius to the ulna. The middle radioulnar joint provides a surface for muscle attachments; also, at the upper end, as at the lower end, there is an opening for blood vessels. The distal radioulnar joint is a pivot joint formed by the articulation of the head of the ulna with a small notch on the radius. It is held securely by the anterior and posterior radioulnar ligaments. The inferior ends of the radius and ulna are bound by an articular, triangular disk that allows a radial movement of 180 degrees into supination and pronation.

The forearm muscles consist of flexors and pronators that are positioned anteriorly and of extensors and supinators that lie posteriorly. The flexors of the wrist and fingers are separated into superficial muscles and deep muscles. The deep flexors arise from the ulna, the radius, and the interosseous tissue anteriorly, whereas the superficial flexors come from the internal humeral condyle. The extensors of the wrist and fingers originate on the posterior aspect and the external condyle of the humerus.

With the exception of the flexor carpi ulnaris and half of the flexor digitorum profundus, most of the flexor muscles of the forearm are supplied by the median nerve. The majority of the extensor muscles are controlled by the radial nerve.

EVALUATING FOREARM INJURIES

Athletic injuries of the forearm are easily detectable because of the amount of exposure of both the ulna and the radius. Recognition of an injury is accomplished mainly through observation of the range of motion present and visible deviations and through the use of palpation. The forearm is first tested as to the amount of pronation and supination possible, 150 degrees being considered average. Next it is tested for wrist flexion and extension, with 150 degrees again considered normal. Injury may be reflected in the visible indications of a deformity or a paralysis. Palpation can reveal a false joint, bone fragments, or a lack of continuity between bones.

INJURIES TO THE FOREARM
Fractures

Fractures of the forearm (Fig. 22-11) are particularly common among active children and youths and occur as the result of a blow or a fall on the outstretched hand. Fractures to the ulna or the radius singly are much more rare than simultaneous fractures to both. The break usually presents all the features of a long bone fracture: pain, swelling, deformity, and a false joint. If there is a break in the upper third, the pronator teres has a tendency to pull the forearm into an abduction deformity, whereas fractures of the lower portion of the arm are often in a neutral position. The older the athlete, the more extensive is the danger to soft tissue and the greater possibility of the paralysis of Volkmann's contractures.

To prevent complications from arising,

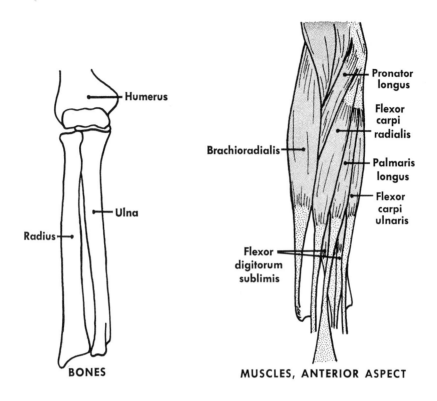

BONES

MUSCLES, ANTERIOR ASPECT

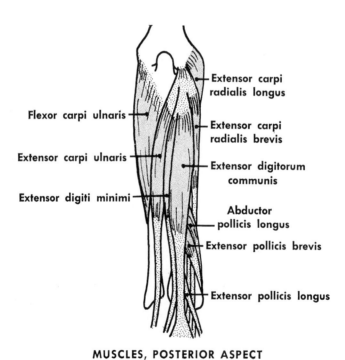

MUSCLES, POSTERIOR ASPECT

Fig. 22-10. Anatomy of the forearm.

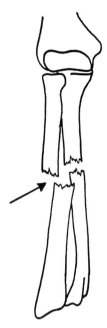

Fig. 22-11. Fracture of the forearm.

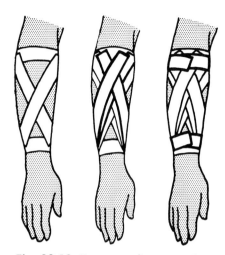

Fig. 22-12. Forearm splints strapping.

the trainer must immediately apply a cold pack to the fracture site, splint the arm, put it in a sling, and refer the athlete to the physician. The athlete will usually be incapacitated for about 8 weeks.

Contusions

The forearm is constantly contused in football. The ulnar side receives the majority of blows in arm blocks and, consequently, the greater amount of bruising. Bruises to this area may be classified as acute or chronic. The acute contusion can, conceivably, result in a fracture; but this happens only rarely. Most often a muscle or bone develops varying degrees of pain, swelling, and hematoma. The chronic contusion develops from repeated blows to the forearm with attendant multiple irritations. Heavy fibrosis may take the place of the hematoma, and a bony callus has been known to arise out of this condition.

Care of the contused forearm requires proper attention in the acute stages by applying cold for at least 1 hour, followed by heat applied by means of the whirlpool and analgesic balm packs the next day.

Protection of the forearm is important for athletes who are prone to this condition. It can best be given by use of a full-length sponge rubber pad for the forearm early in the season.

Forearm splints

The forearm splints, like shin splints, are difficult to manage. They occur most often in gymnasts and particularly in those who perform on the side horse. The main symptom is a dull ache between the extensor muscles crossing the back of the forearm and the radius and ulna. There also may be weakness and extreme pain on muscle contraction. Palpation reveals an irritation of the interosseous membrane and surrounding tissue. The cause of this condition is uncertain; like the shin splints, this usually appears either early or late in the season, which indicates poor conditioning or fatigue, respectively. The pathology is thought to result from the constant static muscle contractions of the forearm for example, those required to stabilize the side horse participant. Continued isometric contraction causes minute tissue tears in the area of the interosseous membrane. For additional discussion refer to Chapter 7.

Care of forearm splints is symptomatic. If the problem occurs in the early season the athlete should concentrate on increasing the strength of his forearm through resistance exercises, but, if it arises late in the season, emphasis should be placed on rest, heat, and use of supportive strapping (Fig. 22-12) during activity.

Forearm splints strapping. Support is given to forearm splints as follows.

Materials needed: One roll of 1½-inch adhesive tape and tape adherent.

Position of the athlete: The athlete stands holding the affected arm in a relaxed position.

Position of the trainer: The trainer stands facing the athlete's affected arm.

Procedure:

1. Two anchor strips are laid loosely, one of them 2 inches above and the other 2 inches below the irritation.

2. A strip of tape is taken from the lower anchor, on the radial side, obliquely upward to the anchor point on the ulnar side. A second strip is taken from the lower anchor on the ulnar side obliquely upward to attach onto the upper anchor on the radial side. This forms a crisscross that should cross below the point of injury and, with the subsequent series, completely cover and support the injury.

The wrist and hand

ANATOMY

The wrist or carpus is formed by the union of the distal aspect of the radius and the articular disk of the ulna with three of the four proximal (of the eight diversely shaped) carpal bones. Appearing in order from the radial to the ulnar side in the first or proximal row are the navicular, the lunate, the triangular (triquetrum), and pisiform bones; the distal row consists of the greater multangular (trapezium), the lesser multangular (trapezoid), the capitate, and the hamate bones (Fig. 22-13).

The concave surfaces of the lower ends of the radius and ulna are designed to articulate with the curved surfaces of the first row of carpal bones, with the exception of the pisiform, which articulates with the articular disk interposed between the head of the ulna and the triquetrum. This radiocarpal joint is a condyloid joint and permits flexion, extension, abduction, and circumduction. Its major strength is drawn from the great number of tendons that cross it rather than from its bone structure or ligamentous arrangement. The articular capsule is a continuous cover formed by the merging of the radial and the ulnar collateral, the volar radiocarpal, and the dorsal radiocarpal ligaments.

The *carpal bones* articulate with one another in arthrodial or gliding joints and combine their movements with that of the radiocarpal joint and the carpometacarpal articulations. They are stabilized by anterior, posterior, and connecting interosseous ligaments.

The *metacarpal bones* are five bones that join the carpals above and the phalanges below, forming metacarpophalangeal articulations of a condyloid type and permitting flexion, extension, abduction, adduction, and circumduction. As is true for the carpals, each joint has an articular capsule that is reinforced by collateral and accessory volar ligaments.

The interphalangeal articulations are of the hinge type, permitting only flexion and extension. Their ligamentous and capsular support is basically the same as that of the metacarpophalangeal joints.

The thumb varies slightly at its carpometacarpal joint and is classified as a saddle joint that allows, besides the other metacarpophalangeal movements, rotation on its long axis.

INJURIES TO THE WRIST
Fractures of the wrist

Colles' fractures (Fig. 22-14) are considered one of the most common types. This kind of fracture involves the lower end of the radius and/or ulna. The mechanism of injury is usually a fall upon the

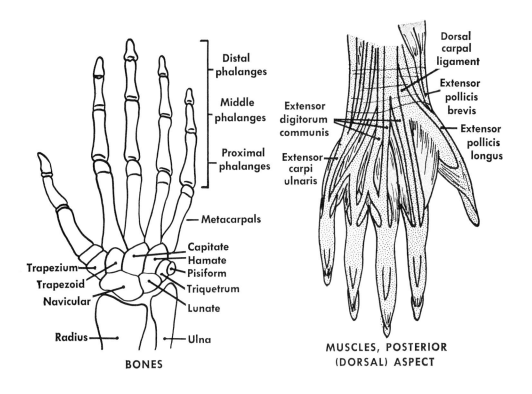

BONES

MUSCLES, POSTERIOR
(DORSAL) ASPECT

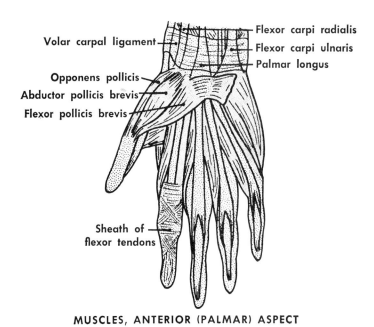

MUSCLES, ANTERIOR (PALMAR) ASPECT

Fig. 22-13. Anatomy of the wrist and hand.

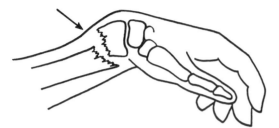

Fig. 22-14. Colles' fracture.

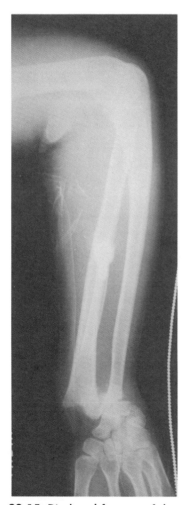

Fig. 22-15. Displaced fracture of the wrist.

outstretched hand, forcing the radius backward and upward. Direct blows to the wrist by a hard object may also cause fracturing, but this is a less common occurrence. In most cases there is a forward displacement of the radius that causes a visible deformity to the wrist (Fig. 22-15). Sometimes no deformity is present, and the injury may be passed off as a bad sprain—to the detriment of the athlete. Bleeding is quite profuse in this area with the extravasated fluids causing extensive swelling in the wrist area and, if unchecked, in fingers and forearm. Ligamentous tissue is usually unharmed, but tendons may be torn and avulsed, and there may possibly be median nerve damage.

The trainer's responsibility is to apply a cold compress, splint, put the limb in a sling, and then refer the athlete to the physician for x-ray examination and casting. Severe sprains should always be treated as possible fractures. Lacking complications, the Colles' fracture will keep an athlete out of sports for 1 to 2 months. It should be noted that what appears to be a fracture of Colles' type in children and youths is often a lower epiphyseal separation.

Carpal navicular fracture

The navicular bone is the most frequently fractured of the carpals, and about 8% of all fractures that occur in athletics are navicular fractures.[2] The injury is caused by a fall on the outstretched hand, which compresses the navicular bone in between the radius and the second row of carpals (Fig. 22-16). This condition is often mistaken for a severe sprain, and as a result the required complete immobilization is not carried out. Without proper splinting the carpal navicular fracture often fails to heal because of an inadequate supply of blood, and degeneration and necrosis occur. This condition is often called "aseptic necrosis" of the navicular bone. The trainer must try, in every way possible, to distinguish between a wrist sprain and a fracture of the navicular bone because in the case of fracture an immediate referral to the physician is necessary. The signs of a recent carpal navicular fracture include a swelling in the area of the carpal bones, severe point tenderness of the navicular in the anatomical "snuffbox" (Fig. 22-17), and navicular pain that is elicited by upward pressure exerted on the long axis of the thumb and by radial flexion. With these signs present, the trainer should apply cold, splint the area, and refer the athlete to the physician for x-ray study and casting. In most cases, cast immobilization lasts for about 8 weeks and is followed by strengthening exercises coupled with protective strapping.

Dislocation of the lunate carpal bone

The dislocation of the lunate (Fig. 22-18) is considered the most common dislocation of a carpal bone. It occurs as a result of a fall upon the outstretched hand, forcing open the space between the distal and the proximal carpal bones. When the stretching force is released, the lunate is dislocated anteriorly (palmar side). The primary signs of this condition are pain, swelling, and difficulty in executing wrist and finger flexion. There also may be numbness or even paralysis of the flexor muscles, because of lunate pressure on the median nerve. This condition should be treated as acute and the athlete sent to the physician for reduction of the dislocation. The usual time of disability and subsequent recovery totals from 1 to 2 months.

Wrist sprain

A sprain is by far the most common wrist injury and in most cases is the most poorly managed injury in sports. It can arise from any abnormal, forced movement of the wrist. Falling on the hyperextended wrist is the most common cause, but violent flexion or torsion will also tear supporting tissue. Since the main support of the wrist is derived from posterior and anterior ligaments that carry the major nutrient vessels to the carpal bones in addition to stabilizing the joint, repeated sprains may disrupt the blood supply and consequently the nutrition to the carpal bones.

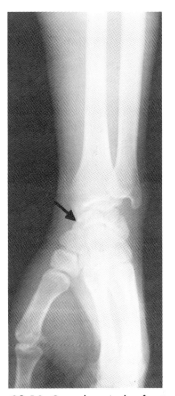

Fig. 22-16. Carpal navicular fracture.

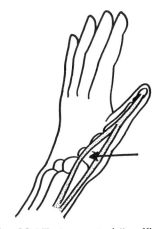

Fig. 22-17. Anatomical "snuffbox."

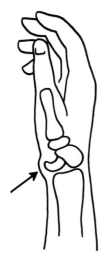

Fig. 22-18. Dislocation of the lunate.

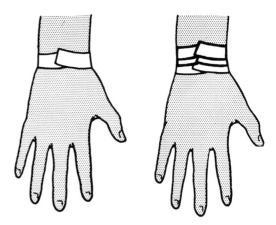

Fig. 22-19. Wrist strapping—Technique 1.

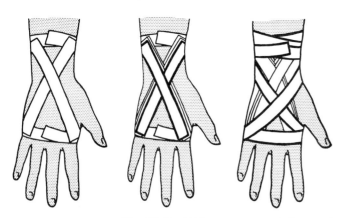

Fig. 22-20. Wrist strapping—Technique 2.

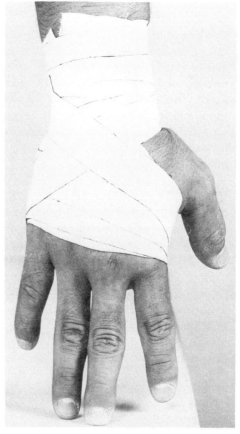

The sprained wrist may be differentiated from the carpal navicular fracture by recognition of the generalized swelling, tenderness, inability to flex the wrist, and absence of appreciable pain or irritation over the navicular bone. All athletes having severe sprains should be referred to the physician for x-ray examination to determine possible fractures. Mild and moderate sprains should be given cold and compression for at least 24 hours, after which there should be a gradual increase in heat therapy. It is desirable to have the athlete start hand-strengthening exercises almost immediately after the injury has occurred (see chapter 15).

Wrist strappings. Strapping support should be maintained until the athlete has regained his full strength and mobility.

Technique 1:

This wrist strapping (Fig. 22-19) is designed for mild wrist strains or sprains.

Materials needed: One roll of 1-inch tape and tape adherent.

Position of the athlete: The athlete stands with the affected hand flexed toward the injured side and the fingers moderately spread to increase the breadth of the wrist for the protection of nerves and blood vessels.

Position of the trainer: The trainer stands facing the athlete's affected wrist.

Procedure:

1. A strip of 1-inch tape, starting at the base of the wrist, is brought from the palmar side upward and around both sides of the wrist.

2. In the same pattern, with each strip overlapping the preceding one by at least one half its width, 3 additional strips are laid in place.

Technique 2:

This wrist strapping (Fig. 22-20) is designed to stabilize and protect a badly injured wrist. The materials and positioning are the same as in Technique 1.

Procedure:

1. One anchor strip is applied around the wrist approximately 3 inches from the hand; another anchor strip encircles the spread hand.

2. With the wrist flexed toward the side of the injury, a strip of tape is taken from the anchor strip near the little finger and carried obliquely across the wrist joint to the wrist anchor strip. Another strip is taken from the anchor strip on the index finger side and carried across the wrist joint to the wrist anchor. This forms a crisscross over the wrist joint. A series of 4 or 5 crisscrosses may be applied, depending upon the extent of splinting needed.

3. Over the crisscross strapping, 2 or 3 series of figure-of-eight strappings are applied. Start by encircling the wrist once, carry a strip over the back of the hand obliquely, encircling the hand twice, and then carry another strip obliquely upward across the back of the hand to where the figure-of-eight started. This procedure should be repeated to ensure a strong strapping.

Wrist ganglion of the tendon sheath

The wrist ganglion (Fig. 22-21) is often seen in athletics. It is considered by many to be a herniation of the joint capsule or of the synovial sheath of a tendon; other authorities believe it to be a cystic structure.[3] It usually appears slowly, after a wrist strain, and contains a clear, mucinous fluid. The ganglion most often appears on the back of the wrist but can appear at any tendinous point in the wrist or hand. As it increases in size, it may be accompanied by a mild pressure discomfort. An old method of treatment was to first break down the swelling by means of digital pressure and then apply a felt pressure pad for a period of time to encourage healing. A newer approach is the use of a combination of aspiration and chemical cauterization, with subsequent application of a pressure pad. Neither of these methods prevents the ganglion from recurring. Surgical removal has been found the best of the various methods of treatment.

INJURIES TO THE HAND
Fractures of the metacarpals

Fractures of the metacarpals (Fig. 22-22) are common in contact sports. They

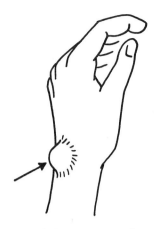

Fig. 22-21. Wrist ganglion.

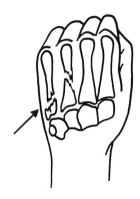

Fig. 22-22. Fractures of the metacarpals.

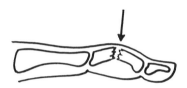

Fig. 22-23. Fracture of the phalanx.

Fig. 22-24. Avulsion of the extensor tendon (mallet finger).

arise from striking an object with the fist or from having the hand stepped on. There is often pain, deformity, swelling, and abnormal mobility. In some cases no deformity occurs, and by palpation one is unable to distinguish between a severe contusion and a fracture. In this situation, the trainer should place digital pressure to the knuckles and the long axes of the metacarpal bones. Pressure will often reveal pain at the fracture site. After the fracture is located, the hand should be splinted over a gauze roll splint (see Fig. 14-24), cold and pressure applied, and the athlete referred to the physician. Uncomplicated metacarpal fractures take approximately 1 month for complete healing.

Fractures of the phalanges

Fractures of the phalanges (Fig. 22-23) are among the most common fractures in athletics and can occur as the result of a variety of mechanisms: the fingers' being stepped upon, hit by a ball, or twisted.

More concern should be given to fractures of the middle and proximal phalanges because of possible involvement with the extensor or flexor tendons. A deformity in an anterior direction usually occurs in proximal fractures. The finger must be splinted in flexion, around a gauze roll or a curved splint to avoid full extension of the digit, which must be avoided at all times. Flexion splinting reduces the deformity by relaxing the flexor tendons. Fracture of the distal phalanx is less complicated than fracture of the middle or proximal phalanges, but it constitutes a painful injury that sometimes becomes complicated by a subungual hematoma. The trainer's major concern is to control bleeding, apply a splint properly, and then refer the athlete to the physician.

Mallet finger (baseball finger)

The mallet finger (Fig. 22-24) is common in athletics, particularly in baseball and basketball. It is caused by a blow from a thrown ball that strikes the tip of the fin-

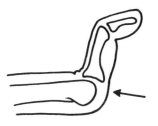

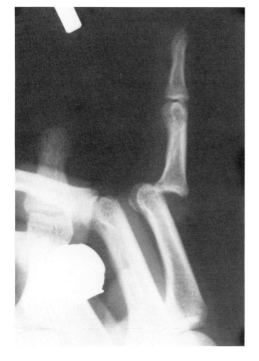

Fig. 22-25. Dislocated finger.

ger and avulses the extensor tendon from its insertion. The athlete is unable to extend his finger and carries it at about a 30-degree angle. Pain, swelling, and discoloration from internal hemorrhage are present. The trainer should immediately splint the distal phalanx in a position of extension, apply cold to the area, and refer the athlete to the physician. Most physicians will splint the mallet finger into extension and the proximal phalanx into flexion for 4 to 6 weeks.

Dislocations of the phalanges

Dislocations of the phalanges (Fig. 22-25) have a high rate of occurrence in ath-

letics and are caused mainly by being hit by a ball on the tip of the finger (Fig. 22-26). The force of injury is usually directed upward from the palmar side, displacing either the first or the second joint dorsally. The resultant pathology is primarily a tearing of the supporting capsular tissue, accompanied by hemorrhaging. However, there may be a rupture of the flexor or extensor tendon and chip fractures in and around the dislocated joint. It is advisable for the trainer to splint the dislocation as it is and refer all first-time dislocations to the team physician for reduction.

To secure the most complete healing of the dislocated phalanx, immobilization should be maintained for about 3 weeks because an immobilization period of too short duration can cause excessive scar tissue and, possibly, a permanent deformity.

Special consideration must be given to dislocation of the thumb (Fig. 22-27). A properly functioning thumb is necessary for hand dexterity; consequently, any traumatic injury should be considered serious. Thumb dislocations occur frequently at the second joint, resulting from a sharp blow to the distal end, with the trauma forcing the thumb into hyperextension and dislocating the second joint downward. Prompt control of hemorrhage, splinting, and physician referral must be executed by the trainer.

Sprains of the phalanges

The phalanges, particularly the thumb (Fig. 22-28), are prone to sprains caused by a blow delivered to the tip or by violent twisting. The mechanism of injury is similar to that of fractures and dislocations. The sprain, however, mainly affects the capsular, ligamentous, and tendinous tissues. Recognition is accomplished primarily through the history and the sprain symptoms: pain, marked swelling, and hematoma. The trainer should attempt to control the bleeding by means of cold and compression applied for at least 1 hour. It is important to minimize the organization of scar tissue so that permanent disability

Fig. 22-26. Volleyball produces a high percentage of finger injuries.

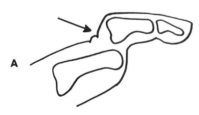

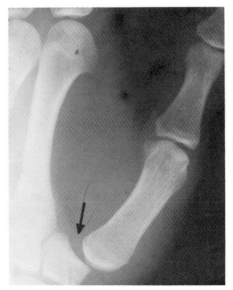

Fig. 22-27. A, Dislocated thumb; **B,** partial dislocated thumb.

does not take place. Heat (in the form of hot packs or the whirlpool) is beneficial after hemorrhage control. A protective strapping should be applied until the sprained phalanx has regained its full range of motion and strength.

Sprained thumb strapping. Sprained thumb strapping (Fig. 22-29) is designed to give both protection for muscle and joint and support to the thumb.

Materials needed: One roll of 1-inch tape and tape adherent.

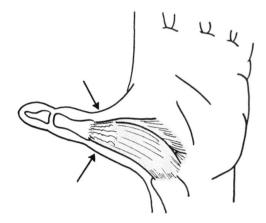

Fig. 22-28. Sprained thumb.

Position of the athlete: The athlete should hold the injured thumb in a relaxed neutral position.

Position of the trainer: The trainer stands in front of the athlete's injured thumb.

Procedure:

1. An anchor strip is placed loosely around the wrist and another around the distal end of the thumb.

2. From the anchor at the tip of the thumb to the anchor around the wrist, 4 splint strips are applied in a series on the side of greater injury (dorsal or palmar side) and are held in place by one lock strip around the wrist and one encircling the tip of the thumb.

3. A series of 3 thumb spicas is now added. The first spica is started on the radial side at the base of the thumb and is carried over the back of the thumb, completely encircling it and then crossing the starting point. The strip should continue around the wrist and finish at the starting point. Each of the following spica strips should overlap the preceding strip by at least ⅔ inch and move downward on the thumb (Fig. 22-30).

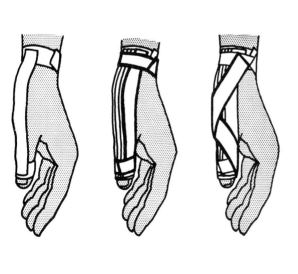
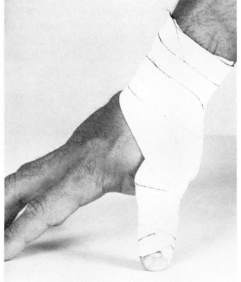

Fig. 22-29. Sprained thumb strapping.

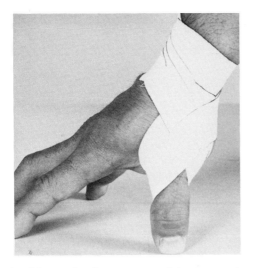

Fig. 22-30. Thumb spica—a useful strapping for minor protection.

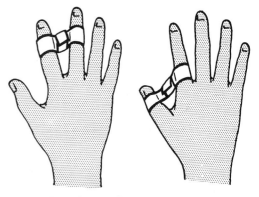

Fig. 22-31. Checkrein for finger.

Finger and thumb checkreins. Fingers and thumb that have been sprained may require the additional protection afforded by a restraining checkrein (Fig. 22-31).

Materials needed: One roll of 1-inch tape.

Position of the athlete: The athlete spreads his injured fingers widely but within a range free of pain.

Position of the trainer: The trainer faces the athlete's injured finger.

Procedure:

1. A strip of 1-inch tape, after encircling the middle phalanx of the injured finger, is brought over to the adjacent finger, which it also encircles. The tape left between the 2 fingers, which are spread apart, is called the checkrein.

2. Additional strength is given by means of a lock strip that encircles the center of the checkrein.

Contusions of the hand and phalanges

The hand and phalanges, having irregular bony structure combined with little protective fat and muscle padding, are prone to bruising in athletics. This condition is easily identified from the history of trauma and the pain and swelling of soft tissues. Cold and compression should be applied immediately until hemorrhage has ceased followed by gradual warming of the part in whirlpool or immersion baths. While soreness is still present, protection should be given by a sponge rubber pad (Fig. 22-32).

Bruised hand strapping. The following method is used to strap a bruised hand.

Materials needed: One roll of 1-inch adhesive tape, roll of ½-inch tape, ¼-inch thick sponge rubber pad, and tape adherent.

Position of the athlete: The fingers are spread moderately.

Position of the trainer: The trainer faces the athlete's hand.

Procedure:

1. The protective pad is laid over the bruise and held in place by 3 strips of ½-inch tape laced through the webbing of the fingers.

2. A basic figure-of-eight, made of 1-inch tape, is applied.

A particularly common contusion of the finger is the bruising of the distal phalanx, which results in a *subungual hematoma* (contusion of the fingernail). This is an extremely painful condition because of the accumulation of blood underneath the finger nail. The trainer should have the athlete place his finger in ice water until the

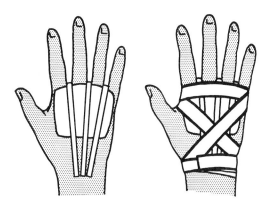

Fig. 22-32. Bruised-hand strapping.

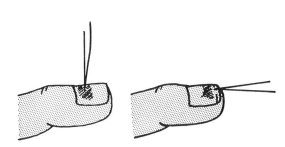

Fig. 22-33. Releasing blood from beneath the fingernail.

hemorrhage ceases and should then release the pressure of blood by the following method (Fig. 22-33).

Releasing blood from beneath the fingernail. The following are two common methods for releasing the pressure of the subungual hematoma.

Materials needed: Scalpel, small-gauge drill, or paper clip, and antiseptic.

Position of the athlete: The athlete sits with his injured hand, palm downward, on the table.

Position of the trainer: The trainer sits facing the athlete's affected finger and stabilizes it with one hand.

Technique 1:

1. The injured finger should first be coated with an antiseptic solution.

2. A sharp scalpel point or a small-gauge drill is used to penetrate the injured nail by a rotary action. If the hematoma extends out as far as the end of the nail, it may be best to release the blood by slipping the scalpel tip under the end of the nail.

Technique 2:

1. A paper clip is heated to a red-hot temperature.[4]

2. The red-hot paper clip is laid on the surface of the nail with moderate pressure.

This results in melting a hole through the nail to the site of the bleeding.

RECONDITIONING OF THE WRIST, HAND, AND FINGER

Reconditioning of the wrist and finger joints must commence as early as possible. Immobilization of the forearm or wrist requires that the muscles be exercised almost immediately after an injury occurs if atrophy and contractures are to be prevented. The trainer should remember that the athlete is not ready for competition until he has regained full strength and mobility of the injured joint. Grip strength is an excellent way to determine the state of reconditioning of the hand, wrist, and forearm. The hand dynamometer may be used to ascertain strength increments during the process of rehabilitation. Exercises for reconditioning the wrist, hand, and fingers are presented in Chapter 15.

REFERENCES

1. King, J. W., and others: Epicondylitis and osteochondritis of the professional baseball pitcher's elbow. In American Academy of Orthopaedic Surgeons: Symposium on Sports Medicine, 1967, St. Louis, 1969, The C. V. Mosby Co.

2. Flatt, A. E.: Athletic injuries of the hand. In

American Academy of Orthopaedic Surgeons: Symposium on Sports Medicine, 1967, St. Louis, 1969, The C. V. Mosby Co.
3. Nichols, H. M.: Manual of hand injuries, Chicago, 1960, Year Book Medical Publishers, Inc.
4. Relieving pain of subungual hematoma, Medical World News, October 9, 1970, p. 30.

RECOMMENDED READINGS

Dayton, O. W.: Athletic training and conditioning, New York, 1965, The Ronald Press Co.
Ferguson, A. B., Jr., and Bender, J.: The ABC's of athletic injuries and conditioning, Baltimore, 1964, The Williams & Wilkins Co.
Flatt, A. E.: The care of minor hand injuries, ed. 2, St. Louis, 1963, The C. V. Mosby Co.
Litton, L. O., and Peltier, L. F.: Athletic injuries, Boston, 1963, Little, Brown & Co.
McLaughlin, H. L.: Trauma, Philadelphia, 1959, W. B. Saunders Co.
Nichols, H. M.: Manual of hand injuries, Chicago, 1960, Year Book Medical Publishers, Inc.
O'Donoghue, D. H.: Treatment of injuries to athletes, Philadelphia, 1962, W. B. Saunders Co.
Thorndike, A.: Athletic injuries, ed. 5, Philadelphia, 1962, Lea & Febiger.

CHAPTER 23

Miscellaneous disorders

In this chapter various conditions, other than athletic traumas, that often affect the health of the athlete will be discussed. It is not our purpose to instruct the trainer in diagnosing particular conditions but rather to help him to recognize gross signs of abnormalities that would justify immediate referral to the athletic physician.

Special attention is given to disorders affecting selected portions of the body (the integumentary, digestive, and upper respiratory systems), and the effect of overexposure to climatic heat. The early recognition of infectious diseases is also extremely important to an athletic program. Highly contagious diseases can infect teams and sometimes result in the disruption or cancellation of an entire season. Because of the importance of such recognition, significant facts concerning common infection and contagion that are relative to the athletic training picture have been discussed at some length.

The integumentary system

The integumentary system consists of the skin and its modifications: the fingernails, toenails, and hair. It is the largest organic system of the body and serves as a protective covering against invasion of bacteria into the underlying tissues; at the same time, it prevents the loss of internal secretions. Other major functions include temperature regulation; relaying impulses of pain, heat, cold, and pressure to the brain; and excretion of waste products.

Protection. The skin offers the body protection by acting as a blockade against mechanical and biological insult. Any fault in the protective continuity of the skin may allow the entrance of pathological organisms into the body.

Temperature regulation. The skin's regulation of temperature takes place by means of two processes. The first process is determined by the blood vessels within the skin, which become dilated to receive more blood when warmth is needed or are constricted to cool the skin by decreasing the amount of blood. A second temperature regulatory process is accomplished by the sweat glands, which function by secreting perspiration that evaporates and thus cools the body surface.

Sensory perception. Sensory perception by the skin helps the body to become aware of its environment. Specialized nerve endings determine heat, cold, touch, pressure, and pain.

Excretion. Excretion of certain waste products from the skin is an important process that is accomplished when fluids containing waste are excreted from the sweat glands through openings in the skin called pores. An oily lubricating material (sebum) is also emitted by the skin from a *sebaceous gland,* an organ that lies next to a hair follicle.

ANATOMY

The average adult skin varies in total weight from 6 to 7½ pounds and in thickness from ⅟₃₂ to ⅛ inch. It is composed of two main layers, the epidermis or cuticle and the dermis or true skin (Fig. 23-1).

The *epidermis* is comprised of the following four sublayers: (1) the *stratum corneum,* the most superficial layer, consisting of dead cells and containing a hardening material called *keratin;* (2) the *stratum lucidum,* a thin layer, found mostly on the palms of the hands and the soles of the feet; (3) the *stratum granulosum,* a thin layer of cells; and (4) the *stratum germinativum,* the innermost epidermal layer, containing the skin pigmentation.

The *dermis* is a skin layer of irregular form, situated underneath the epidermis and made up of connective tissue that contains blood vessels, nerve endings, sweat glands, sebaceous glands, and hair follicles. The dermis forms a series of projections that reach into the epidermis, resulting in an interlocking arrangement and thereby preventing the epidermis from slipping off the dermis. Below the dermis is a subcutaneous fat layer called the *subdermis,* which acts as an insulation for the body.

The *hair* grows from hair follicles that are contained in the skin. It extends into the dermis, where it is nourished by the blood capillaries. The sebaceous glands which surround the hair, secrete an oily substance into the hair follicle. Persons who have overactive sebaceous glands may develop blackheads because of a plugging of the hair follicle. Small muscles called *arrectores pilorum* connect to the hair at its root and when contracted serve to constrict the hair follicles and cause a "standing on end" effect or goose pimples. Such contractions increase the emission of oil, and thereby help to protect the body from cold.

Sweat glands are necessary for cooling the surface of the body and the internal organs. There are two main types of glands: the *eccrine glands,* which are present at birth and are generally present throughout the skin, and the *apocrine glands,* which are much larger than the eccrine and mature at adolescence in conjunction with the axillary and pubic hair. Certain individuals with undersecreting sweat glands (dry skin) may be especially susceptible to various diseases. The fluid of the sweat gland contains antibacterial agents that are essential in controlling skin infections.

The *nails* are special horny cell structures that come from the skin (stratum germinativum) and serve to protect the ends of the phalanges. They are embedded

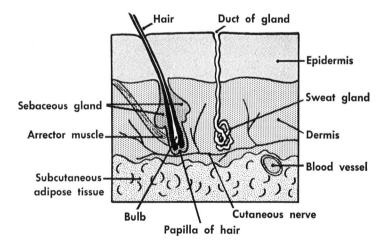

Fig. 23-1. Structure of the skin.

in skin at the base and along their sides and grow about ½ inch in 4 months.

DISORDERS OF THE SKIN—INFECTIONS AND CONTAGIONS

The skin presents the most prevalent site for infections and contagions in athletics. As a result, considerable detail is given in this text to this problem area. A coach or trainer should be able to recognize the more obvious signs of skin disorders.

Skin that is healthy has a smooth, soft appearance. It is colored by a pigment known as melanin. The amount of blood in the skin capillaries may give a ruddy appearance, accompanying an increase, or a pale effect when the amount is insufficient.

The normal appearance of the skin can be altered by many factors, external and internal. Some changes may be signs of other involvements. The different intensities of paleness or redness of the skin, which is related to *redness of superficial capillaries,* may indicate a disease condition. *Excessive oiliness* or *dryness* of the skin may be hereditary, although oiliness can be indicative of a greasy diet. *Pigment variation* may result from an increase of sun exposure or from organic diseases; a yellowish discoloration, for example, is indicative of jaundice.

Some common *lesions* displayed by the skin are as follows:

macule a small, flat, circular discoloration.
papule a small elevation of the skin, varying from a hardly visible size to the size of a pea.
nodule an elevation that is larger than a papule but smaller than a tumor.
wheal an elevation that arises from a local edema of the skin, usually occurring from an allergic reaction.
vesicle a blister that is smaller than a pea.
bulla a blister larger than a pea and containing a serous fluid.
pustule a vesicle containing purulent material (pus).
scale a dry squama or lamina of epidermis that is shed from the skin.
crust a dried, scalelike material produced from blood, serum, or pus.
excoriation a superficial blemish of the skin, caused by scratching.

ulcer an open lesion on the skin surface, extending at least to the corium and usually accompanied by pus.
fissure a groove, cleft, or slit in the skin, penetrating the epidermis and dermis.

Dermatitis or inflammation of the skin may result from numerous causes; burns, physical irritations, infections, plant and insect poisons, nutritional disturbances, and systemic diseases make up an imposing list.

External wounds

All external wounds require good care, and the trainer should have a clear understanding of his responsibilities in this matter.

Wound infection

The kinds of wounds incurred in athletics have been discussed previously. Lacerations and puncture wounds must be handled by the physician, but abrasions may be cared for by the trainer. After proper debridement and cleansing of the abrasion, the trainer should apply either a medicated ointment or a moist dressing. It is advisable that abrasions heal from the inside out to avoid the formation of scabs, which serve only to cover infected areas and are easily torn off in activity, thus causing reinjury of the tissue.

All wounds are subject to infection by external contamination. The organism most often involved is the pyogenic staphylococcus. The trainer should be aware of the following signs of wound infection:

1. Infections become apparent from 2 to 7 days after injury.

2. The wound becomes red, swollen, hot, and tender.

3. Lymph glands near the area of infection (groin, axilla, or neck) become swollen and painful.

4. The athlete may have a mild fever and headache.

Tetanus (lockjaw) is an acute disease causing convulsions and fever. Tonic spasm of skeletal muscles is always a possibility for any nonimmunized athlete. The tetanus bacillus enters an open wound as a spore and, depending upon individual susceptibility, acts on the motor end plate of the central nervous system. Immunization by tetanus toxoid provides protection for several years with a booster given at approximately 4-year intervals. An athlete who is nonimmunized must receive tetanus antitoxin no longer than 24 hours after injury.

Virus infections of the skin

Verruca vulgaris (warts). Warts are common skin conditions and appear as raised, rough-surfaced areas. They are caused by a virus that is both infectious and transferable. Warts are subject to secondary bacterial infections, particularly if they are located on the hands or soles of the feet, where they are subject to constant irritation. The responsibility of the trainer to the athlete who has vulnerable warts is to give protection until they can be removed by the physician. Removal is commonly accomplished by freezing with carbon dioxide or by curettement.

Herpes simplex (cold sore or fever blister). Cold sores or fever blisters are small vesicles that are caused by the herpes simplex virus. They form most often on the nose, face, ears, or genitalia. The groups of vesicles exude their fluid, which produces an itching, yellowish crust. Pain and even lymph gland swelling are also associated with the cold sore. In most cases the condition is self-limiting and will disappear in 1 or 2 weeks. Some individuals are more subject to this condition than are others.

The trainer should be aware that the herpes simplex virus is normally present at the sites of infection but will not erupt unless the athlete's resistance has been lowered by another condition such as fatigue, cold, digestive problems, allergies, or even emotional upsets. If an athlete develops the condition frequently, there may be an underlying predisposing factor that demands medical attention. The usual treatment of choice is application of a coating of camphor, alum, alcohol, or silver nitrate.

Bacterial infections

Bacterial infections are common complications of skin insults. Most of them are associated with staphylococci, particularly the *Staphylococcus aureus* strain, with the resultant production of pus.

Impetigo contagiosa. Impetigo is an acute skin infection caused by staphylococcic and streptococcic organisms. It is characterized by the eruption of small vesicles that form into pustules and, later, yellow crustations. Impetigo can be highly contagious and may spread rapidly through a glymnasium. On the suggestion of the physician the athlete may be requested to remain isolated from the team until the contagious period has passed, particularly in such sports as wrestling in which physical contact is continually made.

The treatment of impetigo requires thorough cleaning of the area and the application of a medicated ointment. The following regimen should be followed by the athlete:

1. Wash vigorously four or five times daily, using a medicated cleansing agent and hot water to remove all the crustations.

2. Dry the area after cleansing by patting gently.

3. When completely dried, an antibiotic or prescribed medicated ointment may be applied.

Every precaution should be taken by the trainer to make sure that the athlete uses isolated gym clothing and towels to prevent the spread of the disease.

Furuncle (boil). Boils are common in athletics. They usually occur from irritations of hair follicles or sebaceous glands. The predominant infectious organism is the staphylococcus, which produces a pustule. The areas of the body most affected are the back of the neck, regions about the face, and the buttocks. The pustule becomes enlarged, reddened, and hard from internal pressure. As pressure increases, extreme pain and tenderness develop. Most furncles will mature and rupture spontaneously, emitting their contents of pus. Boils should *not* be squeezed, since squeezing forces the infection into adjacent tissue or extends it to other skin areas.

The trainer should be aware that furuncles about the face can be dangerous, particularly if they drain into veins that lead to venous sinuses of the brain. Such conditions should immediately be referred to the physician. Care of the furuncle by the trainer involves protection from additional irritation and aid in bringing it to maturity by means of hot compresses or a poultice of ichthammol ointment.

Carbuncle. Carbuncles are similar to furuncles in their early stages, having also developed from the staphylococci. The principal difference is that the carbuncle is larger and deeper than a boil and usually has several openings in the skin. It produces fever and an elevation of white cell count. The site of greatest occurrence is the back of the neck, where it appears early as a dark red, hard area and then in a few days emerges into a lesion that discharges yellowish red pus from a number of places.

The trainer must be aware of the dangers inherent in carbuncles, since they may result in the athlete's developing an internal infection or may spread to adjacent tissue or to other athletes. The most common treatment is surgical drainage combined with penicillin medications.

Folliculitis. Folliculitis is an infection of the hair follicle. It can be caused by comedones (blackheads) or, more commonly, by the "ingrown" hair, which grows inward and curls up to form an infected nodule. The infection occurs most often in areas in which hair is shaved or is rubbed, such as the neck, face, buttocks, or thigh. The trainer should protect the injured area from added irritation and apply a dressing of medicated ointment or a drawing salve (ichthammol). If the infection does not respond to this procedure, the athlete should be sent to the physician for treatment by puncturing, curettage, and removal of the hair follicle.

Many hair follicles may become involved through the extension of infection to contiguous sebaceous glands. Such spreading causes a general condition called *sycosis vulgaris* or "barber's itch." It frequently occurs on the lip and is a red, swollen area, exhibiting tenderness on palpation. Pus collects around the exposed hair, causing it to be removed easily. This condition should be referred to a physician for treatment.

Comedones (blackheads) and pimples. Blackheads and pimples are common skin eruptions, which affect adolescents in particular. Both occur at the hair follicle where the oily secretion (sebum) accumulates. Sebum carries, besides its oily content, waste products that may aid in the initiation of a mild inflammatory condition, if it should stop up a hair follicle. Blackheads arise from external sebum, oxidizing and forming black tips. Blackheads and pimples occur primarily where the skin is oiliest—on the face, nose, chest, and upper back. The oilier an individual's skin, the more prone he is to blackheads. Frequent and thorough cleansing of the skin, using mild soap and hot water, will remove excess oil and consequently help to prevent blackheads.

Pimples may be caused by infected blackheads, skin infections, an inadequate diet, or internal imbalances. The trainer should caution the athlete with pimples or blackheads that squeezing will serve only to cause additional inflammation and infection.

Acne. A skin eruption called *acne vulgaris* occurs during the period of adolescence. This is a chronic inflammatory disease of the sebaceous gland characterized by blackheads, cysts, and pustules. Although most adolescents experience some form of acne, only a few develop an extremely disfiguring case. Its etiology is not definitely known, but food idiosyncrasies and sex hormone imbalance have been offered as possible causal factors. Acne begins as an improper functioning of the sebaceous glands with the formation of blackheads and inflammation, which in turn produces pustules. These occur on the face, neck, and back in varying depths. The superficial lesions usually dry spontaneously, whereas the deeper ones may become chronic and form disfiguring scars.

The athlete with a serious case of acne vulgaris has a scarring disease and because of it he may have a serious emotional reaction. The athlete may become nervous, shy, and even backward, and may develop a feeling of inferiority in his relations with his peer group. The responsibility of the trainer in conditions of acne is to help the athlete carry out the wishes of the physician and to give constructive guidance and counsel whenever needed.

The care of acne is usually symptomatic, with the majority of cases following a similar pattern. Use of a proper diet with avoidance of highly seasoned and fatty foods is important, and the athlete's bowel habits should be well regulated. Hormone therapy may be given by the physician. Cleanliness is essential. The face should be washed twice daily with a mild soap. Other methods may be required, such as the nightly application of keratolytic lotions (sulfur zinc or sulfur resorcinol), individual drainage of cysts or blackheads by the physician, and ultraviolet treatment.

Nail diseases. The fingernails and toenails are continually subject to injury and infection in athletics. A common infection is *paronychia* (Fig. 23-2), which is a purulent infection of the skin surrounding the nail. It develops from staphylococci and streptococcic organisms that accompany the contamination of open wounds or hangnails and appears as a painful, red, and swollen area. The infection may spread and cause *onychia,* an inflammation of the nail bed.

Fig. 23-2. Paronchyia.

The trainer should recognize this condition and have the athlete soak the affected finger in a hot solution of Epsom salts or boric acid three times daily. A medicated ointment, preferably penicillin or 5% ammoniated mercury, should be applied between soakings. Every protection must be given the athlete when he is engaging in his sport. Uncontrollable paronychia may require medical intervention with pus removal by skin incision or the removal of a portion of the infected nail.

Fungous infections

Fungi cause several of the skin diseases found among athletes because athletics produces an environment, at times, which is beneficial to their cultivation. They grow best in unsanitary conditions combined with warmth, moisture, darkness. Most fungous infections in athletics result from the same invading fungi—species of *Trichophyton* or *Epidermophyton*. These organisms are given the common name of ringworm or *tinea* and classified according to the area of the body infected. Infection takes place within superficial keratinized tissue such as hair, skin, and nails. Extremely contagious, the spores of these fungi may be spread by direct contact or contaminated clothing, or dirty locker rooms and showers.

Tinea capitis, beginning as a small papule on the scalp and spreading peripherally, is most common among children. The lesions appear as small grayish scales resulting in bald patches. The primary sources of infection are contaminated animals, barber clippers, hairbrushes, or combs.

Tinea corporis mainly involves the upper extremities and trunk. The lesions are characterized by ring-shaped, reddish, vesicular areas that may be scaly or crusted. Excessive perspiration and friction increase susceptibility to the condition.

Tinea unguium is a fungous infection of the toenails and fingernails. It is often seen among athletes who are involved in water sports or who have chronic athlete's foot. The nail becomes thickened, brittle, and separated from its bed.

Tinea pedis, or athlete's foot, often occurs as a vesicle containing a thin watery fluid that later develops scaling or cracking of the skin between the third and fourth interdigital spaces and plantar aspect of the foot.

Tinea cruris, or more commonly called "jock rash" or "dhobie itch," appears as a bilateral and often symmetrical brownish or reddish lesion, resembling the outline of a butterfly, in the groin area. The athlete complains of mild to moderate itching, resulting in scratching and the possibility of a secondary bacterial infection. A much less common condition that may be mistaken for tinea cruris is candidiasis, caused by the yeast *Candida albicans*. It is more common among individuals who are diabetic or have a tendency toward diabetes. As compared to tinea cruris, candidal infections cause severe itching and discomfort with associated infection of the scrotum.

The responsibility of the trainer is to be able to identify lesions of tinea cruris and handle them accordingly. Conditions of this type must be treated until cured. Infection not responding to normal management must be referred to the team physician. Most ringworm infections will respond to many of the nonprescription medications that contain such ingredients as undecylenic acid, triacetin, or propionate-caprylate compound, which are available as aerosol sprays, liquids, powders, or ointments. Powder, because of its absorbent qualities, should be the only medication vehicle used in the groin area. Medications that are irritating or tend to mask the symptoms of a groin infection must be avoided.

Atypical or complicated groin infections must have medical attention. Many prescription medications that may be applied topically or orally and show dramatic effects on skin fungus are presently on the market.

Arthropod infestations

Several small animals cause severe skin eruptions by burrowing into the skin, biting, or stinging. The most important of these belong in the phylum Arthropoda, which consists of animals without backbones having articulated bodies and limbs. Of the arthropod infestations that cause the most problems in athletics are the mites and lice. They appear as a result of poor sanitation and hygiene.

Scabies (itch). Scabies is a skin disease caused by the mite *Sarcoptes scabiei*, which produces extreme nocturnal itching. The parasitic itch mite is small, with the female causing the greatest irritation. The mite burrows a tunnel about ¼ to ½ inch long into the skin to deposit its eggs. These burrows appear as dark lines between the fingers, toes, body flexures, nipples, and genitalia. Excoriations, pustules, and papules caused by the resulting scratching frequently hide the true nature of the disease. The young mite matures in a few days and returns to the skin surface to repeat the cycle. The skin often develops a hypersensitivity to the mite, which produces extreme itching. The treatment of scabies is as indicated:

1. The entire body should be thoroughly cleansed, with special emphasis placed on the skin lesions.

2. Bedding and clothing should be disinfected.

3. A coating of gamma benzene hexachloride should be applied on the lesions for 3 nights.

4. All individuals who have come in contact with the infected athlete should be examined by the physician.

5. Locker and game equipment must be disinfected.

Pediculosis (lice). Pediculosis is an infestation by the louse, of which three types are parasitic to man. The *Pediculus capitis* (head louse) infests the head, where its eggs (nits) attach to the base of the hair shaft. The *Phthirus pubis* (crab) lives in the hair of the pubic region and lays its eggs at the hair base. The *Pediculus corporis* (body louse) lives and lays its eggs in the seams of clothing. Besides being a carrier for many diseases, the bite of the louse causes an itching dermatitis, which, through subsequent scratching, provokes pustules and excoriations. Treatment of pediculosis involves thorough washing with soap and water, followed by dusting or spraying the body twice weekly with 1% chlorophenothane. After each treatment, clothes and bedding should be disinfected before they are used again. Hairy areas of the body may require shaving for the complete removal of lice and eggs. If a dermatitis is present, it should be treated separately from the delousing procedure.

ALLERGIC SKIN REACTIONS

The skin displays allergic reactions in various ways. An allergy is caused by an allergen, a protein toward which the body is hypersensitive. Causative factors may be food, drugs, clothing, dusts, pollens, plants, animals, heat, cold, or light, or the cause may be psychosomatic. The skin may reflect an allergy in several ways, such as a reddening and swelling, urticaria (hives), or an eczema. Reddening and swelling of the tissue may occur either locally or generally from an increased dilation of blood capillaries. Urticaria occurs as a red or white elevation (wheal) of the skin, characterized by a burning or an itching sensation. Eczema is a skin reaction in which small vesicles are produced, accompanied by itching and a crust formation.

The trainer should be able to recognize gross signs of allergic reactions and should then refer the athlete to the physician. Treatment usually includes avoidance of the sensitizing agents and use of an antipruritic agent (such as calamine lotion) and antihistamine drugs.

MECHANICAL, PHYSICAL, AND THERMAL CONDITIONS

The skin of the athlete is subject to physical, mechanical, and thermal disorders. Outside factors such as heat, cold, and friction can cause varying degrees of inflammation.

Actinic dermatitis (sunburn). Sunburn is a dermatitis caused by the ultraviolet radiation from the sun and varies in intensity from a mild erythema (pink color) to a severe, second-degree burn repre-

sented by itching, swelling, and blistering. Every protection should be given to athletes who have thin, white skin. Such persons are called *heliophobes* and tend to absorb a greater amount of ultraviolet radiation than the more pigmented individuals. If a large area of the skin is sunburned, the athlete may display all the symptoms of a severe inflammation accompanied by shock. A sunburn can cause a malfunctioning of the skin organs, which in turn may result in infection of hair follicles and sweat glands. Prevention of sunburn should be accomplished by a gradual exposure to the rays of the sun, combined with use of a sunburn medication that will filter out a majority of the ultraviolet light.

Once a sunburn has been received, it is treated according to the degree of inflammation present. Mild burns can be aided by a soothing lotion that contains a mild anesthetic. Boric acid solution has also proved beneficial. Moderate and severe burns can be relieved by a tub bath in which a pound of cornstarch is used. A vinegar solution will also aid a severe sunburn.

Miliaria rubra (prickly heat). Prickly heat is common in athletics and occurs most often during the heat of the year to those athletes who perspire profusely and who wear heavy clothing. Continued exposure to heat and moisture serves to cause a retention of perspiration by the sweat glands, resulting in itching and in burning vesicles and pustules. It occurs most often on the arms, trunk, and flexure areas of the body. Care of prickly heat requires the avoidance of overheating, frequent bathing with a nonirritating soap, wearing loose-fitting clothing, and the use of antipruritic lotions.

Intertrigo (chafing). Intertrigo or chafing of the skin is common in athletics and particularly with the heavy or obese individuals. It is caused by a rubbing together of two body parts, which, in combination with perspiration, produces a painful inflammation with an associated burning, itching, moist, and cracking lesion. Treatment of intertrigo consists of frequent cleansing combined with a desciccative (drying), medicated powder.

Chilblains and frostbite. Chilblains is a common type of dermatitis caused by excessive exposure to cold. The tissue does not freeze but reacts with edema, reddening, possibly blistering, and a sensation of burning and itching. The parts of the body most often affected are the ears, face, hands, and feet. Treatment consists of exercise and a gradual warming of the part. Massage and application of heat are contraindicated in cases of chilblains.

Frostbite is a much more serious condition than chilblains, since an actual freezing of the superficial tissue takes place. Mild frostbite is freezing without the formation of blisters and is characterized by itching and numbness. More intensive freezing causes paresthesia, stiffness, blistering, and possibly death of the tissue. Authorities do not agree as to how frozen tissue should be rewarmed. Some indicate that the rewarming should be rapid, with the affected part immersed in water of 108° F. until it is restored to normal temperature; others indicate that a gradual rewarming is best.

Chemical skin irritants. Numerous chemicals are used in athletics that may cause either an allergic or a direct caustic reaction. Overexposure to acids, alkalies, or other irritants may result in a contact dermatitis characterized in the mild form by skin redness and in the severe state by blistering coupled with secretions and crusting. Care includes the elimination of the irritant combined with cleansing and the application of a soothing, medicated ointment (Butesin picrate).

Heat stress. Rising concern is being evidenced over the increase in cases of heat exhaustion and heatstroke, particularly among football players. Since 1964 there have been thirteen deaths in high school and college football, all of which were directly attributable to heatstroke.[1] Findings that uniforms and helmets are major causative factors have led persons in athletics to take a critical look at the type of equipment worn relative to temperature and humidity.[2,3] Murphy and Ashe,[6] who are among the foremost authorities on heat stress, have stated that under certain conditions the uniform can be a death trap. One study showed that water loss resulting from the load imposed by a football suit was 70% over that imposed by a hospital scrub suit.[4]

It is vitally important that the trainer have knowledge of temperature/humidity factors so that he can assist the coaching staff and team physician in planning practice and game uniforming and procedures. He should familiarize himself with the use of the sling psychrometer or the instrument used in establishing the WBGT Index (wet-bulb, globe temperature index).[5] The trainer should be able to determine not only relative humidity but also the danger zones; then he can advise the coaching staff and athletes with a reasonable degree of authority. In addition, he should become familiar with the clinical signs and treatment of heat stress.

Heat is eliminated from the body through conduction, convection, evaporation, and radiation. When temperature exceeds 80° F., the only effective means that the body has of heat dissipation is through sweating. However, when a high temperature is accompanied by high humidity, a condition with serious implications exists, since high humidity reduces the rate of evaporation *without* diminishing sweating. The stage is set for heat exhaustion and/or heatstroke unless certain precautionary measures have been observed. When a person's temperature reaches 106° F., the chances of survival are exceedingly slim.

Sweating occurs whether or not the athlete drinks water, and if the sweat losses are not replaced by fluid intake over a period of several hours, dehydration results. Sweat is always hypotonic, that is, it contains a lower concentration of salt than does the blood, and its loss establishes a deficit of water in excess of the salt deficit. This is reflected in several physiological changes, which may manifest themselves in peripheral vascular collapse, renal decompensation, and uremia. As was indicated in Chapter 8, coaches who fail to permit athletes unlimited access to water will not only undermine their playing potentialities but may be responsible for permitting a dangerous situation to develop that could conceivably have fatal consequences.

Body build must be considered when determining individual susceptibility to heat stress. Overweight individuals may have as much as 18% greater heat production than an underweight individual, since metabolic heat is produced proportionately to surface area. It has been found that heat victims tend to be overweight. Death from heatstroke increases at a ratio of approximately four to one as body weight increases.

Prevention: Mathews[3] uses the term SAW (salt, acclimatization, and water) to designate prevention. The following should be considered when planning a training-competitive program that is likely to take place during hot weather:

1. *Acclimatization.* This is probably the single most effective method of avoiding heat stress. Acclimatization should involve not only becoming accustomed to heat but also becoming acclimatized to exercise in hot temperatures. A good preseason conditioning program, started well before the advent of the competitive season and carefully graded as to intensity, is recommended. During the first 5 or 6 days an 80% acclimatization can be achieved on the basis of a 2-hour practice period in the morning and a 2-hour practice period in the afternoon. Each should be broken down into 20 minutes of work alternated with 20 minutes of rest in shade.

2. *Uniforms.* Select uniforms on the basis of temperature and humidity. Initial practices should be conducted in short-sleeved tee shirts, shorts, and socks, moving gradually into short-sleeved jerseys, lightweight pants, and socks as acclimatization proceeds. All early season practices and games should be conducted in lightweight uniforms, with short-sleeved jerseys and socks. Long sleeves and full stockings are indicated only when the temperature is low.

3. *Weight records.* Careful weight records of all players must be kept. Weights should be taken both before and after practice. Excessive losses (5 pounds or more) should be noted, and the athletes who record such losses should be observed carefully, since such loss often precedes heat exhaustion or heatstroke.[6] Remember that body build may reveal a susceptibility to heat stress.

4. *Salt and water.* Intake of salt and water should be carefully observed. (See Chapter 8.) Athletes should have unlimited access to water, and salt balance should be maintained, replacing 2 grams of salt for

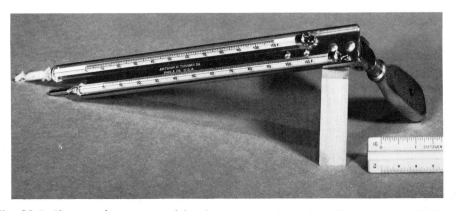

Fig. 23-3. Sling psychrometer used for determining relative humidity. (Courtesy California State University, Long Beach.)

every liter of water lost by sweating. (*Note:* A liter weighs approximately 2.2 pounds.)

5. *Diet.* Vitamin C appears to have some effect in preventing heat exhaustion.[7] Generally, a well-balanced diet is essential. Fat intake should be somewhat minimized.

6. *Temperature/humidity readings.* Dry-bulb and wet-bulb readings should be taken on the field before practice. The purchase of a sling psychrometer for this purpose is recommended (Fig. 23-3). It is relatively inexpensive and uncomplicated to use. The relative humidity should be calculated. The following suggestions regarding temperature and humidity will serve as a guide:

Temp. (°F.)	Humidity	Procedure
80°– 90°	Under 70%	Watch those athletes who tend toward obesity.
80°– 90°	Over 70%	Athletes should take a 10-minute rest every hour and tee shirts should be changed when wet. All athletes should be under constant and careful supervision.
90°–100°	Under 70%	
90°–100°	Over 70%	Under these conditions it would be well to suspend practice. A shortened program conducted in shorts and tee shirts could be established.
Over 100°		

Clinical indications and treatment: The following outline and Table 23-1 list the clinical symptoms of the various hyperthermal conditions and the indications for treatment.*

Environmental conduct of athletics: particularly football

I. General warning
  A. Most adverse reactions to environmental heat and humidity occur during first few days of training.
  B. It is necessary to become thoroughly acclimatized to heat to successfully compete in hot and/or humid environments.
  C. Occurrence of a heat injury indicates poor supervision of the athletic program.
II. Athletes who are most susceptible to heat injury

---

*From Buskirk, E. R., and Grasley, W. C.: Human performance laboratory, The Athletic Institute, The Pennsylvania State University.

A. Individuals unaccustomed to work in the heat.
B. Overweight individuals, particularly large linemen.
C. Eager athlete who constantly competes at his capacity.
D. Ill athlete, one with an infection, fever, or gastrointestinal disturbance.
E. Athlete who receives an immunization injection and subsequently develops a temperature elevation.
III. Prevention of heat injury
  A. Provide complete medical history and physical examination. Include:
    1. History of previous heat illnesses or fainting in the heat.
    2. Inquiry about sweating and peripheral vascular defects.
  B. Evaluate general physical condition.
    1. Type and duration of training activities for previous month.
      a. Extent of work in the heat.
      b. General training activities.
  C. Measure temperature and humidity on the practice or playing fields.
    1. Make measurements before and during training or competitive sessions.
    2. Adjust activity level to environmental conditions.
      a. Decrease activity if hot or humid.
      b. Eliminate unnecessary clothing when hot or humid.
  D. Acclimatize athletes to heat gradually.
    1. Acclimatization to heat requires work in the heat.
      a. Recommended type and variety of warm weather workouts for preseason training.
      b. Provide graduated training program for first 7 to 10 days—and other abnormally hot or humid days.
    2. Provide adequate rest intervals and salt and water replacement during the acclimatization period.
  E. Body weight loss (water and salt loss) during activity in the heat.
    1. Body water and salt losses should be replaced as they are lost.
      a. Supply cold saline—thoroughly mix one teaspoon salt in six quarts of tap water—give 3-4 oz. every 15 minutes or 8 oz. every half-hour.
      b. Allow additional water as desired by player.
      c. Provide salt on training tables and encourage salting of food.
      d. Weigh each day before and after training or competition.

Table 23-1. Heat disorders: treatment and prevention*

Disorders	Cause	Clinical features and diagnosis	Treatment	Prevention
I Heat cramps	Hard work in heat—sweating heavily—salt intake inadequate	Muscle twitching and cramps—spasms—usually after midday—arms, legs, abdomen low serum sodium and chloride	Severe case, I.V., adm. of 500 ml. of normal saline Light case, oral adm. of saline Rest in cool environment, subsequent rest for 24 to 48 hours—Continue with salted foods	Ensure acclimatization—Provide extra salt at meals Drink saline when working
II Heat syncope	Circulatory instability—peripheral vasodilatation—cerebral hypoxia	Syncope—weakness—fatigue—loss of vasomotor tone—peripheral pooling of blood—hypotension—blurred vision—pallor—elevated body temperature	Lower head—place supine rest in cool surroundings—provide oral saline	Ensure acclimatization—lighten work regimen with sudden rise in environmental temperature or humidity
III Water depletion Heat exhaustion	Prolonged sweating—inadequate replacement of body fluid losses—diarrhea—intestinal infection—predisposes to heatstroke	Excessive thirst—dry tongue and mouth—hyporexia—weight loss—fatigue—weakness—disconsolate—incoordination—mentally dull—small urine volume—elevated body temperature high serum protein and sodium—reduced sweating	Bed rest in cool room, I.V. fluids if drinking is impaired—Increase fluid intake to six to eight liters per day—sponge with cool water—keep record of body weight—keep fluid balance record—provide semi-liquid food until salination is normal	Supply adequate water and other liquids Provide adequate rest and opportunity for cooling
IV Salt depletion Heat exhaustion	Prolonged sweating—inadequate replacement of salt losses—inadequate acclimatization—vomiting or diarrhea	Syncope—headache—fatigue—dizziness—anorexia—nausea—vomiting—diarrhea—muscle cramps—low plasma volume—elevated blood urea—hypotension—hemo concentration—low	Bed rest in cool room—high intake of salt and water, I.V. if necessary—Follow urinary specific gravity and chloride, blood pressure and pulse rate—Follow blood urea hematocrit sodium and chloride	Adequate intake of salt, 10-15 gm. day

sodium and chloride in urine and sweat—develops more slowly (3-5 days) than water depletion heat exhaustion

V Heat hyperpyrexia leading to heatstroke	Thermoregulatory failure of sudden onset—	Generalized anhidrosis—hot and dry skin—high body temperatures, over 105° F.—irrational—muscle flacidity—involuntary limb movements seizures—coma—spotty cyanosis—ecchymosis—vomiting diarrhea frequently with blood rapid pulse—rapid breathing	Lower body temperature to 102° F. within one hour with cold water spray (45° F.) and air fan or by placement in ice water bath—massage limbs—strip, fan, wet body surface with water or alcohol on way to treatment station—record rectal temperature continually—use suction equipment to clear airway, tracheotomy if necessary—inject 25-30 mg. chlorpromazine every 30 minutes. Keep under observation after cooling, temperature may rise again. Maintain in cool environment Treat secondary disorders	Educate those supervising activities conducted in the heat Adapt activities to environment Screen participants with past history of heat illness
VI Skin lesions	Constantly wetted skin Overexposure to sun	Erythematous, papulovesicular rash—itchy skin—obstruction of sweat ducts	Maintain dry skin—keep in cool environment	Regular skin examination Air cooling sleeping quarters

*Courtesy E. R. Buskirk and W. C. Grasley, Human performance laboratory, The Athletic Institute, The Pennsylvania State University.

1. Treat athlete who loses excessive weight each day.
2. Treat well conditioned athlete who continues to lose weight for several days.

F. Clothing and uniforms
   1. Provide lightweight clothing that is loose fitting at the neck, waist, and sleeves. Use shorts and T-shirt at beginning of training.
   2. Avoid excessive padding and taping.
   3. Avoid use of long stockings, long sleeves, double jerseys, and other excess clothing.
   4. Avoid use of rubberized clothing or sweatsuits.
   5. Provide clean clothing daily—all items.

G. Provide rest periods to dissipate accumulated body heat.
   1. Rest in cool, shaded area with some air movement.
   2. Avoid hot brick walls or hot benches.
   3. Loosen or remove jerseys or other garments.
   4. Take saline and/or water during the rest period.

IV. Trouble signs: stop activity!

Headache	Diarrhea
Nausea	Cramps
Slow mentally	Seizures
Incoherent	Rigidity
Visual disturbance	Weak rapid pulse
Fatigue	Pallor
Weakness	Flushed
Unsteady	Faints
Collapse	Chilled
Unconscious	Cyanotic
Vomits	

DISEASES ABOUT THE EYES, EARS, AND LIPS

Conjunctivitis. The conjunctiva of the eye is subject to inflammation from various causes in athletics. Colds, excessive light, dust, foreign bodies, and infections about the face may affect the conjunctiva of the eye. Bacteria that enter the eye may result in itching, burning, watering of the eyes, and sensitivity to light. The conjunctiva appears red and swollen with an accumulation of pus. This condition can be highly infectious, spreading to the normal eye or to other individuals. An athlete exhibiting signs of conjunctivitis should be sent for medical care immediately. Conjunctivitis may be an indication of a more serious disease such as iritis or glaucoma.

Hordeolum (sty). Sties are infections of the eyelash follicles or sebaceous glands at the edge of the eyelid. The infection is usually caused by the staphylococcus organism, which has been encouraged by the irritation of rubbing or dust particles. The condition starts as an erythema of the eye, which localizes into a painful pustule within a few days. Treatment consists of the application of hot, moist compresses and an ointment of 1% yellow oxide of mercury. Recurrent sties require the attention of an ophthalmologist.

Ear conditions. The earache is a common symptom for several different ear involvements. It often results from a dermatitis of the external ear canal, from furuncles in the external canal, from a fungous infection, from eardrum inflammation, or from infections of the middle ear.

Infection of the external ear canal can arise from irritation caused by hardened wax (cerumen), foreign bodies, or insult caused by inserting hard objects into the ear. A general dermatitis may result or a localized infection may arise from a furuncle. The inflammation of the outer canal may infect the eardrum, causing a sharp, intermittent pain. Another and more common cause of eardrum infection is an upper respiratory infection, which irritates and closes the eustachian tube, causing increased air pressure within the middle ear. The increased middle ear pressure combines with an inflammation and tends to create a sharp stabbing pain, a difficulty in hearing, and a ringing in the ear. Ear infections require medical attention so that antibiotics and other medical procedures may be instigated.

Otomycosis or fungous infection of the external ear canal is not an uncommon condition among swimmers. It produces crusts and fissures, combined with severe nocturnal itching. The ear may have a fetid odor, a fluid discharge, and hearing may be impaired. Treatment is individual and is determined by the physician.

Cheilitis (dry lips). Cheilitis is an inflammation of the lips, usually caused by the sun, wind, or cold and resulting in cracking and blistering of the lips. Zinc oxide has proved most beneficial in treating cheilitis.

The respiratory tract

The respiratory tract is an organ system through which various communicable diseases are transmitted. It is commonly the port of entry for acute infectious diseases spread from person to person or by direct contact. Some of the more prevalent conditions affecting athletes are the common cold, sinusitis, pharyngitis, and the "childhood" diseases of measles, chickenpox, and mumps.

THE UPPER RESPIRATORY SYSTEM

Colds (coryza). Upper respiratory conditions, especially colds and associated conditions are common in the athletic program and can play havoc with entire teams. They are one of the trainer's greatest problems. The common cold is attributed to a filterable virus, which produces an infection of the upper respiratory tract within a susceptible individual. The susceptible person is thought to be one who has, singly or in combination, any of the following factors:

1. Physical debilitation from overwork or lack of sleep
2. Chronic inflammation from a local infection
3. Inflammation of the nasal mucosa from an allergy
4. Inflammation of the nasal mucosa from the breathing in of foreign substances such as dust
5. Sensitivity to stress

The onset of coryza is usually rapid, with symptoms varying in each individual. The typical effects are a general feeling of malaise with an accompanying headache, sneezing, and nasal discharge. Some individuals may register a fever of 100° to 102° F., as well as chills. Various aches and pains may also accompany the symptoms. The nasal discharge starts as a watery secretion, gradually becoming thick and discolored from the inflammation. A cold may be centered in a specific area or may extend throughout the upper respiratory tract. Sinusitis and pharyngitis often result from the common cold. The trainer should remember that many disorders begin with the same symptoms that a cold presents.

Treatment of the cold is usually symptomatic, with emphasis placed on isolation, bed rest, and light eating. Medications given as palliative aids are aspirin, for relieving general discomfort, rhinitis tablets for drying the secreting mucosa, and nasal drops or an inhaler containing ephedrine to relieve nasal congestion. If a cough is present, various syrups may be given to afford relief. Caution should be taken in disguising basic cold symptoms so that the athlete may return to activity sooner. Activity before complete recovery will serve only to delay full recuperation and may possibly cause chronic associated conditions.

The prevention of colds is much more important than is caring for them after they have become established. The methods of cold prevention that have proved most beneficial are (1) eating regularly of a proper diet, (2) avoiding extreme fatigue, (3) avoiding undue temperature changes without adjustments of clothing to meet such changes, (4) maintaining cleanliness at all times, and (5) attempting to eliminate undue emotional stress.

Sinusitis. There are numerous sinuses in the facial bony structure. These sinuses are hollow cavities lined with a mucous membrane, and each sinus is connected by a canal with the nasal passages. There are two basic groups of facial sinuses: (1) an anterior group made up of the maxillary, frontal, and ethmoid sinuses and (2) a posterior group consisting of the sphenoid and ethmoid sinuses.

Inflammation of the sinuses may be acute, subacute, or chronic and can occur from any condition that hampers normal sinus ventilation and drainage. Sinusitis may follow a cold, an allergy, measles, or other diseases that involve the upper respiratory tract. It can develop gradually or suddenly and is associated with headache,

Table 23-2. Some infectious diseases*

Disease	Sites involved	Mode of transmission	Incubation period	Chief symptoms	Duration	Period of contagion	Treatment	Prophylaxis
Measles (rubeola)	Skin, respiratory tract, and conjunctivae	Contact or droplet	7-14 days	Appearance—like a common cold with fever, coryza, cough, conjunctivitis, photophobia, and spots in throat followed by a skin rash	4-7 days after symptoms appear	Just before coldlike symptoms and about a week after rash appears	Bed rest and use of smoked glasses; symptomatic	Vaccine available
German measles (rubella)	Skin, respiratory tract, and conjunctivae	Contact or droplet	14-21 days	Cold symptoms, skin rash, and swollen lymph nodes behind ear	1-2 days	2-4 days before rash and up to 5 days afterward	Symptomatic	Vaccine available; gamma globulin given in postexposure situations
Chickenpox (varicella)	Trunk; then face, neck, and limbs	Contact or droplet	14-21 days	Mild cold symptoms followed by the appearance of vesicles	1-2 weeks	1 day before onset and 6 days afterward	Symptomatic	None: avoid exposure
Mumps (epidemic parotitis)	Salivary glands	Prolonged contact or droplet	18-21 days	Headache, drowsiness, fever, abdominal pain, pain on chewing and swallowing, and swelling of neck beneath jaw	10 days	1 week	Symptomatic	Temporary immunization by virus vaccine
Influenza (grippe)	Respiratory tract	Droplet	1-2 days	Aching of low back, generalized aching, chills, headache, fever, and bronchitis	2-3 days		Symptomatic	Moderate temporary protection by polyvalent influenza virus

Cold (coryza)	Respiratory tract	Droplet	12 hours-4 days	Mild fever, headache, chills, and nasal discharge	1-2 weeks	Symptomatic	Possible help from vitamins and/or cold vaccine; avoid exposure
Infectious mononucleosis†	Trunk	Contact	7-14 days	Sore throat, fever, skin rash, general aching, and swelling of lymph glands	3-4 weeks	Symptomatic	None; avoid extreme fatigue

*Except as indicated, the common cause of each disease included in this table is a virus.
†Common cause, undetermined; probably a virus.

nasal and postnasal discharge, and a general feeling of malaise. There may also be accompanying fever and sore throat.

Because the infected sinuses lie close to the brain, sinusitis can be extremely dangerous. Cases of sinusitis should be managed by a physician who uses various methods to help evacuate and heal the inflamed sinuses. The most common treatment procedure consists of the inhalation of steam and the use of vasoconstricting nose drops combined with symptomatic therapy such as rest, a light diet, and aspirin.

The trainer can aid the athlete by instructing him as to the proper way to apply nose drops (Fig. 23-4) and the way to blow his nose safely. The nose should be blown with the mouth open and pressure applied to one nostril at a time to avoid additional sinus irritation or the spread of the infection.

Pharyngitis (sore throat). A sore throat usually occurs as a corollary of a common cold or sinusitis, as the result of the postnasal drip. It may also be an indication of a more serious condition. Frequently it starts as a dryness in the throat, progressing to soreness, with pain and swelling. It is sometimes accompanied by a headache, a fever of 101° to 102° F., chills, coughing, and a general feeling of fatigue. On examination, the throat may appear dark red and swollen, and mucous membranes may be coated. In most cases bed rest is considered the best treatment when combined with the use of symptomatic medications such as aspirin and a hot salt water gargle. Antibiotics and a silver nitrate throat swab may be used by the physician if other measures are inadequate.

The digestive system

The athlete, like any other individual, may develop various complaints of the digestive system. So that trainers will be able to (1) give proper counsel on the prevention of mouth and intestinal disorders, (2) recommend a proper diet, and (3) recognize deviations from the normal in these

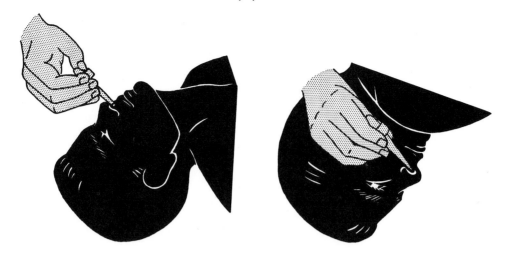

Fig. 23-4. Proper application of nose drops.

areas, the following pages are devoted to the discussion of the digestive system disorders that are common in sports and athletics.

MOUTH DISORDERS

Many different conditions involving the mouth appear during the course of a regular training program. Of these, the most commonly observed is dental caries (tooth decay), which is indicated by a local decalcification of the tooth. Tooth decay is the result of an increase in mouth acids, usually from food fermentation. Any disorder within the oral environment that raises its acid content without adequate neutralization may result in tooth decay. Proper oral hygiene is necessary and should include the following: (1) eating wholesome foods and (2) brushing the teeth properly, directly after meals.

The greatest single cause of tooth loss is gum disease, whose symptoms usually display the following pattern: (1) gingivitis, (2) periodontitis, and (3) pyorrhea. Gingivitis is an inflammation of the gum tissue surrounding the teeth and can arise from irritation brought about by tartar (calculus) or bacterial infection. If not cared for properly, gingivitis can extend to the periodontal tissue and eventually to the alveolar bone that supports the teeth, resulting in eventual loss of the teeth.

Infections associated with dental caries and gum disease can completely debilitate an athlete. Therefore, an immediate referral to the dentist is important.

DISORDERS OF THE GASTROINTESTINAL TRACT

The athlete may, as a result of poor eating habits or the stress engendered from competition, display various disorders of the gastrointestinal tract. The responsibility of the trainer in such cases is to be able to recognize the more severe conditions so that early referrals to the physician can be made.

Indigestion. Some athletes have certain food idiosyncrasies that cause them considerable distress after eating. Others develop reactions when eating prior to competition. The term given to digestive upset is indigestion (dyspepsia). This can be caused by any number of conditions. The most common in athletics are emotional stress, esophageal and stomach spasms, and/or inflammation of the mucous lining of the esophagus and stomach. These conditions cause an increased secretion of hydrochloric acid, nausea, and flatulence. Care of acute dyspepsia involves the elimination of irritating foods, development of regular eating habits, and avoidance of anxieties that may lead to gastric distress.

Constant irritation of the stomach may lead to chronic and more serious disorders such as gastritis, an inflammation of the stomach wall, or ulcerations of the gastro-intestinal mucosa. Athletes who appear nervous and high-strung and suffer from dyspepsia should be examined by the athletic physican.

Constipation. Some athletes are subject to constipation, the failure of the bowels to evacuate feces. There are numerous causes of constipation, the most common of which are (1) lack of abdominal muscle tone, (2) insufficient moisture of the feces, causing it to be hard and dry, (3) lack of sufficient bulk in the diet to stimulate peristalsis, (4) poor bowel habits, (5) failure to eat a sufficient proportion of roughage foods, (6) nervousness and anxiety, and (7) overuse of laxatives and enemas.

An individual's best means of overcoming constipation is to regulate his eating pattern to include those foods which will encourage normal defecation. Cereals, fruits, vegetables, and fats stimulate bowel movement, whereas sugars and carbohydrates tend to inhibit it. The trainer should also realize that some persons become constipated as the result of psychological factors. In such cases, the trainer may be able to help by trying to determine the causes of stress and, if need be, he can refer the athlete to the physician or school psychologist for counseling. Above all, laxatives or enemas should be avoided unless their use has been prescribed by the physician.

Hemorrhoids (piles). Hemorrhoids are varicosities of the hemorrhoidal venous plexus of the anus. There are both internal and external anal veins. Chronic constipation or straining at the stool may tend to stretch the anal veins, resulting in either a protrusion (prolapse) and bleeding of the internal or external veins or a thrombus of the external veins. Most often hemorrhoids are painful nodular swellings near the sphincter of the anus. There may be slight bleeding and itching. The majority of hemorrhoids are self-limiting and spontaneously heal within 2 to 3 weeks.

The treatment of hemorrhoids is mostly palliative and serves to eliminate discomfort until healing takes place. The following measures can be suggested:

1. Use of proper bowel habits
2. Ingestion of 1 tablespoonful of mineral oil daily to assist in lubricating dry stool
3. Application of an astringent suppository (tannic acid)
4. Application of a local anesthetic to control pain and itching (Nupercaine)

If palliative measures are unsuccessful, surgery may be required.

Diarrhea. Diarrhea is defined as the abnormal looseness or passage of a fluid, unformed stool and is categorized into acute and chronic, according to the type present. It is characterized by abdominal cramps, nausea, and possibly vomiting, coupled with frequent elimination of stools, ranging from 3 to 20 per day. The infected person often has a loss of appetite and a light brown or gray, foul-smelling stool. Extreme weakness caused by the fluid dehydration is usually present.

The cause of diarrhea is often difficult to establish. It is conceivable that any irritant may cause the loose stool. This can include either an infestation of parasitic organisms or an emotional upset. Management of diarrhea requires a knowledge of its cause. Less severe cases can be cared for by (1) omitting foods that cause irritation, (2) drinking boiled milk, (3) eating bland food until symptoms have ceased, and (4) using pectins 2 or 3 times daily for the absorption of excess fluid.

Appendicitis. Appendicitis is considered because of the importance of its early detection and the possibility of the trainer's mistaking it for a common gastric complaint. Inflammation of the vermiform appendix can be chronic or acute in nature; it is cause by a bacterial infection. In its early stages the appendix becomes red and swollen; in later stages it may become gangrenous, rupturing into the bowels or the peritoneal cavity and causing peritonitis. The athlete may complain of a mild to severe cramp in his lower abdomen, associated with nausea, vomiting, and a low-grade fever of from 99° to 100° F. Later, the cramps may localize into a pain in the right side, and palpation may reveal tenderness at a point midway between the anterior superior spine of the ilium and the umbilicus (McBurney's point). If appendicitis is suspected, the athlete must be referred immediately to the physician for diagnostic tests. Surgery is the usual treatment in most cases.

REFERENCES

1. Blyth, C. S.: Summary and recommendations of the 40th annual survey of football fatalities, 1931-1971. Committee on Injuries and Fatalities, 1971, American Football Coaches Association.
2. Goldman, R.: The effects of football equipment on heat transfer. In Physiological aspects of sports and physical fitness, Chicago, 1968, American College of Sports Medicine and The Athletic Institute, pp. 38-40.
3. Mathews, D. K.: Recognition and prevention of heat stroke, Mich. Osteopathic J. 31(8):10, 1966.
4. Fox, E. L., Mathews, D. K., Kaufman, W. S., and Bowers, R. W.: The effects of football equipment on thermal balance and energy cost during exercise. In Physiological aspects of sports and physical fitness, Chicago, 1968, American College of Sports Medicine and The Athletic Institute, pp. 41-44.
5. Tait, G. T., Grasley, W. C., and Buskirk, E. R.: Simple surveillance records for prevention of heat injury in football: body weight and environmental conditions. In Physiological aspects of sports and physical fitness, Chicago, 1968, American College of Sports Medicine and The Athletic Institute, pp. 87-90.
6. Murphy, R. J., and Ashe, W. F.: Prevention of heat illness in football players, J.A.M.A. 194: 650-654, 1965.
7. Welt, L. G.: Clinical disorder of hydration and acid base equilibrium, ed. 2, Boston, 1959, Little, Brown & Co.

RECOMMENDED READINGS

Consolazio, C. F., Johnson, R. E., and Pecora, L. J.: Physiological measurements of metabolic functions in man, New York, 1963, McGraw-Hill Book Co.

De Vries, H. A.: Physiology of exercise for physical education and athletics, Dubuque, Iowa, 1966, William C. Brown Co., Publishers.

Forsythe, C. E.: Administration of high school athletics, Englewood Cliffs, N. J., 1962, Prentice-Hall, Inc.

Gordon, J. E., editor: Control of communicable diseases in man, ed. 10, New York, 1965, The American Public Health Association.

James, A. P. R.: Common dermatologic disorders, Clin. Sympos. 19:39, 1967.

Johnson, W. R., editor: Science and medicine of exercise and sports, New York, 1960, Harper & Row.

Lyght, Charles E., and others, editors: The Merck manual of diagnosis and therapy, ed. 11, N. J., 1966, The Merck, Sharp and Dohme Research Laboratories.

Sartwell, P. E., and Maxcy, K. F., editors: Rosenau's preventive medicine and public health, ed. 9, New York, 1965, Appleton-Century-Cofts.

Sauer, G. C.: Manual of skin diseases, Philadelphia, 1965, J. B. Lippincott Co.

Symposium: Sports performance in hot environments. In Physiological aspects of sports and physical fitness, Chicago, 1968, American College of Sports Medicine and The Athletic Institute.

Top, F. H., and others: Communicable and infectious diseases, ed. 5, St. Louis, 1964, The C. V. Mosby Co.

Glossary

abduction movement of a body part away from the median plane.

acidosis increased or excessive acidity in the body.

adduction movement of a body part toward the median plane.

Adrenalin proprietary name for epinephrine, $C_9H_{13}NO_3$.

aerobic requiring the presence of oxygen.

afferent bringing to or leading toward; afferent neuron, sensory neuron, transmits impulses to the central nervous system; opposite of efferent.

agonist muscle which, in moving a part, is resisted by a muscle that relaxes sufficiently to permit the movement.

alkali reserve total of alkaline salts in the blood available for buffering acids other than carbonic acid and acting to keep up the normal blood alkalinity.

ambient environmental; as temperature or air which invests one's immediate environment.

ambivalence coexistence of conflicting and opposite feelings, for example, love and hate.

amine any of a class of organic compounds containing nitrogen.

amino acids basic structural units from which proteins are built; a group of organic compounds.

aminolytic capable of splitting up amines.

amylase any starch-digesting enzyme that converts starch into sugar.

anaerobic nonoxidative; not requiring free oxygen; opposite of aerobic.

anaphylaxis increased susceptibility or sensitiveness to a foreign protein or toxin as the result of previous exposure to it.

andric rating maleness presentation.

androgen any substance that aids the development and controls the appearance of male characteristics.

androgyny hermaphroditism.

ankylosis abnormal immobility of a joint.

anodyne medicine that removes or ameliorates pain.

anorexia lack or loss of appetite; aversion to food.

anoxia oxygen deficiency; inadequate supply of oxygen to the tissues.

antagonist muscle that opposes an action; for example, the triceps functions antagonistically to the action of the biceps brachii during flexion of the elbow joint.

antiphlogistic pertaining to the checking or diminishing of inflammation and fever.

aspirate to remove fluids usually by suction.

ATP adenosine triphosphate; a high-energy phosphate compound stored in muscle; a source of quick energy.

atrophy wasting away of tissue or of an organ; diminution of the size of a body part.

avascular not vascularized; bloodless.

axilla plural form, axillae; armpit.

bacteriostatic halting the growth of bacteria.

bilateral pertaining to both sides.

B.M.R. basal metabolic rate.

buccal pertaining to the cheek or mouth.

buffer compound that minimizes the change that occurs in pH (the degree of alkalinity or acidity) of a fluid, for example, the blood, when alkalis or acids are added.

calorie (large) the amount of heat required to raise 1 kilogram of water 1° C.; used to express the fuel or energy value of food or the heat output of the organism; the amount of heat required to heat 1 pound of water to 4° F.

cancellous latticelike or meshlike structure in bone.

carcinogenic producing or causing cancer.

cardiac cycle total sequence of cardiac movement, including the valve actions and the pressure and volume changes, during one complete period of relaxation and contraction.

cardiac output volume of blood pumped by both ventricles in a 1-minute period.

cardiac reserve ability of the heart to increase its rate and/or its stroke volume, thus increasing its output of blood.

cardiant any medicine stimulating the heart.

catalyst substance that accelerates a chemical reaction.

cicatrix scar or mark, formed by fibrous connective tissue; left by a wound or sore.

circadian rhythm the biological time clock by which the body functions.

circumduction movement in which the part describes a cone with the apex at the joint.

collagen main organic constituent of connective tissue.

colloid liquid or gelatinous substance that retains particles of another substance in a state of suspension.

conduction in therapy, the use of heat transferred by direct contact, as in a hot bath or a whirlpool bath.

convection in therapy, the use of heat transferred by circulation or movement, for example, heated air.

conversion in therapy, the use of heat produced by forms of energy other than air or water, for example, radiowaves, as in diathermy.

crepitus grating sound produced by the contact of the fractured ends of bones.

cubital fossa triangular area on the anterior aspect of the forearm directly opposite the elbow joint (the bend of the elbow).

cyanosis bluish discoloration of lividness of the skin, caused by deficient oxygenation of the blood.

diapedesis passage of blood cells through the walls of the blood vessels; term sometimes used to refer to the oozing of blood.

distal farthest end of a structure or part; opposite of proximal.

diuretic agent or medicinal substance that increases or stimulates the flow of urine.

dorsal from dorsum; combining form, dorsi; pertaining to the back; backward.

dorsiflexion act of bending a part backward; generally used to describe flexion of the ankle joint wherein the angle between the dorsum of the foot and the anterior aspect of the leg decreases.

dyspepsia indigestion.

dyspnea labored or difficult breathing.

ecchymosis extravasation of blood; tissue discoloration caused by the extravasation of blood.

edema swelling as a result of the collection of fluid in the connective tissue.

efferent bearing from; opposite of afferent; efferent nerves, motor neurons, lead away from an organ.

emesis vomiting.

enthesitis group of conditions characterized by inflammation, fibrosis, and calcification around tendons, ligaments, and muscle insertions.

enzyme complex organic substance, originating from living cells, which acts as a catalyst in certain chemical changes; digestive enzyme.

eosinophil white blood cell easily stained by eosin, a red coloring matter.

epiphysis portion of a bone that in early life is formed independently and later is joined to complete the whole bone through further ossification.

estrogen any substance that influences estrus or produces changes in female sexual characteristics.

etiology study of the causes of diseases.

eversion turning outward.

excoriation removal of a piece or strip of skin.

extension straightening out of two parts that have previously been in a position of flexion; opposite of flexion.

extravasation escape of a fluid from its proper vessels into the surrounding tissues.

fascia band or sheet of connective tissue.

fibroblast any cell component from which fibers are developed.

fibrosis development of excessive fibrous connective tissue; fibroid degeneration.

flexion bending of a part, wherein the anterior surfaces on either side of a joint move toward each other, thus decreasing the angle of the joint.

force couple depressor action by the subscapularis, infraspinatus, and teres minor to stabilize the head of the humerus and to counteract the upward force exerted by the deltoid during abduction of the arm.

glucose simple sugar; blood sugar; dextrose.

glycogenesis formation of glycogen from lactic acid or simple sugar.

glycogenolytic splitting of gylcogen.

glycolysis transformation of glycogen to lactic acid during muscle contraction.

glycosuria abnormally high proportion of sugar in the urine.

gynic rating feminine presentation.

hematolytic pertaining to the degeneration and disintegration of the blood.

hematuria passing of blood in the urine.

hemoglobin iron-containing protein which is the coloring matter of the red blood cells.

hip pointer iliac crest contusion.

homeostasis maintenance of a steady state in the body's internal environment.

hook-lying position basic starting position in exercise in which the subject, lying supine and keeping the feet flat on the floor, flexes the knees and brings the heels as close to the buttocks as possible.

hyperemia increase of blood in any part of the body.

hyperextension extension of a joint beyond straight alignment.

hyperglycemia excess of glucose in the blood.

hyperhidrosis excessive sweating; excessive foot perspiration.

hyperpnea hyperventilation; increased minute volume of breathing; exaggerated deep breathing.

hypertension high blood pressure; abnormally high tension.

hypertrophy enlargement of a part, caused by an increase in the size of its cells.

hyperventilation abnormal breathing that is deep and prolonged; hyperpnea.

idiopathic caused by an unknown factor; self-originated.

Indian grip position in which hands are placed palms toward each other, with the fingers of the two pointing in opposite directions and hooked together, that is, the flexed fingers of one hand engaging the flexed fingers of the other.

indurated tissue area of hardened tissue.

inversion turning inward.

ipsilateral situated on the same side.

irritability ability of a muscle to respond to stimulus.

ischemia lack of blood supply to a part.

isometric pertaining to a contraction wherein tension of the muscle is altered and heat is produced but the muscle does not shorten.

isotonic pertaining to a contraction in which the muscle shortens against resistance, thus performing visible work.

keloid fibrous tumor.

ketogenic forming ketones, acids produced during fat metabolism.

kinesthesia; kinesthesis sensation or feeling of movement; the awarness one has of the spatial relationships of his body and its parts.

lactic acid a by-product of muscle contraction, producing fatigue and pain in the muscle; it evolves through glycolysis.

lesion wound or injury.

lipid fat or ester.

menarche onset of the menstrual function.

mesentery fold of peritoneum that supports the intestine from the posterior abdominal wall.

morphology science of form and structure.

motor unit basic unit of neuromuscular function.

muscle viscosity internal resistance factor of the muscle.

necrosis death of a tissue or organ, especially bone.

nystagmus constant and involuntary rolling movement of the eyeball.

parenteral not given through the alimentary canal.

paresthesia abnormal or morbid sensation such as itching or prickling.

pathogenic disease-producing.

phagocytosis destruction of injurious cells or particles by the phagocytes (white blood cells).

phosphocreatine organic phosphate base, which functions as an important source of muscular energy.

placebo medicine given merely to please the patient; in research, an innocuous pill or capsule given a subject to aid in eliminating psychological or other variables.

plantar flexion extension of the ankle joint; that is, the angle between the dorsum of the foot and the anterior aspect of the leg becomes greater.

pledget small tuft of absorbent cotton.

post-parturition the period following childbirth.

prognosis prediction as to probable result of a disease or injury.

proprioceptor one of several receptors, each of which responds to stimuli elicited from within the body itself; for example, the muscle spindles that invoke the myotatic or stretch reflex.

prosthesis replacement of an absent body part with an artificial part; the artificial part.

proteolytic that which brings about the digestion of proteins.

psyche mind or spirit.

psychogenic of psychic origin; that which originates in the mind.

psychosomatic showing effects of mind-body relationship; a physical disorder caused or influenced by the mind, that is, by the emotions.

purulent consisting of or containing pus.

pyrogenic inducing fever.

reconditioning process of restoring the body and its parts after injury or illness to a normal condition, through the use of exercise and other therapeutic modalities.

residual that which remains; often used to describe a permanent condition resulting from injury or disease, for example, a limp or a paralysis.

Romberg's sign (or symptom) experiencing difficulty when standing with the eyes closed.

rotation turning about an axis in an angular motion.

rotator cuff tendinous attachments of the subscapularis, supraspinatus, infraspinatus, and teres minor, on the head of the humerus.

sarcoplasm fluid content surrounding the myofibrils (muscle fibers).

sequela that which results, for example, an affection that follows and is the result of a disease.

somatotype body form classification.

spermatogenesis formation of spermatozoa, male sex cell formed within the testes.

splanchnic pertaining to the internal organs, the viscera.

stasis blocking or stoppage of circulation.

static contraction isometric contraction.

sterol any one of a group of alcohols that are of vegetable or animal origin and have characteristics similar to fats.

stressor anything that affects the body's physiological or psychological condition, upsetting the homeostatic balance.

subacute relatively acute; a stage between acute and chronic.

syndrome group of typical symptoms or conditions that characterize a deficiency or a disease.

testosterone a male sex hormone.

torque anything that causes torsion, the turning moment of force.

torsion act or state of being twisted.

trauma plural form, traumas or traumata; wound or injury.

vascularization process of becoming vascular, that is, having a great many blood vessels.

vital capacity volume of air that can be forcefully expired after a maximal inspiration.

volar referring to the palm or the sole.

Appendixes

APPENDIX **A**

Additional passive mobilization techniques

The following mobilization techniques are included in this text to assist the experienced trainer in managing specific athletic affections.

Rotation stretch

Indications. Use of the rotation stretch (Fig. A-1) is indicated when the athlete complains of discomfort on movement as a result in neck strain or because of muscle spasm. The rotation stretch is safe, since all segments are stabilized and rotation of the head can go no farther than the table, approximately 90 degrees.

Positioning. The athlete lies face down, arms along his sides, and his head turned to one side. The trainer stands at the head of the table with the palm of one hand placed on the side of the athlete's head and the other placed on the scapula of the side toward which the head is turned.

Execution. A mild and steady pressure is applied by both hands in a scissorslike action, resulting in a rotary stretching of the cervical muscles. After the stretch has been applied to one side, the head is turned, the opposite position is taken by the hands, and the stretch is applied.

Precautions. A light massage should be given before the stretch is initiated. Sudden jerks should be avoided and a mild and steady pressure be maintained.

Compression stretch

Indications. Upper back strains, fatigue, or muscle spasms caused by nervousness may warrant a compression stretch (Fig. A-2) as part of the massage procedure.

Positioning. The athlete lies face down, his arms at his side, and rests his forehead on the table. Padding may be placed under the chin and chest for comfort. The trainer stands facing forward at the side of the table, in line with the athlete's hips. He places the heels of his hands at the twelfth rib on each side of the spine, approximately over the transverse processes.

Execution. The trainer pushes gently downward, forward, and outward, depressing the rib cage as the athlete exhales. Each time a stretch is applied the trainer should move slowly upward, initiating successive stretches, until the entire thoracic cage has been covered.

Precautions. Never stretch where there may be torn cartilage or a rib or vertebral fracture. Push gently, but do not stretch hard or suddenly or trauma may be increased. The best results are obtained after the area has been warmed up by massage, whirlpool, or heat lamp.

Low back scissors stretch

Indications. This mild stretch is to be used with an effleurage massage of the back; it helps to relax and loosen contracted tissue.

Positioning. The athlete lies prone with his arms at his side. The trainer stands transversely at the middle of the table, on the side opposite the one to be stretched. With the hand nearest the athlete's feet, the

427

Fig. A-1. Rotation stretch.

Fig. A-2. Compression stretch.

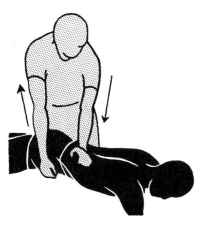

Fig. A-3. Low back scissors stretch.

Fig. A-4. Scapular stretch.

Fig. A-5. Elbow traction stretch.

trainer grasps the anterior superior spine of the ilium; he places the heel of the other hand on the lumbar area of the spine, directly over the transverse process (Fig. A-3).

Execution. The trainer pulls upward on the anterior superior spine as he simultaneously pushes downward on the lower thoracic and the lumbar area of the spine.

Precautions. Do not stretch if there is a possibility of fracture or if the athlete complains of tenderness at the anterior superior spine of the ilium. In the latter instance, a pad should be placed on the site before it is grasped.

Scapular stretch

Indications. The scapula pulls away from the rib cage, giving the sensation of more than normal freedom of movement at the shoulder girdle. This stretch is an excellent adjunct to the shoulder massage.

Positioning. The athlete lies prone, with the arm that is to be stretched at his side in a hammer lock position; this is, the arm is bent at right angles across the back (Fig. A-4). The trainer stands facing the athlete's shoulder and places the hand closest the head underneath the point of the shoulder. He lifts gently upward as the other hand grasps the spinal border of the scapula.

Execution. With a gentle lifting of the hand and grasping the scapula, the trainer pulls outward and away from the rib cage.

Precautions. A pad, placed over the scapula, should be used if irritation is evident upon grasping this area.

Elbow traction stretch

Indications. This procedure can be used to stretch out contracted capsular and tendinous tissue.

Positioning. The athlete, in either a sitting or a standing postion, places the affected arm underneath the trainer's arm (Fig. A-5). The trainer, whose back is to the athlete, clasps his upper arm tightly over the athlete's arm and then with both hands grasps the athlete's wrist.

Execution. In this position the trainer gradually extends the athlete's arm forward, placing traction on the elbow joint. Note that the elbow should never be forced into extension but should be stretched gradually. An increased range of movement can be facilitated if flexion is first initiated through several repetitions before extension is attempted.

Precautions. This traction stretch should be used only in cases of inelastic and contracted tissue, never after a recent dislocation.

Suggested medical record for high school athletes

SUGGESTED MEDICAL RECORD FOR HIGH SCHOOL ATHLETES*
Fill in each space. This part to be retained in physician's office.

HEALTH HISTORY

Identification

Name _____ Address _____

School_____ Grade _____ Date_____

Birthplace_____ Date of birth_____ Sex_____

Father's name_____ Business address_____

Home phone _____ Business phone _____

Date of last dental examination or treatment_____

Date last attended by family physician_____

Name of family physician_____

Physician's address_____ Phone_____

Family history: (If living, state present health; if deceased, cause of death.)

Father_____ Mother_____

Brothers_____ Sisters_____

_____

_____

_____

_____

Record of illness (Check those which occurred at any time; star illness of past 5 years.)

Frequent colds	_____	Diphtheria	_____	Hernia	_____
Influenza	_____	Measles	_____	Chorea	_____
Bronchitis	_____	Mumps	_____	Rheumatic fever	_____
Pneumonia	_____	Whooping cough	_____	Bone & joint disease	_____
Tuberculosis	_____	Scarlet fever	_____	Skin disease (name)	_____
Allergies	_____	Poliomyelitis	_____	Diabetes	_____
Chickenpox	_____	Appendicitis	_____	Kidney disease	_____
Other: (Specify)_____					

*From Committee on the medical aspects of sports: A guide for medical evaluation of candidates for school sports, Chicago, 1965, the American Medical Association, pp. 2-3.

Do any of the following occur? (Yes—No—Doubtful)

Aching eyes	_____	Frequent urination	_____
Sties	_____	Bed wetting	_____
Blurred vision	_____	Painful urination	_____
Inflamed eyelids	_____	Cough (prolonged)	_____
Recurring headache	_____	Hoarseness	_____
Blackouts	_____	Nasal discharge	_____
Fainting spells	_____	Nosebleed	_____
Toothache	_____	Sore throat	_____
Painful joints	_____	Abdominal pains	_____
Backache	_____	Diarrhea	_____
Leg pains	_____	Jaundice	_____
Palpitations	_____	Vomiting	_____
Night sweats	_____	Constipation	_____
Shortness of breath	_____		

Contact with tuberculosis

Tuberculin Test Reaction_____Date_____
Chest X-ray Findings_____Date_____

Specific immunization (Record year of last immunization.)

Smallpox_____Whooping cough_____Typhoid _____
Diphtheria_____Tetanus_____Poliomyelitis_____
Other _____

Record of serious injuries and operations (Record age and state procedure.)

Injuries _____   Operations_____
_____   _____
_____   _____

MEDICAL EXAMINATION

Body type and general appearance_____

_____

Skin _____
Scalp _____
Eyes _____
Vision without glasses   R_____   L_____
Vision with glasses   R_____   L_____
Nasopharynx _____
Tonsils_____
Ears _____
Hearing   R_____   L_____
Nasal obstruction_____
Mouth_____
Teeth _____
Thyroid_____
Lymph glands_____
Other_____
Chest _____
Lungs _____
Observation of posture_____

_____

Heart _____

_____

Blood pressure_____
Pulse_____
Abdomen _____

_____

Hernia _____
Genitalia _____
Nervous system _____

_____

Reflexes_____

_____

Emotional problems _____

_____

SPECIAL TESTS AS INDICATED

X-ray _____

Urine (Albumin)_____(Specific gravity)_____(Sugar)_____(Microscopic)_____
Blood (Red)_____(White)_____(Hemoglobin)_____

This page to be sent to the school. Use space at bottom for remarks.

PHYSICIAN'S REPORT TO SCHOOL
Significant findings of medical examination

Name of athlete_____

School _____Grade_____

Name of parent_____

Address _____Phone _____

Physical findings which are of significance to the school: _____
_____
_____
_____
_____

Recommendations to the school: _____
_____
_____
_____
_____
_____

Is athlete capable of sports competition?   Yes_____   No_____
Should there be restrictions?   Yes_____   No_____
Remarks:

_____M.D.

Date _____   (Signature of examining physician)

Address_____

Phone _____

Author index

Subject index